CHRISTIAN DOGMATICS

CHRISTIAN DOGMATICS

by

FRANCIS PIEPER, D. D.

Volume I

CONCORDIA PUBLISHING HOUSE • SAINT LOUIS

9 780570 067122

MANUFACTUREED IN THE UNITIED STATES OF AMERICA

26 27 28 29 30 31 32 33 34 35 34 33 32 31 30 29 28 27 26 25

Foreword

"HIS lifework was the *Christliche Dogmatik*, a monumental work in three volumes, setting forth the doctrines of Christianity as taught in the Lutheran Church. . . . In the clarity of his style and cogency of argumentation there has not been the equal of Dr. Pieper in the Lutheran Church in America. His literary ability, his eloquence, his deep personal piety, and his endearing traits of humility among his associates and charity towards the erring combined to make him a character rare in the history of a Church which has produced so many noble characters." So read the obituary which announced the death on June 3, 1931, of the eminent churchman who had been the theological leader of the Missouri Synod for upward of four decades.

Called to a professorship at Concordia Theological Seminary, St. Louis, in 1878, Francis Pieper succeeded Dr. C. F. W. Walther as president of the institution in 1887. The outstanding gifts with which he was endowed led to his prompt recognition as the chief dogmatician of the Synod as well as to the presidency of the general body from 1899 to 1911. Through the years the work of training young men for the Gospel ministry was ever the prime area of his labors. To demonstrate how the whole inspired Word comes to its ultimate focus in the revelation of God's grace in Christ Jesus was his unfailing delight. How that perception of divine mercy dominated his thinking and teaching is plainly to be seen also in this dogmatics, with its constant, loving reiteration of the truths of universal grace, the vicarious satisfaction, and justification through faith alone.

As the four-hundredth anniversary of the Reformation approached, Dr. Pieper, now relieved of the arduous duties of the synodical presidency, found opportunity to devote himself to preparation of a Christian dogmatics. It was designed to be an expression of thanksgiving for the Lord's merciful kindness in preserving the full truth of His Word to the Synod Pieper loved so dearly and served so notably. Since the first volume was to appear in the quadricentennial year, the author chose to offer first the *loci* that are the very heart of Scripture's message and were the fundamentals of Luther's glorious testimony: the grace of God in Christ, Christ's person and work, saving faith, conversion, and justification by faith. This volume, issued in 1917, became the second of the whole work. Volume III, treating sanctification, preservation, the means of grace, the Church, the ministry, the election of grace, and eschatology, followed in 1920. With the publication of Volume I, embracing the *loci* on the nature of theology, Holy Scripture, God, creation, divine providence, angels, and man (*anthropologia*), the project was brought to completion in 1924.

The *Dogmatik* was at once hailed as a masterwork. The *Theological*

Monthly commented: "His work will go down to future generations as the dogmatic standard, alongside of the works of Walther and his earlier colleagues, of the Missouri Synod." Theologians of other church bodies characterized it as "monumental," "a veritable treasure house on dogmatic theology," and hastened to emphasize its importance: "Among the newer dogmatical works that are to be warmly commended to our pastors we give first place to this dogmatics of Francis Pieper."

As early as 1924 pastoral conferences and individuals began to voice and to multiply formal requests that this *opus magnum* be made available in an English edition. In 1941 the synodical convention created a committee to formulate plans for a worthy celebration of the centennial of the Evangelical Lutheran Synod of Missouri, Ohio, and Other States – since 1947 The Lutheran Church – Missouri Synod. As one of its basic recommendations the Centennial Committee proposed that a translation of the *Christliche Dogmatik* be prepared. The suggestion was enthusiastically adopted, with the hope that the work might be issued in the centennial year – a hope that could not be realized because of a number of delaying factors.

Dr. Theodore Engelder, the successor of Dr. Walther and Dr. Pieper as senior dogmatician of Synod, accepted the commission to serve as chief translator and supervising editor. Under his skilled hand the major part of the work of planning and translation was executed. Prof. Walter W. F. Albrecht of Concordia Seminary, Springfield, Ill., who had prepared the first English translation of the *Dogmatik* in the late thirties, Dr. Fred E. Mayer of Concordia Seminary, St. Louis, Mo., and Prof. Lorenz F. Blankenbuehler, house editor of Concordia Publishing House, were enlisted as assistants in the project. "Professor Albrecht's translation, prepared in mimeographed form for the use of his students," the chief editor's notes record, "was constantly consulted," and afforded him invaluable aid. Dr. J. T. Mueller's condensation of the Pieper volumes was also used for reference. To all these brethren, as well as to Mr. O. A. Dorn, manager of Concordia Publishing House, the committee and Synod owe thanks for their helpful advice and able collaboration.

In June, 1949, our Lord found it good in His wisdom and grace to call Dr. Engelder home before he could complete the task which had chiefly occupied him during the several past years. We are grateful, however, that time was granted him to carry the translation well into the third volume and that, on the basis of this work, issuance of Volume II and III may be anticipated in the near future.

Explanatory remarks assembled posthumously from the chief editor's notes will, we think, be of interest: "We shall endeavor to offer a passable English translation, preserving as much as possible the inimitable flavor of Pieper's powerful, lucid, and trenchant style. . . . It is not an easy task to make a German theologian speak fluent English (cf. C. T. M., VIII 77). . . . Much of the original beauty of style must inevitably be lost in a translation (cf. Preface to Koeberle)."

"We have condensed some parts, for instance, on the Crypto-Kenotic controversy, on German church conditions at the time of writing, etc., because we feel that they are not of equal interest for the reader today." "But we feel, too, that the constant reiteration of the same truth, from different angles, will prove welcome. That constitutes one of the beauties of the books."

"We had planned to discuss the more recent development in theology, but soon found that it was not feasible without causing an undesirable delay. We therefore give Pieper as he is. Perhaps we can hope that a volume of studies in modern developments will soon be issued."

However, on the general compass of Pieper's DOGMATICS and its utility in meeting modern trends thetically and antithetically Dr. Engelder added: "It was a monumental work for its time, and one who has imbibed the principles of this book is well prepared to meet whatever new forms the most modern error takes. In fact, any up-to-date dogmatics must stand on these principles. Pieper did much for his generation. He kept it straight through his classic. He is doing much for the present generation. It is fine that Synod through its Centennial Committee made it available in English translation. It will do much to keep us straight. They that study it will be prepared to deal with recent developments." He jotted down with full approval Dr. L. Fuerbringer's oft-repeated remark that the DOGMATICS "must be considered and remain a standard work of Lutheran theology," and joined to it as his own estimate of the work words written some years earlier: "It was a power for orthodoxy in its day. And it has not outlived its usefulness. It is a mighty force today to keep Lutherans reminded of the treasure of pure doctrine which God has bestowed upon them."

It will be noted that a few references to translations of older publications which are not readily accessible now have been added to the original text in brackets. Also in a few instances footnote references to materials no longer available or pertinent have been omitted. Long Latin quotations have been translated.

An index of the entire work is planned upon completion of the third volume.

May the issuance of this classic Scriptural theology in English form be indeed a mighty force to assist us in proclaiming our Savior's Word of truth and grace and in repeating the Psalmist's asseveration: "I have stuck unto Thy testimonies"!

THE SYNODICAL CENTENNIAL COMMITTEE

H. W. ROMOSER
A. H. KRAMER
G. A. FLEISCHER
E. T. LAMS
H. M. ZORN

January, 1950

Preface

THE three volumes of my CHRISTLICHE DOGMATIK are now in print. An explanation is in order why the first volume was published last. It had been suggested that the volume containing the doctrines of God's grace in Christ, of Christ's person and work, and of justification be published in 1917, the fourth centennial of the Lutheran Reformation. It was only natural that Volume III, setting forth the results and consequences of justification, should appear next (1920).

More than half of the present volume is devoted to "The Nature and Character of Theology" and "Holy Scripture." This has become necessary because modern Protestant theology has adopted unchristian views regarding the nature and contents of theology. And this again is simply the inevitable consequence when men deny that Holy Scripture is God's own infallible Word. Modern theology has gone the way of Rome. In the Church of Rome, Christian theology has completely broken down, for there the sole authority of Scripture is denied and the subjective opinion of the Pope is made the real authority. Just so modern Protestant theology has abandoned the objective divine authority of Scripture and put in its place "Christian experience," that is, the subjective views of "the theologizing subject," of the theologian. This situation called for the comprehensive treatment given the matter in the first two sections. – In the doctrine of God the difference between the natural and the Christian knowledge of God had to be presented somewhat more fully, because modern theology, represented also by some Lutherans, has become dynamic Unitarianism. – Modern theology has adopted the Romanist-Zwinglian concept of a "guiltless sin." This aberration made it necessary to dwell more extensively on several points of the doctrine of sin in the chapter on "Anthropology."

Considerable space has been given to the charge, raised especially in German dogmatical treatises, that the Missouri Synod teaches a "repristination theology," which must inevitably prove harmful to the Church. The claim is made that by identifying Scripture and the Word of God our theology will lead to an intellectualism which will stifle all true and genuine religion of the heart ("*Herzenschristentum*"). This matter does not properly belong to dogmatics. Nevertheless, I considered it necessary to refute the unwarranted charge and to remove any misgivings concerning the "repristination theology," and have therefore set forth in some detail the religious life of a church body which is definitely committed to the "repristination theology." I also presented the additional historical fact that also other church bodies explicitly adhere to this "repristination theology." I refer to Dr. Hoenecke's exhaustive *Ev.-Luth. Dogmatik* as proof that the doctrinal position of the Joint Synod of Wisconsin and Other States is exactly the same as that of the Synod of Missouri, Ohio, and Other States. This excursus also contains several quotations from a monograph by Franz Delitzsch, published in 1839 for the 300th anniversary of the Reformation of the city of Leipzig. The purpose of these quotations is to show that what God gave also to Germany a century ago has been perpetuated, further elucidated, and applied in practice by the "strictly confessional wing" of American Lutheranism. Let me here repeat a few statements of Delitzsch: "I confess without shame that in matters of faith I am 300 years behind our time, because I came to see, after wandering a long time in the mazes of error, that truth is *one* and indeed eternal, immutable, and that, since it is revealed by God, it is not in need of any sifting and improvement." "I preach *retrogression* to you: Return to the Word of God, which you have forsaken." "What I have voiced and sought to defend is nothing but the faith of our old Lutheran Church, which our forefathers confessed as their faith 300 years ago on Pentecost with fervent thanksgiving to God." And Delitzsch was not an isolated case. The author of this dogmatics has, as student, as pastor, and as theological professor, read with great interest and true joy several smaller monographs of Ernst Sartorius. They are *Die Religion ausserhalb der Grenzen der blossen Vernunft*, 1822; *Die Unwissenschaftlichkeit und innere Verwandtschaft des Rationalismus und Romanismus*, 1825; *Von dem religioesen Erkenntnisprinzip*, 1826. Dogmatically these essays set forth the true nature of Christian theology even more clearly than Delitzsch. And modern German theology would do well to study these products of the "awakening" which Germany experienced a hundred years ago. It should not be deterred from this study by the fact that the writers of these essays themselves, under the pressure of an unscientific theological science, forsook the truth they had confessed.

Also in this volume I have endeavored to be entirely objective. Occasionally strong terms have been used, but they seemed to be demanded by the importance of the matter under discussion. We must state as emphatically as possible that it is neither Christian nor scientific for theologians to accord equal authority to the Scriptures and their own Ego (subjective experience) as the source of Christian doctrine. This statement, of course, does not deny the possibility that a theologian's personal faith may be at variance with his published views. That I admit such a theological inconsistency is stated repeatedly also in this volume.

We American Lutherans of the "strictly confessional wing" do not have the slightest reason to exalt ourselves above others. We owe everything to God's grace. He has placed us, for instance, in the most favorable religious and theological environment. We – the second and third generation – have received our theological training under the most favorable conditions imaginable. We studied the theology of the Early Church, the Reformation, and the dogmaticians on the basis of the sources; we also learned the method and findings of modern theology from the sources. At the same time our teachers constantly admonished us not to substitute any human authority – not even Luther or the Lutheran Confessions – for the authority of Scripture. In the graduate year we were exhorted: "Let none of you enter the ministry with doubts as to the Scripturalness of any doctrine contained in our Lutheran Symbols. If anyone is still in doubt, let him frankly discuss his scruples with his teachers." When we submitted our first sermon in the first seminary year, all high-flown terminology and bombastic rhetoric were mercilessly culled out and eliminated; our professors impressed upon us that the *usus didacticus* of Scripture comes first; that our goal should be so to teach and to preach that through the proclamation of the Law in its full severity the carnally secure would be aroused out of their carnal security, and the terrified consciences would obtain the assurance of the grace of God and of salvation through the preaching of the full and free Gospel (*satisfactio vicaria*). Furthermore, we were constantly engaged in polemics against Rome, the "enthusiastic" ["*schwaermerischen*"] sects, disloyal Lutherans, Unitarians, and the antichristian lodges. As a result we were compelled to occupy ourselves continually and intensively with the Christian doctrine in our congregations as well as at pastoral conferences and synodical conventions. True, our church body is far, far from being perfect. We are not so blind as not to see our weaknesses and shortcomings. We have been and are encountering difficulties in establishing and maintaining correct practice in some congregations. We have even experienced secessions, which deeply humbled us. On the other hand, by God's grace we are certain that the doctrine proclaimed among us is the Christian faith, the faith revealed in Scripture, the faith confessed in the Lutheran Symbols, and that this doctrine demands and must be granted exclusive recognition in the Church. From this viewpoint this CHRISTIAN DOGMATICS, too, desires to be judged in both its thetical and its antithetical statements.

Soli Deo Gloria!

F. PIEPER

St. Louis, Missouri, April, 1924

Contents

Prolegomena

The Nature and Character of Theology

Holy Scripture

The Doctrine of God

The Creation of the World and of Man

Divine Providence, or the Preservation and Government of the World

Angelology

The Doctrine of Man

Prolegomena
The Nature and Character of Theology

(DE NATURA ET CONSTITUTIONE THEOLOGIAE)

1

Our Position

WE take the position that Holy Scripture, in contradistinction to all other books in the world, is God's own infallible Word and therefore the only source and norm of Christian doctrine. Prevailing conditions in the Church make it necessary for the author of a treatise on Christian dogmatics to state clearly and emphatically where he stands on the question of the source and nature of Christian Theology. Until about 1750, Protestant dogmaticians were quite generally agreed that nothing but what Scripture teaches should have a place in Christian dogmatics. But today the situation has changed completely. The representative theologians of modern Protestantism with but a few exceptions deny that Holy Scripture is by inspiration the very Word of God. Accordingly they refuse to regard and employ Holy Scripture as the sole source and standard of theology. A mass movement away from Holy Scripture has set in. The human Ego, euphemistically called the "Christian consciousness," the "regenerate I," "experience," etc., has been made the norm of theology.

This away-from-Scripture movement has created a situation in modern Protestantism which has its counterpart in Romanism. In the Roman Catholic Church the sole source and norm of doctrine is not Holy Scripture but in reality the Ego of the Pope, who "boasts that all rights exist in the shrine of his heart" (Smalc. Art., *Concordia Triglotta,* 495, 4). Modern Protestant theologians do the very same thing when they refuse to derive and determine Christian doctrine from Holy Writ and make "the pious self-consciousness of the theologizing subject" [1] the source and norm of theology. In the Papacy only so much of Scripture is regarded as binding as the Pope approves and confirms; just so modern Protestantism accepts only so much of Scripture as the pious theologizing subject has found acceptable.

This, then, is the sad situation: The overwhelming majority of modern theologians refuses to identify Scripture and the Word of God; and accordingly they do not make Scripture but their own heart the source and judge of Christian doctrine. And this false principle does not merely disturb the order of things in the Christian Church,

---

[1] A phrase employed by Nitzsch-Stephan, *Lehrbuch der ev. Dogmatik,* 3d ed., 1912, p. 13.

but turns it upside down. It is an outright revolt against the divine order.

We, on our part, stand for the supreme and sole authority of Holy Scripture. We maintain that Scripture, by virtue of the singular divine act of inspiration, is *God's own infallible Word,* "God's Book,"[2] from which alone, to the end of time, the Christian doctrine, every single part of it, is to be taken and determined. And we do not ask men to bear with us for taking this position; we insist that it is the only position one may take.

In taking this position we are following great exemplars. There is the example of Christ and His holy Apostles. They fully "identified" Scripture with the Word of God: γέγραπται, "It is written," *Scriptura sacra locuta, res decisa est.* Then there is the example of the Reformer, Luther, who faithfully followed the authoritative norm set by Christ and the Apostles. When Luther declares, "The Word they still shall let remain," he is speaking of the Holy Scriptures. Luther admonishes all readers of the Bible – and he does not exclude the theologians –: "When you read the words of Holy Scripture, you must realize that God is speaking them."[3] And he tells us theologians in drastic words that we shall become theological "monsters" (*portenta*), monsters like the Scholastics, if we depart from Scripture, for Scripture "alone is the fountain of all wisdom."[4] True, in our day men assert, at times very emphatically, that Luther took a "rather free," a "more liberal" attitude toward Scripture than did the later Lutheran theologians. This assertion, however, if made *bona fide,* ignores the historical facts. We shall have more to say on this point in the chapter on "Holy Scripture."

Modern theologians substitute their own "Christian consciousness" for Scripture as the source and norm of theology and claim that it is just this Christian consciousness and their highly developed "sense of realities," based on science, which keeps them from identifying Scripture and the Word of God. If they appeal to their "experience" and "sense of realities," so may we. With millions of Christians we experience, by the grace of God, right along that the Holy Scriptures are indeed the Word of God. And this experience is wrought by Holy Scripture itself. It was the Word itself which produced in the hearts of the Corinthian Christians the experience that the oral word

---

[2] Luther's term for Scripture, St. L. IX:1071.

[3] Sermons on Genesis, St. L. III:21.

[4] Exeg. opp. Lat. Ed. Erl. IV, 328. St. L. I:1289 f.

of the Apostles was the Word of God (1 Cor. 2:1-5). And through the same means we experience that the written Word is God's Word. Since Holy Scripture is God's Word, it does not ask the Pope or any other theologizing individual for its credentials, but through the operation of the Holy Ghost, which is inseparably connected with it, the Word creates the very faith which recognizes it as God's Word. The works of God in the realm of nature present an analogous case. They attest themselves as divine works. They do not need to be certified as such by the naturalists.

And mark well that the experience created by Scripture is a reality, while the experience of those who base their faith on anything else but Scripture and seek to derive the knowledge of the truth from their own hearts is a delusion. Scripture is the sole basis of faith, the sole source of the knowledge of the truth. Christ tells us clearly and definitely that only through His Word can men learn the truth. "If ye continue in My Word . . . ye shall know the truth," ἐν τῷ λόγῳ τῷ ἐμῷ . . . γνώσεσθε τὴν ἀλήθειαν (John 8:31-32). All who imagine that they have found the truth elsewhere are deluding themselves. If we theologians would know and teach the truth and not error, we must continue in the Word of Christ. And we have this Word of Christ in the Word of His Apostles; to the end of time we shall have it in no other way. Christ, too, states this most clearly when He says that all shall believe on Him "through their Word," διὰ λόγου αὐτῶν (John 17:20).

It will, therefore, never do for the theologian to retreat from the Word of the Apostles and Prophets and to seek refuge in the theological Ego. In theology it is absolutely necessary that the theologian disqualify his own Ego. The theologian must disregard all thoughts and opinions of his own, which come to him as unwelcome guests; he will permit only such thoughts, words, and doctrines to make their abode in his heart as are found in Christ's Word.

Some have called the complete submergence of the theologian's Ego a disgraceful "bondage" and a "letter worship." Christ, however, teaches that this is the glorious liberty which we as Christian theologians are privileged to enjoy. "If ye continue in My Word . . . ye shall know the truth, and the truth shall make you free," ἡ ἀλήθεια ἐλευθερώσει ὑμᾶς (John 8:31-32). To be held in bondage by one's own false opinions is the most disgraceful form of human slavery. And the purpose for which Christ gave us His own Word through His Apostles and Prophets is to deliver us from the bondage of our own false notions in matters pertaining to our salvation and that of all men. Therefore our slogan dare never be: "Away from Scripture!" It must remain: "Into Scripture, into Scripture as the sole source and standard of theology!" Luther thanked God for the wonderful grace that he could at once discard all thoughts that came to him "without Scripture."

Furthermore, the results show that the theology which has moved away from Scripture into the domain of the "pious faith-consciousness" is in a bad way. One of the deplorable products of this theology is its denial of the *satisfactio Christi vicaria.* Hofmann, for instance, who has been called the father of the subjective theology (*Ichtheologie*) among the conservative Lutheran theologians of the nineteenth century, has very definitely denied the substitutional atonement of Christ. And today the denial of the *satisfactio vicaria* is about as universal as the denial of the inspiration of Holy Scripture. And right here we have the real reason why Scripture is not recognized as Christ's Word. Whoever denies the *satisfactio vicaria* does not know the Christ whom Scripture shows us. (John 1:29: "Behold the Lamb of God, etc."; Matt. 20:28: "to give His life a ransom for many.") And one who does not know Christ cannot know Christ's Word. Christ Himself makes the statement: "Why do ye not understand My speech? Even because ye cannot hear My Word. . . . He that is of God heareth God's words; ye therefore hear them not because ye are not of God." (John 8:43, 47.)

We do not call into question the personal faith of every theologian who from the safe retreat of his study or lecture room attacks the *satisfactio vicaria.* Luther, too, takes cognizance of such a "felicitous inconsistency" when he says of the theologians whom Erasmus quoted against him that the language they used *inter disputandum* was not the language their heart spoke before God.[5] But our present concern is to show that there is necessarily a causal connection between the denial of Christ's vicarious satisfaction and the rejection of Scripture as the Word of God. And, conversely, the knowledge of Christ as the sinner's Savior and the recognition of Scripture as the Word of God go hand in hand. This will be shown more fully in the chapter on Scripture.

Another evil product of subjectivism (*Ichtheologie*) is doctrinal chaos and discord. There can be no unity of faith in a church body which bases its teaching on the subjective opinions of the theologians and not on the one doctrinal foundation, the Word of the Apostles and Prophets (Eph. 2:20: "And are built upon the foundation of the

[5] Opp. v. a. VII, 166. St. L. XVIII:1730.

Apostles and Prophets"). Men tell us, indeed, that doctrinal unity is possible even though the divine authority of Scripture be surrendered. They are confident that the "purely subjective vagaries" would be easily recognized as such and eliminated by "the communal spirit of the Church." But the same author who makes this statement also reports that while there is a general agreement on the new dogmatical principles, there are also "uncounted divergencies in the application of these principles, these divergencies being due to the differences in the religious individualities of the dogmaticians or in the degree of their scientific consistency." [6]

There is only one cure for this scandalous doctrinal disunity. The theologians must forsake the Ego basis and return to that foundation on which the whole Christian Church is built, namely, the Word of the Apostles and Prophets of Christ, the Word of Christ, the Holy Scriptures. That will make Christian theologians, theologians as described by Luther: "Let that be our boast that we are catechumens and pupils of the Prophets; let us simply repeat and preach what we have heard and learned from the Prophets and be sure that the Prophets have taught it. The Old Testament calls those the children of the prophets who did not produce anything of their own, anything new, as did the Prophets, but taught what they received from the Prophets." [7]

2

Religion in General

The derivation of the Latin word *religio* (whether from *relegere* or *religare*) has always been a debatable question. Latin scholars, both pagan and Christian, are not agreed on the etymology.[8] But this

---

[6] Nitzsch-Stephan, *Dogmatik*, pp. 13, IX.

[7] Exposition of the Last Words of David, 2 Sam. 23:3. St. L. III:1890. Erl. 37, 12.

[8] Cicero derives *religio* from *relegere* or *religere*. *De Nat. Deorum* 2:28: "Men who make all those things that pertain to the worship of the gods the object of diligent study and close scrutiny are called religious because of this close study (*relegendo*), just as the elegant are called thus because of their choosing (*eligendo*), the diligent because of their giving close attention (*diligendo*), the intelligent because of their reflecting (*intelligendo*)." The Christian author Lactantius, on the other hand, derives *religio* from *religare*, in the sense of to bind, place under obligation to God. *Inst. Div.* 4:28: "By this bond of piety we are so obligated and bound [*obstricti et religati*] to God that therefrom religion itself received its name and not, as Cicero would have it, from relegere." Augustine wavers between *religere* and *religare*. (Compare *De Civ. Dei* 10, 4 with *De Vera*

etymological question need not trouble us. It does not affect our religious knowledge, since the meaning of a word is in the last analysis not established by its etymology, but by its usage (*usus loquendi*).[9]

What, then, is the meaning of the term "religion" as established by common usage? There is no common usage. True, heathen and Christians use the word "religion." But the former naturally associate heathen concepts with this word, and the latter Christian concepts. The fact that both Christians and heathen use the same word does not enable us to arrive at a definition of religion comprehensive enough to include both Christianity and the non-Christian religions under one genus. Men are today eagerly searching for such a definition, but it is a futile undertaking. For the concepts which these two groups attach to the word *religion* are absolutely contradictory.

What religion means to the heathen is the exact opposite of what it means to the Christians. Since the heathen know nothing of the Gospel of Christ (1 Cor. 2:6-10: "neither have entered into the heart of man"), but have some knowledge of the Law (Rom. 1:32: "knowing the judgment of God"; Rom. 2:15: "work of the Law written in their hearts"), their entire religious thinking moves in the sphere of the Law. Religion to the heathen means man's endeavor to placate the deity through his own efforts and works, through worship, sacrifices, moral exercises, ascetic discipline, and the like. The religion of the heathen is therefore a religion of the Law.[10]

Relig. c. 55.) Most of the older Lutheran theologians prefer the derivation from *religare:* Quenstedt, *Syst.*, 1715, I. 28; Hollaz, *Examen Proleg.* II, qu. 2. Calov has a detailed account of the various derivations, *Isag.* I, 275 sqq. (See Baier-Walther, I, 14.) Modern theologians accept one or the other of the explanations mentioned or give other explanations; consult the larger encyclopedias. Voigt, *Fundamentaldogmatik*, pp. 1—30, discusses the question at great length.

[9] H. Ebeling cites the axiom: "The etymology of a word usually sheds some light on its meaning but rarely covers the meaning it has acquired in common usage." He adds: "Only in rare cases can the original meaning of a word be absolutely determined, and the historical development of the meaning and of the usage is something different from the etymology and the original meaning." (*Woerterbuch zum N. T.* III, Introd.) Luther says on this point: "It is one thing to speak grammatically, another, to talk Latin. Therefore one must consider not so much the grammatical and regular language as the common usage. . . . In Latin many words have through usage acquired a meaning foreign to the grammatical laws." (Opp. Exeg. Lat. VIII, 69.)

[10] This definition of the pagan religion has always been quite generally accepted. Karl Stange, for instance, says: "The characteristic feature of the heathen religion is that it sees no other way to reconcile God and man than through human efforts and undertakings." "The heathen religion instructs the sinner to remove the consciousness of sin by striving to make amends for his sin." (*Moderne Probleme,* 1910, p. 183 f.) Luthardt: "It is the characteristic of

In the Christian language, religion has an altogether different meaning. The Christian religion is faith in the Gospel, that is, faith in the divine message that through the substitutionary satisfaction of Christ (*satisfactio vicaria*) God is already reconciled to all men. Paul declares in the name of all Christians: "Knowing [εἰδότες] that a man is not justified by the works of the Law, but by the faith of Jesus Christ, even we have believed in Jesus Christ that we might be justified by the faith of Christ and not by the works of the Law" (Gal. 2:16). Apology: "By faith we obtain remission of sins for Christ's sake, and not for the sake of our works that precede or follow" (*Trigl.* 287, 19).

Therefore such religious bodies within external Christendom as teach that man is reconciled to God, wholly or in part, through his own works have reverted to the pagan conception of religion and are, as to their teaching, outside Christendom. "Christ is become of no effect unto you whosoever of you are justified by the Law; ye are fallen from grace" (Gal. 5:4).[11] The Large Catechism: "Therefore all who seek and wish to merit holiness [sanctification], not through the Gospel and forgiveness of sin, but by their works, have expelled and separated themselves [from this Church]" (*Trigl.* 693, 56). Meyer on Gal. 5:4: "Justification by the Law and justification for Christ's sake are *opposita* (works – faith), so that one excludes the other."

3

The Number of Religions in the World

How many essentially different religions are there in the world? The preceding chapter has already shown that there are not a thousand (Meyer, *Grosses Konversationslexikon,* 6th ed., XVI, 784), not

heathenism to base the relation of God and man altogether on a *quid pro quo* arrangement, that is, to achieve salvation through works" (*Glaubenslehre,* 1898, p. 467). Thus also Ihmels (see *Aus der Kirche,* p. 52). And the Lutheran Confessions declare: "Works become conspicuous before men. Human reason naturally admires these, and because it sees only works, and does not understand or consider faith, it dreams accordingly that these works merit remission of sins and justify. This opinion of the Law inheres by nature in men's minds; neither can it be expelled, unless we are divinely taught. *Haec opinio legis inhaeret naturaliter in animis hominum.*" (Apology, *Trigl.,* 197, 144.)

[11] Κατηργήθητε ἀπὸ τοῦ Χριστοῦ — you become severed from Chirst, have no communion with Him. Cp. Cremer sub καταργεῖν. Luther: *"Ihr habt Christum verloren, die ihr durch das Gesetz gerecht werden wollt."* You who imagine that you are justified through the Law. (R. V.: "would be justified.")

even four,[12] but only two essentially different religions: the religion of the Law, that is, the endeavor to reconcile God through man's own works, and the religion of the Gospel, that is, faith in the Lord Jesus Christ, belief wrought through the Gospel by the Holy Ghost that we have a gracious God through the reconciliation already effected by Christ, and not because of our own works (χωρὶς ἔργων νόμου).

Scripture teaches throughout that there are but two essentially different religions. This is apparent from the divine mission of the Christian religion to displace all other religions. The commission given the Church: "μαθητεύσατε πάντα τὰ ἔθνη" (Matt. 28:19), is certainly universal[13] and therefore exclusive. It denies the right of existence to all other religions because only the Christian religion has saving power. All others leave man in darkness and in the power of Satan. Christianity is designed as the world religion, for its charter reads: "to open their" [Jews and Gentiles] "eyes and to turn them from darkness to light and from the power of Satan unto God, that they may receive forgiveness of sins and inheritance among them which are sanctified by faith that is in Me," namely, in Christ (Acts 26:18).[14]

Men do not want to put Christianity and all other religions into diametrical opposition, do not want religions divided into essentially different classes. And so they are searching, particularly in these modern days, for a "general concept of religion," a definition of religion so wide and all-embracing that it expresses the nature both of the heathen religions and of the Christian religion and thus puts Christianity and the non-Christian religions into one genus, one class. But when these definitions which are supposed to cover both Chris-

---

[12] The pagan, the Jewish, the Mohammedan, the Christian religion. Some Lutheran Catechisms, too, make this fourfold division.

[13] This universality and exclusiveness of the Christian religion has already been prophesied in the Old Testament. Ps. 2:8: "I shall give Thee the heathen for Thine inheritance, and the uttermost parts of the earth for Thy possession." Gen. 49:10; Ps. 72:8; etc.; Is. 49:6. Christ the "Light to the Gentiles" and "My Salvation unto the end of the earth."

[14] Compare Luther's comments on Is. 9.2 f., where he convincingly sets forth that all intellectual and moral endeavors of the heathen and unbelieving Jews leave men in darkness and despair. VI:106 ff. — The Lange-Schaff *Commentary* on Acts 26:18 says: "The purpose of Paul's mission is stated in such a manner that it can be understood as referring only to Gentiles." But Meyer's *Commentary* is right when it points out that Paul himself declares that he was sent to the Jews and the Gentiles, v. 20, so that the phrase in v. 17: "Unto whom I now send thee" refers to "the people" (the Jews) and "the Gentiles." — Meyer, however, is in error when he states that on the basis of the "turning from the power of Satan unto God" applies primarily to the Gentiles, since Paul in Eph. 2:3-4 expressly applies to the Jews what he says of the Gentiles in vv. 1 and 2.

tianity and paganism are closely examined, it is clear that men are simply using a common name to designate entirely different things. They are playing with mere "*Verbaldefinitionen*" (Karl Hase's phrase),[15] which make heterogeneous religions appear homogeneous by the simple expedient of ignoring the essence of the Christian religion. Those who accept the basic truth of Christianity, the reconciliation of the world with God through Christ's *satisfactio vicaria,* have no use for such "verbal definitions."

Let us examine some of them. Some propose to define "religion in general" as "the personal relation of man to God." This definition is widely accepted in our day. Macpherson: "The common element in all religions is the recognition of a relation between men and God." [16] Luthardt offers the same definition: "Though the designations of what we call religion may be different, all of them express a relation to the deity of a more or less internal and personal nature. And this, I think, we may call the general concept of religion." (*Glaubenslehre,* 1898, p. 34.) But this does not make the two essentially different religions one. As soon as we get down to the concrete facts behind this abstract concept "relation," as soon as we determine the actual relation of men to God and the nature of this relation, we see at once that this "relation" is twofold.

In the case of all men who seek to placate God by their own efforts we find that their personal relation to God is one of fear, of hopelessness and despair, resulting from an evil conscience, from the consciousness of God's wrath. The reason for this unhappy relation is that the attempt to reconcile God through works is doomed to failure; for "by the deeds of the Law shall no flesh be justified in His sight" (Rom. 3:20; Gal. 2:16). No man has ever eased his evil conscience through his works; Scripture states that all Gentiles without exception "have no hope" and are "without God in the world," Eph. 2:12. ("At that time" – as long as men are Gentiles, unbelievers, they are under God's wrath.) And their many sacrifices did not in the least alter their "personal relation to God," for these sacrifices were not offered to God, but to devils (1 Cor. 10:20). In spite of all his religious endeavors the heathen's personal relation to God is and remains a relation of fear and despair. – This applies, of course, also to those within visible Christendom who seek to establish good relations with God through their own works. Gal. 3:10 applies to them no less than to

---

[15] *Hutterus Redivivus,* 10th ed., p. 11.

[16] *Christian Dogmatics,* Edinburgh 1898, p. 10.

the heathen: "As many as are of the works of the Law (οἱ ἐξ ἔργων νόμου) are under the curse."

The Christians' "personal relation to God," however, is of an entirely different nature. Through faith in the reconciliation effected by Christ they know God as their dear Father, have a good conscience, or the assurance of grace, and enjoy the hope of eternal life, which God has promised all believers in Christ. Voicing his and the Christians' experience, the Apostle Paul thus describes the status of the Christians: "Therefore being justified by faith, we have peace with God through our Lord Jesus Christ . . . and rejoice in hope of the glory of God. . . . We also joy in God through our Lord Jesus Christ, by whom we have now received the atonement." (Rom. 5:1, 2, 11.) – Even though "religion in general" is defined as "the personal relation of man to God," the fact remains that the Christian religion and the religion of the heathen differ essentially.

This applies also to the popular formula that "religion in general" is "the mode and manner of worshiping God" (*ratio Deum colendi sive Deo serviendi*). For the nature and character of Christian worship differs radically from that of the worship practiced in all other religions. Christians worship God as the God who has bestowed His grace upon them not on account of the works of the Law, but for the sake of Christ's vicarious satisfaction. They present their good works to God not as a ransom to pay for their sins, but as a *thankoffering* for the redemption that Christ has effected. Thus Paul says of himself: "The life which I now live in the flesh I live by the faith of the Son of God, who loved me and gave Himself for me" (Gal. 2:20). Only such a worship and service of God is God-pleasing and fitting. Rom. 12:1: "I beseech you, therefore, brethren, by the mercies of God that ye present your bodies a living sacrifice, holy, acceptable unto God, which is your reasonable service." To non-Christians, however, the worship and service of God is the performance of a "religious duty," dictated by the fear of God's wrath and aimed at winning God's favor by keeping the Law. But this *modus Deum colendi atque Deo serviendi*, far from pleasing God, only evokes God's wrath. "For as many as are of the works of the Law are under the curse" (Gal. 3:10).

Others again propose as the common denominator of all religions the striving of man to bring life to its highest fulfillment. Kirn actually declares: "What is common to all religions is the striving of man to establish, broaden, and perfect his own personality and the human relationships with the aid of a higher, superhuman power." [17]

---

[17] *Grundrisz*, 3d ed., p. 10.

But it is only the non-Christian religions that ask men to save and better themselves by their own striving and efforts. Because of the *opinio legis* inherent in man, the religion of all unbelievers is the religion of works. Moreover, there is in no man the "striving" after the way to life which the Christian religion offers, salvation through faith in Christ, crucified for the sins of the world. The way of grace is unknown to man. "Eye hath not seen, nor ear heard, neither have entered into the heart of man, the things which God hath prepared for them that love Him" (1 Cor. 2:9). And when the religion of grace is preached to man, it is to him "a stumbling block and foolishness" (1 Cor. 1:23). He does not strive for it but against it. "The natural man receiveth not the things of the Spirit of God, for they are foolishness unto him" (1 Cor. 2:14).

There are modern theologians who acknowledge that a general definition of religion which would put the non-Christian religions and the Christian religion into one class is not found in Holy Scripture. Thus Nitzsch-Stephan: "The Old Testament does not have a general definition of religion which would also cover paganism." "The New Testament, too, does not have such a general definition."[18]

The "older theologians," therefore, must not be faulted, but rather commended for maintaining that essentially there are but two different religions, that the Christian religion is in a class by itself, and that all non-Christian religions belong in the class of "*falsae religiones,*" from which men need to be delivered through the Christian religion. The same classification is found throughout Luther's writings. He says: "Thus the Prophet warns against the other religions which can do nothing but wear down both body and soul, and all to no avail; and the stricter they are, the more do they fill men with fear and grief and drive them to despair. And just as the woman suffering from an issue of blood only grew worse under the treatment of the doctors (Mark 5:26), so also these undertakings make the evil worse, and the hearts of men are distressed more and more. We have experienced it under the Pope, where the souls found no peace through the countless satisfactions, prayers, fasts, masses, pilgrimages, but were tortured the more. The Word alone gives true consolation, as Scripture says: 'Therefore, being justified by faith, we have peace' (Rom. 5:1). Therefore the true and only religion and the true and only worship is this, that one believes the forgiveness of sins, which God gives graciously and freely, without subsequent or previous good works, from

---

[18] *Ev. Dogmatik,* 1912, p. 112.

pure mercy, just as He freely gives the light of the sun and all other good things. Believing in this good God, who bestows His blessings graciously and freely, is the true religion and the true righteousness." (St. L. VI:540.) [19]

In this connection the objection is raised that the old theologians, including Luther, were not in a position to classify the religions correctly; if they had been acquainted with the psychology of religion, the history of religion, and the philosophy of religion – sciences which have received the proper attention only in recent times – they would not have made the distinction between true and false religions. The findings of these sciences, we are told, establish the homogeneity of the religions of the world. The examination of these "findings," however, will show that they are contrary to the facts.

What has modern psychology of religion found? It is asserted very emphatically that "the psychological phenomena" appearing in both non-Christians and Christians are "of the same kind"; and that it was because the older theologians were not cognizant of these phenomena that they found it impossible to put the Christian religion and the non-Christian religions into one genus.[20] But this asserted similarity and sameness immediately disappears when the two kinds of "psychological phenomena" are compared; what appears is a radical dissimilarity and absolute contrariety. The "psychological phenomena" in the non-Christian soul are these: the feeling of guilt, or the evil conscience, the fear of punishment and with it the inner flight from God, the endeavor to avert punishment through the performance of good works, and, owing to the futility of this endeavor, the fear of death (Heb. 2:15), the state of hopelessness and despair, Eph. 2:12: "That at that time ye were without Christ, being aliens from the commonwealth of Israel and strangers from the covenants of promise, having no hope, and without God in the world." [21] The psychology of the Christian, however, is the very opposite. The Christian has a good conscience and peace with God through faith in the

---

[19] Moritz von Engelhardt also states emphatically that there are only two religions in the world, two essentially different religions. (R. E., 2d ed., XVII, p. 773.)

[20] Thus, e. g., Kirn, *Grundrisz*, 3d ed., p. 9.

[21] Harless is right in putting into the domain of "dreams" the notion of Zwingli, Bucer, and others that an exception must be made in the case of certain individuals among the heathen. Luther against Zwingli's beatification of the pagan heroes Hercules, Theseus, Socrates, etc. St. L. XX:1767. Certain heathen themselves have confessed that their situation is hopeless. See Luthardt, *Apologetische Vortraege*, I, 2, note 11.

redemption that is in Christ Jesus (Rom. 5:1); there is no inner flight from God, but confident access to God (Rom. 5:2); no terror of death and hopelessness, but triumph over death (1 Cor. 15:55; Phil. 1:23); and rejoicing in the hope of the glory of God (Rom. 5:2). Thus the similarity of these two kinds of psychological phenomena dwindles to the fact that the Christians and the non-Christians are alike inasmuch as both have a human soul, and the psychological phenomena are alike inasmuch as both are psychological phenomena. They are alike only formally, in no sense materially. As to their motives, purpose, and nature, they are not alike, but absolutely disparate.

The student of the psychology of religion must also take note of the fact that, as Christ Himself tells us, the souls of the non-Christians are the dwelling place and workshop of the "strong man armed," who "keepeth his palace" so that "his goods are in peace" (Luke 11:21), while the souls of the Christians are inhabited, ruled, and led by the Spirit of God (1 Cor. 3:16: "Know ye not, etc."; Rom. 8:11-14: "But if the Spirit of Him, etc."). But it is impossible that the "psychological phenomena" produced by the Prince of this world should be of the same kind as those produced by the Holy Spirit. St. Paul calls upon the former Gentiles and Jews to bear witness to this when he asks them to contrast their present psychological experiences with the former (Eph. 2:2-3: "walked . . . according to, etc."; 1 Cor. 12:2: "Ye know that ye were Gentiles, etc."; Eph. 2:11-12: "Wherefore remember, etc."). — The examination of the "psychological phenomena" thus demonstrates that the Christian and the non-Christian religions, far from being of one kind, differ essentially.

A critical analysis of the Historico-Religious School brings us to the same conclusion. When we examine the "religious phenomena" in the non-Christian religions and compare them with those of the Christian religion, we find again that the non-Christian religions — the monotheistic religions no less than the polytheistic, animistic, and other forms of religion — seek to establish good relations with the deity by way of works, while the essence of the Christian religion consists in the exact opposite, in the πίστει, οὐκ ἐξ ἔργων, by faith, not of works (Rom. 3:28; Rom. 4:5; Eph. 2:8). The truly scientific historical study of religions leads to the conclusion Monier-Williams reached as the result of his comparative study of religion. He sets forth the essential difference between the Christian and the non-Christian religions in these striking words: "In the discharge of my duties for forty years as professor of Sanskrit in the University of Oxford, I have devoted as much time as any man living to the study of the Sacred Books of the

East, and I have found the one keynote, the one diapason, so to speak, of all these so-called sacred books, whether it be the Veda of the Brahmans, the Puranas of Siva and Vishnu, the Koran of the Mohammedans, the Zend-Avesta of the Parsees, the Tripitaka of the Buddhists – the *one refrain through all – salvation by works.* They all say that salvation must be purchased, must be bought with a price, and that the sole price, the sole purchase money, must be our own works and deservings. Our own holy Bible, our sacred Book of the East, *is from beginning to end a protest against this doctrine.* Good works are, indeed, enjoined upon us in that sacred Book of the East far more strongly than in any other sacred book of the East; but they are only the outcome of a grateful heart – they are only a thank-offering, the fruits of our faith. They are never the ransom money of the true disciples of Christ. Let us not shut our eyes to what is excellent and true and of good report in these sacred books, but let us teach Hindus, Buddhists, Mohammedans, that there is only one sacred Book of the East that can be their mainstay in that awful hour when they pass all alone into the unseen world. It is the sacred Book which contains that faithful saying, worthy to be received of all men, women, and children, and not merely of us Christians – that Christ Jesus came into the world to save sinners." [22]

Finally, can the homogeneity of the religions in the world be established on the basis of the philosophy of religion? Certainly not, for the religion espoused by the philosophers is the very opposite of the Christian religion; it is the religion of works. – Here we encounter the difficulty that the advocates of a philosophical conception of religion are by no means agreed as to what this term means and covers. But a very clear hint as to its meaning is given by those religious philosophers who say that the philosophical conception of religion must be kept "clean and objective," that is to say, in determining "the essence of religion" the teaching of Scripture must be entirely disregarded and its claim to be the Word of God and the source and norm of the Christian religion ruled out. The religious philosophers insist that any definition of religion must be in accord with "the human idea" of religion. They go so far as to say – and from their standpoint they are compelled to say – that there can be no philosophy of religion "in the strict sense" until the human mind has freed itself from all "religious prejudices" and is "unfettered by dogmatism and faith in an external authority," has outgrown the idea that religious

---

[22] F. Pieper, *Das Wesen des Christentums*, p. 5. [Max Mueller: wrong name.]

knowledge comes to man in a miraculous way through divine revelation, and has rid itself of the superstition that the religious dogmas are something sacred, given from above, fixed and inviolable. In a word, the prerequisite of a "genuine," "clean and objective" philosophy of religion is the repudiation of the divine authority of Holy Scripture.

True, such a purely human conception of religion is then attained. But at what a price! It is going to be the pagan conception of religion, the religion, as Max Mueller puts it, of "salvation by works." That is inevitable. Let us bear in mind that the Christian religion, the truth that mankind is reconciled to God through the *satisfactio vicaria* of Christ and that man therefore has a gracious God by faith in Christ without the deeds of the Law, is *terra incognita* to all men, including the philosophers. This truth, the essence of the Christian religion, has never "entered into the heart of man" (1 Cor. 2:9). All men, including the philosophers, know something about the Law of God. "The work of the Law" is written also in the hearts of the philosophers (Rom. 2:15). But that is the limit of their innate religious knowledge. It follows that their religious thoughts are confined within the limits of the Law and the works of man. In his dying hour Socrates directed that a cock be sacrificed to Aesculapius, and Kant, whom some consider to be the first genuine philosopher of religion, made morality, not faith in Christ's reconciliation, the essential thing in religion.[23] Luther saw through this philosophy of religion and disposed of it thus: "From this inherent knowledge originated all writings of the saner philosophers, of Aesop, Aristotle, Plato, Xenophon, Cicero, and Cato. . . . If, however, you seek for peace of conscience and for certain hope of eternal life, such philosophers are like the raven which wanders around the ark, finding no peace outside, but not looking for it within (Gen. 8:7). Paul says of the Jews, 'Israel, following after a law of righteousness, did not arrive at that law' (Rom. 9:31). The reason for this lies in the fact that the Law is like the raven; it is either the ministry of death and sin, or it produces hypocrites." (St. L. I:621.) See also VI:102 ff., on Is. 9:2. In short, any conception of religion which springs from the philosopher's "pure, objective" knowledge of religion and conforms to the "human idea" of religion is sure to by-pass the Christian religion. It will not include the Christian religion but will be diametrically opposed to it. — We repeat: There are but two religions: the religion of works, which the philos-

---

[23] M. Heinze in R. E., 3d ed., XVI, 613 f.

ophy of religion accepts as the true religion, and the religion of revelation, which the religious philosopher rejects as false.

In passing we should like to make a few remarks concerning those religious philosophers who do not indeed permit philosophy to replace the revelation of Scripture as the source of religious knowledge but still give it an important place in theology. They admit that the Christian religion transcends all human ideas of religion. But they also hold that the truths of the Christian religion, first revealed in Scripture, can also be demonstrated as true by rational processes, so that they are no longer merely believed, but also intellectually comprehended, and accepted not merely on the authority of Scripture but also on the authority of reason. That is what Anselm, "the father of Scholasticism," meant when he declared: "*Credo, ut intelligam*" (I believe in order to understand). Anselm, on the one hand, inveighs against the "modern dialecticians" (e. g., Abelard), who place knowledge before faith and consequently reject, *a priori,* what they cannot comprehend (*intelligere*). On the other hand, he demands that the Christian progress (*proficere*) from faith to knowledge. "The Christian should progress through faith to understanding and not through understanding to faith. He must not refuse to believe because he does not comprehend the matter. But when he is able to reach understanding, he is delighted." [24] The "scientific theologians" of our day take a similar position. According to them it is the business of theology to elevate faith to knowledge, to satisfy the "intellectual needs" of the Christian, or, in other words, to establish the Christian religion as the "absolute" truth, to be perceived as such independently of its revelation in Scripture.[25] This move on the part of the scientific theologians to "aggrandize" faith is in reality a form of self-aggrandizement. For at the bottom of it lies the notion that the professional "theologian," in contradistinction to other Christians, possesses already in this life a knowledge of the Christian religion which exceeds mere faith in God's revelation in the Word.

Christ does not approve of such notions. He condemns them as false when He declares that all religious truth is mediated solely by faith in His Word (John 8:31: "If ye continue in My Word"). St. Paul's judgment of the matter is that anyone, particularly a teacher of the Church, is a conceited ignoramus (τετύφωται, μηδὲν ἐπιστάμενος)

---

[24] Mansi, XX, 742.

[25] Compare Luthardt, *Dogmatik,* 10th ed., p. 5 ff., in the chapter "Die Berechtigung der Theologie." Harless had already expressed the same idea, *Theol. Encyclopaedie,* 1837, p. 27.

because he does not consent to the wholesome words of our Lord Jesus Christ (1 Tim. 6:3 f.). And the result of the theology which would elevate faith to knowledge is, as our old Lutheran theologians drastically express it, a monstrosity, a *mixtum compositum* of theology and philosophy, like unto "the biform race of the Centaurs." (Quenstedt, I, 57.) Applying this theological method, Anselm denied that Christ's fulfillment of the Law, the *obedientia activa,* was of a vicarious nature (see "Theories of Atonement"), and later on Abelard eliminated the *satisfactio vicaria* entirely.[26] And it is notorious that among modern theologians the attempt to convert faith into knowledge has resulted in a quite general denial of the *satisfactio vicaria* and of the sole authority of Scripture. This matter will receive further consideration in several of the following sections, particularly in the chapter "Theology and Science."

4

The Sources of the Two Existing Religions

As there are but two religions, of essentially different content, the religion of the Law, or of man's own works, and the religion of the Gospel, or of faith in Christ, so there are but two principles of cognition (*principia cognoscendi*) from which these religions are derived – two essentially different sources.

The religion of the Law, practiced in various forms outside and within visible Christendom, is of human origin. It is a "man-made religion." That is the clear teaching of Scripture. Let us present this matter more fully under three heads. First, Scripture teaches that even after the Fall men still have a knowledge of the divine Law. They "know the judgment of God" (Rom. 1:32).[27] The "work of the Law," that is, what God demands, is "written in their hearts"; though they do not have the Law as written in Scripture ("which have not the Law . . . are a Law unto themselves," Rom. 2:14 f.). Apology: "Human reason naturally understands, in some way, the Law, for it has the same judgment divinely written in the mind" (*Trigl.* 121, 7). – Secondly, the heathen have an evil conscience because of their transgressions of the divine Law. They know "that they which commit such things" – the Apostle is speaking of the sins of the pagans –

---

26 R. Seeberg, too, points out that Anselm and Abelard operate on the same rationalistic basis. Both give *ratio* a place beside faith. *Dogmengeschichte* II, 41 f.

27 δικαίωμα here means God's legislative and judicial righteousness. Cf. on the passage Stoeckhardt, Meyer, Philippi.

"are worthy of death," of eternal damnation (Rom. 1:32).[28] And so, in the third place, they propose to reconcile the Deity through "good works," moral endeavors, self-devised worship and sacrifices, etc. Though they know little about God and inscribe on the altar: "To the Unknown God" (Acts 17:23), they feel sure that they can win God's favor by observing the Law. They know of no other way. "This opinion of the Law" (that works obtain grace) "inheres by nature in men's minds; neither can it be expelled unless we are divinely taught." Thus the Apology (*Trigl.* 197, 144). Again: "Thus the world judges of all works that they are a propitiation by which God is appeased" (*Trigl.* 179, 91).

The religion of the Law is the religion of the flesh. The Apostle Paul expressly calls it that when he reminds the Galatians, who sought to obtain justification through the Law: "Having begun in the Spirit, are ye now made perfect by the flesh?" (Gal. 3:3.) The religion of the Law is the product of the unregenerate, the natural mind. Luther on Gal. 3:3: "Paul setteth here the spirit against the flesh. He calleth not the flesh (as I have said before) fleshly lust, beastly passions, or sensual appetites; for he entreateth not here of lust and such other fleshly desires, but of forgiveness of sins, of justifying the conscience, of obtaining righteousness before God, of delivery from the Law, sin, and death. . . . *Flesh* therefore is here taken for the very righteousness and wisdom of the flesh, and the judgment of reason, which seeketh to be justified by the Law." (St. L. IX:288 f.) Scripture thus clearly teaches that every type of religion which in any way directs men to gain God's grace through human endeavors and accomplishments is not wisdom of God, but wisdom from below, man-made religion.

The religion of the Gospel, on the contrary, is not of man, but of God. It deals with things that "have not entered into the heart of man" (1 Cor. 2:9). The plan of salvation, according to which the Son of God became incarnate and by His work reconciled mankind with God, so that men are now saved without works of their own (χωρὶς ἔργων νόμου, Rom. 3:28), by faith in the work of Christ, was conceived in the eternal counsel of God. The Christian religion, the religion of grace, is very truth, the wisdom of God, and men know of it only

[28] Stoeckhardt on our passage: "Hofmann takes *death* to mean the death penalty inflicted by the government. Such an interpretation is altogether foreign to the text." Philippi refers to the heathen teaching on Hades and its punishments and concludes: "Accordingly θάνατος in our passage should be interpreted as meaning the *mors aeterna.*"

through God's revelation in the Word. Not even the intelligentsia, "the princes of this world," can conceive the idea that God forgives the sins of men not because of their own works, but for the sake of the crucified Christ (1 Cor. 2:8). In short, the religion of grace is in no sense a human product. It is "God-made," and the only source of this knowledge until the end of time is God's revelation in the Word – in the written Word of the Apostles and Prophets. (Rom. 16:25 f.; Eph. 2:20; 1 John 1:1-4.)

Accordingly, various doctrinal systems in visible Christendom which say that God's grace is obtained wholly or in part through human works and "moral achievements" (Pelagianism, Semi-Pelagianism, synergism) are of human origin. They are outside the sphere of the divine religion, revealed in God's *Word,* and must be classified as religions devised by men. The Christian Church would have been spared much confusion, strife, and dissension if the proponents of these theories had always plainly supplied them with the proper trademark: "Man-made."

How old is the Gospel religion? It was revealed immediately after the Fall in the promise that the Seed of the Woman would crush the head of the Serpent (Gen. 3:15).[29] All the Old Testament Prophets taught it *unisono,* and all the children of God in the days of the Old Testament believed it *unanimiter,* as Peter testifies: "To Him give all the Prophets witness that through His name whosoever believeth in Him shall receive remission of sins" (Acts 10:43). Paul, too, declares that the righteousness which is obtained χωρὶς νόμου, "without the Law," by faith in Christ, was witnessed "by the Law and the Prophets" (Rom. 3:21). And he brings the historical proof for this in Romans, Chapter Four. – Luther's writings abound in statements that men derive their knowledge of divine things either from the Law or from the Gospel, that thus there are but two principles of religious knowledge.[30]

5

The Cause of the Divisions Within Visible Christendom

It is nothing strange that the non-Christian religions, which seek to reconcile God through human works, appear in well-nigh countless and diverse forms. For these works do not bring peace to the con-

---

29 Cf. Luther, St. L. I:230 ff., III:650 ff.

30 Luther discusses this matter at greater length in St. L. VII:1704–1712.

science, and the inevitable result is that men keep on devising new works and new forms of worship. That accounts, say the Lutheran Confessions, for the multiplicity and diversity of the religions of the Law. The Apology states: "And because no works pacify the conscience, new works, in addition to God's commands, were from time to time devised" (*Trigl.* 177, 87).

But it is a strange thing that diversities and divisions should appear within Christendom. For the Christian Church has only one principle of cognition, namely, the Word of Christ, given by Christ to the Church through His Apostles and Prophets,[31] only one source of the saving knowledge, therefore only one doctrine, one faith. Moreover, this Word of Christ rejects and condemns in the strongest terms the causes of divisions, namely, the religion of works (Gal. 2:16: "By the works of the Law shall no flesh be justified"; 3:10: "As many as are of the works of the Law are under the curse"), and, on the other hand, teaches most clearly that remission of sins is obtained without the works of the Law, by faith in Christ, whose redemptive work has fully and completely reconciled God with the world (Rom. 3:28: "A man is justified by faith without the deeds of the Law"; Gal. 2:16: "Knowing that a man is not justified by the works of the Law, but by the faith of Jesus Christ"). Furthermore, all Christians experience that faith in the reconciliation accomplished by Christ brings peace to the conscience. "Therefore being justified by faith, we have peace with God through our Lord Jesus Christ" (Rom. 5:1). "We are complete in Him [Christ]" (Col. 2:10). Christians therefore have no need to look about for other means of reconciliation. Finally, Scripture expressly prohibits factions within the Church ("that there be no divisions among you," 1 Cor. 1:10). In view of this, one would certainly expect to find the Christian Church to be free from divisions and factions.

History, however, presents an entirely different picture. Already in the days of the Apostles the Church was troubled with divisions.

What, then, causes the divisions in the Church? They are not the result of climatic influences, as some say, nor of racial differences, as others say.[32] They are due solely to the fact that men arose within

---

[31] John 8:31 f.: "If ye continue in My Word, then are ye My disciples indeed, and ye shall know the truth." – John 17:20: "Which shall believe on Me through their Word." All who come to faith in Christ are brought to faith, now and to the Last Day, through the Word of the Apostles. See also Eph. 2:20: "Ye are built upon the foundation of the Apostles and Prophets."

[32] See on this Nitzsch-Stephan, *Ev. Dogmatik*, p. 270; Hase, *Hutterus Redivivus*, 10th ed., p. 12, note 1.

the Church and gained a following who did not continue in the Word of Christ's Apostles and Prophets, but proclaimed their own word and as a natural consequence impaired, or even wiped out, the *differentia specifica* of the Christian religion, justification by faith, without the deeds of the Law. Divisions in the Apostolic Church arose because men refused to recognize the Word of the Apostles as the Word of God and offered the Church in place of the Word of God their own human notions. That is clearly stated by Paul in Rom. 16:17: "Now I beseech you, brethren, mark them which cause divisions and offenses contrary to the doctrine which ye have learned; and avoid them." In the church at Corinth men engaged in the same business. They regarded themselves as "prophets" and "spiritual," but in spite of this, rather for this very reason, they denied the divine authority of the Word of the Apostles and thus compelled Paul to utter the strong words: "If any man think himself to be a prophet, or spiritual, let him acknowledge that the things that I write unto you are the commandments of the Lord" (1 Cor. 14:37). At the same time these men made it their business to supplant the doctrine of salvation by grace with the religion of works. That is evident from the words in which Paul expresses his amazement over the apostasy of the Galatians: "I marvel that ye are so soon removed from Him that called you into the grace of Christ unto another Gospel" (Gal. 1:6), and from his sharp polemics against the advocates of the gospel of works: "Though we, or an angel from heaven, preach any other gospel unto you . . . let him be accursed" (1:8), and: "I would they were even cut off which trouble you" (5:12). The attempt to get rid of the Word of the Apostles and of the central teaching of Christianity, the doctrine of salvation by grace, has been and still is the sole cause of the divisions in the Christian Church.

This will become evident as we examine the formal and the material principle of the major divisions that disrupt the Church today, the Roman Catholic body, the Reformed communions, the factions within the Lutheran Church, and the modernistic schools. — We here submit in a condensed form what will be more fully presented when we discuss the individual doctrines in detail, thetically and antithetically.[33]

1. The *Roman Catholic* body, the largest in Christendom, acknowl-

---

[33] The point under discussion has been treated in recent textbooks on dogmatics and monographs under titles such as: "Romanismus und Protestantismus," "Der Lutherische und der Reformierte Protestantismus," "Fortbildung des Luthertums," "Moderne Theologie des Alten Glaubens," "Irenic Theology," etc.

edges in principle the divine authority of Scripture. But it sets Scripture aside by insisting that its sense can be ascertained only through the interpretation given by the Roman Catholic Church, the *sancta mater ecclesia*, that is, in the last analysis, by the Pope. "It (the holy and sacred synod) decrees that no one, relying on his own skill, shall in matters of faith and of morals pertaining to the edification of Christian doctrine, wresting the sacred Scripture to his own senses, presume to interpret the Sacred Scripture contrary to that sense which holy mother church, whose it is to judge of the true sense and interpretation of Holy Scripture, hath held and doth hold." (*Tridentinum*, Sess. IV, Decretum de editione et usu sacrorum librorum.) The inevitable result of thus interpreting Scripture according to the sense of "holy mother church," that is to say, of the Pope, is that the Romish Church expressly and emphatically anathematizes the central doctrine of the Christian religion, the doctrine of justification by faith in the Gospel of grace without the deeds of the Law.[34] There are indeed Christians among Roman Catholics, for there are those who in spiritual distress cast aside their good works and, in spite of the interdict of "the Church," put their trust solely in the grace of God in Christ and are true members of the Holy Christian Church.[35] Nevertheless, the fact remains that the Roman Catholic Church *as such* is a separate body destructive of true Christianity, because, in the first place, its formal principle is unchristian. By making the decrees of *sancta mater ecclesia*, that is, of the Pope, the source and basis of religious knowledge it suppresses the Word of Christ, the Word of the Prophets and Apostles, Holy Scripture. Luther gives an exact de-

---

[34] *Tridentinum*, Sess. VI, Can. 11, 12, 20: "If any one saith, that men are justified, either by the sole imputation of the justice of Christ, or by the sole remission of sins, to the exclusion of the grace and the charity which is poured forth in their hearts by the Holy Ghost (Rom. 5:5) and is inherent in them; or even that grace, whereby we are justified, is only the favor of God; let him be anathema. – If any one saith, that justifying faith is nothing else but confidence in the divine mercy which remits sins for Christ's sake; or that this confidence alone is that whereby we are justified; let him be anathema. – If any one saith, that the man who is justified and how perfect soever, is not bound to observe the commandments of God and of the Church, but only to believe; as if indeed the Gospel were a bare and absolute promise of eternal life, without the condition of observing the commandments; let him be anathema." For a further discussion, see Vol. II, "The Papacy and the Doctrine of Justification."

[35] Apology: "Therefore, even though Popes, or some theologians, and monks in the Church have taught us to seek remission of sins, grace, and righteousness through our own works, and to invent new forms of worship, which have obscured the office of Christ, and have made out of Christ not a Propitiator and Justifier, but only a Legislator, nevertheless the knowledge of Christ has always remained with some godly persons" (*Trigl.* 225, 271).

scription of the situation when he says in the Smalcald Articles: "The Pope boasts that all rights exist in the shrine of his heart, and whatever he decides and commands with (in) his church is spirit and right, even though it is above and contrary to Scripture and the spoken Word" (*Trigl.* 495, 4). Secondly, its material principle is unchristian, for in thus setting aside Scripture, Roman Catholicism in fact proscribes the Christian doctrine of grace. The whole colossal machinery of Romanism is geared to establish the absolute authority of the Pope and to serve the religion of works. Remove these two factors, and the Romish group would disappear from visible Christendom.

2. The *Reformed denominations* likewise acknowledge in principle the divine authority of the divinely inspired Scriptures. The inspiration of Scripture has found valiant champions among the Reformed theologians not only in the past, but also today.[36] But in practice Reformed theology forsakes the Scripture principle. It has become the fashion to say that the difference between the Reformed and the Lutheran Church consists in this, that the Reformed Church "more exclusively" makes Scripture the source of the Christian doctrine, while the Lutheran Church, being more deeply "rooted in the past" and of a more "conservative" nature, accepts not only Scripture, but also tradition as authoritative.[37] But this is not in accord with the facts. The history of dogma tells this story: In those doctrines in which it differs from the Lutheran Church and for the sake of which it has established itself as a separate body within visible Christendom, the Reformed Church, as far as it follows in the footsteps of Zwingli and Calvin, sets aside the Scripture principle and operates instead with rationalistic axioms. The Reformed theologians frankly state that reason must have a voice in determining Christian doctrine.

a. Rationalistic considerations have produced, first, the Reformed doctrine of the means of grace. While Scripture teaches that God offers and gives the forgiveness of sins which Christ gained and creates and sustains faith through external means ordained by Him (the Word of the Gospel, Baptism, and the Lord's Supper),[38] Zwingli and Calvin argue that it does not befit the Holy Ghost to make use of external means for the revelation and operation of His grace, that He does not need such external means, and that He does not, in fact, use them

---

[36] Recent theologians: Gaussen, Kuyper, Boehl, Shedd, Hodge.

[37] Statements characterizing the Lutheran and the Reformed Church in Luthardt, *Dogmatik*, 11th ed., p. 26 f.

[38] See the chapters: "The Means of Grace in General" and "All Means of Grace Have the Same Purpose and the Same Effect," in Vol. III.

where His saving grace operates.[39] Modern Calvinists take the same position. And this "holy spirit," which severed the Holy Spirit from the means of grace, caused the division in the Protestant camp at the time of the Reformation; it raised the charge against Luther that he did not understand the Gospel, for by his clinging to the means of grace he showed that he was still in "the flesh." [40]

Separating the revelation and operation of grace from the means of grace is, in effect, a reversion to the Romish "infused grace" (*gratia infusa*) and therefore a defection from the Christian doctrine of justification. For when men set aside the external means of grace, they can no longer base their confidence in God on God's gracious disposition (*favor Dei propter Christum*), i. e., on the forgiveness of sin for Christ's sake, which the grace of God offers in the Gospel promise and which is to be believed on the basis of this objective promise and offer; they necessarily base their confidence in God on an inward transformation, illumination, and renewal, which allegedly is effected by an immediate operation. This reduces grace in the final analysis to *a good quality* in man. Since the Holy Ghost will not deal in such immediate operations, all those who follow Zwingli's and Calvin's instructions and seek an immediate illumination and renewal necessarily substitute for the genuine operation of the Spirit their own human product. – Luther said repeatedly: "Papist and 'enthusiast' are one." That judgment was not an outburst of "the immoderate polemics in the 16th century," but is based on facts.

The fact that despite the Reformed repudiation of the means of grace many Christians are found in the Reformed denominations is due to an inconsistency, to which Luther points frequently, particularly in the Smalcald Articles. If the Reformed would translate their theory concerning the supposed immediate operation of the Spirit into prac-

---

39 Thus Zwingli, *Fidei Ratio*. Niemeyer, p. 24: "The Spirit needs no guide or vehicle, for He is Himself the power and the bearer by whom everything is borne, who needs not to be borne." So also Calvin, *Inst.* IV, ch. 14, 17. "We get rid of that fiction by which the cause of justification and the power of the Holy Spirit are included in the elements as vessels and vehicles." *Geneva Catechism* (Niemeyer, p. 161): "It does not inhere in the visible signs, so that we should have to seek salvation there." Charles Hodge (*Syst. Theol.* II, 684): "Efficacious grace acts immediately." Boehl, too, teaches that the Word is efficacious only in those who have already been regenerated, through the immediate operation of the Spirit. (*Dogmatik*, p. 447 f.)

40 Zwingli's answer to Luther's "That these words, etc.," reprinted in the St. L. ed. of Luther's Works, XX:1131 f.: "I [Zwingli] am going to show you [Luther] that you have never grasped the vast and marvelous glory of the Gospel: and if you have once known it, you have forgotten it."

tice, they would have to refrain from proclaiming the Gospel by the printed or spoken word and keep silence lest they interfere with the operation of the Spirit. But they refuse to do this, and in as far as they teach the Gospel of the Savior crucified for the sins of the world, they give the Holy Ghost the opportunity to create and sustain faith in Christ, not without the Word and alongside the Word, but through the Word, mediately.

b. Again, when the Reformed deny the real presence of Christ's body and blood in the Lord's Supper, they are repudiating the Word of God because of rationalistic considerations. They admit, directly and indirectly, that the Scriptural statements on the Lord's Supper indicate *prima facie* not the absence, but the presence of the body and blood of Christ. But, they say, the words of institution must be so interpreted that they agree with "faith." And when they are asked what this "faith" is which must interpret Scripture, the Reformed theologians of all times do not adduce Scripture but a rationalistic axiom. They insist that since every human body occupies space and is visible, the body of Christ, too, can have only a visible and local mode of presence (*visibilis et localis praesentia*); else it would not be a true human body. The presence of Christ's human nature, says Calvin, cannot extend beyond the natural dimensions of the body of Christ (*dimensio corporis, mensura corporis*), beyond about six feet, and consequently cannot suffice for the simultaneous celebration of the Lord's Supper at many places in the world. Carlstadt and Zwingli, and Calvin, too, deny the Real Presence, clearly taught in the words of institution, on the strength of the rationalistic canon that wherever the body of Christ is, it must necessarily occupy space and be visible.[41] The Reformed denial of the Real Presence is thus based not on what Scripture says, but on what reason dictates; a human judgment counts more than the Scripture statement. Calvin accepts Luther's definition of the *status controversiae:* "Their whole case rests on this, that Christ's body must be at one place only, in a local and tangible

---

41 Calvin, *Inst.* IV, ch. 17, 19: "The presence of Christ in the Supper must be such as neither divests Him of His just dimensions nor dissevers Him by differences of place, nor makes Him occupy a variety of places at the same time." 29: "The essential properties of the body are to be confined by space, to have dimension and form." Calvin adds: "Have done, then, with that foolish fiction which affixes the minds of men, as well as Christ, to bread." In the same paragraph Calvin asserts that John 20:19 cannot mean that Christ with His body "penetrated through solid matter" – an opening had to be provided – and that Luke 24:31 does not say that Christ became invisible; it simply says that "their eyes were holden."

manner." The motive for the Reformed denial of the Real Presence is fully discussed in Vol. III.

c. The false principle, both the formal and the material, of the Calvinistic theologians is evident particularly in their answer to the question: Is the grace of God in Christ universal (*gratia universalis*) or particular (*gratia particularis*)? The Calvinistic Reformed will not permit Scripture to answer the question, though in many passages it teaches the *gratia universalis* (John 1:29; 3:16 ff.; 1 John 2:2; 1 Tim. 2:4-6, etc.); they find the answer in the historical "result" or the historical "experience." Hodge: "We must assume that the *result* is the interpretation of the purposes of God" (*Syst. Theol.* II, 323).[42] The Reformed argue: Since actually not all men are saved, we must conclude that Christ's merit and God's will of grace do *not* extend over all men; to say that God wills something (the salvation of all men) which is only partially accomplished is to make sport of God's wisdom, power, and majesty.[43] The rationalistic conclusions nullify the declarations of Scripture.

In a very pronounced way Calvin rejects the Scripture principle in favor of speculative rationalism when he denies that Matt. 23:37, Luke 19:41 ff., Is. 65:2, and Rom. 10:21 prove that God seriously wills the salvation of all. It would be ridiculous, he contends, to take seriously the plaint and tears of Jesus and the "hands stretched forth" to the people and thus to "transfer to God what is peculiar to man."

---

[42] So also Calvin, *Inst.*, III, ch. 24, 17, 15: "However universal the promises of salvation may be, there is no discrepancy between them and the predestination of the reprobate, provided we attend to their *effect*. – Experience teaches that He does not will the repentance of those whom He externally calls, in such a manner as to affect all their hearts."

[43] Calvin argues against the universality of God's gracious will on the basis of God's omnipotence: "If they obstinately insist on its being said that God is merciful to all, I will oppose to them what is elsewhere asserted, that our God is in the heavens, where He hath done whatsoever He hath pleased, Ps. 115:3" (*Inst.* III, ch. 24, par. 16). Hodge: "It cannot be supposed that God intends what is never accomplished – that He adopts means for an end which is never to be attained. This cannot be affirmed of any rational being who has the wisdom and power to secure the execution of his purposes. Much less can it be said of Him whose power and wisdom are infinite." (*Loc. cit.*) – It should be noted here that in quoting Ps. 115:3 Calvin takes the liberty to change the wording. The words: "But our God is in the heavens; He hath done whatsoever He hath pleased" set forth the omnipotence of God in contrast to the impotence of the idols of the pagans, as set forth in the next verse: "Their idols are silver and gold, the work of men's hands." Calvin's insertion of the *ubi:* "Our God is in the heavens, *ubi faciat quaecumque velit*" (where He does whatsoever He pleases) changes the meaning completely. It makes the text say that God wills and does otherwise in heaven than on earth.

(*Inst.* III, ch. 24, 17.) It will be seen that Calvin is so obsessed with his rationalistic speculations about the absolute God that he becomes the bitter enemy of all Scripture statements that teach universal grace.

The inevitable result of eliminating the *gratia universalis* is that the Gospel is, in effect, paralyzed. The stricken sinner does not believe in the Savior of sinners if he is really convinced that Jesus is the Savior of only some of the sinners (*gratia particularis*). The children of God within the Calvinistic Reformed Church rejoice in the salvation gained for them by Christ only because they never believed in the *gratia particularis;* or if they have accepted it intellectually, they comfort themselves in the *terrores conscientiae* with the *gratia universalis.* – When Reformed theologians, contrary to their own principle, direct the despairing sinner to the *gratia universalis,* they themselves condemn their partisanship for the *gratia particularis.*[44]

The Arminian section of the Reformed Church makes much of the *gratia universalis,* but does so at the expense of the *sola gratia.* Arminianism stands for a human co-operation in conversion.[45] But in thus "limiting" the *sola gratia* it has abandoned the Scripture principle, for Scripture ascribes the conversion and salvation of man to the monergism of God (Eph. 1:19: "who believe according to the working of His mighty power"; Phil. 1:29; 1 Cor. 2:14; 1:23).[46] – At the same time this Arminian faith, which is in part the work of man, strikes at the heart of the Christian doctrine of justification χωρὶς νόμου, οὐκ ἐξ ἔργων, without the Law, not by works. When Erasmus declared that the *facultas se applicandi ad gratiam,* the co-operation of man, is needed to bring about conversion, Luther said: "Du bist mir an die Kehle gefahren" ("*iugulum petisti,*" "you have me by the throat"), "You have attacked the vital part at once" (St. Louis XVIII:1967. Opp. v. a. VII, 367).

3. This criticism applies, of course, also to the synergistic Lutherans. Synergism teaches that man's conversion and salvation depend on his "right conduct," "self-assertion," "self-determination," "lesser guilt in comparison with others," etc. – that is the same as the Ar-

---

44 Schneckenburger shows in detail how in his pastoral practice the Calvinist finds himself operating with the Lutheran *gratia universalis.* (*Vergleichende Darstellung d. luth. u. ref. Lehrbegriffs* I, 260 ff. See Pieper, III, 201.)

45 The *Apol. Conf. Remonstr.* declares (p. 162) that the divine grace working towards conversion "cannot accomplish anything without the cooperation of man's free will and therefore its success depends on the free will."

46 This is presented in detail under "Conversion" in Vol. II and "Final Perseverance" in Vol. III.

minian "co-operation" – and thus blocks the entrance of saving faith into the heart. Faith finds entrance only in crushed hearts,[47] and it is the very nature of the Christian faith to rest on the *sola gratia.*[48] A consistent synergist cannot be a believer. Those synergists who really believe in the *sola gratia* do so because in their private prayer life they do not believe their own doctrine. Frank is certainly right in maintaining that Melanchthon never really believed his synergistic theory.[49] But that cannot undo the evil effects of his synergistic teaching. From his day to the present, synergism has been creating factions and divisions in the Christian Church.

4. At the present time the dissensions and divisions outside and within the visible Church are due to the brazen denial of the divine authority of Scripture on the part of most of the leading theologians. Denying that Holy Scripture is God's own infallible Word, these men naturally discard Scripture as the sole source and norm of the Christian doctrine, and thus they *eo ipso* do away with the principle of unity in the Christian Church. The unity of the Church is a unity in the truth, but only those know the truth who continue in the Word of Christ (John 8:31-32). And as Paul, Christ's Apostle, assures us, he who does not consent to the wholesome words of our Lord Jesus Christ "is proud, knowing nothing" (1 Tim. 6:3 ff.). But our modern theologians, the so-called "positive" theologians no less than the liberals, refuse to accept Scripture as the principle of knowledge, the source and norm of doctrine (formal principle), substituting for it the "experience," or "Erlebnis," of the "theologizing individual," also called "faith consciousness," "Christian consciousness," the "regenerate I," etc. Concerning this theological method there is great unanimity. But it cannot produce unity in the Christian Church. – Nitzsch-Stephan declares that no one bases his dogmatics on the *norma normans,* the Bible, as was the fashion among the Old Protestants

---

47 "As long as man has any persuasion that he can do even the least thing toward his own salvation, he retains a confidence in himself, he does not humble himself before God, but proposes to himself some place, some time, or some work, whereby he may at length attain unto salvation" (Luther, St. L. XVIII:1715).

48 Apology: "As often as we speak of faith, we wish an object to be understood, namely, the promised mercy" (*Trigl.* 136, 55).

49 *Theologie der Konkordienformel* I, 135. In *De Servo Arbitrio* Luther mentions certain advocates of free will who, when dealing with God, forget their synergistic theories. He says (St. L. XVIII:1730): "When they are engaged in words and disputations, they are one thing, but another when they come to experience and practice. . . . When they approach God, either to pray or to do, they approach Him utterly forgetful of their own 'free will' and, despairing of themselves, cry unto Him for pure grace only." See also Mead, *Irenic Theology,* p. 163.

(*Ev. Dogm.*, p. 15). But there the unanimity ends. "In the application of these principles," the same writer tells us (*op. cit.*, p. IX), "there are uncounted divergencies, these divergencies being due to the differences in the religious individualities of the dogmaticians or in the degree of their scientific consistency." But at one point the moderns meet again. As with great unanimity they have discarded Holy Scripture as the only source and standard of the Christian doctrine, so with great unanimity they repudiate the Scripture doctrine of the *satisfactio vicaria* and so necessarily also the Scripture doctrine of justification by faith, "without the deeds of the Law" (οὐκ ἐξ ἔργων).[50]

The question arises here whether the Christian faith can exist side by side with the refusal to accept Scripture as the Word of God and with the denial of the *satisfactio vicaria.* The answer is: No – not if men reduce their teaching to practice. If men refuse to believe Christ and His Apostles when they declare that Scripture is the inviolable Word of God (John 10:35: "The Scripture cannot be broken"; 2 Tim. 3:16: "All Scripture is given by inspiration of God"; 1 Pet. 1:10-12), will they not also, to remain consistent, refuse to believe what Christ and His Apostles teach concerning the Saviorship of Christ (John 3:16; Matt. 20:28: "give His life a ransom for many"; John 1:29; 1 John 1:9; Rom. 3:28; etc.)? It can happen, however, and it has happened, that a person who in theory has denied the inspiration of Scripture and the vicarious satisfaction of Christ does by faith accept the remission of his sins in the hour of affliction and in the agony of death – basing his faith on the Word of Scripture and on the vicarious atonement of Christ. But thereby he relinquishes and disavows his former sectarian belief, by which he had separated himself from the Church, and returns to the one faith of the Christian Church, which continues in the words of Christ and knows of no other foundation for the assurance of God's grace than the redemption (ἀπολύτρωσις) wrought by Christ Jesus.

As our examination of the major divisions in the Church has shown, there is but one cause of the divisions within the visible Church: the refusal to abide by Scripture as the only source and standard of Christian doctrine and, in consequence of this, substitution, in one form or another, of the doctrine of works for the Christian doctrine of salvation by grace.

At this point we must answer the question whether the Lutheran Church should be numbered with the "divisions," "factions," "sects." There are those who insist that the Lutheran Church is a sect like

---

[50] Thieme in R. E., 3d ed., XXI, 120.

all the others. The discussion of this matter will have no point until we are agreed on the meaning of the terms "Lutheran Church" and "sect." By "Lutheran Church" we do not mean all church bodies that call themselves Lutheran, but only those that actually teach and confess the Lutheran doctrine as it is taught and confessed in the Confessions of the Lutheran Church. And by "sects" we mean church bodies which have established themselves as separate organizations on the basis of unscriptural doctrines. The terms being thus understood, the Lutheran Church is certainly not a sect, since it does not stand for doctrines of its own, but simply confesses and teaches that which according to God's will and order all Christians should confess and teach. This is the ecumenical character of the Church of the Reformation. On the one hand, the Lutheran Church does not set itself up as the *una sancta,* but acknowledges that there are children of God also in those denominations in which, besides the doctrines of men, enough Gospel is still proclaimed to produce faith in Christ as the only Redeemer. On the other hand, the Lutheran Church claims to be the Church of the pure doctrine, i. e., it claims that its doctrine agrees in all points with Holy Scripture and should according to God's will be believed and accepted by all. The proof for this ecumenical character of the Lutheran Church, of course, must and can be furnished by way of induction, by submitting every one of its doctrines to the test of Scripture. Luther followed that method. In his confession of faith of 1529 he says: "If after my death anyone should say: 'If Dr. Luther were living now, he would hold this or that article differently, for he did not sufficiently consider it,' against this I say now as then, and then as now, that, by God's grace, I have most diligently compared all these articles with the Scriptures time and again and often gone over them, and would defend them as confidently as I have now defended the Sacrament of the Altar." [51]

We should here like to call attention to the fact that the Lutheran Church has proved its unwavering adherence to the *sola Scriptura* in a matter in which the great majority of theologians from Augustine down to our day have under the stress of rationalistic considerations abandoned the Scripture principle. We refer to what is known as the *crux theologorum.* The question: Are you willing to maintain both the *universalis gratia* and the *sola gratia?* forces men to disclose whether Scripture or reason rules their theology. The Calvinists cannot pass this final examination. They insist, as we have seen, that if the

---

[51] St. L. XX:1094 ff. Erlangen 30, 363 ff. F. C., *Trigl.,* 981 f.

sola gratia is to be saved, the *gratia universalis* must be sacrificed. And the synergists, too, fail in this final test; they demand that in order to save the *gratia universalis,* the *sola gratia* must be surrendered. Both, says reason, cannot be maintained at the same time. The Lutheran Church is fully conscious of the difficulty which the human mind here encounters. But our Church maintains both the *universalis gratia* and the *sola gratia,* fully and without any restrictions, because both doctrines are clearly revealed in Scripture. It leaves the intellectual difficulty unsolved for the present; it awaits the solution in yonder life.[52]

The divisions and factions in the Christian Church are the result of a departure from Scripture doctrine. It is only natural to seek the underlying causes for this abnormal condition. Modern theologians of all shades not only assume a number of noble motives, such as the quest for truth, the scientific spirit, for the deviation from the Scripture doctrine and the incident formation of sects, but even assert that "these divergent trends have been designed by God and are beneficial to the Church." But Scripture states the very opposite and states it most emphatically: that the motives actuating those responsible for this abnormal phenomenon in Christendom are carnal, not noble. As it often and earnestly warns against departing from the doctrine of the Apostles, which is Christ's own doctrine (Rom. 16:17: "Mark them which cause divisions . . . and avoid them"), so it spares no words in condemning the motives behind this sorry business. Those who depart from the teaching of Christ and the Apostles are actuated by self-interest (Rom. 16:18: "They that are such serve not our Lord Jesus Christ, but their own belly") as it shows itself in self-conceit (1 Tim. 6:3 f.: "He is proud"; R. V., "puffed up"); greed for honor (John 5:44); refusal to bear the cross (Gal. 6:12); envy (Matt. 27:18). Nor is it complimentary when Scripture uses the term "ignorance" in this connection (1 Tim. 6:4: "knowing nothing"; John 16:3; 1 Tim. 1:13). – Church history confirms this judgment of Scripture. Novatian would hardly have originated Novatianism and the Novatian schism if he, and not Cornelius, had been elected bishop of Rome.[53] And one reason why Zwingli claimed

[52] The Formula of Concord, *Trigl.,* 1071, 28-29; 837, 17-19 confesses the *gratia universalis,* and 788, 9-11; 1081, 57-64, the *sola gratia,* and forgoes all attempts to ease this *crux theologorum.* Likewise Luther, *De Servo Arbitrio,* St. L. XVIII:1965 f.

[53] Seeberg, *Dogmengeschichte,* I, 138. F. H. Foster in the *Concise Dictionary* by Jackson, Chambers and Foster: "The theoretical difference grew out of a personal one."

to be the Reformer independent of, and in opposition to, Luther may have been jealousy of Luther's leading position; Luther, he said, is only "one honest Ajax or Diomedes among many Nestors, Ulysseses, Meneläuses." (See St. L. XX:1134.)

It does not go beyond the province of a dogmatics if we point out very emphatically that the evil disposition which impels men to depart from Scripture and to create divisions, as exemplified by Novatian, Zwingli, and the founders of sects in the Apostolic period, inheres in every one of us and is ever active. Carnal ambition, envy, personal likes and dislikes, are continually threatening to cause factions and divisions in the local churches, in the synods, and in the church federations. *Multae in ecclesia haereses ortae sunt tantum odio doctorum* (Apol., *Trigl.*, 186, 121). It is clear, therefore, that the unity in the Christian doctrine is in no wise the result of our power, wisdom, and skill; the grace and power of God alone can establish and preserve it. That is what Scripture states (John 17:11, 12, 15, 20, 21; Ps. 86:11, etc.) and what the Church confesses in the liturgy.[54]

6

Christianity the Absolute Religion

The Christian religion is the "absolute," that is to say, the absolutely perfect, religion. It is not in need of any supplementation or improvement, and it cannot be developed to a higher degree of perfection. It is unsurpassable.

By that we do not mean that it presents a "logically complete whole," a system of religious thought in which there are no gaps for the human mind. The Apostle Paul does not claim this sort of perfection for the Christian religion; on the contrary, he calls the religious knowledge of the Christians, including his own, a fragmentary one (1 Cor. 13:12).

Again, Christianity must not be called the absolute religion in so far as it teaches the "most perfect morality." To be sure, the Christian religion teaches the best, the perfect, system of ethics. The Christian morality cannot be surpassed, for it centers in the command: "Thou shalt love the Lord, thy God, with all thy heart and with all thy soul

---

[54] See, for example, the German *Agende* of the Missouri Synod, p. 44 f.; 58 f. See also Walther, *Pastorale*, p. 389 f., Note 1. [Fritz, *Pastoral Theology*, 1945, p. 323 f.]

and with all thy mind," and "Thou shalt love thy neighbor as thyself" (Matt. 22:37-40). But this does not constitute the Christian religion. The love of God and of the neighbor is the daughter of faith. We love because we know that "God loved us and sent His Son to be the Propitiation for our sins" (1 John 4:9-21). Paul motivates his exhortation concerning the Christian moral life thus: "I beseech you, therefore, brethren, by the mercies of God [manifested in Christ] that ye present your bodies a living sacrifice, holy, acceptable unto God" (Rom. 12:1).[55]

Christianity is the "absolute," altogether perfect, and unsurpassable religion for two reasons.

The first reason is that it conveys the perfect salvation. It does not ask man to reconcile God through his own works or own virtues as all non-Christian religions do, but it teaches man to accept and obtain by faith the perfect and unsurpassable reconciliation effected by Christ – "God was in Christ reconciling the world unto Himself" (2 Cor. 5:18-19). In other words, the Christian religion is absolutely perfect because it is not a moral code instructing men how to earn the forgiveness of sin themselves, but rather it is faith in that forgiveness of sins which was gained through Christ's vicarious fulfillment of the Law and His substitutionary suffering of our punishment (Gal. 4:4-5; 3:13; Acts 26:18; Luke 24:46-47). Because through Christ's *satisfactio vicaria* God is reconciled, the sins of the world forgiven, and this forgiveness proclaimed in the Gospel, the person who by the working of the Gospel (Rom. 10:17; 1 Cor. 2:4-5) believes in the Gospel, is through this faith – without the deeds of the Law, χωρὶς ἔργων νόμου – declared righteous before God (Rom. 3:28; 5:1), and that means that he is perfect (πεπληρωμένος, τέλειος) in the sight of God (Col. 2:10; 1 Cor. 2:6).[56] For this is God's method: to him who is

---

[55] Nitzsch-Stephan presents the matter thus: "The primary defect of Kant's [ethical] interpretation of Christianity inheres also in those interpretations which hold that the Christian religion is the perfect religion for no other reason than that it is the religion of love towards God and men. Now, it is true that Christianity stresses the duty of love towards God and all men as no other religion does. But mere obligations do not constitute a religion and the Christian's love is not merely to be patterned after God's love, but according to our Christian faith the love of God is the prerequisite and enabling cause of our love. We love because we know and realize that God, redeeming us and forgiving us our sins, first loved us." (*Op. cit.*, p. 147.) Ihmels, too, states that "the ethical quality of any activity or movement is not determined by the individual external actions but solely by the motives from which the ethical behavior flows" (*Zentralfragen*, p. 51).

[56] Col. 2:10: "Ye are complete in Him." Not only the "more advanced" Christians, but all who have received Christ Jesus the Lord by faith, vv. 5, 7, are

inherently ungodly (ἀσεβής) his faith is counted for righteousness (Rom. 4:5); Christ's perfect righteousness covers the sinner's own unrighteousness (1 John 2:1-2).

It is thus clear that in order to preserve the absolutely unique character of the Christian religion, we must keep the *satisfactio vicaria* inviolate. If we held that the work of Christ did not fully reconcile God but needs to be supplemented by the "infused grace," the keeping of the commandments of God and the Church, as Rome teaches,[57] or by "the reshaping of man's life into its divine form," as the modern Protestants teach,[58] we should thereby divest the Christian religion of its specific character and reduce it to the level of the religions of the Law; and the assurance of grace and of the sonship with God would

---

perfect in Christ. The Apostle is here warning the Christians against the philosophy which belittles our perfection in Christ and sets itself up as the way to greater perfection, v. 8; they must learn that the philosophy which claims authority in the domain of religion is "vain deceit," κενὴ ἀπάτη, being the product of man ("after the tradition of men"), the beggarly wisdom of the world ("after the rudiments of the world"), that is, Law. (See Cremer, *Woerterbuch, sub* στοιχεῖον.) — The Christians, on the contrary, have their "doctrinal norm" in Christ ("after Christ"), and through that they have obtained the highest perfection. Let them realize the glory of Christ's person and the unsurpassable excellence of the benefits they have in Christ. Christ is not a mere man, but one in whom all the fullness of the Godhead dwells bodily and who is exalted above all principalities and powers in heaven; it is therefore impossible that these angelic powers should be the source of a higher perfection, as the false teachers asserted (v. 18). And no greater benefit can come to the Christians than those which they have in Christ; they have been raised from death in sin to spiritual life through "the circumcision of Christ," namely, Baptism, through the forgiveness of their sins. And this remission Christ gained through His death on the Cross ("the objective propitiatory sacrifice of Christ's death," v. 14, Meyer), by which He has blotted out the handwriting of ordinances against us, the penalty exacted by the Law.

The "perfect," τέλειοι, of 1 Cor. 2:6, too ("howbeit we speak wisdom among them that are perfect"), are not the "mature" Christians, those who have penetrated "into the higher sphere of thorough and comprehensive insight," particularly of an insight into "the future conditions of the Messianic kingdom" (Meyer, etc.), but according to the context all those who through the operation of the Holy Ghost believe the Gospel, which is hidden to this world, even to the princes of this world. The "perfect" are all Christians (Luther, Olshausen, etc.). Wolf's *Curae* reviews the various interpretations of our passage and finds with Luther and most other interpreters that the "perfect" are the believers, those who are described in ch. 1:24 as "the called," those who obeyed the call. In the entire context nothing is said of "future conditions of the Messianic kingdom" (an interpretation that is colored by chiliastic notions), nor does the context deal specifically with the future bliss of the Christians (some have thus applied verse 9), but only with what they now have by faith in the Gospel of Christ Crucified.

[57] *Tridentinum,* Sess. VI, Can. 11, 12, 20.

[58] Thus, e. g., Kirn, *Grundriss,* 3d ed., p. 118. This substitutes the "Guarantee Theory" for the *satisfactio Christi vicaria.*

be replaced by the *monstrum incertitudinis.* But as long as we teach and believe that Christ's vicarious atonement has fully reconciled God and that we are thereby fully justified by faith (Rom. 3:28) and have peace with God (Rom. 5:1ff.), Christianity will be for us *eo ipso* the absolute religion; we shall look for nothing better, nothing higher. And it is the sacred duty of theological professors to warn their students most earnestly against the modern "theories of atonement," some of which directly reject Christ's *satisfactio vicaria* as too "juridical" and "perfunctory," while others charge it with insufficiencies.[59]

In the second place, the Christian religion is perfect and unsurpassable because its source and norm is not the word of men, but God's own Word, which is perfect and beyond criticism. For the Church of our day this is the written Word of God, the Holy Scriptures (*sola Scriptura*). Is Scripture indeed the very Word of God? Christ and His Apostles assure us of that (John 10:35; 2 Tim. 3:16-17; 1 Pet. 1:10-12; Eph. 2:20). Though it was written by men, we are bound to receive it not as a mixture of human and divine thoughts and words, but as God's own Word, infallible, inviolable. This point will be elaborated in the chapter on "The Inspiration of Scripture." What we are pointing out here is that if Scripture were a mixture of God's Word and man's word and not God's own infallible Word, it would be subject to human criticism – and that would spell the end of the absoluteness of the Christian religion. The science of criticism is constantly advancing new theories; in twenty-five years, possibly sooner, it may invalidate its present-day findings as to what constitutes the essentials of the Christian religion, having then found that much more will have to be deleted. Adolf Harnack, who will have "historical" criticism decide what is essential or non-essential in the Christian religion, says (and from his point of view he is right): "I imagine that a few hundred years hence there will be found to exist in the intellectual ideas which we shall have left behind us much that is contradictory; people will wonder how we put up with it. They will find much to be hard and dry husks in what we took for the kernel; they will be unable to understand how we could be so shortsighted and fail to get a sound grasp of what was essential and separate it from the rest."[60] And this applies not only to the liberal theology represented by Harnack. It applies also to those modern theologians who are classified as "positive," conservative theologians. For by their re-

---

59 See "Some Modern Theories of the Atonement Examined" in Vol. II.

60 *Wesen des Christentums,* 3d ed., p. 35.

jection of the inspiration of Scripture they have, like Harnack, surrendered its infallible, divine authority; and they are laboring under a delusion when they imagine that one can assume a critical attitude toward Scripture and at the same time maintain the absoluteness of the Christian religion. Making the "Christian ego," the "Christian faith consciousness," the "religious experience," the source of the Christian religion instead of Holy Scripture, the *divine* fountain, removes the Christian religion into the domain of subjective human opinion, and in place of the "absolute" Christian religion there are "uncounted divergencies" of religious opinions. It is, therefore, the sacred duty of the theological professors of our age to warn students most earnestly against all modern theologians who refuse to recognize Holy Scripture as God's infallible Word.

In short, if we would hold the absoluteness of the Christian religion, we must hold to both the doctrine of Christ's vicarious satisfaction and the doctrine that Scripture is the Word of God.

We may also call attention to the fact that, according to Scripture, Christianity did not gradually acquire its "absolute" character but was from the very beginning the "absolute" religion. The objection that the Christian religion is a historical phenomenon and, like all history, cannot have absolute but only relative qualities, is not valid. It operates with a *petitio principii.* It takes for granted that the omnipotent God, He who shapes and rules history, could not or would not intervene in the "history of mankind" in such a way as to reveal to mankind immediately after the Fall that Christ is the Savior from sin and death. But the fact is that God did intervene in just that way, as Scripture states clearly and emphatically. In the promise given immediately after the Fall, God declared that the Seed of the woman should crush the head of the Serpent, that is, destroy the works of the devil, deliver men from sin and death. God announced to the human race that it could be saved in no other way than through the work of the Savior. And the entire Scripture of the Old Testament proclaims this absoluteness and exclusiveness of the Christian religion; Peter plainly states (Acts 10:43) that "to Him give all the Prophets witness that through His name whosoever believeth in Him shall receive remission of sins." And Christ Himself says that the entire Scriptures of the Old Testament testify of Him [Christ] as the Giver of eternal life (John 5:39; John 5:46); and He states particularly that Abraham, the father of the believers, believed in Him (John 8:56). When Scripture speaks of a covenant that had become old (παλαιοῦσθαι) and needed to be changed (Jer. 31:31-34; Heb. 8:6-13), it does not mean the Gospel of Christ, but the covenant of the Law from Mount Sinai, which had come later (Gal. 3:17 ff.). In short, according to Scripture the Christian religion is not, like other religions, the result of a natural historical development; it is not one of many kindred religions; not a religion absorbing and supplementing other religions; but it was from the very beginning the absolute religion, absolute and exclusive in the strict sense of the term, presenting the woman's Seed as the sole Deliverer from sin and death, the one Savior of all mankind, thus declaring all other religions, of whatever name or form, to be delusions and having no right to exist.

It is, therefore, incorrect to speak of the Christian religion as the "highest," the "most perfect" religion, the "acme" of religions. The use of these terms creates the impression as though there were only a difference in degree between Christianity and the non-Christianity religions, while in fact they differ radically. There is an essential difference as respects their origin (God-made, man-made), their nature (Gospel, Law), and their effect (assurance of salvation, hopelessness). Christianity differs from all non-Christian religions not as light differs from dusk, but as light differs from darkness (Eph. 5:8: "Ye were sometimes darkness, but now are ye light"; Is. 9:2 ff.; 60:2). The difference is not that between life and the beginning of life, but between life and death (Eph. 2:1-5: "You hath He quickened who were dead in trespasses and sins"); not between the worship of God and some faint beginning of divine worship, but between the worship of God and the worship of demons (1 Cor. 10:20: "The things which the Gentiles sacrifice, they sacrifice to devils and not to God"; Acts 26:18). Christianity produces not only the "highest satisfaction," but the only satisfaction (Rom. 5:1 ff.: "Therefore being justified by faith, we have peace with God through our Lord Jesus Christ," etc.; Gal. 2:16).

Some have argued against the absoluteness of Christianity on the basis of the difference between the Old and the New Testament. But this difference pertains only to the increasing clarity and the extent of revelation; there is no difference as to the content of the divine revelation. Both Testaments teach that the one and only way of life for men is faith in Christ, salvation without the deeds of the Law. Christ tells the Jews: "If ye believe not that I am He, ye shall die in your sins" (John 8:24). But in order to ward off the idea that He was thereby introducing a *novum*, He declares that He is the true content of the Scripture of the Old Testament: "They are they which testify of Me" (John 5:39). Paul, too, protests against the erroneous idea as though by teaching justification not by the Law, but by grace through faith in Christ, he is teaching a new method of obtaining justification; he shows that the χωρὶς νόμου method had been "witnessed by the Law and the Prophets" (Rom. 3:21 ff.) and that only this conception of the religion of the Old Testament is historically correct (Romans 4).

7

Christian Religion and Christian Theology

In ecclesiastical terminology a distinction is made between Christian religion and Christian theology, religion (in the subjective sense) designating the knowledge of God and divine matters which all Christians have, and theology (in the subjective sense), the special knowledge of the teachers of the Church. We can accept this distinction. Scripture teaches (a) that all Christians have a knowledge of divine matters, for "they shall be all taught of God" (John 6:45); and (b) that the teachers of the Church should possess a special knowledge.[61] But there is no difference between these two kinds of knowledge as to their source. The teachers derive their knowledge of God and divine things from the very same source from which all other Christians derive it – from Holy Scripture. There is no other source open to theologians.

Modern theologians are not agreed on the relation between "religious" and "theological" knowledge. Some want to "connect them as closely as possible," while others want to separate them as widely as possible. At the present time much is being written on the difference between "religious" and "theological" knowledge.[62] According to the Scriptural, the Christian, standard we must maintain that "religious knowledge" and "theological knowledge" do not differ essentially regarding source and medium of cognition. That is to say, theological knowledge begins and ends where all the knowledge of all Christians

---

[61] The rhetorical question: "Are they all teachers?" (1 Cor. 12:29) means that not all Christians are teachers. According to 1 Tim. 3:2 one who would be a bishop must be διδακτικός, "apt to teach," have a special degree of the ability to teach, for, according to verse 5, he is to take care not only of himself and his own house, but also of the Church of God. Paul stresses this once more in 2 Tim. 2:2: "The things that thou hast heard of me among many witnesses, the same commit thou to faithful men who shall be able to teach others also." Therefore men must not be elected to the teaching office by lot or in any other haphazard way; only such may be chosen as possess the qualifications set down in 1 Tim. 3:1 ff.; Titus 1:5-11, one of which is a special aptitude to teach.

[62] See, for instance, Richard Gruetzmacher, *Studien zur dogm. Theol.*, 3, p. 120 ff.

begins and ends – by believing the Word of God as we have it in Scripture. The theologians, the teachers of the Church, do not progress in their knowledge of the Christian doctrine one inch beyond God's revelation in His Word. That is the clear teaching of Scripture.[63]

The textbooks in which the divine knowledge of all Christians is systematically arranged according to the chief parts of the Christian religion (religion in the objective sense, as doctrine) are usually called catechisms, *Religionslehre,* handbooks of the Christian doctrine, etc.[64] The manuals in which the special divine knowledge of the teachers of the Church (theology in the objective sense) is presented are called: Textbooks of Theology, Dogmatics, Systematic Theology, Scientific Theology, *die christliche Lehre in wissenschaftlicher Darstellung,* etc. . . . formerly *loci communes, systema theologiae Christianae,* etc. – May the terms "science" and "system" be applied to theology? Yes and no. Because of its importance this matter will be discussed at length in the chapters "Theology and Science" and "Theology and System."

8

Christian Theology

The etymology of "theology" is not doubtful, as is the case with the term "religion." The original meaning of θεολογία is clearly λόγος περὶ τοῦ θεοῦ. Theology denotes, in its subjective sense, the knowledge of God and of divine matters; in its objective sense it designates the doctrine of God.[65] Analogous terms are psychology, physiology, biology, astrology, etc. Thomas Aquinas: *"Theologia a*

---

63 According to John 8:31-32 the knowledge of the truth is mediated by the Word of Christ, which we have in the Word of His Apostles (John 17:20): "If ye continue in My Word . . . ye shall know the truth." And only by believing Christ's Word do men "continue in it." When a teacher does not continue in Christ's Word, the Apostle does not credit him with knowledge but with ignorance (1 Tim. 6:3-4).

64 Cf. Zezschwitz, R. E., 2d ed., VII, 585 ff. Luther in his "Short Preface" to the Large Catechism defines a catechism as "an instruction for children and the simple-minded," as an "instruction for children, what every Christian must needs know, so that he who does not know this could not be numbered with the Christians, nor be admitted to any Sacrament" (*Trigl.* 575). Cf. F. Bente, in *Concordia Triglotta,* "Historical Introductions," pp. 62–93, on catechisms in general and Luther's Catechism in particular, also for a bibliography of recent literature.

65 Luthardt, *Kompendium,* p. 4. Walther, *Lehre und Wehre,* 14, 5. Augustine, *De Civ. Dei,* VIII, 1: "We understand the Greek *theologia* to mean the knowledge and doctrine of the deity" (*ratio sive sermo*).

Deo docetur, Deum docet, et ad Deum ducit." Similarly Baier: "In the composite term *theology* the name ϑεοῦ denotes the object of the λόγος" (Baier-Walther, I, 2).

As to the usage (*usus loquendi*) of the term "theology," we note that it does not occur in Holy Writ. Our old theologians say: "Theology is a word not ἔγγραφος, but ἄγραφος; however, it is not ἀντίγραφος." In the heading of the Book of Revelation, St. John is indeed called "the theologian"("ἀποκάλυψις Ἰωάννου τοῦ ϑεολόγου"), but, as Gerhard points out, "whoever wrote this heading gave John this title, not he himself." – Note further that the terms "theology" and "theologian" did not originate with the Christians. Even the heathen employed these terms. That fact need not surprise us. Knowing that there is a God (Romans 1 and 2), the heathen would naturally devote earnest study to this subject. In their way they studied "theology.' And they employed this very term.[66] Calov: "We see that the term *theology* was first used by the heathen and then adopted by the Church" (*Isagoge*, 2d ed., I, 8).

Within the Christian Church the word *theology* and its cognate *theologian* are not always used in the same sense. The reminder is here in place that since these terms are not found in Scripture but belong to the vocabulary of the Church, there should be no strife about words. What matters is that the words used should not express any unscriptural ideas. The matter denoted by these words must be contained in Scripture. And that is the case when the Church takes *theology* to mean:

1. The special measure of the knowledge of God and the divine doctrine which public ministers in the congregation should possess. Scripture speaks of this form of theology when it says that the ἐπίσκοπος, who takes care of the church of God (1 Tim. 3:5), must be διδακτικός, "apt to teach" (1 Tim. 3:2). The pastor must have a special

---

[66] Aristotle says that Thales and those who before him speculated on the origin of things "theologized," ϑεολογήσαντες (*Metaph.* I, 3). According to Josephus, Pherekydes of Syros in the sixth century wrote a book with the title *Theologia*, in which he philosophized about the heavens and things divine (*C. Apionem*, I, 2). Cicero writes: "In the beginning there were three Joves — so say those who are called theologians" (*De Nat. Deorum* III, 21). Augustine quotes Varro, a contemporary of Cicero, on three types of heathen theology: "The mythical genus, used mostly by the poets; the physical, used by the philosophers; and the civil, which the people and the priests should know and employ." (*De Civ. Dei*, VI, 5.) – Study Augustine's criticism of the heathen theology in this and the following chapters. See further Buddeus, *Inst.*, 1741, p. 48 sqq. August Hahn, *Lehrbuch d. Chr. Gl.*, 2d ed., I, 104 f.; Walther, *Lehre und Wehre*, 1868, p. 5 f.

teaching ability. This matter will be discussed at length in the next chapter.[67]

2. The knowledge of God and the divine doctrine which is required of those who train the future public teachers. These "theological professors" are called theologians in a special sense. Timothy performed the work of a theological professor when he committed the things he had learned from the Apostle Paul "to faithful men, who shall be able to teach others also" (2 Tim. 2:2).[68]

3. The knowledge of God and the divine doctrine possessed by all Christians. Luther on this point: "These are words ('For God so loved the world,' etc., John 3:16) which no one can exhaust or fathom; and when they are rightly believed, they ought to make one a good theologian, or rather a strong, happy Christian, who can speak and teach aught of Christ, judge all other doctrines, counsel and comfort all men, and patiently bear all ills." (St. L. XI:1103.) [69]

---

67 Quenstedt I, 13: "*Theologia acroamatica* teaches and establishes the mysteries of the faith and refutes the errors contrary to the sound doctrine more accurately and copiously, and is the province of the bishops and preachers in the Church." [According to Koenig, theology is divided into: '*catechetical*, or simple, such as is required of all Christians, and *acroamatic*, or more accurate, which is the province of the learned, the ministers of the Word.' "]

68 Quenstedt, I, 13: "*Theologia acroamatica* is the province of those who in the seminaries instruct, not Christians but the *future teachers of the Christians;* and these are called theologians κατ' ἐξοχήν." – Luther has some interesting remarks on the theological doctorate. He calls the pomp and ceremony connected with the conferring of this degree "*Larven*," mummeries. But he does not condemn the thing outright. It is all right if the recipients of the high degree recognize that while the thing in itself means nothing, the honor conferred on them is the honor of "the service in the Word." (St. L. XXI a:564. II:260.)

69 Luther also calls the centurion at Capernaum a "*theologus*" because he "argued in such a fine Christian way that one who has been a doctor for four years could not have done better" (St. L. XII:1185). And on Rom. 12:7 Luther comments: "Hence you will perceive whom Paul makes doctors of Holy Scripture, namely, all who have the faith, and no one else. They should judge all doctrine, and their decision must stand, even though it be against the Pope, the councils and all the world." (St. L. XII:335.) Gerhard, too, says that the term *theology* is used "for the Christian faith and religion as it is found in all believers, the learned as well as the unlearned, and in this sense all who know and accept the articles of faith" (*locus* "De Natura Theologiae," §4), "who teach and profess these articles" (*locus* "De Ministerio Ecclesiastico," §64), are called theologians. According to 1 Pet. 3:15, Col. 3:16, etc., it is the business of the Christians in general to teach and profess the Christian faith and religion. – There are those among the so-called laymen whose knowledge of the Christian doctrine and whose interest in the affairs of the Church exceeds the average. We like to call them "lay theologians." The Apostolic Church had such lay theologians. The list of greetings in Romans 16 seems to indicate that. In the vast majority of cases the

4. The knowledge and doctrine of certain parts of the Christian religion, namely, of the deity of Christ and, respectively, of the Trinity.[70] This use of the term *theology* has been and is quite general. We, too, call the doctrine of the deity of Christ and of the Trinity "theology in the narrower sense" to distinguish it from cosmology, anthropology, Christology, ecclesiology, etc.

We may use the terms *theology* and *theologia* in this fourfold sense, since the matter itself is found in Scripture. But it is an unscriptural use of language when men define theology as a knowledge of God and divine things which, it is claimed, reaches farther than faith in the Word of Scripture and expands faith into scientific comprehension. This is the πρῶτον ψεῦδος of modern theology in all of its various forms. And we have to keep on insisting that when men imagine that their theological knowledge rises above faith in the written Word, they are deluding themselves; their alleged knowledge is ignorance.

Following the custom of the early Lutheran theologians, we shall here use the term *theology* to denote the divine knowledge necessary for the administration of the public ministry. Theology, then, taken subjectively, or concretely, is the aptitude (ἱκανότης, *habitus*) wrought by the Holy Ghost in a Christian to perform the functions of the pastoral office, i. e., to teach the Word of God, the Word of Scripture, in all its purity, both publicly and privately, to refute all false doctrine,

---

lay theologians have proved a blessing to the Church. *Lehre und Wehre*, 1860, p. 352, shows that the fear of having "laymen at the synodical conventions" is unwarranted.

70 Thus Gregory Nazianzen (d. ca. 390) was called ὁ θεολόγος because in speech and writing he had so ably defended the doctrine of the deity of Christ. And we know that the Church Fathers called the evangelist John ὁ θεολόγος because his Gospel lays particular stress on the eternal, essential deity of Christ. Thus Athanasius (4th century): "As also the theologian says: 'In the beginning was the Word.'" The Church Fathers distinguished between theology as the doctrine of the deity of Christ and οἰκονομία (*dispensatio*) as the doctrine concerning the incarnate Christ. Thus Gregory Nazianzen: "The doctrine of the theology or of the nature is one thing, the doctrine of the economy is another." — By reason of this specific sense of θεολογία the verb θεολογεῖν, to theologize, came to be used in the sense of "confessing as God." Thus Athanasius: "How can you theologize the Spirit (confess the Spirit as God) if you are not ready to say that He has the same essence and glory, will and power, as the Father and the Son?" (*De S. Trin.*, dial. 3. Opp. ed. Bonutius II, 190 sq. Quoted by Walther in *Lehre und Wehre*, 1868, p. 7.) — Basilius uses the word *theology* to designate the doctrine of the mystery of the Trinity: "Had we not better remain silent lest the dignity of theology be endangered because of the poverty and weakness of the language?" (*Sermo de fide et trinitate*. Opp. I, 371. *Lehre und Wehre*, 1868, p. 8.)

and thus to lead sinners to faith in Christ and to salvation.[71] Theology taken objectively as doctrine is the Christian doctrine in its correct oral and written presentation by the public minister of the Church.[72] Both definitions are contained, in substance, in Scripture. The subjective concept of theology is found in 2 Cor. 3:5-6: "Our sufficiency [ἱκανότης: ability] is of God, who also hath made us able ministers of the new testament." We have the objective concept, for example, in 2 Tim. 1:13: "Hold fast the form of sound words which thou hast heard of me." [73] – More on these definitions in the following chapters.

Obviously the first and proper meaning of the term *theology* is theology in the subjective sense, aptitude [ἱκανότης]; only in its secondary, derived meaning does it denote objective theology, doctrine. For, as Walther says: "Theology must first be in the soul of a man before he can teach it, present it in speech and writing" (*Lehre und Wehre*, 14, p. 9).[74]

---

71 Quenstedt: "Theology taken concretely as a *habitus* is the God-given practical aptitude of the mind which the Holy Ghost bestows upon a man through the Word, for the purpose of leading sinful man to faith in Christ, and to eternal salvation" (*Systema* I, 16). Similarly Gerhard (*locus* "De Natura Theologiae," ¶31).

72 Quenstedt: "Theology taken abstractly as a system is the body of doctrine taken from the Word of God, by which men are correctly instructed in faith and life unto salvation; in other words, it is the doctrine drawn from the divine revelation that shows how men are to be trained for the service of God through Christ unto eternal life" (I, 16).

73 "Can you imagine St. Paul writing a normative dogmatics after the manner of Hutter's *Compendium Locorum Theologicorum?*" Thus the advocates of "academic freedom." It is a cheap quip and falls flat in the light of 2 Tim. 1:13. The passage states very clearly, first, that Timothy heard ὑγιαίνοντες λόγοι (sound words) from the Apostle, words that did not express unsound human opinions, but the pure divine truth; and, secondly, that Paul set these "sound words" before Timothy not as matter of passing entertainment or mere amusement, but as the ὑποτύπωσις, copy, model, pattern, *norma sanorum verborum*, by which Timothy should be guided in his teaching. Note also the ἔχε, "hold," "hold fast"; Timothy is not at liberty to depart from the norm set up by Paul. According to this text, then, Paul did write what we would call a "Normaldogmatik." Plitt on our passage: "What I have given you use as a pattern, namely, the sound words, 'the sound doctrine' (Titus 1:9)." Matthies: "ὑποτύπωσις, pattern, as in 1 Tim. 1:16, distinct type, original and model." Huther (Meyer's Commentary) remarks: "Luther translates ὑποτύπωσις by 'pattern' (so, too, De Wette, Wiesinger, and others), but this definition is not in the word itself." But the words of the text plainly show that Paul is referring to a "pattern." The ὑποτύπωσις by which men are to be guided becomes *eo ipso* a pattern.

74 Musaeus: "The doctrine regarding God and divine matters issues from the theological aptitude and is its result" (*Introd. in Theol.* 1679, p. 3). Luthardt holds that the old Lutheran theologians, who defined theology *primo loco* as a personal aptitude, "a personal qualification," meant well, but finds that "this definition is scientifically incorrect" (*Komp.*, 10th ed., p. 4). We fail to see why

9

Theology as Aptitude

Theology in the sense of aptitude, or "personal qualification," is defined in all those Scripture passages which describe the persons to whom according to God's will and ordinance the teaching office in the Church may be committed. Walther, following the earlier Lutheran theologians, correctly says: "Since theology, in the subjective sense, is the proficiency which the incumbents of the teaching office in the Church should possess, it is clear that when Scripture describes the true teacher, it describes the true theologian" (*Lehre und Wehre*, 14, p. 10). These qualifications are described in Scripture as follows:

1. The theological aptitude is a spiritual aptitude (*habitus spiritualis, supernaturalis*), that is to say, an aptitude which in every case presupposes, besides natural gifts, personal faith in Christ (faith in the forgiveness of sins by grace for the sake of Christ's *satisfactio vicaria*). In other words, it presupposes the conversion of the theologian. Unbelievers may be able to apprehend the whole body of Christian doctrine intellectually, and they may be endowed with a natural ability to teach it. But that does not make them theologians in the Scriptural sense. There is no "*theologia irregenitorum.*"[75] Scripture distinctly states that the aptitude to administer the public teaching office is not a natural gift and attainment, but that it is of a spiritual nature, a gift of God: "Not that we are sufficient of ourselves to think anything as of ourselves, but our sufficiency is of God, who also hath made us able ministers of the New Testament" (2 Cor. 3:5-6). And all unbelievers are dwelling places and workshops, not of the Holy Ghost, but of the prince of this world: "In times past ye walked according to the prince

---

this definition should be out of line with scientific thinking. Why, Luthardt himself thinks along the same lines! When he with Kahnis defines theology as "the scientific self-consciousness of the Church," he, too, conceives of theology as a "personal qualification," since every kind of "self-consciousness," including the "scientific" kind, presupposes persons, in whom it inheres as a *personal* attribute. An impersonal self-consciousness is a contradiction in itself. Luthardt will not deny that he, too, has in mind persons within the Church, viz., the theologians who, in distinction from the ordinary Christians, possess a scientific self-consciousness. It is a queer thing by the way, that Luthardt, while thinking of theologians, should define theology as "the scientific self-consciousness of the Church." The theologians, whether they are equipped with scientific self-consciousnes or not, are not the Church.

[75] Cf. Walch, *Bibliotheca Theol.*, II, 667 *sqq.*; Baumgarten, *Theol. Streitigkeiten*, III, 425 f.; there is a wealth of material on the controversy concerning this point in Hollaz, *Examen Prol.*, I, qus. 18—21.

of the power of the air, the spirit that now worketh in the children of disobedience" (Eph. 2:2). Note, too, that when Scripture speaks of the qualifications for the public ministry, it always describes the minister as possessing not only the special pastoral gifts, but also the common Christian virtues; it invariably describes him as a Christian. For example, according to 1 Tim. 3:1 ff. the ἐπίσκοπος must not only be "apt to teach" (διδακτικός), but also must "not be given to wine," etc. And in 2 Tim. 2:1 ff. the aptitude to administer the public ministry is traced back to the grace of God in Christ. "Thou, therefore, my son, be strong in the grace of God that is in Christ." Unbelievers hold the office of the public ministry only by God's toleration, against God's will and ordinance. – A remark: it can and will happen that men are converted and saved through the ministry of an unconverted preacher, provided that he preaches the truth of God's Word. The reason for this is that the efficacy of the means of grace is not affected by the character of the administrant.

Our old theologians expressed the truth that the theological aptitude always presupposes personal Christianity by defining this aptitude as *habitus spiritualis, supernaturalis,* θεόσδοτος, *a Spiritu Sancto per verbum Dei collatus.* Baier, for instance, says: "Theology, then, is essentially a supernatural aptitude, acquired by the powers of grace and through the operation of the Holy Spirit, the theologian himself, of course, making use of these powers" (Baier-Walther I, 69), and then adds the remark that a "theology" which consists merely in an external knowledge and teaching of the Scripture truth and lacks the "genuine," "supernatural" assent wrought by the Holy Ghost, a theology which unregenerate, wicked man may have, is called theology only in an improper sense.[76] Luther on the *spiritual* character of the theological aptitude: "We see that there is more of heathen and human conceit than of the holy, sure teaching of Scripture in the writings of the theologians. What shall we do about it? The only advice I can give is to humbly pray God that He would give us doctors of theology. The Pope, emperor, and the universities can make doctors of art, of medicine, of jurisprudence, of the Sentences; but be assured that no one can make a doctor of Holy Scripture for you but only the Holy Ghost from heaven, as Christ says John 6:45: 'They shall all be taught of God.'" (St. L. X:339 f.) – An important element of the spiritual aptitude is, of course, the Christian conviction that the Holy Scrip-

[76] It is not correct to say that Spener was the first to emphasize this truth. In his tract "Die Allgemeine Gottesgelehrtheit" Spener himself says that others have done that before him. (See Baier, *loc. cit.*)

tures are the infallible Word of God, a conviction wrought by the Holy Ghost through the Word of Scripture. Let us elaborate this point at once.

2. The theological aptitude includes the ability of the theologian to confine himself in his teaching entirely to God's Word; he must be able to suppress his own thoughts about God and divine matters and put aside the thoughts of other men, deriving the doctrine exclusively from the Word of God, from Holy Scripture. The theologian who refuses to do this is, in the words of St. Paul, a bloated ignoramus (τετύφωται, μηδὲν ἐπιστάμενος). "If any man teach otherwise and consent not to the wholesome words, even the words of our Lord Jesus Christ . . . he is proud, knowing nothing" (1 Tim. 6:3). And bear in mind that the "words of our Lord Jesus Christ," according to John 17:20, 1 Pet. 1:10-12, Eph. 2:20, are the writings of the Apostles and Prophets. Scripture thus declares all those to be theologically incompetent and disqualified for the Christian ministry who are not willing to take their doctrine exclusively from Holy Scripture, but in addition set up other sources, such as alleged private revelations ("enthusiasm"), the so-called "Christian consciousness," "faith consciousness," "the regenerate Ego," "the Christian experience," the decretals of the Pope and of "the Church," "history," and so forth. Let us hear Luther on this point: "Jeremiah has an entire chapter on the false prophets (Jeremiah 23). Among other things he says this (v. 16): 'Thus saith the Lord of Hosts, Hearken not unto the words of the prophets that prophesy unto you; they make you vain [they teach you vanity, R. V.]; they speak a vision of their own heart – and not out of the mouth of the Lord!' Behold, all prophets who do not preach out of the mouth of the Lord are deceivers, and God forbids us to hear them. Does not the text state clearly that where God's Word is not preached no one dare, under pain of God's wrath, listen to it, for it is pure deception? O Pope, O bishops, O priests, O monks, O theologians, how are you going to escape here? Do you consider it a trifling matter when the Supreme Majesty forbids whatever does not proceed out of the mouth of the Lord and is something else than *God's Word?* It is not a thresher or herdsman who is saying this. When the servant hears the master say: 'Who told you to do that? It is not what I have commanded,' he will certainly realize that he should not have done it as being contrary to the master's orders." (St. L. XIX:821 f.)

3. Another theological skill is the ability to teach the whole Word of God, the entire truth of Scripture. Only he is an able minister of

the Church who can say with the Apostle Paul: "I have not shunned to declare unto you all the counsel of God" (Acts 20:27). If the minister fails to do this, souls entrusted to his care may be eternally lost. Only he who declares all the counsel of God can say with the Apostle: "I am pure from the blood of all men" (Acts 20:26). – Let us remind ourselves in this connection that since God requires the theologian to teach the entire Christian doctrine, without subtraction or addition, "publicly and from house to house," therefore theological students should apply themselves very diligently to acquire the theological fitness, and pastors in office should strive to retain and increase it. The Apostle admonishes Timothy and all theologians: "Take heed unto thyself and unto the doctrine; continue in them; for in doing this thou shalt both save thyself and them that hear thee" (1 Tim. 4:16).

4. Again, only he is a fit minister of the Church who is able to refute false teachers. That is listed as one of the necessary qualifications of an elder or bishop: "Holding fast the faithful Word as he hath been taught, that he may be able by sound doctrine both to exhort and to convince the gainsayers . . . whose mouths must be stopped" (Titus 1:9-11). The popular demand that the public teacher refrain from polemics is not supported by Scripture. Scripture admonishes pastors to "avoid foolish questions and genealogies and contentions about the law; for they are unprofitable and vain" (Titus 3:9).[77] Nor dare we engage in polemics from carnal motives, in carnal zeal. "For though we walk in the flesh, we do not war after the flesh" (2 Cor. 10:3). It is also to be noted that in Titus 1:9 the words "able by sound doctrine to exhort" precede "able to convince the gainsayer." That means that the clear presentation of the true doctrine must come before the refutation of the false doctrine. The hearers will thus be in a position to see that the polemics are *justified* and will be able to make the condemnation of the false doctrine their own. And they will hardly suspect the teachers of being contentious and unjust. Scripture thus warns us against false polemics. But the demand that polemical theology be excluded from Christian theology is contrary to Scripture. The duty of refuting false doctrine and rebuking false teachers is laid upon the teachers of the Church in Titus 1:9-11 and many other passages of Scripture. All Prophets and Apostles and Christ Himself

---

[77] Quenstedt: "In the field of polemical theology we must take special care not to engage in controversies over useless questions and not to let controversies breed controversies; polemics must not become a quarrelsome and contentious theology, by which the truth is lost through too much disputing" (*Systema* I, 14).

have both proclaimed the true doctrine and condemned the false doctrine.

Walther does not go too far when he writes: "A man may proclaim the pure doctrine, but if he does not condemn and refute the opposing false doctrine, does not warn against the wolves in sheep's clothing, the false prophets, and unmask them, he is not a faithful steward of God's mysteries, not a faithful shepherd of the sheep entrusted to him, not a faithful watchman on the walls of Zion, but, as the Word of God says, an unfaithful servant, a dumb dog, a traitor. The terrible consequences of the minister's failure to use the *elenchus* are before our eyes — many souls lost and the Church deeply hurt. Polemics are absolutely needed. Not only because a doctrine is more fully comprehended in the light of its antithesis, but mainly because the errorists so craftily mask their error behind a show of truth that the simple Christians, if not forewarned, are despite their love of the truth only too easily deceived. The pastor cannot wash his hands in innocence, pleading that he has always preached the full truth, if he did not at the same time warn against the error and, when necessary, identify it by naming the errorist; if his sheep, either while he is still serving or after he had to leave them for another field, become the prey of the ravening wolves in sheep's clothing, he is guilty of their blood." (Walther, *Pastorale*, p. 82 f. [Fritz, *Pastoral Theology*, 1945, p. 336 f.].)

When men here invoke the "spirit of tolerance," we must remind them of the difference between Church and State. Tolerating false teachers in the State is something different from tolerating them in the Church. The Christian Church of the New Testament has no command to expel false teachers from the State or the civil community; that would call for the use of force, and the Church is enjoined from employing force. But the Church may not tolerate the false teachers in the Church. God has commanded the Church to take up arms against them and oppose them with the Word of God. This means that the Church must (a) realize that he who departs from the Word of the Apostles is a false teacher (Rom. 16:17: "Mark them which cause divisions and offenses contrary to the doctrine which ye have learned"); must (b) disprove their teaching (Titus 1:9, 11: "Convince [convict] the gainsayers . . . whose mouths must be stopped"); and finally (c) must isolate them, that is, have no church fellowship with them (Rom. 16:17: "Avoid them"; 2 John 10: "neither bid him Godspeed"), and eventually, if they do not themselves sever their connection with the Church, formally excommunicate them (1 Tim. 1:20:

Hymenaeus and Alexander expelled from the church; cp. 2 Tim. 2:17; 4:14).

5. The theological aptitude includes, finally, the willingness and strength to suffer for the Christian doctrine. Scripture distinctly includes the readiness to suffer for the sake of Christ and His Word as a necessary part of the theologian's equipment. The Apostle Paul tells Timothy: "Thou therefore endure hardness ["hardship," R. V.] as a good soldier of Jesus Christ," "suffer trouble even unto bonds" (2 Tim. 2:3, 9). The minister of the Gospel cannot escape trouble because the Gospel, which he preaches, salvation by faith in the crucified Christ without the deeds of the Law, does not at all appeal to the world, but is "a stumbling block to the Jews and foolishness to the Greeks" (1 Cor. 1:23). The Christians' lot therefore, is described by Christ Himself: "Ye shall be hated of all nations for My name's sake" (Matt. 24:9). It is but natural – and experience confirms it – that this hatred should be directed principally against the teachers of the Church. What Jesus said concerning Paul applies in some degree to all faithful ministers of the Gospel: "I will show him how great things he must suffer for My name's sake" (Acts 9:16; cf. Acts 26:21). And if the minister is not willing to suffer the loss of his goods, of honor and rank, yes, even of his life, he is not a profitable servant of the Church: he will, for the sake of ease, compromise with error; he may even deny Christ, and thus be denied by Him (2 Tim. 2:12). – The Christian ministry requires strong men, men able to "endure hardship": "Thou, therefore, my son, be strong in the grace that is in Christ Jesus" (2 Tim. 2:1).

10

Theology as Doctrine

Since subjective theology is the aptitude to teach no more and no less than God's Word [78] as the Church of our day possesses it in the written Word of the Apostles and Prophets,[79] objective theology, theology in the sense of doctrine, is nothing more and nothing less than the presentation in oral and written form of the doctrine presented in Holy Scripture. The Christian doctrine is not produced by the

[78] 1 Pet. 4:11: "If any man speak, let him speak as the oracles of God." No doctrine may be preached in the Church but "the doctrine of God our Savior" (Titus 2:10).

[79] What the Apostles taught orally, that (ταῦτα) they also set down in writing (1 John 1:3-4).

theologian; all that the Christian theologian does is that he compiles the doctrinal statements contained in Scripture (in the text and context), groups them under their proper heads, and arranges these doctrines in the order of their relationship. Accordingly, objective theology (*theologia positiva*) is, as our old Lutheran dogmaticians say, nothing else than Scripture itself arranged according to doctrines; hence all the parts that go to make up this body of doctrine (*corpus doctrinae*), the least important no less than the most important articles, must be based on Scripture.[80] All theologians since the days of the Apostles, says Luther, must confine themselves in their teaching to the teaching of the Apostles: "We are catechumens and pupils of the Prophets. Let us simply repeat and preach what we have heard and learned from the Prophets and Apostles" (St. L. III:1890). Luther enforces the demand that the theologians simply "repeat the words of the Apostles after them" with the solemn warning: "Neither ought any doctrine be taught or heard in the Church but the pure Word of God, that is to say, the Holy Scriptures; otherwise accursed be both the teachers and hearers together with their doctrine."[81] The same truth is expressed in the well-known axiom: *Quod non est biblicum, non est theologicum.*

It follows that (Christian) theology is not made up of the variable notions and opinions of men, but is the immutable divine truth or God's own doctrine (*doctrina divina*). It has this quality because of the source from which it is drawn. According to the witness of Christ and His Apostles and its own self-attestation in the hearts of the Christians, Holy Scripture is God's infallible Word, and therefore the doctrine taken from the Scripture is not "after the tradition of men" (Col. 2:8), not man's doctrine, but God's own doctrine, "the doctrine of God our Savior" (Titus 2:10). And in God's Church nothing but God's own doctrine may be preached and heard. The door of the Church is closed to all doctrines devised by men.

This truth needs to be stressed in view of the contrary claims of

---

80 Aug. Pfeiffer: "*Theologia positiva,* theology in the form of doctrine, is, correctly speaking, nothing else than Holy Scripture itself arranged according to doctrines, its statements set down in the various *loci* according to a proper method and in fitting order; it follows that in this body of doctrine there is no place for even one article, and be it the least one, which is not based on Scripture" (*Thesaurus hermeneut.*, p. 5, quoted in Baier, I, 43, 76).

81 *Comment. ad Gal.*, see Erl. I, 91: "*Neque alia doctrina in ecclesia tradi et audiri debet quam purum Verbum Dei, hoc est, Sancta Scriptura, vel doctores et auditores cum sua doctrina anathema sunto.*" St. L. IX:87.

modern theology. The moderns have nothing to offer but human doctrine. Refusing to accept Scripture as the Word of God, they have found it theologically unreliable and have substituted for it as the source of doctrine the human heart, the theological Ego. And they insist that the Church accept the results of their theological cogitations as the true theology. They are virtually demanding that theology be removed from the realm of the objective divine truth into the sphere of subjective human opinion. Because of the insistent claims of the modern theologians that the Church is well served by this human theology we shall have to insist that what the Church needs is God's theology and that the theology, the doctrine drawn by the theologian from Scripture (*doctrina e Scriptura Sacra hausta*), is divine doctrine, *doctrina divina.* And this not merely in the sense that it tells of God and divine things but particularly and *primo loco* in the sense that such doctrine, in contrast to all human doctrines, views, and judgments, is God's own doctrine, view, and judgment.

To illustrate: Concerning the creation of the world and man the Christian theologian teaches what God has told him in Genesis 1 and 2 and elsewhere in Scripture; and so his doctrine is divine doctrine. When he is forced to take note of the stories told by human cosmogonists, he rejects whatever does not agree with the Biblical cosmogony as worthless human speculation. – Concerning the Fall and the nature of sin the Christian theologian teaches no more and no less than what God reports, pronounces, and teaches on this matter in Holy Scripture. He must here, too, take note of a great mass of human speculation on the origin of sin, its nature, and its consequences. But whatever is contrary to the teaching of Scripture, which cannot be broken, he rejects at once as man's antithesis to God's own thesis. – Concerning the redemption of fallen mankind, i. e., the incarnation of the eternal Son of God, the person and work of the Savior, the Christian theologian teaches only what God Himself teaches concerning these great things (τὰ μεγαλεῖα τοῦ θεοῦ, Acts 2:11). These wonderful things never entered into the heart of man (1 Cor. 2:9; John 1:18). They constitute a "mystery which was kept secret since the world began," but are "now made manifest by the Scriptures of the Prophets," by God Himself (Rom. 16:25-26; Eph. 3:7-12). Therefore the Christian theologian renounces all human speculations and insists that God be heard. Modern theology insists on the right of man to judge these matters, finds fault with the divine method of redemption, particularly with the substitutionary satisfaction of Christ, as being too "juridical," and refuses to teach it. However, this attempt to silence God's voice and suppress the divine doctrine of redemption can have only one effect on the Christian theologian: He will the more loudly proclaim what the Scriptures of the Old and the New Testament teach, redemption through the vicarious satisfaction of Christ.[82] – On the *articulus stantis et cadentis ecclesiae*, the doctrine of justification before God, the Christian theologian teaches that man obtains the forgiveness of sins by faith (πίστει), that is, through faith in the Gospel, which forgives sins for the sake of Christ's atoning sacrifice, without the Law and without the works of the Law (χωρὶς νόμου, χωρὶς ἔργων νόμου), that is, without demanding any moral quality in man or any ethical achievement as contributing factors in justification. Neither Rome's anathema nor the protests of degenerate Protestantism, which reject the divine mode of justification as too external and juridical, nor the antagonism of his own natural heart, in which the *opinio legis* inheres *naturaliter*, can induce the Christian theologian to change the Scripture doctrine of justification, "even though heaven and earth and whatever will not abide, should sink to ruin" (Smalc. Art., *Trigl.*, 461, 5). The Christian theologian as such is a realist. He knows from his own experience what the disquieted sinner needs. He realizes what a terrible thing it would be if the terrified sinner, who wants to know about the way of salvation, had to rely on human opinions. The sinner wants absolutely reliable information on the question of justification. Nothing but God's own doctrine will serve him. – And this applies to all parts of the Christian doctrine, including the doctrines of eternal damnation and of eternal salvation. In short, the Christian theologian teaches only God's doctrine, as set down in Holy Scripture, "God's Book" (Luther's phrase; St. L. IX:1071). He does not deal with human thoughts and opinions.

Holy Scripture holds him to such teaching. Holy Scripture makes the absolute demand that the doctrine taught in the Church be *doctrina divina.* The Holy Scriptures of the Old and the New Testament are full of warnings against those teachers who will not confine themselves to teaching God's Word, but feel free to proclaim their own thoughts. Read the solemn words of Jer. 23:16: "Thus saith the Lord of Hosts, Hearken not unto the words of the prophets that prophesy unto you; they make you vain [R. V., they teach you vanity]; they speak a vision of their own heart [חֲזוֹן לִבָּם: they tell you fancies of their own] and not out of the mouth of the Lord." [83] In like manner

---

[82] This will be presented in detail in the section "The Vicarious Satisfaction" in Vol. II.

[83] Parallel passages: Jer. 14:14; 27:14-16; Lam. 2:14; Ezek. 13:2 ff.

the entire New Testament proscribes the teaching of human thoughts and opinions and enjoins all teachers to speak out of the mouth of the Lord. Whoever opens his mouth to teach in the Church, which is "the house of God" (1 Tim. 3:15), should speak God's Word, λόγια θεοῦ (1 Pet. 4:11).[84] Whoever teaches otherwise [ἑτεροδιδασκαλεῖ] and does not adhere to the wholesome words of our Lord Jesus Christ, as we have them in the Word of His Apostles (John 8:31-32 compared with John 17:20), is unfit for the office of teaching in the Christian Church; for in place of teaching the divine truth such a one is bloated (τετύφωται) with his own human opinion, and he knows nothing (μηδὲν ἐπιστάμενος) but is sick with disputations and strifes about words (1 Tim. 6:3 f.). The Christians are therefore forbidden, both by the Old and the New Testament (2 John 8—11; Rom. 16:17), to fellowship those teachers who do not bring Christ's doctrine (τὴν διδαχὴν τοῦ Χριστοῦ), that is, God's doctrine, because such teachers by bringing in their own doctrine "cause divisions and offenses" in the Church, rob the Christians of their Christian treasures (2 John 8), and do not perform the "good work" of a Christian teacher (1 Tim. 3:1), but are engaged in "evil deeds" (2 John 11). Scripture thus declares in the strongest possible way that the doctrine proclaimed in the Christian Church must be God's own doctrine, *doctrina divina.*

Luther upholds this demand of Scripture with might and main. Recall his urgent words: "O theologians, how are you going to escape here? Do you consider it a trifling matter when the Supreme Majesty forbids whatever does not proceed out of the mouth of the Lord and is something else than God's Word?" (On Jer. 23:16. St. L. XIX:821.) Feeling deeply about this matter, Luther stressed the *necessitas doctrinae divinae in ecclesia tradendae et audiendae* from various points of view. He points, for instance, to the difference between State and Church and says that in "the government of the world and the home" human opinions and the word of man are in place, for this territory is ruled by the "natural light," that is, by human reason. But teaching in the Church is a different matter: "If any man would preach, let him suppress his own words. . . . Here in the Church he must utter nothing but the words of the rich head of the family; otherwise it is not the true Church. Therefore it must be thus: God is speaking." (St. L. XII:1413.) Luther expresses this same thought in his somewhat paradoxical statement that the Christian doctrine "does not belong in the Lord's Prayer." The meaning is that it should not be necessary

---

84 "Let him speak as the oracles of God." Luther: "He should be certain that what he is speaking is God's Word and not his own word" (XII:443).

for the preacher to ask God's forgiveness for the doctrine he has preached; he should rather be in a position to say: "It is God's Word and not mine, and so there can be no reason for His forgiving me; He can only confirm, praise, and crown what I have preached, saying, 'Thou hast taught correctly, for I have spoken through thee, and the Word is Mine.'" Luther adds the weighty words: "Whoever cannot truthfully say that of his sermon should quit preaching, for he must surely be lying and blaspheming God when he preaches." (St. L. XVII:1343 f. Cp. VIII:37.)

Luther takes this matter up again when he discusses the authority of the Christian Church. He denies that the Church has the authority to make Christian doctrine or to decree articles of faith, because the Church has and proclaims no word of its own, but only Christ's Word. The Church repudiates every teaching which is not Christ's Word, "Though a lot of this gabbling is going on, the Church has no part in the prattle. Let them cry and rave, 'Church, Church!'; without God's Word it amounts to nothing." (St. L. XII:1414.)

And Luther applies this also to those teachers who are held to be theologians *par excellence*, the professors of theology. Some modern theologians take the position that while the ordinary preacher should content himself with teaching the doctrine as Scripture presents it, this restriction must not be laid upon the divinity professors, who owe a duty to the scientific method.[85] Luther does not share that view. He tells the university theologians that they, too, must exercise the strictest mental discipline; they must, without mercy, banish from

[85] Kahnis, for instance, is very outspoken on this point. In his *Zeugnis von den Grundwahrheiten des Protestantismus gegen D. Hengstenberg*, Leipzig, 1862, p. 133, he says: "I have not written my dogmatics for the general public, not for the educated laymen, but only for scientific theologians. However, after Dr. Hengstenberg and Dr. Muenkel have, in a most unwarranted manner, brought the matter to the attention of wider circles, I have been forced to address, at least in this essay, a wider circle than the readers of my dogmatics." Again on page 118 f.: "I cannot believe that Pastor Muenkel, who signs himself Th. D., knows so little of theology that he does not know that there are difficulties in theology which have to be discussed. These investigations and discussions are of course not meant for the common people. But who is spreading them there? Why, periodicals like Pastor Muenkel's paper. Do not charge me with confusing the people; the blame rests with this man, who, while he is neither a man of science nor a man of the people, goes about like a telltale and scares people by telling them things which they need not know. If Pastor Muenkel cannot stand the mountain heights with their avalanches and landslides, he had better stay on the *Lueneburger Heide* and tend sheep, raise bees, and grow asparagus." — It is only natural that Kahnis, who denies that the Holy Scripture is "the inspired textbook of the pure doctrine" (p. 127), would insist that it requires the scientific apparatus of the theologians to establish what is Christian doctrine.

their minds all thoughts about God and divine matters which are not clearly expressed in the words of Scripture. Luther adduces his own example. It is inevitable, he says, that our own thoughts intrude into our study of the high matters pertaining to God and divine things; he, too, found all sorts of notions arising in his mind, but God had granted him the grace to submerge all thoughts that were outside Scripture. Zwingli and his associates said that Luther was without "spirit"; they condemned this clinging to the words of Scripture as mere intellectual knowledge, letter worship, dead theology; the "spirit" must be given the reins. Luther replied that if he had wanted to give free play to the "spirit," he could perhaps have originated more thoughts of his own than all "enthusiasts" together, but he had no right to foist his own notions on the Church. "Oh, how many fine ideas occurred to me which I had to dismiss! If an 'enthusiast' had so many fine notions, he would not find enough printing presses to tell the Church about them." (St. L. XX:792.) Moreover, says Luther, it is not the Holy Spirit that urges you to have your own thoughts about God and divine matters. The Holy Spirit would have us be "catechumens and pupils of the Prophets"; "we repeat and preach what we have heard and learned from the Prophets and Apostles." (St. L. III:1890.)

To some the use of the word "repeat" (*nachsagen*) in this connection is offensive. Now, Luther does not mean that the Christian teacher "must not use more words and other words than are found in Scripture," for that is untenable. (St. L. XVI:2212.) But he purposely uses the strong word "repeat"; he would emphasize as strongly as possible that the Christian teacher "should teach nothing in divine matters outside Scripture." His doctrine should be, as to its content, simply a reproduction of the doctrine of the Prophets and Apostles, without any admixture of his own human views. All true teachers of the Church are so constituted, says Luther, that "they present nothing original or new, as the Prophets did, but teach only what they get from the Prophets" (St. L. III:1890). — The teachers at the theological schools of the Missouri Synod are not overdoing it when they ask their students to examine and re-examine their completed sermons for the purpose of detecting, and mercilessly deleting, any non-Scriptural thought that may have crept in, because it has no right to be heard in the Church of God, which is built on the foundation of the Apostles and Prophets.

Our old Lutheran theologians, too, insist on the *doctrina divina*. For them theology is simply the compilation, systematizing of the divine doctrine contained in Scripture. The Christian doctrine is *doctrina e revelatione divina hausta; doctrina ex Verbo Dei exstructa,* etc. Nothing must be injected into the *corpus doctrinae* of the Church which is not contained in Scripture. And in order to accentuate this characteristic feature of the Christian doctrine, they have called objective theology *theologia* ἔκτυπος, ectypal, or derived, theology, that is, a reproduction, re-presentation, of the *theologia* ἀρχέτυπος, the archetypal, or original, theology, which is that knowledge of God and divine things originally found only in God, but which God has graciously communicated to man through His Word.

Some think that this terminology serves no purpose and is outmoded.[86] But it is thoroughly Scriptural, and the theologians of all ages can profit by it. Rudelbach says: "I do not know whether anyone has pointed out that this distinction (between *theologia* ἔκτυπος and ἀρχέτυπος), which brings out the true nature of theology, is based on Scripture. Nevertheless it is clearly taught in the words of the Lord (Matt. 11:27): 'No man knoweth the Son but the Father; neither knoweth any man the Father save the Son and he to whomsoever the Son will reveal Him.'"[87] Our old theologians furnish abundant proof for the Scripturalness of this distinction. Scherzer, for instance, writes: "*Theologia* ἀρχέτυπος is God's own knowledge of Himself (Matt. 11:27; 1 Cor. 2:10 f.)."[88] The old theologians develop the following thoughts: (1) Only God knows God; God dwells in a light which no man can approach unto (1 Tim. 6:16; 1 Cor. 2:10-11; John 1:18 a; Matt. 11:27). (2) God stepped out of this unapproachable light and revealed Himself to man, so that man can, in a measure, know God. He reveals Himself to man in the realm of nature and through His Word. God's self-revelation in nature (Rom. 1:19 ff., 32; 2:14-15; Acts 14:17; 17:26-27) is the source of natural theology, of the natural knowledge of God. God's revelation of Himself in the Word (John 1:18 b; 8:31-32; Eph. 2:20) is the source, and the only source, of Christian theology, of the saving knowledge of God. Since man can know God only as He has revealed Himself, and since He has revealed Himself as the God of our salvation in the Word, Christian theology must be ectypal; it cannot be anything else than an exact replica of the divine doctrine contained in Scripture. Gerhard's presentation of this matter is worth

---

[86] Bretschneider, *Systematische Entwicklung aller in der Dogmatik vorkommenden Begriffe,* 3d ed., p. 68.

[87] *Zeitschrift f. luth. Theol. u. Kirche,* 1848, I, 7; quoted in Baier-Walther, I. 5.

[88] *Systema, Proleg. de Theologia,* p. 2, in Quenstedt, *Syst.,* I, 5 *sq.,* under Thesis IV.

reading.[89] Luther is describing the *theologia* ἔκτυπος when he says that the Christian teachers are not "Prophets," but "children of the Prophets," "catechumens and pupils of the Prophets," who simply repeat and preach what they have heard and learned from the Prophets. And when Scherzer, for instance, classifies the theology which does not conform to the original type (*theologia* ἀρχέτυπος) as *mataeologia* (vain theology), as heretical, empty babbling,[90] that was not a *novum* in Lutheran theology. Already Luther had said: Whatever is taught in the Church without Scripture is not the Church's doctrine; it is silly "prattle."

Modern theology flatly rejects the thesis that the Christian doctrine is *doctrina divina* and in no way *doctrina humana.* It must do so because it no longer believes that Scripture is the Word of God. When Luther requires the theologian to discard every thought that is not taken from the words of Scripture, and when the dogmaticians recognize only that teaching as Christian which is *theologia* ἔκτυπος, the reproduction of the Scripture doctrine, that is due to the fact that they – both Luther and the dogmaticians – regard Scripture as God's own Word, as "God's mouth." But the modern theologians refuse to recognize Scripture as God's Word.[91] They insist that the only scientifically correct method is to draw on "the pious self-consciousness of the theologizing individual."[92] Thus they do not base their theology on the objective divine truth, but on subjective human

---

[89] He writes in the *locus* "De Natura Theologiae," §15 *sqq.*: "The archetypal, or prototypal, theology is in God the Creator, inasmuch as God knows Himself in Himself and knows the universe through Himself by one immutable act of knowing. Ectypal theology is the outgrowth of archetypal theology (a copy, so to say, of it), communicated to man through God's grace." The means by which this knowledge, original only in God, is communicated, is the external Word, "by which God here in time speaks to men." It follows that Christian theology takes its teaching exclusively from Scripture: "The supernatural, adequate, and proper principle of theology is the divine revelation; and because we today have this divine revelation nowhere else than in the sacred writings, that is, in the prophetic books of the Old Testament and the apostolic books of the New Testament, we say that the written Word of God, that is, Holy Scripture, is the only and the proper principle of theology." Cp. also Quenstedt, *Syst.*, I, 5 *sqq.*

[90] *Systema*, p. 2: "So far as it [the theology of the "pilgrims"] reproduces and expresses the archetype revealed to us in the Word, it is true theology. Whatever deviates from that archetype is false theology and heretical mataeology."

[91] Nitzsch-Stephan, p. 258: "In our day the orthodox doctrine of inspiration has hardly any standing in dogmatics." Horst Stephan: "Today the doctrine of inspiration is discarded by scientific theology; it has retained its hold – a strong one at that – only in the theology of the laymen" (*Glaubenslehre*, 1921, p. 52).

[92] Nitzsch-Stephan, p. 12 ff. 15: "No one bases his dogmatics on the *norma normans*" (the Bible), "as was the fashion among the old Protestants."

opinions. That has produced the situation so aptly described by Luther in the well-known words which Hase made the motto of his *Hutterus Redivivus:* "They all have something to sell. Their aim is not to reveal Christ and His mystery, but their own mystery. They think more of that than of the mystery of Christ. Their own beautiful thoughts must not go to waste. Through them they hope to convert even the devils, while they have never yet converted a gnat. And the worst of it is, all they do is pervert the truth." (St. L. XIV:397.) Naturally, everyone prefers his own brand. And so there is in modern theology no longer any unanimity of doctrine. The moderns do not attempt to hide this situation. Recall the statement of Nitzsch-Stephan: The unanimity in the acceptance of the principle that the Christian doctrine must not be taken from the Bible but out of the pious self-consciousness is accompanied by "uncounted divergencies" of theological trends (*Lehrbuch,* pp. 16 and IX). Nor does modern theology deplore the chaotic condition that has resulted from the repudiation of the Scripture principle. It has sunk so far below the Christian level that it prizes "the divergent trends" in theology as embellishments of the Christian Church and brands the agreement in doctrine and faith, which Scripture clearly demands,[93] as an abnormality, as a "repristination" of an outmoded theological position.

The Erlangen professor Hofmann, of the "conservative" school, has been a most zealous exponent of the Ego theology. In fact, he has been called by some the father of the Ego theology in the Lutheran Church of the nineteenth century. The Leipzig *Theologisches Literaturblatt,* edited by Ihmels, said in its issue of Dec. 8, 1922: "Hofmann, and still more Frank, have come out squarely for the principle of the 'self-assurance of Christianity and its theology' as the all-sufficient source of religious knowledge." Hofmann tells the theologian that in studying and presenting the Christian doctrine he must, for the time being, completely ignore not only what the Church has taught, but also what the teaching of Scripture is; he must train the theological Ego to form its doctrinal conclusions "in exclusive independence." We quote from his *Schriftbeweis* (2d ed., I, 11): "After God has established relations with a man [in Christ], the

---

[93] Scripture demands 1 Cor. 1:10 that "ye all speak the same thing: . . . that ye be perfectly joined together in the same mind and the same judgment"; Eph. 4:5: "one faith." The "sound words," 2 Tim. 1:13, the "sound doctrine," ἡ διδασκαλία ἡ ὑγιαίνουσα (Luther: "*die heilsame Lehre*"), Titus 1:9; 1 Tim. 6:3; 2 Tim. 1:13; 4:3; 1 Tim. 1:10, is the "pure doctrine" (*reine Lehre*), God's own doctrine, unmixed with human thoughts; as the Apostle himself explains the term (1 Tim. 6:3).

believer is on his own; that is to say, that after he has been brought into communion with God – and only within the Church, which has the Scriptures, can this be effected – his relationship with God no longer depends on the Church nor on Scripture, to which the Church appeals; it does not look to the Church nor to Scripture for the primary and real confirmation of its truth, but it rests in itself and has an immediate assurance of the truth. The Ego has within itself the Spirit of God to certify the truth. Accordingly, in giving expression to the truth the Ego must remain the only source. Let it speak for itself, unaffected and undisturbed by anything whatever that lies outside itself, that is, outside ourselves. And though that which is outside us stands in close relation, yea, in a causal relation to that which is within us, and though it proves to be the very same truth: nevertheless, that which is within us must be permitted to perform its function in exclusive independence. To be sure, under normal conditions that which Scripture and the Church offers will be the same as what we have found in ourselves. And it is our business to show this agreement. However, that only follows after the performance of our chief task."

These last statements of Hofmann seem to indicate that he is willing to revise the product of the Ego according to Scripture as the final norm. For that he has been charged with inconsistency, as having abandoned the Ego principle and reverted to "Biblicism" and "intellectualism." Just recently Horst-Stephan censured Hofmann for adding a "Scripture proof – *Schriftbeweis*," "thereby destroying the uniformity of the dogmatic method and returning, in fact, to Biblicistic and Confessionalist dogmatics." [94] There is something in this charge of inconsistency. Hofmann cannot make Scripture a norm if he would remain true to the principles of his experience theology. Hofmann denies very emphatically that the Holy Scriptures are by inspiration God's infallible Word. He insists that it is the business of the theologian to separate the truth from the error in Scripture. In that case Scripture cannot remain the norm; it has become a *norma normata*, which the Ego of the theologian has censored and corrected. If Hofmann really did subject the findings of his Ego to the test of Scripture, if his book really was a "*Schriftbeweis*," he was inconsistent.

However, he did not do that. He did not let Scriptures revise, censor, and correct what his theological Ego, working "in exclusive independence" of Scripture, had found to be the true doctrine. On the contrary, he defended even such products of his Ego as the denial

---

[94] *Glaubenslehre*, Giessen 1921, p. 21.

of the *satisfactio vicaria* with the zeal of the fanatic, defended them in spite of the warnings of his friends, defended them as "the enraged lioness protects her cub." Hofmann was consistent.

He could not pursue a different course. It is impossible to separate these two functions of Scripture: to be the source of the Christian doctrine and to be its norm. The Holy Scriptures are the norm of the Christian doctrine only because they are its only source. And anybody who is in the abnormal state that, in looking for the truth, he compels himself to ignore the Bible completely for the time being and to look exclusively into his own Ego will hardly turn to the Bible later on and ask it to function as the norm and corrective of his Ego product.

Every theologian should be able to see that we are here confronted with an *aut-aut.* Either we accept Scripture as God's own Word and, emphasizing it as the sole source and norm of theology, teach *doctrinam divinam,* or we deny that Scripture is God's infallible Word, distinguish in it between truth and error, and teach, in God's Church, the "visions of our own heart," the *doctrina humana* of our Ego. The divine authority which we take away from Scripture we necessarily assign to our own human mind. We are adrift on the sea of subjectivism. Human opinion occupies the rostrum in the Church. Theology is no longer theocentric, but has become anthropocentric.

The moderns are determined to establish their anthropocentric theology in the Church – not content with defending it (claiming, e. g., that they are teaching "the old truth" in "a new way"), they launch vicious attacks against those who insist on taking the Christian doctrine from Scripture, on teaching the *doctrina divina;* they denounce the absolute dependence on Scripture as "intellectualism," "Biblicism," *"Buchstabentheologie,"* "mechanical treatment of Scripture," treating it as "a manual of dogmatic statutes," "a codex of laws fallen from heaven," "a paper pope," etc. They cannot find invectives enough to apply to the theocentric theology. They employ just about the same abusive vocabulary as the Romanists and the Reformed "enthusiasts" hurled against Luther and the Lutheran Church. Romish theologians have ridiculed the idea as though the Church gets its doctrine from "paper" and "parchment." [95] They did that in the interest

[95] They even quoted 2 Cor. 3:3: "Ye are . . . the epistle of Christ ministered by us, written not with ink, but with the spirit of the living God." Francis Coster asserts in his *Enchiridion Controversiarum Praecipuarum,* c. 1, p. 43, that "Christ did not want to have His Church depend on something written on paper, nor would He entrust His mysteries to parchments." (See Quenstedt, I, 90, 92.)

of the principle that the Ego of the Pope is the source and norm of Christian doctrine. The Reformed "enthusiasts," in like manner, berated Luther's firm adherence to the Word of Scripture as dead *Buchstabentheologie* (literalism) and unevangelical Christianity. Their aim was to clear the way for that "Holy Spirit" who does not need a "vehicle" (*vehiculum, plaustrum*) and finds the use of it beneath His dignity.[96] But since it is the way of God's Holy Spirit to use a "vehicle," namely, the means of grace, they were in reality – whether they were conscious of it or not – enthroning in God's Church their own spirit, which was supposed to deal with the Holy Ghost immediately. And that exactly is the aim of the moderns. When they designate the use of Scripture as the sole source and norm of the Christian doctrine as intellectualism, *Buchstabentheologie,* etc., speak of a "paper pope," and make the "experience" of the theologian the source and norm of doctrine in place of Scripture, they are actually – whether they are doing it consciously or unconsciously or semiconsciously – setting up the product of their own spirit as the supreme authority in God's Church. The divine authority which is taken away from Scripture is actually awarded to the Ego of the theologian. The severe words which Luther uses to characterize the animus back of the papistical discrediting of Scripture: "They speak such things only in order to lead us away from Scripture and make themselves masters over us that we should believe their dream sermons (*Traumpredigten*)" (St. L. V:334), apply in their full force to the moderns. So also what Luther wrote against the Reformed "enthusiasts," who set the judgments of their own "spirit" against Scripture: "Because of their conceited notion that one must disregard these words, 'This is My body,' and first study the matter spiritually, they presume to correct the Evangelists. . . . This devil goes about without a mask and openly instructs us to disregard Scripture,[97] just as Muenzer and Carlstadt also did; they, too, got their wisdom from the witness of their own heart (*"Inwendigkeit"*); they did not need Holy Scripture for themselves but for others, merely using Scripture as an external witness of the witness in their heart." (St. L. XX:1022 f.)

This rejection of the Scripture principle is quite general today. The Ego theology has a monopoly on the modern theological market.

---

96 See the quotations in chapter 5: "The Cause of Divisions."

97 Compare Zwingli's admonition that "no one should permit the anxious searching of the words [the words of institution] to raise scruples in his mind; for we do not base our doctrine on them" (reprinted in Luther's Works, St. L. XX:477).

The outspoken liberal theologians are not the only ones who sell it. There are many "conservative," "positive" theologians, too, who do not want to take the Christian doctrine directly from Scripture; that would be, they say, "intellectualism." Ihmels, for instance, charges that the Early Church and the Church of the Reformation, particularly the dogmaticians, made this mistake. There was, indeed, Ihmels says, some excuse for that. The Early Church had to deal with men "of a religious disposition," and it was but natural that its "immature theology" would appeal to a special supernatural revelation – meaning the appeal to the Word of the Prophets and Apostles as God's Word and doctrine. But it was a mistake to employ this "essentially intellectualistic" method. The Church of the Reformation was in a similar situation. Its opponent, the Church of Rome, claimed divine authority for its traditionally accepted teaching, and the Church of the Reformation "calculated that it could establish the truth of its doctrine most effectively by supporting it, in the most direct way, with the authority of divine revelation." The same wrong method, declares Ihmels, the same intellectualism! Like the Early Church, "the spirit of the Reformation and especially of later Lutheran dogmatics was in the main satisfied with an intellectualistic understanding of revelation." (*Zentralfragen*, 2d ed., p. 56 ff.) According to Ihmels, therefore, one must not take the Christian doctrine solely and exclusively from Scripture, for such an intellectualistic use of Scripture (Biblicism) can produce only a dead Christianity, a Christianity of the intellect.

One wonders how the modern theologians get the strange notion that adherence to the Scripture principle necessarily results in intellectualism, dead orthodoxy, lacking inner warmth. And what they offer as proof for their thesis only increases our wonder. They argue that the old method violates the laws of psychology; it fails to establish the "psychological contact." Richard Rothe describes the situation, as he sees it, thus: "The old dogmatics was wrong in assuming that when God gave His revelation, He at once communicated the supernatural truths. This compelled it to conceive of this communication as a mechanical infusion of such truths and this infusion would necessarily be a magic affair, since the psychological contact with man would be missing." [98] That certainly would be a bad situation. The truth of the matter, however, is that the premise of our old dogmaticians did not compel them to draw Rothe's deduction, nor did they ever operate with the idea of a mechanical transmission of the super-

---

[98] Quoted in Ihmels, *Zentralfragen*, p. 60; Ihmels discusses this "psychological point of contact," p. 78.

natural truths. What they said about the "psychological contact" is exactly the same as what the Apostle Paul said about it. He says in 1 Corinthians 2 that when men "declare the testimony of God," the Holy Ghost is present and psychologically active, that is, the Holy Ghost, by creating faith, moves the psyche, the hearts of the hearers, to accept the testimony of God. And that is exactly what Quenstedt, as spokesman for the old dogmatics, teaches: "The Gospel of Christ is attested as the truth through the testimony of the Holy Spirit in our hearts. In this manner the Holy Ghost bears witness that His doctrine is the truth, that He, through the doctrine revealed by Him in Scripture, inwardly works so that they accept and believe this doctrine as coming from God, as truly divine doctrine." (*Systema*, 1715, I, 145.) Rest at ease; the old dogmaticians and St. Paul did not neglect the matter of the "psychological contact"; everything is in good psychological order.

And let us add that the only way of transmitting the supernatural truths to man is through this creation of a new psychology in him. There is nothing in the psychology of the natural man that will respond to these truths. The Gospel of Christ Crucified has never "entered into the heart of man" (1 Cor. 2:9; Rom. 16:25). And worse, it is to every natural man a "stumbling block" and "foolishness" (1 Cor. 1:23; 2:14). The arguments supplied by the science of apologetics – and there is a great wealth of them – cannot change the human heart, cannot produce an inner acceptance of the Gospel. Accordingly, St. Paul refused to employ the "psychological contact point" of "enticing words of man's wisdom" (ἐν πειθοῖς σοφίας λόγοις); he simply preached the Gospel – with its "demonstration of the Spirit and of power" – in order "that your faith should not stand in the wisdom of men, but in the power of God" (1 Cor. 2:5).

It is certainly a strange aberration to hold that teaching the divine truths directly from Scripture produces mere historical faith, merely an intellectual apprehension, and involves a "mechanical infusion of supernatural truths." – Note, in passing, the conceit of the Ego theology. Most men will agree with us when we say: If the written Word of the Apostles and Prophets of Christ cannot win the hearts of men, cannot establish the "psychological contact," much less will that word do it which modern theologians have evolved out of their "experience." Let the Ego theologians study the forceful words which Luther (in the Smalcald Articles) addressed to all "enthusiasts": "All this is the old devil and old serpent, who also converted Adam and Eve into 'enthusiasts,' and led them from the outward Word of

God to spiritualizing and self-conceit, and nevertheless he accomplished this through outward words. Just as also our 'enthusiasts' [at the present day] condemn the outward Word, and nevertheless they themselves are not silent, but they fill the world with their pratings and writings, as though, indeed, the Spirit would not come through the writings and spoken Word of the Apostles, but [first] through their writings and words He must come" *Trigl.*, 495, 5-6).

That is a bad case of self-deception. And it is not an isolated phenomenon. The entire terminology of the theologians who would procure the Christian doctrine from their own heart moves in the sphere of self-deception, and that means in the sphere of untruthfulness. An examination of the pertinent vocabulary will expose the deception lurking in these phrases. And it is certainly imperative that the theological students of the present age be in a position to detect it.

a. It is sheer delusion to make the Christian "experience" take the place of Scripture. It is a delusion, because without Scripture there can be no Christian experience. Needless to say, there is a Christian experience. Without the personal Christian experience there can be no Christianity. Everyone who is a Christian has experienced, and daily experiences, both sin and grace. He knows and realizes that on account of his sin he is subject to eternal damnation. And he knows and realizes that on account of Christ's *satisfactio vicaria* his sins are forgiven. But this twofold experience of the Christian is wrought solely through the preaching and teaching of God's Word, of the Law and of the Gospel – certainly not through his experience. In order to create this experience of repentance and of the forgiveness of sins, Christ commands that repentance (μετάνοιαν) and remission of sins (ἄφεσιν ἁμαρτιῶν) be preached in His name among all nations (Luke 24:46 f.), and Paul, by Christ's command, proclaimed to Jews and Gentiles "that they should repent and turn to God" (μετανοεῖν καὶ ἐπιστρέφειν ἐπὶ τὸν θεόν, Acts 26:20). This Word, the Word of the Law and the Word of the Gospel, the Church has in the recorded Word of the Apostles, and when the Church preaches this Word, which is God's own Word and pronounces God's own verdict *in re* "sin" and "forgiveness of sins," men learn to know what repentance (*contritio*) and forgiveness of sins (*remissio peccatorum sive fides in Christum*) is. The ideas of sin and salvation which the "grandfather" and the "father" of the Ego theology of the 19th century, Schleiermacher and Hofmann, evolved out of their own heart will never cause a man to experience *contritio* and *fides, fides in Christum crucifixum.* As for Schleiermacher, it is quite generally admitted that his Reformed-pantheistic theology ignores the concept of sin completely. And when Hofmann, guided by his faith consciousness, which operates "independently" of Scripture, denies original sin,[99] he, too, is a poor preacher of repentance. Furthermore, both Schleiermacher and Hofmann, drawing upon their Ego, deny the *satisfactio vicaria.* And such teaching and preaching certainly cannot produce the experience of *fides,* of faith in the Savior crucified for us.

In order to bring about *contritio,* something other than human opinions concerning sin, even though they be "scientifically mediated," must be taught. God's Holy Law alone can do it. God's Law, as the Church has it to the end of time in the written Word of Scripture, must be preached without additions or subtractions. (Matt. 5:17-19; Gal. 3:10, 12.) That, "then, is the thunderbolt of God by which He strikes in a heap [hurls to the ground] both manifest sinners and false saints [hypocrites], and suffers no one to be in the right [declares no one righteous], but drives them all together to terror and despair. This is the hammer, as Jeremiah says, 23:29: 'Is not My Word like a hammer that breaketh the rock in pieces?' This is not *activa contritio,* or manufactured repentance, but *passiva contritio* [torture of conscience], true sorrow of heart, suffering, and sensation of death. This, then, is what it means to begin true repentance; and here man must hear such a sentence as this: You are all of no account, whether you be manifest sinners or saints [in your own opinion]; you all must become different and do otherwise than you now are and are doing [no matter what sort of people you are], be you as great, wise, powerful, and holy as you may. Here no one is [righteous, holy] godly." (Smalc. Art., *Trigl.,* 479, 2-3.) Nor will human opinions concerning the forgiveness of sins, even if they be "scientifically mediated," bring about faith, which must be added to *contritio,* to the *terrores conscientiae.* God's opinion must be taught, God's Word, which the Church, thanks to God, possesses in the Gospel written down in Scripture. That, then, is God's Gospel, εὐαγγέλιον τοῦ θεοῦ, unto which Paul was separated (Rom. 1:1) and which he faithfully proclaimed, suffering neither theologizing men nor an angel from heaven to change it (Gal. 1:7-9). If this Gospel of God is proclaimed and taught in the Church, then we have there, as Luther says, "the consolatory promise of grace through the Gospel" (Smalc. Art., *Trigl.,* 481, 4). Through the Word of the Gospel, faith is produced. The object of faith is the Word of the Gospel, for in the Word of the

---

[99] *Schriftbeweis,* 2d ed., I, 562.

Gospel it apprehends the forgiveness of sins gained by Christ. Luther: "This is the faith that apprehends Christ, who died for our sins and rose again for our justification. This is the faith which Paul preaches and which the Holy Spirit gives and preserves in the hearts of the believers in order to accept the Gospel." (Opp. v. a. IV, 486.)

To repeat, the Christian experience of sin and grace is wrought solely through God's revelation in His Word, in no way through an immediate operation of God or through God's operation in the realm of nature and of history. To the extent that men – "laymen" or "theologians" – separate themselves from Holy Scripture as God's own Word, addressed to us, to that extent they are cut off from the Christian "experience." Men deny this and assert that God powerfully influences our lives through certain occurrences in nature and certain events in history. We answer that God certainly makes use of these events – makes use of them to direct man's external attention to the proclamation of the Word of Christ. But that experience of sin and grace whereby man becomes a Christian and remains a Christian is effected only through the teaching of the divine Word, whether Scripture be directly quoted or not. Without the preaching of Christ's Word darkness covers the earth and gross darkness the people, even though the nations are surrounded by "history," even though God speaks to them with a loud voice in earthquakes, war, famines, etc.[100] For this reason the Church of Christ must continue her mission work among all nations, to the ends of the earth, to the end of time, no matter what and how much is happening among them in history and in the realm of nature. For "how shall they believe in Him of whom they have not heard? . . . So, then, faith cometh by hearing, and hearing by the Word of God. (Rom. 10:14, 17.)

b. Again, the modern theologians are dealing with a delusion when they refuse to derive the Christian doctrine from Scripture but make "faith" or the Christian "faith consciousness" supply it. Not only the radical but also the conservative modern theologians are doing that.[101] To be sure, there is a Christian faith consciousness, and out of it the Christians speak and teach. "I believed, and therefore have I spoken" (2 Cor. 4:13; Ps. 116:10). But this Christian faith has its

---

[100] For further discussion of this point see Vol. II, the last section of the chapter "The Personal Union and the Christological Theories of Modern Theology," and chapter 8 of "Saving Faith."

[101] Nitzsch-Stephan, p. 7: "Julius Kaftan and Herrman are the most radical proponents of this view. But also Ihmels insists that 'only those things need to be sharply defined of which faith is immediately certain' (*Zentralfragen*, p. 101)."

being exclusively in the Word of the Apostles (John 17:20). The Christian faith knows nothing but God's Word. That "faith," however, which is not faith in the Word of the Apostles, which declares its independence of the Word, rejecting it as the sole source and norm of faith, is *ex toto,* in every respect, human delusion; as Paul puts it (1 Tim. 6:3), the teaching of those who do not abide by the wholesome words of Christ proceeds out of conceited ignorance. Luther indeed says: "Faith teaches and holds to the truth," but he adds at once: "For faith clings to the Scriptures; they do not lie and deceive." (St. L. XI:162.) "Faith" and "God's Word" are certainly inseparably joined together, but not in this wise that faith comes first and doctrine follows, faith making the doctrine, but in this wise that the Word is first and fixes and determines faith. As Luther says: "The Word of God is first, and out of it flows faith." "Whatever does not have its origin in Scripture is surely of the devil himself." Because the theologians, says Luther, had gotten away from Scripture, "which alone is the source of all wisdom in theology," such "monstrosities (*portenta*)" arose in theology "as Thomas, Scotus, and others." (St. L. XIX:34; 1080; I:1289 f.) This severe judgment of Luther applies to its full extent to modern theology in so far as it will not permit God's Word, Holy Scripture, to be faith's source of knowledge and its object, but wants faith to be its own source and its own object.

Some advocates of the Ego theology have gone even farther. They set up the monstrous proposition that the Christian religion is not "in real truth" concerned with doctrine and hence Scripture must not be regarded as "a divine manual of religion" (Nitzsch-Stephan, p. 249). This notion, they say, is a papistical remnant still clinging to the dogmaticians. And to Luther, too. Also Meusel's *Kirchliches Handlexicon* places doctrine and Christian religion in opposition. "What the New Testament, and also St. Paul, is primarily concerned with is not doctrine, but revelation and religion. What Grau (in Zoeckler, *Handbuch der Theologischen Wissenschaft,* I, 561) says concerning Paulinism – that its tenor is religion and life, not dogma or system of doctrine – holds true of the entire New Testament." (IV, 209, *sub Lehrbegriff.*) This view, though unscriptural and unreasonable, is shared also by Ihmels. He makes statements like this: "The essential thing about revelation is not that it imparts doctrine, but that it is a self-disclosure of God. Clearly only such an understanding of revelation is in accord with evangelical faith."[102] But Christ's Word, which

[102] Ihmels, *Aus der Kirche* etc., 1914, p. 18.

we have in the Word of His Apostles, is exactly that: in it God both manifests Himself and imparts the doctrine, the doctrine on which alone the faith that knows the truth is based. Christ states distinctly: "If ye continue in My Word (λόγος) . . . ye shall know the truth."

Depriving faith of its object, namely, the doctrine presented in Scripture, has, as Eduard Koenig said, fatal results: It destroys the Biblical concept of "believing" and does away with the Christian religion as a positive religion.[103] Indeed, it is due to an astounding aberration of the human mind that men can assert that "doctrine" or the "communication of doctrine" is not a "prime" concern of the Christian religion; we cannot comprehend how they can claim in all seriousness that what is to be preached is not "doctrine," but "faith," arguing that only in this way "a living Christianity can be produced" and "dead orthodoxy," "intellectualism," warded off. The stubborn fact is that from its very beginning the Christian religion dealt with doctrine and the impartation of doctrine. The Word spoken in the very beginning about the Seed of the woman, who would crush the head of the Serpent (Gen. 3:15), what is it but doctrine? And the entire Old Testament was written, as the Apostle Paul assures us, for our learning, εἰς τὴν ἡμετέραν διδασκαλίαν (doctrine), Rom. 15:4, and is profitable πρὸς διδασκαλίαν (doctrine), 2 Tim. 3:16. When in the fullness of the time the Son of God appeared in the flesh and walked here on earth, He engaged in teaching. He teaches from the ship (Luke 5:3), on the mount (Matt. 5:2), in the synagogs (Luke 4:15), went about the land teaching (Matt. 4:23). He also makes use of the forty days between His resurrection and ascension to teach (Acts 1:3), and before His ascension He gives His Church the commission to teach all nations to the Last Day: "Teaching them to observe all things whatsoever I have commanded you" (Matt. 28:20). And the Apostles executed this commission. Paul declared, taught, publicly and from house to house, all the counsel of God (Acts 20:20, 27). Teaching the saving doctrine was his chief business, and he tells his successors in the ministry that it must be their chief business. He bids Timothy and Titus to hold fast the form of sound words, the doctrine, which they had heard from him (2 Tim. 1:13; Titus 1:9; 2 Tim. 2:2) and requires of the bishop that he should be apt to teach, διδακτικός (1 Tim. 3:2). Teachers should know that Scripture is given first of all "for doctrine" (2 Tim. 3:16). The members of the congregations, too, are bidden,

---

[103] See his book *"Der Glaubensakt des Christen, nach Begriff und Fundament untersucht,"* 1891, p. 119. Also his *Theologie des A. T.*, 1921, p. 313.

like the teachers, to continue in the doctrine and to apply the doctrine to one another. Col. 3:16: "Let the Word of Christ dwell in you richly in all wisdom, teaching and admonishing one another." 2 Thess. 2:15: "Therefore, brethren, stand fast, and hold the traditions which ye have been taught, whether by word or our Epistle." It is said in praise of the Christians at Jerusalem that they continued steadfastly in the Apostles' doctrine, διδαχή (Acts 2:42); and the Apostle John deems the adherence to the doctrine of Christ of such great importance that he instructs the churches to deny Christian fellowship to all who do not bring the doctrine of Christ (2 John 9-11). When in spite of all this modern theologians insist that Holy Scripture must not be regarded as "doctrine" nor received as a "manual" of the Christian religion, it is evident that their conception of the Christian religion is diametrically opposed to that of Christ and His Apostles and Prophets.

c. The moderns are deluding themselves when they imagine that the "regenerate Ego" or the new man in the theologian can and will serve as the source of Christian doctrine. Surely, the regenerate Ego, the new man, speaks and teaches. And it is the will of God that all teachers of the Church should be reborn, new men (see chap. 9). But you are insulting the new man if you consider him capable of committing the folly of disregarding Scripture, even though only "for the first," and seeking some other source and norm of the Christian doctrine. Where this method is employed, the old Adam is playing the theologian. There the revolutionist is at work, breaking down the foundation on which the Christian Church is built (Eph. 2:20). There Nietzsche's "Superman" has taken over. Nietzsche placed his Ego above God's Moral Law, "beyond good and evil"; even so the moderns place themselves as "supermen" above God's Word by asserting that it is for the theologian to determine what is true and what is false in Scripture and that only so much of Scripture is true as has approved itself as the truth to the theologian's Ego, his "experience," etc. The new man, however, does not engage in that kind of theology. The new man in the theologian has too much sense for that. He knows Scripture to be the Word of God, subjects himself to it unconditionally, regulates and forms his thoughts and judgments according to the "It is written," and with Luther submerges all thoughts that emerge in his old Adam contrary to Scripture. The new man has learned from John 8:31-32 that only by continuing in Christ's Word can the truth be known, and he is therefore guided by the general rule binding all teachers: "If any man speak [that is, in the Christian Church], let him speak as the oracles of God" (1 Pet. 4:11).

We are not impugning the personal faith of everyone who is enmeshed in the Ego theology. Here, too, a "felicitous inconsistency" may obtain. It will happen, too, that one and the same theologian contradicts himself in one and the same writing; on the one hand he declines to base his faith on "doctrines communicated" in Scripture, and on the other hand he practically admits that faith without the Scripture basis is not faith but delusion. A Christian theologian may forget for a time what the true situation is; but when his Christian intelligence asserts itself, his new man clearly sees that it is a trick of the old man to play up the "regenerate Ego" and "faith" and "faith consciousness" against the Word of Scripture, the only source and norm of theology.

d. It is hard to understand how men can make themselves believe that in ascertaining the Christian doctrine one must look not so much to the words (usually they say "the letter") of Scripture as rather to the "content," the import. Here we have one of the many catch phrases which despite their inanity endure from generation to generation. It is a formula which requires us to perform a logical and psychological impossibility. You cannot understand the content of a message without the words which express that message. And since the meaning of Scripture, like that of any other writing, lies solely in the words of Scripture, this meaning is certain only because the words are certain and reliable. If we cannot rely on the words of Scripture, the doctrinal content of Scripture will ever remain a matter of conjecture and doubt. But in order to save us from this condition of uncertainty, which to the anxious soul is more bitter than death (cp. *Trigl.*, 291, 31), the Savior assures us that Scripture cannot be broken and directs us to the words of His Apostles. The instruction given John 8 does not say: "If ye continue in the content of My Word," but "If ye continue in My Word (λόγος), then . . . ye shall know the truth." So also the instruction Christ gives in John 17:20 does not separate content and words, but declares that men will believe in Him through the word of the Apostles (διὰ λόγου αὐτῶν). — This matter will be taken up again in the *locus* "Holy Scripture," particularly in the chapter on the "*variae lectiones*," which some adduce as disproving the trustworthiness of the Word of Scripture.

Take note that also the Christian experience (*Erlebnis*) protests most emphatically against this proposed separation of the contents and the words of Holy Scripture. In the seclusion of his study the theologian may be satisfied to say: "Not the words but the contents of Scripture is what counts." He will not say it when his soul is battling for its life. Consciences stricken by the Law of God can find peace only when they take their stand on the unshakable foundation on which the whole Christian Church is built, on the Word of the Apostles and Prophets (Eph. 2:20), on Christ's own Word (John 8:31). Lessing, indeed, cried out: "Who will deliver us from the intolerable yoke of the letter!" (meaning the words of Scripture), and modern theology, separating the import of Scripture and the words of Scripture, fulfilled his wish. But remember, Lessing preferred a state of doubt to the state of certainty; as witness his well-known declaration: "If God held in His right hand all truth and in His left only the ever-active impulse to search for truth, even with the condition that I must always make mistakes, and said to me: 'Choose!' I should humbly bow before His left hand and say: 'Father, give me this. Pure truth belongs to Thee alone.'"[104] That is in accord with Lessing's religious position, his "experience." "Lessing did not treat the concepts 'sin' and 'redemption' as matters concerning him personally; as a consequence a supernatural revelation, the Word of Scripture, had no value for him."[105]

e. The contention, finally, that because of the "historical character" of the Christian religion the philosophy of history must determine the Christian doctrine is not in accord with the facts of history.[106] To be sure, the Christian religion bears a "historical character," and preeminently so. Scripture testifies that the eternal Son of God became man and thus entered "history." The Eternal became temporal. Scripture furthermore tells us that this wonderful divine mystery was revealed by the command of the eternal God, through the prophetic writings, in human language and thus became a part of recorded history. "According to the revelation of the mystery . . . now made known to all nations" (Rom. 16:25 f.). And here is another historical fact with which the philosophy of history must deal: "the revelation of salvation" has been completed with the Word of Christ, which we have in the Word of His Apostles. It is so fully finished and closed that all subsequent history cannot change it in the least. Richard Gruetzmacher is perfectly right in saying: "For us the historical revela-

---

104 See Ed. Koenig, *Der Glaubensakt*, p. 63; *Concise Dictionary of Rel. Knowledge*, by Jackson, *sub* "Lessing."

105 Bertheau in R. E. 2d ed., VIII, 611.

106 Before there was a written Word, the spoken Word of God served the same purpose. God has always accompanied the historical facts through which He effected our redemption with His historical Word, lest men indulge in their own thoughts about the appearance of the Son of God in the flesh.

tion of salvation is contained solely in the record of it given in Holy Scripture." [107] Now, the position of the moderns is not in accord with this historical fact. When they operate with the "historical character" of Christianity for the purpose of setting aside Scripture as the only source and norm of the Christian doctrine from their own cogitations, they are engaged in an entirely unhistorical attack on the true history of Christianity. They are simply deluding themselves with their talk about evaluating Christianity "historically." Moreover, by making the "philosophy of history" a source and norm of the Christian doctrine, they are infringing on the authority of Christ: Christ in His Word is the one and only Teacher (εἷς ὁ διδάσκαλος) in the Church to the end of days (Matt. 23:8; 28:19-20; John 8:31-32; 17:20).

To sum up: If we, the theological teachers, refuse to recognize Scripture as God's own Word and to employ it as the sole source and norm of theology, we shall not be teaching God's doctrine (*doctrinam divinam*), but our own opinions (*proprias opiniones*). It is immaterial whether we call this subjective source and norm Christian experience or faith or faith consciousness or the regenerate Ego or the historical understanding of Christianity, etc. All roads that by-pass Scripture as the one and only source and norm of theology lead into the Ego theology. And we, as Christians, should remind ourselves of the words of Luther, already quoted: "They speak such things only in order to lead us away from Scripture and make themselves masters over us, that we should believe their dream sermons (*Traumpredigten*)" (St. L. V:334). Employing drastic language, Luther says (col. 336): "They would lead us away from Scripture, obscure faith, lay and hatch their own eggs, and become our idol."

The situation, then, is this: Modern theology must execute a complete change of base before it can claim to be Christian theology. It must abandon its basic principle that Scripture is a human book and must learn again to "identify" Scripture and the Word of God. It must recognize the claim of Scripture that it is God's own infallible Word. It must declare with Christ and His Apostles: "All Scripture is given by inspiration of God" (2 Tim. 3:15, 16); "The Scripture cannot be broken" (John 10:35); "It is written" (Matt. 4:4, 7, 10). (See also Luke 24:25; John 17:12; Matt. 26:54; Rom. 16:25-26; 2 Thess. 2:15.) It will then have learned the only correct theological method, the method according to which we refuse to draw the Christian doctrine

---

[107] *Studien zur systematischen Theologie*, Vol. III, p. 40. Gruetzmacher unfortunately does not always apply the truth he so well expresses.

either out of the Ego of other men or out of our own Ego but accept Scripture unreservedly as the "divine manual of religion" and stand squarely on the proposition: *Quod non est biblicum, non est theologicum.* Then, too, there will be an end to the nasty talk about *Buchstabentheologie,* intellectualism, Biblicism, paper pope, codex of dogmas fallen from the skies, etc. No, we have learned and joyfully proclaim that the doctrine taken from Scripture, being God's own doctrine, *doctrina divina,* has the benign power to win its way into the hearts of men and that, far from inducing "dead orthodoxy," it produces "living" Christianity, Christianity pulsating with divine warmth and strength. Likewise the multiform gibes about "pure doctrine" will disappear; coming under the rule of the Scripture principle, men no longer ridicule "the sound doctrine" (ὑγιαίνουσα διδασκαλία, Titus 1:9; 2 Tim. 1:13), but realize with holy fear that this is the only kind of doctrine permissible in God's Church, the only kind befitting the Christian teacher.

The conviction that Holy Scripture is God's own Word and the sole source of the divine doctrine, produces these three chief virtues in the theologian: (1) He will despair of his wisdom and approach Scripture with the humble spirit that prays: "Speak, Lord; for thy servant heareth" (1 Sam. 3:9). (2) He will not seek other textbooks of the Christian doctrine, but will receive the doctrine revealed in Scripture by faith, the only *medium cognoscendi* of the divine doctrine, and faithfully teach it; he will pray God to keep him from mixing the chaff of his own foolish thoughts with the wheat of the divine thoughts (Jer. 23:28). (3) He will through the grace of God have the courage and strength to demand exclusive authority for the doctrine taken from Scripture as being God's own doctrine and thus do his part to check the ravages of indifferentism, doctrinal chaos, and confusion. – Theodore Kaftan has been charging certain men whom he classes with the "old theologians" with a "deficiency in confidence and strength." He says: "It is very noticeable that the attitude of these representatives of the old theology, taken as a whole, is that of despondency; a sort of discouragement, a feeling of weakness frequently prevails; they say, in effect: We are a failure." [108] If these old-school theologians have indeed, as Kaftan asserts, become disheartened and weak-spirited, it is only because the pressure of the *Zeitgeist* has shaken their conviction that Scripture is by inspiration God's own infallible Word. But as soon as these men become aware

---

[108] *Moderne Theologie des Alten Glaubens,* 1906, p. 120 f.

of the real situation and again realize on what their faith and the faith of all Christendom is founded (Eph. 2:20) and what they absolutely need in their temptation from within and without, they will again with Christ and His Apostles confidently utter the γέγραπται, "It is written," and repeat, not merely with the mouth, but from the depth of their hearts, the word of Luther: *"Das Wort sie sollen lassen stahn."* They will then also know how to appraise the "greater confidence" which Kaftan finds in himself and other modern theologians; it is the "confidence" of men who are "puffed up with conceit" (1 Tim. 6:4, R. S. V.), the "confidence" of the Pope and the "enthusiasts" of all times. Luther describes it thus: "All confidence which is not based on the Word of God is vain" (St. L. VI:70. on Is. 7:9). "Solely through His Word, God would declare to us His will and His counsels, not through our notions and imaginations" (St. L. III:1417 on Deut. 4:12).

11

Divisions of the Christian Doctrine

In this chapter we shall discuss: (A) Law and Gospel; (B) Fundamental and Non-fundamental Doctrines; (C) Open Questions and Theological Problems.

A. LAW AND GOSPEL

Fr. H. R. Frank has called attention to the fact that the doctrine of Law and Gospel and in particular of the difference between Law and Gospel – a doctrine which Luther and the old theologians treated most thoroughly – has practically disappeared from modern theology. Modern theologians have no use for it.[109] Frank says: "Ritschl has declared most emphatically that the customary distinction between Law and Gospel with all that it implies is incorrect." And Horst Stephan made a similar statement: "There is no sense, after the manner of the old dogmatics, in dividing the 'Word of God' into Law and Gospel."[110] Frank is right in saying: "It characterizes the present state of affairs that men find also this part of the evangelical doctrine objectionable and declare it to be in conflict with the true evangelical spirit" (*loc. cit.*, p. 104). It does not surprise us that modern theology would have no use for the distinction between Law and Gospel. That

---

[109] *Dogmatische Studien*, Erlangen and Leipzig, 1892, pp. 104–135.

[110] *Glaubenslehre*, 1921, p. 183.

idea is the inevitable result of the denial of the *satisfactio Christi vicaria,* which characterizes modern theology. Certainly, if God did not fully reconcile mankind unto Himself through Christ's vicarious satisfaction, if Christ has not, in our stead, fulfilled the requirements of the Law which binds mankind, and suffered its punishment in our stead, it necessarily follows that man must somehow by his own work and his own virtues either effect his reconciliation with God or complete the reconciliation begun by Christ. That is just what modern theologians teach. The "conservatives" among them, too, hold that the Savior's work of reconciliation must be supplemented by man's holiness. One of them states it thus: "We are compelled to make the transformation of man a factor in the work of the atonement."[111] That does away with the difference between Law and Gospel. What we get, as Frank puts it, is "a veritable hodgepodge" (*Glaubenslehre,* 1921, p. 124).

This "hodgepodge" is not a harmless matter. Scripture warns us that the commingling of Law and Gospel has fatal results. It definitely tells the sinner who is seeking remission of his sins and eternal salvation that he can obtain this in no other way than by completely eliminating the Law from his consideration and placing himself under the Gospel. This is God's method of forgiving sins and bestowing salvation: "without the Law," χωρὶς νόμου (Rom. 3:21); "by faith . . . without the deeds of the Law," πίστει . . . χωρὶς ἔργων νόμου (Rom. 3:28); "by faith in Jesus Christ," διὰ πίστεως Χριστοῦ Ἰησοῦ (Gal. 2:16; Rom. 3:22); "through faith," διὰ πίστεως (Eph. 2:8); "through the Gospel," διὰ τοῦ εὐαγγελίου (1 Cor. 4:15). All who refuse to eliminate the Law in the matter of obtaining grace and salvation remain under the curse of the Law, since the Law pronounces the curse on everyone who has not continued in all things which are written in the book of the Law to do them (Gal. 3:10). Luther is therefore right in saying that every Christian must know the art of separating Law and Gospel. "If this is lacking, one cannot tell a Christian from a pagan or a Jew" (St. L. IX:798). There is only one way to be and remain a Christian: Man must silence his conscience against the accusations of the Law with the Gospel, which assures him of the forgiveness of sins "without the Law." And only those men are able to lead a holy life according to the Law who "are not under the Law, but under grace" (Rom. 6:14). All this will be treated in detail in the chapter on the means of grace

---

[111] Kirn, R. E., 3d ed., XX, 574; also in his *Ev. Dogm.,* 3d ed., p. 118. Cp. the section "Some Modern Theories of the Atonement Examined" in Vol. II.

under the heading "Law and Gospel," in Vol. III. Here we are presenting only so much as bears on the matter before us – the "division" of the doctrines of Scripture and the characteristics of true "theology" and the true "theologian."

Holy Scripture, the Word of God, is divided into Law and Gospel.[112] The theologian must teach both, without curtailment or alteration. He dare not discard any part of the Law nor make any alterations in the Gospel. As for the Law, God declares: "Till heaven and earth pass, one jot or one tittle shall in no wise pass from the Law," and adds the warning: "Whosoever therefore shall break one of these least commandments and shall teach men so, he shall be called the least in the kingdom of heaven" (Matt. 5:17-19). And as for the Gospel, the Apostle Paul pronounces the curse on everyone who teaches any other Gospel than he himself taught (Gal. 1:7-9). But now Law and Gospel are absolute opposites, "*plus quam contradictoria*" (St. L. IX:447). The Law curses everyone who has not kept it perfectly (Gal. 3:10; Rom. 3:9-19) and is "the ministration of condemnation" (2 Cor. 3:9). But according to the Gospel, God does not impute to man the transgression of the Law (2 Cor. 5:19). This is "the Gospel of the grace of God" (Acts 20:24), also "the ministration of righteousness" (2 Cor. 3:9). How shall the theologian meet this seemingly confusing situation? He will preach both Law and Gospel in their full force; but no confusion can arise if he keeps Law and Gospel separate. He does that when he confines each to its own particular sphere. He who knows when and where to apply the Law, when and where to apply the Gospel, is indeed a Christian theologian.

1. According to God's will and order, as set down in Scripture, the knowledge of sin must be taught from the Law, for "by the Law is the knowledge of sin" (Rom. 3:20), while the remission of sins, or justification, must be taught solely from the Gospel, for "we conclude that a man is justified by faith, without the deeds of the Law" (Rom. 3:28). Whoever teaches that forgiveness is obtained also by observing the Law is no Christian theologian, but a deceiver, who seduces men away from Christianity, for "Christ is become of no effect unto you whosoever of you are justified by the Law; ye are fallen from grace"

---

[112] Throughout Scripture God's Law is taught (Matt. 22:37-40), and throughout Scripture God's Gospel is taught (Rom. 1:1-2; 3:21; Acts 10:43). The Apology states: "All Scripture ought to be distributed into these two principal topics, the Law and the promises. For in some places it presents the Law, and in others the promise concerning Christ." (*Trigl.* 121, 5.)

(Gal. 5:4). The evil work of such calls forth the imprecation of the Apostle: "I would they were even cut off which trouble you" (Gal. 5:12). It follows that the Law, by which the knowledge of sins is produced, must be preached to the self-righteous and secure sinners, to those who will not acknowledge that they deserve God's wrath and eternal damnation. "We know," says the Apostle, "that what things soever the Law saith, it saith to them who are under the Law, that every mouth may be stopped and all the world may become guilty before God" (Rom. 3:19). The Gospel, on the other hand, should be preached to those whom the Law has humbled and who therefore are contrite and brokenhearted and poor in spirit (Matt. 11:5; Luke 4:18). The spiritual condition of the persons dealt with determines when the Law and when the Gospel is to be applied.

2. The Law is the only source from which the Christian theologian teaches what good works are, even as Christ Himself pointed to the Law when He answered the question which works are commanded by God and are therefore God-pleasing (Matt. 15:1 ff.; 22:35 ff.; 19:16 ff.). Christians, too, need the Law in this respect, for, because of their old Adam, they are prone to take commandments of men, such as the commandments concerning meat and drink, celibacy, etc. (Col. 2:16-22; 1 Tim. 4:1 ff.), to be commandments of God. But the Law cannot produce the works which are commanded by God and are good in His sight. The Christian theologian knows and ever bears in mind that only the Gospel can create in man the will and strength to do good works. The Apostle knew of no other way: "I beseech you, therefore, brethren, by the mercies of God, that ye present your bodies a living sacrifice, holy, acceptable unto God" (Rom. 12:1). Axiom: *Lex praescribit, evangelium inscribit* (Jer. 31:31-34). Luther: "The lawmonger compels by threats and punishments; the preacher of grace persuades and incites men by setting forth the goodness and mercy of God" (St. L. XII:318). Learn to preach the Gospel, and you have learned the art of making your people zealous of good works.

3. The Christian theologian knows, too, that he cannot successfully combat sin by means of the Law. The Law can, indeed, check sin outwardly, but inwardly it only activates and multiplies sin. Paul speaks from experience: "For when we were in the flesh [under the Law], the motions of sin which were by the Law did work in our members to bring forth fruit unto death" (Rom. 7:5). It is the Gospel alone which slays the sin in man. "But now we are delivered from the Law, that being dead wherein we were held; that we should serve in newness of spirit and not in the oldness of the letter" (Rom. 7:6).

And Rom. 6:14 declares: "Sin shall have no dominion over you; for ye are not under the Law, but under grace." Axiom: *Lex necat peccatorem, non peccatum; evangelium necat peccatum, non peccatorem.* – "Therefore place him who is well versed in this art of dividing the Law from the Gospel at the head and call him a Doctor of Holy Writ" (St. L. IX:802).

B. FUNDAMENTAL AND NON-FUNDAMENTAL DOCTRINES

The distinction between fundamental and non-fundamental doctrines and the further distinction between primary and secondary fundamental articles is not a dispensation from accepting certain doctrines of the Bible. No man has the right to discard any Scripture teaching. Scripture expressly forbids it. Christ gave His Church the specific commission: "Teaching them to observe all things whatsoever I have commanded you" (Matt. 28:20). And Paul declares (Acts 20:27): "I have not shunned to declare unto you all the counsel of God." In the Old Testament, too, men were forbidden to add to the written Word or to take anything away from it (Joshua 1:8; Deut. 17:19). That means that nothing in Scripture may be regarded as superfluous or worthless. "Whatsoever things were written aforetime were written for our learning" (Rom. 15:4; 2 Tim. 3:16; 1 Cor. 10:11; Rom. 4:23-24). But while all doctrines of Scripture are important and binding, we do well to distinguish between fundamental and non-fundamental doctrines, as Scripture does. And this distinction has great practical value.

It will become clear that this distinction is Scriptural and of practical value when, for example, the doctrine concerning Christ and the doctrine concerning Antichrist are compared. Both doctrines are revealed in Scripture. But their relation to saving faith differs radically. The doctrine concerning Christ is the foundation of this faith, for saving faith has as its object Christ in His vicarious satisfaction; it is faith in Christ. "Ye are all the children of God by faith in Christ Jesus" (Gal. 3:26). The doctrine concerning Antichrist, however, is not fundamental to the Christian faith. Scripture nowhere says that men obtain forgiveness of their sins and are saved by knowing who the Antichrist is. What it does say, everywhere and always, in the Old and in the New Testament, is that salvation comes through the knowledge of Christ, through faith in Christ. This does not mean, however, that the doctrine of the Antichrist, as set down in Scripture, serves no purpose. It serves saving faith inasmuch as it warns against the dangers threatening the Christian faith through Antichrist's seductions. We shall discuss this self-evident truth more fully later on. — A remark in passing: The old Lutheran teachers did not, as some have stated, classify the doctrine of the Antichrist as a "fundamental article." Rather they have expressly declared that before as well as after the unveiling of the Antichrist by the Reformation many Christians did not, and do not, recognize the Papacy as the Antichrist.

The question which articles are "fundamental articles" as distinguished from non-fundamental articles must be answered by Scripture. And Scripture clearly states which articles constitute the foundation of the Christian faith. Some say that in the interest of freedom of doctrine the concept "fundamental doctrines" cannot be clearly defined; they point to the fact that there is no general agreement among theologians on this question. The Erlangen theologian Hofmann, for instance, thinks that "the dispute about the distinction between fundamentals and non-fundamentals has up to this day yielded no results" (*Der Schriftbeweis*, 2d ed., I, 9. 10). Our reply is that where the Scriptural concept of the object of saving faith is accepted, there can be no doubt as to which are the *articuli fundamentales.* According to Scripture, saving faith is faith in the remission of sins for the sake of Christ's vicarious satisfaction, faith in the grace of God, who justifies the sinner without the deeds of the Law, by faith. Scripture teaches that only he who through the operation of the Holy Ghost accepts this forgiveness, this justification, is a true believer, a "believer" in the Scriptural sense of the term (Gal. 2:16: "Knowing that a man is not justified by the works of the Law, but by the faith of Jesus Christ, even we have believed in Jesus Christ"). Only such a one is a member of the Christian Church. Believers in the Lord were added to the Church (Acts 5:14).[113] One who does not believe the article of justification by faith is not, as Scripture plainly states, a "child of Abraham," is not numbered among the believers, is outside the Christian Church (Gal. 3:6-10). Luther puts it thus: "This article [of justification] is the head and cornerstone which alone begets, nourishes, builds, preserves, and protects the Church; without it the Church of God cannot subsist one hour" (St. L. XIV:168). Again: "All people in the world who do not hold this article [*doctrinam justificationis*] are either Jews or Turks or Papists or heretics" (St. L. IX:24). The dogmaticians have called the doctrine of justification *articulum omnium fundamentalissimum.* (See the quotations in Baier-Walther, III, 245 sq.)

---

[113] Luther: *"Die da glaubeten an den Herrn."*

But Scripture informs us further that faith in the forgiveness of sins for Christ's sake presupposes and includes certain other doctrines. Scripture teaches clearly:

1. That the knowledge of sin and of the consequence of sin, eternal damnation, is a prerequisite of saving faith. As long as men fail to realize that their sins merit eternal damnation and as long as they trust in their own goodness for eternal salvation, they have no interest in the forgiveness of sins obtained by Christ for the condemned sinner. The only effective way of dealing with sinful man is therefore to preach first repentance and then forgiveness of sins. Christ prescribed this method in Luke 24:47. The story of the Pharisee and the publican (Luke 18:9-14) teaches the same truth. Christ rejects very definitely the faith of the Pharisee, who refused to believe that he was under God's wrath, guilty of eternal damnation, but who thanked God that he "was not as other men are" and believed that in God's sight he was better than the extortioners, unjust, adulterers, or "this publican." Christ's method is shown in all those Scripture passages which declare that the grace of God is nigh unto the "brokenhearted" and dwells with them (Is. 66:2; 57:15; Ps. 34:18; 51:17; Luke 4:18).

2. Scripture furthermore teaches very definitely that saving faith includes the knowledge of the Person of Christ; it knows that Christ is θεάνθρωπος, God and Man. Christ's question, "What think ye of Christ? whose Son is He?" (Matt. 22:42) has not merely academic, but a very practical value. Christ Himself declares that unless men believe in the essential deity of Christ, they do not believe in Christ. He rejects the belief of the Jewish people, who took Him for John the Baptist, Elias, Jeremias, or one of the Prophets; and He commended the faith of His disciples who, through the revelation of the Father, knew Him as the Son of the living God (Matt. 16:13-17; 1 John 1:1-4). The fact that men are ready to give Jesus the title of God *honoris causa* does not make them believers; as long as they deny His eternal godhead, they do not possess the saving faith. The Unitarians and the Unitarian Modernists are placed by Scripture *extra ecclesiam.* (See 1 John 5:12-13; *Trigl.* 103, 2.) — The same is true of the Trinity. Because the *unus Deus* is Father, Son, and Holy Ghost, faith in the three Persons is, according to Scripture, so closely interwoven that there can be no knowledge of the Son without the Father (Matt. 16:17: "Blessed art thou, Simon Barjona; for flesh and blood hath not revealed it unto thee, but My Father which is in heaven";

11:27 a: "No man knoweth the Son but the Father"); there is no knowledge of the Father without the Son (Matt. 11:27 b: "Neither knoweth any man the Father save the Son and he to whomsoever the Son will reveal Him"); and there is no knowledge of the Father and the Son without the Holy Ghost (Rom. 8:15: "Ye have received the Spirit of adoption, whereby we cry, Abba, Father"; 1 Cor. 12:3: "No man can say that Jesus is the Lord but by the Holy Ghost"; John 16:13-15). – For the purpose of invalidating these New Testament statements on the Trinity the moderns contend that such "reflections" on Father, Son, and Holy Spirit were far beyond the first Christians. They even challenge the historicity of the Trinitarian baptismal formula of Matt. 28:19 on the ground that the early Christians were totally unaware of the doctrine of the Trinity. The truth of the matter is, as will be shown in the *locus* on Baptism, that modern theology is, in a most unhistorical manner, foisting its own deficiency in Christian knowledge upon the early Christians. Not only the early Christians, but also the Old Testament believers accepted the revelation of the Trinity as will be shown in the *locus* "De Deo."

3. The *fides salvifica* includes also the knowledge of the work of Christ. According to Scripture, Christ is the object of saving faith, not in so far as He is a Teacher of the divine Law, nor in so far as He is the "ideal man," the perfect Pattern of morality, but only in so far as He is the Mediator between God and men, who gave Himself a ransom (ἀντίλυτρον) for all (1 Tim. 2:5-6), the Lamb of God which taketh away the sin of the world (John 1:29). One who does not believe Christ's *satisfactio vicaria* is not a believer in the Scriptural sense; he bases – *tertium non datur* – his reconciliation with God in some way on his own work and his own worthiness and thus *eo ipso* excludes himself from the grace earned by Christ. That is the express verdict of Scripture. "Christ is become of no effect unto you . . . ye are fallen from grace" (Gal. 5:4). True, there are children of God, true believers, within such communions as ban the teaching that justification for the sake of Christ's perfect merit constitutes the foundation of saving faith (Rome); but that is due to the fact that these men, in spite of the Church's interdict, put their trust solely in Christ, crucified for their sins. The Apology therefore declares, on the one hand, that the Roman Church does indeed subvert the foundation of the Christian faith: "Most of those errors which our adversaries defend overthrow faith, as their condemnation of the article concerning the remission of sins, in which we say that the remission of sins is by faith. Likewise it is a manifest and pernicious error when

the adversaries teach that men merit the remission of sins by love of God, prior to grace. For this also is to remove the 'foundation,' i. e., Christ. Likewise, what need will there be of faith if the Sacraments justify *ex opere operato,* without a good disposition on the part of the one using them? [Now, a person that does not regard faith as necessary has already lost Christ. Again, they set up the worship of saints, call upon them instead of Christ, the Mediator, etc.]" (*Trigl.* 233, 21.) On the other hand, the Apology says: "Nevertheless, the knowledge of Christ has always remained with some godly persons" (*Trigl.* 225, 271).

4. Scripture teaches, furthermore, that saving faith is always faith in the Word of Christ, faith in the external Word of the Gospel, which Christ commanded His Church to preach and to teach (Mark 16:15-16; Rom. 1:1-2). This external Word is both the object of faith ("Believe the Gospel," Mark 1:15) and the means by which faith is created ("Faith cometh by hearing," Rom. 10:17). A belief whose object is not the Word of Christ as we have it in the Word of His Apostles (John 17:20) and which is not the product of this Word, is according to the Scriptures a delusion, ignorance, and a human fabrication (1 Tim. 6:3-4; 1 Cor. 2:1-5: "faith in the wisdom of men"). The faith which is not based on the external Word is, as Luther puts it, nothing but an air castle.[114] True, there are children of God within those communions which officially reject the external Word of Christ as the medium of the forgiveness of sins; but that is due solely to the fact that there are always those who in spite of the official teaching of their Church base their faith on the written Word. (On the "felicitous inconsistency" found within the Reformed communions more will be said later.)

5. Scripture teaches, finally, that the denial of the bodily resurrection of the dead and of the eternal life subverts the Christian faith. This is done by the radical wing of modern Protestantism which says that it is sufficient to believe in Christ for this life; the "hereafter,"

---

[114] See the section "Saving Faith Is Trust in the Grace That is Offered to Us in the Gospel" in Vol. II, p. 446 ff. — The old distinction between the *fundamentum substantiale* [Christ] and the *fundamentum organicum* [the Word of the Gospel] does not set up two separate and distinct foundations of faith, but simply emphasizes, as Hollaz points out (*Examen,* Proleg., C. 2, qu. 19), the all-important truth that faith can lay hold of Christ only by way of laying hold of the Word. The modern theologians who refuse to accept the Word of the Apostles and Prophets of Christ as God's Word substitute for the *fundamentum organicum* "the Person of Christ," "the living Christ," etc., as the foundation of faith. But he who by-passes Christ's words also misses the "living Christ."

the resurrection, heaven and hell, need not concern us.[115] But even such conservative "liberals" as Horst Stephan declare: "The strong interest in the human body and its glorified entrance into eternity, which marks the belief in the resurrection, should not be considered an absolutely necessary part of the Christian faith; rather it seems to be an outgrowth of the Jewish ideas of a future recompense" (*Glaubenslehre*, 1921, p. 119). But Holy Scripture declares that those who, like Hymenaeus, Alexander, and Philetus, denied the future bodily resurrection of the dead and sought to "spiritualize" the resurrection, "saying that the resurrection is past already," have made shipwreck concerning their faith and erred concerning the truth (1 Tim. 1:19-20; 2 Tim. 2:17-18). Such men do not belong in the Christian Church, but must be excommunicated: "Whom I have delivered unto Satan that they may learn not to blaspheme."[116] When some of the Corinthians declared that "there is no resurrection of the dead" (1 Cor. 15:12), the Apostle informed them that they knew nothing of God (1 Cor. 15:34) and denied the entire Christian religion by denying one of its essential teachings. Christ said the same thing to the Sadducees (Matt. 22:29: "Ye do err, not knowing the Scriptures nor the power of God").[117]

These "fundamental doctrines" did not, of course, originate with the Church. They existed in full force before the Church formulated them in dogmatical terms. The old dogmaticians frequently point that out (see Baier-Walther, I, 61, note e). Luther, too, shows at length that the councils "have proposed nothing new" in their ecclesiastical *termini*, but have merely maintained "with and through Holy Scripture" the old faith which the Christians held before all councils. This applies also to the Nicene Creed. The Christians, says Luther, have always believed that the Son is of the same essence with the Father, even before the term ὁμοούσιος was adopted over against Arius. ("*Von den Conciliis u. Kirchen*," St. L. XVI:2233, 2214.)

Primary and Secondary Fundamental Doctrines

This further division of the fundamental doctrines is not an invention of the orthodox dogmaticians to plague the theologians. It is theologically correct and extremely practical. To illustrate, in the

---

115 *Lehre und Wehre*, 67, p. 1 ff.

116 Huther on the words: οὓς παρέδωκα τῷ σατανᾷ: "It is the same excommunication as in 1 Cor. 5:5."

117 The Biblical doctrine of the resurrection of the dead is fully presented in the chapter on "The Resurrection of the Dead," in Vol. III.

controversies between the Lutheran and the Reformed Church, one of the disputed questions was whether Baptism and the Lord's Supper belong to the foundation of the Christian faith.[118] Scripture has decided this question. Baptism and the Lord's Supper certainly do belong to the foundation of the Christian faith, together with the Word of the Gospel, for Baptism is given "for the remission of sins" (Acts 2:38), and in the Lord's Supper Christ's body and blood are imparted as "given for you" and "shed for you for the remission of sins" (Luke 22:19 ff.; Matt. 26:26 ff.). The promise and offer of the forgiveness of sins, which is the foundation of faith, is contained also in the Sacraments.[119] Hence the doctrines of Baptism and the Lord's Supper are certainly fundamental doctrines. – But why do we call them *articuli fundamentales secundarii?* A man may, through ignorance of the nature and benefit of the Sacraments, lack that foundation of his faith which the Sacraments supply, but still have the true faith in the forgiveness of sins if he trusts in the Word of the Gospel, as heard or read. The reason is that the Gospel Word gives the full remission of sins gained by Christ, and Baptism and the Lord's Supper give the same grace only in another and in a particularly consoling way (*verbum visibile – applicatio individualis*). The Christian who does not make the right use of the Sacraments, but trusts in the Gospel, has the true saving faith though he lacks the additional support for his faith which God has provided in the Sacraments.[120] Baptism and the Lord's Supper, important as they are, do not have the same importance and necessity as basis of faith as the Word in the form of the Gospel and are therefore appropriately called secondary fundamental articles. The one is essential to faith, the other is intended to support faith. What is absolutely necessary is the hearing of the Word. The *articuli fundamentales secundarii* are, in the words of Quenstedt, those *qui non simpliciter fundamentales seu causa salutis sunt, ad fundamentum tamen pertinent* (*Systema* I, 355).

---

[118] Nikolaus Hunnius' Διάσκεψις *Theologica de Fundamentali Dissensu* (1626) and Joh. Huelsemann's *Calvinismus Irreconciliabilis* (1646). Walch, *Bibliotheca Theologica,* II, 486 ff., discusses the complete bibliography, covering also the Reformed writings.

[119] This is fully discussed in the section "Baptism a True Means of Grace," in Vol. III.

[120] This is the case with the children of God in the Reformed bodies, who, misled by their teachers, fail to use Baptism and the Lord's Supper as divinely appointed means of justification. Believing the Gospel, they have the full forgiveness of their sins, full salvation. Both Luther (St. L. XVII: 2212) and the Preface to the Book of Concord (*Trigl.* 19 f.) call attention to this.

In view of this relation between the primary and secondary fundamental articles one should exercise due restraint in judging the personal state of faith of those individuals who deny the secondary articles. On the one hand, it must be said that because of the close connection between the secondary and the primary fundamental articles one who denies the former would, for the sake of consistency, also have to deny the latter. To illustrate, whoever denies that God can forgive sins through Baptism and the Lord's Supper on the ground that these are only external means, must, to be consistent, also deny that God forgives sins through the Word of His Gospel, because that, too, is an external means. Another example: One who denies the communication of attributes (*communicatio idiomatum*) in Christ on the basis of the axiom that the finite is not capable of the infinite (*finitum non est capax infiniti*) will, if he is consistent in his reasoning, also deny the communication of the Person of the Son of God to the human nature and thus deny the incarnation of the Son of God. However, we here meet with a "felicitous inconsistency," not only among laymen, but also among learned theologians. Since the Fall man's logic is, as we note again and again, in a bad way, and the heat of controversy plays further havoc with it. This prompted Luther to temper his judgment concerning Nestorius. He says: "Though it necessarily and logically follows from Nestorius' teaching that Christ is a mere man and two persons, Nestorius did not mean to teach that. The crude, unlearned man did not see that he was proposing the impossible when he honestly held that Christ is God and Man in one person and at the same time would not ascribe the *idiomata* of the two natures to the Person of Christ. He wants to hold the first statement as true, but he will not grant that which follows from that first statement. Thus he shows that he does not really understand what he denies." (St. L. XVI:2230.) Luther adduces further instances of the same kind, for "such unreason is not rare in the world" (St. L. XVI:2238). The Roman doctrine of the Mass overthrows *per se* the foundation of faith, the *sola gratia.* Nevertheless, there are those who believe in the Mass and still believe in the *sola gratia.* Luther writes in his dissertation "Of the Abuse of the Mass" (1521): "No doubt it still happens to many pious Christians that in the simple faith of their heart they observe Mass and regard it as a sacrifice. But because they do not [before God] rely on the sacrifice, yea, hold that all they do is sin, and cleave solely to the pure mercy of God, they are preserved, so that they do not perish in this error." (St. L. XIX:1131.) And in the year 1539 Luther says in his book *Of the Councils and Churches:*

"There are today many great lords and scholars who confess freely and firmly that our doctrine of faith which justifies without merit, by pure grace, is true, yet they resent the thought that therefore monasticism and the worship of saints, and the like, must be discarded as of no value, though logic compels that conclusion. For no man can be justified except by faith; it follows that one cannot be justified by the monastic life." And honest Luther (*"damit ich mich selbst bei der Nase nehme"*) confesses to the same inconsistency. Twenty years before, he had taught "that faith alone justifies, without works," and nevertheless he had clung to monkery and nunnery. "Thoughtless fool that I was, I could not see the consequence, which I ought to have admitted, viz., that if faith alone does it, monkery and Mass could not do it" (St. L. XVI:2238). Synergism, the teaching that man possesses a *facultas se applicandi ad gratiam* (Erasmus' phrase), confirms man, as Luther points out, in his trust in his own ability in the matter of obtaining salvation and thus rules out the Christian faith in the remission of sins without the deeds of the Law.[121] But at the same time Luther grants the possibility of a "felicitous inconsistency" in the case of individuals. In theory, in their writings and disputations, they hold that man still possesses some spiritual powers; but in practice, "whenever they deal with God, when they stand before Him in prayer, they completely forget their 'free will,' despair of themselves, and cry unto Him for pure grace only" (St. L. XVIII:1730). Later Lutheran theologians have made similar statements. Thus Huelsemann says that not every false doctrine which by its nature is destructive of the foundation of faith, has this effect in the case of every erring individual; the "felicitous inconsistency" may prevent that.[122]

This truth has at all times been abused in the interest of indifferentism. There are those who hold that because certain errors do not in every case cause the Christian to lose his faith, these errors may be tolerated in the Church. Catholic theologians so argued against Luther. When he insisted that the Romish errors must be abolished, they contended that these doctrines had been taught by "saints," by men whom Luther himself held to be true children of God. This same

121 "As long as he [man] is persuaded that he can do even the least thing towards his own salvation, he retains some confidence in himself, he does not humble himself before God, but proposes to himself some place, some time, or some works whereby he may at length attain unto salvation" (*The Bondage of the Will*, St. L. XVIII:1715).

122 *Calvinismus Irreconciliabilis*, p. 432, quoted in Baier-Walther, I:62: "Not every teaching which in its nature adds or destroys some prerequisite necessary to faith or some consequence of it, also has this effect in the mind of every man."

line of argument is employed when men claim the right to teach certain errors in the Lutheran Church because outstanding theologians of the Lutheran Church had taught these errors. Over against such notions we need to perceive clearly and to maintain firmly that the "felicitous inconsistency," through which by the grace of God an erring Christian is kept from losing his personal faith, in no way extenuates the error, much less legitimizes it. Those who defend their false teaching by citing the case of pious erring fathers are reminded by Luther of a possible eventuality: they follow the pious fathers indeed, but "will not be with them at the end" (St. L. XIX:1133). Teaching in the house of God, the Church, is a most serious matter. The teachers of the Church must never forget:

1. Scripture nowhere gives any man the license to deviate in any point from God's Word. On the contrary, the regulations governing the household of God until the end of time read: "Teaching them to observe all things whatsoever I have commanded you" (Matt. 28:20).

2. Every departure from the Word of Christ, as found in the Word of His Apostles, is expressly designated an offense (σκάνδαλον ποιεῖν, Rom. 16:17: "Mark them which cause divisions and offenses contrary to the doctrine which ye have learned"). Through a special gracious intervention of God the error may not harm its author, but it is and remains an offense to others, to those who, unable to discount the error, embrace it in its full implications and, spreading it, in some cases under the aegis of the "fathers," cause further division in the Church. In order to remove, as far as possible, the offense resulting from the departure from the Word of God, public teachers have felt the need of publicly retracting the errors they formerly taught. This caused Augustine to write his *Retractationes;* [123] and Luther asked that his early writings be read "with much charity," since they were not yet entirely free from Romish errors (St. L. XIV:439; see also XIX:293, 296, and many other places).

3. Everyone who rejects the testimony of Scripture concerning one doctrine, actually, though he is not fully aware of it, invalidates

---

[123] In the Prologue to his *Retractationes* Augustine says: "From ever so many of my disputations many things could be collected which, if not false, still certainly appear so or, in other cases, do not necessarily prove convincing. But what faithful servant of Christ does not tremble at this word of Christ: 'Every idle word that men shall speak, they shall give account thereof in the Day of Judgment'? (Matt. 12:36.)" Augustine continues: "It behooves me therefore that I judge myself under the one Master whose judgment of my offenses I desire to escape." (Ed. Basil. I, 1.)

the Christian principle of cognition. We must never forget that all articles of the Christian doctrine have a common source, Holy Scripture, and that the authority of Scripture applies with equal and undivided force to all doctrines. If we, then, had the right to set aside, for reasons of "inconceivability," irrationality, or any other reason urged by our Ego, the authority of Scripture with respect to one doctrine, e. g., the doctrine of Baptism, of the Lord's Supper, of conversion, of election, of the inspiration of Holy Scripture, there is no reason why we should bow to the authority of Scripture when it speaks of the Lamb of God that bears the sins of the world (John 1:29) and of the blood of Christ that cleanses us from all sin (1 John 1:7). Luther has this in mind when he utters the warning: "The Holy Ghost [speaking in all words of Scripture] cannot be parceled and divided. He will not have men accept His Word on one point and reject it on other points." (St. L. XX:1781.)

Here, too, Luther makes the reservation: "Except where there are weak Christians who are ready to receive instruction and do not stubbornly contradict." The willingness to be further instructed shows that despite their error faith in the forgiveness of sins for Christ's sake still dwells in the hearts of these weak ones. But the situation is always fraught with danger, particularly so when controversies arise. Luther reminds us that not only secular wars, but also spiritual wars are dangerous. The spiritual wars, too, have their casualties. The greatest danger sets in when in doctrinal controversies the erring Christian, confronted with the clear Word of Scripture, clings to the error in spite of the clear Scripture and the power of the Holy Ghost active in it. Then it may easily happen that the "Christian erring," i. e., erring from weakness, in which faith still survives, ceases, and the "unchristian erring," the will to err, takes its place, which renders faith impossible.[124] That is the case described Titus 3:10-11: "A man that is an heretic after the first and second admonition reject, knowing that he that is such is subverted and sinneth, being condemned of himself." [125]

---

[124] Luther's classical dictum on "the Christian error": "You cannot say, I am going to err after the manner of a Christian; a Christian errs unwittingly" (St. L. XIX:1132).

[125] The meaning of the *hapax legomenon* αὐτοκατάκριτος is clear beyond any doubt. It designates the inner self-condemnation, *suopte judicio condemnatus*. God's Word, with which he has been confronted, has condemned him, and he has felt this condemnation in his conscience. Huther on this passage: "He sins, being conscious of his guilt and condemnation."

4. Finally, we should always bear in mind that, like sin in the sphere of morality,[126] so every error in the sphere of doctrine has the tendency to spread and to infect other doctrines with its virus. Unchecked, it will corrupt the entire body of doctrine. That is the meaning of Gal. 5:9: "A little leaven leaveneth the whole lump." [127] Luther illustrates the evil effect of any false doctrine when he compares the Christian doctrine to a ring, which is no longer whole if it has only one break. To put it epigrammatically: "One article is all articles, and all articles are one, and (that) if one article is lost, gradually all will be lost" (St. L. IX:642 ff., on Gal. 5:9). The history of the Church substantiates this in all its periods. The "felicitous inconsistency" is superseded by the "unfelicitous consistency." Moved by rationalistic considerations, the Reformed reject Baptism and the Lord's Supper as means of grace; and some of them, in harmony with their principle, have rejected also the external Word of the Gospel as a means of grace and substituted for it an alleged "immediate inner illumination," and then have fallen prey to outright rationalism. The denial that a communication of attributes in the Person of Christ was possible led others of the Reformed to deny the incarnation of the Son of God, thus landing in Socinianism.[128] The synergistic notion of Melanchthon that in order to safeguard universal grace the "different conduct" must be made the decisive factor in man's conversion and salvation was responsible, in part, for his later vacillations. Furthermore, the error of synergism dulled his discernment in matters of the Christian truth to such a degree that he collaborated on the Leipzig Interim, a document which G. Plitt characterizes as "a veritable travesty, yea, a repudiation of the Reformation and the Evangelical Church. – Deeply depressed, Melanchthon returned to Wittenberg." [129]

Non-Fundamental Doctrines

Non-fundamental doctrines, as distinguished from the fundamental doctrines, are those Scripture truths which are not the foundation or object of faith in so far as it obtains forgiveness of sins and makes men children of God, but with which the faith of those who

---

[126] 1 Cor. 5:6: "A little leaven leaveneth the whole lump." Hence 2 Cor. 7:1 admonishes us to "cleanse ourselves from all filthiness of the flesh and spirit."

[127] Meyer, too, like Luther and our old theologians, refers Gal. 5:9 to the domain of doctrine.

[128] See the case of Adam Neuser, in Vol. II, in the section "The Doctrine of Christ" (p. 273 f.).

[129] R. E., 2d ed., VI, 777 (*Trigl.*, "Historical Introductions," p. 98).

have already obtained the forgiveness of sins should and does concern itself. The Christians need to learn also these for their spiritual welfare. Such doctrines are, for instance, the doctrine of the Antichrist and the doctrine of the angels. The doctrine of the Antichrist does not, as we have already pointed out, belong to the foundation of the *fides salvifica.* And the faith which appropriates the forgiveness of sins is not faith in the angels but solely faith in Christ. But the Christian faith should concern itself also with these non-fundamental doctrines. The knowledge of them serves faith, inasmuch as the truth concerning Antichrist warns the believers of a grave danger, and the doctrine of the angels sheds additional light upon the goodness of God, causing faith to sing anew of the goodness and grace of Him who made the angels "ministering spirits, sent forth to minister for them who shall be heirs of salvation" (Heb. 1:14). Faith certainly profits by the *articuli non-fundamentales. "All* Scripture," including these non-fundamental articles," is given by inspiration of God and is profitable" (2 Tim. 3:16).

Furthermore, the denial of non-fundamental doctrines endangers faith. It involves the denial of the divine authority of Scripture. One who knows that the doctrine concerning the angels and their work is taught by Scripture and still refuses to believe in angels, is certainly rejecting the authority of Scripture. But where Scripture has lost its authority, the source of Christian knowledge is stopped up, and there is nothing left for faith to build on. Though we know that these articles are not fundamental, says Baier, "we must be at the same time on our guard lest by embracing and teaching error we rashly sin against the divine revelation and against God Himself" (*Compendium* I, 65).

This applies also, of course, to the historical, geographic, archaeological, and similar statements of Scripture. While they are not the object of faith in so far as faith obtains forgiveness of sins,[130] they cannot be denied without endangering saving faith. If a man will not believe Scripture in minor matters, such as its historical and geographical statements, how shall he in the *terrores conscientiae* believe Scripture in the great things which tell of the incarnation and the *satisfactio*

---

130 Cardinal Bellarmine taught a grave error when he said: "Catholics extend the object of justifying faith as far as the Word of God extends" (*Lib.* I, *De Justif.*, c. 4. See Quenstedt, II, p. 362). That would make saving faith a work. Over against this error it needs to be stressed that the only object of the *fides justificans* is the promise of the Gospel, offering the remission of sins for Christ's sake. See the section "The Sole Object of Saving Faith Is the Gospel" in Vol. II.

vicaria of the Son of God, things which run counter to every religious conception of the natural man (1 Cor. 1:23; 2:14)? – On this account Philippi felt that he must formally retract, in the third edition of his *Dogmatics*, the doubt that he had previously voiced with regard to the reliability of the historical, etc., statements in Scripture.[131]

C. OPEN QUESTIONS AND THEOLOGICAL PROBLEMS

Open questions must not be defined as points of doctrine on which men cannot agree or which the Church has left undecided in the Symbols, but as questions which Scripture leaves open, unanswered.

The principle that no doctrine can be universally binding until it has gained universal consent deposes Scripture as the source and norm of Christian doctrine. That principle changes Christ's instruction: "Teaching them to observe all things whatsoever I have commanded you" to read: "Teach them to observe those things for which you can obtain common consent." This anti-Scriptural idea is responsible for the numerous attempts to bring about church union without unity in the Christian doctrine.[132]

In our day some Lutheran theologians have set up the strange principle that any article may be treated as an open question, binding no one, so long as the Church has not decided the matter in the Symbols. That is in reality the same Romish error which Luther rejects in the familiar statement: "The Christian Church [therefore also the Lutheran Church] has no power to set up a single article of faith, has never done so, and nevermore will do it" (St. L. XIX:958). It is practically the position taken by the Dorpat Opinion of 1866. It is a plain disavowal of the Scripture principle.[133]

Correctly defined, open questions are such questions as inevitably arise in our study of the Scripture doctrines but are not answered by Scripture at all or at least not clearly. And Scripture enjoins us to let them remain open questions. If we presume to answer them and ask men to accept our opinion as divine truth, we would be rejecting those Scripture passages which forbid us to add anything to God's

---

131 See the addition to the third edition of his *Glaubenslehre* I, 279; also *Proceedings of the Synodical Conference*, 1886, p. 35.

132 Compare F. Bente, *American Lutheranism*, II, p. 9. The same unionism and indifferentism infected the former General Synod, pp. 19, 48, 170; the General Council, pp. 195, 224; and the United Synod of the South, p. 232 ff.

133 More on this in the *locus* on "Holy Scripture," in the chapter "The Authority of Scripture and the Confessions."

Word (Deut. 4:2; 12:32; 1 Pet. 4:11). Every true theologian must learn not only to speak, but also to keep silence. He should speak where and as far as God's Word speaks; he should hold his tongue where God's Word is silent. He who has not learned this art of silence and dares to speak where God's Word is silent is condemned by Jer. 23:16: "Thus saith the Lord of Hosts, Hearken not unto the words of the prophets that prophesy unto you; they make you vain; they speak a vision of their own heart and not out of the mouth of the Lord." He should also study 1 Tim. 6:3 ff.

Open questions may also be called "theological problems" if such problems are meant as cannot be solved on earth because God has not given us the solution in Scripture. A theologian may with a good conscience reply to many questions with an "I do not know" – *nescio*.

We cannot, for instance, answer the question how sin could originate, seeing that all creatures, including all the angels, were originally created "very good." [134] Another open question: Is the soul of each individual created by God immediately (creationism) or mediately through the parents (traducianism)? [135] In the list of problems which cannot be solved in this life the *Cur alii, alii non* question occupies a prominent place. How shall we account for the fact that, as the Formula of Concord puts it, "one is hardened, blinded, given over to a reprobate mind, while another, who is indeed in the same guilt (*in eadem culpa*), is converted again"? (*Trigl.* 1081, 57.) The Formula of Concord warns against any attempt to solve this

---

[134] The attempt to solve this problem has led to Dualism in its various forms, and to the denial of sin. Nitzsch-Stephan, *Ev. Dogmatik*, 3d ed., p. 438. More particulars in section "The Doctrine of God."

[135] This question was discussed at great length during the Pelagian controversies, but also in later periods. See Chemnitz, *Loci*, I, "De Peccato Originis," ed. 1599, I, 567 *sqq.*, for the historical material. On Luther's position Chemnitz says: "Luther declared that publicly he would assert nothing in answer to this question, but that he, for himself, favored traducianism; furthermore, that the Papists must be censured for their audacity and presumptuousness in creating an article of faith in an obscure matter, without one clear testimony of Scripture, in order to subvert the Scripture doctrine of original sin." Chemnitz adds: ". . . let us learn from this example to cut short, piously, firmly, and in well-founded simplicity, these subtle disputations which endanger faith. As to the *causa efficiens* [of original sin], it is sufficient to know that the fall of our first parents justly resulted in this, that they transmitted to all their offspring the very same nature, both as to body and as to soul, as was theirs after the Fall. In what manner, however, the soul contracts this evil, faith can safely ignore, because the Holy Spirit did not want to make it known to us through certain and clear Scripture testimonies." Cf. also Baier's brief historical remarks, I, 67, *nota* c; Luthardt, *Dogmatik*, 11th ed., p. 168 f.

question, the *crux theologorum,* in this life; the life to come will bring the answer.[136]

In short, all theologians who attempt to answer the real "open questions" in theology or to solve real theological problems (a) disagree with Scripture, because they refuse to abide by 1 Pet. 4:11: "If any man speak, let him speak as the oracles of God," and (b) are unscholarly, because they pretend to know what they cannot know. The knowledge of Christian truth is obtained only by continuing in the Word of Christ (John 8:31-32). Whatever is palmed off as Christian knowledge alongside the sound words of our Lord Jesus Christ is nothing but conceit and ignorance (τετύφωται, μηδὲν ἐπιστάμενος, 1 Tim. 6:3).

Now, since Scripture furnishes no information on these open questions and theological problems, it is foolish to spend much time and energy on them.[137] We surely have enough to do if we study and teach what is clearly revealed in Holy Writ. If we do not make that our sole business, but take time to discuss useless questions, we are, as Luther points out, "hindering the Gospel." The great matters which should be man's sole concern are pushed into the background. And experience shows that the interest of the crowd is too easily won for human speculations; it will have its curiosity satisfied. Luther adduces the example of the Jews, who bothered about the genealogies, and of the Papists, among whom there was endless wrangling about useless

---

[136] The attempt to answer this question must lead either to Calvinism (the denial of the *gratia universalis*) or to Semi-Pelagianism and synergism (the denial of the *sola gratia*). – It is, of course, not sinful nor indicative of false teaching to pose the problem. In practically all periods of the Church the problem has been stated in various forms (*Cur alii, alii non? Cur non omnes? Cur alii prae aliis?*) But they sin and teach false doctrine who, with Melanchthon, the father of synergism in the Lutheran Church, would solve the problem by means of the "dissimilar conduct." The Formula of Concord does not warn against acknowledging the problem, but it warns against any attempted solution of it. "In these and similar questions Paul fixes a certain limit (*certas metas*) to us, how far we should go, namely, that in the one part we should recognize God's judgment . . . which we all have well deserved," and that in the other part, "we acknowledge and praise God's goodness to the exclusion of, and contrary to, our merit," since God "does not harden and reject us," who are certainly in the same guilt. – See the fuller discussion of this matter in the *locus* on "Conversion" and the *locus* on "The Election of Grace," in Vols. II and III.

[137] Reusch in his *Annotationes* in Baieri *Comp.*, p. 52: "Reflection upon them is useless, the disputations about them unprofitable." In recounting the futile labors of the Scholastics on the many questions which Scripture leaves unanswered, Dannhauer summarizes the result and practical benefits of their labors in the words: "The one milks the billy goat, and the other holds a sieve," *"unus hircum mulget, alter supponit cribrum" (Hodosophia, Phaen.* XI, p. 667).

fables and empty trifles, and everyone wanted to be in the right. (See St. L. IX:863 f. on 1 Tim. 1:3-4.) Let us heed Luther's warning: "There are two hindrances to the Gospel: the first is teaching false doctrine, driving the consciences into the Law and works. And the second is this trick of the devil: when he finds that he cannot subvert the faith by directly denying the Gospel, he sneaks in from the rear; raises useless questions and gets men to contend about them and meanwhile to forget the chief thing; and gets them to contend about dead saints and departed souls, where they abide, whether they sleep, and the like.[138] One question follows the other in endless succession. Wretched curiosity busies itself about unnecessary and useless things that are neither commanded nor serve any purpose. Thus Satan comes in the back way, people gape with wide-open mouth at these things and lose the chief things. A man does not need much wit to gain the popular applause; let him but preach new and strange things, and people will say that he is more learned than others; they come in droves, with eyes and ears and mouth widely opened. They do not care to have faith and love preached to them; that is too common; they heard and know enough about that; it irks them always to hear the same thing." [139]

12

The Church and Its Dogmas

The question as to the essence and value of dogmas has in reality been disposed of in the previous chapter, where we have demonstrated that the Church is obligated to teach only the *doctrina divina,* the truths set down by God in Holy Scripture. But the need of Christian dogmas has been challenged, especially on two fronts.

There are those who insistently call for an "undogmatic," a creedless, Christianity. They reduce the Christian faith and the "real" work of the Church to the "social gospel." This "social gospel" would have the Church forget the "other world" (*das "Jenseits"*), including heaven and hell, or at least put it into the background, and instead of that concentrate on the "present world" (*das "Diesseits"*), on "heaven on

---

[138] What Scripture has revealed concerning the condition of the soul between death and the resurrection will be presented in Vol. III.

[139] In the language of the modern theologians who deny the inspiration of Scripture and want to draw the Christian doctrine out of their own Ego, the term "theological problems" has a different meaning. See Chapter 16, "Theology and Certainty," p. 110.

earth." The social gospel regards "Boston as of equal importance with the New Jerusalem because it takes, almost literally, the vision of St. John, who saw the 'New Jerusalem coming down out of heaven' to occupy this earth."[140] Others admit the necessity of dogma. But since the old dogmas have outlived their usefulness, they must be supplanted by a new set of dogmas, such as will be suited to present conditions, their exact form being, in the nature of the case, still under discussion. Others, again, think that the old dogmas can well be retained, but, of course, they must be "further developed" or "liberalized." The advocates of an undogmatic Christianity, of course, have no need of any kind of dogma.[141]

In establishing the definition of dogma,[142] we must examine the validity of the claim that all those doctrines should be recognized as church dogmas that "ask for or claim to have the sanction of the Church." This definition, though widely favored, is unsatisfactory. History shows that it was particularly the "unchurchly" dogmas which most insistently demanded recognition as dogmas of the Church. But the mere claim for recognition does not establish that claim. To illustrate, one of Rome's dogmas declares that the sinner obtains the forgiveness of his sins not by faith in the Gospel, but by keeping the commandments of God and the Church, and Rome demands in the strongest terms possible that this dogma be accepted; Rome goes so far as to anathematize all who believe that the sinner is justified solely through God's mercy in Christ without the deeds of the Law.[143] As a matter of fact, however, this Romish dogma is a most "unchurchly" thing; so much so that it excludes from the Church all who believe it. "Christ is become of no effect unto you, whosoever of you are justified by the Law, ye are fallen from grace" (Gal. 5:4). "As many as are of the works of the Law are under the curse" (Gal. 3:10;

---

140 Thus Winchester Donald, *The Expansion of Religion*, 1896, p. 125. This matter is fully presented in *Lehre und Wehre*, 1920, p. 270 ff.: "*Die moderne Diesseitstheologie*," and in *Lehre und Wehre*, 1921, p. 2 ff.: "*Das Christentum als Jenseitsreligion*." Here also the pertinent literature is mentioned. Cp. also *Proceedings of the Michigan District*, 1919, p. 44 ff. The creedless character of the modern social gospel will be discussed later.

141 Cp. R. Seeberg, *Brauchen wir ein neues Dogma?* 1892, and: *Grundwahrheiten der chr. Rel.*, 5th ed., 1910, p. 61 ff. Theodore Kaftan, *Moderne Theologie des alten Glaubens*, 2d ed., 1906; Loofs, in R. E., 3d ed., IV, 753 ff., *sub v. Dogmengeschichte*. Nitzsch-Stephan *Dogmatik* 3d ed., p. 2 ff.; 47 ff.; Horst Stephan, *Glaubenslehre*, 1921, p. 19 ff.

142 In Scripture the term is used to designate ordinances of both the Church and the State. Cf. Luke 2:1; Acts 16:4.

143 *Trid.*, Sess. VI, can. 10, 11, 12, 20.

Gal. 4:21-31). Then there is the dogma of the supremacy and infallibility of the Pope.[144] For this dogma, too, Rome demands recognition by all men, under pain of eternal damnation; it anathematizes all who reject it.[145] Nevertheless, it is not a church dogma, but is banned from the Church, whose sole head and authoritative Teacher is Christ (Luke 22:25; Matt. 23:8, 10).

Other illustrations. There is the Reformed dogma of the immediate revelation and operation of divine grace. "*Dux et vehiculum Spiritui non est necessarium*" (the Spirit needs no guide or vehicle). "Efficacious grace acts immediately."[146] The Reformed strive with might and main for its acceptance and vehemently demand the rejection of the contrary Lutheran doctrine as derogatory of the majesty of God and as fostering a mere intellectual Christianity (intellectualism). But it cannot qualify as a church dogma; it is a pure delusion, for which there is not a shadow of Scripture proof, but which directly contradicts Scripture (John 17:20: "through their Word"; 1 Cor. 4:15: "through the Gospel"; Rom. 10:17: "by hearing"; Tit. 3:5: "by the washing of regeneration"; Eph. 5:26: "with the washing of water").

The Arminians and the synergistic Lutherans bring great pressure to bear to have the teaching of human co-operation in conversion accepted by the Church. They raise the cry that unless the *sola gratia* be "restricted," a compulsory conversion, a *gratia particularis,* and other evils will result. However, synergism is not a church dogma, because Scripture throughout teaches the *sola gratia.*

One more example. While there is wide doctrinal divergence among modern theologians, they are agreed that the Christian doctrine must not be drawn from Holy Scripture, but from the bosom of the theologian, from his "experience." The supporters of this peculiar dogma will brook no opposition. They declare that the inevitable result of "making the Bible an infallible book," "the only source and norm of the Christian doctrine," is Biblicism, dead orthodoxy, and the like. But the preceding chapter has shown that this dogma, far from being a church dogma, destroys the foundation of the Church.

It will certainly not do to define as "dogma" any doctrine which merely "asks for, or claims to have, the sanction of the Church." The

---

144 Guenther, *Populaere Symbolik,* 3d ed., p. 378 f.

145 See the decree of the Vatican Council, *Popular Symbolics,* p. 162.

146 See the chapters "The Means of Grace According to the 'Enthusiasts'" and "Comprehensive Characterization of the Reformed Teaching of the Means of Grace," in Vol. III.

correct definition is: that dogma is a church dogma which is taken from the "manual" of the Christian Church, from Holy Scripture, and every dogma which does not have its origin in Scripture is unchurchly. As matters stand, it cannot be otherwise. The Christian Church has no doctrine of its own; it possesses, teaches, and confesses only Christ's doctrine. Luther: *Ecclesia Dei non habet potestatem condendi ullum articulum fidei, sicut nec ullum unquam condidit, nec condet in perpetuum.* The Church, indeed, teaches, confesses, and approves the articles of faith or the Scriptures, not as lord and judge, as though she had authority over Scripture (*more majoris sive auctoritate iudiciali*); she does it in subjection to Scripture (*more minoris*) – just as the servant acknowledges the seal of his lord. (St. L. XIX:958.) And this applies not only to the local congregations, but also to the larger church organizations, general bodies, synods, councils, and the like.[147]

The question has been raised whether such ecclesiastical terminology as expresses the exact sense of Scripture without employing the express words of Scripture may be termed a dogma. To put it concretely, Are the doctrines expressed in the terms "Trinity" and "*homoousia*" (consubstantiality) dogmas of the Church? We shall have to say with Luther: "It is certainly true that in matters concerning God nothing should be taught except the Scriptures, as Hilary says in his *De Trinitate.* But that means only that nothing should be taught which is different from the Scriptures. It does not mean, and it cannot be held, that one cannot use more words or other words than those that are in the Scriptures. Especially in controversies, when the heretics opposed the true doctrine with all manner of sophistries and evasions and perverted the words of Scripture, it became necessary to comprise what Scripture says in many passages in a short word of summary and to ask them whether they held Christ to be *homoousios;* for that word expresses the true meaning of all those words of Scripture which they perverted." (St. L. XVI:2212.)

What is true of synods and councils and of all large and small church assemblies certainly applies also to the individual theologian and his theology, particularly also to the dogmatician and his dogmatics. Theologians (and dogmaticians) are church theologians only in so far as they recognize Scripture as the sole source and norm of theology, only in so far as their theology is not a *mixtum compositum* of Scripture doctrine and human opinions, but *theologia* ἔκτυπος,

---

147 More on this point under "The Representative Church" in Vol. III.

simply the reproduction of the doctrine revealed and presented in Scripture. The theologian (and the dogmatician) dare not make human teachers of the Church the source and norm of doctrine. Even when they teach the pure Scripture doctrine, these human teachers serve only as *testes veritatis,* "as witnesses which are to show in what manner after the time of the Apostles, and at what places, this [pure] doctrine of the Prophets and Apostles was preserved" (*Trigl.* 777, 2). The genuine Lutheran dogmaticians apply this also to the Symbols of the Lutheran Church, for they confess, "first, the Prophetic and Apostolic Scriptures of the Old and New Testaments as the pure, clear fountain of Israel, which is the only true standard by which all teachers and doctrines are to be judged" (*Trigl.* 851, 3).

In passing we may say a word for the "old dogmatics." It is claimed quite generally that the old dogmaticians, in presenting their doctrine, did not start with Scripture, but with the *corpus doctrinae* fixed by the Church, using Scripture merely as a "collection of proof-texts" for what they had already accepted as the true doctrine. The assertion is historically untrue, and those that make it *bona fide* are ignorant of the facts. In the old dogmatics, as represented, for instance, by Quenstedt, Scripture serves not only as the norm but, first of all, as the source of the doctrine. Just take time to study Quenstedt's *Systema Theologicum,* its ἔκθεσις and θέσεως βεβαίωσις, the presentation and the corroboration of the various doctrines. – Modern theology, by the way, fighting *pro domo,* denounces the old method of establishing doctrine by the direct statements of Scripture and asks us to operate instead with the "Scripture as a whole." What an inconceivable concept this "Scripture as a whole" is will be shown later.

Church Dogma and the Theological Disciplines. Theology is commonly divided into dogmatic, historical, exegetical, and practical theology. And it is the dogma, that is, the doctrine of Scripture, which stamps these various branches of theology as theological disciplines and unifies them. It is the function of historical theology not only to give a historically true picture of the events, but also to evaluate these established facts in the light of Scripture. Historical theology is the divinely taught art of ascertaining from Scripture God's verdict on the historical events and conditions. That is what makes church history a theological discipline. When the church historian judges events according to his subjective view or any other extra-Biblical norm, church history is no longer a theological discipline. A Christian church history shows, says Luther, "how the dear Gospel fared in the world." Where things are as they should be, the Church will, therefore, elect only such men as professors of church history as are thoroughly conversant with the Scripture doctrine in all its parts, well informed in dogmatics, in order that the instruction in church history will not confuse but aid Christian understanding. The final aim of church history is not to "awaken reverence for history," but to instill and strengthen reverence for God's Word. – Exegetical theology deals exclusively with the words of Holy Scripture. It is the divinely taught art which binds the teacher and the learner to the sense expressed in the words of Scripture and compels him to expose as false all interpretations contrary to text and context. Exegesis loses its theological character if the exegete does not adhere throughout to the "*Scriptura Scripturam interpretatur*" and "*Scriptura sua luce radiat.*" No extra-Biblical material, philological or historical, may determine the exegesis. That holds true particularly with regard to historical circumstances. Interpreting the words of Scripture according to a "historical background" not furnished by Scripture itself but, wholly or in part, by contemporary secular writers, is false exegesis. All the historical background necessary for the correct understanding of Scripture is given by Scripture itself.[148] Practical theology is the ability to apply the pure Christian doctrine, learned from Holy Scripture, in the work of the public ministry, in preaching, in ministering to souls, in catechetical instruction of young and old, etc. In so far as the minister yields to non-Biblical considerations in the performance of his ministerial functions, in so far his practical theology is no longer theological.

From the foregoing it is evident that the dogma is the unifying core of the various theological disciplines. The dogma, the Scriptural doctrine, is the essential element in every discipline, which integrates all branches of sacred theology. The dogmatician must also be an exegete, historian, and practical theologian; and likewise the exegete, the historian, and the practical theologian must also be a good dogmatician. Each must be well acquainted with the Scripture doctrine in all its parts. – In spite of the demand for an "undogmatic" Christianity, we declare: "Only dogmatics is edifying," namely, dogmatics as *doctrina divina* revealed in Scripture, the only doctrine which may be taught in Christ's Church. In the Christian Church, doctrine is the all-important thing. The general orders issued by Christ (Matthew 28) read: "Teaching them to observe all things whatsoever I have commanded you." Let no minister of Jesus Christ, be he theological professor or pastor of a church, forget this. The theologian

---

148 More on this point in the chapter "Holy Scripture and Exegesis" in the *locus* on "Holy Scripture."

who no longer believes that "supernatural truths" are imparted through Scripture, through the doctrine of Scripture, but denounces that as conducive to "intellectualism," has lost sight of the obligations of his sacred office. And the pastors, yes, they especially, dare never forget that their paramount business is to preach doctrine, the divine doctrine of Holy Scripture. Their sermons must be what we commonly call "doctrinal sermons." Dr. Walther's plea for doctrinal sermons deserves careful attention. He says: "Let a sermon be ever so rich in exhortation, rebuke, and comfort, if it be devoid of doctrine, it is a lean and empty sermon; its exhortation, rebuke, and comfort float in the air. It is almost beyond belief how many preachers sin in this respect. Hardly has the preacher touched his text and theme when he starts exhorting or reproving or consoling. The sermon consists almost entirely of questions and exclamations, beatitudes and lamentations; there is so much calling for self-examination and such a belaboring of the feeling and conscience that the hearers have little opportunity for quiet reflection. But far from reaching the heart and producing true life, such preaching is more likely to talk people to death, to destroy any existing hunger for the bread of life, to produce disgust with, and loathing for, God's Word. It cannot but nauseate the hearers to be forced to listen to everlasting exhortations and reproofs and consolations which, because the doctrinal foundation is lacking, are pointless and saltless. It is, of course, much easier to shake this sort of thing out of one's sleeve, and thus give the sermon the appearance of vivacity and power, than to present a doctrine lucidly and thoroughly. This may be the chief reason why many preach doctrine so sparingly, and as a rule deliberately choose such topics as are already well known to hearers and therefore call only for practical applications. There are many, however, who shy away from doctrinal preaching simply because they themselves have no thorough knowledge of the revealed doctrines and so are unable to present them clearly and thoroughly to others. And then there are those who do not care to preach much doctrine because they are laboring under the illusion that detailed doctrinal discussions are too dry, leave the hearers cold, and contribute nothing to the awakening of the conscience, to conversion, and to a living, active Christianity of the heart. This, however, is a gross mistake. The very opposite is true. The eternal thoughts of God, revealed to us in Scripture for our salvation, these divine truths, these divine counsels, these mysteries of faith, which had been kept secret since the world began but are now made manifest to us through the writings of the Prophets and Apostles, are the heavenly seed which must be planted in the hearts of the hearers in order to produce the fruit of a sincere repentance, an unfeigned faith and a sincere, active love. There can be no true growth of the spiritual life in a congregation if the preaching is not rich in doctrine. The preacher who skimps on the doctrine is not faithful in his office, even though his continuous fervid admonitions, earnest reproofs, and the consolations which sound so evangelical give him the reputation that he is consuming himself in faithful care of the souls entrusted to him." [149]

13

The Purpose of Christian Theology for Man

The purpose which theology is to accomplish in man after the Fall is to save men from eternal damnation, incurred by every member of the human race, or, to state it positively, to lead men to eternal salvation (σωτηρία, *salus aeterna*). This purpose is stated by St. Paul when he says (1 Tim. 4:16): "In doing this [taking heed unto the doctrine, performing the office of a Christian teacher] thou shalt both save thyself and them that hear thee." So also Jesus: "Every scribe . . . is instructed unto the kingdom of heaven" (Matt. 13:52). Because of this high purpose of theology the ministry of the Christian teacher is the most important office on earth, the "good work" (καλὸν ἔργον) *par excellence* (1 Tim. 3:1).

The theologian must continually be on his guard lest he entertain false notions as to the purpose of his theological activity. The purpose of theology is not the spread of culture or the establishment of civil righteousness – though Christianity is the one thing that really makes good citizens and promotes true culture. Nor is it the purpose of theology to "satisfy the intellectual craving of the human mind" or to enrich human knowledge in general – though theology does answer from Scripture many questions which baffle all human wisdom and research.[150]

We can well understand why Luthardt would fault the old Lutheran theologians for "relating theology immediately to salvation," since from his point of view this is "scientifically incorrect." Luthardt

---

149 Walther, *Pastorale*, p. 81 f. [Fritz, *Pastoral Theology*, 1945, p. 334 f.]

150 Thus Scripture gives us reliable information on the metaphysical problems concerning the nature and the origin of things (Col. 1:16-17; Gen. 1:11-12), for which the philosophers have not yet found a satisfactory answer.

represents a theology which has lost sight of the true aim of theology; his theology aims to supplant faith with understanding and therefore insists on deriving the Christian doctrine not from Scripture, but from the Ego of the dogmatizing subject. Such a theology is, of course, not related to salvation "immediately." In fact, it has no relation whatever to man's salvation. It would be a terrible situation if our salvation depended in the least degree on a theology which is determined to speak not out of the mouth of the Lord, but out of the mouth of the theologian. And certainly this sort of theology cannot claim that its "inner life, its rights and strength are lodged" in the Christian Church.[151] A theology which does not want to speak out of the mouth of the Lord and have as its direct aim eternal salvation has no place in the Christian Church and has forfeited its right to be heard. It is an exotic plant, not one which the heavenly Father has planted (Matt. 15:13). In the Church only God's Word (λόγια θεοῦ) should be heard, and that for the purpose of saving men (1 Pet. 4:11; 1 Tim. 1:4; 6:3). From Meisner's *Philosophia Sobria* Walther quotes the pointed statement: "The theologian who does not continually pursue this purpose and does not make the salvation of men the objective of all his study and teaching, does not deserve to be called a true theologian."[152]

The old theologians define the purpose of theology quite well when they say: "The subject of the operation of theology is *homo peccator* in so far as he is to be led to eternal salvation" (Baier, I, 40). Also society or the State concerns itself with the *homo peccator*, not for the purpose of saving souls, but only for the purpose of protecting by means of temporal punishment the bodily life and temporal goods of its members against the outbursts of the wickedness inherent in human nature. Theology, however, is not concerned with the civil punishment to be meted out to the evildoer. Rather it is the business of the theologian and of the Christian Church, through the preaching of the Law, to convince the *homo peccator* of his guilt before God and of the certainty of the eternal punishment to be meted out to the transgressor and, through the preaching of the Gospel, to bring him the remission of sins and eternal salvation.

And this ultimate purpose of theology [*finis ultimus*], the *salus aeterna*, can be achieved in only one way. Eternal salvation is obtained only through faith in Christ, through faith in the Gospel of the grace of God in Christ, as we read in John 3:36: "He that believeth on the

---

151 Luthardt, *Kompendium*, 11th ed., pp. 4, 6.

152 *Lehre und Wehre*, XIV, 76 f.

Son hath everlasting life; and he that believeth not the Son shall not see life, but the wrath of God abideth on him." Hence the intermediate purpose of theology (*finis intermedius*) is, primarily, the creation and preservation of faith in Christ. Rom. 1:5 names this as a *finis theologiae.* Paul received his apostleship "for obedience to the faith."

Sanctification and good works, of course, is another objective of theology. Theology teaches the believers to "be careful to maintain good works" (Titus 3:8) – not as though good works were the cause or prerequisite or means of obtaining the forgiveness of sins and salvation (those who teach such a thing are cursed by the Apostle, Gal. 1:8), but because good works are a result and effect of the faith which has obtained the forgiveness of sins and salvation without works. In this way the theologian achieves both the right quality and a gratifying quantity of good works.

14

The Means by Which Theology Accomplishes Its Purpose

Ever mindful of the purpose of theology, which is to bring men to faith and thus lead them to heaven, the theologian must concern himself with the means by which this purpose is accomplished. He must not be beguiled into employing the means suggested by carnal wisdom, such as worldly might, external compulsion, state support, "social affairs," and the like. Men are strongly tempted to employ these unchurchly means.[153] But the only thing that achieves the purpose of theology and builds the Church is the Gospel, and only he is fitted for the ministry (ἱκανότης ἐκ τοῦ θεοῦ – "our sufficiency is of God," 2 Cor. 3:5) of the Church who firmly relies, for his success, on the divinely ordained means and knows that the "Gospel of the grace of God" (Acts 20:24), though mean and contemptible in the eyes of the world and his flesh, is the power of God unto salvation. That is what Christ has commanded His Church to teach and to preach. That is how Paul achieved his success. Bidding farewell to the pastors

153 The flesh of the theologian would persuade him that his office as pastor or theological professor would be safer and be more respected if it were supported by the authority and power of the State. That is the reason why so many favor the "State Church" and are against the "Free Church," despite the fact that according to God's will the Church should function externally as a free Church. And the free Church theologians, too, are ever exposed to the temptation to resort to unchurchly means for the building of the Church, as witnessed by the "social affairs" in vogue here in the United States, the community churches, the clamor for a "strong church government," and other phenomena.

and churches of Ephesus, he said: "And now, brethren, I commend you to God and to the Word of His grace, which is able to build you up and to give you an inheritance among all them which are sanctified" (Acts 20:32). That is the lesson which all of us, pastors and professors, must ever learn anew in faith.

A word on church government in this connection. Schleiermacher states that one of the purposes, the final purpose of theology, is "the government and rule of the Church."[154] We could subscribe to that with the understanding that it is God's Word alone that rules and governs the Church. The regulations made by smaller or larger church bodies, which concern the externals of their common work, ought not to be called "means of governing the Church." Luther: "Christians cannot be ruled by any other means than the Word of God. For Christians must be ruled in faith, not by outward works. Faith, however, can come through no word of man, but only through the Word of God, as Paul says Romans 10: 'Faith cometh by hearing, and hearing by the Word of God.'" (St. L. X:406.)

15

Theology and Science

Before we discuss the question whether theology is a science, we shall have to agree on the meaning of this term; it is used in more than one sense, frequently without any sense at all.

If "science" is defined as "a systematized natural knowledge," meaning a knowledge of nature and of man which is not derived from the revelation of Holy Scripture, but is obtained through human observation, then Christian theology is not a science. For neither nature, in all its wide reaches, nor the voice of conscience tells anything about the specific content of the Christian doctrine, about the Gospel of Christ. That is the clear teaching of Scripture (1 Cor. 2:6-16). The natural religion, the knowledge of God derived from what God has revealed concerning Himself in nature and in man's conscience, is not the Christian religion, but the religion of the Law. That is the clear teaching of Scripture (Rom. 1:20: "The invisible things of Him from the creation of the world are clearly seen"; Rom. 2:14-15: "The work of the Law written in their hearts . . . their conscience also bearing witness . . . their thoughts accusing or else excusing one another").

---

[154] *Der Christliche Glaube, nach den Grundsaetzen der evangelischen Kirche im Zusammenhange dargestellt*, I, 16.

Nor is theology a science in the sense that "theological science" represents a higher form of knowledge than the knowledge of faith.[155] The simple fact is that the theologian, with all his learning, cannot acquire more knowledge of spiritual things than the revelation of Holy Scripture provides. There is but one organ for apprehending things spiritual (*medium cognoscendi*), and that is faith, the simple faith of the Christian man; the theologian is not equipped with some other, more highly developed organ for this purpose. In other words, the theologian, like any other Christian, knows of spiritual things only so much as he believes on the basis of the revealed Word of God (John 8:31 f.: "If ye continue in My Word," etc.; 1 Cor. 13:12; Rom. 1:5). "To believe God's Word is the beginning, middle, and end of theology." True, the theologian, as a rule, has a wider knowledge of the Bible than the layman. He devotes more study to it and knows much more about the details and minor circumstances of the Biblical facts. His knowledge is greater extensively. But it is not true that his knowledge of the mysteries of faith is of a different nature from that of his fellow Christians. It is not true that he comprehends what the ordinary Christian merely believes. Also in the case of the theologian, knowledge is faith, and faith is knowledge. And his greater philological, philosophical, and historical learning is merely a part of the external theological apparatus. It is not a source of the spiritual knowledge. It does, indeed, when properly applied, serve this knowledge of faith; it helps him to ascertain the exact meaning of a passage of Scripture, that is, to understand exactly what God has revealed. But it does not give the theologian the ability to generate of himself spiritual thoughts; it does not give him the right to think his own theological thoughts. Some modern theologians like to define theology as the "science of Christianity" ("of the Christian faith"), meaning that theology aims at elevating faith to knowledge. But that is nothing else than self-deception and direct rejection of the principle of cognition in theology, of the Scripture principle.

If the term "science" denotes a *certain* knowledge, in opposition to mere opinions, views, hypotheses, etc., theology is the perfect science, the only reliable science on earth. All other sciences are based on human observations and human deductions, and in the nature of the case– *errare humanum est*– the information offered by philosophy, astronomy, medical science, etc., is more or less unreliable. But the Christian theologian gets his information from the Bible, which

---

[155] See p. 18.

is God's Word, the depository of God's own observation, opinion, and doctrine. Such a science cannot contain any error — *errare in Deum non cadit* — and cannot give any unreliable information (John 17:17: "Thy Word is truth"; John 10:35: "The Scripture cannot be broken").

An objection is raised here: Objective certainty does not guarantee subjective certainty. The teaching of Scripture may be the absolute truth, but it will always be doubtful whether one has correctly apprehended and understood Scripture. Thus Nitzsch-Stephan: "The pure objectivity of those who insist on relying solely on Scripture, on making Scripture not only the norm but also the source, is pure illusion," because, says our objector, the thought of Scripture must necessarily pass through the subjective understanding of the theologian. We reply: The faith by which the Christian theologian, just as every Christian, apprehends and knows God's own doctrine in Scripture, is not a knowledge or conviction gained by the use of his own natural powers (*fides humana*), but is a knowledge and conviction wrought by the Holy Ghost through the divine Word itself (*fides divina*); it is therefore a sure knowledge; it is absolute certainty. Faith is the product not of "the wisdom of men," but of "the power of God" (1 Cor. 2:5); it is therefore, in contrast to worldly knowledge, the one certain knowledge, as Scripture itself declares (1 Cor. 2:12): "We have received not the spirit of the world, but the Spirit which is of God, that we might know the things that are freely given to us of God." Theology deals with certainties. In the words of Luther: "The Holy Ghost is not a skeptic, nor are what He has written on our hearts doubts or opinions, but assertions more certain and more firm than life itself and all human experience."[156] Also later Lutheran dogmaticians who refused to classify theology as one of the sciences were ready to apply this term to theology in the sense that theology deals with certainties, not with mere opinions. Thus Calov: "It is to be noted that the question is not whether theology may be called a science in the wider sense of the term nor whether theology, because of its perfection, ought not be called a science rather than an opinion or an imperfect aptitude. We readily admit both, because it is called a science, in the wider sense, by the Spirit of God (1 Cor. 12:8), and Thomas (of Aquino) as well as Augustine, in various places, correctly teach that theology is not merely an opinion, but also science."[157]

---

[156] *The Bondage of the Will*, St. L. XVIII:1680. — More on this in the next section.

[157] *Systema* I, 42.

We prefer not to call theology a science because today an evil odor attaches to this term, due to its use in modern theology. Modern theologians call theology a science in the sense that it is the business of theology to elevate faith to knowledge, to demonstrate the truth of the Christian doctrine before the forum of human reason. That is impossible, since the natural man cannot apprehend the truth of the Gospel: "the natural man receiveth not the things of the Spirit of God . . . neither can he know them" (1 Cor. 2:14; 1:23). Christ therefore does not ask the Church to prove the Gospel to men; His orders are to proclaim it (Mark 16:15). The Apostle Paul certainly knew his science and philosophy. But this same Apostle Paul would have us know that he never resorted in his preaching, even when dealing with a highly educated public, to scientific demonstrations. He would not offer his hearers such false props for their faith. He told the Corinthians: "My speech and my preaching was not with enticing words of man's wisdom, but in demonstration of the Spirit and of power, that your faith should not stand in the wisdom of men, but in the power of God" (1 Cor. 2:4-5). Our old theologians expressed this truth in the terse and pointed phrase: *Theologia non est habitus demonstrativus, sed exhibitivus.* That means: Christian theology is the ability to present, or preach, the Christian doctrine to the world; Christian theology does not attempt to prove its truth by rational or philosophical arguments. As for proving its truth, the Holy Spirit, united with the Word, takes care of that when He crushes secure hearts through the preaching of the Law and creates faith in the Gospel through the preaching of God's Gospel. That absolutely settles the case. Just deal with realities! The man in whom the Law of God has wrought *contritio* has lost all interest in rational and philosophical proofs, because he is crushed and "knocked into a heap." And when the Gospel has wrought faith in the Savior of sinners in him, he rejoices in the saving divine truth and does not ask to have this truth demonstrated to him scientifically. That is the meaning of the axiom: "The best apology of the Christian religion is its proclamation." [158]

---

[158] In this connection we call attention to Kirn's idea that a man is sufficiently prepared for understanding the Gospel if he "seeks God and strives for moral perfection" (*Ev. Dogmatik* 3d ed., p. 37). The very opposite is true. Only he who despairs of achieving any kind of moral perfection, only he who knows that because of his moral disability and turpitude he is subject to eternal perdition (*terrores conscientiae, contritio*), is prepared to "understand" and appreciate the Gospel.

A word on the rational proofs for the Christian religion, as employed in apologetics. The Christian apologist is in a position to show any rational man, particularly if he have a well-trained mind, that after all it would appear more reasonable to accept the claims of Christianity as true than to reject them as false. But he must ever keep in mind that his real business is not to demonstrate the truth of the Christian religion to the unbeliever, but to uncover the insincerity of unbelief, for all who reject Christianity do so, consciously or unconsciously, because of their evil will and not because of their pretended "intellectual honesty." So Christ declares: "Men loved darkness rather than light. . . . Everyone that doeth evil hateth the light, neither cometh to the light, lest his deeds should be reproved" (John 3:19-20). There are no scientific reasons or rational proofs against the truths of Christianity. This matter will be discussed further in the chapter "The Divine Authority of Holy Scripture," particularly under "*fides humana*."

16

Theology and Certainty

The question how the theologian attains subjective certainty, how he attains personal assurance of the truth of the Christian doctrine (*erkenntnis-theoretische Frage*), is much discussed today. The moderns, both of the "conservative" and the "liberal" wing, raise the "problem," and some of their spokesmen are free to confess that it is a difficult problem.[159] But the difficulty they encounter is of their own making. It is due to their repudiation of Scripture as God's Word.

Scripture gives a clear and simple answer to the question concerning subjective certitude. Christ tells all Christians, including the theologians: "If ye continue in My Word . . . ye shall know the truth" (John 8:31-32). Christ here states two things. First, there is such a thing as Christian certainty, "Ye shall know the truth," and, second, that this certain knowledge of the truth (*Wahrheitsgewissheit*) is identical with continuing in the Word of Christ, believing His Word. Faith is certainty. And when we ask further how this faith, which continues in Christ's Word, is brought about, Scripture again gives us a clear and definite answer. It is the Word of Christ itself which works

---

159 Frank, *System der Christlichen Gewissheit*, 2d ed., I, 128. Ihmels, *Die Christliche Wahrheitsgewissheit*, 1901, p. 8. Horst Stephan, *Glaubenslehre*, 1921, p. 66.

faith in the Word of Christ (Rom. 10:17: "Faith cometh by hearing, and hearing by the Word of God"). The reason for this is that the Word of Christ, when we hear and read it and thus apprehend it with our mind, carries with it the power of the Holy Ghost. Our Christian faith, as Paul declares (1 Cor. 2:5), is not produced by, and does not stand in, "the wisdom of men, but in the power of God." So, then, it is the sure Word which produces the Christian assurance. As Luther's axiom has it: "Man is *certus passive, sicut Verbum Dei certum est active.*" Elaborating this statement, Luther says: "Where this Word [of God] takes possession of the heart by true faith, it makes the heart as firm, sure, and certain as it is itself, unmoved, stubborn, hard, in the face of temptation, the devil, death, and anything whatsoever, in proud confidence laughing to scorn all that spells doubt and fear, ire and wrath, for it knows that the Word of God cannot lie" (St. L. III:1887).

And only by continuing in the Word of Christ is the Christian certainty mediated. Particularly the teachers of the Church need to learn this lesson. The Apostle Paul informs every teacher who will not abide by the wholesome words of the Lord Jesus Christ that he is given to hallucinations, knows nothing, is sick with the disease of question and strifes of words (1 Tim. 6:4), and thus shuts out all Christian assurance. The matter of Christian certainty, of personal assurance of the truth, is, as we see, fully settled by Scripture.

What Scripture says concerning the nature and source of Christian certainty is of great practical value for all Christians, particularly also for the theologian. Following the directions given by Scripture, they will, as often as their assurance wanes, at once flee into the Word of Christ, into Holy Scripture, hear, read, and ponder the Word in their hearts, accept the Word through the influence of the Holy Spirit active in the Word, completely subjecting themselves to it, and humbly praying: "Speak, Lord, for thy servant heareth" (1 Sam. 3:9). Luther did that. Whenever he found that his Christian certainty, both the "assurance of salvation" and the "assurance of the truth," was about to vanish, he fled into Scripture. He says: "I do not know how strong in the Spirit others are; as for me, I could never be so holy as some feel themselves to be, even if I were ever so learned and full of the Spirit. Yet this is constantly happening to me that when I am without the Word, do not meditate on it, and occupy myself with it, there is no Christ at home, no fervor and Spirit; but as soon as I take up a Psalm or a passage of Scripture, it shines and burns into the heart and gives me new courage and a new mind. I know, too, that everyone will daily experience the same thing." (St. L. VIII:749 f.) Luther therefore gives every Christian and every theologian the further advice to "take hold with his thoughts of the letters [of Scripture] as one clings with his hand to a tree or a wall, in order that he may not slip and flutter around and go astray with his own thoughts. That is the trouble with our 'enthusiasts': they imagine that their high spiritual thoughts will do it, and they do not see that without the Word they must lose their way, letting will-o'-the-wisps lead them hither and yon." It is the wrong attitude towards Scripture, Luther here tells us, which precludes the Christian certainty. If we neglect Scripture, opining that we have advanced beyond it and no longer need it, we shall remain, or again become, the prey of uncertainty; we are not listening, not even outwardly, to the voice of Scripture and thus deny it the opportunity to attest itself as the divine truth. Then there are those who take a critical attitude toward Scripture. Their case is infinitely worse. They may experience the blinding effect of the Word of Christ, which Christ describes in the words: "I thank Thee, O Father, Lord of heaven and earth, because Thou hast hid these things from the wise and prudent and hast revealed them unto babes" (Matt. 11:25); and again: "For judgment I am come into this world, that they which see not might see and that they which see might be made blind" (John 9:39). Such a one is absolutely cut off from all Christian knowledge.[160] This warning, too, is a necessary safeguard of the Christian certainty.— We shall take up this point again later on.

If we keep in mind what Scripture teaches concerning Christian certainty, we shall know how to evaluate the "theory of cognition" set up by the moderns and their quest for "the assurance of truth." Though they speak glibly of an "immediate" Christian assurance, they search for a reliable foundation or basis for their assurance, for an "impregnable fortress" [their phrase] into which the Christian "ultimately retreats" and in which he will be safe against all hostile attacks. But Christ directs us to His Word, the Word of His Apostles and Prophets, as the one strong fortress, indestructible, outlasting heaven and earth (Matt. 24:35; Mark 13:31; Luke 21:33). And the Christian Church has understood these orders. It has taken its stand on Scripture, and making Scripture the basis of certainty, it has withstood all assaults of the enemy. Standing on this basis, Luther, too, stood his ground against the whole world. But the moderns insist that Christ, the Christian Church, and of course also Luther, were in error. They hold that

[160] Cp. Luther on Matt. 13:15. St. L. VII:194 f.

the fortress so long regarded as "impregnable" has in our day been captured and demolished, never to be restored. They protest that their keen "sense of realities," as developed by modern scientific methods, forbids them to accept Scripture as God's own Word.[161] The modern theologians are sure they have found that basis in man himself, in something within the Christian. They are, indeed, not sure what constitutes this "impregnable fortress," whether it is the pious self-consciousness of the theologizing subject, or the regenerate self, or the Christian faith consciousness, or the Christian experience, etc. Nor have they yet settled the question among themselves in which region of the Ego the actual seat of assurance is located, whether in the feeling or in the intellect or in the will or in a combination of these three activities of the soul. And they are still arguing the question whether the basis of assurance is the moral ("ethical") condition or the "faith" of the Christian. But of one thing they are sure: the basis of assurance must be located within the "Christian subject" and not outside of it. And since all of them have given up Scripture as the Word of God, it is but natural that on this point they should be in full accord.

It was Schleiermacher who in the first quarter of the last century sold the theological world on this theology of "self-assurance" (*Selbstgewissheit*).[162] Both the liberal and the conservative camps rang with the praises of Schleiermacher's great achievement. Nitzsch-Stephan hailed his "*Glaubenslehre*" as "a reformatory deed," an "achievement of the utmost spiritual importance," "by far the most important dogmatics in recent theology." "In it and through it man's self-consciousness has reached its highest development."[163] And R. Seeberg fully agrees with this appraisal. He acclaims Schleiermacher as "the Reformer of the theology of our century" and calls his "*Glaubenslehre*" "the most perfect, the grandest dogmatics produced by the Evangelical Church up till now"; "this book has taught the nineteenth cen-

---

[161] They say: "In our day the orthodox doctrine of inspiration has hardly any significance in dogmatics. True, it is still being upheld by a few, e. g., Koelling and Noesgen, with some modifications. A theologian, strictly conservative, says concerning these laggards: 'Their number is small, their labor unsuccessful, and their indignation at the comrades who are pressing forward on new paths impresses no one.' . . . The rest of the theologians, including the conservatives, reject the old doctrine." (Nitzsch-Stephan, p. 258.)

[162] *"Der Christliche Glaube, nach den Grundsaetzen der evangelischen Kirche im Zusammenhange dargestellt von D. Friedrich Schleiermacher,"* appeared in print in 1821.

[163] *Ev. Glaubenslehre,* p. 43 ff.

tury true theology."[164] Pupils and admirers of Schleiermacher were found even in what is known as the "confessional Lutheran" group. "The entire dogmatic labor of the Church of the nineteenth century has followed," as Seeberg points out, "the guidelines laid down by Schleiermacher" (*loc. cit.*, p. 84). That applies, and particularly so, to what is known as the "Erlangen Theology." This school stands squarely and unalterably on the theology of self-assurance. Hofmann declared that the Christian consciousness "does not look to the Church nor to Scripture for the primary and real certification of its truth, but it rests in itself and has an immediate assurance of the truth; it has within itself the Spirit of God to certify the truth to it."[165] And Frank says: "We deal with the central and specific essence of the Christian certainty, where no authority coming from without but the Christian personally determines the ground and validity of his certainty."[166]

That Frank includes Scripture among the "authorities coming from without" which cannot serve as the foundation of Christian certainty is evident from his somewhat brusque reply to Philippi: "With him, however, who opposes to me the 'objective' act of redemption and the Word of God in place of my 'subjective' starting point, I am not able to find terms of agreement, because he has not understood the position of the question" (*op. cit.*, p. 115. – Engl. ed., p. 111). Frank certainly comes out squarely for "the full self-assurance of Christianity and its theology." This agrees with Ph. Bachmann's judgment, the last outstanding representative of the Erlangen School, when he says: "Hofmann and still more Frank have as a matter of principle espoused the principle of the full self-assurance of Christianity and its theology."[167]

---

164 *Die Kirche Deutschlands im 19. Jahrhundert*, pp. 90, 84.

165 *Schriftbeweis*, 2d ed., p. 11.

166 *System der chr. Gewissheit*, 2d ed., I, 49. [In the English translation, *System of the Christian Certainty*, p. 46.]

167 *Theol. Literaturblatt*, Leipzig, 1922, p. 395. As to Bachmann's phrase "as a matter of principle," we would say that Frank certainly believed in this "full self-assurance" while he was lecturing to his students and writing books in his study. But from what we have heard concerning him and from what he wrote elsewhere we feel justified in assuming that his communion with God did not take place on the basis of his "self-assurance," but on the basis of the "objective act of redemption" and the objective "Word of God." Just as Frank assumes, in his *Theologie der Konkordienformel* (I, p. 135), that Melanchthon never believed in his synergism, so we assume that Frank never really believed in "the self-assurance of Christianity and its theology." It should be noted, in passing, that we are not impugning the personal Christianity of all advocates of the self-assurance theory. While it is certain, according to Scripture, that this

We must now proceed to an examination of the real nature of this "self-certainty" of theology. We maintain that a certainty which in principle rejects the Word of God as the foundation of assurance is (1) not Christian, (2) not certain, (3) not scientific.

1. All are agreed that only what Christ teaches and does is Christian. And Christ definitely teaches, as was shown at the beginning of this chapter, that the method we must employ if we would know and be sure of the truth is to continue in His Word. Now, since Christ is always right, Schleiermacher, Hofmann, Frank, and all who employ their method, all who ask the "Christian subject" to furnish independently of the Word of Christ full assurance or, at least, half assurance, are in error. Their theological method is not Christian but unchristian. Every theologian who ascribes to a self-mediated consciousness such fine-sounding appellatives as the "Christian self-consciousness," the "pious" self-consciousnes of the "regenerate I," deceives only himself and others.

2. This vaunted "self-certainty" is anything but certainty. It is pure illusion. It cannot be anything else, because the Word of Scripture is the sole foundation of certainty. The notion that one does not need the Word of Christ in order to obtain the knowledge and the assurance of the truth had appeared already in the Apostolic age of the Church. There were men in the Corinthian congregation who ignored the Word of the Apostle and still claimed to be "prophets," the possessors and dispensers of "spiritual" truth. But Paul tells these men plainly that his Word is the Word of Christ ("the things I write unto you are the commandments of the Lord"); furthermore, that they must root out all notions of "self-certainty" and take for their basis the Word of the Apostle, and, finally, that if a man persists in his rejection of this basis, his case is hopeless. That is the meaning of the sharp words: "If any man be ignorant, let him be ignorant" (1 Cor. 14:37-38; 2 Cor. 13:3). "Self-certainty men" appeared in other congregations, too, and all of them had to be told by the Apostle that their assurance was a self-delusion: "If any man teach otherwise and

---

theory, when consistently applied in practice, precludes personal Christianity, it is also true, on the other hand, that in the field of theology, too, "felicitous inconsistency" plays a role; men do "keep a double set of books." A few years ago German periodicals reported that a theologian who had been cultivating this same theology of self-assurance declared on his deathbed that now he found his entire theology summarized in John 3:16. He thus found it necessary to go beyond his own I, "beyond himself," as Luther expresses it; he actually took his stand on a foundation outside himself.

consent not to wholesome words, even the words of our Lord Jesus Christ . . . he is proud, knowing nothing, but doting (νοσῶν, sick) about questions and strifes of words" (1 Tim. 6:3-4). In short, the "knowledge" that is not based on the Word of Christ, that is, on the Word of the Apostles, is ignorance, the pretended "certainty," a sham.

And this applies to the whole group of the modern theologians who have definitely rejected the Word of Christ as the source and basis of certainty and therefore have done away with all real assurance. By erecting a barricade between themselves and Scripture, which is God's Word, they also erect a barricade against the Holy Spirit's testimony to the truth, for Scripture, because it is the Word of God, carries this testimony. They are thus forced to furnish their own *testimonium veritatis* on the basis of intuition, reflection, or self-analysis which they feel in themselves, do of themselves, or judge concerning themselves. It is therefore not surprising that the advocates of "self-certainty" have little use for the testimony of the Holy Spirit. Some of them reject it outright as involving a logical fallacy, "arguing in a circle." The others declare it to be insufficient. That is only consistent with their theological position. One who believes in "self-certainty" will see in this witness of the Holy Spirit an unfair competitor, an unwarranted meddling in what is the theologian's own business. The moderns actually hold that the theologian must bring about the certainty himself. Zoeckler, for instance, who belongs to the right wing of modern theology, says concerning "the appeal of the old Protestant dogmaticians to the *testimonium Spiritus Sancti*," that while it is not to be rejected altogether, it is faulty, and then he makes the plain statement: "A free act is needed, one depending on ourselves, the responsibility for which devolves upon us, an achievement which is morally necessary and for that reason left to our free choice. *Only by this free act do we create the certainty.*" [168] But this self-created certainty is nothing but an illusion. Everything in theology that is built on man himself, whether it be the "assurance of salvation" or the "assurance of the truth," collapses at once when the thunderbolt of the divine Law strikes it, which hurls both sinner and "saint" into a heap "and suffers no one to be in the right but drives them all together to terror and despair" (Smalc. Art., *Trigl.*, 479, 2).

Frank refers in his *System of the Christian Certainty* to the

---

[168] *Handbuch der theol. Wissenschaften*, 2d ed., III, 65. The last sentence italicized by Zoeckler.

Archimedian ποῦ στῶ. We thank him for this reference. The famous saying, rightly or wrongly ascribed to Archimedes: "Δὸς ποῦ στῶ, καὶ τὸν κόσμον κινήσω – give me a place to stand, and I will move the world" – dealing with a physical law, furnishes a fine analogy to the spiritual law which we are studying. Just as Archimedes required a position outside the world to move the world, just so we require a foothold outside ourselves and all the world in order to be able to maintain ourselves against the world, the devil, and our own *I*. All these powers, including our Ego, oppose us, particularly in the matter of the assurance of our salvation and of the assurance of the truth.[169] There is such a position, lying outside of ourselves, providing a firm and safe footing. That is the Word of Christ, concerning which Christ says, as we have already pointed out: "Heaven and earth shall pass away, but My words shall not pass away." And this Word, which is firmer than heaven and earth, Christ designates as the basis on which all must stand who would be His true disciples and know the truth. Luther understood and followed Christ's instruction and command. And as one well experienced in this matter he incessantly calls upon all Christians and particularly all theologians to step out of their own *I* and "through the Word ascend above themselves" (St. L. XI:1727, 1736). In this way, in direct opposition to the ways of the self-certain theology, Luther gained an assurance of the truth that stood unmoved, unshaken in the face of all attacks, and that emboldened him to speak to King Henry VIII thus: "As the Lord liveth, if any king or prince imagines that this man Luther humbles himself before him in the sense that he repents of his doctrine, pleads guilty of false teaching and begs for mercy, such a one is deceiving himself badly, and the gold he was dreaming of turns out to be nothing but filth. In the domain of doctrine the greatness of men means nothing to me; there the greatest of them is a mere bubble or even less. That is not going to be changed. Whoever rues it, let him give up; whoever is afraid, let him flee. My Supporter is strong enough and safe enough for me; that I know. Whether all the world follows me or deserts me, that is all the same to me; for I recall that it did not side with me when I stood alone. Any man that wants to may quit; if he does not care to remain, he is free to go." ("Antwort auf des Koenigs zu England Laesterschrift," St. L. XIX:413, 422.)

---

[169] Frank asks the Christian to base his assurance on something within himself. His statement reads: "With the breaking through and the installation of the new *I* in the center of the personal nature, the ποῦ στῶ is gained" (*op. cit.*, p. 133; Engl., p. 128).

That is certainty, that is assurance of the truth! And this assurance of Luther was the result of the fact that he stood on Scripture as God's own Word, and thus he had a foothold outside his *I*, outside the whole world. Nothing in the world, nothing in us, can give us the needed assurance. Only the Word can do it. Says Luther: "It is greater than a hundred thousand worlds, yea, greater than heaven and earth. That Word shall be my faithful counselor and sturdy tree to which I will cling in order that I may bear and stand it. If we do not cling to that tree, our nature is much too weak to bear the burning hatred and envy of the world and to withstand the crafty plots and fiery darts of the devil." (St. L. XIII:2621.) Recall once more Luther's remarks on 2 Samuel 23: God's Word alone makes certain, *certum est active;* man, however, is made certain by God's Word, he is *certus passive;* but so certain that "the heart in proud confidence laughs to scorn all that spells doubt and fear, ire and wrath, for it knows that the Word of God cannot lie" (St. L. III:1887).

That is the voice of assurance. What about the assurance of the theology of self-certainty? We find that it is a theology of "self-uncertainty" (*Selbstungewissheit*). That is evidenced by a number of facts. There is the indifference to doctrine which prevails today. It has come to such a pass that agreement in doctrine is looked upon as an abnormality, while "pure doctrine" is disparaged as "so-called pure doctrine" and is made the object of ridicule. But indifferentism is the signature of uncertainty. One who is certain of the truth is never indifferent to doctrine, but insists uncompromisingly on pure doctrine, even as Scripture, both in the Old and in the New Testament, insistently demands that the doctrine be "pure," uncontaminated by any human Ego product. (See Chapter 10: "Theology as Doctrine." Jer. 23:16; 1 Pet. 4:11; 1 Tim. 6:3; 2 John 8–11; Rom. 16:17.)

Another symptom of uncertainty is unionism, which pervades the life of the Church today. Unionism has no scruples about practicing church fellowship with spirits that are not of God. But one who is sure of the divine truth thinks and acts according to the order of Christ: "Beware of false prophets" (Matt. 7:15), and the admonition of Paul: "Avoid them" (Rom. 16:17), and the instruction given by "the Apostle of love" with regard to Christian fellowship: "If there come any unto you and bring not this doctrine, receive him not into your house, neither bid him Godspeed; for he that biddeth him Godspeed is partaker of his evil deeds" (2 John 10-11).

Again, modern theology betrays its uncertainty by treating Christian doctrines as "problems." There are, indeed, *sano sensu* open questions and problems in theology,[170] questions which arise in connection with the doctrines revealed in Scripture but concerning which Scripture either is silent or does not speak with sufficient clarity to warrant the careful theologian to say: "Thus saith the Lord," "It is written." Scrupulous theologians, like Luther, would not dare to rank a human opinion with the divine doctrine clearly revealed in Scripture, even though this human opinion is probably correct, as for example, traducianism. Luther says on occasion: "What I do not know for certain [from Scripture], I will teach no one" (St. L. XX:1062). Such theologians are certainly not to be censured; they deserve praise, for their refusal to affirm what Scripture has not clearly affirmed brings into bold relief the majesty of Holy Scripture and its unique divine authority, which does not tolerate any human authority to be set up beside it. The Christian theologians speak and assert where Scripture speaks and asserts; where Scripture does not speak and decide, they humbly step aside and keep silence, for what God has not decided in Scripture must remain a problem. Modern theologians, however, have an entirely different concept of theological problems. They have reduced such doctrines as are clearly revealed in Scripture to "problems." They speak of the "problem" of creation and the preservation of the cosmos, the "problem" of the person and office of Christ, of conversion and justification, of the inspiration of Holy Scripture, of the relation of the Christian religion and the non-Christian religion; everything has become a "problem." And, indeed, on the basis of their principle of cognition, everything must be treated as a problem. In the first place, their source and norm of theology, the human subject, is fallible. They say so themselves, either implicitly or explicitly — and this in spite of the claim of the "immediate certainty" of their theology. But a fallible source and norm can never beget certainty. In the second place, also their secondary and ancillary source of religious certainty is fallible. Modern theology admits — contrary to its principle of a self-mediated assurance — that "Christian experience" is subject to "self-deception."[171] Therefore it advises and enjoins the theologian to test his own findings according to several objective factors, such as the principal world views, man's cumulative religious knowledge, the results of scientific research in the field of anthropology, sociology, comparative religion, and the natural sciences. But if these factors are needed to establish certainty, no man can tell when the

170 See the section above, "Open Questions and Theological Problems."

171 See Ihmels, *Zentralfragen*, pp. 159–166. Also Kirn, *Dogmatik*, pp. 1–6.

quest for certainty will end; to date no absolute finality in any of these fields has been achieved. The "Christian subject," seeking certainty, is thus wandering about in a labyrinth of uncertainties. In addition, he is asked to "form a unified system" out of this tangle of uncertainties. That certainly spells toil and moil; it is indeed a "problem" in the strict sense of the term. And this "laborious search for certainty," as they themselves call it, is altogether profitless. It is rolling the stone of Sisyphus and drawing water, after the manner of the Danaides, with a sieve. – In short, the theology which spurns Scripture as the only source and norm of theology and sets up its tents in the "pious self-consciousness of the theologizing subject" is a theology of uncertainty. But does not Scripture itself teach us to follow the method of the self-certainty theologians when it tells us that we should gain the assurance of our faith and of our continuance in the truth by reflecting on our good works, i. e., our own Ego? Now, it is true that our good works do assure us that we have passed from death unto life. That is the teaching of Scripture (John 8:47; 1 John 3:14; 2:3-4; Matt. 6:14; 2 Pet. 1:10) and of the Lutheran Symbols (*Trigl.* 199, 154 f.). But we must always bear in mind that when "stormy weather sets in," and that happens very often, the Christian is driven, lest he perish in uncertainty, to rely solely and exclusively on the objective word of Scripture as the immovable basis of his assurance. Nevertheless, it is God's will that the Christians should always be in a position to bring in their works as a *testimonium* of their standing in grace and in the truth.[172] But note well that obviously this applies only to the good works of the Christians. But when we examine the works or the fruits produced by the tree of the "pious self-consciousness of the theologizing subject," we see at once that they are evil works. Schleiermacher, the "father" of the nineteenth-century theology of self-consciousness, denies the guilt of sin and its expiation through the vicarious satisfaction of Christ, he denies the eternal deity of Christ, the Trinity; in a word, he denies all fundamentals of the Christian religion. There are theologians among the moderns who acknowledge the evil nature of the fruits of Schleiermacher's self-consciousness. They admire, indeed, Schleiermacher's method and apply it, but they view the products of Schleiermacher's self-consciousness with "grave

[172] With our old theologians we call the good works the *testimonia Spiritus Sancti externa* in distinction from the *testimonium Spiritus Sancti internum,* which consists in faith in God's Word wrought by the Holy Ghost. The internal testimony of the Spirit and faith are one and the same thing. Cf. the fuller presentation in the chapters "Faith and the Testimony of the Holy Ghost" and "Justification on the Basis of Works," in Vol. II.

misgivings." And what do we find when we examine the doctrinal fruits produced by the "Confessional Lutheran" theologians who had adopted Schleiermacher's experience method? With malicious glee the radical wing of the moderns noted and published the fact that the Lutherans have in the Schleiermacher tradition also discarded the Scriptures as the Word of God and Christ's work as *satisfactio vicaria,* also original sin and the eternal, immutable deity of Christ and the "two-nature doctrine" and justification as *actus forensis* and the means of grace as the only means by which the forgiveness of sin is obtained and faith produced and preserved. But these are all evil works. The Holy Ghost in the heart of the Christians views them with horror. They cannot support the "Christian certainty," but can serve only as props for the imaginary certainty of the "human self-consciousness," that has cut loose from Christ's Word and thus erected a barricade against the cognition of the truth.[173]

3. But even if the theology of self-certainty does not serve the cause of certainty – it works the other way – is it not at least scientific? When Frank's *System der christlichen Gewissheit* appeared in its first edition, it created a great stir. But there was also some sharp criticism. In particular one whom Frank himself in the second edition of the book calls an "eminent theologian" suggested to Frank that on his own theory "the profit" of his large book "must be but small." If the

---

[173] Also in Frank's theology the articles of the Christian faith "have been mutilated and crippled" by his use of the Ego method. That has been demonstrated in the article "*Franks Theologie,*" *Lehre und Wehre,* 1896, pp. 65 ff., 97 ff., 129 ff., 161 ff., 201 ff., 262 ff. The writer, Dr. Stoeckhardt, does not place Frank outright in the liberal wing of the theology of self-certainty. He acknowledges that "Frank permits certain elements of the Christian truth to remain." That, however, is, as Stoeckhardt points out, "not due to his system, but to his inconsistency. This residue of Christianity has maintained itself against the antagonistic principle of the system. Frank and his system deserve no credit for these good features in his theology." Stoeckhardt brings proof that Frank does away with the infallible divine authority of Holy Scripture at the behest of the Ego principle. While Christ and His Apostles unhesitatingly identify the Scriptures and God's Word, Frank says: "I would not like to assume the responsibility of teaching a Christian that faith in the saving truth involves faith in the absolute inerrancy of Holy Scripture" (*op. cit.,* p. 97). Frank also discards the *satisfactio vicaria* of Christ. Though Scripture expressly teaches that Christ suffered the punishment which we should have suffered (Is. 53:5; 2 Cor. 5:21; Gal. 3:13), Frank declares: "If substitution is made to mean that Christ suffered whatever condemned mankind would have had to suffer, the *satisfactio vicaria* falls to the ground, for the simple reason that that is not what Christ suffered" (*op. cit.,* p. 138). Frank presents the doctrine of justification correctly when he describes the righteousness involved as the *iustitia extra nos posita,* but he falsifies it when he says that faith comes into consideration in justification, not merely as *medium* ληπτικόν, but also as the conduct of man, as an act of free self-determination. (*Ibid.*)

"Christian certainty," as Frank claims, really is entirely independent of everything lying outside itself, then Frank's book, too, being one of the things lying outside the Christian, would be of no help towards producing and preserving Christian certainty; it could help neither Frank himself nor any other person in the world. This objection certainly puts the self-assurance men into a tight place. Here the Ego theology faces an insurmountable difficulty. When the "enthusiasts" of the sixteenth century (the Ego theology did not originate with Schleiermacher; there was plenty of it before his days) boasted that their "spirit" – and that included, of course, their assurance of the truth – did not need the "external word," Luther told them that then they would have to desist from their own pratings and writings, unless, indeed, they were puffed up with the thought that "the Spirit could not come through the writings and spoken Word of the Apostles, but through their (the enthusiasts') writings and words He must come" (Smalc. Art., *Trigl.* 495, 6). Frank concedes the force of this objection. He admits that his *System of the Christian Certainty* cannot help anyone to attain certainty; nor was it intended for that purpose. But, says Frank, there are other interests in the world besides Christian certainty. There is the scientific interest, and to serve this interest his *System* was written. We quote from the second edition: "If, then, it is further objected – as was done by an eminent theologian, now some years dead – that if such is our meaning, the profit must be but small, for he who had such experience and stands assured, does not need that proof, and for him who has not had it and does not stand in this assurance, it is of no help; I answer that I should desire nothing more than to understand in some measure that which is really present, the certainty actually existing. . . . A small task it may be, but yet a task, namely, a scientific one: he who, standing in the certainty, has no desire for this understanding may let it alone; and he who does not stand in the certainty may also let it alone!" [174]

But Frank is wrong again. When he says that his work serves at least the scientific interest, we shall have to tell him that his method and his work do not meet the requirements of science. It is not easy to gain a clear picture of Frank's line of reasoning owing either to his involved language or his failure to keep in mind the train of thought by which he arrived at his "self-certification." As we and others understand Frank, the way to arrive at scientific certainty is for the subject to "objectify" itself, that is, to make itself the object of in-

[174] *Op. cit.,* 119, resp. 114.

vestigation. And from this rather arbitrarily fixed object the subject receives "impressions," studies these impressions until they become "knowledge," and thus obtains a sound scientific basis for its assurance. But throughout this process the subject dare not look for an object outside itself; not even Holy Scripture and the *testimonium Spiritus Sancti*.[175] That is like advising a man looking for a support (the scientific certainty is never meant to be anything else than a quest) to take a firm hold on some part of his own body; that will give him the necessary means of support. But this method of attaining certainty by grasping one's own Ego and disdaining every "outside" support is as scientific as when Baron Muenchhausen pulled himself and his horse out of the quagmire by his own bootstraps. The self-certainty theologians claim that their method is a masterstroke of systematic theology, because it brings into a perfect unit all Christian knowledge and experience. Yes, it is a perfect unit, as when the playful kitten chases its own tail and revolves around itself. That describes the situation exactly. The theologian who actually cuts loose from Scripture is no longer in contact with God and the divine truth; he is communicating only with himself and his own human thoughts; he is, as has been aptly stated, in communication with "the projections of his own Ego." And that is what the *I* theologians call scientific thinking! [176]

It follows that if modern theology wishes to serve the cause of real, not imaginary, Christian certainty and if it wants to meet the requirements of real science—science certainly calls for orderly thought processes—it must—there is absolutely no other choice—completely reverse itself. It must renounce the unchristian and illogical idea of self-certainty and place itself on the objective foundation on which the Church is actually built, on the Word of the Apostles and Prophets,

---

175 Frank declares: "To the Holy Ghost I cannot appeal in connection therewith, since, of course, it is first a question whether what I receive is testimony of the Holy Ghost; exactly as I cannot appeal to sacred Scripture when it is in question how I come to admit the claim of Scripture to be sacred to me" (*op. cit.*, p. 143).

176 Frank cites Fichte's Idealism, according to which the subject posits the object, in support of the scientific character of self-certainty. He says: "That is the abiding truth in the Idealism of Fichte" (*Christliche Gewissheit*, I, 61). O. Fluegel describes Fichte's Idealism thus in *Probleme der Philosophie und ihre Loesungen*, p. 96: "Fichte holds, with Berkeley, that things exist merely in the mind, but he goes beyond Berkeley in that he no longer seeks an external cause which produces these conceptions of the mind but, expressly denying any such external cause, makes the mind itself the sole originator of the things which seem to exist outside of it." Fluegel finds "only about two" inconsistencies in Fichte; H. Ulrici calls Fichte's Idealism a "senseless one-sidedness" (R. E., 2d ed., XV, 381).

that is, on the Word of Christ (Eph. 2:20; John 8:31-32; 17:20). There is no self-certainty in the Christian theology, but, as Luther says: *Homo est certus passive, sicut Verbum Dei est certum active.* — Modern theology asks us, in this connection, to make Christ's person, and not Christ's Word, our foundation. That will not do. To be sure, Christ's person is the cornerstone of His Church (Eph. 2:20; 1 Pet. 2:6). But we find Christ nowhere else than in His Word. Only as we believe, and stand on, the Apostolic and Prophetic Word, which is Christ's Word, are we built on Christ the Cornerstone. That is clearly stated in the words immediately preceding: "built on the foundation of the Apostles and Prophets." Whoever pushes the Word of the Apostles and Prophets away is not standing on Christ; Christ is not there. "When I am without the Word, do not meditate on it, and occupy myself with it, there is no Christ at home" (Luther).

The spiritual and intellectual collapse of the theology of self-certainty, of experience, etc., is inevitable, because this theology does not take a believing but a critical attitude toward God's Word, that is, toward God Himself. This critical attitude is its *raison d'être.* Because the experience theology rejects Scripture as the infallible Word of God, it has taken its stand on the "religious experience" of the theologizing subject and assumes the right to examine and criticize Holy Scripture. While Christ says: "I have given them Thy Word" and certifies this Word as the truth: "Thy Word is truth" (John 17: 14, 17), the experience theologians, from the extreme left to the extreme right wing, declare either openly or subtly, but *unisono:* Thy Word is not the truth; it is mixed with error. And while Christ instructs His Church to take its stand on His Word for the purpose of gaining the knowledge of the truth, and thus be delivered from all subjectivism, particularly also from the subjectivism of the theologians, the experience theology directs the Church to free itself from the Word of Christ, given the Church, and retreat into the "impregnable fortress" of the self-consciousness of the Christian subject. It goes so far in its censure as to charge that those theologians bring disaster upon the Church who, like the Early Church, the Church of the Reformation, and "especially the old dogmaticians," make Holy Scripture, and not "experience," the source and norm of Christian doctrine. Yes, it goes so far as to claim that such theologians do not foster a "living Christianity" and "living faith," but "intellectualism," dead orthodoxy. In their critical attitude the experience theologians set themselves above God's Word. It is Nietzsche's "superman" in the sphere of theology. But we know from Scripture that it is a most dangerous thing for men to criticize the Word of God. God cannot brook criticism of His Word. Christ has given men God's Word that they should believe. All who criticize it instead of believing it call down upon themselves the judgment of which Christ speaks Matt. 11:25: "Thou hast hid these things from the wise and prudent and hast revealed them unto babes." They become incapable of knowing the truth. The Word of God has a twofold effect on man. *Primo loco,* it illumines; *secundo loco,* it blinds. Whoever, through the power of the Holy Ghost, operating in the Word, receives it not as the word of man, but, as it is in truth, the Word of God, as the Thessalonians did (1 Thess. 2:13), him it illumines; whoever opposes it with the criticism of his Ego, him it blinds.

It blinds his natural judgment, too. We point, first, to the efforts on the part of practically all experience theologians to make Luther the protector of the Ego theology. They insist that Luther had already before them directed the theologians to break away from the Scripture word and had made the pious Ego the judge of the Scripture word. Statements of Luther declaring that faith must be added to the external Word of Scripture are made to mean that Luther declared faith to be independent of the external Word of Scripture. This is a glaring misconception and misinterpretation of Luther's statements.

In the second place, we note the fact that the advocates of the experience theology charge one another with "subjectivism." And that makes no sense, since invariably both parties of the dispute are sick with the same disease, subjectivism. W. Herrmann accuses Frank of "subjectivism" while he himself asserts that the assurance of the truth is based on the fact that the human subject imitates "the inner life of Jesus."[177] As if that were not "subjectivism" in a pronounced degree! Ihmels, too, takes Frank to task for his subjectivism, for making the "ethical approach" (the moral transformation of the Christian) "the foundation of the whole Christian state." Ihmels correctly holds that the ethical condition of the Christian is subject to "frequent fluctuations," a fact which Frank himself admits, and that justification, and nothing else, constitutes the foundation of the Christian state. On the other hand, Ihmels himself has not been able to remain free from subjectivism; he, too, like Frank, weaves human work into justifying faith. If the concluding words of his *Zentralfragen* mean what they say, then man's coming to the gracious God and his cognition of the truth depend on the right action of the human will. These

---

177 See Ihmels, *Die christliche Wahrheitsgewissheit,* pp. 124–167.

are his words: "In the final analysis this truth [the Christian truth] is God, and God can reveal Himself only to him who wills to have Him." [178] That clearly puts both the assurance of salvation and the assurance of the truth on a subjective basis. That was also Chrysostom's view: *"Trahit Deus, sed volentem trahit; tantum velis et Deus praeoccurrit,"* – God draws, but He draws the willing one; only be willing and God anticipates – and the Formula of Concord warns against such expressions, because they "have been introduced for confirming the natural free will in man's conversion, against the doctrine concerning God's grace," and "are not in harmony with the form of sound doctrine" (*Trigl.* 913, 86). Salvation depends not upon man's will or effort, but upon God's mercy (Rom. 9:16, 30-33). What fools we poor mortals are – seeking a subjective foundation of certainty! That gets us nowhere. The ground of our certainty lies outside us, in the Word of God, in the Word of the Apostles and Prophets, on which the Christian Church is built. The moment you base your certainty on something within yourself, your certainty becomes uncertainty, call this Ego basis what you will – regeneration, or ethical transformation, or self-determination, or self-positing, or human conduct, or lesser guilt, or prevenient willing, etc. Luther had learned that well, so well that when Erasmus urged him to subscribe to the thesis that salvation depends on the right use of the *facultas se applicandi ad gratiam,* he declared: *"Jugulum petisti!"* (*Du bist mir an die Kehle gefahren.* You've got me by the throat; i. e., You have attacked the vital part at once.) In the matter of the "assurance of truth," Luther clung to the axiom: *Homo certus est passive, sicut Verbum Dei est certum active* – man's certainty is not of his own making, he is made certain by God's Word.

Luther the patron of subjectivism? Luther opposed subjectivism in whatever form it appeared. Thus he warned against making true faith, wrought by the Holy Spirit, the foundation of certainty and thereby founding faith on faith. Luther calls such subjectivists "idolatrous, apostate" Christians. He writes: "It is certainly true that one should have faith for Baptism" [and this applies according to Luther also to the external, objective Word]; "but one is not to be baptized on his faith. There is a very great difference between having faith and relying on one's faith and thus being baptized on it. Whoever is baptized on his faith is not only uncertain, but an idolatrous, apostate Christian, for he trusts and relies on what is his, namely, on a gift

---

[178] *Zentralfragen,* 2d ed., p. 166.

given him of God, and not alone on God's Word, just as another trusts and relies on his strength, wealth, power, wisdom, sanctity, which indeed also are gifts, given him of God." (St. L. XVII:2213.)

In this chapter we have passed a sharp judgment on the "theology of self-consciousness." But that is not our judgment, but God's. And in passing this sharp judgment we are looking also at ourselves. This wicked disposition, which asserts itself in the theology of the "human self-consciousness," inheres in all Christians because of their wicked flesh, which retains all the evil qualities of fallen human nature. It is the nature of fallen man, just because he has fallen away from God, the Center of all things, to make himself the center of things; self-assured, self-centered, self-assertive, he sets himself above God's Word — he is the "superman." Whoever keeps this evil disposition in subjection will extol the unmerited grace of God that has placed him in such religious environment as does not impede but foster true theology. The man who boasts: "God, I thank Thee that I am not as other men are" has *eo ipso* reverted to the theology of self-certainty, in spite of his external association with church circles which emphatically reject the doctrine of self-certainty. But the fact that the theology of self-assertion is but an outgrowth of the evil disposition inhering, since the Fall, in all descendants of Adam, certainly does not release us from the duty of waging grim war against it. Viewed from every angle, this theology is not what it pretends to be.

Let us recapitulate: Invented for the purpose of insuring the scientific character of theology, this theology makes its advocates play the role of the man who, in order to brace his toppling Ego, takes a tight hold of his Ego. Furthermore, the Ego theology is a form, the worst form, of idolatry — self-deification. The authority which the *I* theologian denies to Holy Scripture he claims for himself. And as every other idol leaves the supplications of his votaries unanswered (Ps. 115:4-8), so the idol set up by the *I* theologians makes fools of them. The result of the theology of self-certainty is, as we have shown at length, not certainty, but illusion, self-delusion, uncertainty. We also saw that the *I* theology is most contagious. Schleiermacher is today [at least in some quarters] still hailed as the Reformer of the 19th century. There is a twofold reason for that. Separated from the Center through the Fall, man makes himself the center of things and is therefore easily won for an Ego theology. Secondly, the Ego theology always covers its wickedness with the cloak of piety. The "enthusiasts" of the 16th century would not have won so great a following if they had openly declared that their vagaries were the product of their human Ego. But they labeled them as products of the Holy Spirit. And they shed, as Luther on occasion remarks, "troughs of tears" as evidencing their piety. In the same manner Schleiermacher and his followers speak of the pious self-consciousness of the theologizing subject, of the regenerate Ego, of the Christian experience, etc. And though they reject Scripture as the Word of God and deny the *satisfactio vicaria,* they talk about the great progress of exegesis and a deeper comprehension of the meaning of Scripture. All this is deceptive, apt also to deceive "the simple" (Rom. 16:18). In the realm of nature Fichte's method of having the subject posit the object creates no trouble, because the irrational creatures do not order their life according to the ideas of Fichte, Plato, or any man's Ego. In the spiritual realm, however, the situation is quite different. There the notion that the subject posits the object is much admired and does a thriving business. It is therefore the duty of all those who by the grace of God see clearly in this matter to uncover the fraud practiced by the theology of self-consciousness and war against it.

This unchristian and pernicious theology is not restricted to Germany; here in the United States, too, it dominates practically the entire Protestant theology. Here, in the land of the Reformed sects, it has found a most congenial environment. Zwingli and Calvin, teaching the immediate operation of the Spirit, represented in principle the *I* theology. Owing to the powerful influence of Luther this theology did not attain its full growth in those days. But it is not surprising that when Luther's influence had waned at the beginning of the 19th century, Schleiermacher and his Reformed-pantheistic theology should find admirers and adherents in this country, even though it was criticized in some details.[179] The situation at present is this, that all our large universities, with the partial exception of Princeton, stand for the theology of the self-consciousness, if they deal with theology at all. Some time ago we reported on an "organization of laymen," set up for the purpose of defending the Christian fundamentals.[180] These laymen charge that the universities and most theological seminaries have been training a generation of preachers who deny these fundamentals. They specify that these preachers have substituted for the divine authority of Scripture the consciousness of the individual and for the vicarious satisfaction of Christ moral en-

---

[179] The influence of Schleiermacher in the United States is set forth in Strong's long article on "The Theology of Schleiermacher as Illustrated by His Life and Correspondence," in his *Miscellanies,* II, 1–57.

[180] *Lehre und Wehre,* 1923, 89 f.

deavors conforming to the example of Christ, the ideal man.[181] Whether this "organization" of laymen will check the destructive flood, only the future will show. – In our church body – the Synodical Conference – there has been up to now, thanks be to God, no need of organizing the laymen against the pastors. Among the thousands of our pastors there is to our knowledge not a single one who questions the inspiration of Scripture and, as a result, would be forced to espouse the Ego theology. But we must never overlook the danger threatening us from our American surroundings.

17

Theology and Doctrinal Development

In accord with its principle of continuity in revelation, modern theology holds that development in doctrine is essential to a living and dynamic Christianity. Also within the Lutheran Church of America men had gone in for the further development of the Lutheran doctrine.[182]

There can be no development of the Christian doctrine, because the Christian doctrine given to the Church by the Apostles is a finished product, complete and perfect, fixed for all times. It is not in need of improvement and allows no alteration. Christ's mandate (Matt. 28:

---

[181] We quote from *The Fundamentalist*, Vol. II, No. 1: "The Radicals are set on substituting 'evolution' for creation, 'the principle animating the cosmos' for the living God, consciousness of the individual for the authority of the Bible, reason for revelation, sight for faith, 'social service,' for salvation, reform for regeneration, the priest for the prophet, ecclesiasticism for evangelism, the human Jesus for the divine Christ, a man-made 'ideal society' for the divinely promised kingdom of God, and humanitarian efforts in this poor world for an eternity of joy in God's bright home." Particular attention is called to a widely publicized sermon of Dr. Fosdick: "Dr. Harry Emerson Fosdick, for example, not only preached his now famous sermon here in New York on the question, 'Shall the Fundamentalists Win?' in which he repudiated the inspiration of the Scriptures, the virgin birth, the vicarious atonement, and the second coming of our Lord, but this sermon was then put into pamphlet form, and has been broadcast throughout the nation."

[182] The theologians who are opposed to "doctrinal progress" and "progressive theology" have been branded "repristinating theologians," particularly the so-called Missourians (Preface to *Lehre und Wehre*, 1875, 1 ff., 33 ff., especially 65 ff.), but also others, for example, Philippi. Referring to Philippi, Hofmann gibes: "Let him who likes to take things easy keep on sleeping" (*Schutzschriften*, I, p. 2). – See the articles, "Die falschen Stuetzen der modernen Theorie von den offenen Fragen," *Lehre und Wehre*, 1868, 97 ff. and "Die moderne Lehrentwicklungshaeresie," *Lehre und Wehre*, 1877, 129 ff.

18-20) extends over the entire New Testament era to Judgment Day. According to this mandate the Church is to teach the nations all things whatsoever Christ has commanded. And Christ declares further that the Church has His doctrine in the doctrine of His Apostles when He declares (John 17:20) that all members of His Church to the Last Day will believe on Him through the Word of the Apostles. The Apostles, too, insisted on the finality and immutability of their doctrine. Paul exhorted the churches to retain the doctrine which they had received from him. "Therefore, brethren, stand fast, and hold the traditions which ye have been taught, whether by word or our epistle" (2 Thess. 2:15). And this injunction was addressed not only to the Apostolic Church, but to the Church of all times. That is evident from the passages in which Paul expressly refers to the future. "After my departing shall grievous wolves enter in among you, not sparing the flock. Also of your own selves shall men arise, speaking perverse things, to draw away disciples after them" (Acts 20:29-30). "In the latter times some shall depart from the faith, giving heed to seducing spirits and doctrines of devils" (1 Tim. 4:1; also 2 Tim. 3:1 ff.). Paul left no room for an interim theology. "Keep this commandment . . . until the appearing of our Lord Jesus Christ" (1 Tim. 6:14 f.; 2 Tim. 4:1 ff. See also 1 Pet. 5:1-4). Paul's doctrine is the immutable divine truth; so much so that Paul pronounces a curse upon everyone who dares to change his Gospel (Gal. 1:6-9; 5:12). Because the Apostolic doctrine is immutable, Paul commands the Christians to avoid all who teach otherwise (Rom. 16:17) and to regard them as bloated babblers and ignoramuses (1 Tim. 6:3-4). – The theologians of our day and age should note that Paul maintains the perfection of the Apostolic doctrine especially over against those who claim to possess higher philosophical knowledge and deeper spiritual insights and presume to supply alleged deficiencies in the doctrine of Christ. He declares that those who believe the doctrine of Christ, as proclaimed by the Apostles, "are complete in Him." "Beware lest any man spoil you through philosophy and vain deceit. . . . And ye are complete in Him" (Col. 2:7-10; also 16-20).[183]

---

[183] Peake on Col. 2:8: "There is no condemnation of philosophy in itself, but simply of the empty but plausible sham that went by that name in Colossae" (in *The Expositor's Greek Testament*, p. 522). Thus also, in substance, Meyer and perhaps the majority of the modern exegetes. However, according to the text and the context, the Apostle warns against all philosophy in so far as it meddles with the Christian doctrine and proposes to supplement or improve it. That is, says the Apostle, "vain deceit," since philosophy is nothing but human wisdom, "after the tradition of men," while the Christians are taught "after Christ,"

The advocates of the doctrinal development theory appeal to the fact that the Church in the course of time found it necessary, as new errors arose, to give expression to the Christian doctrine in such new formulations as ὁμοούσιος, θεοτόκος, *homo mere passive se habet.* The point is not well taken. These new formulations did not develop or change the Christian doctrine. On the contrary, they maintained the old doctrine against new errors; employing them, the Church continued in the Word of Christ (John 8:31). Luther proves conclusively that the old "chief councils" with their ὁμοούσιος, θεοτόκος, etc., did not make new doctrines, but simply confessed the doctrines which, on the basis of Scripture, Christendom had believed from the very beginning.[184] Nor did the Reformation in any way develop the Christian

---

who is not a mere man, but He in whom "dwelleth all the fullness of the Godhead bodily," which means that the Christian doctrine, in contradistinction to all human doctrine, is divine doctrine. Cf. Note 56. In short, our passage absolutely excludes from theology all philosophy, because philosophy is made up of the thoughts of men. Meyer thinks that when "Luther so often condemned philosophy," he had in mind "the degeneration of philosophy in the Aristotelian scholasticism." But see Luther's statement, St. L. I:621, quoted on page 17. Luther praises the philosophers in so far as they taught parts of the Law, their natural reason being their guide. Nevertheless he maintains: "The philosophers are not theologians; with good reason Paul therefore warns us against philosophy (Col. 2:8), that is, against all philosophy, because the philosopher has nothing but words of human wisdom, which certainly do not agree with the Gospel and cannot agree with it." (St. L. XXII:1932.) Again: "The philosophers have here and there spoken of God, of His providence, which rules all things, in a way which is not at all inept; to some these words seem so Christian that they are ready to place Socrates, Xenophon, Plato, etc., among the Prophets. Yet, because in these discussions the philosophers are ignorant of the fact that God sent His Son into the world to save sinners, these fine and beautiful pronouncements are, according to our text (Gen. 6:5-6), consummate ignorance of God and plain blasphemies, for the text states bluntly that all imagination and effort of the human heart is only evil." (St. L. I:484 f.)

[184] In his treatise *On the Councils and Churches* he writes: "This, then, was the purpose for which the four chief councils were held. The first, at Nicea, defended the deity of Christ against Arius; the second, at Constantinople, defended the deity of the Holy Ghost against Macedonius; the third, at Ephesus, defended the one person of Christ against Nestorius; the fourth, at Chalcedon, defended the two natures in Christ against Eutyches; but they did not thereby establish any new articles of faith. For these four articles are established far more abundantly and powerfully in St. John's Gospel alone, even though the other Evangelists and St. Paul and St. Peter had written nothing about them, though all these, together with the Prophets, teach them and testify mightily to them. These four councils the bishops of Rome, according to their decree, hold to be like the four Evangelists, as though these matters, together with all articles of faith, did not stand far more richly in the Gospels, and as though the councils had not taken them from the Gospels; so finely do these asses of bishops understand what the Gospels and the councils are. And if these four chief councils do not intend to make or establish anything new in the way of articles of faith, and cannot do so,

doctrine. It added nothing; it only extricated the old doctrine of Scripture out of the rubble of the popish doctrines of men and again taught and confessed the old doctrine. Luther did not set out to improve the old doctrine. "We fabricate nothing new, but retain, and hold to, the old Word of God as the ancient Church confessed it; hence we are, with it, the true ancient Church, believing and teaching one and the same Word of God. Therefore the Papists blaspheme, once more, Christ Himself, the Apostles, and the whole Christian Church when they call us innovators and heretics. For we teach, as they must know, nothing but the old doctrine of the old Church." (St. L. XVII:1324.) All those theologians fail to understand the Reformation who appeal to Luther as an advocate of the doctrinal development theory and who say that the Reformation is a "new interpretation of Christianity." The Augsburg Confession, too, proudly proclaims that it has introduced nothing new into the Church: "This is about the Sum of our Doctrine, in which, as can be seen, there is nothing that varies from the Scriptures, or from the Church Catholic, or from the Church of Rome, as known from its writers. . . . Our churches dissent in no article of faith from the Church Catholic, but only omit some abuses which are new. . . ." (*Trigl.* 59.) Likewise the Formula of Concord has no intention of setting up new doctrines; it declares for the principle "that the sole rule and standard according to which all dogmas together with (all) teachers should be estimated and judged are the Prophetic and Apostolic Scriptures of the Old and of the New Testament alone. . . . Other writings, however, of ancient or modern teachers, whatever name they bear, must not be regarded as equal to the Holy Scriptures, but all of them together be subjected to them, and should not be received otherwise or further than as witnesses (which are to show) in what manner after the time of the apostles and at what places this (pure) doctrine of the Prophets and Apostles was preserved." [185]

That there can be no development of the Christian doctrine is, finally, evidenced by the patent fact that whenever men set out to

---

as they themselves confess, how much less can such power be ascribed to the other councils, which must be held of smaller account, if these four are to be called the chief councils. . . . And if they do establish new things with regard to faith and good works, be assured that the Holy Spirit is not there, but only the unholy spirit and his angels." (St. L. XVI:2248 f.)

[185] Epitome, *Trigl.*, p. 777. The *Catalogus Testimoniorum* (*Trigl.* 1107–1149) brings historic proof that the Formula of Concord brought no new doctrine on the Person of Christ, and particularly on the *communicatio idiomatum*, but the doctrine of orthodox antiquity.

develop the doctrine, they invariably pervert and destroy the Christian doctrine. Not only Luther and the so-called repristination theologians, but all sincere theologians of the nineteenth century who were concerned about the preservation of the Christian doctrine have condemned the doctrinal development theory. The *Evangelische Kirchenzeitung* of Berlin, founded by Hengstenberg and continued by Tauscher, declared in its April issue of 1870: "We must say that the present age, with its theological and ecclesiastical chaos, is not at all suited for a development of the churchly doctrine. For even the most churchly theologians of modern times, such as von Hofmann, Thomasius, even Hengstenberg, have had no success in this business; their attempts to develop this and that doctrine of the Church have been — *sit venia verbo* — a dismal failure. . . . The new impetus given to the development of the Christian doctrine by Schleiermacher has proved to be disastrous for doctrine as well as for life." [186]

---

[186] Quoted in *Lehre und Wehre,* 1875, p. 70. The evidence that the doctrinal development attempted by modern theology does not represent an improvement of the Christian doctrine, but a defection from it is brought by Walther, in a most detailed form, in the series of articles which appeared in *Lehre und Wehre,* 1875, 1876, 1878, entitled: "Was ist es um den Fortschritt der modernen Theologie in der Lehre?" Walther calls the theory that the dogmas are the result of a gradual development a "sister of Romanism in a Protestant mask," a theory which turns the Church "into a school of philosophy, whose task it is to search for the truth eternally, while the Church, according to God's Word, is the bride (*Hausehre*), to whom the truth has been entrusted as her most precious treasure, as the 'good thing' which she is to keep by the Holy Ghost, 2 Tim. 1:13-14; 1 Tim. 6:20." Walther also, together with the old theologians, calls attention to the fact that the Church, in the course of its history, does not exhibit a development of doctrine, progressive and tending upwards, but rather resembles, as touching the public teaching of the true doctrine, the waxing and waning moon, "sometimes experiencing seasons of special visitations of grace, sometimes eclipses." (*Lehre und Wehre,* 1868, p. 136 f.) In 1862 Dr. Muenkel, in the preface of his *Neues Zeitblatt,* wrote: "There is hardly one doctrine left which has not in a marked degree been subjected to recastings, additions, and eliminations. Starting with the Trinity, proceeding to the doctrine of the Person and of the office of Christ, to the doctrines of faith and justification, of the Sacraments and of the Church, down to eschatology, you will scarcely find anything in its old form and with its former value. Often it is changed to such a degree that only the old frame still reminds one of the old picture, and at times even the frame has been smashed as being entirely too narrow and old-fashioned. A small sample to illustrate this: While Christ, according to the Church doctrine, is true God also in His state of humiliation, they now have emptied Him of the divine attributes, without which no man can conceive of the deity, or they let Him gradually grow into His deity and achieve it in His rising from the dead. The death of Christ is no longer permitted to be taught as satisfying for our sins and reconciling us to God. The righteousness of faith, consisting in God's declaring us righteous, is said to be too wooden and externalistic; in a covert manner the works are again drawn in. Law and Gospel are again churned to-

Recall, finally, what has been said in the chapter "Christianity the Absolute Religion." We will engage in the business of developing the doctrine only so long and in so far as we do not know the Christian doctrine. As soon as, and in so far as, we have by God's grace learned to know it by faith in God's Word, we bow our heads and knees in adoration, admiring its unchangeable divine grandeur. That is also the attitude of the holy angels toward the things which the Apostles have proclaimed to us by the Holy Spirit, sent from heaven: "Which things the angels desire to look into" (1 Pet. 1:12). The theology of repristination is the theology of the Church; any other theology has no right of existence (John 8:31-32; 17:20; 1 Tim. 6:3 ff.; Eph. 2:20).

18

Theology and Doctrinal Liberty

Christian liberty consists in this, that Christians are freed from their own will and are now servants of God (Rom. 6:22). Likewise, doctrinal liberty consists in this, that Christian teachers are freed from human opinions and bound only by the Word of God. That is Christ's

---

gether. The Word of God and preaching are pushed back in such a way as to make it appear that the Sacraments did the real work or, at least, must bring life into the Church. They are again attributing to the Visible Church the attributes of the Invisible Church, as though the Visible Church were indeed the one true Church. And what about the relation of the churches, about the public ministry and church government and eschatology and the eternal life? Everybody knows what the issues in these controversies are, and if they were of no importance, the controversy would not be so sharp. . . . Suppose all Lutherans were agreed on making all these changes, including those we have not listed, would that still be the Lutheran doctrine? Would anyone dare to call that an improvement of the Lutheran doctrine which sweeps the most essential portions of the Lutheran doctrine outdoors like old rubbish? I, for my part, would not have the heart to call myself a Lutheran but frankly confess: We have all gone astray. . . . We are ready to predict that before long the scientific theology will lose its standing. While the other sciences with their genuine and undeniable advances are gaining the respect of the world, theology exhibits the utmost confusion; and while it boasts of its progress, nobody knows exactly wherein the progress consists, since one party calls the other party's progression retrogression; the Church gains nothing from all this progress, nothing but quarrels and bruises and wounds. And so it has come about that the other sciences have united all the cultured nations with a common bond and work with united forces, while theology causes splits and ruptures of every sort instead of carrying out its mission, and that is to unite all nations with its proclamation of the one salvation, which is for all nations. That is a most lamentable and discouraging situation; it surely will not encourage men to entrust themselves to the bewildering mazes of theological science." (Quoted in *Lehre und Wehre,* 1875, p. 71 ff.)

own definition of the freedom of doctrine: "If ye continue in My word, then . . . ye shall know the truth, and the truth shall make you free" (John 8:31 f.). When the theologian accepts and regards as Christian doctrine what the human Ego, his own or that of other men, has produced, he has become the slave of men. Under the watchword "academic freedom" our age demands for the theologians freedom from the bondage of the Word, Holy Scripture, "submission to the letter," "shameful academic coercion," "legalism," etc. But this is the liberty of the flesh, the license demanded by the "superman," who sets himself above God's Word and will.

The following considerations will set forth the monstrosity of the universal demand for theological freedom.

1. Until the end of time the Christian Church has but one Teacher, Jesus Christ. "One is your Master (διδάσκαλος), even Christ, and all ye are brethren. One is your Master (καθηγητής), even Christ" (Matt. 23:8, 10). What He, Christ, has commanded His disciples, they are to teach all men to the end of time (Matt. 28:20). Even though Christ in the state of exaltation has withdrawn His visible presence from the Church, He is and remains the one Teacher of His Church; through His Word, which He gave the Church in the Word of His Apostles, He teaches the Church to the end of time (John 8:31-32; 17:20). The Apostles, too, declare that Christ is the sole Teacher of the Church. They bind the Christians to their doctrine (2 Thess. 2:13-15; Gal. 1:6-9), but do that only because they know that their word is Christ's Word (1 Cor. 14:37: ". . . the things that I write unto you are the commandments of the Lord"; 2 Cor. 13:3; 1 Tim. 6:3). And after the days of the Apostles all orthodox teachers of the Church viewed the situation in the same way. Luther: "If any man would preach, let him suppress his own words. He may speak them in the family and State. But here in the Church he must speak nothing but the Word of the rich Head of the family; else it is not the true Church. In the Church the rule should be: God is speaking." (St. L. XII:1413.) It is thus a monstrous thing when men who would be the teachers of Christendom demand "academic freedom." Whoever demands doctrinal license places himself on a level with Christ and, *eo ipso,* in opposition to Christ. For that reason all false teachers are called antichrists (1 John 2:18): "Even now there are many antichrists." [187]

2. The Christians are commanded by Scripture to hear only such

---

[187] This point will be discussed at length in the chapter "The Execution of the Prophetic Office in the State of Exaltation," in Vol. II.

preachers as speak out of the mouth of the Lord — in our day that means: out of Holy Scripture — and not out of their own spirit (Jer. 23:16: "They speak a vision of their own heart and not out of the mouth of the Lord"; v. 31). It is a clear command and repeated again and again. The Christians must deny the greeting of Christian fellowship to all those who do not bring the doctrine of Christ (2 John 7-11), must regard them as bloated ignoramuses (1 Tim. 6:3 ff.), and avoid them (Rom. 16:17). It is, therefore, a stupendous folly for preachers to refuse to subscribe to the Confessions of the Christian congregation on the ground that that would unduly restrict their doctrinal freedom. They reveal by such an attitude that they do not know the first thing about the regulations God made as to what should be preached in the Christian Church. And the theological professors who claim "academic freedom" as their privilege are in worse condemnation. They are to train the future teachers of the Church and do not know the prime qualifications of the Christian teacher! He is not qualified for a theological professorship who claims "academic freedom" in the name of "theological science" contrary to Christ's clear statement that the truth is learned and known only by continuing in His Word.

The history of the Church reveals the fact that in the European State churches the so-called scientific theology has been enjoying this freedom of doctrine for a long time and quite generally. That has been one of the main causes of the chaos prevailing in these churches. And what is the situation in the American "free" churches? There, too, "academic freedom" has made great headway in the schools controlled by the churches, even in circles claiming the name Lutheran. And professors of State universities, which naturally do not have theological faculties, claim the right to make propaganda for their "religious convictions." [188]

In recent times it has almost become axiomatic to say that unqualified subjection to Christ's Word is incompatible with the "inward freedom" which the theologian requires. They say that if the theologian must regard himself as absolutely bound by the word of Scripture, Scripture would become for him a codex of laws fallen from heaven, a paper Pope, etc., in short, a return to Catholic authoritari-

---

[188] See James H. Baker, *American University Progress*, 1916. In the chapter "Academic Freedom," p. 84 f., we read: "Problems may arise in the discussion of . . . religious and political beliefs." "The university is responsible for pioneer thought and must adhere to facts, and, like Huxley, let them lead where they will." The Board of Trustees is said to have done its duty "when they appoint able and fearless men to the faculties and attend to the business details of university management."

anism. If the "evangelical" spirit of Protestantism is to remain unhampered, it must abandon Holy Scripture as the source and norm of theology and rely upon the "living," "ardent" Ego of the theologizing subject. That is the position taken by the entire modern theology; here all parties, from the extreme left wing to the extreme right, are in substantial agreement. It has been said that the right thing for present-day theology to do is to shed "the armor of Saul worn by the old theology," especially the verbal inspiration of Scripture. Then it will be able, like David, to "leap over a wall." [189] The answer to this is, first, that according to Christ's view – which certainly should be authoritative – submission to God's Word and doctrinal freedom agree very well with each other, in fact, they go together, that is to say, only continuance in the Word of Scripture will lead to the knowledge of the truth and theological freedom. Christ states this expressly: "If ye continue in My Word, then . . . ye shall know the truth, and the truth shall make you free" (John 8:31-32). Second, Christ points out, in this connection, that there are two classes of hearers of His Word: The first class knows and willingly accepts His Word as God's Word; the second class refuses to accept His Word as God's Word, but regards it as an oppressive "external authority" and rebels against it. And the reason for this dissimilar attitude towards His Word is stated in these words of Christ: "He that is of God heareth God's words" (John 8:47); in figurative language: "The sheep follow Him [Christ], for they know His voice, and a stranger will they not follow, but will flee from him; for they know not the voice of strangers" (John 10:4-5). Of the other class, of those among the Jews who turned away from His Word as an intolerable "external authority," Christ says: "Ye therefore hear them not because ye are not of God" (John 8:47); "Why do ye not understand My speech? Even because ye cannot hear My Word" (John 8:43). Briefly, Christ says: God's children know Christ's Word to be God's Word; those who are not yet God's children are not in a condition to know and receive God's Word in Christ's Word. There is but one way to stop the Jews from murmuring at the Word of Jesus. Jesus tells them: "Murmur not among yourselves. No man can come to Me except the Father which hath sent Me draw him" (John 6:43-44).

In dealing with an unbeliever we cannot begin with an attempt to convince him of the divine authority of Scripture. We must first bring him to the knowledge of his sins and to faith in Christ, the

---

[189] Theodor Kaftan, *Moderne Theologie des alten Glaubens,* 2d ed., p. 121.

Redeemer from sin. We should preach to him on the basis of Scripture — without discussing the authority of Scripture — repentance and remission of sin. If a man has in this way — and there is no other way — become a Christian, a sheep of Christ's flock, a child of God, then he will know that the Word of Scripture is God's Word, just as the children of God among the Jews knew and received the word Christ spoke as God's Word. If the camel has first gone through the eye of the needle (Hofacker's phrase), that is to say, if a man has by way of the *contritio* and *fides* wrought by the Holy Ghost become a Christian, he will refrain from criticizing anything in Scripture, even if he does not understand certain portions of it; the truth of the entire Scripture is guaranteed to him by the authority of Him (John 10:35; 17:14, 17) whom he adores in faith as his Lord and Redeemer. That is the Christian attitude toward Scripture. Luther describes it thus: "If you cannot understand how it could have been six days [at creation], then accord the Holy Spirit the honor that He is more learned than you. For you are so to deal with the Scriptures that you bear in mind that God Himself is saying this." (St. L. III:21.) And this submission to God's Word is not an "enforced" subjection to an "external authority," unbefitting the Christian, but a childlike, willing, glorious submission to God; even as the Christian in his entire life submits to God's ways and permits God to guide him.

19

Theology and System

Does theology constitute a system? The answer depends on the definition of the term *system*.[190]

If by system we mean an integrated, organized whole, the Christian doctrine is indeed a system. Inasmuch as the Christian doctrine is taken solely from Scripture, it forms a complete, unified, homogeneous whole in a twofold respect; namely, as to its source [formal principle] and its *Leitmotif* [material principle]. (1) Scripture does not contain varying human types of doctrine (e. g., a Mosaic, Johannine, Petrine, Pauline type), but presents the uniform theology of God, since

[190] On the different connotations of the term see Bretschneider, *Systematische Entwicklung*, 3d ed., p. 39; Baier-Walther, I, 76; any larger encyclopedia, e. g., *Century Dictionary*, VII, 6142, *s. v. system;* Kliefoth, *Der Schriftbeweis des Dr. J. Chr. K. von Hofmann*, Schwerin, 1859; pp. 173—190; Nitzsch-Stephan, *Ev. Dogm.*, p. 10 f.; 18.

it is divinely inspired and absolutely errorless.[191] (2) Since the Christian doctrine is taken solely from Scripture, the doctrine of justification διὰ τῆς πίστεως χωρὶς ἔργων νόμου is the central doctrine, of which all other doctrines are either antecedents (*articuli antecedentes*) or consequents (*articuli consequentes*).[192] Such an integration and correlation of the Christian doctrines was not devised by Luther and the Lutheran dogmaticians, but is set down in Holy Scripture as a fact. When Paul asserts, on the one hand, "I have not shunned to declare unto you all the counsel of God" (Acts 20:27), and declares, on the other hand, "I determined not to know anything among you save Jesus Christ and Him Crucified" (1 Cor. 2:2), he thereby teaches that the forgiveness of sins gained by the reconciling death of Christ is the center of the entire Christian doctrine. Peter likewise declares that justification by faith in Christ is the central teaching of the whole Old Testament Scripture. He says: "To Him [Christ] give all the Prophets witness, that through His name whosoever believeth in Him shall receive remission of sins" (Acts 10:43).

Furthermore, the close inner connection of the whole Christian doctrine is evident from the fact that the perversion of any part of the Christian doctrine will in the natural course vitiate the whole body of doctrine.[193] For instance, the denial that Scripture is God's own infallible Word affects the whole body of the Christian doctrine. For if Scripture is not God's Word, it is no longer God and His Word that determines what is Christian doctrine, but the theologizing human Ego. Again, if the metaphysical deity of Christ is denied, the *satisfactio vicaria* falls (Rom. 5:10; 8:32; 1 John 1:7), and if the *satisfactio vicaria* is denied, there can be no forgiveness of sins by faith without the deeds of the Law; no means of grace, means which *ex parte Dei* convey the forgiveness of sins and *ex parte hominis* require nothing but faith; no Christian Church, for the Christian Church is the communion of believers; no salvation, for salvation is obtained by faith in Christ.[194] Luther: "In philosophy a small error in the beginning is a very serious error in the end. So also in theology a slight error

---

[191] See chapter 10, "Theology as Doctrine."

[192] Cf. the chapters "Justification the Central Doctrine of the Christian Religion," in Vol. II; "The Postulates of Justification by Faith Without Works," in Vol. II; "The Relation of Justification to Sanctification," in Vol. III.

[193] That is also stated in Gal. 5:9: "A little leaven leaveneth the whole lump." Meyer: This is said "in regard to doctrine." Luther stresses that point, St. L. IX:642 ff.

[194] That is fully presented in the chapter "Objective and Subjective Reconciliation," in Vol. II.

will destroy the whole doctrine. . . . For the doctrine is like a mathematical point; it cannot be divided, that is, it cannot brook either subtraction or addition. . . . Hence the doctrine must be one continuous and round golden ring, in which there is no break. If even the least break occurs, the ring is no longer perfect." (St. L. IX:644 f.) Luther thus declares, most emphatically, that the Christian doctrine is a unit, all its parts closely interconnected, and in this sense, a "system."

Another fact which shows that the Christian doctrines are a unit, with the doctrine of justification by faith the unifying factor, is this, that unless a man believes the article of justification, he actually does not believe any of the other articles of the Christian faith. He may accept the articles, for instance, of the Trinity and of the Person of Christ, with a *fides humana*, but he cannot accept them with the *fides divina*, which the Holy Ghost produces, unless he believes in justification by faith, for only through faith in justification does the Holy Spirit enter the heart (Gal. 3:1-3). Only he who believes through the operation of the Holy Ghost that God has forgiven his sins for the sake of Christ's *satisfactio vicaria* will also believe, through the operation of the Holy Ghost, that there is none other God but one, that God is triune, that Christ is God and Man, that there is a resurrection of the dead and an eternal life, etc. Most assuredly, the Christian doctrine, in which everything hinges on the article of justification, is "one continuous and round golden ring," a perfect "system."

However, we prefer not to call the Christian doctrine a "system," because modern theology commonly uses this term in a sense in which theology definitely is not a system.

If by "system" is meant the logical arrangement of certain laws which have been derived and deduced from one fundamental principle by pure thought, in disregard of the actual facts (speculative system), then theology certainly is not a system. Systems of that kind are in place only where one is not dealing with things as they actually exist but only with ideal things, as is the case in "pure" mathematics, as distinguished from "applied" mathematics. They are not in place in the field of natural science and history, much less in theology. To apply the methods of the speculative systematizer to science and history is not only unscientific, but also downright nonsensical, because it proceeds on the assumption that facts are obedient to human thinking. Philosophical idealism has been justly called a derangement of the human mind, in which man labors under the obsession that his thoughts (ideas) are the rule and measure of things. Edm. Hoppe remarks in *Der Alte Glaube:* "Nature" [and he might have added history] "is not so obliging as to follow the diagram of the textbook." [195] Much less may the speculative systematizer intrude into the field of theology, because the Christian doctrine is fixed by Scripture. It is a finished product, which no human thinking may or can change in the least. Here every addition and every subtraction is absolutely and expressly forbidden (Joshua 23:6; Matt. 5:17-19; John 10:35; 8:31; Gal. 1:6-9). It is not the business of the theologian to deduce, through a process of thought, the Christian doctrine from some one fundamental principle or from some one fact, e. g., from the fact of regeneration, nor to construct it from the so-called "whole of Scripture," which is a logical monstrosity. His work is limited to drawing the Christian doctrine in all its parts directly from those Scripture statements that treat the respective doctrine (*sedes doctrinae*). When we arrange all the Scriptural statements concerning the various doctrines under the proper heads, we have that well-ordered system of Christian doctrine which we need in this life; and God will not have us ask for something better.

It is, of course, not our business to construct a perfectly logical system and harmonize the various doctrines to suit human reason. We take the doctrines as Scriptures present them. Under this method, gaps (*lacunae*) remain in this life for our human understanding. Take, for example, the Scripture doctrines of salvation *sola Dei gratia* and damnation *sola hominum culpa,* a matter we have already discussed. Both doctrines are clearly revealed in Scripture. But whoever attempts to harmonize these two doctrines in the interest of a logical system will adulterate either the one or the other and will become either a Calvinist or a synergist. The attempts to remove the contradiction which reason finds in the Scripture statements on the Trinity have led to monarchianism on the one hand and to tritheism on the other. Most modern theologians have tried to unify "rationally" what Scripture says concerning the person of Christ (*verus Deus* and *verus homo*). As a result they have rejected the "two-nature doctrine" and occupy a position *extra ecclesiam.* Whoever seeks to "unify" the theological knowledge over and beyond the revelation of Scripture forfeits *eo ipso* the knowledge which deserves the designation "theological." In order to forestall any attempts on our part to supply these "gaps," Paul reminds the theologians of all times that our knowledge of divine

---

[195] Quoted in *Lehre und Wehre,* 1907, p. 316.

matters in this life is a fragmentary one: "We know in part, and we prophesy in part" (1 Cor. 13:9).

Because of the importance of this subject, we shall expand some of the points already touched upon.

1. There is only one book in the world which possesses the quality of perfect unity, and that is the Bible. Though its writers were men of widely different culture and a period of about 1,500 years separated the last from the first writer, the Bible owes its perfect and inerrant unity to the fact that it was written by the inspiration of God. For that we have the authoritative declarations of Christ and His Apostles relative to both the New and the Old Testament in all their parts (John 10:35; 2 Tim. 3:16; 1 Pet. 1:10-11; 2 Pet. 1:21; John 17:14, 17; 8:31-32).

2. Since modern theology denies that Scripture is a "harmonious whole," it calls upon the "pious consciousness," the "religious experience," the "regenerate Ego" of the human subject, to construct this "harmonious whole" of theology. It is confident that this "pious self-consciousness" can do that and has done it. But a closer examination of their pronouncements reveals that they are not so sure after all that the thing has been accomplished. They admit, first, that the pious Ego or the religious experience, which was to take the place of the allegedly unreliable Scripture, is, after all, also somewhat unreliable; they realize that where the human factor enters, one must always reckon with the possibility of self-delusion. They admit, furthermore, that the Ego method has produced uncounted divergencies and that this cornucopia of divergencies will certainly continue to pour out its wealth. Would you call this heterogeneous conglomeration a "harmonious whole"? What is more, they concede both that Holy Scripture should be regarded as an "authentic record" of God's revelation in history and that the writers of the holy books were at any rate "nearer" to God's revelation than we, who have appeared upon the scene so much later, after so many centuries. These admissions certainly suggest that for the purpose of obtaining a "unified whole" it might well be more sensible and safer to abide by Scripture than to take recourse to the pious self-consciousness of the theologizing subject, which is subject to self-delusions and actually has given birth to uncounted divergencies.

3. If we would escape the deceptions which are involved in the attempts to construct a human system of theology, we must ever bear in mind that in theology we deal with given and unalterable facts,

which human reasoning and the alleged needs of the "system" cannot change in the least. There is, as has been pointed out, an analogy here between natural history and theology. Natural history studies the observable data in the realm of nature; its business is to observe the facts. All human knowledge of natural phenomena extends only so far as man's observation and experience of the given facts extends. The true scientist does not determine the nature and characteristics of plants and animals according to a preconceived and hypothetical system. In other words: the naturalist does not make or construct his system, but he finds it and adopts it as it has actually impressed itself on the plants or animals to be classified. Where the conjecture, theory, and speculation of the naturalist begins, there the science of natural history ends. Recall Hoppe's remark: "Nature is not so obliging as to follow the theory of the textbook."

This matter has been aptly illustrated by contrasting railroad systems and mountain systems. A railroad system is conceived in the mind of the builders before it exists; its construction follows the blueprint drawn up by the engineers. The mountain system, on the other hand, does not follow our blueprints. We can only report our findings regarding its characteristics, the relation of the different mountain ranges to each other, etc., as we find them. The theologian is dealing with a fixed and unchangeable fact, the Word of God which Christ gave His Church through His Apostles and Prophets. God's Word is a constant, as the laws of nature are constants. As little as we can change those laws, but accept them as they are, so little can we alter the Word of Christ; the Church and its teachers must receive it as it is. It is the business of the scientist to "observe the data." And the "datum" which the theologian "observes" is the Word of Christ. There are no other "data." It is God's ordinance that we continue in the Word of Christ, teach solely out of the mouth of the Lord, and not out of our Ego or the Ego of others (John 8:31-32; Jer. 23:16). The teaching that comes from any other source than the mouth of God is chaff among the wheat, a delusion and deception, and cannot be tolerated in God's house, in the Christian Church. It is certain, then, that in theology there is no room whatever for human speculation or — and this amounts to the same thing — for the systematizing of theology in the interest of a rational comprehension of the truths of Christianity. Let us not attempt to use our own thoughts to fill the gaps which the revealed Word of God presents to our limited understanding. From 1 Cor. 13:9 we learn that the fragmentary knowledge of divine things is the normal state of the Christian in this life.

One more remark on this point. The modern theologians are inconsistent when they claim that the theologian can construct a unified system on the basis of his subjective experience. Before the scientist can construct a unified system, the scientist must know his subject thoroughly and be fully acquainted with all the facts. All theologians are agreed that the subject of theology is God, who, as even natural reason testifies, is infinite and incomprehensible. From their own Ego standpoint the moderns should see that the attempt to construct a unified system of the divine truth is a titanic undertaking, one that is doomed to failure, and therefore they should abandon it.

4. In his examination of the systematizing method of Hofmann, Kliefoth has clearly shown when the term *theology* can be called a system and when not.[196] Kliefoth writes: "Starting with the fact of his personal faith, in the simplest form of its self-expression, Hofmann would deduce from it, with absolute necessity, the whole of the Christian doctrine; not only the doctrine of the Church, but also Holy Scripture must be totally disregarded. In other words, this fact (personal faith), as it expresses itself, must unfold itself into the entire body of the Christian doctrine, and this with absolute necessity, without adding anything from any other source. Thus I have understood von Hofmann's method, and I have shown from his own statements that I have understood him correctly. Now, there are only two modes of systematic treatment. The one aims merely to arrange the facts logically, in agreement with their nature. It deals with empirical [existing, actual] material. It thus has these two characteristics: First, it always works vis-à-vis its empirical material; its sole province is to observe this empirical material and put it into the proper order. Secondly, an orderly arrangement of the empirical material will produce a homogeneous whole, that is, a system only if this material itself is a whole. . . . The speculative philosophers of all times employ a radically different mode. They start with some fundamental principle and, rejecting all empiricism, would have this fundamental thought unfold into an entire system of propositions, hoping that this process of development, working by absolute necessity, will make the system and its component propositions so correct and certain that it not only agrees with all that we learn through empiricism, but also provides the right key to the empirical knowledge. . . . We see at once

---

196 In the *Kirchl. Zeitschrift*, published by Kliefoth and Meier, Vol. VI reprinted in book form, with the title: "*Der Schriftbeweis des D. von Hofmann,*" Schwerin, 1859, 174 ff.

that the speculative mode of building a system, which on principle ignores empiricism, is something entirely different from the first mode, which simply arranges the knowledge gained by observation in conformity with its subject matter. There is no doubt in my mind that the speculative method cannot be applied, either wholly or in part, to the doctrine of salvation, for God has revealed His salvation historically, by Word and work; it is therefore His will that we obtain the knowledge of it in the empirical way. And it is just as certain and self-evident that only the first, the empirical method of systematic treatment, can be applied to the doctrine of salvation; indeed, more than any other branch of knowledge the doctrine of salvation calls for the empirical method; because the words and works of God for our salvation certainly are in themselves a harmonious whole. That is the reason why all Christian dogmaticians of all times have employed this method. And together with these dogmaticians I insist upon the observance of all the laws of this method, viz., in forming a Christian system of theology the theologian is bound, absolutely, by God's revelation. . . . Von Hofmann, as his own statements show, has no use for the empirical mode of systematic treatment; it is not sufficiently scientific. He recommends the speculative mode. He really attempts to develop the whole of the Christian doctrine from some certain fundamental thought, he really believes that from it all the rest follows with absolute necessity, he actually demands that Scripture and the doctrine of the Church be disregarded in this process and assures us that the results produced by his method will agree with the teaching of Scripture and the Church. . . . Hofmann claims that his systematic method is essentially the same as the scientific method which Augustine employed. However, there is not a word in Augustine's theology about 'this deducing and self-unfolding with absolute necessity' and this 'disregarding Scripture,' not one word. Nor can Hofmann's systematic mode be regarded as an intensification of the method of the earlier dogmaticians. There is a difference in kind between these two methods. The earlier dogmaticians were empirics; Hofmann speculates."

5. The modern systematizers claim Luther as a protagonist of their method. They claim that the Reformer of the Church "genetically developed" the entire body of the Christian doctrine from the article of justification. Thus, for instance, Luthardt: "If dogmatics is to be the systematic presentation of the Christian faith, it must genetically develop the entire body of the Christian doctrine from one fundamental unit. It must not merely deduce it from some first principle, but must

unfold the truths of Christianity as summarized in this first principle. This genetic principle is for Luther the article of justification by faith: 'In it,' Luther says, 'David holds before our eyes the sum of the whole Christian doctrine; it is the dear bright sun which illumines the Christian congregation. If this article is grasped and retained in sure and firm faith, the others, too, will come and gradually follow, as the article of the Trinity, etc.' 'If this doctrine stands, the Church stands, etc.' On Gal. 3:13: 'We must therefore diligently learn the article of justification, as I often admonish you. For all the other articles of our faith are comprehended in it, and if it remains sound, then all the rest are sound.' [St. L. IX:376.] But the later dogmaticians did not follow through with this thought; they designated the Scriptures (in opposition to the Roman fundamental article of the infallibility of the Pope; cf. Gerhard, *Conf. Cathol.*, I, 2, 1, p. 71) as *unicum principium cognoscendi,* from which the doctrines were not only proved, but also developed." [197] It is a fiction that Luther and the "later dogmaticians" are at variance. In the first place, what Luther says about the central position of the doctrine of justification, viz., that this article contains the sum of the whole Christian doctrine, that it illuminates all other doctrines and secures their integrity, etc., is exactly what the Lutheran dogmaticians say when, e. g., they relate all other articles to the doctrine of justification and describe them as *articuli antecedentes* and *consequentes.*[198] And in the second place, Luther proclaims, if anything more forcefully, the very teaching which according to Luthardt distinguishes the dogmaticians from Luther, viz., that for them Scripture was *unicum principium cognoscendi,* not only the norm of doctrine, but also the sole source of doctrine. Luther had no patience with those who by-passed Scripture and "constructed" doctrines, nor did he "construct" the articles of faith from the central article of justification, outside Scripture. Scripture is the only source of the Christian doctrine, says Luther. He says it not only in those numerous statements in which he rejects every thought that is not taken from Scripture (*"schriftlos"*) and advises every theologian to submerge as quickly as possible all thoughts that arise in his mind "without Scripture," but also in those statements in which he compares the Christian doctrine to a "golden chain" and an "unbroken ring." The basic presupposition for Luther in this description of the Christian doctrine is that every link in this "golden chain," every article of the Christian doctrine, is

---

197 *Kompendium,* 11th ed., p. 30.

198 Quenstedt, *Systema,* I, 352 *sqq.,* theses 6–8.

taken directly from the Word of Scripture. For Luther adds that whoever denies any one of the articles of the Christian faith thereby denies God in His Word and makes Him a liar. Luther writes: "It is certain that whoever does not rightly believe one article or refuses to accept it (after he has been admonished and instructed), certainly believes none sincerely and in true faith. And whoever is so presumptuous as to dare to contradict God or call Him a liar in one word [of Scripture], and does this willfully, persisting in it, though he has been admonished and instructed once or twice, he is ready (and he does it, too) to deny God and accuse Him of lying in all His words. There are no two ways about it: either all and everything is believed, truly and fully, or nothing is believed. The Holy Ghost [who wrote all of Scripture, St. L. III:1890] cannot be separated or divided, so that we would be free to teach and believe one article as true and another as false. This does not apply to the weak, who are ready to receive instruction and do not offer stubborn opposition." (St. L. XX:1781.) Luther was fully acquainted with the construction method of Hofmann, according to which, as we have seen, the theologian, totally disregarding Scripture, first constructs the doctrine from his own thoughts and then looks for this Ego product in Scripture and revises it accordingly. For that was the method which the sacramentarian "enthusiasts" asked Luther to employ. The doctrine of the Lord's Supper must not be drawn from the words of Scripture pertaining to the Lord's Supper, but from "faith," and the Scripture passages must be "interpreted" accordingly. What Luther thought of this construction method is expressed in these sharp words: "It is the wantonness of the devil himself, who makes sport of us in this great matter through these 'enthusiasts'; he is very willing to submit to Scripture; however, only in such a way that for the time Scripture be laid aside." Luther demands that the "enthusiasts" do not construct the doctrine of the Lord's Supper from "faith," but show that it is set down in the Scripture passages that deal with the Lord's Supper. "It comes to this, that we have the clear, simple Scripture on our side, which reads: 'Take, eat; this is My body.'" Let Zwingli and Oecolampad "adduce Scripture that reads thus: 'This signifies My body,' or: 'This is the sign of My body.'" (St. L. XX:780, 782.) Luther's powerful sermon on "The Christians' Armor and Weapons" (St. L. IX:810 ff.) is a warning against all doctrinal "construction"; it warns against a "faith" that does not rest, in all its parts, on the express words of Scripture. Its leading thought is: "We have shown that all the articles of our faith are well grounded in Scripture. Cling to that, and permit no one to distort it for you with glosses and to explain and harmonize it according to reason." Answering the objection that the Christian doctrine, if based on the words of Scripture, would not constitute a harmonious whole but would contain contradictions, Luther answers: "Scripture will not contradict itself or any single article of faith, even though in your head it is contradictory and does not harmonize." In short, according to Luther the Christian doctrine certainly constitutes a "unity," not, indeed, a unity "in the head" of the dogmatizing human subject according to the requirements of the construction method, but a unity which results from the fact that the Christian doctrine, in all its parts, is taken directly from Scripture, which is the Word of God and is therefore not self-contradictory, but completely integrated. "The good man Oecolampadius was led astray by his notion that the Scripture passages which contradicted one another [in his head] must be harmonized and one passage be so interpreted that it agrees with the other. . . . If they would only first consider the matter and determine to speak nothing but God's Word, as St. Peter demands, and be done with their speaking and determining, they would not cause so much disaster." (St. L. XX:798.)

6. It should be noted, finally, that the systematization which would "eliminate all contradictions and gaps," and produce an unbroken "logical whole," has been severely criticized also in our day. It has been said that this speculative systematizing, with which Schleiermacher, "the Reformer of the 19th-century Church," has inoculated the theology of the 19th century, is on closer examination found to be simply a sleight-of-hand feat. In their attempt to make the Christian faith acceptable to an unbelieving generation the Schleiermacher-Hofmann-Frank systematizers actually cancel or at least modify the incomprehensible, which after all is inseparable from the Christian religion. Someone has compared this widely admired scheme to the bed of Procrustes.

There are modern theologians, too, who object to this elimination of what is incomprehensible in the Christian religion. They would retain it. But they go about it in the wrong way. They say: it must be accepted as a fact that everything that "faith" declares in this eon with regard to the Christian doctrine must take the form of the "irrational" or the "paradox." That sounds good and seems to agree with 1 Cor. 13:9: "We know in part [in this life], and we prophesy in part." But as long as the representatives of the theology of the "irrational" refuse to accept Holy Scripture as God's Word and as the only source and norm of theology, they do not make Scripture but the *I* of the theologian the judge of what is "irrational" or superrational in the Christian faith. We have here the same human systematizing under a new label. Subjectivism has not been discarded, but remains the ruling principle. The "Christian Ego" is still revolving about its own axis.

And this is true of every form of subjectivism. The *sola Scriptura* and the *sola gratia* are at stake, for subjectivism supplants the *sola gratia* with the self-determination, the self-assertion, the self-decision, the human conduct, the *facultas se applicandi ad gratiam,* etc.; and, further, subjectivism substitutes for the *sola Scriptura* the "pious" self-consciousness, the religious experience, the religious cognition, the "faith," etc., of the theologian. Not only is this a revolving about one's own axis, an unscientific and stupid procedure, but its result is uncertainty of salvation and uncertainty of the truth. On that account Luther fought so relentlessly for the *sola gratia* and the *sola Scriptura* both against Rome and the Reformed "enthusiasts." On that account the Formula of Concord warned so earnestly against making anything in man (*aliquid in homine*) the foundation of salvation. On that account we had to give battle here in the United States against the Ego theology of the Reformed sects and the Ego theology of synergism, which has always claimed, and still claims, the right of existence within the Lutheran Church. The Christian certitude of salvation and the Christian certitude of the truth can be attained only if, with Luther, we rise "above ourselves" or, in other words, find a footing outside the world. And this is accomplished only if, in agreement with the order established by Christ, we continue through faith in His Word, as we have it in the Word of His Apostles and Prophets, in Holy Scripture.

20

Theology and Method

This chapter on theological "methods" is not concerned with the question of the *principium cognoscendi* in theology. That matter has been fully treated in the preceding chapters. Every method, under whatever name, must be rejected which sets up another principle of cognition outside Scripture (*extra Scripturam*), be it the church dogma or the "faith consciousness" of the theologian. In this chapter we shall discuss the order in which the doctrines of Scripture should be presented for the purpose of instruction (*docendi causa*). We might have given this chapter the heading "Theology and the External Arrangement of the Several Scripture Doctrines." But we retain the term *method* because it is customary to speak especially of the synthetic and the analytic method. In this connection we shall also discuss the importance or relative unimportance of thus grouping the doctrines within a *corpus doctrinae*.

Among the old Lutheran theologians some favor the synthetic, others the analytic method. Flacius holds that "theology is most fittingly presented *per synthesin*"; [199] Baier, on the other hand, asserts that "the parts of the revealed theology should be grouped *iuxta ordinem analyticum*." [200] In arranging the subject matter the synthetic method proceeds from cause to effect or by composing the whole from the given parts. The analytical method, however, proceeds from effect to cause or seeks to derive the whole from a particular part, e. g., from the purpose (*finis*).[201]

Applied to theology, the synthetic method treats first of God, the source of all things, including the salvation of man, then of the causes and means by which fallen man is led to salvation, and, finally, of the last things, concluding with eternal life. The analytical method begins with the last things, eternal life, next considers man, who is to be led to salvation, and finally presents the causes and means of salvation (*Patris gratiosa voluntas, Filii redemptio, Spiritus Sancti gratia applicatrix, media gratiae*, etc.). The later theologians preferred the analytical method. They held that since theology is a practical aptitude, the goal (*finis:* salvation) must be the first consideration; next, the subject who is to be brought to this goal (*subiectum operationis:* man); and, finally, the causes and means by which the *subiectum operationis* is brought to the goal.[202]

The synthetic method has been used, generally speaking, by the dogmaticians from Melanchthon to Gerhard, the chief representatives of this period being Melanchthon, Chemnitz, Hutter, Gerhard, Brochmand.[203]

---

199 *Clavis Scripturae*, 5th ed., 1674, II, 54 ff. Flacius also appends a table showing where according to the various methods each doctrine will have its place.

200 *Compendium* I, 76.

201 Flacius, *op. cit.*, quoted in Baier-Walther, I, 29.

202 Quenstedt, I, 25.

203 Melanchthon, *Loci Communes Rerum Theologicarum seu Hypotyposes Theologiae*, 1521. Later editions (1535, 1543, and especially 1548) sacrificed the *sola gratia*, and Melanchthon thus became the father of synergism and Majorism in the Lutheran Church. That is conclusively shown by F. Bente in the *Concordia Triglotta*, "Hist. Introductions," p. 128 ff. – Chemnitz, *Loci Theologici*, published after the death of Chemnitz (1586) by Polycarp Leyser, 1591. These *Loci* are not only an amplification, but also a correction of the later

The dogmaticians of a later period used the analytical. Among them are Dannhauer, Friedrich Koenig, Calov, Quenstedt, Baier, Hollaz.[204] But the advocates of the analytical method are not agreed in

---

editions of Melanchthon's *Loci*. Chemnitz' mastery of theology is evident in his *Examen Concilii Tridentini* and in his treatise *De Duabus Naturis in Christo*, 1571. – Leonhard Hutter, *Loci Communes Theologici, Sacris Literis diligenter eruti. . . .* This, too, is a sort of commentary on Melanchthon's *Loci*. It was published after his death (1616) by the Wittenberg faculty, 1619. Hutter calls Melanchthon "that great Phoenix of our Germany, a most learned man, a man of outstanding merit in the whole field of literature." At the same time he calls attention to the deplorable (*tristis*) defection of the later Melanchthon from the pure doctrine. He adds the remark: "By no means, however, do we doubt that toward the end of his life he, in sincere repentance, sought and obtained from Christ the remission of this sin." These *Loci*, a textbook for theological seminaries, are an expansion of the *Compendium Locorum Theologicorum*, a textbook for colleges (*Gymnasien*). – Gerhard, *Loci Theologici cum pro adstruenda veritate tum pro destruenda quorumvis contradicentium falsitate*, 1610—1622, 9 volumes, with a supplement in 1625. The Cotta edition (1762—1781) has 20 volumes, with two index volumes. The Ed. Preuss edition (Berlin, 1863–1865; Leipzig, 1875) has nine volumes, with an index volume. – Brochmand (Denmark) *Universae Theologiae Systema*, 1633; 6th ed., 1658, published in Ulm. Walch praises this work and rightly so (*Bibliotheca Theol.*, I, 57). His censure: "Though we can hardly deny that the discussion of cases of casuistry does not belong in dogmatic theology," is unfounded. Any full presentation of the Christian faith must also deal with questions of conscience.

[204] Dannhauer, *Hodosophia Christiana*, 1649, presents, in Scriptural imagery, the Christian doctrine in twelve Phaenomena: Man a pilgrim, Scripture the light, the Church the candlestick, God the goal, etc. The best edition is that of 1713. – Koenig, *Theologia Positiva Acroamatica*, 1664. A brief compend for theological lectures, which Quenstedt made the basis of his *Systema*. – Calov, *Systema Locorum Theologicorum*, 1655–1677, 12 vols. The first volumes show careful work, the last volumes less. Calov is the most discerning theologian of the 17th century, a real Scripture theologian, and his *Biblia Illustrata* is still a classic exegetical work. Tholuck's judgment of Calov is unjust, spiteful, and even abusive (R. E., 1st ed., II, 506); J. Kunze's judgment is much fairer (R. E., 3d ed., p. 653 f.). – Quenstedt, *Theologia Didactico-polemica sive Systema Theologiae*, 1685, 1696, 1702, 1715. Tholuck calls him "the bookkeeper and secretary" of the orthodox theology (R. E., 1st ed., XII, 421). This verdict does not agree with the facts, for Quenstedt was independent in his judgment. To be able to pass a proper judgment on Quenstedt, one must have read him and compared him with other dogmaticians. Also Walch's opinion (*Bibliotheca Theol.*, I, 58) that Quenstedt classified "the most deserving doctors of our Church" with the opponents "because of their slight dissent" is unjust. The synergism of the Helmstedt theologians and of Musaeus is not a "slight dissent." Walch is an indifferentist and, besides, has written too much. Even Tholuck, though he cannot entirely suppress malicious remarks, describes Quenstedt as an unassuming, pious character, without a "sharp temper" (R. E., 1st ed., XII, 422). Walch, too, acknowledges that Quenstedt spent great care on the Scripture proof. (*op. cit.*) – Baier, *Compendium Theologiae Positivae;* published 1686, saw many editions. Baier is infected with the synergistic bias of his father-in-law Musaeus. The edition of Walther, St. Louis, 1879, is not a mere reprint of Baier's compend, but by the addition of quotations has been expanded to three volumes.

the sequence of the doctrines. Baier, e. g., discusses the last things: death, resurrection, the Judgment, and the destruction of the world immediately in connection with salvation, the *finis theologiae ex parte hominis,* before speaking of the doctrine of sin and of redemption by Christ. Quenstedt, however, places the doctrines mentioned at the end of his dogmatics.

The important matter is not which method is employed in grouping the doctrines. The all-important point is that the theologian observe the principle of divine revelation and that he take all doctrines solely from Scripture, lest, a la Procrustes, he trim them to suit his opinion or the "faith" of the theologian.[205] The theologian must reject every method, by whatsoever name it may be known, which disregards the Word of Scripture and invents something. No questing method has a place in theology, either as to the content or as to the correlation of the doctrines. Only that method has a place in theology which as a matter of principle limits itself to arranging the matter given in the revelation of Scripture, as is done in the so-called local method, according to which all Scripture revelation on a certain doctrine is collocated at one place, *locus* (hence the several doctrines are fittingly called *loci*). And this is the underlying principle of the synthetic method.

The numerous quotations not only of Luther and our old theologians, but also of the theologians of the 19th century offer source material which enables students to judge fairly both the old and the modern theology. Prof. Theo. Buenger's index of subjects and persons to this Walther edition shows great diligence and a thorough understanding. — Hollaz, *Examen Theologicum Acroamaticum,* 1707. "The last genuinely Lutheran dogmatician." Hollaz did not simply copy, but in his own manner presents what has been taught in the Lutheran Church by its representatives from Luther down to his day. Following the analytical method, he treats the doctrine of eternal salvation in the first part and closes the fourth part with the doctrine of the Church, of the ministry, of civil government, and of the family. Krakewitz, in the preface of the *Editio tertia,* justly praises Hollaz for bringing a carefully chosen Scripture proof. It is unhistorical to charge Hollaz with peculiarities of which he was not guilty, e. g., the statement concerning the *theologia irregenitorum.* (Wagenmann, R. E., 2d ed., VI, 266 f.) That only a regenerate person can be called a theologian in the proper sense of the term has been taught abundantly by Luther and by the "orthodox" teachers, as Hollaz himself establishes (Proleg. I, qu. 18-21). Hase's remark (*Hutterus Red.,* 10th ed., p. 44) that Hollaz recognizes the "religious interest" only "by bringing it in as an afterthought in pious ejaculations" is due in part to Hase's unchristian viewpoint, in part to his bad habit of coining witty catchwords — a habit which caused much harm among the theological students of the 19th century. Most moderns, too, have an altogether different opinion of Hollaz. Cf. Wagenmann, *loc. cit.*

[205] Rudelbach, *Zeitschrift fuer luth. Theologie und Kirche,* 1857, p. 382; quoted in Baier-Walther, I, 77.

Modern theologians charge that those dogmaticians who use the local method atomize the dogmatical material and do not properly set forth the inner unity of the system, while the later theologians, who used the analytical method, seem to be more scientific.[206] It must be granted that the analytical method in its outward form meets the demands of modern theology better; for just this, that the Christian doctrine is not taken from Holy Scripture, but is developed from the Ego of the theologian, constitutes the scientific character of this theology. Thus the analytical method applied to theology would seem to deduce the Christian doctrines through logical deductions from the purpose, that is, to develop them, instead of taking them from Scripture. Walther used to say in his lectures: "The analytical method attempts to find the truth. But in theology we cannot deduce the means from the purpose." However, in vindication of the later theologians it must be said that they follow the analytical method merely for the external arrangement of the doctrine, while in presenting the individual doctrines they maintain the Scripture principle. Baier (I, 79) expressly emphasizes this: "It is the very nature of things that the knowledge of the purpose, obtained from the divine revelation, is naturally prior to the knowledge of the means, likewise obtained from the divine revelation." For that reason Kirn is not ready to differentiate between the "Old Protestant" theologians; they all maintain the Scripture principle. He says: "Though some of the old Protestant dogmaticians prefer the synthetic, others the analytic method, nevertheless all employ essentially the same method, which may be designated briefly as the method of the formal [?] authority of Scripture. It consists in this, that the individual Biblical statements which are understood to be a revelation of doctrine . . . directly determine content and form of the dogmatic statement. This method finds its support in the theory [?] of the verbal inspiration of Scripture." [207]

Kirn is right in saying that the uniform method of the old Protestant dogmatics has its support in the verbal inspiration of Scripture. The old dogmaticians would not have insisted so strongly on the *sola Scriptura* — also against dissenters in their own midst, e. g., against Calixt's *Consensus quinquesaecularis* — if they had not been convinced

---

206 Dorner says: "Geo. Calixt established the analytical method, which soon found favor also with his opponents, such as Calov, Dannhauer, and Huelsemann. It [the analytical method] seeks to deduce from some principal truth (the highest good of mortal man) the several dogmatic statements as members and instrumentalities of the prime purpose. This prime purpose is the blessedness of man in the enjoyment of God." *Geschichte der protestantischen Theologie*, p. 531.

207 *Grundriss der ev. Dogmatik*, 3d ed., p. 4.

that Holy Scripture is God's inspired Word. But Verbal Inspiration is not, as Kirn holds, a "theory," that is, the private opinion of the old Protestant dogmaticians, but the determinative opinion of Christ and His Apostles. It is therefore imperative for the sake of clarity in our theological instruction to divide the Protestant theologians of our day into two classes, according to their declared attitude towards Holy Scripture. The question is not whether they employ the synthetic or the analytic method, nor whether, within these methods, they use also the definition method or the causal method or both. The question is whether they still regard Holy Scripture as the Word of God and let Scripture alone be the source and norm of Christian doctrine, or whether they have already become so liberal that they no longer regard Scripture as the Word of God and the only source and norm of theology and have resolved to offer the Christian Church an Ego product. With the first class a discussion and understanding is possible even where error exists. With the latter class an understanding is impossible, because there is no common ground. *Contra principium negantem disputari non potest* — with him who denies the principle one cannot argue. At the same time we shall charitably give credit to certain modern theologians who have drifted away from the Scripture principle for what they inconsistently still retain as Christian doctrine. However, it is our duty emphatically to remind students of theology that all theologians who have relinquished the Scripture principle belong, according to Scripture, in one class.[208]

In order to wean the Christian Church from the Scripture method to the Ego method, modern theology raises the objection that in presenting the Christian doctrine from Scripture the theologian would not know where to begin.[209] It would, indeed, be an embarrassing situation if those who abide by the Scripture principle did not know at all where to begin in writing a dogmatics, for if it had no beginning,

---

208 We would unnecessarily burden the study of theology and cause confusion if we required our students to consider it a matter of theological importance whether a certain theologian who on principle has declared himself independent of God's Word and intends to furnish an Ego product is influenced more toward the left by Ritschl or toward the right by Frank.

209 As we have shown, Frank has raised this argument. Ihmels, too, argues similarly, when he says: "It [dogmatics] dare not be content with simply collocating the Biblical doctrinal statements. It ought to be possible to make clear to anyone without further ado, no matter how much he may be inclined to such a conception, that this question would already perplex him, at which point he ought to begin with the presentation of the Scripture statements and how he ought to connect them." *Aus der Kirche, ihrem Lehren und Leben*, in the chapter "Aufgabe und Bedeutung der Dogmatik," p. 121.

it would have neither a middle nor an end. In short, all who cling to the Scripture principle in dogmatics would actually be without dogmatics and, no doubt, rightly so. In answer we point, first, to the fact that Luther and the old dogmaticians, though they adhered stubbornly to the Scripture principle, were not at all "perplexed" about the beginning. It is well known that Luther at the end of his "Confession Regarding Christ's Supper" recites his faith "before God and all the world," "point by point." (St. L. XX: 1094 ff.) He begins with the "sublime article of the divine Majesty, that Father, Son, and Holy Ghost, three distinct Persons, are the one single, natural, true God." Then follow the doctrines of the Person of Christ, of the office of Christ, of sin, of justification (by faith in Christ in contrast to all work righteousness), of the means of grace, of the Church. He closes with the resurrection of the dead. The joyous and confident manner in which Luther confesses his faith "point by point" dispels the thought that Luther was puzzled as to a starting point. In his Catechisms Luther uses still another point of departure, viz., the Ten Commandments.

The old dogmaticians do indeed employ opposite poles as points of departure, because some use the synthetic method, others the analytic. As Flacius points out, the former begins where the latter ends; and while he prefers the synthetic method, he finds value also in the analytic method, for in both the *finis theologiae,* eternal life, is presented as man's greatest concern (Matt. 19:16).[210] Thus we, too, would not dare to deny the right of dogmatic existence to the one or the other because he employs a different grouping of the several doctrines. For both groups, as Kirn admits, "follow an essentially uniform method," namely, they take the several doctrines from Scripture. That being the case, it matters not whether we start at the beginning, at the end, or in the middle. If we begin with Scripture and abide by Scripture, we shall soon arrive at the heart of the Christian doctrine, namely, the doctrine of the remission of sin by faith in the incarnate Son of God, who is the Propitiation for our sin and that of the whole world. The reason for this lies in the compact inner unity inherent in the theology taken from Scripture. We could begin with eternity, with the eternal Gospel of Christ, which was kept secret since the world began but now is made manifest and by the Scriptures of the Prophets, according to the commandment of the everlasting God, is made known to all nations for the obedience of faith (Rom. 16:25-26).

---

[210] *Clavis* II, 58.

St. John thus begins both his Gospel and his First Epistle with the eternal Son of God made manifest in time, and from here he soon arrives at the center, namely, the remission of sins by faith in the blood and death of the Son of God. We could also begin with that eternity which follows for us human beings in time, namely, with the bliss of those "which came out of great tribulation and have washed their robes and have made them white in the blood of the Lamb" (Rev. 7:14-17; Matt. 25:34). Here, too, we would have no difficulty in connecting what Scripture says of man and his wretchedness in sin, as also of the redemption which is in Christ Jesus, with the appropriation of the finished redemption. We might also begin in the middle, e. g., with the angel's message: "Fear not; for, behold, I bring you good tidings of great joy, which shall be to all people. For unto you is born this day in the city of David a Savior, which is Christ the Lord" (Luke 2:10-11). Going from here back to the beginning and forward to the end, we could incorporate what Scripture teaches of man's mortal guilt and of God's saving grace. In short, it is immaterial where one begins in presenting the Christian doctrine, provided he begins, continues, and ends with Scripture.

Only one point of departure is ruinous and forbidden within the Christian Church, and that is "the religious experience," "the pious self-consciousness of the theologizing subject." The theologian who rejects Holy Scripture as God's infallible Word and draws and regulates his teaching not from Holy Scripture but from his own Ego, acts contrary to the instruction of Christ to continue in His Word and the Apostle's denial of the *licentia docendi* to every teacher not consenting to the wholesome words of our Lord Jesus Christ. Such a one is suffering from delusion and ignorance. Also Ihmels represents this unscriptural starting point as the only feasible one. He writes: "Even if Scripture intended to give a uniform body of doctrine,[211] and if it therefore would be possible for the dogmatician simply to copy this body of doctrine, still he could not on that account be content with this, since dogmatics as a matter of principle aims at presenting the knowledge of faith." Certainly, dogmatics aims as a matter of principle at presenting the knowledge of faith, but the knowledge of that faith which continues in the Word of Christ, in the Word of the Apostles and Prophets, in the Word of Scripture, of that faith which always

---

211 "Intended?" Scripture does intend to be "uniformly" God's Word — θεόπνευστος, 2 Tim. 3:16: τά λόγια τοῦ θεοῦ, Rom. 3:2; οὐ δύναται λυθῆναι, John 10:35, the Old and the New Testament are "uniformly" the Holy Spirit's Word, 1 Pet. 1:10-12.

speaks only vis-à-vis with Scripture. Faith without Scripture is a faith without foundation. It is not a faith that says, "Speak Lord, for Thy servant heareth," but it is unbelief, for it "believeth not the record that God gave of His Son" and thus "hath made God a liar" (1 John 5:10).

This may suffice on the external grouping of the Christian doctrines within the *corpus doctrinae*. In this connection, however, we ought to review the charges which modern theology raises against all champions of Scriptural theology.

The Christian Church of our day dare not forget that the modern theologians who draw their teaching from their own consciousness instead of from Scripture are deadly enemies, who aim to dislodge the Christian Church from its position on the Word and thus from the foundation of its faith. Modern theologians manifest their hostility toward the Scripture principle by casting aspersions upon the old Scripture theologians and their writings, as well as upon the modern representatives of the *sola Scriptura* principle, whom they stigmatize as "repristination theologians." This censure is directed also against the Missouri Synod and its sister synods. Naturally, these aspersions are in the form of definite charges. This, we feel, ought to be pointed out here specially, though the matter has been often discussed in other connections.

The charge is preferred against the theologians of the sixteenth and seventeenth centuries that they considered Holy Scriptures to be God's Word, or, as it is usually expressed, that they "identified" Scripture and God's Word. We read in Nitzsch-Stephan: "The fault . . . lies in this, that they distinguished imperfectly or not at all between the Bible and the Word of God." "The doctrine of inspiration was fully developed by the Protestant scholastics of the seventeenth and eighteenth centuries ever since the example set by Johann Gerhard as early as 1610 in his *Locus de Scriptura* and continued in 1625 in his *Exegesis Uberior Loci de Scriptura.* They thought they could oppose the Catholics, the Socinians, the Arminians, and other factions successfully only if the divine authority of Scripture were extended to the letter [to the words of Scripture]. The Bible was . . . a divine textbook of religion."[212] This led to the second accusation that because they derived their doctrine solely from Scripture, the old theologians exerted a baneful influence on the Christian Church. They are said to have fostered "intellectualism," a lifeless formal Christianity, whereas a vital Christianity can be attained only when the teacher

---

212 *Op. cit.*, pp. 245, 249.

draws from his "Christian experience" or his "pious consciousness." A further accusation is that there is practically no doctrinal disagreement among the old theologians, from Luther to Hollaz. In other words, the individual dogmaticians did not reproduce the Christian doctrine independently; they operated on the premise that in the content of the inherited doctrine "nothing could be changed and that progress could consist only in a more precise elaboration of the terminology of sacrosanct statutes." Even Quenstedt produced "hardly anything" new.[213] We can understand that this absence of disagreement seems strange to modern theology, for in its own midst it notes a "seemingly endless amount of differences," after it had agreed on a "uniform method" – the method not to take the Christian doctrine from the one Holy Scripture, but to procure it from the "religious experience" of the many theologizing individuals. Even the conservatives among the experience theologians regard agreement in the Christian doctrine as an abnormality. "Pure doctrine" is introduced with a "so-called." That is the reason why the "essential agreement" of the old theologians through two centuries appears uncanny to the modern theologians.

They seek therefore, and also find, an explanation for this fact. But their explanation is historically incorrect. For they claim that the old dogmaticians had universally become guilty of "dogmatical exegesis," had interpreted Scripture according to a "churchly system of doctrine," particularly according to the Formula of Concord. Not only Quenstedt is charged with a lack of a "healthy research in Scripture," but also Chemnitz is accused of "interpreting Melanchthon's *Loci* according to the canon of the Formula of Concord." The same accusation is raised by the great majority of modern theologians against the entire "old Protestant dogmatics." [214] We quote here what we have presented at length in another place:[215] "We cannot but term this talk current fiction that is being circulated with no effort at verification, viz., that the Lutheran dogmaticians were men who merely recorded dogmas according to the traditional dogmatics and the lead of the Confessions, and that they were little concerned about Scriptural evidences and the extraction of doctrines from Scripture. Whoever has taken the pains to study, even superficially, such works as

[213] Nitzsch-Stephan, p. 26 ff.

[214] Kirn, *Grundriss*, 3d ed., p. 4; Nitzsch-Stephan, p. 25 ff. Dorner, *Gesch. d. prot. Theologie*, p. 559; Gass, *Gesch. der prot. Dogmatik*, I, 338.

[215] *Zur Einigung der amerikanisch-lutherischen Kirche*, 2d ed., p. 61. [*Conversion and Election*, p. 90 f.]

those of Gerhard, Quenstedt, Calovius, had his opinion of these men changed completely, if he studied so much as a single *locus*. With Gerhard the presentation of the doctrine from Scripture is the beginning, the middle, and the end. The passages adduced in their defense by the heretics are considered by Gerhard so thoroughly according to their context and the *usus loquendi* of Scripture that, if anything, he overdid a good thing. Quenstedt, who has been called the great 'bookkeeper of Lutheran theology,' in his great dogmatic work offers in the notes to the ϑέσις and in the sections βεβαίωσις (corroboration) and ἐκδίκησις (refutation) principally exposition of Scripture. Calov's greatness as a Scripture theologian is evident not only in his *Biblia Illustrata,* but in all his major works. It was Calov, too, who over and over impressed it on the mind of his students of theology that knowledge of Hebrew and Greek was far more necessary than the study of the Fathers and the Scholastics. Thesis 4 of his *Theol. Antisyncretistica* reads: 'For the student of theology the knowledge of the Hebrew and the Greek language is far more necessary than the study of scholastic theology or of the Fathers or of philosophy.' Meusel's *Lexikon* very aptly remarks on the fashionable disparagement of the old theologians as exegetes: 'The Scripture proof occupies a prominent and extended space in the old Lutheran dogmatics. Especially the authors of the *Loci,* but also those of the later *Systemata* are fully in earnest in regarding Holy Scripture not merely as a touchstone for testing the doctrine derived elsewhere, but as its principle and source, and from it derive the truths of dogma, which they prove logically and defend against the objections of the opponents, so that the dogmatic writings of, e. g., Chemnitz and John Gerhard are a mine of most thorough exegetical investigation." (*Sub voce* "Schriftbeweis," VI, 93.) The home of the "dogmatical exegesis" is not to be found in the theology of the 16th and 17th centuries, as the accusation reads, but is found in the accuser, in the camp of modern theology. This theology emphatically refuses to permit the teaching of Scripture to be the source and norm of its faith. That would be, according to their own express declarations, an "intellectualistic" use of Scripture. This theology interprets and judges the Scriptures according to its own view, according to the pious self-consciousness of the theologizing subject. That is certainly "dogmatical exegesis" in the full sense of the word. And this "dogmatical exegesis" is the mother of the "seemingly endless amount" of doctrinal differences which are causing modern theology some embarrassment – in spite of the occasional expressions of joy over "the multitude of individualistic faiths." That there is no such doctrinal difference during the period from Luther to Hollaz is due to the fact, as Kirn pointed out, that "the old Protestant dogmaticians, though some prefer the synthetic method, others the analytic, all follow an essentially uniform method," namely, the method of taking the Christian doctrine out of Holy Scripture. This uniform method results in a uniform product, scil., unity of doctrine. God has given Holy Scripture such a form that the knowledge of the truth is not only possible, but that straying from the truth is impossible as long as we continue in the words of Scripture. – So much on the derogatory criticism leveled by modern theology against the persons and writings of the old Lutheran dogmaticians.

The same scathing criticism is leveled against those theologians and church bodies of our day that still accept Scripture as the Word of God and therefore insist upon taking the Christian doctrine solely from Scripture and having it judged solely by Scripture. This disapproval becomes all the more vehement because of the fear that the Church of today may again receive Scriptures as the Word of God and thus discredit the theology of the pious self-consciousness. On the one hand, modern theology, as has been stated repeatedly, speaks with great self-assurance. For example: "The dogmatic method is today comparatively uniform." "No one bases his dogmatics in the old Protestant manner on the *norma normans,* the Bible." "In our day the orthodox doctrine of inspiration has hardly any significance in dogmatics." The few theologians who still advocate it are "laggards," "their number is small, their labor unsuccessful, and their indignation at the comrades who are pressing forward on new paths impresses no one." On the other hand, we hear the fear expressed that what has been abolished and lies prostrate might awaken to new life, for while the few theologians who as "laggards" make no impression on their professional comrades, they are "not without danger for the Church." Horst Stephan first quieted the camp of modern theology with the assurance: "Today the doctrine of inspiration has been given up by the scientific theology," but he added immediately: "Only among the lay orthodoxy . . . it still has a strong hold." [216]

---

[216] *Glaubenslehre,* 1921, p. 52. There is the fear, therefore, of a reaction proceeding from the laymen. In a recent number of the *Neue Kirchliche Zeitschrift,* 1923, p. 110, a contributor is weighing the possibility that in our day "a retreat to an unevangelical authority-standpoint [he means a retreat to Scripture as God's Word] might take place in a similar manner as could be observed in the repristination theology of the first half of the 19th century." At the same time we see from these expressions of fear that modern theology has lost the Christian knowledge to such an extent as to regard the return to Scripture as

We need not be surprised, therefore, that particularly also those American Lutherans who cling to the Scripture principle and consequently are united in the Christian doctrine are regarded as an undesirable part of the Christian Church and, as champions of the "repristination theology," are relegated to the background. This criticism is aimed particularly at the Missouri Synod and its publications. Dr. Walther, who is rightly regarded as the leader among the fathers of the Missouri Synod, is stigmatized in Zoeckler's *Handbuch der theologischen Wissenschaften*[217] as a curiosity beside Kohlbruegge, Gaussen, and Kuyper because he taught the inspiration of Holy Scripture "in the old orthodox sense." Walther is classified with the "repristination theologians" of the nineteenth century. Others have called him the "citation theologian," and by that they meant to indicate – though not always – that he is not to be classified as a Scripture theologian. In the United States as well as in Germany and other countries Walther has been both severely censured and also praised, the latter, however, with reservations.[218] In the Preface to *Lehre und Wehre*, 1875, Walther discusses and refutes the charge that the old Protestant theologians from Luther to Hollaz lacked a scientific spirit in the apprehension of theological problems, were guilty of a mechanical use of Scripture by their direct appeal to the "It is written," advocated mere intellectualism, accepted the traditional doctrines without investigation, etc. All these accusations Walther proves false not only by adducing counterarguments, but by pointing out that the much-maligned theology has produced results, as is evident in the Christian activity in congregations, pastoral conferences, and synodical meetings of the Missouri Synod. Walther showed which science the Church must zealously cultivate and which science it must bar according to God's will. The science which the Church should foster and regard as a precious gift of God includes all secular knowledge which the Church needs as

---

the Word of God as a disaster that must be fought strenuously. For this fact the article in the *Neue Kirchl. Zeitschrift* just mentioned furnishes the proof. It is regarded as a striving for the objectionable repristination theology that, according to a report of Ebrard, the Lutheran students of theology at the university of Erlangen during the '30's of the previous century bought the Book of Concord already in their first year of study.

217 Second ed., III, 149.

218 See R. E., 2d ed., IX, 85; XVIII, 687 ff. If we are briefly to express our own opinion of Walther, we would call him the apologist of the Scripture theology of Luther and of the old dogmaticians, so far as they have proved themselves to be true representatives of the Scripture theology of Luther. Thereby Walther at the same time becomes the apologist of those theologians of our day who are designated "repristination theologians."

an external apparatus to carry out its commission in the world, the teaching and preaching of the Gospel. This includes whatever serves for the general training of the mind – what we usually call the "humanities," classical learning. In particular Walther stresses with Luther the study of history, the classical languages, and for fully equipped theologians the study of the original languages of Holy Scripture. He says: "The spirit of Carlstadt, the Anabaptists, and other 'enthusiasts,' who despise science as something worthless, yes, dangerous and carnal, and, instead, pride themselves on the impulses of the 'spirit,' has no place among us. We are not of the mind that the Church should flee into the desert and for its self-preservation isolate itself from the unbelieving world so that the enemies have their way with the educated unbelievers who can be reached by the Gospel only in a certain form and ultimately lead them to destruction, while the Church restricts its work exclusively to the uneducated people. No, we recognize it as our sacred duty to become all things unto all men, in order by all means to save some. We heartily agree with Melanchthon when on one occasion he wrote: 'An Iliad of evils is an unlettered theology' (*Corpus Ref.* XI, 278)." Walther points out how earnestly Luther urged the education in all "free arts" as valuable for all ranks and adds: "How could we call ourselves Lutherans, yes, even Christians, if we were despisers of science?" [219]

Walther also speaks at length on the question in what sense science is not to be granted the right of existence in the Church. He writes: "We will have nothing to do with a science which would play the lord and master over Scripture, which instead of serving to ascertain the meaning of the Scripture truths wants to sit in judgment on it and correct it according to science, which, instead of remaining in its sphere, wants to make the laws that happen to apply to its domain universally applicable, including the domain of Scripture. Such a μετάβασις εἰς ἄλλο γένος we regard as both idolatrous and unscientific. We agree fully with Melanchthon when he says: 'As it would be insanity to say that the Christian doctrine could be judged according to the rules of the cobbler's trade, so they are in error who invest philosophy with the ability to judge theology' (*Scholia in epist. ad Col.*, p. 68). Though science may consider the results of its research as absolutely certain truths, we do not regard science, but the Scriptures as infallible. If the results of scientific research contradict the clear Scriptures, we are *a priori* certain that they are nothing but

---

[219] *Op. cit.*, pp. 3–4.

positive error, even though we are not able to prove them erroneous except by an appeal to the Scriptures. When we must choose between science and Scripture, we say with Christ, our Lord: 'The Scripture cannot be broken' (John 10:35) and with the holy Apostle: 'We bring into captivity every thought to the obedience of Christ' (2 Cor. 10:5). We do not wait for science to establish a foundation for us. We have it already; and prior to all scientific investigation and scrutiny it stands as firm as our God, who has laid it. The findings of science can neither give us the faith nor rob us of it. We stand on a rock; we know that not even the gates of hell, much less human science, can prevail against it. Therefore we laugh at all enemies and their scientific battering rams and siege artillery with which in insane rage they attack this rock towering over the turbulent waters of this world, towering as high as heaven. For thus says the Lord: 'Whoever shall fall on this Stone shall be broken; but on whomsoever it shall fall, it will grind him to powder' (Matt. 21:44)." [220]

Walther also exposes the abuse which modern theology practices with the so-called regenerate Ego or with the illumined reason. He says: "Illumination does not provide reason with a light alongside of Scripture. Illumination rather consists in this, that through the working of the Holy Ghost the Word of the Prophets and Apostles has become its only light in matters of faith. . . . In so far as it tries to argue against the articles of faith from its own premises, it is not regenerate, since the regenerate reason argues from the premises of God's Word." [221] Walther also warns the Christian Church earnestly against the opinion that the methods of modern science can augment the content of theology. He enforces the warning thus: "We consider the Holy Scripture as so clear in regard to the objects of our faith that we cannot entertain the faintest hope that any article of faith until now unknown and hidden will be, or has even now been, disclosed to us through the great advances which modern science has made. We do not believe that the Church grows in knowledge through the gradual construction of dogmas. Rather we believe that the Church of the first century was already in possession of all truly Biblical doctrines. We do not regard the Apostolic Church as a Church in its infancy, growing gradually to manhood through the labor of scientifically trained theologians; on the contrary, we are firmly persuaded that the Church, in regard to the clarity and purity of its knowledge, resembles

---

220 *Op. cit.*, 34–36.

221 *Op. cit.*, p. 35.

the moon, that now waxes, now wanes, and at times even experiences sad eclipses. We disavow not only such scientific contributions as directly contradict the Biblical truth, but also such as are meant to augment our Biblical theology; for God does not only forbid men to contradict His Word, but just as strictly forbids them to add anything to it (Deut. 12:32)."[222]

Regarding the attempt to harmonize theology and science Walther has this to say: "We are certain that there cannot be or ever is a real contradiction between Christian theology and true science, science *in abstracto.* But we are equally certain that it is not nor can it be the task of a theologian to reconcile our Biblical theology and science *in concreto.* The charge is indeed valid that in our efforts to lead the present unbelieving generation back to faith we make no attempt to demonstrate to the world the harmony of faith with science. But we see no reproach in this charge; rather we glory in it, and we will not, by the grace of God, permit anyone ever to rob us of this glorying. For we are very certain that it is not possible to help the present apostate world with the lie that the divinely revealed truth is in perfect accord with the wisdom of this world; only the preaching of the divine foolishness, of the old unaltered Gospel, can help the world. Paul as well as the history of the Church of all ages and of every Christian testifies that the 'foolish Gospel' is the power of God unto salvation to all that believe, to the Jew first and also to the Greek (Rom. 1:16). A person who has been won for Christianity by showing him that Christianity can pass the sharpest probe of science is not yet won; his faith is no faith."[223]

To refute the charge that a return to the theology of Luther and the dogmaticians is "a slavish subjection to the doctrinal decision of the dogmaticians or of Luther or of the Symbols," Walther extends the following general invitation: "Come and see! Go into our church body from parish to parish, from church to church, and see whether you there find a so-called dead orthodoxy ruling and not rather a living knowledge derived from experience and matured by internal struggles. Visit our pastoral conferences and observe whether you find there that attitude which regards the public ministry merely as a means for a livelihood, or not rather an active theological life and the concern to know how a servant of Christ should comport himself in the house of God, which is the Church of the living God (1 Tim. 3:15). Take

[222] *Op. cit.*, pp. 37–40.
[223] *Op. cit.*, p. 41.

part in our synodical conventions, and note whether you there find a *iurare in verba magistri* and not rather that mind of Luther: 'Unless I am overcome and convinced with testimonies of Holy Scripture or with manifest, clear, and plain arguments and reasons, I can and will retract nothing.'"[224]

Because of the array of quotations from Lutheran dogmaticians in his book *The Voice of Our Church on the Question Concerning the Church and the Ministry*,[225] Walther was branded a "citation theologian." He refutes this charge as follows: "When we Lutherans in America again unfolded the good old banner of our Church and closed ranks around it, while roundabout us Zwinglianism, 'enthusiasm,' and rationalism were sailing under the Lutheran colors, the cry immediately went up: Another new sect! Some cried: You are on the way to Rome! Others: You are unionistic! Still others: You are independents! Others again: You are Pietists, Enthusiasts, Donatists, Calvinists! – And who can name all the sects that were said to have arisen and been reborn in us? In short, we were said to be anything except what we expressly declared ourselves to be: Confessors of the doctrine of the Reformation, Lutherans. What could we do under these circumstances if we did not want to bear the name of a sect? As long as men denied that we were true Lutherans, we were obliged to appeal constantly to our precious Confessions and the old faithful teachers of our Church as our witnesses. And we are of the opinion that we have done it in a manner that whoever was open to conviction was also compelled to see that we did not follow those faithful fathers of our Church blindly but from personal conviction, that we do not mechanically repeat and imitate, but that we are their sons, so that at all times we could say: 'I believed, therefore have I spoken.'"[226]

On the charge that the Lutheran Church in America had substituted the Symbols for the Scriptures or interpreted Scripture according to the Symbols, thus committing "symbolatry," Walther answers: "Incomparably valuable though the pure Confessions of our Church have been to us, still we never submitted even to them as to a law of dogma imposed upon us, but we rather received them with joyous thanksgiving to God for His unutterable grace because we found in them our own confession. Our Lutheran Church in America had to fight many a strenuous battle with the proud sects, whom, of course, we could not persuade with the testimony of our fathers, but whoever

---

[224] *Op. cit.*, p. 65.

[225] First edition, 1852; 3d ed., 1874; 4th ed., 1893.

[226] *Op. cit.*, p. 66.

has witnessed these battles knows that God's written Word has proved to be a victorious weapon also in our weak hands. The fact is that those who call our theology the theology of the 17th century do not know us. Highly as we value the immense work done by the great Lutheran dogmaticians of this period, still they are not in reality the ones to whom we returned; we have returned, above all, to our precious Concordia and to Luther, whom we have recognized as the man whom God has chosen to be the Moses of His Church of the New Covenant, to lead His Church out of the bondage of Antichrist, under the pillar of the cloud and the pillar of fire of the sterling and unalloyed Word of God. The dogmatic works of the 17th century, though storehouses of incalculably rich treasures of knowledge and experience, so that with joy and pleasure we profit from them day and night, are nevertheless neither our Bible nor our confession; rather do we observe in them already a pollution of the stream that gushed forth in crystal purity in the sixteenth century." [227]

Walther's description agrees with the facts. The author of this dogmatics can testify on the basis of his long experience with our Church's congregational synodical life that there is no foundation for the charge that our Church has fallen prey to a mere "repristination theology" plus a "mechanical apprehension of Scripture" and a "dead

---

[227] *Op. cit.*, p. 67. When Walther published a new edition of Baier's *Compendium Theologiae Positivae*, some seemed to think that the old dogmaticians, and particularly Baier, were regarded as the "standard theologians" by Walther and within the Missouri Synod generally. Nitzsch-Stephan: "Baier wrote the *Compendium Theologiae Positivae* (1686), which represents the mild orthodoxy of Musaeus; it found instant and wide favor, and even today it transmits the old Protestant dogmatics to the neo-orthodox Lutherans [?], especially of America: new editions by Preuss, Berlin, 1864, and by Walther, St. Louis, 1879 ff." *Lehrbuch der ev. Dogmatik*, 3d ed., 1912, p. 29. We have stated above that Walther's edition is not a mere reprint of Baier's *Compendium*, but has been enlarged by many, and often very extended, quotations to an entirely new book. Not only Luther and the representatives of the old Protestant dogmatics, but also the chief representatives of the 19th century dogmatics are given the floor. The purpose of Walther's edition is to furnish the students of theology the necessary source material for their information on the state of theology in the past and present. Walther on this point: "We [American Lutherans] seek to gain an exact understanding of the things written in our age against the Christian truth, and we do not hide the current attacks with their specious arguments even from our students of theology; we are confident that whoever has come to a thorough and living knowledge of the truth has in that knowledge the sure preservative against infection by the most plausible error." (*Lehre und Wehre*, 1875, p. 68.) A number of quotations inserted by Walther are intended as corrections of Baier's position. "The mild orthodoxy of Musaeus" ascribed to Baier by Nitzsch-Stephan, which is evident in the synergistic expressions of Baier, Walther used to explain with the remark that Baier was the son-in-law of Musaeus. (Cf. *Zur Einigung*, 2d ed., p. 38.)

orthodoxy." That weaknesses and faults in greater or lesser degree became apparent, and appear also today, is self-evident in the *ecclesia militans*.[228]

It might appear to be somewhat out of place in a dogmatic work to give such a rather detailed description of the state of our Lutheran Church in America. However, it should be borne in mind, in the first place, that the charge is frequently made that by its adherence to the Scripture principle our Church has actually propagated a dead orthodoxy and hence must be regarded as an evil in the Church. An *oratio pro domo* is therefore in place. Moreover, this self-defense must also constantly lead to a self-examination. If we recall the treasures which God gave our fathers and which through His grace are still considered our greatest heritage, we shall at the same time urgently admonish ourselves, the present and the future generation, to continue in the ways of the Early Church, of the Church of the Reformation, and of the fathers of our Synod. Finally, we dare not lose sight of the welfare of the Church Universal. Present-day theologians rightly insist that dogmaticians dare not isolate themselves, but must come to grips with current theological thinking and the resultant church life. As we examine the present state of the Church and its theology, we cannot but notice that it is in a state of great perplexity. True, the flight of theology from Holy Scripture and its withdrawal into the "impregnable fortress" of the pious self-consciousness has been called a necessary advance in the theological method. But this shift in theological fronts has caused considerable uneasiness because of the resultant confusion in doctrine. This chaos is regarded as an ideal condition only by the extreme left which with Lessing does not desire any "certainty of the truth" at all; still there are voices in the camp of modern theology asking whether, after all, a return to the forsaken fortress of the divine authority of Scripture ought not to be considered. These voices have to date made no noticeable impression on the mass of the Ego theologians. In strong self-delusion they ever again express

228 We should like to advert here to one more point concerning the unity in doctrine. This complete agreement in doctrine has been attributed to various factors, especially to the submission of the majority to the authority of one man. Nothing could be farther from the truth. We have known most of the fathers of our Synod personally. They were not only unlike characters, but in part also very strong and independent personalities, so that, humanly speaking, one would expect violent disagreements. These did not occur, and the longer we studied it, the more we saw in it a witness for the unifying power of the Word of God. Also divergent political opinions at the time of the Civil War could not destroy the divinely wrought unity of faith. There was the mutual agreement: "Political opinions did not unite us, neither should they divide us."

the fear that with the return to the Scripture principle, "dead orthodoxy" would move into the Christian Church. Lutherans in other lands should note Walther's detailed description of the situation in our Lutheran Church in America, which has remained in the old fortress and in it and from it gained its victories. What had proved its worth in the Lutheran Church of America might also prove to be the right means to build the Church in other lands. *Experto crede Ruperto,* Luther was accustomed to say when he extolled the power of God's Word.

If the theological professors and pastors in Germany would by God's grace return to the theological method of Luther and the Lutheran dogmaticians (*sola Scriptura* and *sola gratia,* resp., *satisfactio vicaria*), there would, according to the divine promise, also in Germany again bloom forth a truly Lutheran church life, and in place of the confusion of doctrine there would be again agreement in doctrine; for "if ye continue in My Word, then . . . ye shall know the truth" (John 8:31-32). The theologians of Germany must return to the theology which they censure in the "strictly confessional Lutheran Church of America" as repristination theology. Franz Delitzsch († 1890) had the same conviction. In the preface of a work published by him in 1839 for the 300th anniversary of the Reformation in the city of Leipzig and bearing the title *Luthertum und Luegentum*[229] he answers the charge that he practices a repristination theology: "I confess without shame that in matters of faith I am 300 years behind our time, because I came to see, after wandering a long time in the mazes of error, that the truth is but one, and indeed a truth eternal, immutable, and, since it is revealed by God, in no need of sifting or improvement," and then goes on to say of Holy Scripture: "It alone is the foundation on which the Christian Church bids defiance to the gates of hell, the touchstone distinguishing truth from error, according to which the Church judges but should also itself be judged. . . . The Church is placed over this Word not as judge, but as steward, of whom God will demand account. . . . You [neologists] flatter yourselves with having Luther as patron. Never, however, does Luther by the term 'Word of God' understand anything else than the letter of Holy Scripture, never the inspiration of the inner light, the vagaries of blind reason, or the illusions of the mistaken feeling, but always the written Word, according to the simple sense of the words, according to its

---

[229] The full title: *Luthertum und Luegentum.* Ein offenes Bekenntnis beim Reformationsjubilaeum der Stadt Leipzig. Von Franz Delitzsch. Grimma, 1839.

clear meaning, to the exclusion of all human mediation, falsification, and spiritualization. . . ." Of the old Lutheran theologians Delitzsch says: "Those old Lutheran teachers were not merely erudite, but also sanctified theologians, trained in the school of the Holy Ghost, filled with heavenly wisdom, sweet consolation, and a living knowledge of God; God's Word was implanted in their hearts, it was fused with their faith, and turned into sap and strength in them. . . . 'Ask thy father, and he will show thee; thy elders, and they will tell thee' (Deut. 32:7). 'Thus said the Lord: Stand ye in the ways, and see, and ask for the old paths, where is the good way, and walk therein, and ye shall find rest for your souls' (Jer. 6:16). I preach retrogression to you: Return to the Word of God, which you have forsaken. Your 'enlightenment' is to me a dark, starless, frightful night; infatuated, you have gotten your terms mixed, else you could not compare your Egyptian darkness, which is God's punishment for your rejection of the light of the Reformation, to a sunny day." After discussing the doctrines of justification and the means of grace, which were brought to light again by the Reformation, Delitzsch closes his jubilee essay with these words: ". . . What I have voiced and sought to defend is nothing but the faith of the old Lutheran Church, which our forefathers confessed 300 years ago on Pentecost Day with fervent thanksgiving to God as their faith. Search the Scriptures; you will find and see that this faith is the Lutheran, the Christian faith, based on the immutable and imperishable Word of eternal truth. This faith has nothing in common with confused doubt, brooding gloom, and sickly decadence, as many imagine; no, indeed, it produces bright eyes, good cheer, and strong vigor. The enlightened reason recognizes its incontestable truth; the regenerate heart finds in it celestial consolation, blessed peace, and rich solace. This faith prevails against the gates of hell and leads an eternal triumphal march through the portals of death. Should we, my friends, relinquish such a tried and firm and joyous and victorious faith for a Christianity that is cut in half, lamed on both sides, and attempts to combine Christ and Belial, or even for an 'enlightenment' that is proud of its folly, that gives God's Word the lie and idolizes reason, that can amuse us in life, but in death cannot console us? We would be acting foolishly towards ourselves and inexcusably towards our descendants." And even ten years later (1849), when he was professor of theology in Rostock, Delitzsch not only sent his greetings to his American friends of "strictly confessional trend," but he also renewed his confession to the Lutheran Confession and added the admonition to cling to this faith, because in it lay the "future" of the Lutheran Church. "What a glorious future is in store for our Church if it provides the lamps of its good confession with the oil of the Spirit and without halting hurries to meet the coming Lord! All you beloved brethren across the sea, let us watch and pray in order not to lose the heritage of this future!" Under the pressure of the "unscientific science," as Walther used to express it, the later Delitzsch forsook his own testimony of the truth. But that does not deprive his earlier testimony of its truth, as little as the later Melanchthon's deviation from the right way made the truth originally confessed by him impotent.

The theology of Germany relinquished Scripture as the Word of God more and more and walked in the footsteps of Schleiermacher, the "Reformer of the 19th century," who did not lead the Church and its theology back onto the rock of God's Word, as the Reformer of the 16th century did, but dragged Church and theology into the slough of subjectivism by giving out the slogan that the Christian doctrine must not be drawn out of Scripture, but from the allegedly pious Ego of the theologizing subject, from the "experience," etc. In this slough of subjectivism well-nigh the entire theology of Germany, as far as the public teachers are concerned, is at present floundering.

In the *Neue Kirchliche Zeitschrift* (1923, p. 116), a layman (a lawyer) writes: "The German nation has sunk as deeply as in the period after the Thirty Years' War. But let us bear in mind that at that time the life of faith in our Evangelical Church showed its richest development. At that time our choicest hymns were written, hymns that have been since our childhood the inalienable treasures of our soul. Let us hope that just in the storms and trials of the new era our Church will prove itself to be a great power of life." That would take place and the Church would today, too, by faith and prayer make the political distress disappear as it did after the Thirty Years' War if the conditions in the Church were now as they were then. At that time the teachers of the nation, practically without exception, clung to the Holy Scriptures as God's Word and clung to the Christian doctrine as taken from Scripture. Out of this faith the God-endowed singers of the Lutheran Church sang those beautiful hymns which still refresh our hearts today. Today, unfortunately, the situation is different. The public teachers of the Church with hardly any exception deny the infallible divine authority of Scripture and reject as repristination theology the Christian doctrine which formed the theme of those glorious hymns. This is done, also in this very number of the *Neue Kirchliche Zeitschrift*, by a theologian who displays his great ignorance of the facts by speaking of an "irreparable fall of the old-fashioned dogma of inspiration" and who with a corresponding lack of the sense of truth points to a "Lutheran Judaism," "where they believe their task already completed if they mechanically, externally, adopt the authority of Scripture as well as of the Confessions." We theologians are, as experience teaches, very hard to convert when once we have thoroughly gone off the right track, when, for example, we no longer know whether we should teach out of Holy Scripture or out of our own Ego. For that reason a turn for the better in Germany will have to come also at this time, as it did in the last century, principally from "lay circles," perhaps under the leadership of pastors who were not up till now in the public eye.

What has been said about the doctrinal position of the Missouri Synod applies also to the other synods in church fellowship with it. This is evident especially in the large dogmatical work by Adolf Hoenecke (d. 1908).[230] Hoenecke, like Walther, arrives at the conclusion that the doctrine which the Lutheran Church confesses in its Symbols is the doctrine of Holy Scripture. And this doctrine he both presents from Scripture and defends victoriously in keen polemics against the old, the later, and the most recent errorists. In the elaborate and detailed Prolegomena the author also analyzes the modern experience theology. He proves that this experience theology, which on principle will not draw and determine the doctrine from Scripture but from the heart of the theologian, is both unscriptural and self-

---

[230] *Ev.-Luth. Dogmatik* von D. theol. Adolf Hoenecke, formerly president and professor of the seminary of the General Ev. Luth. Synod of Wisconsin, Minnesota, Michigan, and Other States, at Wauwatosa, Wis. Prepared for publication by his sons Walther and Otto Hoenecke, 1909, 4 volumes. Northwestern Publ. House, Milwaukee, Wis. In the preface to Hoenecke's dogmatics (p. IX f.) Professor J. Schaller says: "The issue at that time was to provide the Wisconsin Synod with a clear doctrinal position and to clarify its relation to other American church bodies as well as to the Church of Germany. At that time the Wisconsin Synod was a member of the General Council, which indeed in its profession of the Lutheran doctrine was far more positive than the General Synod, but because of its unionistic practices offended the Lutherans belonging to the Wisconsin Synod. On the other side stood the Missouri Synod with its unequivocal acknowledgment of the Symbolical Books of the Lutheran Church and its outspoken testimony against those who did not seriously practice the Lutheran Confession. In the discussions regarding the Confessions young pastor Hoenecke participated actively and soon exerted a decisive influence. His influence contributed in a marked degree to the Wisconsin Synod's severance of its connection with the General Council and also made itself strongly felt in 1868 in the discussion with the Missouri Synod which resulted in mutual recognition of the two bodies."

contradictory.[281] We call special attention to a few main points in Hoenecke's dogmatics which show the character of the author as a dogmatician. Hoenecke identifies Scripture and God's Word without equivocation, and because Scripture and God's Word are interchangeable terms, Scripture is to him also the only source and norm of theology. (I, 329 ff.) Scripture, and not a systematic construction, determines the content of dogmatics. Every other method leads astray, as, for example, the Calvinistic doctrine of predestination or the synergistic Lutheran doctrine of election and conversion. (I, 259 ff.) Hoenecke describes the synthetic and the analytic method, mentions also Coccejus' federal, or covenant, method and the Bible-history method, which makes the Bible history the basis of the dogmatic material. None is to be rejected outright. "But the method used by moderns (Frank, etc.), who develop doctrine from the Christian consciousness, etc., is to be rejected." "Dogmatics is solely the systematic, that is, the well-ordered presentation of the theological knowledge drawn from God's Word in faith. It is therefore continually engaged in bringing its reasons and proofs from God's Word. The Word of God is not only its source (*principium cognoscendi, norma causativa*), but also its standard, according to which it is continually gauged." (I, 325 ff.) Of the Symbols, Hoenecke says: "Our [Lutheran] Church has deposited its knowledge derived from God's Word in its Symbols, and hence a Lutheran dogmatics must meet the standard of the Symbols. But that does not set up a second standard; for the Symbols themselves have their criterion in Scripture; they are therefore themselves a standardized standard (*norma normata*)." Hoenecke also comes to the defense of the old Protestant dogmaticians: "The old dogmatics is theocentric, recent conservative dogmatics is anthropocentric" (I, 315). For the much-maligned Calov, Hoenecke pleads in these words: "In the opinion of the moderns he is a man who, like a watchdog, stands constantly before his master's house and snappishly barks at all who try to break off anything, even what is growing along the fence. Such a man, of course, is not to the liking of such theologians as are ready to sacrifice almost everything in the doctrine, even the fundamentals. In Calov's day, just as in ours, men began, with right-sounding phrases, softly and quietly to break off a little from

281 Hoenecke discusses at length also Frank's *System der chr. Gewissheit.* "This detailed discussion is by no means prompted by the importance of this system. However, the work made quite a stir and gained influence. Accordingly, the interest of the Lutheran Church demands that we consider his work more closely."

what is on the periphery; then he could not, as a faithful watchman, keep silence, and he must therefore suffer much maligning today."

We find no doctrinal difference between Walther and Hoenecke. And in this we see another evidence for the unifying power of God's Word. As the fathers of the Missouri Synod differed from one another in character, so also Walther and Hoenecke were men of pronounced and divergent characters. They also came from different church circles. But they were one in faith and doctrine, as is evident in Hoenecke's characterization of Walther as a theologian. He says of Walther (I, 320 ff.): "Carl F. W. Walther was a Scripture theologian. What the Ritschlian Kattenbusch (*Von Schleiermacher zu Ritschl*, p. 3) presents as a weakness of Walther, namely, that he issued the slogan for dogmatics: Only *loci!* since it is the characteristic of revelation that we know only disconnected pieces of God's mysteries, that redounds to the credit of Walther. He is thereby aligning himself with the genuinely Lutheran theologians, while the so-called 'confessional' theologians across the water, since they actually attempt to construct systems, are under the influence of Schleiermacher, as Kattenbusch also tells them. According to Walther, it is not the task of the theologian to fabricate systems, to harmonize seemingly contradictory doctrines. He holds with Luther: 'If harmonizing were in order, we could not retain one single article of faith.' Nor did he regard it to be the task of the theologian to reconcile Scripture with science, faith with knowledge, even though the moderns strive to do this. When that is attempted, Scripture and faith must suffer. – In spite of his great respect for genuine science (*Lehre und Wehre,* Vol. 21, Preface), he looks upon 'scientific' theology as something foreign. Science should serve merely as the maid of theology; if it arrogates more to itself, it should be cast out. Even the thought of bolstering the Scriptural theology by scientific proofs spoils theology. – For Walther the only principle of knowledge in theology is Scripture. Whatever does not spring from Scripture does not belong to theology. He writes: 'We therefore agree with Johann Gerhard: the only principle of theology is the Word of God; therefore whatever is not revealed in God's Word is not theological.' He therefore rejected absolutely all theologizing on the basis of enlightened reason. (*Lehre und Wehre* 21, 225 ff.) 'All such apologetics we detest with all our heart, for it presupposes that there is something still more certain than God's Word, from which more certain principle the mysterious content of revelation can be derived' (*Lehre und Wehre* 34, 326). – While modern confessional theologians across the sea define theology as the 'churchly science of

Christianity' (thus Luthardt, *Kompendium*, p. 2) and speak of its 'close relation to philosophy' (Oettingen, *Dogm.* I, 411), Walther defines it with Chemnitz and the other old theologians as '*habitus practicus*,' a view which Oettingen regards as primitive (*loc. cit.*, p. 397). He says: 'Whatever is the aim of the ministerial office is also the aim of theology. This aim is the true faith, the knowledge of the truth unto godliness, and, finally, eternal life.' (*Lehre und Wehre*, 14, 73.) – A man becomes a theologian, according to Walther, only through the Holy Ghost, from the Word of God. Only he is a genuine theologian who has been born again of the Spirit by means of the Word. In his edition of Baier (p. 69) he quotes, in support thereof, Luther's word: 'A doctor of the Holy Scriptures no one can make for you but alone the Holy Ghost from heaven, as Christ says John 6:45.' The Word makes the theologian, and in turn the theologian is occupied with the Word. – To Walther, Scripture was God's Word and nothing else. He would permit no man to tamper with the old orthodox doctrine of inspiration. Rohnert praises him for this, that in the last decades he was perhaps the most eminent modern exponent of the doctrine of inspiration as taught by the old dogmaticians (*Dogm.*, p. 105). Walther clung firmly to the inspiration of Scripture because he saw clearly that if one here yielded in the least, he was surrendering the principle that Scripture alone is the source and norm of theology. – Walther does not recognize 'open questions,' as the Iowa Synod understood the term. The Confessions do not make new dogmas; they merely exhibit them as doctrines of Scripture. Scripture is the deciding factor. Therefore the doctrine of the Bible is the doctrine of the Church even though it is not treated in the Symbols. (*Lehre und Wehre* 14, 133 ff.) Still, Walther esteemed the Confessions highly. He constantly quotes them as well as statements of the orthodox Lutheran teachers. Nevertheless, his theology is not a repristination theology in the evil sense, for Walther neither the old dogmaticians nor the Symbols, but Scriptures decide the issues. – As a Scripture theologian he did not unduly emphasize certain doctrines, though conditions demanded that at times certain doctrines be given special attention: the doctrine of the Church and the ministry over against the Buffalo Synod, the doctrine of election and conversion over against the Ohio and Iowa Synod, the doctrine of justification and reconciliation over against the Erlangen theology and the sects of this country."

Though the controversy on the doctrine of the Church and the ministry was virtually ended when Hoenecke landed in the United

States, he still bears witness to the Christian truth over against the errors that had arisen on the right hand and on the left. He teaches (*Dogmatik* IV, 146 ff.): The Church in the proper sense of the word consists only of the believing Christians, and only they are originally invested with all spiritual gifts and privileges. Hence they are also the persons who by the call "confer" (*uebergeben*) the public office of the ministry on qualified persons. In regard to the question whether the public office of preaching is of divine or human ordinance, he emphatically teaches the divine institution of it. (IV, 175 ff.) He opposes, on the one hand, Grabau, Loehe, Kliefoth, Muenchmeyer, and others, who in a Romanizing manner made of the public office a means of grace in addition to Word and Sacraments, and, on the other hand, he opposes Hase, Koestlin, Hoefling, Luthardt, and others, who deny that the public ministry is divinely instituted in the sense that there is an express divine command for it and who claim that the office *in concreto* grows out of the Christian congregation by an inner necessity without an express divine command.

The charge has been advanced not only in America but also in Europe that in the doctrine of conversion and election Hoenecke, resp., the Wisconsin Synod and other synods in the Synodical Conference, "readily swallowed the bitter Missouri-Calvinistic pill." [232] In plain language the accusation means these men sided with the Missouri Synod without a personal conviction, yes, contrary to their personal conviction. What about the allegation that Wisconsin swallowed this "bitter Missouri-Calvinistic pill"? From certain quarters in the Iowa Synod and about eight years later from the Ohio Synod the charge was raised that Missouri had fallen into a "fundamental error," namely, into "Calvinism." Well, what had happened? In dealing with the so-called *crux theologorum:* "Why one is hardened, blinded, and another, in the same guilt, is converted again?" the Missouri Synod summarized its position in three statements: (1) We know very definitely from Scripture the cause of conversion: it is God's gracious operation alone; (2) we also know from Scripture very definitely the cause of non-conversion: it is solely man's resistance against the operation of the Holy Ghost (*sola hominis culpa*); (3) but since the grace of God is both universal and efficacious, and all men are involved in the same total corruption, it remains a mystery for our human comprehension in this life why only some are converted and not all. This question was discussed in the Apostolic

---

[232] Thus the Leipzig *Allgemeine Ev.-Luth. Kirchenzeitung*, 1893, No. 2.

Church (Romans 9–11), in the Pelagian and Semi-Pelagian controversies of the fourth, fifth, and sixth centuries,[233] and particularly at the time of the Reformation, e. g., in the pointed question why Saul was rejected and David accepted, why Peter returns and Judas is lost.[234] We await the solution of this mystery in eternal life. Every attempt at solving it in this life brings us into conflict with Scripture. The mystery would be solved quickly if we dared, with Erasmus and the later Melanchthon, to assume something in man (*aliquid in homine*) as a cause or the explanation of the conversion of man, or if we were permitted to teach in the Christian Church that conversion depends not alone on God's grace, but also on the conduct of man (*facultas se applicandi ad gratiam*). But this solution contradicts all those Scripture passages which so clearly ascribe the generation of faith to the gracious and omnipotent working of God and not only deny to man any inclination toward the Gospel, but ascribe to him enmity against the Gospel. Again, the mystery would be completely solved if we were permitted to substitute, with Calvin, as the cause of non-conversion for the *gratia universalis* the *gratia particularis*. But also this solution is prohibited, because it brings us into conflict with all those Scripture passages which so clearly and powerfully teach the *gratia universalis, seria, et efficax,* and expressly extend the operation of the Holy Ghost, efficacious for conversion, also to those men who are not converted and saved. Therefore, in view of the equal grace of God and in view of the equal total depravity of man, we must desist from attempting to find an answer to the question: *Cur alii, alii non?* which is satisfactory to reason. Thus Luther, thus Chemnitz, thus very outspokenly also the Formula of Concord, which, after stating the fact: "One is hardened, blinded, given over to a reprobate mind, while another, who is indeed in the same guilt, is converted again," immediately adds that here we face a "question" the answer to which is impossible in this life, since the revelation of Scripture does not extend beyond Hos. 13:9: "O Israel, thou hast destroyed thyself; but in Me is thine help." And the Formula very definitely sets forth that, in comparing the saved with the lost, we must teach that Scripture ascribes an equal guilt and an equally wicked conduct to both.

---

[233] The Scriptural position was taken in the 25 canons of Orange, 529. See Mansi, VIII, 712 ff. I have had the 25 canons reprinted in *Die Grunddifferenz,* 1903, p. 34 ff. See also *Zur Einigung,* p. 4. [English: *Conversion and Election,* p. 5.]

[234] The antagonism between Luther and the later Melanchthon and between Melanchthon and Chemnitz. See, in Vol. II, the section "The True Reason for Opposing Divine Monergism in Conversion."

Contrariwise, the Ohio and Iowa Synods claimed that it is not true that the Lutheran Church leaves the question unanswered why death and resistance in the case of one is removed, in the case of another not. Their answer was that the fact "that of two men who hear the Gospel, resistance and death in the case of one is removed, in the case of the other not – has its reason in the will of man; it has this reason that the one persistently, stubbornly, and willfully resists God's grace, while the other permits his natural resistance to be overcome by the Holy Ghost. The reason lies in the free self-decision of man."[235] Because the Missouri Synod clung to the universal grace as well as to the *sola gratia*, the fable of the Missourian "Calvinism" has been broadcast, and the *Allgemeine Ev.-Luth. Kirchenzeitung* speaks of the "bitter Missouri-Calvinistic pill" which the synods of Wisconsin and Minnesota supposedly have swallowed.

The report of their synodical convention of 1882,[236] however, shows with what a clear knowledge of the doctrine of Holy Scripture, of Luther, and of the Lutheran Confessions these synods discussed the relevant doctrines. The position of both synods on this doctrine of the Scriptures and the Lutheran Confessions is plainly seen from the following conclusive statements: "Man can contribute not the least bit to his conversion, neither by his actions nor by his attitude; and the fact that some are converted, while others remain obdurate is to be explained neither by assuming a difference in men nor by denying the universal gracious will of God." "When this double question is asked: Whence is it that the one is converted and the other not? one cannot answer: 'That is of God,' or 'That is of man.' But that a man is converted is the result of the powerful operation of God's grace in the Gospel, which has taken effect on him; that another is not converted is the result of the mighty power and operation of his wicked heart, which has resisted the grace of God." In his dogmatics (I, 260) Hoenecke classifies all who insert into the *ordo salutis* a "dissimilar human conduct" as "fabricators of systems," i. e., as such

---

[235] *Monatshefte,* 1872, p. 80, 87, 103. *Zeitblaetter,* 1911, p. 526. This doctrine, employing the "dissimilar conduct" of men as explanation for the fact why of two men hearing the Gospel the one comes to faith and the other does not, is the doctrine of the later Melanchthon, which the Formula of Concord so emphatically rejects. It is also the doctrine of modern Lutherans, like Dieckhoff and Luthardt, who imagine that the *sola gratia* must be stricken in order to preserve the Church from Calvinism.

[236] *Verhandlungen der 32. Versammlung der Synode von Wisconsin in Gemeinschaft mit der Synode von Minnesota* in La Crosse, Wis., vom 8. bis zum 14. Juni 1882. See especially p. 34 f.

as in the interest of a rational system pretend to be wise beyond Scripture. The "dissimilar conduct" theory was thrown upon the theological market in order to give a rational answer to the fact: "One is hardened, blinded, given over to a reprobate mind, while another, who is indeed in the same guilt, is converted again." In doing this, the Scripture passages that state the equal total depravity of all men are canceled. "Where they sought to proceed in a strictly systematic manner, the result has been the gravest departure from Scripture. Such a system, no matter what kind it is, always demands an answer to the question why many are called but few are saved. It is at this point that the fabricating of a system leads astray: either to the predestinarian doctrine of Calvinism or to the synergistic doctrine of election and conversion."

The two representatives of the "strictly confessional trend" in the Lutheran Church of America were, in spite of the difference in their character, the course of their life, and the sphere of activity, united and remained united to their death in the bond of complete agreement in doctrine. Both were "repristination theologians" in the right, God-pleasing sense of the word and serve as a concrete example of such words of Luther as this: "The Word and the doctrine must effect the Christian fellowship and unity; when these are alike and one, the rest will follow of itself." Again: "Let one church follow the other [in external matters] of its own will, or let each one keep its own customs; if only the unity of the Spirit in the bond of faith and the Word is preserved, the difference and diversity in mundane and visible matters will do no harm." Finally: "None of that peace and unity for me by which one loses God's Word; for then eternal life and everything else would already be lost. Here I dare not yield or concede anything to please you or any man, but all things must yield to the Word, be they friend or foe. For it is not given for the sake of external or political unity and peace, but for the sake of eternal life." [237]

---

[237] St. L. IX:831; XVIII:1985; IX:831. It is a pity that the Lutheran Church in America "of strictly confessional trend" and the Church in Germany became estranged. The original unity of spirit between Walther and Franz Delitzsch is expressed beautifully by Delitzsch in his letter of condolence at Walther's death. *Lehre und Wehre,* 1887, 289 f. In a like vein Delitzsch wrote the author of this dogmatics in 1887. That the two old friends in late years could not come to an agreement "in some matters" was due to the fact that Delitzsch under the pressure of "science" forsook his former position. As a "scientific theologian" he placed "science" as the determining principle between himself and Holy Scripture. He abandoned the inspiration of Scripture. That Delitzsch as a Christian clung to the *satisfactio vicaria,* as we, too, charitably assume, was due to a "felicitous inconsistency." That the denial of the Inspiration, if

It has been asked what influence the "strictly confessional trend" of the Lutheran Church in America has exerted on others, first on the older branches of the Lutheran Church in America, which had hardly more than the name Lutheran, and then on the Church of Germany and other lands. And in connection with this question it has also been asked whether a "repristination theology," holding in all points to Scripture as God's infallible Word (Verbal Inspiration) and consequently also to the Confessions of the Lutheran Church, could endure here and elsewhere.

First, the influence on other Lutheran church bodies must be appraised neither too low nor too high. A strong influence has indeed been exerted on the older Lutheran church bodies in America, even though the fathers of the Missouri Synod did practically their entire work by means of the German tongue. The most eminent theologian of the English-speaking Lutheran Church in America, Charles Porterfield Krauth (d. 1883), has repeatedly and in various ways expressed the opinion that the "Missourians" must be regarded as the benefactors of the Lutheran Church in America. Krauth felt constrained in his conscience to renounce his former lax, unionistic position. Among other things he wrote in 1865: "Our Church can never have genuine internal harmony except in the confession of these articles (the doctrines of the Augsburg Confession), of all of them together, without reservation and equivocation. This is our deep conviction, and we herewith solemnly retract before God and His Church, as we have already earnestly and repeatedly done in an indirect manner, whatever we have written or uttered in conflict with this our present conviction. We are not ashamed to do this. We thank God who has led us to understand the truth." [238] And in the preface to his most important book he states: "The positions taken in this book are largely counter, in some respects, to the prevailing theology of our time and our land. No man can be more fixed in his prejudice against the views here defended than the author himself once was; no man can be more decided in his opinion that those views are false than the author is now decided in his faith that they are the truth. They have been formed in the face of all the influences of education and of bitter hatred or of contemptuous disregard on the part of nearly

---

consistency prevails, leads to denial also of the *satisfactio vicaria*, Delitzsch saw actually occurring even in his day (Hofmann, Frank), and since then has become manifest almost universally.

[238] *Lutheran and Missionary*, July 13, 1865; also *Lehre und Wehre*, XI, 1865, p. 278.

all who were most intimately associated with him in the period of struggle."[239] But because of unyielding resistance Krauth's theological position did not become dominant in his own circles.

The next important English Lutheran dogmatician is Henry E. Jacobs. His *A Summary of Christian Faith* (1905) is written in expert catechetical form. And the endeavor to arrive at the Scriptural Lutheran position is plainly evident from the copious quotations from Luther, the Confessions, and the dogmaticians. But he inserted the "difference in man's attitude" into the order of salvation as the answer to the question: *Cur non omnes?* and thereby definitely turned into the synergistic channel. He writes: "The differences in results in the call do not depend upon differences in God's will or upon the call having an irresistible efficacy attached to it in one case and having no efficacy attached to it in the other. The efficacy of the Word and call is constant; the difference in results is determined by a difference in man's attitude towards the call."[240] The last statement is the doctrine of the later Melanchthon. And when Dr. Schmauck, the president of the General Council, sought to eliminate this synergism,[241] he was censured and reprimanded by members of his own church body.[242] But where the conversion and salvation of man is based, in the final analysis, on man's conduct, self-decision, self-assertion, and not solely on God's grace, there the nature of the Christian religion in its radical difference from all man-made religions, is surrendered in principle. Where this doctrine actually reigns, there the conflict with Rome and the struggle against the work-righteousness of the sects and the lodges are unwarranted and futile. Luther knew well what he was saying when he said to Erasmus: *"Jugulum meum petisti!"* Jacobs has also surrendered the doctrine of the verbal inspiration of Scripture. On the one hand, he calls Scripture the "inerrant record" of divine revelation; on the other hand, he nevertheless speaks of the "discrepancies" of the holy writers. He says, for example: "But there is a true sense in which we may say not only that 'the Bible is,' but 'that

---

[239] *The Conservative Reformation and Its Theology,* 1871, Preface, p. xiii. In many respects this is a classic dogmatical work. In it Krauth masterfully defends also the Lutheran doctrine of Christ's person and of the Lord's Supper and shows their Scripturalness over against the attacks of Shedd. Cp. the pertinent sections in this dogmatics.

[240] *A Summary of the Christian Faith,* p. 216 f.

[241] "Man's will is able to decide for salvation through new powers bestowed by God. This is the subtle synergism which has infected nearly the whole of Evangelical Protestantism, and which is or has been taught in institutions bearing the name of our church." (*The Confessional Principle,* 1911, p. 752.)

[242] See F. Bente, *American Lutheranism,* p. 217 f.

the Bible contains, the Word of God.' This occurs when each part, even the most insignificant and seemingly trifling, even the discrepancies between various human inspired writers, and all that pertains to the limitations of their nature and environment and age and language, are regarded as bearing on the one great end and one great theme of revelation and its clear and inerrant record." [243] Questions which have nothing to do with the inspiration of Scripture, e. g., the historical question whether the Hebrew vowel points were found in the original text (Gerhard) or not (Luther), Jacobs mingles into the doctrine of inspiration.[244] Jacobs gives expression to his rejection of the inspiration of Scripture in a very decided way. While Christ says of the whole Scripture and every single statement of Scripture: "The Scripture cannot be broken," and the Apostle Paul says without distinction of the entire Scripture: "All Scripture is given by inspiration of God," and Peter assures us that the word of the Prophets of the Old Testament and of the Apostles of the New Testament are equally the words of the Holy Ghost, Jacobs assumes that there are degrees of inspiration in the various parts of the Old and the New Testament.[245] Jacobs employs nearly all the arguments which modern theology uses in its attack on the inspiration of Scripture. He appeals, for example, to the fact that the Augsburg Confession contains no article on inspiration and that the Formula of Concord formulates no definition either of revelation or inspiration. In order to discredit Verbal Inspiration, he insinuates that its advocates hold the mechanical conception of the inspiration theory.[246]

---

243 *A Summary of the Christian Faith*, p. 284.

244 "But are not some of the most conservative defenders of traditional theories of inspiration also open to criticism? Yes, when they ignore or endeavor to conceal the human element in Scripture or, what is the same, raise the human factor to an equality with the divine, as when it is claimed that the Hebrew vowel points are inspired." *A Summary of the Christian Faith*, p. 281.

245 In his introduction to J. A. W. Haas, *Biblical Criticism*, Jacobs writes: "A text from Genesis and one from John, one from the Psalms and one from the Romans, cannot stand upon the same footing. There are few theorists [!] who would assign the same degree of inspiration to the statistics and rolls in Ezra or Chronicles as to those parts of the New Testament for whose reading the dying ask when all other earthly words have lost their interest. Even the distinction between the Petrine and the Pauline theology, which the Tuebingen School so greatly exaggerated, contains within it an element of truth, when the difference is found to be one of degree, but not one of kind." Quoted in F. Bente, *American Luth.*, II, 220 f.

246 "If the verbal theory of inspiration means that every word and letter are inspired, so that the writer was purely passive and performed a merely mechanical office, as 'the pen of the Holy Ghost,' this, we hold, is an assumption for which we have no warrant" (*loc. cit.*).

While Krauth advocated the strictly confessional principle represented by the Missourians [247] and denounced every church union without doctrinal unity as displeasing to God,[248] the General Council united with the General Synod, the United Synod of the South, and other Lutheran Synods to form the United Lutheran Church of America without regard for the principles of Krauth. We cannot escape the conviction that neither Walther's nor Krauth's influence had gained the ascendancy.[249]

---

[247] Krauth said: "I have been saddened beyond expression by the bitterness displayed toward the Missourians. So far as they have helped us to see the great principles involved in this disputation [on altar- and pulpit-fellowship with non-Lutherans, Chiliasm, and the lodges], they have been our benefactors, and although I know they have misunderstood some of us, that was perhaps inevitable. They are men of God, and their work has been of inestimable value." Quoted in F. Bente, *American Luth.*, II, 185, from A. Spaeth's *Dr. Charles Porterfield Krauth*, II, 236.

[248] In his presidential address before the Pittsburgh Synod in 1866 he declared: "There can be, there is, no true unity but in the faith. . . . The one *token* of this unity, that by which this internal thing is made visible, is the one expression of faith, one 'form of sound words,' used in simple earnestness, and meaning the same to all who employ it. . . . You may agree to differ; but when men become earnest, difference in faith will lead first to fervent pleadings for the truth, and, if these be hopelessly unheeded, will lead to separation. All kinds of beliefs and unbeliefs may exist under the plea of toleration." Quoted in *op. cit.*, II, 184.

[249] Besides Jacobs' book there are a number of larger and smaller dogmatical works in the English language. To name a few: Milton Valentine, *Christian Theology*, 1905–1907, 2 vols.; Revere F. Weidner, *Introduction to Dogmatic Theology*, 2d ed., 1895; Andrew Voigt, 1916. All are more or less infected with the modern "scientific" theology, but Weidner and Voigt oppose its coarsest excrescences. The false witness borne against the old dogmaticians is, we presume, copied *bona fide* from famous modern theologians. Voigt says, for example, in his Introduction, XVIII: "Confessionalism does not mean that it is the office of dogmatics simply to reproduce and defend the accepted doctrine of the Church. This was the conception in the seventeenth century." Whoever is familiar with the theologians of the seventeenth century knows that they take and prove the Christian doctrine directly from Scripture — for which other modern theologians acknowledge and fault them ("intellectualism," etc.). Valentine's dogmatics may serve as proof how effectually the theologians in the General Synod rebuffed not only the influence of the Missouri Synod, but also Dr. Krauth's endeavors. Valentine espoused nearly all of the errors of modern theology together with the Arminian-Reformed 'enthusiasm.' He rejects the inspiration of Scripture and the substitutional punitive sufferings of Christ. He weakens the doctrine of original sin, rejects the "*mere passive*," and adopts the human will as the third cause of conversion (free self-decision). Children cannot believe and are saved without faith. Heathen are saved "if they lived according to the light afforded them." (II, 405 ff.)

We have in Dr. A. L. Graebner's (d. 1904) *Outlines of Doctrinal Theology*, 1898, an English dogmatics which is entirely correct and Biblical in doctrine. These outlines are, as the author says in the preface, "a brief thetical compend of the outlines of Christian doctrine, consisting of concise definitions and an

It is difficult to evaluate the influence of the "strictly confessional trend" of the Lutheran Church in America on world Lutheranism. Walther attempted to maintain fairly close contacts with European Lutherans and no doubt exerted a wholesome influence.[250] But gradually the breach between us and European theologians widened.[251] Instead of reading our literature, they seemed to believe what our American opponents had to say about our "strictly confessional trend," viz., our alleged Calvinism, our idolizing of the dogmaticians, and our dishonoring of the dogmaticians, our unity and our mutual strife, the congregations' democratic enslaving of the pastors.[252] This need not surprise us, for we are theologically divided by a gulf so wide and deep that it cannot be bridged. We regard Holy Scripture as God's infallible Word and therefore as the only source and norm of theology, while the modern theologians regard the "identification" of Scripture and "Word of God" as an outmoded position that is taken today only in "lay circles" and among theological "laggards." An agreement cannot be reached by theologians who represent such antipodal positions.

---

array of texts from which the various points of doctrine are derived as from their theological source, the written Word of God." That no quotations from the Symbolical Books are added "must not be construed into a disparagement of the Lutheran standards or of any point of doctrine therein contained. With an emphatic refusal to apologize for having nowhere, from the first point in Bibliology to the last in Eschatology, progressed beyond the theology of our orthodox fathers, and with the fervent prayer that God would graciously keep him and his brethren in the faith from any such progress, this humble contribution toward the theological literature of our Church in America is dedicated to the service of our Lord and Savior Jesus Christ and commended to His divine blessing."

250 At the time of Walther's death, General Superintendent Ruperti wrote: "In Walther one of the great men of the Church of Christ has gone home, a man who was an epoch-making personality not only in the history of the Church in America, where he was the outstanding leader and gatherer of Lutherans, but whose activity has made itself felt in the Lutheran Church of all continents as a powerful incentive. The success of his activity is almost without parallel in the recent history of our Church." *Allgemeine Ev.-Luth. Kirchenzeitung*, July 22, 1887.

251 The fathers of the Missouri Synod were surely in no hurry to break off intercourse with the Church in Germany. As they continually endeavored to come to doctrinal agreement with the various Lutheran synods of this country, so they repeatedly sought to come to an agreement with church circles in Germany and in other countries. We, on our part, have kept up the contact by carefully taking cognizance of events in the German Church, particularly also of their literary products. The many volumes of *Lehre und Wehre* and of the *Lutheraner* offer perhaps the richest mine of current church history covering the whole world obtainable today.

252 Kurtz, *Kirchengeschichte fuer Studierende*, 1890, II, 2, p. 262. R. E., 2d ed., IX, 85 f.; partial correction in R. E., 2d ed., XVIII, 687 ff.

Still, amid the terrific convulsions that today are shaking the whole world, God's grace can bring about a change also in this respect.

Will the "strictly confessional trend" of the Lutheran Church as represented here in the United States by the Synodical Conference be able to survive here and in other countries? Our answer may be submitted in the following points:

1. It is not left to our discretion whether we want to abide by the doctrine of the Lutheran Church, as it is declared in its Confession, or whether we should choose a different doctrine. The doctrine of the Lutheran Church agrees perfectly with the doctrine of Christ as we have it in the Word of His Apostles and Prophets (John 8:31; 17:20; Eph. 2:20; 1 Cor. 14:37; 2 Cor. 13:3), and no other doctrine is permissible in the Christian Church to the Last Day. In so far as a man does not consent to the wholesome words of our Lord Jesus Christ, he is proud, knowing nothing, since no man knows anything of God and divine matters beyond God's Word. (1 Tim. 6:3 ff.) Orthodoxy is the divinely intended form of the Christian Church on earth. Of course, whoever has not come to see that the Lutheran doctrine, as presented in the Confessions of that Church, is the doctrine of Scripture, cannot contend for this doctrine. But this lack of knowledge does not change the fact that the Lutheran Church of the Reformation is the Church of the pure, that is, the Scriptural, doctrine, as the Scripture proof furnished by the Confessions themselves shows. The Lutheran Church in its original, unchangeable form of doctrine should therefore not act timidly among men, as though it had to apologize for still existing, but it should by God's grace step before the Church and the world with that confidence which the knowledge of the divine truth flowing from the continuance in the Word of the Apostles and Prophets inspires.

2. The history of the Church shows that by God's grace and power a Church which continues in the immutable Word of the Prophets and Apostles has vitality. The church at Jerusalem continued steadfastly in the Apostles' doctrine, and the Lord added daily such as were saved (Acts 2:42-47; 4:4; 5:14; 11:21; 14:1). Also the Church of the Reformation held its ground against the whole world by taking the position characterized in the axiom: "The Word they still shall let remain." And as to the Lutheran Church in America, a speedy extinction had been prophesied for its "strictly confessional trend" by both the Reformed sects and the liberal "American Lutheranism." The fathers of the Missouri Synod were given the advice from all sides to cast aside the "Symbol theology" and instead to adopt the fashion-

able "revival method," in case they wished to keep their Church alive. Our fathers refused to be confused by such talk. They fought every form of the man-made movement of holding revivals, and in a quiet and clear manner, publicly and privately, in the home, the school, the church, and the higher institutions of learning, kept on teaching the pure divine truth, as it is revealed in God's infallible Word and confessed in the Symbols of the Lutheran Church. And God has blessed the "repristination theology" of our fathers with success also in this country, in spite of vehement opposition. But whether there be success or not, God has commanded His Church to preach His Word without subtraction or addition. Farther than that the responsibility of the Church does not go. The success rests in God's hands. In this conviction the entire Synodical Conference is by God's grace united and active as one Church. To this end God, of course, must give and preserve teachers who are not only scholarly but have also been trained in the school of the Holy Ghost, so that they know by their own experience how absolutely necessary it is for the Church steadfastly to cling to the *sola gratia* and the *sola Scriptura*. Modern theology has unfortunately given up both these truths.

3. Finally, we must keep in mind that in its antithesis to Lutheran theology modern theology takes virtually the same position as Reformed theology. The fact is that modern theology is walking not in Lutheran, but in Reformed paths. The method of Schleiermacher, which would take the Christian doctrine not from Holy Scripture, but from the pious self-consciousness of the Christian "experience," is the method of Zwingli and Calvin, in so far as both taught an immediate operation of the Holy Spirit which is not bound to the written Word. The fact that Zwingli and Calvin did not consistently apply their unscriptural theological principle finds its explanation in part in the powerful influence of Luther, and in part in this, that in dealing with men they were forced back to the Lutheran doctrine of the means of grace in contradiction to their real theological principle of an immediate operation of the Holy Ghost. We have no quarrel with the Reformed theology in regard to the external arrangement of the Christian doctrines within the *corpus doctrinae*. The fact is that the Reformed theologians use both the synthetic and the analytic method.[253] Even according to the federal, or covenant, method the

---

253 Calvin in his *Institutes* (last edition by him, 1559) has the lucid external arrangement: I. The Knowledge of God the Creator. II. The Knowledge of God the Savior. III. The Manner of Receiving Christ's Grace. IV. The External Means or Instruments.

Christian doctrine could be presented exactly according to Scripture. What we object to in the Reformed theology is this, that in all doctrines in which it differs from the Lutheran Church and on which it has constituted itself as the Reformed Church alongside the Lutheran Church, it denies the Scriptural principle and lets rationalistic axioms rule. This has already been treated in the chapter "The Cause of the Divisions Within Visible Christendom."

21

The Attainment of Theological Aptitude

Luther writes in the preface to the first part of his German books in 1539 (St. L. XIV:434ff.): "Let me show you a right method for studying theology, the one that I have used. If you adopt it, you will become so learned that if it were necessary, you yourself would be qualified to produce books just as good as those of the Fathers and the church councils. Even as I dare to be so bold in God as to pride myself, without arrogance or lying, as not being greatly behind some of the Fathers in the matter of making books; as to my life, I am far from being their equal.[254] This method is the one which the pious king David teaches in the 119th Psalm and which, no doubt, was practiced by all the Patriarchs and Prophets. In the 119th Psalm you will find three rules, which are abundantly expounded throughout the entire Psalm. They are called: *Oratio, Meditatio, Tentatio.*" Matthias Hafenreffer, professor of theology and chancellor of the university of Tuebingen (d. 1619), places this axiom of Luther at the head of his dogmatics,[255] at the same time expanding it on the basis of Scripture and applying it to conditions of his day. Among the theologians of the last century Rudelbach (d. 1862) had this to say in an address on Luther's instruction as to the study of theology: "You are familiar with the great word of Luther: *Oratio, meditatio, tentatio faciunt theologum.* This word comprises our entire theological methodology. Here, just as is the case with every thought sealed by the Spirit of God, there is nothing to add, nothing to subtract." [256] There can be no doubt that the distressing lack of true teachers would be quickly ended if Luther's methodology were observed everywhere.

---

[254] Walther used to comment here: "O you humble Luther!"

[255] *Loci Theologici,* Tubingae, 1601; 1603; 1606, and later editions.

[256] Quoted in Walther's *Pastoraltheologie,* p. 9.

Luther explains the necessity of the *oratio* thus: "First, you should know that Holy Scripture is a book such as will make the wisdom of all other books appear as folly, since no book teaches anything concerning eternal life but this one alone. Therefore you should straightway despair of your own wit and intellect, for with them you will attain nothing, but by such arrogance you will cast yourself and others with you from heaven into the abyss of hell, as happened to Lucifer. But enter into thy closet and kneel down and implore God with all humility and earnestness that by His dear Son He would grant you His Holy Ghost, who will enlighten you, guide you, and give you understanding. As you observe that David in the 119th Psalm continually prays: Teach me, O Lord, make me to understand, guide me, show me! and many more such words, though he knew well the text of Moses and of many more such books, also daily heard and read them; still he wants to have the true Master of the Scripture at his side in order that he may not plunge into them with his reason and become master himself. For that is what turns men into unruly fanatics who imagine that Scripture is subject to them and easily attained by their reason, as though it were the fables of Marcolfus or Aesop, for which they need no Holy Ghost nor prayer." What Luther here says of the need of prayer rests on the conviction wrought by the Holy Ghost that there is no other book in the world like Holy Scripture. It is God's own majestic Word. For that reason it is the only book which teaches eternal life, since all the world is held captive in the *opinio legis*. When other books do teach of eternal life, namely, teach that salvation is obtained without the works of the Law, by faith in Christ's *satisfactio vicaria*, this is derived from Scripture. And since Scripture is the very Word of God, it is proper for the theologian that as often as he opens Scripture, he put no faith whatever in his wit or intellect and ask from God His Holy Spirit, who alone teaches one to understand God's Word and creates that spirit which subjects itself to the Scriptures. Without this operation of the Holy Spirit man will arrogantly deem himself superior to Scripture, will make Scripture not the object of his faith, but of his criticism, an arrogance that will finally lead himself and others into perdition and will cause factions and divisions in the Church. And this is true of modern theology, because it will not accept Scripture as the Word of God, but places itself above Scripture. The Ego of the theologian becomes the dominating factor, and since there is many an Ego, the result is not unity in the Christian doctrine, but hopeless dissension and factionalism.

Of the *meditatio* Luther says: "Secondly, you should meditate, that is, not in the heart alone, but also externally, work on and ply the oral speech and the lettered words in the Book, read them and re-read them again and again, noting carefully and reflecting upon what the Holy Ghost means by these words. And have a care that you do not tire of it or think it enough if you have read, heard, said it once or twice and now profoundly understand it all. For in that manner a person will never become much of a theologian. He will be like worm-eaten fruit that drops from the tree before it is half ripe. Therefore you see in this Psalm how David over and over glories in the fact that he will speak, compose, declare, sing, hear, read, day and night and evermore; however, nothing but the Word and precepts of God alone. For God will not give you His Holy Spirit except through the external Word; be guided by that. For He has not without purpose commanded to put things down in writing, to preach, read, hear, sing, recite, etc." In this exposition of the *meditatio* Luther tells what constitutes the study of theology, namely, not the meditation of what the theologizing Ego speculates about God and divine things, but the reflection upon what the Holy Ghost means and teaches in "the lettered words in the Book," in the letters of Scripture, which is not the word of man, but the Word of the Holy Ghost. Modern theology, however, holds that Luther's method demands a theology which is unworthy of theology and leads to intellectualism which is detrimental to piety. But the only method is the continual occupation with the "lettered words in the Book." Without this method a person will "never become much of a theologian." Luther wants no "rustication of the pastor," as Walther used to say, but continued diligent study on his part.

Luther's explanation of the *tentatio* reads thus: "Thirdly, there is *tentatio*, affliction. This is the touchstone; this teaches you not merely to know and understand, but also to experience how right, how true, how sweet, how lovely, how mighty, how consoling, God's Word is, wisdom above all wisdom. That is why you observe how David in the 119th Psalm so often complains about all sorts of enemies, about nefarious princes and tyrants, about false prophets and factions, whom he must endure because he meditates, that is, as stated, is occupied with, God's Word in every way. For as soon as the Word of God blooms forth through you, the devil will visit you, make a real doctor of you, and by his affliction will teach you to seek and love God's Word. For I myself – if I may refer to my humble example (*dass ich Maeusedreck auch mich mit unter den Pfeffer menge*) – owe very much to my Papists, because through the raging of the devil they have so buffeted, distressed, and terrified me that they have made me a fairly good theologian, which I would not have become without them. And what they have, in turn, gained from me, they are heartily welcome to that honor, victory, and triumph, for they were bound to have it so." Luther's entire theology grew out of the *tentatio*, *tentatio* from within and from without. First came the *tentatio* from within. After years of uncertainty and terrors of conscience under the Roman doctrine of works God led him to an understanding of the Gospel of the free grace of God in Christ. Thus he tasted in his own heart and conscience "how right, how true, how sweet, how lovely, how mighty, how consoling, God's Word is, Wisdom above all wisdom." Then came the *tentatio* from without. When Luther taught the Word of God, the Papacy, yes, most all the world, got in his way and declared his eternal life as well as his temporal life forfeited. In this affliction he learned "to seek and to love God's Word," and this with such success that he could exclaim: "Here I stand; I cannot do otherwise." Thus, by way of affliction, Luther became "a fairly good theologian." And let us not be deceived! Also in our day the theological aptitude is attained in no other way than this, that in the distress coming from within and without we are driven into the Word of Scripture and cling to it as the only immovable divine force in the universe. The entire recent scientific theology has a different spirit. It does not employ God's Gospel to bring peace to consciences stricken by God's Law; it does not suppress the wisdom of the world with God's Word, "the Wisdom above all wisdom." It sees its task in satisfying the "craving of the intellect" and in harmonizing the Christian doctrine with the "scientific world view."

Finally, Luther describes how continuance in the Word of Scripture creates those attitudes which are essential for the theologian, namely, grateful delight in the written Word, serene confidence in his ability to teach young and old in all stations of life, lasting and increasing humility to check the pernicious, ever-menacing pride which causes so much havoc in man's own soul and among others. Luther closes thus: "Behold, here you have David's rule. If you now will study well according to this example, you will also sing and glory with him, 'The Law of Thy mouth is better unto me than thousands of gold and silver,' Ps. 119:72; again (vv. 98-100): 'Thou through Thy commandments hast made me wiser than mine enemies; for they are ever with me. I have more understanding than all my teachers; for Thy testimonies are my meditation. I understand more than the ancients, because I keep Thy precepts.' And you will experience how flat and stale the books of the Fathers will taste to you; and not only will you despise the books of the opponents, but your own writings and teachings will please you the longer, the less. When you have arrived at this point, then you can confidently hope that you have made a beginning of becoming a real theologian, who can teach not only the young and immature Christians, but also the more mature, even the perfect Christians; for Christ's Church contains all sorts of Christians, young, old, weak, sick, sound, strong, alert, lazy, foolish, wise, etc. But if you feel and think that you know it all and are tickled with your own booklets, your teaching and writing, as if you had produced something very precious and had preached admirably, and it pleases you much to be praised before others, yes, even expect such praise, so that you do not become depressed and lose interest: if you have that sort of a pelt, my friend, then take hold of your ears; and if you grab right, you will find a fine pair of large, long, shaggy ass's ears; then risk the full cost and decorate yourself with golden bells, so that, wherever you walk, people can hear you, point you out, and say: 'Look, look! There goes that wonderful creature that can write such fine books and deliver such eloquent sermons.' Then you are happy, and superhappy in heaven; ay, where the fire of hell is prepared for the devil and his angels! To sum up, let us seek honor and be elated where it is in place. In this Book the glory belongs entirely to God, and it says: '*Deus superbis resistit, humilibus autem dat gratiam. Cui est gloria in saecula saeculorum. Amen!*' " We advise all theologians and those who would become such to read Luther's theological methodology repeatedly, in order to follow it by God's grace, at all times.

Holy Scripture

(DE SCRIPTURA SACRA)

1

Holy Scripture the Only Source and Norm of Christian Doctrine for the Church Today

THE Christian Church is indeed older than Holy Scripture, that is, older than the written Word of God. Until the time of Moses, God called His Church into existence and preserved it by His oral Word (*viva voce*) The Christian Church came into existence immediately after the Fall, when God, having applied the Law to fallen men orally (Gen. 3:8-14), gave mankind the oral promise of the Woman's Seed, who was to destroy the works of the devil, that is, free men from the guilt of sin and all its consequences (Gen. 3:15), and Adam and Eve believed the "first Gospel." Through the oral Word, proclaimed in various ways, God continued to build His Church until the days of Moses.[1]

But after God had chosen to transmit His Word in writing, the Church of every age was strictly bound to the written Word of God.[2]

---

1 Gen. 4:26: "Then began men to call upon the name of the Lord," plainly refers to meetings held for the purpose of preaching and hearing the Word of God. Cf. Luther on this passage, St. L. I:398 ff.; likewise J. P. Lange on the passage; Calov, *Bibl. Illustrata,* remarks: "Most exegetes accept this passage as referring to the beginning of public preaching." Lucas Osiander comments: "Worship before the birth of Enos was less solemn and was practiced in a somewhat private manner." Further on Scripture reports that God spoke to Noah (ch. 6 ff.) and to Abraham (ch. 12 ff.), etc. And they spread the Word of God that came to them. Abraham is called "a prophet" (Gen. 20:7), and Gen. 13:4 we are told that he "called on the name of the Lord," i. e., preached the name of the Lord. The "name of the Lord" is primarily that whereby God has made a name for Himself among sinful men: the redemption of mankind from the guilt of sin and its consequences by the Seed of the Woman, Christ. What Peter says Acts 10:43 of all Prophets of the Old Testament includes also the passages Gen. 4:26; 13:4; etc.

2 As reasons which may have induced God to substitute the fixed Scriptures for the oral transmission of His Word, Baier gives the following (I, 106): "(1) The growth of the human race; (2) the shortening of man's span of life, it being no longer possible to instruct all men in the same manner, orally and personally, as formerly the patriarchs, who received their instruction by direct revelation of God; but also (3) the infiltration of much corruption of doctrine; in addition (4) the feebleness of the mortals to be instructed and the frailty of their memory required a revelation to which recourse could be had in every case of need, and therefore a written record was considered advantageous." If the objection is raised that the almighty and all-wise God could no doubt have continued to preach to His Church and preserve it without a written

No man was permitted to add anything to the written Word nor to subtract anything from it (Joshua 23:6; Deut. 4:2). The Church of the Old Testament was rigidly bound to the written Word of God as its complete canon, to which only God could add from time to time.[3] In the time of the New Testament God added the writings of the Apostles to the books of the Prophets as the foundation of faith. Of the Church of the New Testament Paul says Eph. 2:20: "Ye are built upon the foundation of the Apostles and Prophets."[4] The Scriptures of the Apostles are co-ordinated with those of the Prophets because it is one and the same Spirit of Christ speaking through both. "Not unto themselves, but unto us, they [the Prophets, who had "the Spirit of Christ"] did minister the things which are now [in the days of the New Testament] reported unto you" (1 Pet. 1:10-12). With the Word of the New Testament Apostles, God's revelation of the doctrine to His Church is entirely completed, for when Christ in His high-

---

transmission of His Word, we answer with Baier: "It has pleased divine Providence that the chief parts of the divine revelation be comprehended in writing" – God willed it so. Moreover, we know that God loves fallen mankind and that therefore, like the gift of His incarnate Son (John 3:16), also the gift of His written Word serves His saving love of sinners (2 Tim. 3:15-17). God's children gratefully acknowledge this love (Ps. 119) and shun the sin of setting aside the written Word or of even denying outright that it is the infallible divine truth. Expressing it according to the causal method: "The internal impelling cause of the reduction to writing, in Holy Scripture, by the divine will, is God's goodness; the external (προκαταρκτική) is the need of mankind to be saved" (Baier I, 105). That, however, no *necessitas absoluta* may be ascribed to Scripture, is maintained also by the old Lutheran theologians and will be brought out more fully when the use to be made of Scripture is treated.

[3] Quenstedt, I, 51: "We must distinguish between the time before and the time after Moses, or between the revelation which was given by God to the patriarchs without the recording of any Scriptures through 2,454 years (after the calculation of Calvisius), namely, from the beginning of the world down to Moses, and which was spread by word of mouth, and that revelation which was recorded in books by Moses and the Prophets. The former was the theological principle up to Moses, the latter after Moses. For immediately after the first canon was constituted, which consisted of the Pentateuch, the Book of Job, and the Song of Moses (Psalm 90), the revelation transmitted by word of mouth was no longer the norm and principle of religion, but solely the revelation recorded in books." That the Scriptures of the Old Testament are the complete canon for the Church of the Old Testament is indicated also by Christ, when He says (Luke 16:29): "They have Moses and the Prophets; let them hear them."

[4] Stoeckhardt's comment on this passage: "The Apostles come into consideration here not as persons, but according to their office, namely, as Apostles, and as such in their relation to the Church of all ages. . . . Though long dead, they live on for us and speak to us in their writings. And so the second genitive, προφητῶν, can mean only the Old Testament Prophets and the writings of the Prophets, which occupy the same rank as the writings of the Apostles and form with them one genus; therefore ἀποστόλων and προφητῶν have but one article."

priestly prayer (John 17:20) says: "Neither pray I for these alone," the Apostles, "but for them also which shall believe on Me through their Word," through the Word of the Apostles, He is thereby making the Word of His Apostles the basis of faith for the entire New Testament era. That through the ministry of hundreds of thousands who are not Apostles men are brought to faith in Jesus has its cause in this, that these hundreds of thousands, yes, millions, of men, do not speak their own words, but the Word of the Apostles and Prophets. We quote once more Luther's remarks on the words of David: "The Spirit of the Lord spake by me" (2 Sam. 23:2): "Such a boast neither we nor anyone who is not a Prophet may utter. What we may do if we are also sanctified and have the Holy Ghost, is this, that we boast of being catechumens and pupils of the Prophets – we repeat and preach what we have heard and learned from the Prophets and Apostles, and are also sure that the Prophets have taught it. In the Old Testament such men are called 'the children of the prophets' who offer nothing of their own and nothing new, as the Prophets do, but teach what they have learned from the Prophets, and they are the 'Israel,' as David calls them, for whom he writes the Psalms." (St. L. III:1890.)

Only one question remains: Where does the Church of the New Testament find this Word of the Apostles with certainty? The Apostles themselves point us to their Scriptures. They declare, in the first place, that their written Word is in content identical with their spoken Word. The Apostle John says: "That which we have seen and heard declare we unto you . . . and these things write we unto you" (1 John 1:3-4). Paul also co-ordinates his oral and his written word: "Hold the traditions which ye have been taught, whether by word or our epistle" (2 Thess. 2:15). Not everything that Christ and the Apostles taught has been recorded (John 21:25), but the instruction given in the writings of the Apostles is abundant, yea, superabundant, since the same thoughts are stated not only once but often. "To write the same things to you, to me indeed is not grievous, but for you it is safe" (Phil. 3:1). In the second place, we see that the Apostles insisted already very firmly on the *sola Scriptura.* Even in the days of the Apostles the same false sources of knowledge and the same false norms were prevalent which later on and down to our day have plagued Christendom, such as spurious prophecy or "spirits," alleged word of the Apostles, or "tradition," alleged epistles of the Apostles. Over against all such claims Paul points to his written Word as the safe source and norm of the true Apostolic doctrine. Genuine "prophecy" and "spirit" were indeed present in the Apostolic Church; therefore

Christian congregations were instructed not to reject *a priori* this Spirit and prophecy, but to apply to them the test of the Apostle's Word. When in the congregation at Corinth "prophecy" and "spirit" placed themselves alongside, and even above, the Apostolic authority, Paul wrote to the congregation (1 Cor. 14:37 f.): "If any man think himself to be a prophet or spiritual, let him acknowledge that the things that I write unto you are the commandments of the Lord. But if any man be ignorant, let him be ignorant." This means that whoever will not acknowledge as divine norm what Paul had written should be recognized as a pseudo prophet and be treated as an ignoramus. The passage 2 Thess. 2:2: "That ye be not soon shaken in mind or be troubled neither by spirit nor by word nor by letter as from us, as that the Day of Christ is at hand," is important because here the Apostle sets his written instruction against "spirit," against the alleged word of the Apostle (tradition), and against the alleged epistle of the Apostle. Christians should not permit themselves to be "shaken in mind or troubled" by any such pretensions.[5] In order that the congregations might be able to distinguish spurious from genuine epistles of the Apostle, Paul wrote the greeting with his own hand (2 Thess. 3:17): "The salutation of Paul with mine own hand, which is the token in every epistle: so I write."

The Scripture principle is rejected and, instead, the human Ego installed as teacher in the Church in the following instances:

1. When natural reason is made the judge. By "natural reason" we mean here man's natural knowledge of God and of divine things, which, without the revelation of Scripture, is limited to a knowledge of God's existence only and of the divine Law, as we have shown repeatedly, and this knowledge leaves man under God's wrath and curse, since man cannot keep the Law. Concerning the Gospel, which brings men the forgiveness of sins for the sake of Christ's vicarious satisfaction and constitutes the very essence of the Christian religion, man himself knows absolutely nothing. 1 Cor. 2:9: "Eye hath not

---

[5] Luenemann: "'Ὡς δι' ἡμῶν ('as from us') is to be connected with διὰ λόγου ('by word') as well as with δι' ἐπιστολῆς ('by letter'), and the former expression is to be understood as referring to oral statements which were falsely ascribed to the Apostle, and the latter to written statements that were attributed to the Apostle by means of a spurious letter. However, to refer διὰ πνεύματος also to ὡς δι' ἡμῶν ('by spirit') as does Erasmus, is impossible. For while one might circulate 'words' or 'letters' as coming from an absent person, this could not be done with Spirit-inspired Prophetic lectures, since such a case required the personal presence of the speaker." Also in v. 15 Paul's "word" and "epistle" are joined: "whether by word or our epistle."

seen nor ear heard neither have entered into the heart of man the things which God hath prepared for them that love Him." It has already been shown that not only the illiterate, but also the cultured, especially the philosophers, whose reason has been trained, lack this knowledge.[6] Making natural reason the judge of matters religious is a μετάβασις εἰς ἄλλο γένος, is the attempt to set up human unreason as teacher in the Christian Church in place of the Word of God. This is done by the Unitarians of all ages, who openly avow that they reject such doctrines as the holy Trinity, the metaphysical deity of Christ, and the *satisfactio vicaria* because they are "unreasonable" (this error will be discussed in greater detail when these doctrines are treated). The Unitarians are *extra ecclesiam.* The same error is committed by all those within external Christendom who reject some parts of the Christian doctrine because, as they say, they are unreasonable. We have already shown that in those doctrines in which the Reformed Church differs from us and by which it has divided Protestantism it does so because it has put rationalistic axioms in the place of the Scripture principle. (See p. 25 ff.) It has also been shown that nothing else than rationalism is the mother of synergism (denial of the *sola gratia*) as well as of Calvinism (denial of the *universalis gratia*). (See p. 32 ff.)

However, the term "reason" has a second meaning, in Scripture as well as in secular usage. It means also the mental or rational nature of man, that is, the capacity of man to receive the thoughts of another into the mind, the ability to perceive and think. This is the so-called ministerial use of reason (*usus rationis ministerialis, organicus*), as distinguished from the magisterial use of reason (*usus rationis magisterialis*). The ministerial use of reason is, of course, legitimate in theology because the Holy Ghost works and sustains faith only through the Word of God as it is correctly perceived by the human mind. Scripture therefore very emphatically enjoins this use of reason Rom. 10:14: "How shall they believe in Him of whom they have not heard?" Rom. 10:17: "Faith cometh by hearing." John 5:39: "Search the Scriptures." Matt. 24:15: "Whoso readeth [what Daniel says of the abomination of desolation] let him understand." Luke 2:19: "Mary kept all these things and pondered them in her heart." This *usus instrumentalis* of reason as a tool to hear, apprehend, and ponder the words of Scripture includes also the observance of the laws of language (grammar) and the laws of human thinking (logic) as used in Scripture, for God

---

[6] See p. 16 ff. on the philosophy of religion.

has adopted the human tongue and the human manner of thinking. God has deigned, as Luther again and again reminds us, to "become incarnate" in Scripture (*Scriptura Sacra est Deus incarnatus*). In this sense the axiom holds good: *Theologia debet esse grammatica;* that is, the theologian who would understand and teach the doctrine revealed must adhere most accurately to the linguistic usage present in Scripture. Luther again and again remarks, especially in his polemical writings, that everyone who blunders in grammar must necessarily also blunder in theology. The orthodox Lutheran dogmaticians take the same view. As emphatically as they reject reason as principle in theology, so emphatically they urge the *usus instrumentalis* of reason, inclusive of the entire philological and logical material, so long as this serves solely to understand the contents of Scripture and does not add its own content. Quenstedt says (*Systema* I, 55 ff.): "One must distinguish between 'reason' used passively as the subject absorbing the information and 'reason' taken in the sense of norm as the approving principle. . . . The first is necessary for the cognition of everything and so also of divine things, as *principium quo,* for in no other way than by his intellect or reason does man understand; the latter, however, is not admitted in the cognition of divine things, as *principium quod.* . . . Without the use of reason or intellect no one can occupy himself with theology; for theology is not to be presented to the brutes and animals, which lack reason. As man therefore cannot see without eyes, cannot hear without ears, cannot taste without a tongue, so he cannot without reason – without which, of course, he is no human being (*homo*) – perceive what faith (which Augustine calls the 'soul of the soul,' *sermo* 250. *de tempore*) encompasses within its periphery. . . . One must distinguish between organic principles, such as grammar, logic, rhetoric, the study of languages, etc., and philosophical principles strictly so called. The first are to be employed in theology (namely, as a means to acquire theology), since without them neither the sense nor the meaning of the words can be found (grammar), nor the forms or modes of speech can be weighed (rhetoric), nor the connections or consequences be perceived nor the discourse undertaken (logic). Dr. Balthasar Meisner in his *Disput. de Calvinismo fugiendo,* Thesis 83, has aptly said: 'Who among us has ever denied the proper use of reason in theology? Do we not use reason as often as we give attention to the peculiarity of the language or the structure of the entire context? "Faith cometh by hearing" (Rom. 10:17). But for hearing the use of reason is required, to distinguish word from word and to perceive the sense. Thus we do not deny that the use of reason is necessary in confirming, in disproving, in explaining, because in all things the method of instruction and the mode prescribed in logic must be observed.' One must distinguish between the *ministerium* of reason, when like a maid it gives way to the mistress and madam (from the old comparison of Ambrosius, 2. *de Abrahamo,* c. 10) and the *magisterium* of reason, when it arrogates to itself judgment in things about which it is ignorant and which exceed its comprehension. . . . We must distinguish between reason left to itself, or judging according to its natural principles, and reason held locked within the circle of the divine Word and kept under discipline, or illumined by Holy Scripture. That the latter can judge in matters of faith, we do not deny; but we deny that judgment in matters of faith belongs to the former."

By distinguishing between the *usus rationis ministerialis* and *magisterialis* the old theologians also decide the question whether there is a real contradiction between theology and reason, or human science (philosophy). They answer: The truth is but one. A contradiction arises only when reason, gone mad, presumes to judge things that transcend its sphere. Quenstedt writes (*Systema* I, 62): "The opponents raise the objection: religion contains much that is above but nothing that is contrary to reason. We answer: (a) In themselves the articles of faith are not against reason, but solely above reason; *per accidens,* however, it happens that they are also against reason, inasmuch as reason presumes to judge of them according to its principles and does not follow the light of the Word, but denies and impugns them. (b) The articles of faith are not only above, but contrary to, corrupt reason, which judges them to be foolishness. Smalzius insists, Disp. IV, contra Franz., p. 137: 'Let one teach that one sentence of the Sacred Scriptures is opposed to reason and therefore reason is to be silent in the Church.' We answer: Reason remaining in its boundaries, no truth of the Sacred Scriptures conflicts with it, but if reason leaves its boundaries, all mysteries of faith, as the Trinity, the Incarnation, etc., conflict with it." We dare not lull ourselves into believing that the struggle of men against Scripture and the Christian religion with its appeal to reason (science) will ever cease, since "the natural man" (1 Cor. 2:14) is God's enemy (Rom. 8:7) and can only regard what is the essence of Christianity, the Gospel, as foolishness ("they are foolishness unto him; neither can he know them," 1 Cor. 2:14). This being the case, man cannot fail, as long as he has not become a Christian through *contritio* and *fides,* to contend with both his utter ignorance and his limited natural knowledge against Holy

Scripture and the Christian doctrine. Quenstedt says regarding this point (*Systema* I, 63): "We must distinguish between philosophy considered *abstracte* and according to its essence, and philosophy considered *concrete* and according to its existence in the person corrupted by sin. According to the former mode it never is opposed to the divine truth, for there is only one truth . . . harmonious in regard to the objects which are subordinate to it; according to the latter mode, however, it is, because of the ignorance of the intellect and the perversion of the will, frequently employed wrongly by the philosopher for distortion and vain deception."

2. The Scripture principle is abrogated by substituting for it the regenerate reason, or, as it is also called, pious self-consciousness, Christian experience, Christian Ego, faith consciousness, faith, spirit, etc. We have already seen (p. 66 ff.) that all these sources and norms, when they are used alongside and apart from the Bible, are simply illusions. To ascribe to the new, or regenerate, man the folly of disregarding Scripture and teaching his own ideas is to insult him. Where that is done, the old man, not the new man, is playing the theologian. The new man knows the Scriptures to be the very Word of God (John 8:47: "He that is of God heareth God's words") and follows the general rule given the Church: "If any man speak, let him speak as the oracles of God" (1 Pet. 4:11). Whenever the Christian recollects what his real nature is, he recognizes that the inclination to teach from his own Ego instead of from Scripture is an erring, yea, wicked self-consciousness, for which he implores God's forgiveness. Following the example of Luther and the old Lutheran theologians, Walther unceasingly inculcated this truth. He wrote for example: "Also the illumined and regenerate reason cannot be made the principle of knowledge alongside Scripture, co-ordinate with it, since the very essence of the illumined, or regenerate, reason consists in this, that it makes the Scriptures and not itself the principle of knowledge in matters of faith (2 Cor. 10:5), not to mention the fact that on this side of heaven there is no man with a perfectly renewed and illumined reason (Gen. 18:10-15)." (*Lehre und Wehre* 13, 99.)[7] In

---

[7] Quenstedt also points this out over against the Calvinists, who likewise appealed to the regenerate reason as source and norm of the Christian doctrine: "The Calvinists urge that they here understand the regenerate reason, or human reason after spiritual regeneration has taken place. Thus Calvin, *Inst.* IV, 17, 26. . . . B. Dannhauer answers: 'This objection would have some weight if reason in man had remained pure, without the streaming into it of a spring that has remained sin-stained unto this hour; but the water is polluted, similar to sweet water which is at least suspected of being poisonous, because every

short, the attempt of modern theology to make the "regenerate Ego" the principle of knowledge of the Christian doctrine, while at the same time rejecting Scripture as the Word of God and the only source and norm of theology, amounts in fact to an attempt to make the natural human Ego, the flesh, ruler in the Church. It is plain rationalism in the mantle of Christianity. The opinion voiced by Dr. Stoeckhardt in a discussion of Frank's theology (*Lehre und Wehre* 42, 74 f.) is perfectly correct: "Frank's theology, which battles against the rationalism of Ritschl, is itself nothing but a new style and edition of rationalism, rationalism in churchly dress. It is the natural reason which in Frank's systems plucks apart, dismembers the Christian realities, and then again joins and harmonizes them. It is a miracle that the mill of Frank's reason has not ground up all Christian dogmas, that Frank still permits certain elements of the Christian truth to stand. That is not due to the system, it is inconsistency. . . . This 'I,' which by its own authority passes judgment in matters of faith and truth, which fabricates and sets up dogmas, which from within constructs God, heaven, earth, and everything, in an arbitrary manner, is at bottom the 'I,' the 'spirit,' the 'inner light,' of the 'enthusiasts.'" Whatever is vaunted as the Spirit without the Word is never the Holy Ghost. Luther: "The Holy Spirit does not work without the Word or before the Word, but He comes with and through the Word and never goes beyond the Word" (St. L. XI:1073).

3. The Scripture principle is rejected by the demand that the Christian doctrine must not be taken from the passages that treat of the individual doctrines (*sedes doctrinae*), but from "the whole of Scripture." This phrase, which certainly makes no sense, has been given currency again by "the Reformer of the 19th century," Schleiermacher. He says (*Glaubenslehre* I, § 30): "Quoting individual Bible passages in dogmatics is a very precarious, yes, in and by itself an unsatisfactory procedure." But this senseless phrase has been adopted by practically all chief representatives of modern theology, from the extreme left to the extreme right wing. We find it in Ihmels (*Zentralfragen*, 2d ed., p. 88 f.) and prior to that in Hofmann (*Schriftbeweis*, 2d ed., I, p. 671 ff.). Kliefoth is right when in his criticism of Hofmann's *Schriftbeweis* he calls this contrast between the whole of Scripture and the individual passages an "inconceivable concept."[8]

---

imagination of man's heart is only evil continually. And was not Sarah regenerated? And still she laughed at and even derided the promise of God as a paradox.'"

[8] *Der Schriftbeweis des Dr. J. Ch. K. v. Hofmann*, p. 32.

In fact, we can obtain the whole body of the Christian doctrine only by taking each doctrine from those passages – considered of course in their context – which treat of that specific doctrine. The "whole of Scripture," or the "whole of the Christian doctrine," which is constructed without considering the individual passages that treat of the doctrine, is purely man's own product. This queer talk of the "whole of Scripture" as opposed to the *sedes doctrinae* was invented to block the authority of Scripture entirely, while making a pretense of strict conformity to Scripture, and to make room in the Church for the theology of the "pious self-consciousness" of the theologizing subject. Kliefoth has uttered the warning that this "inconceivable concept" of the whole of Scripture is no "harmless" phrase "if it happens to enter into brainless heads, as examples show." Kliefoth's expression is strong and discourteous, but no stronger and more discourteous than the terms we find, e. g., in 1 Tim. 6:4: "He is bloated, knowing nothing." To complete the picture, it should be added that not only the heads into which that "inconceivable concept" enters, but also the heads in which it originated belong in the category of the heads mentioned by Kliefoth. For this phrase owes its origin solely to the blindness – one might call it the blindness κατ' ἐξοχήν – in which a person who claims to be a teacher in the Christian Church does not yet recognize, or no longer recognizes, God's Word as God's Word, rejects it as the source and norm of the Christian doctrine, and is therefore engaged in substituting for the εἷς διδάσκαλος, who is Christ in His Word (Matt. 23:8; John 8:31-32), the self-consciousness of the theologizing human subject. This ignorance is so great that even Christ is amazed over it: "Why do ye not understand My speech?" (John 8:43.)

4. The Scripture principle is denied by making the Church, the doctrinal decrees of the Church (councils, synods), the Pope, etc., the arbiters of truth. According to Scripture the Church has no doctrine of its own, no doctrine alongside and without Christ's Word. Christ is her εἷς διδάσκαλος, εἷς καθηγητής (Matt. 23:8, 10). The Church is commanded to teach the Word of Christ (Matt. 28:20). The Church has Christ's Word in the Word of His Apostles and Prophets (John 17:20; Eph. 2:20; 1 Pet. 1:10-12), and in this Word the Church continues at Christ's express command (John 8:31-32; John 15:7: "If ye abide in Me and My words abide in you"). In so far as the Church does not continue in Christ's Word, but teaches the word of man, it forgets its calling and is "prattling," as Luther drastically puts it.[9]

---

[9] This has been fully discussed p. 55 ff.

The teachers who do not bring Christ's doctrine, or, in other words, the doctrine of the Apostles, are not to be received as brethren in the faith, but are to be carefully and strictly avoided as sectarians (2 John 9-11; Rom. 16:17). That the voice of the Church and the voice of Holy Scripture are not two different voices, but one and the same voice, Luther showed conclusively when Erasmus offered to subject his understanding to the Church, even if he did not understand Scripture. Luther tells him: "What is that you say, Erasmus? Is it not enough that you subject your mind to the Scriptures? Do you subject it to the decisions of the Church also? What can the Church decide that has not previously been decided in the Scriptures?" (St. L. XVIII, 1678.) The Apology calls what the Apostles and Prophets teach in their Scriptures the *consensus ecclesiae,* the harmonious doctrine of the whole Christian Church. "He [Peter, Acts 10:43] cites the agreement of all the Prophets. This is truly to cite the authority of the Church." "The consensus of the Prophets is assuredly to be judged as the consensus of the Church universal." "For Peter clearly cites the consensus of the Prophets, and the writings of the Apostles testify that they believe the same thing." (*Trigl.* 145, 83; 271, 66; 273, 73.) We know, then, what to think of those who place the consensus of the Church on the level with the Scriptures as source and norm of doctrine, be it the consensus of the Church of all ages or only the consensus of a few centuries.[10] All are *eo ipso* renouncing the Scripture principle. That is the case even when they want to call the consensus of the Church the "secondary principle." In practice the secondary principle becomes the primary principle. For the secondary principle has been invented for the purpose of interpreting Holy Scripture or of limiting it. Whatever is made the arbiter of interpretation is placed above Scripture and is used to restrict its authority. Scripture sinks to the level of a *norma normata.* That was the intention, in spite of their protestations to the contrary, of both Vincens of Lerinum (d. 450) and of Geo. Calixt (d. 1656) and other Helmstedt theologians.[11]

With respect to the testimony of the Church two extremes must be avoided. First, Christians and Christian theologians do not despise

---

[10] William Laud, Archbishop of Canterbury, d. 1645. R. E., 2d ed., VIII, 485 ff. On Calixt's *Consensus quinquesaecularis* see Quenstedt, I, 65 *sq.* Kahnis, *Innerer Gang,* 3d ed., I, 105: "When Calixt spoke of two principles in the Church, namely, Scripture and tradition, this was manifestly done at the cost of the Protestant Scripture principle and was again a leaning toward the Roman Church" (Baier-Walther, I, 87).

[11] Quenstedt, I, 65 *sq.* Kahnis' judgment in the preceding note is very mild.

this testimony, but take note of it, rejoice over it, and are confirmed in their faith when they see that God also in former ages raised up witnesses of the truth revealed in Scripture.[12] Secondly, they do not overestimate the witness of the Church, as though it could be the foundation of the Christian faith without or alongside Scripture. Rather do they maintain that neither the pronouncements of individuals nor the resolutions of any number of persons *(ecclesia repraesentativa)* can make doctrines of faith or be their basis.[13] The old Lutheran teachers also, by the way, refer to the fact that there is no consensus of the Church at all outside and alongside the Scriptures, not even if the consensus is limited to the first 500 years. Quenstedt gives the following reasons for this: "Many writings of the old teachers have never been published; few of those that have been published have

---

[12] Thus the Augustana repeatedly pleads that it teaches no novelties but is professing only such doctrines as have had the testimony of the ancient Church (*Trigl.*, pp. 51, 59, 61, 93). Likewise the Formula of Concord. (*Trigl.* 1037, 64; cf. the Catalogus Testimoniorum, p. 1107 ff.) – Chemnitz says in his *Examen Concilii Tridentini,* Geneva, 1667, p. 71, in the chapter De Traditionibus: "Andradius has done us wrong in that he claims that in general we make nothing of the testimony of antiquity, that the authority of the Fathers means nothing, that we impair the approbation of the Church, its faith, and its majesty. However, with a good conscience we can affirm that after the study of Holy Scripture we have in our inquiry and investigation of the consensus of the true and purer antiquity stood for as much as agreed with the grace of God and do stand for that today. For we give to the writings of the Fathers their proper and honorable place, which is due them, as men who have explained many passages of Scripture very clearly and defended the ancient doctrines of the Church against the new corruptions of the heretics, and that from Scripture, explaining many doctrinal passages correctly." Chemnitz then demonstrates this by particular instances.

[13] Cp. the relevant words of the Smalcald Articles: "The Papists quote here Augustine and some of the Fathers who are said to have written concerning purgatory, and they think that we do not understand for what purpose and to what end they spoke as they did. St. Augustine does not write that there is a purgatory, nor has he a testimony of Scripture to constrain him thereto, but he leaves it in doubt whether there is one, and says that his mother asked to be remembered at the altar or Sacrament. Now, all this is indeed nothing but the devotion of men, and that, too, of individuals, and does not establish an article of faith, which is the prerogative of God alone. Our Papists, however, cite such statements [opinions] of men in order that men should believe in their horrible, blasphemous, and cursed traffic in masses for souls in purgatory. . . . For it will not do to frame articles of faith from the works or words of the holy Fathers; otherwise their kind of fare, of garments, of house, etc., would have to become an article of faith, as was done with relics. [We have, however, another rule, namely] The rule is: The Word of God shall establish articles of faith, and no one else, not even an angel." *Trigl.* 465, 13 ff. See also the clear-cut and concise declaration of the F. C., both in the Epitome and in the Solida Declaratio, regarding the specific difference between Holy Scripture and all other writings, the Symbols included (*Trigl.* 777, 1, 2, 7, 8; 851, 3).

come down to us, most of them having been lost; many of the Fathers, especially of the earliest times, wrote little or nothing, and what is left is mutilated, falsified, and corrupted." And as the last and chief reason Quenstedt mentions: "The consensus of a few Fathers does not at once become the consensus of the whole Church." [14] The rule of Vincens of Lerinum that "*quod ubique, quod semper, quod ab omnibus creditum est*" must be accepted as truth [15] cannot be carried out in practice. The Romanists cut the Gordian knot by withdrawing behind the Pope as the authoritative interpreter of the doctrinal tradition. Protestant representatives of the principle of tradition, as Calixt, for instance, are obliged to depend on the writers of the histories of dogma; they thus miss Scripture and land in the sphere of human authority.

The Roman theologians enumerate as principles of theology Holy

---

[14] The entire section in Quenstedt (I, 66) is instructive and interesting. "The conclusion is proved: By the nullity or nonexistence of that consensus. Many writings of the ancient doctors of the Church were never published; few of those that were published have come down to us; very many have perished; also many of the Fathers, particularly of the earliest antiquity, wrote little or nothing, and whatever is now left as writings of the Fathers is mutilated, interpolated, and corrupted. The consensus, however, of a few Fathers is not immediately the consensus of the whole Church. – The adversaries counter: The best writings of the Fathers, however, have been preserved by the providence of heaven, while the less valuable have perished. But who will convince us of this? Who writes the laws for divine providence? Or who will convince us that in the burning of the Alexandrian library, which Gallius reports lib. VI, Noc. Att. c. ult., or in the burning of the Diocletian library, of which Dr. Dannhauer tells in *Christeid.*, p. 231, only the less valuable documents perished while those worthy of immortality escaped the teeth of fate. Luther rather ascribes more to divine providence in his preface to the First Wittenberg Part, namely, 'that by no means a small part of the ecclesiastical writers perished, so that men would not find the time which they should devote to the reading and scrutiny of Scripture taken up by the study of the wallowing of the Fathers and the councils.' – They insist that from the published writings we can satisfactorily estimate the consensus of the ancient Church. I answer: I concede that it is possible to estimate *particulariter et probabiliter*, but I deny this with reference to the Christian faith; it is possible in those cases in which there appears a unanimous decision, not in others, where they themselves are divided; it is possible to estimate it if in any one tradition of the faith they manifestly, universally, and constantly agree in one and the same sense: Thus, for example, on the Canon of Scripture we have a very fine agreement of the old doctors if you take the testimonies collectively through five or more centuries; but this consensus is not in like manner apparent in the doctrines. How much discrepancy in the writings of the Fathers also in regard to the sense of Scripture! How great often the gulf of time! What empty spaces where no books have appeared! That consensus of five centuries deals solely with co-eval controversies, not with heresies born after the five centuries."

[15] R. Seeberg, *Dogmeng.*, 1895, I, 328 f.

Scripture, tradition, the Councils, the Pope.[16] In the *Tridentinum*, Sess. IV, we read: "This truth and discipline are contained in the written books and the unwritten traditions, which . . . [the Synod], following the examples of the orthodox Fathers, receives and venerates with an equal affection of piety and reverence. But if anyone . . . knowingly and deliberately contemn the traditions aforesaid, let him be anathema." But since the final interpretation of Scripture, tradition, the decrees of Councils, etc., rests in the hands of the Pope, he is in the end the only principle of papistic theology.[17] The Papal infallibility had long ago been asserted by individual theologians and whole groups. But they disagreed on the question whether the Pope was infallible together with the Church (i. e., the Councils and the teachers of the Church) or whether he was infallible by himself. The latter view, espoused by the Jesuits, won and in 1870 was made the dogma for the whole Church. Pius IX declared: "We, the sacred Council approving, teach and so define as dogma divinely revealed, that the Roman Pontiff, when he speaks *ex cathedra* – that is to say, when in the discharge of his office of pastor and teacher of all Christians, by virtue of his supreme Apostolic authority, he defines a doctrine regarding faith and morals to be held by the universal Church – is, through the divine assistance promised to the blessed Peter himself, possessed of the infallibility with which the divine Redeemer willed that His Church should be endowed for defining doctrine concerning faith and morals; and that therefore such definitions of the Roman Pontiff are of themselves, and not from the consent of the Church, unalterable." [18] Roman theology, in so far as it is determined by the "infallibility" of the Pope, has as its principle the Satanic insolence of him who as God sits in the temple of God and acts as though he were

---

[16] Thus Bellarmine, *De Conciliis*, II, 12, 1, states the four principles: "The written Word of God, the unwritten traditions, the authority of the Councils, and the Roman Pope" (see Quenstedt, I, 53). In the *Roman Catechism, Prooem.*, qu. 12, we read: "The contents of every doctrine which is to be communicated to the faithful are contained in the Word of God, which is divided into Scripture and the traditions."

[17] Huelsemann: "Though they pretend that their faith rests on Sacred Scripture and the prime truth, understood according to the sense of the Church Universal, they nevertheless make the interpretation of the Church Universal depend on the interpretation of one man, who is called by them the Roman Pontifex" (*Anti-Bellarminus*, cap. I, thes. 20, quoted by Quenstedt, I, 53).

[18] Constitutio dogmatica prima de ecclesia Christi, edita, in Sess. IV, Concilii Vaticani: "Pastor aeternus." A. 1870, d. 18 Iulii. See *Die Kanones und Beschluesse des Vatikanischen Konzils*, deutsch-lateinische Ausg. von G. Schneemann, 1871, p. 45 *sq.* – Baier-Walther, I, 81.

God (2 Thess. 2:4). Instead of continuing, according to the divine order, in Christ's Word, Roman theology sets above Christ's Word the monstrous lie of Papal infallibility, which infallibility was conceived by Satan and finds acceptance among men through the working of Satan (2 Thess. 2:9-12). – This matter will be treated more fully in the chapter on "The Public Ministry," under "The Antichrist" in Vol. III.

Roman theologians, particularly, appeal to Matt. 28:20 as proof that the testimony of the Church is a theological principle alongside the Word of Scripture. The argument runs thus: Here Christ promises His gracious and sustaining presence to His Church "unto the end of the world"; therefore it were but reasonable to assume that the Church would not err in the proclamation of the truth which it is commissioned to teach. This argument has confused some. But the very passage cited shows the futility of the argument. Christ promises, in Matt. 28:20, the Church His gracious presence after He has directed it to teach only His Word: "Teaching them to observe all things whatsoever I have commanded you." Christ is present with His Church through His gracious revelation and His gracious help in His Word, which the Church is commanded to teach. In so far, therefore, as the Church teaches and confesses Christ's Word, it can, indeed, not err; in so far, however, as it teaches anything without and alongside Christ's Word, it is not only not infallible, but also certainly errs.

5. The Scripture principle is abrogated and natural reason substituted through the appeal to private revelations, also called "immediate revelations," or "new revelations" (*revelationes immediatae, revelationes novae*). By private revelations are meant such revelations regarding the Christian doctrine as some people are supposed to have received by visions, appearances, inner voice, inner light, etc. Through these private, or immediate, revelations the doctrinal revelation contained in Scripture is supposed to be explained, corrected, and supplemented. The Christian Church has in all ages been disturbed by persons who boasted new revelations alongside the Word of the Prophets and Apostles. This was the case already in the Apostolic Church. We see from such passages as 1 Cor. 14:37 and 2 Thess. 2:2 that in the Apostolic congregations "prophets" and "spiritual persons" appeared who pretended that their word was co-ordinate with the Word of the Apostles and for that reason were sharply called to order by Paul. Later there arose the Montanists, the Donatists, the Messalians, and others. At the time of the Reformation the Anabaptists, Schwenkfeldians, and others made their appearance, who rejected

Luther's insistence on the sole authority of Holy Scripture as "letter worship" and opposed the "external word" of Scripture with their so-called "inner" word as a higher revelation.[19] In the era following up to the present time are found the Quakers, Labadists, Swedenborgians, Irvingites, Amana Society, Mormons, etc.[20] In general, all who divorce the operation of the Holy Ghost from the Word of Scripture make private or immediate revelations their principle in theology. It is essentially correct to embrace them all under the general title *Schwaermer*, or "enthusiasts" (*fanatici, enthusiastae*).

a. This includes, first, the Papists, in so far as they make the Pope an infallible teacher outside and beyond the written Word of God. Luther depicted the situation correctly when he wrote in the Smalcald Articles: "For (indeed) the Papacy also is nothing but sheer enthusiasm, by which the Pope boasts that all rights exist in the shrine of his heart (*in scrinio sui pectoris*), and whatever he decides and commands with (in) his Church is spirit and right, even though it is above and contrary to Scripture and the spoken Word." And again: "Enthusiasm . . . is the origin . . . of the Papacy." (*Trigl.* 495, 4; 497, 9.)

b. All Reformed, like Zwingli and Calvin and recent Reformed theologians, such as Shedd, Hodge, and Boehl, inasmuch as they maintain that the Holy Spirit works with His saving operation immediately, outside and apart from the Word. Efficacious grace acts immediately. (See "The Cause of the Divisions Within Visible Christendom.")

c. All modern theologians, in so far as they deny that the Scriptures are God's infallible Word and hence, as a matter of principle,

---

[19] Luther describes the nature of Carlstadt and his ilk in his book *Wider die himmlischen Propheten* (St. L. XX:202 ff.) as follows: "What God ordains externally as the adjunct to the Spirit inwardly, as we have said, oh, how disdainfully and scoffingly does he [Carlstadt] cast that aside and wants to get into the Spirit *beforehand*. . . . If you ask them: How does one get that high Spirit? they do not direct you to the external Gospel, but to a utopia and say: Stand and wait, as I have waited for a long time; then you will experience it; the heavenly voice will come and God Himself will speak to you. . . . Do you not see the devil here, that enemy of divine order, how he gets you to gape by his shouting: 'The Spirit, the Spirit, the Spirit!' and all the while he is tearing up the bridges, highway and by-way, ladder, and everything by which the Spirit is really to come to you, namely, the external ordinances of God in the material Baptism, the written and oral Word of God, and wants to teach you, not how the Spirit will come to you, but how you should come to the Spirit, that you should learn to float on the clouds and ride the wind; and still they will not tell you how or when, where or what, but tell you that you must experience it yourself just as they."

[20] For proofs see Guenther, *Symbolik*, p. 90 ff. (*Popular Symbolics*, p. 378 ff.; 388 ff.; 323 ff.; 423 f.; 440 ff.)

make the "pious self-consciousness," the "religious experience," etc., the source and norm of the Christian doctrine. This false teaching regarding the principle of theology coincides in its nature with the "*in scrinio pectoris papae*" and with Zwingli's: "For the Spirit no guide or vehicle is required, for He is Himself the Power and Conveyer who bears all things; He Himself does not need to be borne." Accordingly we noted that the invectives used by modern theologians (paper pope, letter theology, intellectualism, etc.) for the purpose of holding up to suspicion and of rejecting the Scripture principle coincide in kind with the invectives which the Roman theologians and the Reformed 'enthusiasts' employed against Luther and the Lutheran Church. (See the section "Theology as Doctrine.") So also the outcome of the modern theology, in so far as it replaces the Scripture principle with the principle of experience, is identical with that of the Papistic and Reformed "enthusiasts." Luther: "They speak such things only in order to lead us away from Scripture and make themselves masters over us, that we should believe their dream sermons." (St. L. V:334.) [21]

---

[21] Quenstedt (I, 70 *sq.*) lists the "enthusiasts" up to his day. This list, because of the remarks interspersed, is interesting and informative. He writes: "Antithesis: 1. Various fanatics who state: 'The knowledge of God and of all the doctrines to be believed must be sought not in the written Word of God, but from the exclusive revelation given specially to the individual and from the congenital light, from raptures, dreams, conversations with angels, from the internal word, from the inspiration *(Einsprechen)* of the heavenly Father, from the information given them internally by Christ, who is essentially united with them, from the teaching of the Holy Ghost, who is speaking from within them – all of which constitutes a higher wisdom than that contained in the Holy Scriptures.' It is certain that ever so many fanatics, ancient and modern, were seized by such 'enthusiasm'; among the ancients can be named the Montanists, Donatists, Adelphius. . . . The words of the *Hist. Tripart.* are these: 'This heresy came from the disturbance of the Messalians, who were called the εὐχήτας, i. e., the "pray-ers" *(orantes)*. They were, however, also called by the other name of ἐνθουσιασταί, i. e., men breathed upon, and *divini*. For they expect the operation of some demon, whom they call the presence of the Holy Spirit. Those who have given themselves over entirely to this disease, despise any manual labor as evil, give themselves over to dreaming, and call their dreams and phantasies prophecies. The leaders of this heresy were Dadoes and Sabbas and Adelphius, Hermas and Symeones, and others.' More recent 'enthusiasts' are those who . . . came forth out of the nether world . . . under the leadership and auspices of Thomas Muenzer, that seditious forerunner of the Anabaptists, in Thuringia, Caspar of Schwenkfeld in Silesia, Theophrastus Paracelsus in Switzerland, Coppinus and Quintinus in Picardy, Valentin Weigel in Meissen. All these contended that not merely the written Word of God, but also revelations, enthusiasms, dreams, and the immediate voice of God were to be heard and according to these things the government of the Church was to be organized. . . . To these add the Rosicrucian brethren and the recent prophets John Warner and George Richard, the Quakers, or Tremblers, in England, who also dream

Scripture has definitely decided the question what one is to think of doctrinal revelations which are above and beyond Scripture. There is no promise of such revelations; on the contrary, God has directed and bound all Christians to the Last Day to the Word of the Apostles and Prophets. With this Word the period of divine revelation is closed. All Christians to the end of time come to faith through the Word of the Apostles (John 17:20). The Church is built on the foundation of the Apostles and Prophets (Eph. 2:20). Our old theologians are right in calling attention, again and again, to the axiom which holds true of all pretended sources of theological knowledge, distinct and independent of Scripture: "New revelations in regard to the Christian doctrine either coincide with the doctrine contained in Scripture, and then they are superfluous, or they offer something else than is recorded in the Word of the Apostles and Prophets, and then they are to be rejected" (Rom. 16:17; 1 Tim. 6:3 ff.; Luke 16:29-31).

The question has often been asked whether divine revelations pertaining to external events in Church or world might not be given to individual persons in our time. It does not contradict Scripture to

---

of divine raptures and immediate revelations. Thus also Jean de Labadie has publicly boasted of heavenly revelations, of talks with the blessed saints, and of appearances of the blessed Virgin Mary granted him while praying, and also his followers; they assert that God often deals with the faithful without the Word of God and accordingly admonish men 'to seek refuge in the internal revelations of the Spirit and give diligent attention to them.' Also Anna von Schuermann attempts to prove in her *Eukleria*, p. 80, that 'besides Scripture there are also given today doctrinal prophecies and internal revelations.' 2. The Papists, of whom Dr. Dannhauer (*Hodom. Spiritus Pap. Phantasm.*, I, p. 61 *sq.*) shows that they admit among the fundamentals of faith revelations given to individuals, e. g., Brigitta, Catherine of Siena. . . . 3. The Socinians. Thus Faustus Socinus expresses it as his opinion, against Joh. Erasmus, p. 166, that Laelius Socinus . . . by many prayers obtained from Christ Himself the interpretation of those words of Christ, John 8:52: 'Before Abraham became the father of many nations, I am the light of the world,' and that this was revealed to him by God Himself. Osterodus, *Instit. Germ.*, c. 1, regards immediate revelations or special internal illuminations necessary for understanding the prophetic Scripture and the largest part of the Apocalypse of John. . . . 4. Some of the Calvinists. Thus Andrew Carlstadt regarded private revelations and visions highly; Luther refuted him in his book *Contra coelestes prophetas*, Tom. III, Ienens.; cf. Sleidanus, III, 61; V, 117, where he says: 'This man of whom we spoke above, Carlstadt, disagreeing with Luther, left Wittenberg and became very friendly with those secret teachers who simulated visions and talks with God.' And Huld. Zwingli, who claims that the Spirit revealed to him through a special revelation that the word *'est'* in the words of the institution of the Lord's Supper is written there for *'significat.'* For this reason Dr. Dannhauer, *Hodom. Spirit. Calv. Phantas*, I, 9, p. 59 says: 'If you look at the beginning, Calvinism owes the fanatical enthusiasm of Carlstadt and Zwingli not a little, although later this seems to have died out.'"

admit the possibility and fact of such revelations.[22] But it is contrary to Scripture to assume that new revelations on doctrine will be given; the revelation of doctrine has come to an end with the Word of the Apostles and Prophets.[23]

6. The Scripture principle is denied by the demand that the Christian religion be interpreted "historically." We have already shown, in the chapter on "Christianity the Absolute Religion," and more particularly in the chapter on "Theology as Doctrine," in what sense Christianity can very well be called an historical phenomenon and in what sense the "historical interpretation" is definitely to be declined. The latter must be done when the so-called "historical interpretation" is used to criticize the Christian doctrine, which is contained in Holy Scripture. This is done on the part of modern theologians when they set aside Scripture as source and norm of Christian doctrine and offer us in place of that their "historical interpretation." We have already quoted Richard Gruetzmacher's correct remark that "for us the historical revelation of salvation is contained solely in the record of it given in Holy Scripture." What we know of Christ and His doctrine we know solely from Christ's Word, which we possess in the written Word of His Apostles and Prophets and to which Christ so emphatically directs us as to the sole medium of knowing the truth (John 8). Whoever discards this sole source and norm of the Christian doctrine and instead directs us to the historical interpretation of the student of history, is asking us to substitute human authority for the divine authority of Holy Scripture. The neologists who misuse the term "history" by opposing the Christ in His Word with the "historical Christ" ought to be able to see that they are offering the Church a product of the human Ego. The actual "historical Christ" is Christ in His Word. Luther says in his "Word of Warning to the People of Frankfurt on the Main": "Outside His Word and without His Word we know of no Christ, much less of Christ's teaching. For the 'Christ' who pretends to bring His teaching without His Word is the abomi-

---

22 Examples in Scripture (Acts 11:27-28; 21:10-11). In church history: John Hilten's prophecy of the coming of Luther (*Trigl.* 419, 1–4). It is added: "The outcome will teach how much weight should be given to this declaration."

23 Quenstedt says on this score (I, 75): "We must distinguish between revelations which pertain to, or attack, an article of faith, and those which concern the state of the Church or the State, social life,. and future events; the first we repudiate; the latter, however, some hold, are not to be urged with any necessity of believing, nevertheless are not to be rashly rejected. B. Balduin says in his Commentary on 1 Tim. 4, P. I, q. 1: 'We do not doubt that God to this day at times reveals to some men future things pertaining to the state of the Church or the State, to be announced for the use of men.'"

nable devil out of hell, who uses Christ's holy name and under it is peddling his infernal venom" (St. L. XVII:2015). That is a hard saying which our modern ears can hardly stand. But it states the full truth. It applies fully to the modern theologians who separate the "historical Christ" from the Christ in His Word. – In this connection we ought to recall the admission made by the modern theologians who consistently stand for the historical interpretation of Christianity. They admit that their historical interpretation can never lead to certainty, but would necessarily leave the contents of the Christian doctrine in doubt. (See the chapter "Christianity the Absolute Religion.")

From the above it is clear that the number of essentially different sources and norms of religious knowledge is exactly two. Whatever is not taken entirely from Scripture has its origin in the human Ego and is fittingly given the general name rationalism, whether it is called that outright or whether some euphemistic circumlocution is used. Whoever appeals to natural reason as the source and norm of theology appeals to his natural human Ego, since natural reason knows nothing of the Gospel and, when it does stray into theology (μετάβασις εἰς ἄλλο γένος), necessarily reduces the Christian religion to a system of morality (ethics, *"opinio legis"*), for all that is left to reason is a little knowledge of the divine Law. Whoever appeals to the illumined reason, the regenerate Ego, etc., is likewise appealing to the natural reason, since the illumined reason – or the new man – is so constituted that it will take the Christian doctrine solely from Scripture and judge it solely by Scripture. Whoever attempts to draw the Christian doctrine from the so-called "whole of Scriptures," and not from the specific passages in which the Christian doctrine is revealed, thereby actually declares that he is offering solely a product of his own thoughts to the Church and the world. Whoever appeals to the Church, tradition, the Pope, etc., as source and norm of theology apart from and alongside Scripture, is likewise appealing to human authorities, since the Christian Church has no doctrine whatever apart from and alongside Scripture. Whoever appeals in matters of the Christian doctrine to private revelations apart from and alongside Scripture is likewise making his human Ego the source and norm of Christian doctrine, because the Christian doctrine is set down in the Word of the Apostles and Prophets as a fixed quantity, adding to or subtracting from which is forbidden to all men. And we have seen that also by the so-called "historical interpretation" of Christianity fallible human opinion is made the teacher in the house of God instead of the certain infallible Word of God.

We conclude this section with a remark of Luther in the Smalcald Articles: "In a word, 'enthusiasm' inheres in Adam and his children from the beginning [from the first fall] to the end of the world, [its poison] having been implanted and infused in them by the old dragon, and is the origin, power [life], and strength of all heresy" (*Trigl.* 497, 9). Whoever is no longer dominated by the 'enthusiasm' should in no wise credit that to himself, but should ascribe it alone to the gracious working of God, just as Luther ascribed to the grace of God his ability to dismiss all thoughts that arose in his mind without God's Word.

2

Holy Scripture Identical with the Word of God

The chief fault which modern theology finds in the Early Church, in Luther, and in the Lutheran dogmaticians, is that they "identify" Scripture with the Word of God. We have already heard the remark of Nitzsch-Stephan: "The fault [of the old dogmaticians] . . . lies in this, that they did not at all distinguish between the Bible and God's Word, or did so imperfectly" (*Ev. Dogmatik*, p. 245). Ihmels subscribes to this verdict, extending the censure at the same time to the Early Church and the Church of the Reformation. He says: "The old dogmatics sought to safeguard the uniqueness of Christianity by basing Christianity on a most unique supernatural revelation. . . . Revelation is thereby taken by it in an essentially intellectualistic meaning and is virtually *identified* with Scripture. . . . That is the fruition which descended from the first age of the Church. . . . The Church of the Reformation was much concerned about the pure doctrine, and this interest would seem to be best guaranteed by protecting this doctrine directly with the authority of the divine revelation. A second consideration was added, which more than ever seemed to be demanded by the immediate practical need of the Reformation. The Church of the Reformation rejected absolutely the authority of Rome, but it had no substitute but the authority of Scripture; and this authority seemed to be best safeguarded by identifying Scripture with God's Word. However, as understandable as all this may be, considered historically, nevertheless, considered *fundamentally*, the verdict stands that there is an incongruity between the conception of Scripture by the Church of the Reformation [which identified Scripture with God's Word] and revelation." (*Zentralfragen*, 2d ed., p. 56 ff.) But what modern theology so unanimously, on the part of both the liberal and the "positive," "conservative" wing, stamps as a "fault" in the Apostolic Church, in Luther, and in the old dogmaticians, that is the only correct position. It is what Scripture teaches of itself. Scripture teaches the identity of Scripture and God's Word in several ways.

a. The Scriptures of the Old Testament are quoted in the New Testament plainly as God's Word. The words of Is. 7:14: "Behold, a virgin shall be with Child and shall bring forth a Son," are quoted in Matt. 1:22-23 as "spoken of the Lord by the Prophet." When Hos. 11:1: "Out of Egypt have I called My Son," is adduced in Matt. 2:15, it is at once stated of these words that they were "spoken of the Lord." Ps. 2:1: "Why do the heathen rage and the people imagine a vain thing?" is quoted in Acts 4:25 with the remark that God spoke this by the mouth of His servant David. When Is. 6:9-10 is brought to the attention of the Jews in Rome: "Go unto this people and say, Hearing ye shall hear and shall not understand; and seeing ye shall see and not perceive," it is plainly stated in Acts 28:25 ff.: "Well spake the Holy Ghost by Esaias the Prophet unto our fathers." Heb. 3:7 it is said of a quotation from Psalm 95: "As the Holy Ghost saith, Today if ye will hear His voice, harden not your hearts." Rom. 3:2 the entire Scriptures of the Old Testament, committed to the Jews, are called "the oracles of God," God's sayings, God's words. And because the entire Scripture of the Old Testament is God's Word, Christ says of it (John 10:35) that it cannot be broken in one single word – the one single word here being the word *elohim*, אֱלֹהִים, θεοί, gods, as used of government officials.

There is another lengthy series of Scripture passages which must not be overlooked when the question is raised whether Scripture and the Word of God are one and the same or not. These are the passages which state that all events in the world are directed by the Word of Scripture. All that has taken place and will take place, from the beginning to the end of the world, takes place because it is so written. Thus the birth of Christ from the Virgin Mary occurred "that (ἵνα) it might be fulfilled which was spoken of the Lord by the Prophet" (Matt. 1:22). John 17:12 Jesus speaks of the defection and end of Judas and adds: "That (ἵνα) the Scripture might be fulfilled." When Peter seeks with the sword to prevent the arrest of Jesus in the Garden, Jesus intervenes with the words: "But how then shall the Scriptures be fulfilled, that thus it must be?" (Matt. 26:54.) And of all that happened to Christ, especially His suffering and the ensuing glory, Christ says: "All things must be fulfilled which were written in the Law of Moses and in the Prophets and in the Psalms concerning Me" (Luke

24:44). If all things written in Scripture must be fulfilled, Scripture cannot be the word of man, but must be the Word of Him who holds everything in heaven and on earth in the hollow of His hand, who guides all events, without whom nothing in heaven and on earth can occur, who is omnipotent and all-knowing, who is, in short, the great majestic God Himself. – Olshausen says concerning the quotations from the Old Testament in the New Testament: "The quotations from the Old Testament in the New Testament are not adduced as mere corroborations drawn from humanly important writings, but as irrefutable proofs from divine books. They possessed this convincing power because they proceeded not from human sages, but from men who were moved by the Holy Ghost." [24]

b. The same applies to the writings of the Apostles of the New Testament. 1 Pet. 1:10-12 proves that these writings, too, were God's own Word. Peter first states concerning the Prophets of the Old Testament that they prophesied by "the Spirit of Christ, which was in them," of the grace that should come in the New Testament era, but then adds concerning the Apostles of the New Testament: "which are now [in the New Testament era] reported unto you by them that have preached the Gospel unto you with the Holy Ghost sent down from heaven." It is here clearly taught that, like the Word of the Prophets of the Old Testament, so also the Word of the Apostles of the New Testament is the Word of the Holy Ghost. The objection that Peter here refers only to the preached word and not to the writings of the Apostles is not valid, since the Apostles expressly declare that they wrote the identical things which they preached. Thus the Apostle John (1 John 1:3-4): "That which we have seen and heard declare we unto you . . . and these things write we unto you." In like manner the Apostle Paul admonishes the Thessalonians not to make a distinction between his oral Word and his written Word. He says (2 Thess. 2:15): "Therefore, brethren, stand fast, and hold the traditions which ye have been taught, whether by word or our Epistle." The Apostles were also fully aware of speaking and writing not their own, but Christ's Word. We saw above that Paul demands of the "prophets" and "men with the Spirit" in Corinth that they be subject to His Word because, as he says, "the things that I write unto you are the commandments of the Lord" (1 Cor. 14:37). In his Second Epistle to the Corinthians (13:3) he reminds the entire congregation

---

[24] *Nachweis der Echtheit saemtlicher Schriften des Neuen Testaments*, 1832, p. 168.

of the fact that Christ is speaking through him. And when Paul (Gal. 1:8-9) pronounces a curse on everyone preaching "another Gospel" than he himself taught, we have, as has been correctly stated, the choice between but two things: either we must assume that Paul's Word is actually Christ's Word, as he himself asserts in the passages from First and Second Corinthians, or we must assume that he was deranged when he cursed every departure from the Word as proclaimed by him. A third assumption, or a middle course, is out of the question. So abundantly do the Scriptures themselves testify that the Scriptures of both the Old Testament and the New Testament are God's Word. Scripture and God's Word are therefore actually to be "identified."

The Bible is a book truly unique. It is, in distinction from the millions of other books in the world, God's Word. It is in a class by itself. If we, in the external arrangement of the books in a library, wished to show the importance and authority of the books, we should have to place the Holy Scriptures on one side and all the other books on the other side. True, many other books contain God's Word; for example, the writings of Luther. But what there is of God's Word in the other books is taken from the Bible. It is entirely true when Luther in his methodology for the study of theology says that no other book teaches eternal life (namely, correctly) but Scripture alone. (St. L. XIV:434). Scripture is neither a human nor a "divine-human" report on God's Word and the "facts of the revelation," but is itself the Word of God. That is Luther's position as to Scripture. To quote, for the first, only two short words of Luther. He says: "You are so to deal with the Scriptures that you bear in mind that God Himself is saying this" (St. L. III:21). And: "The Holy Scriptures did not grow on earth" (St. L. VII:2095). As spokesman for the old Lutheran dogmaticians, Gerhard writes: "There is no real difference (*non est reale aliquod discrimen*) between God's Word and Holy Scripture" (*locus "De Scriptura Sacra,"* § 7). There is no real difference, but only a difference in expression, between the two terms "Holy Scripture says" and "God says." "Holy Scripture and the Word of God are interchangeable terms."

We are at times apt to lose sight of this truth because the Holy Scriptures speak to us in such simple human terms and also dwell – especially in the Old Testament – on such ordinary affairs of life as the household, agriculture, stock raising, clothes, food, etc. For this reason Holy Scripture fares as did Christ in the days when He walked upon this earth. Because Christ was found in fashion as a man, the

Jewish public took Him for a mere man, like John the Baptist, Elias, Jeremias, or one of the prophets (Matt. 16:14). The same thing happens to Scripture. Because the Scriptures are written in human language, they are not regarded as God's Word, but placed in one class with human books and are even criticized by men. For this reason Luther warns in the preface to the Old Testament: "I beg and faithfully warn every pious Christian not to stumble at the simplicity of the language and the stories that will often meet him here. He should not doubt that however simple they may seem, these are the very words, judgments, and deeds of the high majesty, power, and wisdom of God. For this is Scripture, and it makes fools of all the wise and prudent and is an open book to the small and foolish, as Christ says Matt. 11:25. Therefore dismiss your own thoughts and feelings, and think of the Scriptures as the loftiest and noblest of holy things, as the richest of mines, which can never be exhausted, so that you may find the wisdom of God that He lays before you in such foolish and simple guise, in order that He may quench all pride." (St. L. XIV:3 f.)

3

The Verbal Inspiration of Holy Scripture

The Scriptures not only tell us that they are the Word of God, but they also teach very clearly why they are the Word of God, namely, because they were inspired, or breathed into the writers, by God. 2 Tim. 3:16: "All Scripture is given by inspiration of God." 2 Pet. 1:21: "Holy men of God spake as they were moved by the Holy Ghost." This divine act of inspiration establishes the fact that the Holy Scriptures, though written by men, are the Word of God. The Scripture passages speaking of inspiration contain the following truths:

1. Inspiration does not consist in the so-called subject inspiration *(Realinspiration)*, inspiration of the matter merely, nor in the so-called inspiration of persons (*Personalinspiration*), but it is verbal inspiration, *suggestio verborum*, since the Scriptures, which are said to be inspired, do not consist of things or persons, but of written words. As surely as 2 Tim. 3:16 predicates the θεόπνευστος of the γραφή as subject, so certainly Verbal Inspiration is not a "subtle theory" of the old dogmaticians, but the plain teaching of Scripture itself. 2 Pet. 1:21 teaches the same thing. According to this passage, the holy men of God, being moved by the Holy Ghost, did not merely think or meditate,

but they "spake," that is, uttered words. And the preceding verse (v. 20) expressly states that the reference is to the written words of Holy Scripture; the words uttered by the holy men are defined as the "prophecy of the Scripture." And, according to 1 Cor. 14:37, the Apostle Paul did not merely think or meditate in his heart on the commandments of the Lord, but wrote them to the Corinthians: "The things that I write unto you are the commandments of the Lord." When Hastings says: [25] "Inspiration applies to men, not to written words," he is asserting the very opposite of what Scripture teaches concerning inspiration. Hiley, as quoted by Gaussen,[26] has the correct view: "The miraculous operation of the Holy Ghost [namely, the divine act of inspiration] had not the writers themselves for its object — these were only His instruments, and were soon to pass away — its objects were the holy books themselves." Whoever rejects Verbal Inspiration and will accept only an inspiration of general ideas or of persons, thereby denies — from dogmatic bias — the Scripture doctrine of inspiration. To repeat, Scripture affirms of Scripture, which admittedly consists of words (*verba*), that it is inspired. Quenstedt (I, 107): "The Apostle does not say: 'Everything in Scripture, πάντα ἐν γραφῇ. θεόπνευστα,' but 'All Scripture, πᾶσα γραφὴ, θεόπνευστος,' in order to show that not only the things written about, but also the writing itself is θεόπνευστον. And whatever is said of the whole Scripture must of necessity be understood also of the words, not the most insignificant part of Scripture. For if one little word occurred in Scripture that is not suggested or divinely inspired, it could not be said that 'All Scripture is given by inspiration of God.'" [27]

We are unable to see that the rejection of Verbal Inspiration, while the inspiration of the subjects or of the thoughts is assumed, is based on sound thinking. We can get at the thoughts contained in a book only by means of the words it contains. The situation is the same in a book as in the case of a speech. We get at the thoughts of the

---

[25] *Encyclopedia of Religion and Ethics*, by James Hastings, II, 589.

[26] Richard W. Hiley, *The Inspiration of Scripture*, 1885, p. 50.

[27] The statement in Meusel, *sub* "Inspiration der Heiligen Schrift," is entirely correct: "More or less all the polychrome, modern theories amount to a transformation of the inspiration of Scripture into an illumination of the writers, which differs from the illumination of every believing Christian only in degree." For a while it was the fashion to translate θεόπνευστος (2 Tim. 3:16) not as passive, "breathed by God," but as active, "breathing God." This fashion has died out. Nitzsch-Stephan, p. 263, note 1: "Today the interpretation of θεόπνευστος as *inspired* is universally accepted; cf., e. g., Winer-Schmiedel, *Grammatik des neutestamentlichen Sprachidioms*, 1894, p. 135.21."

speaker only by means of the words he uses, so far as the speaker is able and willing to clothe his thoughts in words. In the same manner we discover the thoughts of the author of a book only by means of the words he uses in that book, so far as the author is able and willing to express his thoughts in the written words. The same thing applies to God's speech and God's Scripture. Presupposing that God wants to deal with men by word of mouth, men have to take note of God's words. Presupposing that God wants to deal with men by the written Word, men must take note of the written words. And since God is the Author of Scripture, we have the great advantage that He is perfectly capable and willing to clothe His thoughts in fully adequate words. Therefore Luther so consistently urges upon every Christian and every theologian to adhere to the exact wording of Scripture. He felt as if every passage of Scripture made the world too narrow for him (St. L. XX:788). He therefore gives the advice, as we have already heard, to cling to the words of Scripture as we cling with our hand to a wall or a tree. But why talk of Luther? Christ Himself has directed us to the words of Scripture. In His temptation He thrice opposes Satan with the words of Scripture and obtains the victory. Furthermore, referring to an individual word of Scripture (*elohim*, θεοί, gods, John 10), He says that Scripture cannot be broken. And He binds us to His own words when He says (John 8): "If ye continue in My Word, then . . . ye shall know the truth." But Christ's words – we have to call attention to this truth again and again – we have in the words of His Apostles, as He expressly says in His high-priestly prayer (John 17) that all Christians to the end of time will believe on Him through their Word, through the Apostles' Word. And the Apostle Paul says (1 Tim. 6:3) of all teachers who do not consent to the wholesome words of our Lord Jesus that they are proud and know nothing and only cause pernicious dispute and strife in the Church. The denial of Verbal Inspiration is unscriptural, foolish, and harmful.

2. Inspiration does not consist in mere divine guidance and protection against error (*assistentia, directio,* or *gubernatio divina*), but is a divine supplying or divine giving of the very words that constitute Scripture. The predicate θεόπνευστος, applied to Scripture, teaches unmistakably that God not merely directed the writing of Scripture, but inspired the Scriptures. Within the Lutheran Church the Helmstedt theologian George Calixt (d. 1656) held that in regard to facts already familiar to the holy writers or to facts of less importance the Holy Ghost merely guided and protected the writers against error. Calixt's doctrine was justly rejected by his Lutheran contemporaries

as unscriptural, because "guided and directed by God" and "θεόπνευστος – given by inspiration of God" are two entirely different concepts. And it is of great practical importance that we permit no one to substitute a mere guidance and preservation from error for the θεόπνευστος. This substitute would at best make Scripture an errorless human word, but never the living, majestic Word of God, throbbing with divine power. Scripture is God's own Word only because of inspiration. Quenstedt (I, 98 *sq.*) writes against Calixt and some Romanists (Bellarmine): "One must distinguish between mere divine assistance and direction by which the holy writers in speaking and writing were only prevented from departing from the truth, and divine assistance and direction which included the inspiration and the dictation of the Holy Ghost. Not the former, but the latter makes the Bible θεόπνευστον."

3. Inspiration covers not only a part of Scripture, e. g., the chief matters, the doctrines, and such things as were before unknown to the writers, etc., but the entire Scriptures. Every part of Scripture is inspired. That, and nothing less, is the meaning of "All Scripture is given by inspiration of God." We would be doing violence to this statement of God if we excepted from inspiration those parts of Scripture that contain historical, geographical, scientific, etc., information or relate matters well known to the holy writers. It is by no means a clever objection to the inspiration of Holy Scripture when modern theologians remark that the Bible is no textbook of history or geography or natural science and that for that reason inspiration could not pertain to the historical, geographical, and scientific data.[28] Of course, it is not the chief purpose of Scripture to give information on such points. The real purpose of Scripture is indicated in passages like John 5:39; 2 Tim. 3:15 ff.; 1 John 1:4. Scripture is to bring us human beings to the knowledge of Christ and thus to salvation. But also the historical data which are found in Scripture (for with His Word God has entered the history of mankind), though mentioned only incidentally, are inspired and infallible, because they are a part of Scripture. More about this later. Quenstedt (I, 98) does not go beyond 2 Tim. 3:16 when he says: "In the manner of inspiration we acknowledge no distinction (among the matters in Holy Scripture) and assert that the divinity inheres uniformly in the entire Scriptures. . . . The Scriptural matters differ in three ways: 1) Some were naturally utterly unknown to the sacred writers, either because of their sublimity, like the mys-

---

[28] Thus also Ihmels, *Zentralfragen*, p. 72.

teries of faith, or because of non-existence, like contingent future events, or because of their being imperceptible to the senses, like the secrets of the heart. 2) Some were naturally indeed knowable, but actually unknown to the sacred writers, because of the antiquity and remoteness of the times and places, unless they accidentally became known to them in some other way, either by rumor, or by tradition, or by some human writing, like the history of the Deluge. . . . 3) Some were not only knowable, but were also naturally known to the public notaries of God through the proper search (historical research of Luke, ch. 1:1 ff.) and by their own observation, as the exodus of Israel from Egypt and the journey in the desert were known to Moses, the history of the Judges to Samuel, the life and deeds of Christ to the Evangelists and Apostles. Certainly not only first-class matters, but also second- and third-class matters were in the very act of writing immediately dictated and breathed into the holy amanuenses by the Holy Spirit, so that they would be attested by these and no other circumstances, in this and no other mode or order."

4. The statement of Scripture that inspiration extends not merely to a part, but to the entire Scriptures, together with the fact that Scripture does not consist of persons or things, but of words, declares at the same time that Scripture is perfectly inerrant in all its words and in every one of its words. That is the meaning of Christ's testimony to the Scriptures when He declares (John 10:35) concerning the use of a single word (Ps. 82:6; אֱלֹהִים θεοί): "The Scripture cannot be broken." Stoeckhardt is entirely right in saying: [29] "When Christ and the Apostles appeal to Scripture, they adduce not merely general Scripture thoughts, they are not even satisfied to quote single passages, but they often lay their finger on a single word of Scripture to prove their point. Paul writes Gal. 3:16: 'Now to Abraham and his Seed were the promises made. He saith not, And to seeds, as of many, but as of one, And to thy Seed, which is Christ.' To this single word: 'And to thy Seed' (Gen. 22:18), the singular of this noun, he attaches all weight and proves by it that Christ was already promised to Abraham, and he declares that God chose this term intentionally. In Matt. 22:43-44 Christ attests and proves to the Pharisees His deity from Ps. 110, and note that He proves it from the single word: 'my Lord.' In John 10:35 the entire emphasis lies on the term θεοί, *elohim*, 'gods,' that being the title given by Psalm 82 to the government. . . .

---

[29] *Lehre und Wehre*, 32, 255 f., in his comprehensive essay: "*Was sagt die Schrift von sich selbst?*"

If even the government officials are entitled to this name, how much more He whom the Father has sanctified and sent into the world! For Christ and the Apostles every sentence, every word they found and read in Scripture, was God's Word in the strictest sense of the term. – Verbal Inspiration, which is so defamed in our day and is called 'an invention' of the dogmaticians,[30] has a firm basis and support in Scripture. Every word of Scripture is an inviolable sanctuary, is the infallible, unchangeable Word of God. Scripture insists on that. . . . Scripture contains the earnest warning not to add to, nor to take away from, what God has commanded and spoken (Deut. 4:2; 12:32; Prov. 30:5-6; Rev. 22:18-19). Every addition is a sacrilege, since it dilutes God's Word with the word of men. And the warning has the threat attached: 'Add thou not unto His words, lest He reprove thee' (Prov. 30:6). . . . Christ raises His voice and declares: 'I am not come to destroy, but to fulfill. For verily I say unto you, Till heaven and earth pass, one jot or one tittle shall in no wise pass from the Law, till all be fulfilled. Whosoever therefore shall break one of these least commandments, and shall teach men so, he shall be called the least in the kingdom of heaven; but whosoever shall do and teach them, the same shall be called great in the kingdom of heaven.' (Matt. 5:17-19.) Cp. Luke 16:17. We take Christ's warning to heart and confess with Paul: 'I believe all things which are written in the Law and in the Prophets' (Acts 24:14)." Likewise Luther confesses: "The Scriptures have never erred" (St. L. XV:1481) and "One little point of doctrine is of more value than heaven and earth; and therefore we cannot abide to have the least jot thereof corrupted" (St. L. IX:650). The context shows that Luther has in mind every tittle of doctrine, inasmuch as the doctrine is expressed in the definite, inviolable words of Scripture. The point at issue over against the Sacramentarians was the words of the institution of the Lord's Supper, and Luther adds: "If they believed that the Word is God's, they would not play with it in such a manner, but would hold it in highest esteem and without any dispute or doubt regard it as credible, and would know that one word of God is all words of God and all words of God are one word of God." Quenstedt has made statements with regard to the infallibility of the words of Scripture at which the camp of modern theologians throws up its hands in horror. And yet Quenstedt

---

30 Also Luthardt (*Komp.*, 10th ed., p. 332) does not hesitate to say that Verbal Inspiration has no basis in Scripture, but is "a purely mental construction." Theodor Kaftan (*Moderne Theol. d. alten Glaubens*, 2d ed., p. 109) speaks of Verbal Inspiration as a "theologumenon" – having no basis in Scripture.

does not say one whit more than what the Scriptures say of themselves. He writes (*Systema* I, 112): "The canonical Holy Scriptures in the original text are the infallible truth and free from every error, or, in other words, in the canonical Holy Scriptures there is found no lie, no falsity, no error, whether in the things or in the words; but all things, and each single one, that are handed down in them are the most true, whether they pertain to doctrine or morals or history, chronology, topography, or nomenclature; no ignorance, no thoughtlessness or forgetfulness, no lapse of memory, can or dare be ascribed to the amanuenses of the Holy Ghost in their penning of the sacred writings." Likewise Calov (*Systema* I, 551) says: "No error, even in unimportant matters, no lapse of memory, not to say untruth, can have place in the whole of Scripture."

These words of Quenstedt and Calov have sounded so strange to even a man like Philippi that he felt constrained to express his dissent from them. He wrote in the first edition of his *Kirchliche Glaubenslehre* (I, 1st ed., p. 208 f.) that one should not at the outset exclude the possibility that some few minor discrepancies actually are present, that there is here a territory of unimportant accidents, just as the resemblance of a portrait does not depend on the exactly corresponding length of the fingernails or the hair, that the question how far inspiration has overcome human weakness can be decided not *a priori*, on the basis of what Scripture says of itself, but only *a posteriori*, on the basis of human investigation, and that "we therefore would not like to declare with Calov, at least not *a priori*: 'No error, even in unimportant matters, no lapse of memory, . . . can have place in the whole of Scripture.'" But Philippi did not feel at ease in admitting this possibility of errors in unimportant details in Holy Scripture. He remarks that experience has shown it to be a rash assumption when in a concrete case this or that difference had been regarded as absolutely unsolvable, that (on page 197) the corrosive poison of subjectivism has eaten into the spiritual marrow and bone of faith to such a degree that it appears a trifling thing to us to break the objective, infallible, and eternal Word of God, that the truthfulness and certainty of the revelation of Scripture in no wise depends on the success of the attempts to harmonize Scripture and the natural sciences, so that the believing theologian should not rejoice so much when the scientific hypotheses agree with Scripture and not grieve so much when they do not agree: "The actually assured results do not contradict Scripture, and the hypotheses are but hypotheses." One of the strongest indications of Philippi's perplexity is this, that he felt impelled to make the senseless distinction between "*Wortinspiration*" and "*Woerterinspiration*" and was ready to accept the former and to reject the latter (pp. 184, 191) – a distinction which called forth much derision even among the neologists. But no sane person ever taught a "*Woerterinspiration*," least of all the Lutheran dogmaticians. Dr. Ebeling correctly remarks: "The Bible does not contain '*Woerter*' (disconnected words) like a dictionary, but '*Worte*' in a certain connection and sense." [31] Philippi finally saw his error, and in the third edition of his dogmatics (3d ed., I, p. 279) he expressly retracted his former opinion that in minor matters an error is possible. These are his words: "I am now ready to admit that according to my own theory of inspiration even the possibility of errors in Scripture in minor matters and unimportant accidentals must be denied *a priori*." Modern theologians were glad to take notice of Philippi's former position. Thus Grimm wrote: "Philippi, if we correctly understand him, teaches that the manner and form of the diction, not, however, the single words, are due to the Holy Spirit [*Wortinspiration*, not *Woerterinspiration*]; also he concedes discrepancies of very slight importance in the narrations." [32] We do not find the same eagerness to report Philippi's retraction, even after it had become known. In 1912 Nitzsch-Stephan still talks of Philippi as though there had been no change from his former position (*Ev. Dogmatik*, 3d ed., 1912, p. 253).

5. The inspiration of Scripture self-evidently includes also the impulse and command to write (*impulsum et mandatum scribendi*). When Roman theologians, on the one hand, are ready to admit that the Evangelists and Apostles wrote according to God's will and by God's inspiration (*Deo volente et inspirante*), but, on the other hand, claim that a command (*mandatum*) to write cannot be found, this claim amounts to a self-contradiction.[33] Quenstedt correctly says: "They [the Roman theologians] are perpetrating a joke (*nugantur*)." If God willed that the Evangelists and Apostles should write and at

---

[31] *Die Bibel Gottes Wort und des Glaubens einzige Quelle*, 2d ed., p. 18.

[32] *Institutio Theologiae Dogmaticae Evangelicae, Historico-critica*, 2d ed., p. 122.

[33] Thus Bellarmine says: "It is wrong to say that God commanded the Apostles to write. For in the last chapter of Matthew we read that they should preach the Gospel; but we read nowhere that they should write. Therefore God neither commanded expressly that they should write, nor did He command that they should not write. Still we do not deny that the Apostles wrote what they wrote by the will and inspiration of God." (Quoted in Quenstedt, I, 94, from Bellarmine, *De V. D.*, 1, 4, c. 3.)

the same time inspired what they wrote, this act of inspiration constituted also the impulse and command to write. The Lutheran theologians therefore say: "Inspiration itself, by which the things were suggested that were to be set down in writing, implies the impulse of executing the act of writing" (Baier-Walther, I, 99). Quenstedt (I, 96): "The inspiration of the things to be written and the inner impulse to write amount to the same thing. It involves a *contradictio in adiecto* to say that the Apostles wrote by the will and inspiration and suggestion of God and nevertheless not by His command." The reason why the Roman theologians burden themselves with this self-contradiction is manifest. They bring this *sacrificium intellectus* in the interest of supreme authority of the Pope, *ad summam papae potestatem stabiliendam.* The claim that the Gospels and the Apostolic Epistles are indeed inspired, the inspired Word of God, but were not written by the express divine command, is meant to lower the value and necessity of the Holy Scriptures and, *per contra,* to exalt the value and necessity of the "unwritten Word of God," which under the name of "tradition" is administered, controlled, and manufactured by the Pope (Luther: "the magician's bag, *Gauckelsack,*" of the Pope). According to the Roman doctrine the written Word of God, Holy Scripture, is not a complete standard of faith and life, but needs to be supplemented by tradition, which is to be "received and to be venerated with an equal affection of piety and reverence."[34] The "equal affection of piety and reverence" naturally, however, changes into an unequal affection of piety and reverence, and tradition is to be placed above Scripture if the Evangelists and Apostles have written without a divine mandate. Then the matter assumes this aspect: The Holy Scriptures are really not a divine institution, since the *mandatum scribendi* is lacking. But the holy father Pope, as the visible head of the Church appointed by Christ, is a divine institution in the eminent sense, and thus the supreme authority in the Church rests in the Pope, respectively in the tradition controlled by the Pope. These views are expressed in such *dicta* of Romish theologians as the following: the Christian doctrine is preserved purer by tradition than by Holy Scripture; the Church could exist very well without Holy Scripture, but not without tradition; Christ did not want to make His Church dependent on a paper Scripture or a lifeless parchment; they went so far as to say that the Scriptures are, because of the human weaknesses clinging to them, not at all a dependable guide and the Church

---

[34] *Trident.*, Sess. IV, decr. de canon. Script. Cat. Rom., praef. 12.

would have been served better if there had been no Scripture at all.[35] This explains the interest Roman theologians have in denying the *mandatum scribendi* and in speaking as though the Evangelists had written merely "by accident," "for accidental reasons," etc. Their concern is to have the Ego of the Pope acknowledged as the supreme authority of the Church.

The close relation of modern theology to the theological principle of Rome will be seen at once. Although the modern theologians deny the inspiration of Holy Scripture, they are nevertheless ready to admit that God's Word is in Scripture. Even radical neologists still concede that the Apostles in their writings "stand closer" to the divine revelation than the later generations. But what they strongly protest against, just like Rome, is that the divine revelation is to be restricted to the "book revelation" of Holy Scripture, to a "paper Pope," to a codex of dogmas fallen from heaven. – Modern theology has the same interest as Rome. According to its own declaration it desires freedom from Scripture as the only source and standard of theology and in place of Scripture would make the decisive factor in the Church, indeed not the Ego of the Pope, but the "experience" or – what amounts to the same thing – "the pious self-consciousness," the Ego of the theologizing subject. When Theodor Kaftan says: [36] "The modern theology that I stand for bows to no mere external authority," he means by that "external authority" to which he will not bow Holy Scripture, the written Word of the Apostles and the Prophets. And when he adds that he bows to "God's Word" "as to an authority that has proved itself, and maintains itself, in its own power," he means to say that he will accept only so much of Scripture as valid as has given satisfactory proof of being the truth before the judgment seat of his "ex-

[35] Quenstedt, I, 90, brings the documentary proof: "Antithesis: 1. Of the Scripture-hating Papists who assert that the Holy Scriptures are not necessary and the Church could do without the Scripture; thus Gregory of Valencia in *Anal. Fid.*, p. 388, where he says 'that the heavenly doctrine can be preserved purer by tradition than by Scripture.' Bellarmine, IV, *De V. Dei*, c. 4, contends 'that the Church can subsist without the Scriptures but not without tradition.' Costerus asserts 'that Christ did not want His Church to be dependent on paper Scriptures or commit His mysteries to parchments.' Petrus a Soto: 'This should be held as most certain that this plan of writing the divine words and revelations has been devised by God because of the human imperfection and infirmity, and so it is of great help to the more infirm and imperfect; but for the more sanctified and purer ones it is either less or not at all necessary.' Of the same nature is that impious remark of some cardinal, related by Tilenus, P. 1, disp. 2, th. 35: 'The Church would have been better served if no Scriptures had ever appeared.'"

[36] *Moderne Theologie des alten Glaubens*, 2d ed., p. 112 f.

perience" or his "pious self-consciousness." Ihmels means the same thing when he calls it a "fatal mistake" that the Early Church, the Church of the Reformation, and the old dogmaticians retreated into Scripture as the sole source and norm of the Christian doctrine and when he sees in Schleiermacher's theology, and particularly in the Erlangen theology, an "immense advance" in the right direction, because this theology has brought to the fore the "experience" or the "Christian Ego." (*Zentralfragen*, 2d ed., p. 56 ff.) What we get is this: Rome is concerned with the Ego of the Pope, modern theology is concerned with the Ego of the theologizing individual.

Scripture has already ended the whole dispute by stating that the Christian Church is built to no extent whatever upon the pious Ego whether of the Pope or of other theologizing individuals, but to the Day of Judgment is built solely on the foundation of the Apostles and Prophets, i. e., the Word of Scripture. We have already seen that Christ directs His Church and all the world to the Word of His Apostles, that the Apostles point to their written Word over against all spurious sources of knowledge and all spurious norms, that the Apostles knew that they had taught all of Christ's Word, and that they accordingly instruct all Christians to deny Church fellowship to all who depart from the doctrine of the Apostles. We have also noted that the Apostles claimed not only temporary and local, but permanent validity for what they wrote, even when their writing was prompted "by accidental reasons" (1 Cor. 1:11). Luther discusses this point in dealing with a Roman opponent who would grant only temporary and local validity for the Lord's Supper *sub utraque specie;* in this connection he insists most emphatically that the epistles of Paul are binding on all Christians, of all times, and of all places. He writes: "What could be more ridiculous and more worthy of this friar's brain [37] than this saying that the Apostle wrote these words and gave this permission (namely, to celebrate the Lord's Supper under both kinds) to a particular church, i. e., the Corinthian and not to the Church Universal? Where does he get his proof? Out of his usual storehouse, namely, out of his impious head. If we admit that any epistle, or any part of any epistle, of Paul does not apply to the Church Universal, then the whole authority of Paul falls to the ground. Then the Corinthians will say that what he teaches about faith in the Epistle to the Romans does not apply to them. What

---

[37] The unknown Italian monk of Cremona who had written an article in which he sought to bring Luther back into the Roman Church. Several pages later Luther describes him.

greater blasphemy and madness can be imagined than this? God forbid that there should be one jot or tittle in all of Paul which the whole Church Universal is not bound to follow and keep! Not so did the Fathers hold, down to these perilous times, in which, as Paul foretold, there would be blasphemers and blind and insensate men, of whom this brother is one, nay, the chief." (St. L. XIX, 19 f.) [38]

4

The Relation of the Holy Ghost to the Holy Writers

Modern theologians speak as though this relationship were left indeterminate. They present it as a "difficult problem" for the solution of which no suitable formula has to date been found. Luthardt, for example, remarks: "On the whole, conservative theology is still searching for a formula giving expression to the 'divine-human' character of Scripture. Philippi, too, speaks of an 'organic union of the Spirit of God and the spirit of man' in the act of inspiration, claims a '*Wortinspiration*' but not a '*Woerterinspiration,*' and grants 'the possibility of minor discrepancies.'" [39] Again, when Grau says:[40] "The boundaries between the divine and the human in Scripture cannot be determined mechanically and quantitatively," his meaning is that it cannot be determined what in Scripture is to be attributed to the Holy Ghost and what to the human spirit of its writers. If this were actually the case, Horst Stephan would be right in again advising the theological

[38] With this "God forbid, etc." Luther does not contradict 1 Cor. 7:26. There Paul does not give a commandment (v. 25), but only the advice to young women not to marry "by reason of the present distress." The sophistry of Papistic theologians that the Apostles wrote "by accidental reasons" *(ex occasione accidentaria, fortuito)*, hence not by divine command and accordingly not as binding all Christians, is shown up by Quenstedt thus: "The Apostles wrote sometimes prompted by the occasion; however, not by a casual happening, but by one sent by God. God so guided everything that we should have a complete and perfect canon of faith and life – the Prophetic and Apostolic Scriptures." Quenstedt quotes from Tertullian, *Contra Marcionem*, 1, 5: "The Apostles, in writing to certain people, wrote to all," and from Cyril, *Proleg. in Ioh.*: "Moved by this thing, John believed it to be meet to provide by the composition of his Gospel for his contemporaries as well as for future generations."

[39] *Kompendium,* 10th ed., 1900, p. 338. By the way, also Luthardt, in 1900, fails to take notice of Philippi's retraction, 17 years before, in his *Glaubenslehre,* 3d ed., 1883, I, 279, of the statement concerning "the possibility of errors in Scripture in minor matters."

[40] The entire quotation is given in Baier-Walther, I, 102, taken from Grau's *Entwicklungsgeschichte des neutestamentlichen Schrifttums,* I, 11, 12, 18.

world: "It would be better for us to abandon entirely the idea of inspiration, in spite of all modern attempts at a good evangelical interpretation of it." [41] A Bible in which the boundaries between divine truth and human error would forever be uncertain would indeed be a fitting controversial subject for theologians of the school of Lessing, but would certainly not be the Book of which David says: "The testimony of the Lord is sure, making wise the simple" (Ps. 19:7), and: "Thy Word is a lamp unto my feet and a light unto my path" (Ps. 119: 105). But all this talk about the relation of the Holy Ghost to the holy writers being left indeterminate in Holy Scripture is contrary to the facts in the case. It is but an attempt to muddy the clear waters. The Scriptures define the relation of the Holy Spirit to the human writers of Scripture very exactly when, for example, they say that "the Lord" or "the Holy Ghost" spoke "by the Prophet," "by the mouth of David," "by the mouth of His holy Prophets" (Matt. 1:22; 2:15; Acts 1:16; 4:25; Luke 1:70), with the result that the Word spoken by them was not their word, but entirely God's Word, or the Word of the Holy Ghost, τὰ λόγια τοῦ θεοῦ (Rom. 3:2). In exactly the same manner Paul expressly declares the Word he wrote to be God's Word, in distinction from the word of men (1 Cor. 14:37: "The things that I write unto you are the commandments of the Lord"), just as he says of the Word he had spoken: "When ye received the Word of God which ye heard of us, ye received it not as the word of men, but, as it is in truth, the Word of God" (1 Thess. 2:13).

With regard to the relation of the Holy Ghost to the holy writers we shall therefore have to say: God employed the holy writers as His tools, or instruments, in order that men might have His Word fixed in writing. In order to express this relation between the Holy Ghost and the human writers, the Church Fathers as well as the old Lutheran dogmaticians call the holy writers *amanuenses, notarii, manus, calami,* clerks, secretaries, hands, pens, of the Holy Spirit. Philippi rightly calls the derision heaped upon these terms by the neologists "senseless derision" (*Glaubenslehre* I, 177). For these terms are perfectly Scriptural as long as we observe the point of comparison (*tertium comparationis*), the mere instrumentality. The expressions state no more and no less than the fact that the holy writers did not write their

---

[41] *Glaubenslehre,* 1921, p. 52. This advice is nothing new. Many years before, Bretschneider had written in his *Dogmatik,* 4th ed., I, 394: "In general, all inspiration of the New Testament, and particularly of the words, appears useless for the reason that it presupposes a mechanism of instruction which is entirely inapplicable to human souls."

own word, but God's Word, τὰ λόγια τοῦ θεοῦ; and that is, as we have seen, the authoritative judgment of Christ and His Apostles. These terms should therefore not be subjected to ridicule but rather acknowledged as Scriptural.

That in this relationship the writers were not lifeless machines, but living, personal instruments, endowed with intellect and will and equipped with their own distinct style (*modus dicendi*), is evident from the very nature of the case. For God did not first kill or "dehumanize" Isaiah, David, and all the Prophets in order to speak or write through (διά) them, but He carefully preserved their lives and their genuine human way of expressing themselves in order that they might in their speaking be understood by men. And precisely this, and only this, was most definitely taught and set forth by the Church Fathers and the old dogmaticians when they spoke of *amanuenses, calami*, etc. It is to be noted that the Church Fathers and the old dogmaticians had two things in mind when they used these phrases.

First, since God gave His Word through the Apostles and Prophets, or, in other words, since the Apostles and Prophets wrote not their own, but God's Word, the Church Fathers and dogmaticians call the Apostles and Prophets God's hands, penmen, secretaries, etc. Augustine, *De Consensu Evangelistarum*, I, 35: "While they [the Apostles] wrote what He [Christ] showed and said, it dare by no means be said that He Himself [Christ] did not write, since, after all, His members performed that which they learned from the dictating head. For whatever He wanted us to know about His deeds and words, this He commanded them as His hands to write." Cyprian, *Serm. de Eleem:* "The Holy Ghost was the writer, the Prophets were His pens, to whom the Holy Ghost dictated what to write" (quoted in Quenstedt, I, 80). The old dogmaticians speak in the same way. Gerhard: "With good reason we call the Prophets in the Old Testament and the Evangelists and the Apostles in the New Testament the penmen, the hands of Christ, the letterwriters, or the clerks of the Holy Ghost, because they did not speak or write from their own human will, but φερόμενοι ὑπὸ τοῦ πνεύματος ἁγίου, activated, led, impelled, inspired, and governed by the Holy Spirit. They wrote not as men, but as men of God, that is, as God's servants and the peculiar organs of the Holy Ghost. When therefore any canonical book is called the book of Moses, the Psalter of David, the epistle of Paul, etc., that is done simply because they were the instruments, not because they were the principal cause." (*Loci, locus "De Scriptura Sacra,"* § 18.) Quenstedt says of the Prophets of the Old Testament and the Apostles of the New Testament: "Just as the Prophets and the Apostles were the mouth of God in speaking or preaching, so they also were the hands and pens of the Holy Ghost in writing. For, as the Holy Spirit spoke through them, so He wrote through them. For there is no difference as to the fountain of the spoken Word and the written Word. For this reason they were also called the amanuenses, the hands of Christ, the letterwriters, or clerks, or actuaries, of the Holy Ghost." (*Systema* I, 80.)

But, in the second place, both Church Fathers and dogmaticians decidedly reject any mechanical or external concept of the "διά," of the relationship of the writers to the Holy Ghost. The Church Fathers expressly repudiate the notion of the Montanists that the holy writers wrote in a state of trance. This also Cremer admits when he writes: "Miltiades, also an apologete, wrote, according to Eusebius' *Hist. Eccl.* 5, 17, against the Montanists that 'it dare not be maintained that a prophet speaks in ecstasy,' Clemens of Alexandria declares ecstasy to be a mark of the false prophets and the evil spirit (*Strom.* 1, 311), and since Origen the rejection of the ideas of paganism is characteristic of the teaching of the Church Fathers. In absolute contrast to Montanism they refused to acknowledge in the prophets any unconsciousness." (R. E., 2d ed., VI, 752.) Cremer refers also to Chrysostom, Epiphanius, Athanasius, etc., to the same effect. And as to the old dogmaticians, they utterly repudiated the false notion that the Prophets and Apostles performed only a mechanical labor when they wrote the Holy Scriptures. On the contrary, they show that the amanuenses performed their service willingly and fully conscious of the fact that they were writing God's Word. Quenstedt (*Systema* I, 82 sq.), in explaining the φερόμενοι (2 Pet. 1:21), states very clearly in what manner the will and the understanding of the holy writers participated in the composition of Holy Scripture. The amanuenses participated not according to their natural will, according to which man is actuated by God in the natural domain; nor according to their regenerate will, according to which all Christians are impelled by God to do good works; but according to the extraordinary impulse, according to which they were impelled by the Holy Ghost in their special calling and office, namely, as Prophets and Apostles, to reduce God's own Word to writing (*in literas redigere*). Quenstedt shows in what respect the human will of the writers was by no means excluded in composing the Holy Scriptures, namely, not *materialiter et subiective sumta,* that is, "as though the holy writers had written without and against their will, without consciousness and unwittingly; for they wrote voluntarily, willingly, and knowingly." And with the Church Fathers,

Quenstedt, in explaining the term φερόμενοι, rejects expressly the ecstasy. He writes: "The holy writers are said to be φερόμενοι, actuated, moved, impelled, by the Holy Ghost; by no means as though they were in a trance (*mente fuerint alienati*), as the 'enthusiasts' say of themselves and as the heathen fable of such an 'enthusiasm' in their prophets. Nor by any means as though even the Prophets themselves did not understand their prophecies or the matter which they were to write, which was the error once held by the Montanists, Phrygians, or Cataphrygians, and the Priscillianists."

Hence it is not historically true when Luthardt (*Kompendium*, 10th ed., p. 332) describes the orthodox doctrine of inspiration thus: "The relation of the Holy Ghost to Scripture is not conceived as taking in the personal mental activity of the Biblical authors (!), but as taking in merely the external use of the hands of the writers." Cremer departs from the path of historical truth still farther when he says: "This doctrine of inspiration was an absolute *novum*. True, it lacked only the concept of ecstasy to be a renewal of the magic doctrine of inspiration of Philo and the old apologetes, which has been universally rejected by the Church in its opposition to Montanism. But the very absence of this concept only made the situation worse, for it reduced the magical inspiration to a mechanical one." It is evident that Cremer had entirely lost control not only of the historical facts, but also of himself, when he wrote the above. The ridicule heaped by the modern theologians on the terms *amanuenses, calami*, etc., does credit neither to their intellect nor to their veracity. Philippi is using a mild term when he calls it "foolish."

5

Objections to the Doctrine of Inspiration

The objections raised against the inspiration of Holy Scripture constitute an exceedingly sad chapter. They are as harmful as the objections voiced against the *satisfactio vicaria* of Christ. Whoever denies the substitutional satisfaction of Christ denies the very essence of the Christian faith, because only the reliance on Christ's vicarious satisfaction (1 Cor. 2:2; 15:1-3; John 1:29) is the Christian faith. And whoever denies the inspiration of Scripture, i. e., denies that the Word of the Apostles and Prophets is God's own infallible Word, destroys, as far as lies in his power, the foundation of the Christian Church, because, according to Eph. 2:20, the Christian Church is built on the foundation of the Apostles and Prophets. Nor dare we forget that everyone who denies the inspiration of Scripture *eo ipso* becomes a critic of Scripture and as a critic of Scripture – which as God's Word is not to be criticized but believed – is subject to the divine judgment described in Matt. 11:25. None of us, even though he were a doctor in all four of the learned professions, can deny the inspiration of Holy Scripture without suffering an impairment of his natural mental powers. The arguments advanced against the inspiration of Scripture are below the level of the natural powers of mind which mankind still possesses since the Fall. Among the arguments against the inspiration of Holy Scripture we note:

1. The different style in the various books in the Scripture.[42] The different writers do have different styles. Isaiah writes in a style different from that of Amos; the style of John differs from that of Paul, etc. The old dogmaticians point out this difference. Quenstedt (*Systema* I, 111) writes: "Great is the diversity among the sacred writers as to style and manner of speech." One need not be conversant with the Hebrew and the Greek original text in order to recognize such a diversity; the translations, too, show this difference of style. This difference of style is said to contradict the inspiration of Scripture. The argument runs thus: If God were the true Author of the Scriptures, or, in other words, if the Scriptures actually were the Word of the one God, there would have to be one and the same style in all books of Scripture; the difference in the style – that has been the emphatic declaration – gives the doctrine of the divine inspiration of the Scriptures the deathblow. In Nitzsch-Stephan (p. 251) one finds the ironical remark that the old Lutheran theology was not in the least disconcerted by the variety of styles, but clung to the Verbal Inspiration without faltering. We say: That was very sensible on the part of the old Lutheran theologians. For, as a matter of fact, the diversity in the style does not contradict inspiration, but is demanded by it. God did not speak through one man, but through a number of them, each one of whom had his own distinctive style, which God used in communicating His Word. There is, to resort to more learned language, no human style *in abstracto* but only *in concreto,* that is, the style of individual persons. No man has ever observed a style which was severed from the person who used it. But why did God not have the Scriptures written in His own divine style? Would that

---

[42] Nitzsch-Stephan, p. 251. Grau, according to Hofmann, calls it "the literary diversity" of the various authors; see Baier-Walther, I, 101 f.

not have been the incontrovertible external proof that "all Scripture is given by inspiration of God"? Scripture has the answer. Scripture tells us that God could not use His own divine, or heavenly, style because it was a celestial style, unsuited to men here on earth. According to 2 Cor. 12:4 Paul was caught up into the heavenly Paradise and heard words there. But they were "unspeakable words, which it is not lawful [margin: possible] for a man to utter" (Luther: *"welche kein Mensch sagen kann"*). This celestial style of speech, which is not fitting for this world, we shall someday understand in heaven. It follows that the objection to inspiration taken from the diversity of styles reveals anything but good reasoning.

Our old dogmaticians take a very sensible view of the matter. Quenstedt says (*Systema* I, 109): "According as the holy writers were trained or accustomed to speak or write either in an elegant or in a simpler style, so the Holy Ghost used them and was ready to accommodate Himself to the natural aptitude of the men and to condescend to it." [43] We have an analogy to this "condescension" in Christ's humbling Himself while in the State of Humiliation. If Christ was to fulfill the Law and suffer and die in our stead, it was necessary that He go about in Palestine not in His divine glory (else everyone from Dan to Beersheba would have fled from Him), but that He humiliate Himself and "become in fashion as a man" (Phil. 2:7). Similarly, if God would speak to men, He had to refrain from using His divine, or celestial, style and condescend to use the human style (*condescendere, attemperare*). How this was possible is, indeed, beyond our "rational discernment" (*"erkenntnismaessigen Erfassung"*), just as the *unio personalis* of God and man, and particularly the fact that the Son of God could condescend to die on the Cross without renouncing or reducing His deity, remains an impenetrable mystery to us. But as this latter fact is incontrovertibly true – for the Lord of glory, God's Son, was crucified (1 Cor. 2:8; Rom. 8:32) – so, too, this fact is incontestable that God's speech in Scripture, through His condescension to human speech and the human style of the writers, does not cease to be fully and entirely God's Word, as is evident from all passages that identify the Word of Scripture and God's Word.

It is certain, then, that God has given us through men (διὰ τοῦ προφήτου κτλ.) a Word which is not, as modern theology claims, in

[43] Quenstedt adds: "One and the same thing is expressed by some in more magnificent language, by others in more lowly language; but that these and no other phrases, these and no other words or synonyms were used by the holy writers, was due entirely to the divine impulse and inspiration."

part the Word of God and in part the word of men, but so wholly and entirely God's Word that not one word of it can be broken (John 10:35); on which, as on an adamantine foundation, the whole Church rests with its faith to the Last Day (Eph. 2:20); in compliance with which all events in the world take place, or, to use Rudelbach's striking phrase: "The Scriptures are, so to say, the spiritual hour hand in the Kingdom of God; the strokes of the clock of the world correspond to it or rather are determined by it." [44]

Modern theology raises the charge against the old dogmaticians that they emphasized the "divine side" of Scripture so strongly that they neglected the "human side." Even Philippi was misled into joining, at least to some extent, in this accusation (*Glaubenslehre* I, 179 f.). Now, it is a fact that the dogmaticians placed a strong emphasis on the divine side of Scripture. But in doing that they merely followed the example of the Evangelists and Apostles of Christ and of Christ Himself. In the first four chapters of the Gospel according to Matthew, for instance, Scripture is quoted nine times, and every time the "divine side" is emphasized. For it is certainly stressing the divine side of Scripture when we are told that what is reported in those chapters from the life of Jesus happened in order that the Scriptures might be fulfilled. In obedience to the word of men no events occur; events occur only in obedience to the Word of God. And the fact that Christ overcomes the temptations of the devil, as reported in the fourth chapter, with the "It is written," again definitely stresses the divine side. For by the word of man the devil cannot be vanquished; the Word of God, however, is the sword of the Spirit, with which the fiery darts of the devil are victoriously beaten back (Eph. 6:16-17).

If we ask why Scripture itself so strongly emphasizes the divine side of Scripture, the answer is simple. There is no danger that the "human side," rightly understood, will be overlooked. Everyone sees the human side, because the Scriptures are written in the human language. But the "divine side" was and is in danger of being overlooked. Because our human understanding since the Fall is darkened in spiritual things and we are alienated from the life of God through the ignorance in us, through the blindness (πώρωσις) of our heart, this fact that the Word written through men, entirely in the human language, is not the word of men, but altogether God's Word, τὰ λόγια τοῦ θεοῦ, is apt to recede into the background, yes, to fade out en-

[44] *Zeitschrift f. luth. Th. u. Kirche,* 1841, Section 4, p. 34.

tirely — just as the Jews did not recognize Christ's Word as God's Word, just as the modern theologians do not recognize the Holy Scriptures as God's Word and have therefore deposed Scripture from its office of being the source and norm of theology. — By the way, the modern theologians do not really mean the "human side" of Scripture when they say that the human side has been overlooked by the dogmaticians. By the human side, about which they are so concerned, they mean the alleged errors in Scripture. They want Scripture to be broken in order that the Scriptures will not be regarded as the "textbook" of the Christian religion, but that "the pious self-consciousness of the theologizing subject" may have liberty of action.

2. The appeal of the holy writers to their historical research has been advanced against the inspiration of the Bible. True, the holy writers did make historical research. The Evangelist Luke refers to the fact that he had "traced the course of all things accurately from the first" (Luke 1:3, R. V.). And Paul refers to historical facts communicated to him by others (1 Cor. 1:11: "For it hath been declared unto me of you, my brethren, by them which are of the house of Chloe, that there are contentions among you"). This is turned into an argument against inspiration: "If God gave the holy writers by inspiration what they were to write, why do they appeal to their own research and to communications given them by others?" This argument lies on the same plane as the one regarding the different styles. As the Holy Ghost employed the literary style which the several writers possessed, so He also used the historical knowledge which they had acquired by their own experience or by their own research or by communications from others. Take what happened on the first Pentecost. By their own experience the Apostles knew of the resurrection of Christ before Pentecost. Yet on the day of Pentecost they preached of this event, as of the other great deeds of God, "as the Spirit gave them utterance" (Acts 2:4). Again, it has been urged against the inspiration of the Psalms that it would be absurd to assume that the Holy Ghost spoke through David what he, David, felt in his heart. Thus Kahnis says: "Should we assume that the Holy Ghost dictated to David in the form of a Psalm the emotions David experienced in his heart?" [45] But that the experience of his own heart does not cancel the inspiration David himself affirms when he says (2 Sam. 23:1-2): "David, the son of Jesse, said, and the man who was raised up on

---

[45] The complete quotation is given in Baier-Walther, I, 102. Later on we shall have something to say on the abuse of this term "dictated" and of the ridicule heaped upon it.

high, the anointed of the God of Jacob and the sweet Psalmist of Israel, said: The Spirit of the Lord spake by me, and His Word was in my tongue." For this reason also Luther saw no contradiction between the "feelings of the heart" and "inspiration," but rather praised this combination highly as the Holy Ghost's method of teaching; and at the same time he warns us all against casting aside David's Psalms, so filled with his heart's feelings, as containing only human instruction. Luther comments on 2 Sam. 23:1-2 as follows: "What an excellent, bold glorying that is! Whoever can boast that the Spirit of the Lord speaks through him and that his tongue speaks the words of the Holy Ghost, he must be very sure of his case. That cannot be David, the son of Jesse, born in sin, but he who has been raised to be a Prophet by God's promise. Should you not expect delightful Psalms from him who has such a Teacher to teach him and speak through him? He that has ears to hear, let him hear. My speech (*nota bene* in the Psalms) is not my speech, but whoever hears me hears God; whoever despises me, despises God. For I see that many of my descendants will not give ear to my words, to their great harm. Such a boast neither we nor anyone who is not a Prophet may utter. What we may do if we are also sanctified and have the Holy Ghost is this, that we boast of being catechumens and pupils of the Prophets, who repeat and preach what we have heard and learned from the Prophets and Apostles and are also sure that the Prophets have taught it. Such men are called in the Old Testament 'the children of the prophets' as offer nothing of their own and nothing new, as the Prophets do, but teach what they have learned from the Prophets, and they are the 'Israel,' as David calls them, for whom he writes the Psalms." (St. L. III:1890.)

3. The variant readings (*variae lectiones*) found in the copies (ἀπόγραφα) of the originals (αὐτόγραφα) are said to disprove the doctrine of inspiration. Variant readings in the copies do exist. But, first of all, let us bear in mind that it is not fair to argue from the variant readings in the copies against the inspiration of the originals. We have never held that the copyists of the holy writings were inspired. Spelling mistakes or slips or attempted corrections in the copies have absolutely nothing to do with the inspiration of the originals. To adduce an analogous case: If it is discovered that in copying or printing an act of the legislature, say of the State of Missouri, mistakes crept in, no sensible person would conclude that the act was never adopted with a definite wording. That is generally admitted. Accordingly, men ought not to argue from the mistakes

which are found in the copies of the Bible against the inspiration of the originals.

But now the objection to the inspiration of Scripture assumes another form, namely, that an inspired Scripture becomes useless and should no longer be urged, since the presence of variant readings makes it, after all, uncertain which is the original Word of God. The critics make much of this objection. Theodor Kaftan claims in his *Moderne Theologie des alten Glaubens,* 2d ed., p. 96 f.: "Every theologian knows that there is no authentic text," "that the number of variant readings is legion," and "that it must give the verbal inspirationist quite a jolt when he realizes that no one, not even he himself, is able to tell which text is the one that is verbally inspired." The exact opposite is true! In spite of the variants in the copies of the Bible we have a reliable Bible text. Referring to this reliable Bible text, Luther uttered the words: "The Word they still shall let remain." With reference to the text of the New Testament (of which in particular the "legion of variant readings" is asserted) we have two ways of knowing that in the copies the Word of the Apostles or, what is identical with it, the Word of Christ, has been preserved for us.

a. We know we have this Word *a priori,* that is, prior to any human investigation, on the basis of the divine promise. When our Savior says in His high-priestly prayer (John 17:20) that all those who will come to faith to the end of time will come to faith through the Word of the Apostles, He therewith promises us that the Word of the Apostles will be present in the Church to the Last Day. Again, when Christ admonishes all believers to continue in His Word (John 8:31-32: "If ye continue in My Word, then are ye My disciples indeed, and ye shall know the truth"), He guarantees that His Word will be present for us to continue in it. If there are such as do not recognize the Word of Christ which they have as Christ's Word, such failure is certainly due to their blindness, that, seeing, they do not see and, hearing, they do not hear, because they do not understand. (Matt. 13:13 ff.) Again, when Christ instructs not only the Apostles, but His Church (Matt. 28:20) to teach all nations all things (πάντα) whatsoever He has commanded them, He gives the Church the guarantee that His doctrine in all its parts will be clearly and surely known to it to the end of time. Christ also comes to the defense of the text of the Old Testament. When Christ says in particular of the entire Scriptures of the Old Testament that they cannot be broken (John 10:35), He is certainly affirming that the text of the Old Testament is reliable. Similarly He states (Luke 16:29): "They have (ἔχουσιν)

Moses and the Prophets, let them hear them." Likewise in His temptation (Matthew 4) Christ operates with the γέγραπται as with an immovable certain text. We do not read that the devil brought up the matter of "variant readings." So we know *a priori,* before any investigation, from the promise and the testimony of Christ, that in the Scriptures now at the disposal of the Church we have a reliable text, or, in other words, the authentic doctrine of the Apostles and Prophets, that is, of God, in spite of the *variae lectiones* in the copies.

b. We reach the same result also *a posteriori,* on the basis of scientific investigation. Human scientific investigation establishes the fact that not a single Christian doctrine has been rendered doubtful in any point by the "legion" of variant readings. Also neologists have said as much. Luthardt (*Komp.,* 10th ed., p. 334): "We may be certain, and investigation confirms it, that the text of the Bible has been preserved for us in all essentials." This is admitted also by the genuine textual critics, those who are to be taken seriously. Luthardt's remark that the Biblical text has been preserved "in all essentials" might be understood to say, and has been so understood, that on the basis of the Biblical text, as we now have it, the Christian doctrine could be determined merely approximately, not in all its parts or with complete certainty. But that is a mistake. Exactly the opposite holds true. Compare, e. g., the newer critical editions of the New Testament text, those by Tischendorf or by Westcott and Hort or by Nestle, with the *textus receptus* of Erasmus in the sixteenth century, which was established "when the science of textual criticism was unborn," as A. B. Bruce of Glasgow expresses it in *The Expositor's Greek Testament* I, p. 52, and you will be completely cured of the fear that the collection of many thousands of variant readings [46] which modern textual criticism has recorded demand a change in a single Christian doctrine. There is much in the five volumes of the *Expositor's Greek Testament* of which we cannot approve. It is written from the modern theologian's standpoint. But we have no fault to find with the action of the editor and his collaborators in agreeing to reproduce the *textus receptus,* "representing the Greek text as known to Erasmus in the sixteenth century." Variations from the *textus receptus* are added in notes. Two reasons are advanced for retaining the old text: 1) the fact that this text is the basis of the Authorized Version, and 2) the fact that "while the modern textual critics have done much to provide a purer

[46] Bruce calls them, *op. cit.,* p. 55, "a formidable affair" and refers to Tischendorf's "eighth edition in two large octavos."

text," "their judgments in many cases do not accord and their results cannot be regarded as final" (*loc. cit.*, p. 52). Bruce is an out-and-out modern theologian and has given up the "inerrancy" of Scripture. Still he insists that a great number of the variations are of so little weight that they can be entirely disregarded since they do not affect the sense.[47] In short, the situation is this: A comparison of recent critical editions of the text of the New Testament with the *textus receptus*, which is also substantially the basis of Luther's translation, convinces us of the fact that the establishing of the Christian doctrine does not depend in the least on modern textual criticism.

We are not saying, however, that textual criticism should be eliminated entirely from our theological curriculum. We, too, in our theological seminary at St. Louis introduce our students to modern textual criticism. That is a part of the complete external equipment of a theologian of our day. But we point out two things to our students: 1) We know *a priori* from the divine promise that in our present Bible we have the Word of Christ which is to be taught in the Church and by the Church to the Last Day. 2) We recognize, too, *a posteriori*, that the divine providence has so wonderfully held its protecting hand over the Bible text that in spite of the *variae lectiones* not a single Christian doctrine has become a matter of doubt.

This, then, is the situation: God has arranged the Bible so that one and the same doctrine is set down in several, usually in numerous places. That is also brought out by the words of the Apostle (Phil.

---

47 Well-intentioned men, who in other respects are theologically well trained, harbor distorted conceptions of the "legion" of variations. The "legion" dwindles decidedly when we scrutinize the nature of these variations. Take, by way of example, two German Bibles, the one having the old and the other the new orthography, and compare merely the New Testament text of both. The difference in orthography will at once reveal thousands of *variae lectiones*. The same thing applies to the thousands of variations in the transcripts of the Greek New Testament that have come down to us; the variants pertain solely to the orthography. Also Bruce points this out when he speaks of variants "not affecting the sense, but merely the spelling and grammatical form of words." Such, for instance, is the large number of variations in the spelling of proper names: Ναζαρέτ – Ναζαρέθ, Δαβίδ – Δαυείδ, 'Ηλίας – 'Ηλείας, Μωσῆς – Μωυσῆς, 'Ιωάννης – 'Ιωάνης, etc. Among other insignificant variations Bruce mentions the presence or absence of the final ν in verbs (ἔλεγε – ἔλεγεν); the omission or insertion of μ (λήψομαι – λήμψομαι); the assimilation or non-assimilation of ἐν and σύν in compound verbs (συζητεῖν, συνζητεῖν; ἐκκακεῖν, ἐνκακεῖν); the doubling of μ, ν, ρ or the reverse (μαμμωνᾶς, μαμωνᾶς; γέννημα, γένημα; ἐπιρράπτει, ἐπιράπτει); the conjunction or disjunction of syllables (οὐκ ἔτι, οὐκέτι); οὕτως for οὕτω; the aorist forms εἶπον, ἦλθον, etc., replaced by forms in α (εἶπαν, ἦλθαν); single or double augment in certain verbs (ἐδυνάμην, ἠδυνάμην; ἔμελλον, ἤμελλον). Anyone interested in the variations of this kind will find rich material in Winer, *Grammatik d. neutest. Sprachidioms*, 6th ed., p. 39 ff.

3:1): "To write the same things [τὰ αὐτά, one and the same] to you, to me indeed is not grievous, but for you it is safe." Now, if because of a variant we must relinquish a certain prooftext for a certain doctrine – which, by the way, is seldom the case – we have ample proof for that doctrine in other passages which have not been touched by textual criticism. Here is a precaution which is important in disputing with opponents: *Disputandi causa* refrain from establishing a challenged reading. To illustrate, in a dispute with Unitarians on the doctrine of the Trinity relinquish 1 John 5:7-8 as prooftext. The words which mention the three witnesses in heaven: "The Father, the Word, and the Holy Ghost," are not found in the older Greek transcripts. One may indeed be convinced, on the basis of scientific investigation, that these words are nevertheless genuine, that is, that they were in the original autographs. We personally hold this conviction, because Cyprian quotes these words as Scripture.[48] But in a dispute with a Unitarian, who denies the authenticity of 1 John 5:7, we at once disregard this passage as prooftext. That does not make the doctrine of the Holy Trinity doubtful in any way, since this doctrine is taught clearly – also with the co-ordination of the three persons in God – in such passages of Scripture as are not questioned by the critics, e. g., Matt. 28:19: "Baptizing them in the name of the Father and of the Son and of the Holy Ghost," and 2 Cor. 13:13: "The grace of the Lord Jesus Christ and the love of God and the communion of the Holy Ghost be with you all."

4. The alleged contradictions in Scripture and erroneous statements in general are stressed particularly by the opponents of inspiration. At the time when Philippi had not yet gained the right attitude toward Scripture and still admitted the possibility of errors in Scripture, he nevertheless censured the "furious search for discrepancies" on the part of the moderns, which was "due primarily to the wicked attitude

---

[48] We are of the opinion that J. E. F. Sander's position on the passage has yet to be proved wrong. And Stroebel's criticism of Sander (*Zeitschr. f. luth. Theologie*, 1854, p. 135 f.), that "abysmal arbitrariness in criticism" would prevail if the old codices were not made the judge in textual criticism, is not cogent. Modern criticism is right in insisting that a quotation from the Fathers is often of decisive importance over against even the oldest codices. If Schoemann in his edition of Cicero's *De Natura Deorum* (3d ed., Berlin, 1865, p. 99) has seen correctly, we have an analog to 1 John 5:7-8 in the field of secular literature. Schoemann in his edition of *De Natura Deorum* I, 41, inserts the words "*ne intereat*" and adds a note: "These words are, it is true, lacking in the codices, but are preserved in a quotation of this passage in Augustine, *Epist.* 56, tom. II, p. 267, ed. Basil, 1569." We shall have to take up this subject again in the section on "The Integrity of the Biblical Text."

which boasts of having eliminated all assumptions and presuppositions; they claimed the right to cut loose from the presupposition that Scripture is the Word of God, but in place of that sat down in the temple of God and presupposed that they were God" (*Glaubenslehre*, 1st ed., I, 199). With regard to the alleged contradictions in Scripture the situation is briefly this: if only there is some readiness to come to an understanding, the possibility of harmonizing the seemingly contradictory statements can easily be shown; and no fair-minded person will ask more than that. Ebrard [49] should not have reproved Chemnitz for "offering the probable when he could offer nothing certain." Chemnitz's principle is the only sensible one. In recent years A. T. Robertson has written these apt words: "In explaining a difficulty, it is always to be remembered that even a possible explanation is sufficient to meet the objector. If several possible explanations are suggested, it becomes all the more unreasonable for one to contend that the discrepancy is irreconcilable. It is a work of supererogation to show that this or that explanation is the real solution of the problem. Sometimes, owing to new light, this might be possible, but it is never necessary. And by reason of the meager information we have on many points in the Gospel narrative, it may always be impossible in various cases to present a solution satisfactory in every point. The harmonist has done his duty if he can show a reasonable explanation of the problem before him. It is to be remembered also that there is as much prejudice against the supernatural element in the Gospels as there is a favorable opinion for the accuracy of the narratives." [50] We shall have to agree with Robertson. This might be added: If we should meet with a case where we can discover no way of adjusting the difference, we leave the matter in abeyance, since as Christians we believe, on the authority of the Son of God, in the infallibility of Scripture – "the Scriptures cannot be broken" (John 10:35). All objections against the inerrancy of Scripture disgrace the Christian, because they oppose a human judgment to Christ's judgment.

Luther knew very well how to deal with the unbeliever and the Christian according to his flesh in an apologetic way, but when he describes the attitude toward the Scriptures which is becoming to the Christian, he uses firm, yes, strong language. He says, for example: "They [the sophists] say the Scriptures are far too weak that we should silence heretics with them; reason must do it, and it must come forth

[49] *Wissenschaftliche Kritik der evangelischen Geschichte*, 2d ed., p. 59.
[50] Quoted in Broadus, *A Harmony of the Gospels*, 8th ed., p. 232.

from the brain; thus one must prove that the faith is the right one. But our faith is above all reason, and it alone is the power of God. Therefore, if the people will not believe, then be silent; for you are not held to compel them to receive Scripture as God's book or Word; it is enough if you give the reason therefor. But if they take exceptions and say: You preach that one should not hold to man's doctrine, and yet St. Peter and Paul, and even Christ, were men — when you hear people of this stamp, who are so blinded and hardened as to deny that what Christ and the Apostles spoke and wrote is God's Word, or doubt it, then be silent, speak no more with them, and let them go. Only say: I will give you reasons enough from Scripture; if you will believe it, it is well; if not, go your way. Will you say: Then God's Word must suffer defeat? Leave that to God!" (St. L. IX:1238 f.) According to Luther, it is utterly unworthy of a Christian to refuse to accept as God's Word and inerrant what Christ and the Apostles spoke and wrote. This judgment Luther also applies to the historical trustworthiness of Scripture in all cases where there is a discrepancy between secular writers and the statements of Scripture. He says: "I make use of the secular writings in such a manner that I am not forced to contradict Scripture. For I believe that in the Scriptures the God of truth speaks; in the histories good people display, according to their ability, their diligence and fidelity (but only as men) or at least that their copyists have perchance erred" (St. L. XIV:491). Likewise Luther maintains the inerrancy of the Scriptures when they differ with the natural scientists. He says with regard to the doctrine of the creation of the world: "When Moses writes that God created heaven and earth and all that is therein in six days, then let it stand that it was in six days, and you dare not find a gloss how six days were one day. And if you cannot understand how it could have been done in six days, then accord the Holy Ghost the honor that He is more erudite than you" (St. L. III:21). As to the accommodation of the differences in the reports of the Gospels, Luther (just like Chemnitz in his *Evangelienharmonie*) is content with pointing out several possible ways of solving the apparent discrepancies. (St. L. VII:1780 f.) He is so far from doubting the correctness of the reports that he even declares the apparent disorder in them to be God's work and wisdom (St. L. VII:1297).

The right attitude toward the apparent contradictions in Scripture was set forth about thirty years ago at the "August Conference" by Pastor Schulze of Walsleben. He said among other things: "As the historical person of Jesus Christ, so also single historical events may be considered from various viewpoints. It is pettiness to construct contradictions out of this. Other things we leave in abeyance and patiently wait for the time when they will be clarified and, even if that does not take place, die in peace, our lips and our hearts bearing testimony to the truth of Scripture. . . . We find no cause to give up the attitude toward Scripture which the Church has taken toward it from the beginning, and we shall continue to praise as its glory that through it God is speaking to men and that it is His infallible Word. That is also the position of Christ and His Apostles." (See *Lehre und Wehre,* 1891, p. 379.) Philipp Schaff (*Geschichte der apostolischen Kirche,* 1854, p. 101) said: "The full and perfect awe for the Word of God, which we miss more or less among the entire school of Schleiermacher, demands in such cases where science cannot yet dispel the darkness a humble bringing into captivity of every thought to the obedience of Christ or suspension for the time being of any definite judgment, in the hope that a further and deeper research will succeed in arriving at satisfactory results" (quoted in Philippi's *Glaubenslehre,* 1st ed., I, 200). Just recently we read in the *Deutsche Lehrerzeitung* the following on "contradictions" in Scripture: [51] "You point to contradictions that you cannot solve with your reason; but you also emphatically state that you are convinced of the conditionality of your knowledge. The same holds true of me. The 'facts' you mention — I could easily increase the number — are not unfamiliar to me nor to any attentive reader of the Bible. But can and dare we positively claim that everything which appears as a contradiction to your reason and to mine will under no circumstances ever be harmonized, that the things which at present appear discordant to us will not, in the light of a better and unconditional knowledge, after all pass from dissonance to concord? 'Now we see through a glass, darkly; but then face to face; now I know in part, but then shall I know even as also I am known.' Might this word of the Apostle not be applicable to our case and your 'facts'? We both acknowledge that Holy Scripture contains 'contradictions' for our reason, but the deductions which we draw from these premises are diametrically opposed to each other. You conclude on the basis of the 'primitive' use of your reason: there appear contradictions in Scripture, therefore Scripture cannot be inerrant. I conclude: the Scriptures are according to the statements of Him of whom they bear witness inviolable truth;

---

[51] Vol. 36, No. 17, Berlin, April 28, 1923. The quotation is from a letter addressed by Rector, *em.,* August Gruenweller in Rheydt to a teacher in Saxony.

therefore the 'contradictions' must resolve themselves in the light of a higher or more perfect knowledge. You, though you are convinced of the insufficiency and conditionality of your knowledge, take the rationalistic standpoint. I, because I do not believe my limited reason capable of a reliable judgment in divine matters, take the standpoint of my Lord and Master, Jesus Christ. For you the question at issue is a matter of reason, for me it is a matter of faith."

The neologists certainly cannot blame Philippi for speaking of a "furious search for discrepancies" on their part. Take the case of the difference in the numbers given 1 Cor. 10:8 – 23,000; and Num. 25:9 – 24,000. Men like Volck of Dorpat find a plain contradiction here, while, in fact, the solution of the apparent contradiction is clearly indicated in these very passages. *Lehre und Wehre,* 1886, p. 319 f., says of this case: "If one reads these two passages and dispenses with all further reflexion, the thought may take root that only one of the two sums can be correct. But on closer examination of the narrative in Numbers 25 one observes a difference among those struck down by the wrath of God. The heads of the people, the real instigators who had misled Israel to commit whoredom and idolatry, were to be hanged, others to be slain by the judges with the sword (Num. 25:4-5). Most of them were swept away by the plague, possibly a pestilence. How now, if Paul in 1 Cor. 10:8 had in mind those stricken down directly by God, the 23,000, in distinction from those slain by human hands, of which there may have been a thousand, while Num. 25:9 gives the total number of those who perished? Or if the entire 24,000 mentioned by Moses died of the pestilence, still it is not said that the 24,000 died on one day, while according to Paul the 23,000 fell on one day. Paul describes the scourge of that one day, while Moses speaks in general of the punishment provoked by the whoredom of Israel. It is plainly a rash judgment, also according to the reckoning of natural reason, if the one figure is made to contradict the other. And the same holds true in other cases."

Lehre und Wehre goes on to call attention to the thought we expressed above, namely, that common reason demands that we be content with a possible solution of apparent contradictions. "When one and the same event is described in two different places in the Bible in two different ways, it is manifest that different features, different aspects of the same thing are brought out in the two reports. We should have to know exactly all minor circumstances and particulars of the central fact spoken of to recognize how these various features fit together. Since, however, as a rule, only a few data are given, since various circumstances are unknown to us, since all kinds of links are missing, it is often impossible for us to say definitely how the various circumstances fit together and find room in one frame. Here various possibilities suggest themselves. And it is subjective arbitrariness, yes, a crying wrong is inflicted on the Scriptures if the difference in the reporting is turned into a dissension and contradiction of the reporters. As long as proof is not furnished that the two reports are diametrically opposed, the recognition of contradictions demanded by the scientific theology of our day is nothing less than a scientific swindle. . . . Harmonistics is confined within narrow limits. In numerous cases it is impossible to construct from the different statements of the Evangelists concerning one and the same miracle of Jesus a complete and exact picture of the whole event and assign to each of the minor circumstances reported by the individual Evangelist its place in the whole structure. It is much better to answer the question what the connection between the various individual circumstances is and what the sequence of the individual incidents had been with a *non liquet* [it is not clear] than to palm off a self-conceived combination as evangelical truth. But as long as the various features do not mutually cancel and exclude one another – and it will never be possible to prove that they do – so long, even from a purely human standpoint, it is foolish and foolhardy to stamp the variations as contradictions." After exemplifying this procedure in the case of the Easter Story, the article finally states: "Moreover, we see from this dissimilarity in the reports of the Evangelists that the holy writers were not led in composing their writings by cunning calculation and consideration of the impression their readers might gain from their Gospels. Else they would have practiced more harmonization. The second writer would have followed more closely and more scrupulously the writing of the first. No, a higher hand has been here arranging and forming things. The Spirit of God has here managed and governed things as He saw fit, entirely unconcerned und unaffected, so to say, by any fear that the future criticism of His holy work might in some way harm His authority." [52]

5. Furthermore, a whole series of real or merely assumed facts has been advanced against the inspiration of Holy Scripture, for ex-

---

[52] A very thorough discussion of the "alleged contradictions in the Bible," in connection with the controversy in the Baltic provinces, is found in *Lehre und Wehre*, 1893, pp. 33–273 *passim*. Cp. also the *Proceedings of the Ev. Luth. Synodical Conference*, 1902, pp. 5–56. In these two essays practically all essential passages in which contradictions have been found have been considered.

ample, "inaccurate quotations" from the Old Testament by the writers of the New Testament, insignificant matters unworthy of the Holy Ghost, solecisms and barbarisms, etc., also single passages, like 1 Cor. 7:12, and longer passages from Scripture.

As to the inaccurate quotations, Kahnis asks whether it comports with the dignity of the Holy Ghost to ascribe to Him "all the inaccurate quotations" from the Old Testament found in the New.[53] And the Englishman Row says: "The mode in which the Old Testament Scriptures are referred to and quoted in the New is fatal to all theories of mechanical [!] or verbal inspiration" (quoted by Dr. R. Watts, *The Rule of Faith,* p. 233). We insert here, in a somewhat abbreviated form and with a few additions, what we wrote in *Lehre und Wehre* 32, 77–82, at the time of the Bible controversy in the Baltic provinces under the heading *"Die Form der alttestamentlichen Zitate im Neuen Testament":* When the Evangelists and Apostles narrate those things which happened "among us" (Luke 1:1), or when they present the saving doctrine, they introduce statements of the Old Testament with an "as it is written," "as the Scripture hath said," thus showing the fulfillment in the New Testament of events prophesied in the Old Testament or adducing the testimony of the Old Testament for their doctrine. Here, however, it is surprising to note the phenomenon, at first sight somewhat disturbing, that the words expressly quoted as the words of the Old Testament by the clauses "as it is written," "as the Scripture hath said," frequently depart in form, and that quite considerably, from the exact reading in the Old Testament. Luther writes: "We see again and again that the Evangelist quotes the Prophet in a somewhat altered form" (St. L. XI:12). According to our count, there are in the Epistle to the Romans forty-seven quotations from the Old Testament, only twenty-four of which can be classed as literal. The deviations in form from the wording of the Old Testament texts are of various kinds. In some cases the New Testament writers have expanded the Old Testament text (e. g., Is. 61:1; Luke 4:18); in numerous other cases contracted it (Is. 8:22; 9:1 f.; Matt. 4:15); in several instances the order of the sentences has been inverted (Hos. 2:23; Rom. 9:25); frequently several passages are blended into one (Jer. 32:6 ff.; Zech. 11:12-13; Matt. 27:9). That this method of quoting always preserved the original sense of the Old Testament words is *a priori* certain to all who believe that the Evangelists and Prophets spoke and wrote as they were moved by the Holy Ghost. It can also

[53] The long quotation from Kahnis is found in Baier-Walther, I, 102 f.

be proved *a posteriori,* in the light of the New Testament, that the intended sense of the Old Testament text is none other than the one expressed in the New Testament. Luther writes in the place quoted above: "One must know that the evangelists are not concerned about citing every last word of the prophets; they were satisfied if they gave the same sense and showed the fulfillment. . . . But it is all done without prejudice to the sense and the meaning." [54]

But still the question remains as to the true reason why the writers of the New Testament frequently chose a form which departed so strikingly and radically from the wording of the Old Testament. If a preacher today quotes Scripture with an express: "Thus writes St. Paul, or St. John," etc., we expect him to give the exact words of the passage. We would consider it improper if he were to disregard the form of the words he is quoting – and that is exactly what the Evangelists and Apostles did in quoting from the Old Testament. Various explanations of this procedure have been offered. Some have advanced the opinion that the form as given in the New Testament is the original one, that the text of the Old Testament has been – at least in these passages – very much corrupted.[55] That would, indeed, explain the difference in the wording. But this explanation is inadmissible. Disregarding other considerations, we find that the textual criticisms of the Old Testament know of no such corruption of the text. Others have sought the reason in a lapse of memory on the part of the holy writers, who imagined that they were quoting the Old Testament – but were mistaken in that. Just recently these "inaccurate quotations" have been advanced as disproving the inspiration of Holy Scripture (Kahnis, Row). But disregarding the fact that such an assumption of "mistakes" on the part of the Apostles contradicts their own statements that the Holy Ghost is speaking

---

[54] Cf. the series of articles by Dr. Stoeckhardt in *Lehre und Wehre* 30, p. 42 ff. and 31, p. 220 ff., with the heading: "Weissagung und Erfuellung." In these articles all the "misquotations" found in Matthew are treated: Is. 7:14 – Matt. 1:18-23; Micah 5:2 – Matt. 2:5-6; Hos. 11:1 – Matt. 2:15; Jer. 31:15 – Matt. 2:17-18; Is. 11:1 and Zech. 6:12 – Matt. 2:23; Is. 40:3 – Matt. 3:1-3; Is. 8:22 and 9:1-2 – Matt. 4:12-16; Is. 53:4 – Matt. 8:17; Is. 42:1 ff. – Matt. 12:15-21; Is. 6:9-10 – Matt. 13:13-15; Ps. 78:2 – Matt. 13:34-35; Zech. 9:9 – Matt. 21:1-5; Ps. 118:26 – Matt. 21:9; Ps. 118:22-23 – Matt. 21:42-44; Ps. 8:2 – Matt. 21:16; Ps. 110:1 – Matt. 22:43-46; Ex. 3:6 – Matt. 22:31-32; Dan. 9:23 ff. – Matt. 24:15; Zech. 13:7 – Matt. 26:31 ff.; Zech. 11:12-13 and Jer. 32:6 ff. – Matt. 27:3 ff. (Here it is demonstrated that Matthew also quotes Jeremiah.) Ps. 22:18 – Matt. 27:35; Ps. 22:1 – Matt. 27:46.

[55] Thus Ludovicus Capellus II. Cf. Pfeiffer, *Critica Sacra,* Leipzig, 1712, p. 105 ff.

through them (1 Cor. 2:13; 14:37; 2 Cor. 13:3; 1 Pet. 1:12), even a purely human reflection must regard the theory that the deviation from the Old Testament was due to "slips" or "lapses of memory" as untenable, as will be shown hereafter.

There is but one explanation for this often bold manner of quoting the wording of the Old Testament in the New Testament. This explanation is found in such passages as 1 Pet. 1:10-12, which expressly state that the same Spirit of Christ who spoke through the Old Testament Prophets also testified through the Evangelists and Apostles. And this testimony naturally included the explanation of the Old Testament passages. Thus in quoting the Old Testament the Holy Spirit is in a manner quoting Himself. And He has the authority to use His own words as He chooses; in quoting He makes of the Old Testament Scripture passage, so to say, a "new text" (Luther's phrase), which at the same time explains the Old Testament text. The Evangelists and Apostles, inspired by the Holy Ghost, are therefore not so much quoting as rather "taking hold" of the Scriptures. Luther says of the Pentecost sermon of the Apostles: "How amazingly they take hold of Scripture, as though they had studied it a thousand years and knew it inside out. I could not take hold of Scripture with such certainty, although I am a doctor of the Holy Scriptures. . . . Thus God displays the greatest wisdom that has come into the world through the foolishness and ignorance of these miserable weak beggars, so that no one can do what they did, neither Annas nor Caiaphas nor any man on earth." (St. L. XIII:2053 f.) Flacius writes: "It must be maintained that the Old Testament is usually cited by the holy writers of the New Testament in such a manner that they observed the sense and produced rather the fulfillment of the prophecy than the words of the prophecy. That will not appear strange or rash to him who takes the right view of the matter and is convinced that the Spirit who spoke through the mouth of the Evangelists was the same who opened the mouth of the Prophets and, furthermore, that the function of the Prophets was to foretell the future, the function of the Evangelists, however, to narrate the fulfillment. Since therefore the Spirit of God does not write out, but expounds the prophecies of the former in the New Testament, the demand must not be made that He enumerate the exact words." (*Clavis Scripturae Sacrae,* P. II, p. 103.) A. Pfeiffer remarks: "That the passages of the Old Testament are not always adduced verbatim (αὐτολεξεί) in the New Testament is not due to a corruption of the text as we have it, but is due to the fact that by inspiration of the Holy Ghost an explanation of the true sense of the passage is given" (*Thesaurus Hermeneuticus*, 1704, p. 59). The same writer says: "In the New Testament the statements of the Old Testament are not always quoted according to the wording, but often according to the sense, and that freely, sometimes from the Hebrew text, sometimes from the Septuagint, sometimes from both. Why make much ado about it, since there is here no contradiction? The Holy Spirit has revealed the Old Testament, and He has reserved the right to interpret it in the New. Where this was done by the Septuagint, its translation was retained; where this was not the case, the original text was quoted. Repeatedly the Holy Ghost has bound Himself neither to that translation nor to the words of the original text, but has given the sense in new words. Whatever may be the case, the same Holy Ghost, the best Interpreter of His own words, spoke in both places." (*Critica Sacra*, p. 109 f.)

Dr. Watts (in *The Rule of Faith*, London, 1885, p. 236 ff.) has well said: "The New Testament writers often vary the language of the passages they quote from the Old Testament in order to give an authoritative interpretation of them. It is true they might have given the sacred text as it stood, and then have added their own explanatory comments; but in this, as in other matters, the Apostolic admonition may not be out of place for those who would prescribe rules for men acting under the special guidance of the Holy Spirit: 'For who hath known the mind of the Lord? or who hath been his counselor?' (Rom. 11:34.). . . . Inspired by the free Spirit . . . they reveal that freedom wherewith the indwelling Spirit, by the very fullness of His habitation, has made them free, and they quote from the Septuagint where it differs from the Hebrew, and from the Hebrew where it differs from the Septuagint, and often cite a passage in a form in which it is not found in either the Hebrew or the Greek. In moving the New Testament writers to deal in this manner with the Old Testament, the Spirit, who is the Author of both the New Testament Revelation and that of the Old, was but asserting His own authority, while He was acting in conformity with a law of authorship which no one ever thinks of questioning as applied to uninspired writers. No one ever holds that an author, when reiterating a statement, must keep the exact phraseology of the first utterance of it. Surely, if such license is given to man, and is considered almost the birthright of human authorship, it is as irreverent as it is unreasonable to abridge, by such limitations as the objector would impose, the liberty of the Spirit of the Lord."

The form of the Old Testament quotations as given in the New

Testament does therefore not prove "fatal" to the theory of "verbal inspiration," but is, on the contrary, a mighty proof of inspiration. Suppose that the Evangelists and Apostles had not been inspired, but, like other writers, had only their own good judgment to fall back on. Would that not have affected the form of their citations? Would they not have carefully refrained from shocking men with their free manner of quoting and have quoted more literally? To say that the exact context and the exact wording of the quoted passage were not present at the moment to the mind of the Apostles, is a rather weak objection. Suppose they had forgotten context and wording, a simple means of supplying the want was at hand. They could simply look up the matter! That is what we do, and the Apostles had the Old Testament at hand. Or could anyone reasonably assume that the Apostles did not take the trouble to assist their faulty memory by consulting the text, hoping that their readers would not notice their inaccurate citations? St. Paul knew better than that; he knew that his readers knew the Law (Rom. 7:1). We are of the opinion that human reason, if it be reasonable, must refrain from explaining the departure of the New Testament quotation from the wording of the Old Testament by assuming "mistakes" or "slips of memory" in the holy writers. There is but one explanation: the Holy Ghost is speaking through the Apostles and is "taking liberties" with His own Word. And as the apparent contradictions in the Scriptures prove that the Scriptures are not a fabrication of designing men, so particularly the manner in which the Evangelists and Apostles quote the Old Testament is a powerful proof that they have not spoken and written of themselves, not by purely human deliberation, but that they wrote by inspiration of the Holy Ghost.

The many "unimportant human matters" or the "trivialities" *(levicula)* mentioned in the Bible are said to impeach the inspiration of Holy Scripture: it does not comport with the divine dignity of the Holy Ghost to mention such things. Paul's cloak and the parchments he had left in Troas (2 Tim. 4:13) are usually designated as such trivialities; and special emphasis is laid on the prescription Paul gave Timothy for his diet, that Timothy should drink not only water, but use a little wine for his "stomach's sake" (1 Tim. 5:23). This objection reveals an entirely wrong conception of the "ethical principles" of the Holy Ghost. The Holy Ghost is of the opinion that faithfulness in small matters is decidedly proper and necessary. We read Luke 16:10: "He that is faithful in that which is least (ἐν ἐλαχίστῳ) is faithful also in much (ἐν πολλῷ); and he that is unjust in the least is unjust also in much." Even the unbelieving world, when it uses its reason, pays tribute to this virtue; it recognizes the great man by his trustworthiness in small matters. And the Christian ought to agree with Luther when he writes: "You should not wonder or ask in surprise why the Holy Ghost took pleasure in describing such common and contemptible things [in the life of the patriarchs], but you should listen to what St. Paul says Rom. 15:4: 'Whatsoever things were written aforetime were written for our learning, that we through patience and comfort of the Scriptures might have hope.' If we firmly believed, as I believe, though weakly, that the Holy Ghost Himself and God, the Creator of all things, is the true author (*auctor*) of this Book [The Bible] and of such mean and despicable things – mean and small to our carnal eyes – we should, as St. Paul says, derive the greatest comfort therefrom. . . . This is what the Holy Ghost would teach us when He condescends to write about the saints and their petty affairs: the lowliest works of the saints please God. Behold the glory and worth of a Christian man: there is nothing so lowly about him but it pleases God. To shed one's blood, to die, to sweat, to strive and battle against the devil is in truth a great thing and pleases God much. You must conclude thus: After you have come to faith, then also the natural, carnal, and physical works please God, whether you eat or drink, are awake or sleep, these are surely nothing but bodily and natural works. Such a great thing is faith. Therefore see to it first that you become a Christian and that your person becomes acceptable and pleasing to God through the Word, through Baptism and the Sacrament. When the person believes and becomes attached to the Word, no longer persecutes it, but thanks God for it, then all you are to do is what Solomon tells you in Eccl. 9:7-8: 'Go thy way, eat thy bread with joy, and drink thy wine with a merry heart; for God now accepteth thy works. Let thy garments be always white; and let thy head lack no ointment.'" (St. L. II:469 ff.)

Accordingly, also the teachers of old, including the old dogmaticians, point out what weighty lessons are contained in these insignificant matters mentioned by the Apostle Paul in 2 Tim. 4:13 and 1 Tim. 5:23. We see from these and other passages that the Apostle Paul was no "Enthusiast." He might have asked God to have angels bring him the coat and the parchments he left in Troas. But because the Apostle knows that God asks us to use the natural means appointed by Him, as long as such means are at our command, he instructs Timothy to bring along the cloak and the parchments. The same applies to his dietary advice. In Timothy's illness and bodily weakness Paul directs not only to prayer: "Praying always with all prayer and supplication in the Lord" (Eph. 6:18) and: "Cast thy burden upon the Lord and He shall sustain thee" (Ps. 55:22), but also to the use of natural remedies: Timothy is to refrain from the exclusive use of water and use a little wine.[56] In Paul's concern about his cloak old teachers find an indication of his poverty, which, however, did not make him weary and unwilling to perform the duties of his apostleship. They have also found that Paul's desire for the parchment revealed his zeal in the performance of his office. (*Lehre und Wehre,* 32, p. 297.) The Apostle's statement (1 Tim. 5:23) is, further, a warning against imposing Prohibition, a law of men, upon the Church as a law of God. The State, or, as Luther usually expresses it, the "Kaiser," may enact laws concerning meat and drink, and the Christians will obey such laws. But when "the Church" presumes to make such laws, it falls under the sharp judgment of the Apostle (1 Tim. 4:1-5): "Some shall depart from the faith, giving heed to seducing spirits and doctrines of devils," since in that case "the Church" is "commanding to abstain from meats, which God hath created to be received with thanksgiving of them which believe and know the truth. For every creature of God is good, and nothing to be refused, if it be received with thanksgiving." The practical result of the imposition of such commandments of men by "the Church" is stated by Christ Matt. 15:6: God's doctrine and commandment is displaced by the commandments of men. The sectarian bodies of our country furnish plenty of examples of such aberrations. In short, in these "trivialities" in the Bible there are important lessons for eyes that are able to see. Whoever imagines that these *levicula* are unworthy of the Holy Ghost knows little about the Holy Ghost or about the Christian life or conduct.[57]

In general, he who talks as though it were beneath the dignity

---

[56] Huther comments: "Of course the Apostle does not mean to forbid Timothy to drink water at all, but only urges him not to avoid wine altogether. ὑδροποτεῖν does not exactly mean 'to drink water,' but 'to be a water drinker' and is only used of a man who makes water his special and exclusive drink." Similarly Winer, *Grammar,* 6th ed., p. 442. The verb ὑδροποτεῖν occurs in the New Testament only here; it is, however, not a word coined by the Apostle, but is genuine Greek. Ebeling, *s. v.*, furnishes the proof of this.

[57] Hoenecke says (*Dogmatik* I, p. 351) that these passages [1 Tim. 5:23 and 2 Tim. 4:13] yield two important principles for our Christian life; the first, that an overstrained asceticism is foreign to the spirit of the Gospel; the second, that it is a false spirituality which despises the insignificant things of this life and regards itself as superior to them; and that statements of Scripture which are so edifying are not unworthy of being inspired by the Holy Ghost. Quenstedt

of the Holy Ghost to refer to such small matters as eating, drinking, clothing, etc., in the Scriptures must have completely forgotten that the eternal Son of God did not consider it beneath His dignity to assume a true human nature from the Virgin Mary into His divine person, to be wrapped in swaddling clothes and laid in a manger. He who stands in adoration before the miracle in the manger of Bethlehem will not consider it strange, but altogether in order that mention is made in the Scriptures, which are God's Word, of "human trivialities." For God loves men and their trifles. Luther: "Moses says to Pharaoh (Exodus 10): 'Our cattle also shall go with us; there shall not a hoof be left behind.' Not only are the men, women, and children, and the cattle to leave Egypt, but we shall leave nothing behind, not even one mean hoof. . . . Yes, and hear what Christ says, who uses stronger language (Matthew 10): 'But the very hairs of your head are all numbered.' Friend, what can be more insignificant and of less account on the body of men than a hair or a nail? But they are all counted, and the Father in heaven cares about them. In this manner we are to consider the examples of the lowly and ordinary works of the saints in order that we may be instructed and comforted by them." (St. L. II:470.) When we take offense at these human trivialities in Scripture, that is proof positive either that we do not at all believe

---

says (I, p. 103) that it is one thing to regard a thing unimportant when it is considered in itself, and another thing to regard the same thing as unimportant when you consider its purpose and the wise counsel of God; that many things in Scripture seem of little importance, such as Paul's leaving his cloak at Troas (2 Tim. 4:13); and that these things, which some think are contrary to the majesty of the Holy Spirit, are nevertheless of great import if we look to the end (Rom. 15:4) and the most wise counsel of God by which these things were inserted into the divine writings. Philippi (*Glaubenslehre,* 3d ed., I, 261): "But what of that cloak at Troas, worn threadbare by modern criticism, with which the Anomians loved to cloak their unbelief, and the books, especially the parchment of 2 Tim. 4:13? And, to crown all, the dietary advice of the Apostle (1 Tim. 5:23)! We should not be surprised if our modern naturalists, who set such store by eating and drinking, by clothing, and by books, especially their own, and parchments, as being absolutely necessary for the welfare of the human race would one of these days make a complete about-face and rate only these passages as inspired. But as pertaining to the matter itself, the higher, ethical import of both statements is easily recognizable. The second passage guards against a false overstrained asceticism as well as an immoderate use of God's earthly gifts, teaches in a concrete way both that every creature of God is good and nothing is to be rejected, if it be received with thanksgiving (1 Tim. 4:4), and that we are to make provision for the flesh, but not in such a manner as to fulfill the lusts thereof (Rom. 13:14). The first passage shows us how faithful attention to seemingly insignificant matters comports well with even the most zealous devotion to the highest calling in the Kingdom of God, that the one does not exclude, but include the other."

the incarnation of the Son of God or that this central truth has so far receded into the background as to be almost forgotten. This matter Luther had in view when he wrote the well-known monitory warning: "I beg and faithfully warn every pious Christian not to stumble at the simplicity of the language and the stories that will often meet him there. He should not doubt that however simple they may seem, these are the very words, works, judgments, and history of the high majesty and wisdom of God. For this is the Scripture that makes fools of all the wise and prudent and is open to the small and foolish, as Christ says in Matt. 11:25. Therefore let your thoughts and feelings go, and think of the Scripture as the loftiest and noblest of holy things, as the richest of mines, which can never be worked out, so that you may find the wisdom of God that He lays before you in such foolish and simple guise, that He may quench all pride. Here you will find the swaddling clothes and the manger in which Christ lies, to which also the angel directs the shepherds (Luke 2:11). Simple and lowly swaddling clothes they are, but precious is the treasure, Christ, lying in them." (St. L. XIV:3–4.)

The foes of inspiration make very much of the "solecisms," "barbarisms," faulty sentence construction, and similar things which they find in Scripture. Kahnis, who has drawn up a lengthy list of all those matters which according to his notion conflict with the dignity of the Holy Ghost, writes: "Is not that conception of inspiration which ascribes all solecisms and barbarisms of the Apostolic Scriptures, all faulty constructions of Paul, to the Holy Ghost derogatory of the Holy Ghost?" [58] The dogmaticians are charged with narrowness because they are ready to admit Hebraisms in the Bible, but no solecisms and barbarisms.

As to solecisms, it should be noted that this term *solecism* has not always been employed in the same sense. Quenstedt already observed and proved that.[59] If by it is meant a "faulty dialect," or a departure from the so-called classical Greek, we shall take care of that when we discuss the "barbarisms." But if by "solecism" is meant a violation of the grammatical rules of a language, Winer answers the objection in his *Grammatik des neutestamentlichen Sprachidioms* (6th ed., p. 36) thus: "The New Testament is written in correct Greek and

---

[58] Quoted in Baier-Walther, I, 102 f., from the 1st ed. of his *Dogmatik*. These words are somewhat toned down in the 2d ed., I, 281, 284 ff., 293 ff.

[59] *Systema* I, 119. *The Century Dictionary and Cyclopedia* has some interesting remarks on the use of the term *solecism*.

observes the Greek grammar." Whoever tests the New Testament in this respect will agree with Winer. But also the wild talk of "barbarisms" makes no sense. The New Testament, as everyone knows, is written in the so-called κοινὴ διάλεκτος, the language of international intercourse since Alexander the Great. Ebeling writes: "The New Testament writers wrote in Hellenistic Greek, in the language used in their day by the people throughout the entire Roman Empire." "The vocabulary and grammatical usage of the New Testament presents no isolated case, but belongs to the κοινή and is found, above all, in letters, reports, applications, bills, contracts, testaments, and the like, in the language of daily intercourse and of the people." [60] Robertson states: "It is not speculation to speak of the κοινή as a world speech, for the inscriptions in the κοινή testify to its spread over Asia, Egypt, Greece, Italy, Sicily, and the isles of the sea. . . . The κοινή was in such general use that the Roman Senate and imperial governors had the decrees translated into the world language and scattered over the empire. It is significant that the Greek speech becomes one instead of many dialects at the very time that the Roman rule sweeps over the world." [61] The reason is thus clear why the holy writers wrote in the κοινὴ διάλεκτος, in the world language, or the vernacular of the people, and why they should write in that language according to the intention of the Holy Ghost, who was in them (1 Pet. 1:12; 1 Cor. 2:15; 2 Cor. 13:3). For they had a call into all the world (Matt. 28:18-20; Mark 16:16; Luke 24:46-47). They desired to be understood, as in their preaching, so in their writing, not only by a part of the people, the people, for instance, with a classical training, but by all the people. The salvation of all the people, of the whole human race, was at stake! [62]

How well the use of the universal popular speech served the purpose of the Apostles of being generally understood is apparent from the fact that they did not deem it necessary to send commentaries along with their letters. The epistles of the Apostles were understood

---

[60] *Woerterbuch zum Neuen Testament*, 1913, Preface, III.

[61] Grammar, 3d ed., p. 54. Regarding the term *Hellenistic* compare Winer, p. 26 f.; Blass-Debrunner, *Grammatik des neutest. Griechisch*, 5th ed., p. 1.

[62] Dr. A. L. Graebner calls the New Testament Greek "a type of Greek which rendered the New Testament highly adapted to its intended use for doctrine, reproof, correction, and instruction in righteousness, not to men of polite education only, but to the people at large, to entire congregations of hearers to whom these books were to be read and interpreted, and who should themselves be readers searching the Scriptures of the New Testament as well as of the Old" (*Theological Quarterly*, 1897, p. 146).

not only by the teachers of the congregations, but by the congregations themselves, by the common people, when the epistles were read to them. St. Paul writes to the Christians at Colosse: "When this epistle is read among you, cause that it be read also in the church of the Laodiceans; and that ye likewise read the epistle from Laodicea" (Col. 4:16). And to the Thessalonians he writes: "I charge you by the Lord that this epistle be read unto all the holy brethren" (1 Thess. 5:27).

But even apart from the fact that the Apostles made use of this language for the purpose of being understood in their letters by all, it reveals great foolishness to call deviations from the "classical Greek" barbarisms. The folly is so great that one takes notice of it only reluctantly. To call the deviations from classical Greek barbarisms amounts to the absurd thought, contrary even to the natural reason, that it would have been more becoming to the Holy Ghost to talk like Demosthenes or Plato than to use the language of the common people. It is certainly also true of language: "Before God nothing is small, since before Him nothing is great." And therefore the dogmaticians are right when they maintain that all opinions of the New Testament Greek which express a censure are improper and should not be found among Christians.[63] The Greek language as we have it in the New Testament and of course also the Hebrew language of the Old Testament are holy languages, above all other languages which the world contains. Even Cremer[64] says of the New Testament Greek that it "became the organ of the Spirit of Christ" – though these words hardly fit the position which Cremer takes toward the inspiration of Scripture. And even Rothe declares: "One can, in fact, on good grounds speak of a language of the Holy Ghost."[65] We should never forget this: The Hellenistic Greek of the New Testament is that Greek which God speaks to the world to the end of time and to which God binds all the world to the Last Day; it is God's original text, which, of course, all translations must follow. Finding fault with the New Testament Greek is therefore indeed offensive, because it is finding fault with God. For this reason the dogmaticians, as already stated, are so sensitive when men speak of solecisms and barbarisms in the New Testament; for in their days, as also in our day, these terms were

---

63 Quenstedt, I, 118 *sq.*, under *status controversiae.*

64 *Woerterbuch der neutest. Graezitaet,* 3d ed., Preface, V.

65 Quoted by Cremer, *op. cit.*, Preface, VI, from Rothe's *Zur Dogmatik,* Gotha, 1863, p. 238.

used in a derogatory sense.[66] As insulting and offensive as it would be to call the Son of God a "barbarian," because in the fullness of (the) time He assumed the human nature from the Virgin Mary, so insulting and offensive it is to speak of "barbarisms" in Holy Scripture, because this Word appeared in the fullness of the time, in the dress of that Greek which was then the universal language of the people.[67]

The so-called "Hebraisms" (*"das juedische Kolorit"*) which we find in the New Testament [68] properly belong there. The New Testament does not bring a new religion, but is the fulfillment of the Old Testament. Dr. A. L. Graebner (*Theol. Quarterly,* 1897, p. 22) writes: "The Greek of the New Testament was to bear the stamp and imprint of the country where Jesus lived and died, and of that Church and people of which New Testament Christianity is, not in form, but as to its spiritual nature, the true continuation, its adherents living by the same faith in the same Savior as Abraham their father according to the faith." The dogmaticians also point this out when they show that Hebraisms in the New Testament are a matter of course and entirely in order because of its connection with the Old Testament, while they deny solecisms and barbarisms since they imply a censure of God.[69]

---

[66] Quenstedt, I, 119, under θέσις: "The style of the New Testament is free from every blot of barbarism and solecism." Robertson reports in his *Grammar* (3d ed., p. 50): "Deissmann strongly disapproves the term 'vulgar Greek,' 'bad Greek,' '*Graecitas fatiscens*' in contrast with 'classic Greek.'" The objectionable terms are not only linguistically improper but, above all, offensive to the Christian, because the Christian knows that the New Testament Greek is "the organ of Christ." However, the term *vulgar Greek* is in our day not always used in a derogatory sense; at times it is synonymous with "popular language."

[67] A word of caution is here in place. One who is versed in the vocabulary and diction of the New Testament Greek will find every point of agreement with the classical Greek interesting, but it would be going too far to speak of such agreement as enhancing the dignity of the language of the New Testament. We should thereby be surrendering the true criterion of excellence. The unique dignity of the New Testament Greek consists in its being "the Greek organ of the Spirit of Christ," as Cremer expresses it. Moreover, it should not be forgotten that in the case of such terms as ἀλήθεια, εὐαγγέλιον, χάρις, πίστις, etc., there is no more than an agreement in sound, since the specifically Christian meaning of these words was utterly unknown to all authors of the classical period of Greek (1 Cor. 2:9). The same is true also of expressions such as ἅγιος, δίκαιος, etc., in reference to life and conduct, since the conceptions which these terms awaken in the unbelievers are distinctly unchristian.

[68] Their number has been exaggerated. Cf. Winer, *Grammar,* 6th ed., p. 26 ff., ¶3: *"Hebraeisch-aramaeisches Kolorit der alttestamentlichen Diktion."*

[69] Quenstedt, I, 119: "'Ἑβραΐζειν is one thing, βαρβαρίζειν is another. The former we affirm concerning the New Testament; the latter we deny. . . . For it pleased God to connect the two covenants and to preserve in the Old and the

The "faulty constructions of Paul," which according to Kahnis' view conflict with the dignity of the Holy Ghost, are, we imagine, mainly the so-called anacolutha (Gal. 2:6; 1 Tim. 1:3 ff.; Rom. 5:12). We call an anacoluthon the forsaking of the grammatical sequence in a sentence by a speaker or writer under the rush of strong emotions. It is a legitimate figure of speech. As to the genesis of thus breaking off the sentence structure, Winer says (*Grammar*, 6th ed., p. 500): "Lively intellects, concerned more with the thought than with the grammatical expression, are the more apt to resort to such anacolutha." In popular language it is known as *"aus der Konstruktion fallen"* — to forsake the construction of the sentence. The sensible speaker or author will, instinctively or intentionally, violate the coherent sentence structure when he feels that this will contribute to the clarity of his presentation or help to stress important thoughts. We find plenty of anacolutha in the Greek and Roman classics, and old and modern grammarians have much to say in favor and praise of the anacolutha. They do not call them blunders, but point out the psychological reason for them and then also their benefit: they serve to clarify the presentation and to emphasize important thoughts. And now, since the Holy Ghost is concerned with the clarity of the presentation and the emphasis of especially important thoughts, He certainly did not consider it beneath His dignity to use not only the human language in general but also, in particular, the anacolutha.[70] What the grammarians say in

---

New Testament, in things as well as in words and phrases, a conformity which is truly admirable and in no wise accidental. . . . He who dares to accuse Holy Scripture of barbarisms must himself be a barbaric despiser of Holy Scripture."

70 Illustrations in Winer, *op. cit.*, p. 500 ff. There is in Gal. 2:6 an anacoluthon also in Luther's translation. In regular grammatical sequence the sentence beginning with ἀπὸ δὲ τῶν δοκοῦντων εἶναί τι ought to have an apodosis of passive construction, e. g., οὐδὲν ἐδιδάχθην (Winer). But induced by the inserted clause, ὁποῖοί ποτε ἦσαν, etc., an apodosis in active (medial) construction follows. Robertson, *Grammar*, 3d ed., p. 438: "One of the most striking anacolutha in Paul's epistles is found at the end of Rom. 5:12, where the apodosis to the ὥσπερ clause is wanting. The next sentence (ἄχρι γάρ) takes up the subordinate clause ἐφ' ᾧ πάντες ἥμαρτον, and the comparison is never completed. In v. 18 a new comparison is drawn in complete form." The more recent New Testament philologists, such as Winer, Blass (Blass-Debrunner, *Grammar*, 5th ed., 1921, p. 269 ff.), differ very considerably in their explanation of the New Testament anacolutha. There is no harm in this difference, because the attentive Bible reader understands the passages very well without having the anacolutha explained. Gal. 2:6, for example, is understood by every reader of the Bible without any dissecting of the sentence structure. While Winer, Robertson, Buttmann, and others speak very sensibly of these irregular sentence structures, Blass-Debrunner unfortunately does not. Compare, for example, p. 271: "The sentence structure of 1 Tim. 1:3 ff. turns out to be a real jumble, because

explanation and in praise of the anacolutha the reader may look up in the advanced grammars, old and new. We would like to submit here what the venerable Matthiae says in his *Ausfuehrliche Griechische Grammatik* (p. 1296) on the "deviations from the regular construction." He writes: "The best Greek writers very often deviate from the order or relation of the words in a sentence which is demanded by logic or else sanctioned by usage, in order either to increase the emphasis upon some word or words or the clarity or to give the speech the unconstrained lightness of the conversational tone and thus to heighten the charm. The classical Attic authors always do this for one of those considerations; the later stylists, however, lose the sought-for elegance by the very striving after it. Such deviations from the grammatical sequence are called anacolutha, that is, constructions in which a sentence ends differently than one would expect, or wherein that which the initial structure calls for, does not follow (ἀκολουθέω with the ἀ *privativum*). Such departures from the grammatically or logically correct construction are not due to an oversight, but to the intention of the author and always have a cause." [71]

Certain Scripture statements are said to contradict inspiration. Thus 1 Cor. 7:10, 12, 25, where, they tell us, Paul expressly says that not everything he is writing is the Lord's command. While we read in v. 10: "Unto the married I command, yet not I, but the Lord," he adds in v. 12: "To the rest speak I, not the Lord," and in v. 25: "Concerning virgins I have no commandment of the Lord." Luther's words on this passage will suffice to refute this objection. "When St. Paul here testifies that in this matter not the Lord, but he is speaking, he would have us understand that God did not command to do so or so, but left it free. For he distinguishes his own word from the Word of the Lord, making the Lord's Word a commandment, his own word, however, only advice." (St. L. VIII:1058.) In other words, the Apostle

---

of the ceaseless intercalations and appendages." The "jumble" has its source elsewhere than in the words of Paul. In spite of the anacoluthon every thought in the entire mighty chapter is clearly attached to the preceding thought until the Apostle closes, v. 17, with ἀμήν. Buttmann (*Grammar*, p. 331) is right in classing the passage 1 Tim. 1:3 ff. with the passages in which the initial sentence structure is not completed "because of the wealth of thoughts and the fullness of the heart."

[71] Alex Buttmann, in his *New Testament Grammar*, which closely follows Ph. Buttmann's *Griech. Grammatik*, also discusses extensively the anacoluthon, p. 324 ff. Robertson, in part following Winer, deals very thoroughly with this subject, *Grammar*, 3d ed., p. 435 ff.: "The very jolt that is given by the anacoluthon is often successful in making more emphasis. The attention is drawn anew to the sentence to see what is the matter."

is here not distinguishing between inspired and non-inspired portions of his epistle, but between an inspired divine command, binding the conscience, and inspired apostolic advice which does not bind the conscience. Luther's distinction between command and advice in this passage must be observed; otherwise the passage will be misunderstood, and the inattentive reader will be perplexed. Philippi first makes the entirely correct statement that the Apostle here distinguishes between an "unconditional commandment of the Lord in regard to an ethical *necessarium* and free advice on his part regarding an ethical ἀδιάφορον." But when Philippi adds that the δοκῶ δὲ κἀγῶ, etc. (v. 40: "I think also that I have the Spirit of God"), "in the mouth of the Apostle admits of no contradiction in the contents," he labors under a misunderstanding which makes the Apostle contradict himself. Paul declares repeatedly and expressly that everyone who does not consider his advice good is free not to take it.

The objection against the inspiration of Scripture taken from 1 Cor. 1:16 is due to a confusion of two things which have nothing in common. It has been said that since the Apostle in this passage concedes the possibility of a *lapsus memoriae* with regard to the number of those whom he baptized personally, his epistles could not have been written by inspiration of the Holy Ghost, since the Holy Ghost is not subject to *lapsus memoriae*. This objection has been answered briefly and pointedly: As inspiration did not make the holy writers personally sinless in their lives, so it also did not make them infallible or omniscient as to their past lives.

The brief personal letter to Philemon has also been used as an argument against the inspiration of Scripture, because this letter has been written in such a tender and courteous tone. Kahnis: "Would you have us believe that when the Apostle wrote that tender urbane letter to Philemon tinged as it is with some humor [!], he recorded what the Holy Ghost dictated to him?" (Quoted in Baier-Walther, I, 102.) Indeed we believe that; for we know that the Holy Ghost makes it His business to teach Christians tender, gracious, courteous, well-sounding speech. Col. 4:6: "Let your speech be alway with grace." Phil. 4:8: "Whatsoever things are lovely, whatsoever things are of good report; if there be any virtue and if there be any praise, think on these things." The gentle "humor" which Kahnis considers beneath the notice of the Holy Ghost, he most likely finds in vv. 18-20, where Paul asks Philemon to charge any debt the runaway slave might owe his master to Paul's account. The Apostle here uses a term which reminds one of a business transaction. "I, Paul, have written it with mine own hand, I will repay it" – that sounds like our: "I promise to pay." But to Christians this "business" ought not to be entirely unfamiliar, and they ought not to take offense at it. The "I will repay" is simply a concrete way of expressing the universal Christian obligation of love: "Bear ye one another's burdens, and so fulfill the law of Christ" (Gal. 6:2). And this commandment of the love with which Christians love one another flows from the love shown us by Christ, since the debt of all sinful mankind was charged to His account. Paul unites the two kinds of love that assumes the other's burden when he writes: "And walk in love, as Christ also hath loved us and hath given Himself for us an offering and a sacrifice to God for a sweet-smelling savor" (Eph. 5:2). If we were to call what Paul says concerning the transfer of debt "humor" which is not worthy of the Holy Ghost, we would be passing a judgment which does not flow from the knowledge which is of God. The ancient Church has therefore, without hesitation or opposition, granted the Epistle to Philemon a place in the canon.[72] In his Preface to the Epistle to Philemon, Luther has this to say: "This Epistle gives us a masterly and tender illustration of Christian love, for here we see how St. Paul takes the part of poor Onesimus and advocates his cause with his master all he can and acts no differently than if he were himself Onesimus, who has done wrong. And yet he does this not with force or compulsion, as he had a right to do, but he lays aside his rights and thus compels Philemon also to waive his rights. What Christ has done for us with God the Father, St. Paul does for Onesimus with Philemon. For Christ laid aside His rights and overcame His Father with love and humility, so that He had to put away His wrath and rights and receive us into favor, for Christ's sake, who so earnestly advocates our cause and takes our part so tenderly." (St. L. XIV:122.)[73]

Finally, the evil consequences which allegedly follow the "old

---

[72] Cf. Fuerbringer, *Einleitung in d. N. T.*, p. 71.

[73] One might speak of a "pleasantry" here on the part of the Apostle, as a number of exegetes do. But it is a "refined spiritual" humor. Thus, for example, Vilmar writes in his *Erklaerung des Neuen Testaments*, II, 427: "Finally the Apostle jokes in a refined manner, saying that he is ready to have charged to his account any damage Onesimus may have caused Philemon by absconding; he will, even as he was writing this with his own hand, personally square this account with him and will not take into account at all that Philemon owes himself to him," the Apostle, by whom he had been converted. See in Calov, *Biblia Illustrata*, on this passage, the testimonies of the Church Fathers on the fine spiritual tone of the Epistle to Philemon.

doctrine of inspiration" are marshaled against the inspiration of Holy Scripture. Modern theology, including the "positive" wing, sees, as we have repeatedly pointed out, in the identification of Scripture and God's Word an "evil heritage," bequeathed to us by the Apostolic Church, the Church of the Reformation, and particularly by the dogmaticians. "Intellectualism," a Christianity which is lodged merely in the mind, is said to be the natural product of Verbal Inspiration or the equating of Scripture and God's Word. At present we wish to call attention to two evil consequences which Professor Zoeckler of Greifswald, in the Kier controversy, especially emphasized and used as an argument against "a return to the 17th century treatment of Scripture." These evil consequences are said to be the downfall of "scientific theology" and the transformation of the State Churches into Free Churches. Pastor Schulze of Walsleben had declared in an essay read at the "August Conference" in 1891: "There is no reason for us to give up the position toward Scripture which the Church has from the beginning taken toward it, and we shall persist in praising as its glory the fact that God speaks through it to men and that it is God's infallible Word." In answer to this statement Professor Zoeckler wrote a lengthy article in the *Evangelische Kirchenzeitung,* whose editor he was at that time, and closed his discussion with these words: "Do not entertain the hope of obtaining from the universities of our State Churches men who will be fitted out to put such repristination plans into execution, or of being able at all to keep up contact with the theological science of the State Churches, if you seriously intend to take the road leading back to Lutheran scholasticism and to absolute 'theopneusty.' The end result of believing in an absolute Verbal Inspiration is the 'free church.' Adopt the position which at the present time is so earnestly maintained in the American West [the "Missourians" are meant], and soon the separation from our State Churches would take place." If we recall what Zoeckler and the entire modern theology mean by "theological science," they have reason to fear for it. They mean by it that theological science which no longer accepts the Word of the Prophets and Apostles as Christ's Word and which has therefore undertaken a change of base – which refuses to derive and determine the Christian doctrine from the Word of Christ, the Holy Scripture, but makes the heart of the theologian its source and norm.[74]

---

[74] How emphatically Zoeckler denies the inspiration of Scripture and hence also questions its "judicatory authority," its "perspicuity," and its "sufficiency" becomes evident from his presentation of these matters in his *Handbuch der theol. Wissenschaften,* 2d ed., III, 148–151.

A scientific theology of this sort does not, of course, agree with a γραφή which is θεόπνευστος. Holy Scripture, which is by inspiration God's infallible Word, condemns every theological science which engages in any way in an away-from-Scripture movement. Scripture says: "If any man consent not to the wholesome words of our Lord Jesus Christ . . . he is proud, knowing nothing" (1 Tim. 6:3-4). This scientific theology, which has made the "impregnable fortress" of the theologian's Ego instead of Scripture its basis, fares as did the idol Dagon: "And when they of Ashdod arose early on the morrow, behold, Dagon was fallen upon his face to the earth before the ark of the Lord. And they took Dagon and set him in his place again. And when they arose early on the morrow morning, behold, Dagon was fallen upon his face to the ground before the ark of the Lord; and the head of Dagon and both the palms of his hands were cut off upon the threshold; only the stump of Dagon was left to him." (1 Sam. 5:3 ff.) One can easily see why the people of Ashdod said in a spirit of self-preservation: "The ark of the God of Israel shall not abide with us; for His hand is sore upon us and upon Dagon, our god." It is easy to see that the modern theologians are urged by the spirit of self-preservation not to permit the Scriptures to prevail in the Church as God's infallible Word; such a Scripture would be too hard on them and their "theological science." As for the Church, let her retain the Word of the Apostles and Prophets, for that is her one foundation [θεμέλιος, Eph. 2:21], and let her get rid of modern theology with its "theological science," for in forsaking the wholesome words of our Lord Jesus Christ, this "science" is based on illusion and ignorance (τετύφωται, μηδὲν ἐπιστάμενος, 1 Tim. 6:3-4).

The fear, too, that "the end result of the absolute 'theopneusty'" may be the Free Church is not without basis. For the inspired Scriptures teach two things that must be considered here, (1) that the "Free Church," that is, the Church independent of the State, is God's ordinance;[75] (2) that Christians are under the divine command to avoid all teachers who cause divisions and offenses contrary to the doctrine which the Christians have learned from the Apostles, that is, from Christ (Rom. 16:17; 2 John 9-11). But it is generally admitted that the State Churches are full of such ἑτεροδιδασκαλοῦντες (1 Tim. 1:3; 6:3). And that applies at present in the same degree to the "People's Churches" (*"Landes-Volkskirchen"*) in those localities where

[75] Luke 22:25-26: "The kings of the Gentiles exercise lordship over them. . . . But ye shall not be so." Matt. 23:8: "One is your Master, even Christ." John 18:36: "My kingdom is not of this world."

the separation of Church and State has been officially declared. "The end result of believing in an absolute Verbal Inspiration" – and that is the true faith – impels Christians at all places and at all times, also under a Free Church constitution, to cling to the unadulterated doctrine of Christ, as it is expressed clearly and inerrantly in the inspired Holy Scriptures and to deny church fellowship to all false teachers.

6

On the History of the Doctrine of Inspiration

Christ and the Apostles taught the verbal inspiration both of the Old and the New Testament, a fact we have repeatedly demonstrated in defining Christian theology and particularly in the chapters "Holy Scripture Identical with the Word of God" and "The Verbal Inspiration of Holy Scripture." Rothe, too, whom many regard as a leader in establishing the modern, the "correct," view of Scripture (Nitzsch-Stephan, p. 255 ff.), admits that the Apostles identified Scripture and the Word of God – though he stands sufficiently far toward the left to confess openly that he does not accept the opinion of the Apostles as authoritative.[76] When Hofmann, following Schleiermacher, claims in his *Schriftbeweis*, 2d ed., I, 671 ff., that Christ and the Apostles did not appeal to "single statements" or "individual words," but always only to "the whole of Scripture" or "the organic whole of Scripture," hence did not teach Verbal Inspiration, Kliefoth, as already stated, correctly calls this an "inconceivable concept." Hofmann's assertion belongs to the class of absolute dicta that nonplus one because of their boldness. Every reader of the Gospels and the Epistles of the

[76] Cp. Philippi, *Glaubenslehre*, 3d ed., p. 299: "The fact that the Apostles regard the entire Scriptures of the Old Testament as the Word of God, inspired by the Holy Ghost, and hence regard God Himself as *auctor primarius Scripturae Sacrae* is a fact so undeniable that even Rothe (in his book *Zur Dogmatik*, 1863, p. 180 ff.) dares not deny, yea, even admits, that the Apostles themselves can be cited as authority for the doctrine of inspiration as taught by our Church and dogmaticians. Nevertheless he does not want to be bound by the doctrine of the Apostles in general nor by their particular doctrine regarding the source and the nature of the Old Testament." Also Meusel (III, 459) calls attention to this concession of Rothe: "Rothe acknowledges that the entire exegesis and hermeneutics of the New Testament in reference to the Old Testament rests on such a view of the inspiration. For that very reason his exegetical conscience forbids him to be bound here by the doctrine of the Apostles, and he proposes another theory of inspiration in opposition to theirs. For us the testimony of the Scripture itself counts for more."

Apostles knows that the opposite is the fact (Matt. 4:4, 7, 10; John 10:35, etc. – Rom. 4:3, 6, 7; Gal. 3:16, etc.).

The Church Fathers, too, taught the Verbal Inspiration. That is so evident that Cremer raises the charge that "they have the same doctrine of inspiration as the older Protestant dogmaticians" (R. E., 2d ed., VI, 751). Among recent theologians Rudelbach furnishes the same proof with regard to the Church Fathers, not in a spirit of criticism, however, but of approval and praise.[77]

Regarding Luther and the dogmaticians, modern theology generally acknowledges and deplores that they have "identified" Scripture with the Word of God, thus taking over an evil heritage from the ancient Church and, unfortunately, passing it on, to the harm of the Church. (Ihmels, *Zentralfragen,* 2d ed., 56 ff. See above.) In order to gain a *particeps criminis in nuce* in the Reformer of the Church, most modern theologians insist that one finds here and there in Luther a tendency toward a "more liberal conception of Scripture." (Thus also R. Seeberg, *Dogmengeschichte,* II, 285 ff.) This assertion is in conflict with the historical facts, as the next chapter will show. As to the Symbols of the Lutheran Church, it is generally admitted in our day that they presuppose Verbal Inspiration as an unquestionably established doctrine, since they use "Scripture" and "Word of the Holy Ghost" as synonymous terms. Augsburg Confession: "Why does Scripture so often prohibit to make, and to listen to, traditions? . . . Did the Holy Ghost in vain forewarn of those things?" (*Trigl.* 91, 49.) Apology: "Do they think that these words fell inconsiderately from the Holy Ghost?" (*Op. cit.,* 153, 108.) "They have condemned several

[77] *Zeitschrift fuer d. luth. Theol. u. Kirche,* 1840, 1st section, p. 18 f. Baier's *Compendium Theologiae Historicae* (published posthumously by his son, 1690) contains sufficient quotations from the Church Fathers to prove that they taught Verbal Inspiration. Quenstedt on Augustine's doctrine of the Scriptures, *Systema* I, 116. Cp. in Chemnitz' *Examen* the lengthy section *"Testimonia veteris ecclesiae de Scriptura,"* p. 39 *sqq*. In the preceding pages Chemnitz sets forth what Scripture teaches regarding itself, and this presentation clearly shows Chemnitz' view of Scripture. Concerning the proof from Scripture for Scripture Chemnitz remarks, *loc. cit.:* "These testimonies which we have adduced so far from the very words of Scripture are the strongest kind of testimonies, on which the pious mind can safely rely. For they set before us the verdict of the Holy Spirit Himself regarding the Scriptures. For just as the ancient teachers say that nothing is to be believed regarding God except what God Himself has revealed and testified, so we are also to believe regarding the Scriptures just what Scripture itself says concerning itself, yea, rather what the Holy Ghost Himself judges and pronounces regarding His work." Chemnitz is therefore certainly not "hesitant," as has been here and there asserted by modern theologians, in expressing his position as to the inspiration of Scripture.

articles contrary to the manifest Scripture of the Holy Ghost" (*op. cit.*, 101, 9). When those Lutherans who deny inspiration find comfort in the fact that the Lutheran Symbols indeed presuppose Verbal Inspiration as an undeniable truth, but contain no separate article which teaches it, neither logic nor psychology shows how there can be any comfort for them in this observation. – It cannot be denied that among the Lutheran dogmaticians George Calixt (d. 1656) gave up the Scriptural doctrine of inspiration; he limited inspiration to the chief matters and the things not previously known to the holy writers; in minor matters and in the things previously known to them he assumed only a preservation from error (Quenstedt, I, 100). It must also be admitted that John Musaeus (d. 1681) on occasion voiced the opinion that Verbal Inspiration was a hypothesis not yet sufficiently proved. Musaeus retracted this statement and declared that it did not express his view but that of the opponents.[78]

When rationalism, which wielded a mighty influence after the middle of the 18th century, discarded the Christian doctrine in general, namely, the *satisfactio Christi vicaria*, it also discarded the inspiration of Holy Scripture.[79] The denial of the *satisfactio vicaria* is a surrender of the *differentia specifica* of Christianity and puts the Christian religion in a class with the pagan religion of works. What need is there after that of a God-inspired Holy Scripture? The whole theological activity of the rationalists consists in proving that Scripture, correctly understood, that is, interpreted according to reason, is nothing more than a sublime code of morals, exemplified in Jesus of Nazareth. "The Reformer of the Church of the 19th Century," Schleiermacher, did not, like the Reformer of the 16th century, lead theology back into Scripture, but into the morass of emotional rationalism. To him the source and determining norm of theology are no longer Scripture, but the

---

[78] Quenstedt reports (I, 106): "See the treatise of Musaeus on the style of the New Testament, which he wrote against the Apology of M. Iac. Gross in 1641 and in which he says, par. 16: 'The argument of Gross will meet the reply of the opponent that it rests upon a hypothesis which is not yet conceded nor satisfactorily proved, scil., that the Holy Ghost breathed into the Apostles not only the matter, but also the very words.' Likewise, par. 39: 'An utterance of the Apostles is not an utterance by God pertaining to the *materiale*, or the words themselves, but only to the *formale*, namely, that which is revealed through the utterance.' See *der Jenaer Theologen ausfuehrliche Erklaerung, locus* I, De Scriptura Sacra, p. 31 *sq.*, where the same Musaeus declares that he said this not from his own viewpoint, but from the viewpoint of the opponent." Regarding Musaeus see Philippi, *Glaubenslehre*, 3d ed., I, 252.

[79] Nitzsch-Stephan, p. 33 ff., 556. As to Toellner, see also R. E., 2d ed., XV, 711 ff. Toellner argues in a manner that indicates his rejection not only of the *obedientia activa*, but of the substitutional satisfaction of Christ in general.

pious self-consciousness of the theologizing subject, the Christian experience, etc. It is a fact admitted by all that the entire modern theology, liberal and conservative, practices theology according to the method of Schleiermacher, though there are differences among them as to what belongs to the "pious self-consciousness." Because it has not returned to the Scripture doctrine of the vicarious satisfaction of Christ, modern theology stands outside the sphere within which the Word of Christ, which we have in the Scriptures of the Apostles and Prophets, is recognized as Christ's, that is, God's Word. Whoever will not believe what Christ and the Apostles teach of the reconciliation of the world by the substitutional satisfaction of Christ will naturally also not believe what Christ and the Apostles say of Holy Scripture. Whoever rejects God's thoughts and entertains his own thoughts on Gods' reconciliation of sinful mankind will naturally also entertain his own thoughts on God's Word, Holy Scripture, even to the extent of rejecting what God says regarding Scripture.[80]

---

[80] Attention has been called to this point in *Lehre und Wehre* (1893, p. 163 f.) in connection with the trial of Dr. Briggs: "If a person denies the inspiration of Scripture as definitely as Dr. Briggs, there is every reason to ask whether Briggs still believes anything at all of the Christian doctrine. By Christian doctrine we do not, of course, mean the Law – for all pagan religions still contain parts of the Law – but the Gospel, that is, the doctrine that man is saved by grace, for Christ's sake, through faith and not through works of his own. If a person actually believes the Gospel, if he believes that God has saved mankind from eternal damnation by the substitutional suffering and death of His Son, he will not be inclined to doubt that God has in addition given man the Holy Scriptures as His infallible Word. Whoever really believes the doctrine of justification may indeed for a time be assailed by doubts regarding the divinity of Scripture, but it is hard to assume that he could persistently deny it and still cling to the Christian doctrine of the remission of sins by faith in the merit of Christ. Dr. Briggs has – so he has himself declared – thrown the Christian faith overboard. . . . He explicitly states this in his presentation of the doctrine of 'progressive sanctification.' To prove his doctrine that the 'sanctification' of the soul is progressive after death, he states that it is impossible to assume that 'father and child, mother and infant, teacher and pupil, the self-sacrificing missionary and the new convert, the zealous evangelist and the thief and murderer who on the gallows, in his last hour, turns to Christ – that all these should receive the same treatment.' This argumentation involves a denial of Christianity, namely, of the doctrine: 'There is no difference; for all have sinned and come short of the glory of God; being justified freely by His grace through the redemption that is in Christ Jesus.' Dr. Briggs will not let the malefactor on the cross enter Paradise at once together with the 'zealous evangelist,' but makes him first go through the 'progressive sanctification,' because Briggs does not believe that all sins are remitted solely for the sake of Christ's merit and that therefore for the believer, as soon as he believes, all transgressions are blotted out like a thick cloud and all his sins like mist. Briggs therefore has renounced the very center of the Christian faith. It need not surprise us, then, that also those passages which testify that Holy Scripture is the Word of God no longer make any im-

We might summarize the position of modern theologians toward Scripture in these words: modern theologians refuse to believe what Scripture says of itself, but would determine the character of Scripture *a posteriori*, by way of human investigation and criticism.[81] Applying this *modus procedendi*, they reach the conclusion that the Scriptures are not God's infallible Word, but a report, more or less divinely influenced, on God's revelation by word (account of the revelation). In this historical report, which originates in part with the Holy Ghost and in part with men (*"Urgemeinde"* – primitive Church, hence "divine-human" report), errors are naturally not excluded. Hence it is said to be the office of modern theology, which possesses in a high degree a sense of "reality," to subject Scripture, in its contents and wording, to criticism, even though it has not yet succeeded in defining the boundaries between truth and error in the Bible. But as to the chief point they are agreed: Scripture cannot be regarded as God's infallible Word; Scripture, if regarded as the infallible Word of God, cannot produce "warm-blooded" Christianity; the natural consequence of the old conception of Scripture is "intellectualism." When the modern theologians still speak of "inspiration," they do not mean the unique divine act by which He breathed His Word into the holy writers and made it the foundation of faith for His Church unto the Last Day (Eph. 2:20; John 17:20), but they take it to mean merely an intensified spiritual enlightenment of a kind which all Christians possess. As the illumination possessed by all Christians does not include perfect inerrancy, so neither did the intensified illumination of the holy writers make them inerrant.

Another characteristic of modern theology is the claim of a majority of its representatives that "manifestly" degrees of the inspiration of Scripture must be assumed. But this assumption of degrees in inspiration has as little sense as the assumption of ranks in the Godhead. When the subordinationists call God's Son God "in the secondary sense of the word," they destroy the concept "God"; and when modern theologians speak of degrees of inspiration, they discard the Scriptural concept "inspiration." Kahnis actually combines these two things, ranks in the Godhead and degrees in the divine inspiration of Holy Scripture. He assumes three degrees of inspiration, though he confesses

---

pression on him. His teaching concerning the way of salvation would have caused him to forsake the Christian faith, even if he outwardly believed that Scripture were the Word of God."

[81] Hastings, VII, 346, gives an apt description of this *a posteriori* method of modern theology.

not to be entirely sure of it. He writes (the quotation is given in Baier-Walther, I, p. 103): "Among these Prophetic and Apostolic writings we find differences, from the viewpoint of both origin and content. We cannot place Deuteronomy on the same level with the first four books. Among the Prophets, Obadiah and Jonah stand beneath Isaiah, Jeremiah, and Ezekiel. In the New Testament the Pastoral Epistles and the Epistle to Philemon stand in the second row. The word of revelation given within the kingdom of the Old and the New Covenant can be understood only in connection with its history. Accordingly the historical books of the Old and the New Covenant have their place in the canon, but only one of second rank. As their content is the combined activity of the divine and the human in the Kingdom of God, so also the sacred historical writers are not necessarily men who received revelations, but only men animated by the Spirit of the Kingdom of God. This class is made up in the Old Testament of the prophetic-historical books as of the first rank; the hagiographa Ruth, Ezra, Nehemiah as of the second rank; the books Esther and Chronicles as of the third rank. In the New Testament this second class includes the first three Gospels as of the first rank, the Acts of the Apostles as of the second rank. In the third class are the Old and New Testament hagiographa, the contents of which are neither revelation nor history of the Kingdom, but which depict the life in the Kingdom of God as it appears in the individuals. This class includes in the Old Testament the Psalms as of the first rank, the Proverbs of Solomon, Job, and the Lamentations of Jeremiah as of the second rank, the Song of Solomon, Ecclesiastes, and Daniel as of the third rank; in the New Testament the Epistle to the Hebrews and the Second and Third Epistles of John (which very probably but not positively are of Johannean origin and in addition are of a more personal nature) as of the first rank, the rest of the Catholic Epistles and the Apocalypse as of the second rank. While in the first class the person is of prime importance, the individual recedes in the second class, since here everything depends on the objective truth and the spirit in which things are presented. But it lies in the nature of the third class that here the subject becomes important. It is not immaterial whether a Psalm was written by David or not, whether the Proverbs were written by Solomon or others, whether Daniel is authentic or not, etc. But in the case of these Scriptures of the third rank one must guard well against giving authenticity too much weight. Faulty as this attempt to divide Scripture into three classes may be from the viewpoint of inspiration, nevertheless a distinction of degrees is in accordance with the sense of Scripture; it also has renowned authorities of ancient and modern times in its favor." Manifestly this distinction is not in accordance with Scripture. Scripture says 2 Tim. 3:16 πᾶσα γραφὴ θεόπνευστος. This statement places all writings of the Old Testament (τὰ ἱερὰ γράμματα, v. 15) without any distinction into one class. Christ quotes John 10:34 from the Psalms (Ps. 82:6; "Ye are gods"). But He does not add that this is a "third-class" word of Scripture, as Kahnis holds; rather He says: "The Scripture cannot be broken." . This whole distinction of degrees of inspiration is a human fabrication, the purpose of which is to free the human theologizing subject from the irksome bond of the divine authority of Scripture.

Sad to say, it is true what Nitzsch-Stephan says of the "present situation" (p. 258): "In our day the orthodox doctrine of inspiration has hardly any significance in dogmatics. It is, true enough, still being upheld by a few, e. g., Koelling and Noesgen, with some modifications. . . . The rest of the theologians, including the conservatives, reject the old doctrine." Zoeckler mentions (*Handbuch der theol. Wissenschaften,* 2d ed., III, 149) as lonely defenders of the old doctrine: Kohlbruegge, Gaussen, Kuyper, and, "among the Lutherans, Walther in St. Louis and with him the Missouri Synod." Also most of the present-day Reformed theologians have given up the inspiration of Scripture.[82] Well-known exceptions are Charles Hodge of Princeton; Wm. Shedd of Union Seminary, New York; Benj. B. Warfield of Princeton.[83] Of

---

[82] This caused the appeal of "the Fundamentalists" to "the laymen" to organize an alliance against the unbelieving generation of the ministers trained in the "skeptical schools and seminaries of today." Cf. *Lehre und Wehre,* 1923, 89 f. John Horsch, a fundamentalist, recently wrote an excellent book, in which he courageously attacks American Liberalism. Its title is *Modern Religious Liberalism.* The Destructiveness and Irrationality of the New Theology. Fundamental Truth Depot, Scottdale, Pa. 331 pages. Cp. the review in *Lehre und Wehre,* 1922, p. 179 f.

[83] Charles Hodge, *Systematic Theology,* 1873, 3 vols. He says (I, 170): "Admitting that the Scriptures do contain, in a few instances, discrepancies which, with our present means of knowledge, we are unable satisfactorily to explain, they furnish no rational ground for denying their infallibility. 'The Scripture cannot be broken' (John 10:35). This is the whole doctrine of plenary inspiration, taught by the lips of Christ Himself." Hodge, however, now and then does make uncalled-for obeisances before geologists and astronomers, thus weakening his position. — William Shedd, *Dogmatic Theology,* two volumes and one supplementary volume, 2d ed., 1889, says (I, 93, 103): "Scripture itself asserts verbal inspiration. . . . Those who contend that the Bible is fallible because it contains a human element commit the same error in kind with those who assert that Jesus Christ was sinful because He had a human nature in His complex person. The human element . . . is not a fallible element, because it is blended with the divine element of inspiration and kept free from human error." But our note

the more widely known theologians in Germany it is only Philippi who in the last years of his life returned to the Scripture doctrine of inspiration.[84]

In the Roman Catholic Church some theologians of note have limited inspiration to the mysteries of faith or the chief matters; concerning other matters, however, they have assumed a mere preservation from error.[85] A few others have gone further and expressly admitted the actual occurrence of errors.[86]

The Socinians and the Arminians assume errors in "minor matters." [87] – This would be the place to advert to the essential agreement

---

regarding Hodge applies also to Shedd. – Benj. B. Warfield has to our knowledge, up to his recent demise (d. 1921), taught the inspiration and absolute infallibility of Scripture, a position he already took in his inaugural address at Princeton, 1887. (Published in the *Presbyterian Quarterly*, p. 389 *sqq.*) Because of this stand he had to endure opposition and derision from many in his own church body; in these trials he found much comfort in the fact that "an entire Lutheran Synod" unanimously subscribed to the doctrine of the inspiration of Scripture.

[84] We have already stated that he revoked his former error regarding the possibility of errors in Scripture. Of the lesser known German theologians Wilhelm Rohnert (*Dogmatik der ev.-luth. Kirche*, 1902) subscribes to "the much-maligned doctrine of inspiration held by the old Church." – A complete presentation and review of the doctrine of inspiration held by modern theologians is found in the 11th report of the Synodical Conference, 1886.

[85] Thus the Jesuit Franz Suarez (d. 1617). Quenstedt (*Systema* I, 106) quotes him to the effect that this method, according to which the Holy Ghost furnished also the words, is the most appropriate where the mysteries of faith were recorded, but that it does not seem necessary that the words were always dictated by this peculiar method; for where the canonical writers wrote of things that were known by means of the senses, it would appear sufficient that the Spirit assisted them and preserved them from all error. Quenstedt adds: "Suarez' opinion is lauded and approved by Dr. Geo. Calixt in *Exercit. de auctoritate Scripturae*, thes. 47."

[86] Quenstedt (I, 114) quotes Pighius (d. 1542) to the effect that the Evangelists could have a lapse of memory and lie, and Erasmus, he says, taught that the Evangelists, trusting to memory, made mistakes. On the other hand, Quenstedt reports (I, 117) that Dr. Eck, "at other times the most violent defender of Papistic errors and superstitions," attacked Erasmus sharply in a public letter and stated: "By these words you seem to insinuate that the Evangelists wrote as other men do, that they wrote these things trusting to their memory, but that they neglected to look up these things in the books and thus made mistakes. Listen to me, Erasmus, do you hold that a Christian will patiently accept that the Evangelists made mistakes in their Gospels? If the authority of the Holy Scriptures becomes shaky here, what other part will be above suspicion of error, as Augustine concludes in a most beautiful argument?" This fact has correctly been adduced as proof (also by Walther in *Lehre und Wehre*, 1886, p. 35 f.) that the inspiration of Scripture was acknowledged in the Papacy as a firmly established doctrine.

[87] Faustus Socinus says in his *De Auctoritate Scripturae*, c. 1, p. 15: "Certain things in Scripture – such as are of little moment – are in themselves plainly

of the ancient and modern "enthusiasts," the Quakers, and the like, with modern theology. Just like the modern theologians, the "enthusiasts" refuse, in the interest of their "inner life" or their "immediate revelation," to "identify" Scripture with the Word of God. Their talk of "spirit," of "inner light," of "immediate revelation," lies on the same plane as the talk of modern theologians about a "self-certainty" of Christianity and its religion, a certainty which does not depend on Holy Scripture, but "rests in itself and is immediate truth" (Erlangen theology). Again, when the "enthusiasts" declare the "spirit," or the "inner light," etc., to be the "chief source" or the "real source of the truth" and acknowledge Scripture only as a "subordinate norm," this corresponds exactly to the position of modern theology, which likewise turns everything topsy-turvy in the Christian Church by casting aside Scripture as the source and norm of doctrine, withdrawing into the "pious self-consciousness" of the theologian, the "experience," as constituting the allegedly "impregnable fortress," and from this vantage point correcting Scripture.[88]

---

false" (see Quenstedt, I, 114; the full quotation is given in Guenther, *Pop. Symbolik*, p. 97). Schneckenburger, "*Kleinere protest. Kirchenparteien*," p. 34 f.: "The dependability [of Scripture] according to Socinus is limited to matters pertaining to doctrine. . . . In minor matters he grants that there are errors." But it is just in "matters pertaining to doctrine" that Socinus goes against Scripture; he denies the deity of Christ and the substitutionary satisfaction; and this results most naturally in the denial of the inspiration of Scripture. – The teaching of the modern Unitarians regarding Scripture is in complete agreement with that of modern theologians, including the positive wing. Guenther, *op. cit.*, p. 96 f.: "In C. W. Wendt's *What Do Unitarians Believe?* it is stated: 'We do not regard the Bible as a fetish, as a verbally inspired and infallible oracle of God.' In *Unitarian Principles and Practices* it is stated: 'Unitarians regard the books of the Bible as the record of the doctrine of God. . . . The inspiration which they find in the Bible is an inspiration of men, whose history is told, not an inspiration of words and letters. . . . The Unitarians think as highly of the Bible as any sect . . . but they do not make more of it than it actually is, nor do they assert it to be something that it never claims to be.' In *Scriptural Belief of Unitarian Christians* we read: 'Unitarians believe that the Bible contains the Word of God.' " – Regarding the Arminian doctrine of Scripture consult Schneckenburger, *op. cit.*, p. 10 f., and Guenther, *op. cit.*, p. 97. Episcopius asserts (*Inst. Theol.* IV, 1, 4: "The holy writers were fallible and suffered lapses of memory in unimportant matters not pertaining to salvation."

88 Schneckenburger, *op. cit.*, p. 67 ff., has some trenchant remarks on the relationship of the Quakers to the "orthodox-Reformed" position. According to the Reformed position the gracious operation of the Holy Ghost proceeds not through the external Word, the Scripture, but without it and alongside it. "The Quakers go a step farther and come very close to the line beyond which Scripture as a historical book really becomes something irrelevant, accidental, immaterial, over against the immediate granting of the Spirit" (p. 71). "It [Scripture] stands lower than this higher thing [the immediate Word], without

Calvin's position toward Scripture has been also much debated in recent times. Seeberg says (*Dogmengeschichte* II, 385): "Calvin, then, is the creator of the so-called old dogmatical theory of inspiration"; and to prove his assertion, he shows that Calvin not only calls the Scriptures of the Old and New Testaments God's "oracles," but also expressly states that the Scriptures, including the historical parts (*historiae*), were written *dictante Spiritu Sancto* (*Inst.* IV, 8, 6), and the holy writers were His amanuenses (*Inst.* IV, 8, 9). Seeberg also points to the fact that Calvin called the critics who asked: "How do we know that Moses and the Prophets wrote the books which now bear their name?" and who even dared to question whether there ever was a Moses, "*nebulones*" (miscreants) and their wisdom "*insania*" (*Inst.* I, 8, 9). Seeberg declares that he does not agree with Heppe, who says (*Die Dogmatik der ev.-ref. Kirche,* 1861, p. 16 f.): "There is [here in Calvin] no thought of a real inspiration of the recording." — It will have to be admitted, however, that Calvin, contradicting his direct statements that Scripture is written *dictante Spiritu Sancto* and that the holy writers must be called *Spiritus Sancti amanuenses,* occa-

---

which it would have no authority" (p. 73). According to Robert Barclay, the dogmatician of the Quakers, the Scriptures are the product of the revelation by the Holy Ghost, but he adds: "Nevertheless, as they are only the declaration of the fount and not the fount itself, so also they are not to be rated as the principal source of all truth and knowledge nor the adequate primary rule of faith and morals, although, since they give true and trustworthy testimony of the prime source, they can be rated as a secondary rule, subordinate to the Spirit." Barclay does not want the inner light tested by the Scriptures, as though the Scriptures were a more certain norm, since immediate revelation brings with it its own certainty: "From this it does not follow that these divine revelations should be examined according to the external testimony of the Scriptures . . . as a higher and surer norm and rule. For divine revelation and internal illumination is something evident and clear *per se,* the mind, well informed through proper evidence and clarity, being forced to assent and in an insuperable manner moved and bent." Therefore Barclay directs the Christians to look, not upon the Bible, but upon the inner immediate revelation as their mighty fortress or last resort. "That must be the only very sure and immovable foundation of the entire Christian faith. It is the internal, immediate, objective revelation of the Spirit to which all who profess Christianity ultimately have recourse." It is a sad self-deception, but its agreement with modern theology is manifest; modern theology declares the "experience" or the "self-assurance" of the theologian, not Scripture, to be the "invincible fortress" of Christianity. Barclay therefore, just like the modern theologians, would hear nothing of identifying Scripture and the Word of God. He says in his *Animadversions* against Nic. Arnold that the Bible "is not properly and without qualification the Word of God and should not be called the Word of God." See the quotation in Guenther, p. 97. There also, p. 93, is a quotation from the *American Christian Record,* which shows that the Hicksites likewise employ the terminology of the modern theologians.

sionally speaks of the Evangelists as incorrectly quoting from the Old Testament.[89] Here, then, there is an inconsistency on the part of Calvin.

And, what is worse, it has little practical value when the older and the more recent Calvinists (Hodge, Shedd, Boehl, etc.) teach Verbal Inspiration and at the same time teach the doctrine peculiar to Calvinism. Calvinism teaches that the redemption which is in Christ Jesus does not extend over all men, but only over a part of mankind. It teaches with Calvin that the purpose of the written Word is not to lead all men to faith and salvation, but to harden the hearts of the majority of the hearers. Calvin teaches (*Inst.* III, 24, 12): "Those, therefore, whom He has created to a life of shame and a death of destruction, that they might be the instruments of His wrath and examples of His severity, He causes to reach their appointed end, sometimes depriving them of the opportunity of hearing the Word, sometimes, by the preaching of it, increasing their blindness and stupidity." Furthermore, the old and the more recent Calvinists teach that those who are actually illuminated unto faith and salvation do not receive this illumination through the external Word, the Scriptures, but receive it without this Word, through an immediate illumination of the Holy Ghost. It is obvious that such teaching makes the truth that Scripture is God's inspired Word entirely worthless for practical purposes. Calvinists must become, as has been pointed out by men in their own midst, Lutherans in practice, that is, they must forget their *gratia particularis* and their *immediata Spiritus Sancti operatio* if, terrified by the Law, they desire to derive any consolation from the written Word as the Word of God. And the grace of God leads many a Calvinist to forget his Calvinism in the time of need.[90]

The synergists, too – those that still teach the inspiration of Scripture – make this doctrine practically worthless. Because the synergists make the obtaining of God's grace dependent on an achievement of man (self-decision, self-determination, "different conduct," lesser guilt in comparison with others), and because this required achievement is found in no man (Rom. 3:19: "That all the world become guilty before God"; v. 22: "There is no difference"), by their obstruc-

[89] Calvin remarks in his *Comment. super Ioh.*, p. 346: "When David there (Ps. 22) complains that he became the prey of his enemies, he metaphorically designates by the name 'clothes' all his possessions, as though he had said in one word that he was robbed and made naked by the godless. Because the Evangelists neglect this figure, they depart from the native sense."

[90] This matter has been discussed, in another connection, in chapter 4 of the Prolegomena.

tion of the *sola gratia* raise as strong a barrier against the obtaining of God's grace as do the Calvinists by their obstruction of the *universalis gratia.* The Christian faith which is counted by God for righteousness is convinced that God "justifieth the ungodly" (Rom. 4:5). Whoever considers himself as being better before God, or less guilty than other men, is *eo ipso* excluding himself from grace (Luke 18:9-14; Rom. 11:22). A synergist can be saved, just like the Calvinist, only if he becomes inconsistent. As the Calvinists must forget their limitation of the *universalis gratia,* so the synergists must forget their limitation of the *sola gratia* if the truth that the Scriptures are God's own Word is to be of any practical value for them. And here, too, this forgetting, no doubt, occurs in many instances. It is solely the grace of God which saves from an error which is fatal in itself.[91]

It goes without saying that the Romish theologians, too, completely destroy the practical value of their profession of the inspiration of Scripture by assigning the authoritative interpretation of Scripture to the Pope. The result of this exegetical method is that it is no longer God who through His Word, the Holy Scriptures, speaks to men, instructs, and rules them, but that the Pope – pretending to speak in the name of Scripture – subjects the Church and the State to his papal Ego. Luther is right in declaring that the principle of the "Romanists" that "the interpretation of Scripture belongs to no one except the Pope" is one of the "three walls" behind which the Papacy has entrenched itself and seeks to set up and maintain its rule. (*An den christlichen Adel deutscher Nation,* St. L. X:269 f.)

7

Luther and the Inspiration of Holy Scripture

Luther a *particeps criminis* in the denial of the inspiration of Scripture – that is the cry of modern theology. The later dogmaticians, it is quite generally asserted, devised the "artificial theory" of an inspiration according to which Scripture and God's Word were identified outright, but Luther took a more liberal attitude toward Scripture. Cremer calls the dogmaticians' doctrine of inspiration "an absolute *novum*" (R. E., 2d and 3d ed., VI, 755). Because of certain remarks of Luther, Seeberg cannot conceive that Verbal Inspiration was in his

---

[91] On this point see Vol. I, p. 29; Vol. II: "The Pernicious Character of Synergism"; and Vol. III: "The Synergists on the Means of Grace."

mind (*Dogmengesch.*, 2d ed., II, 289, note 1). In Nitzsch-Stephan there is, on the one hand, the admission that Luther "substituted for the church authority [under the Papacy] the authority of Holy Scripture," and, on the other hand, the assertion that in Luther "pronounced traces" of a more liberal conception of the inspiration of Scripture are found. "In the Lutheran Church the intensification of the concept of inspiration began with Flacius and Chemnitz. This was completed by the Protestant scholastics of the 17th and 18th centuries after the model set by John Gerhard as early as 1610 in his *locus 'De Scriptura'* and completed by him in 1625 in his *Exegesis Uberior Loci de Scriptura*. It was thought that the battle against the Catholics, Socinians, Arminians, and other parties would prove successful only if the divine authority of Scripture were extended to the letter [the words of Scripture]. The Bible was considered not so much the record of the divine revelation or of the Word as rather a divine textbook of religion. . . . We meet this fully developed theory of inspiration in its most pointed scholastic form in those dogmaticians who sought to uphold the old orthodox system against Calixt and the syncretists" (*Ev. Dogmatik*, 3d ed., p. 249). That Luther took a more liberal attitude toward the doctrine of inspiration has been asserted not only by theologians of Germany, but also by American theologians, e. g., by Dr. Charles A. Briggs.[92]

But this assertion is void of all historical truth. The alleged difference between Luther and the Lutheran dogmaticians is pure fabrication. The real difference between Luther and the dogmaticians is this, that the dogmaticians but weakly stammer and echo what Luther taught much more powerfully about Scripture from Scripture itself. Recall what Quenstedt, for instance, states concerning Scripture as the inspired Word of God: "The canonical Holy Scriptures in the original text are the infallible truth and are free from every error, or, in other words, in the canonical Holy Scriptures there is found no lie, no falsity, no error, not even the least, whether in subject matter or words, but all things and all the details that are handed down in them are most certainly true whether they pertain to doctrine, or morals, or history, or chronology, or topography, or nomenclature; no ignorance, no thoughtlessness or forgetfulness, no lapse of memory, can and dare be ascribed to the amanuenses of the Holy Ghost in their

---

92 Cp. *Presbytery of New York*. The Presbyterian Church in the United States of America against the Rev. Charles A. Briggs, D. D. Argument of the Rev. J. J. Lampe, D. D., a member of the Prosecuting Committee, p. 54 *sqq.* – Likewise the rebuttal: *The Other Side*, by S. A. Farrand, Ph. D., 1897.

penning of the sacred writings." (*Systema* I, 112.) – This statement of Quenstedt has been called a *dictum horribile*. But everything that Quenstedt says concerning Scripture is said also by Luther, including the details mentioned by Quenstedt, only that Luther states these things with incomparably greater force. To demonstrate this, we shall record here, first, what Luther says regarding the entire Scriptures, and, then, what Luther says on the details concerning which it is claimed that he taught differently from the dogmaticians. To repeat here certain statements of Luther which have been already adduced in another connection will do no harm.

Concerning the entire Scriptures Luther says: "So, then, the entire Scriptures are assigned to the Holy Ghost" (St. L. III:1890). "The Holy Scriptures did not grow on earth" (St. L. VII:2095). "The Holy Scriptures have been spoken by the Holy Ghost" (St. L. III:1895). It is "the book of the Holy Ghost" (St. L. IX:1775). It is "God's Epistle" addressed to men (St. L. I:1055). Hundreds of similar statements from Luther could be quoted.

But what Luther asserts of the entire Scriptures he asserts, consistently, regarding individual portions of the Scriptures, whose divine authority has been denied. Modern theology, it is well known, insists strongly that the "human side" of Scripture be duly recognized, this "human side" having been neglected by the old theologians, and it is the particular *donum* of modern theology, whose sense of "realities" has been so strongly developed, to bring out this "human side." Now, Luther, too, was well acquainted with the "human side" of Scripture, but only in the sense that God caused His Word to be written by men in the human tongue. Luther is horrified at people who dare to claim that Scripture is not entirely and in all its parts the Word of God because the writers, such as Peter and Paul, after all, were men. Luther remarks on 1 Pet. 3:15: "But if they take exception and say: You preach that one should not hold to man's doctrine, and yet Peter and Paul, and even Christ, were men – when you hear people of this stamp, who are so blinded and hardened as to deny that what Christ and the Apostles spoke and wrote is God's Word, or doubt it, then be silent, speak no more with them, and let them go." (St. L. IX:1238.) And Luther maintains that just those parts of Scripture which appear rather "human" to us must be "identified" with the Word of God. A few examples: While Kahnis thinks it is hardly credible to assume that the Holy Ghost inspired David to say what David felt in his heart in the form of a Psalm, Luther says of the Psalms: "I think the Holy Ghost Himself wanted to take the trouble to compile a short Bible and book of illustrations from all Christendom and all saints" (St. L. XIV:21). And concerning those who would assign the Psalms, which describe the emotions of the human heart, not to the Holy Ghost, but to the man David, Luther concludes that they have a "carnal heart" (St. L. III:1894).

While modern theologians, together with some older theologians, hold that it would not be worthy of the Holy Ghost to recount the seemingly ordinary human things (*levicula*), Luther warns, in his preface to the Old Testament (St. L. XIV:3), "every pious Christian" against being misled into thinking that "the high Majesty of God" would not bother about the lowly things described in the Bible. Luther has much to say on this point. "God takes pleasure in describing such lowly things [as, e. g., Jacob's domestic economy and married state] to show and testify that He does not despise or abhor the household, nor be far away from it and from a pious husband and from wife and children." (St. L. II:537 ff.) One feels as if Luther could not do enough to stress and impress upon us how important and full of wholesome doctrine these seemingly ordinary things are. For this reason these lowly things should not be thought too trivial in the church either, but "they should always be dealt with and taught the people, namely, why the Holy Spirit, who certainly has a very clean mouth, speaks with such diligence of these things, of which the Most Holy Father, the Pope, with his chaste monks and nuns, is unwilling even to think, as of things that are utterly filthy and carnal in his sight. For they move about on the high level of their celibacy and single blessedness. The filth, however, that wives became pregnant, children were born, and that the spouses perhaps quarreled with each other, they do not regard as worthy of reading. The Holy Ghost might, they say, in keeping with His holiness, have spoken of celestial and other higher things, and not of such lowly carnal things. He should have become a monk or a nun; but now He tells merely how things stood in the household and how Jacob fared in marrying. That offends us holy and angelic men, who walk above the clouds in the wisdom and spirituality of the angels. But because they despise these ordinary things and look upon them with loathing, the Holy Ghost on His part turns away from these proud and boasting saints and will not acknowledge them as His; He abandons them to their glorying, pride, and vanity, and descends to His creatures; for them He provides and them He adorns. For He has made the earth, He has created man and wife and blessed them that they be fruitful; He has subjected the world unto them, and it is He who still preserves all things; He nourishes and gives the mother milk to nourish and sustain her child. . . . Hence the Holy Ghost would here teach and assure us in speaking of these lowly, human, and ordinary things that we should know that He is minded to be with us, to provide for us and to prove that He is our Creator and Ruler. This the Papists do not see, but despise it; therefore they must justly bear the punishment for such contempt. . . . What better or more profitable thing can be taught in God's congregation than the example of a God-fearing housewife and mother, who prays, sighs, implores, thanks God, rules the house, does what the duty of a pious wife calls for, desires to have children, in great chastity, gratitude, and godliness. What more could be expected of her? But the Pope, cardinals, and bishops are not to see that, for they are not worthy of it. The Holy Ghost lets them roam on in their fanciful, great, and supercelestial things, lets them admire nothing but their chastity and highly extol it (which really is only fit for the brothel), but these things they are by no means to see. Meanwhile the Holy Ghost so guides and rules the pious wives that thereby He proves that they are His creatures, whom He would govern not alone according to the spirit, but also according to the flesh, that they should call on Him, pray, and thank Him for the children and be obedient to their husbands," etc.

There are passages in the Old Testament containing the record of gross sexual sins. Earlier and recent theologians have said that we must not make the Holy Ghost responsible for the telling of such "filthy stories." Luther remarks in his commentary on Genesis 38, where the sin of Judah and Tamar is related: "The Holy Ghost is wonderfully diligent in narrating this shameful, adulterous history; He describes everything to the last detail. . . . What induced the most pure mouth of the Holy Ghost to condescend to such low, despised things, yea, even unchaste and filthy, even to damnable things, as though such things might be of value to teach something to the Church and Congregation of God? What has the Church to do with such things?" (St. L. II:1200 ff.) Luther then shows at length how full of doctrine, reproof, admonition, and consolation also such Scripture passages are for the Church of all ages.

Whether a person takes the Christian attitude toward Scripture and lets Scripture be the Word of God, is seen at once from the attitude he takes as to the possibility of error in Scripture. Christ very definitely rules out the possibility of an error in Scripture when He says: "The Scripture cannot (οὐ δύναται) be broken." Philippi had not yet reached the Christian attitude toward Scripture when he wrote: "We would not like to say *a priori* with Calov that no error can have a place in Scripture." He had reached the attitude befitting the Christian when he retracted his statement in the third edition of his *Glaubenslehre* and declared Calov's *a priori* position to be the correct one. This *a priori* position is Luther's position. Luther has no thought of ascertaining the inerrancy of Scripture by human investigation (*a posteriori*), but before all investigation he is convinced that there can be no error in Scripture.

Luther maintains this throughout. If there seems to be a conflict between Scripture and human science, he is firmly convinced from the outset that human science is in error and Scripture in the right. Thus Luther says of the hexaemeron: "If you cannot understand how it could have been done in six days, then accord the Holy Ghost the honor that He is more erudite than you. When you read the words of Holy Scripture, you must realize that God is speaking them." (St. L. III:21.) Luther maintains this also with regard to all chronological data in Scripture, and he thus places himself in direct opposition to all modern theology. Examples: Professor Hausleiter of Greifswald prefers Josephus' account of Herodias to the account given in Scripture. (*Lehre und Wehre*, 1907, p. 426.) A. B. Bruce, in *The Expositor's Greek Testament*, on Mark 6:17, at least admits the possibility that the Biblical report is in error, even though the error cannot be established definitely. Also Ihmels assumes from the outset that at any rate the chronology of the Bible is not infallible (*Zentralfragen*, 2d ed., p. 72). Luther takes a different stand. Luther is certain, *a priori*, that in every case where the chronological data of Scripture differ from those of secular historians, the Holy Scriptures are correct. He says: "I make use of the secular writers in such a manner that I am not forced to contradict Scripture. For I believe that in the Scriptures the God of truth speaks, but in the histories good people display according to their ability their diligence and fidelity (but only as men) or at least that their copyists have perchance erred." (St. L. XIV:491.) This is a popular theme with Luther, who was devoted to the study of history.[93] On Gen. 11:27-28 he remarks that "in the case of Abraham sixty years are lost" according to the Biblical figures. At the same time he censures the "daring people" who assert that an error has occurred here. He, Luther, had likewise "diligently compiled and added the years of the world." He protests against the assumption that he "knew nothing or had read nothing on such questions." But he will not make common

---

93 *Schrift an die Ratsherren*, St. L. X:483 f.

cause with these daring people who charge the Holy Scriptures with a chronological error; rather he closes with the humble confession of his "ignorance, as is fitting; for the Holy Ghost is the only One who knows and understands everything." Luther adds that such obscurities in the chronology as the disappearance of the sixty years in the case of Abraham are intended by the Holy Ghost "in order that no one will undertake to prophesy, as from the exact figures of the age of the world, something definite as to the end of the world. For though God truly sets signs (*signa*) of the Judgment Day and also wants them to stand before our eyes and be noted, still He does not want us to know anything certain (*certum aliquid*) of this Day, not even the year, in order that pious Christians may feel bound, in expectation of this most delightful and joyous Day, continually to exercise their faith and fear of God." (I:721 f.) In connection with Gen. 11:11 Luther deals with the question how Arphaxad could have been born two years after the Flood. He points out possible ways of harmonizing, but then adds that our faith is not endangered if the attempts at harmonizing have no assured result. The reason why faith is not endangered is given in these words: "For that is certain that the Scriptures do not lie." (St. L. I:713 f.)

As Luther *a priori* takes all chronological data of Scripture to be correct, so, too, he *a priori* considers any contradictions in Scripture to be utterly impossible. And Luther took this attitude toward Scripture not only at the beginning of his public career, as neologists have asserted, but he maintained this position to the end of his life. He wrote in 1520: "The Scriptures cannot err" (St. L. XIX:1073). In the same year: "The Scriptures have never erred" (St. L. XV:1481). In 1524: "Scripture agrees with itself everywhere" (St. L. III:18). In 1527: "It is certain that Scripture cannot disagree with itself" (St. L. XX:798). In 1535: "It is impossible that Scripture should contradict itself, only that it so appears to the senseless and obstinate hypocrites" (St. L. IX:356). And Luther's *Chronikon* dates from the years 1541 and 1545; in this he states, as we saw above, that the chronology of Scripture is absolutely dependable (St. L. XIV:491).

The apparent disorder in the chronology of Scripture also dates, according to Luther, from the Holy Ghost. In his commentary on the Prophet Habakkuk he remarks that the Prophets seemingly observe no order in that, while speaking of the Jewish kingdom, they suddenly break off and begin to speak of Christ. But this, too, is due to the Holy Ghost. Luther says: "The Holy Ghost has been blamed for not speaking correctly; He speaks like a drunkard or a fool, He so mixes up things, and uses wild, queer words and statements. But it is our fault, who have not understood the language nor known the manner of the Prophets. For it cannot be otherwise; the Holy Ghost is wise and makes the Prophets also wise. A wise man must be able to speak correctly; that holds true without fail." (St. L. XIV:1418.) Of the Evangelist Matthew, Luther says that in chapter 24 he "mixes and blends together" the destruction of Jerusalem and the end of the world, but he adds at once: "And this is also the Holy Ghost's manner of speaking in the Holy Scriptures" (St. L. VII:1297). The statements of Luther concerning the mixing together, the nonobservance of the proper order, etc., modern theologians employ as proofs that Luther thus "provided for the possibility of inaccuracies and contradictions" (Nitzsch-Stephan, p. 268). But they fail to add that Luther traced this "mixing together," etc., to the intention of the Holy Ghost. Against the inspiration of Scripture Kahnis also advances this fact, that the Evangelists do not use the identical words in their report of the institution of the Lord's Supper.[94] Luther, however, writes against the Papists, who declared the administration of the Lord's Supper invalid if a single word in the canon of the Mass were omitted: "They did not observe that the Holy Ghost intentionally so arranged it that no Evangelist agrees with the other in using the same words" (St. L. XIX:1104).

We have seen that it is characteristic of modern theology to place the inspiration of Scripture essentially on the same level with the illumination of all Christians; to assume with reference to the knowledge and the teaching of the truth, not a specific difference, but only one of degree between the writers of Holy Scripture and all Christians with their teachers; and to argue that as the illumination does not make Christians and their teachers inerrant, so, too, the inspiration of the holy writers does not guarantee the inerrancy of Scripture, though, of course, the writers of Scripture did enjoy a richer measure of the Holy Ghost. Luther, on the other hand, holds that there is not merely a difference in degree, but a specific difference between illumination and inspiration, between illuminated teachers of the Church and the inspired writers of Scripture. What the inspired writers of Holy Scripture teach is out and out God's own Word; as to the enlightened teachers of the Church, such as Luther and the rest, they teach God's Word only inasmuch and in so far as "we repeat and preach what we have heard and learned from the Prophets and Apostles." (St. L. III:1890.)

---

[94] Quoted in Baier-Walther, I, 102, from Kahnis, *Dogmatik*, 1st ed., I, 666.

In his *Disputatio de Fide* of the year 1535 Luther indeed first says that it is one and the same Holy Ghost who was active in the Apostles and is now active in illuminating all Christians and their teachers. But then he draws a sharp line of distinction between the Apostles on the one hand and all Christians with all later teachers on the other hand, "in order that the Church might not be divided" (St. L. XIX: 1442). For he adds: "We are not all Apostles, who were sent by a firm decree of God (*certo Dei decreto*) to us as infallible teachers (*infallibiles doctores*). Hence they cannot err, but we can, and we can be deceived in our faith, since we lack such a decree of God." The same distinction Luther makes when he defines a Prophet as distinguished from all later teachers. He says in his commentary on several chapters of Exodus, 1525: "A Prophet is one who gets his understanding immediately from God, into whose mouth the Holy Ghost puts the right word. . . . No one can make a Prophet by human instruction; and though it be God's Word and I [Luther] preach the Word most purely, still I cannot be a Prophet; a learned and wise man I can be. For example, in Matthew 23 those are called 'wise' who derive the doctrine from the Prophets, for God speaks through men and not without means. But Prophets are those who have their doctrine from God without any means." (St. L. III:785.) Also what the Prophets and Apostles knew before or what they took from the Scriptures already written was given them "immediately," inasmuch as the Holy Ghost "put the right words" regarding the familiar things or thing taken from Scripture "into their mouth," as happened to the Apostles at Pentecost, when they so "amazingly take hold of Scripture as though they had studied it 100,000 years and knew it inside out." Luther adds: "I could not take hold of Scripture with such certainty, although I am a doctor of the Holy Scriptures." (St. L. XIII:2053.)

Modern theologians furthermore distinguish degrees in inspiration. We mentioned Kahnis above and Henry E. Jacobs. Kahnis attempts to divide the Bible into three classes, according as he regards them more or less inspired. Jacobs says: "A text from Genesis and one from John, one from the Psalms and one from Romans, cannot stand on the same footing." That means the complete abandonment of the Scriptural concept of inspiration. According to Scripture, inspiration is a concept which admits of no increase or decrease. Quenstedt, taking issue with the Jesuit Bonfrère (d. 1643) and others, correctly states that nothing at all can be found in Scripture (*nec vola nec vestigium*) to indicate that one part of the Scriptures is more divine (*divinius*) than another.[95] Christ ascribes the same divinity to all the parts of Scripture when He says John 10:35 that "the Scripture" cannot be broken. And, according to 2 Tim. 3:16; Rom. 3:2; 2 Pet. 1:21; 1 Pet. 1:10-12; Eph. 2:20; etc., all parts of Scripture are equally a divine product. And so Luther will accept no degrees in inspiration: "So, then, the entire Scriptures are assigned to the Holy Ghost" (St. L. III:1890). Of course, Luther does make a distinction between the books of Holy Scripture as to their relative importance for the generation and preservation of Christian faith. In this sense he calls the Gospel according to St. John the "one tender, truly chief Gospel," because it is occupied chiefly with doctrine, while the other Gospels deal more with deeds and events from the life of Christ. For the same reason, too, he gives first place in the epistles of the Apostles to "St. Paul's epistles, especially that to the Romans, and St. Peter's First Epistle," "the true kernel and marrow of all books. They ought rightly be the first books, and it would be advisable for every Christian to read them first and most and, by daily reading, to make them as familiar as his daily bread." (St. L. XIV:90 f.) Modern theologians think they can prove from these words that according to Luther's "real opinion" the Scriptures were not in all parts equally the words of the Holy Ghost. But this is a misunderstanding and misuse of Luther's words. Though Luther calls the Gospel according to St. John the "tender, truly chief Gospel," because it is occupied principally with doctrine, still he assigns also the other Gospels in all their parts to the Holy Ghost. We heard above that he declares the external arrangements of the events in Matthew, according to which this Evangelist "mixes or blends together" the destruction of Jerusalem and the end of the world (chapter 24), the Holy Ghost's manner of speaking (St. L. VII:1297). Again, concerning the institution of the Lord's Supper, which is found not in John, but in Matthew, Mark, and Luke, Luther says that the Holy Ghost has intentionally so ordered it that no Evangelist agrees with the other in the words of the institution (St. L. XIX:1104). Quenstedt has been charged with an almost unbelievable exaggeration of the concept of inspiration because he does not leave the choice of the words (*voces*) and manner of expression (*phrasis*) to the discretion or the human consideration of the holy writers, but ascribes that to the divine inspiration. Quenstedt teaches, in the first place, as we saw in Section Five, that in inspiring Scripture the Holy Ghost did not create a new language in

---

95 *Systema* I, 101 f. On Bonfrère compare W. S. Reilly in *The Catholic Encyclopedia*, II, 655 *sq*.

vocabulary and mode of expression, but accommodated Himself to the usage (*genus loquendi*) known and familiar to the writers. He says: "According as they were trained or accustomed to speak or write either in an elegant or in a more simple style, so the Holy Ghost used them and was ready to accommodate Himself to the natural aptitude of the men and condescended to it and so to express the same things by some in more magnificent, by others in more simple language." But then Quenstedt adds, in the second place: "The fact that the holy writers, however, used these and no other phrases, these and no other words (*voces*) or equivalents (*aequipollentes*) resulted solely from the divine impulse and divine inspiration." But in exactly the same manner Luther describes inspiration. He, too, makes the choice of definite words and of a definite mode of expression depend on inspiration. He says on Ps. 127:3: "Not only the words (*vocabula*), but also the mode of expression (*phrasis*), which the Holy Ghost and Scripture use, are divine" (St. L. IV:1960). On top of all this there are the familiar words from Luther's "Direction How to Study Theology," which establish the fact that when Luther spoke of inspiration he meant "Verbal Inspiration." He says in explanation of *meditatio:* "Secondly, you should meditate, that is, not in the heart alone, but also externally, work on and ply the oral speech and the lettered words in the Book [scil., in Holy Scripture], read them and reread them again and again, noting carefully and reflecting upon what the Holy Ghost means by these words [scil., by the 'lettered words']. And have a care that you do not tire of it or think it enough if you have read, heard, said, it once or twice, and now profoundly understand it all; for in that manner a person will never become much of a theologian." (St. L. XIV:435.) In this forceful way, Luther ties all theological study and all endeavor to perceive the divine truth with "the lettered words in the Book," with Verbal Inspiration. We repeat what we have said in the beginning of this chapter: if we wish to speak of a difference between Luther and the orthodox Lutheran dogmaticians, then the difference does not consist in Luther's taking a "more liberal" attitude toward Scripture, but in his teaching with much more force and more fully than the dogmaticians that Scripture and the Word of God are identical.

We cannot close this chapter on "Luther and the Inspiration of Scripture" without considering several statements of Luther that are adduced with great confidence by nearly all modern theologians as proofs for Luther's "liberal attitude" toward Scripture. When we examine these statements, we shall see that they do not prove Luther's "liberal" attitude toward Scripture, but the unscientific and loose manner of the neologists in quoting Luther. In part the statements quoted do not at all deal with the inspiration of Scripture, and in part they have been torn out of the context entirely and invested with a sense that is the opposite of what Luther said. They belong to that class of quotations which without investigation have been passed down from one generation to another.

This applies in full measure to the quotation which is perhaps the one most widely known and which has given many men a false opinion on Luther's attitude toward Scripture — the "hay, straw, and stubble" quotation. To prove that Luther "concedes errors in Scripture," Tholuck wrote in the first edition of Herzog's *Realenzyklopaedie* VI, 695: "In his preface to Link's *Annotations on the Five Books of Moses,* Luther says: 'Without doubt the Prophets studied Moses, and the later Prophets studied the first Prophets and wrote their good thoughts, inspired by the Holy Ghost, into a book. But though some hay, straw, and stubble slipped in at times (into the writing) of these good faithful teachers and searchers of the Scriptures and they did not build purely silver, gold, and precious stones, still the foundation remains; the rest the fire consumes. (St. L. XIV:150.)'" In the second edition (1880) of the *Realenzyklopaedie* (VI, 753), Cremer, following Tholuck, writes: "On the one hand Holy Scripture is for Luther a book in which 'one letter, yes, one tittle, is of greater importance than heaven and earth'; on the other hand he knows and tells of hay, straw, and stubble that in the case of the Prophets slipped in with their own good thoughts." Errors in the Scriptures! Cremer's article has been reprinted in the third edition (1901) of the *Realenzyklopaedie* (IX, p. 191). Also Kahnis claimed: "Luther says concerning the Prophets that they studied Moses and their predecessors and built thereon not always gold and silver, but also hay, straw, and wood" (*Die luth. Dogmatik,* 2d ed., I, 275). Kahnis' words were reproduced in Nitzsch-Stephan, in 1912 (*Ev. Dogmatik,* 3d ed., p. 268). The facts in the case are that in this passage, so generally and even recently quoted, Luther does not at all speak of the writing of Holy Scripture and therefore also not of the inspiration of Scripture, as has been shown *in extenso* in *Lehre und Wehre,* 1885, p. 329 ff., and 1886, p. 8 ff. Also the tenth edition of Luthardt's *Kompendium* admits that Luther here has been misquoted. While the text gives the "hay, straw, and stubble" passage as proof for Luther's liberal attitude, a footnote on p. 328 says: "These words, however, as Luther meant them, do not refer to the Biblical authors, but to the exegetes; cp. Kawerau, *Theol.*

Lit. Ztg., 1895, p. 216." As a matter of fact, it is utterly impossible to refer Luther's words to the "Biblical authors," that is, to the Prophets, in so far as they wrote the Bible of the Old Testament. Luther is rather speaking of those periods in the lives of the Prophets when they were not moved as the infallible organs of the Holy Spirit to write the Holy Scriptures, but when outside the state of inspiration, they, just like other people, made the Scriptures of the Old Testament the object of their study and, in doing this, entered "in a book" the good thoughts the Holy Spirit awakened in them during this study. To this study and this writing, which took place when they were not inspired to write the Holy Scriptures, Luther's words refer: "Though some hay, straw, and wood slipped in at times, etc." What Luther teaches is that the Prophets of the Old Testament did not always infallibly speak and write God's Word, but only at times, temporarily, namely, when inspired by the Holy Ghost. Read his remarks on Gen. 44:18: "The theologians have a common proverb: 'The Holy Ghost did not always touch the hearts of the Prophets.' [96] The inspiration of the Prophets does not continue forever, on and on, without stopping. Isaiah did not continuously and forever receive revelations of high and great things, but only at special times. We have also the example of the Prophet Elisha, who says of the Shunammite (2 Kings 4:27): 'Let her alone; for her soul is vexed within her; and the Lord hath hid it from me and hath not told me.' There he confesses that the Lord does not at all times move the hearts of the Prophets. The Spirit did come at times when they played the harp or Psalter and sang several Psalms and spiritual hymns." (St. L. II:1645.)

Tholuck overlooks the words *"auf diese Weise"* in the quotation from Luther; otherwise he could not have failed to see that Luther is speaking of the Prophets apart from their specific prophetic office, of the times when they were on a level with other "good, faithful teachers and searchers of Scripture" who were mediately illuminated and could err. Luther's words read: "In this manner, without doubt, the Prophets studied Moses and the last Prophets the first," and with the phrase "in this manner" he refers to his preceding remarks about Scripture study, which God enjoins upon all Christians and all teachers, as he himself [Luther] and also Augustine read and studied the Scriptures. Such "searching and reading" cannot be done "unless one is there with the pen and jots down the special thoughts with which

96 In *Lehre und Wehre*, 1886, p. 9, note 7, attention is called to the fact that also Quenstedt and Calov show the Scriptural basis for the *"Spiritus Sanctus non semper tangit corda prophetarum."*

he is inspired while reading and studying, so that he can hold and retain them." Also in the words following the remark quoted by Tholuck, Luther speaks of writings as they have been written by all teachers in the Church, also by his "dear sir and friend Dr. Wenzeslaus Link."

Lehre und Wehre, 1885, p. 329 ff., reprints Luther's entire preface to Link's *Annotationes* and then says: "From this it is evident that Luther is not speaking of the Prophets as writing the Scriptures, but as writing such books as his friend Wenzeslaus Link wrote and for which he [Luther] composed the prefaces. Luther is not speaking of writing under the influence of 'inspiration,' as we use the term when we speak of the doctrine of inspiration, but of a study of Scripture and noting 'in a book' the good thoughts which the Holy Ghost inspires in a Christian while reading Scripture. . . . Luther is speaking here – to use that expression – of the daily private study of the Prophets, 'for they were not men of a kind that would put Moses on the shelf and dream their own visions and preach their dreams, but men who daily and diligently studied Moses.' And in this sphere it was possible, says Luther, that 'also hay, straw, wood, at times slipped into the writings of these good, faithful teachers and searchers of Scripture.' . . . It is clear, then, that in this passage, so persistently quoted to prove Luther's 'liberal' position in the doctrine of inspiration, Luther is not at all speaking of inspiration. Luthardt, Kahnis, Cremer, etc., have either not looked up the passage in Luther at all or have read the passage inattentively."

Walther therefore addresses the following words of earnest reproof to Luthardt and Cremer (*Lehre und Wehre,* 1886, p. 10 f.): "Professor Luthardt and Professor Cremer may, on the one hand, be excused to a certain extent, since they manifestly have not looked up the passage in its context but copied Tholuck in good faith; but it is, on the other hand, inexcusable that in so important a matter they relied on a man like Tholuck, who even says of Christ 'that the exegetical equipment, which must be merely memorized, can have been known and accessible to Him (Christ) only according to the general level of education in His day and the educational facilities supplied in His training and from His surroundings' [!], from which Tholuck draws the conclusion: 'Though no hermeneutical blunder is found in the extant speeches of the Redeemer, the impossibility of one cannot be asserted from the outset, as little as the impossibility of a grammatical or a chronological error.' (See Tholuck, *Das Alte Testament im Neuen Testament,* Gotha, 1861, p. 59 f.)" In this connection,

Walther points out that a twofold sin is here being committed: the modern theologians are doing this evil work by appealing to the authority of Luther, whose doctrine they misrepresent in order to destroy the faith of Christians in the divine authority of Scripture. "They commit, in the first place, a grave sin against the dear man of God, Luther, in ascribing to him, without looking up the reference, an opinion which would, if one compares a hundred other statements of his, make him out to be the most confused brain in all the world, yes, an opinion that he would condemn to the abyss of hell. But, in the second place, it is an even far more terrible sin against the thousands who have recognized in Luther the greatest witness of the truth since the day of the Apostles and Prophets, but who are now, contrary to all truth, shaken in their faith by the appeal to Luther's authority."

Next to the "hay, straw, and stubble" quotation the moderns like to use the "too weak for a thrust" passage to prove Luther's vacillating attitude toward Scripture. But here, too, the context is utterly disregarded. When Cremer writes (R. E., 2d ed., VI, p. 753): Luther speaks "of an inadequate proof of the Apostle (Gal. 4:21: *'zum Stich zu schwach'* – too weak for a thrust, i. e., unconvincing)," the impression is created – and Cremer intended to create that impression – as though Luther denied that the allegory used by Paul in Galatians 4 (Sarah and Isaac represent the Christian Church, Hagar and Ishmael the people of the Law) had any validity whatever, while Luther, in fact, merely says that in a controversy with the Jews (*contra Iudaeos*), for whom the Apostle was not yet an authority, the allegory was "too weak for a thrust." It is too bad that Cremer and all those who make so much of this expression in order to prove Luther's vacillating attitude did not regard it worth while to look up the Latin original. In Luther's *Commentary on Genesis* (written in Latin) the expression translated with *"zum Stich zu schwach"* reads: *"in acie minus valet"* – "it has less convincing power in a controversy." The phrase "in controversy" should have reminded these men that Luther does not say that the allegory of Galatians 4 has no convincing power whatever (it convinces the Christians, for whom Paul is an inspired Apostle of Christ), but that it does not have this power in a certain respect, namely, in controversy with the Jews.[97] Therefore Walther

97 In the entire discussion, Luther draws attention to the fact that a preacher proceeds differently when he teaches his Christian hearers than when he argues with the enemies of the Church. Luther says: "The godless Jews deride us that our Fathers [the Church Fathers are meant] sought to prove the Trinity from this text [Gen. 18:1 ff.] that three men appeared to Abraham and he never-

wrote these words against Cremer: "Luther never had the notion to deny that for Christians, who recognized Paul's authority as that of an inspired writer, a doctrine presented by Paul by means of an allegorical interpretation of a story is just as conclusive as any other doctrine presented by him directly, in line with the established hermeneutical rule: '*Sensus allegoricus non est argumentativus, nisi a Spiritu Sancto traditur,*' that is, the allegorical sense is not conclusive unless it is taught by the Holy Ghost Himself" (*Lehre und Wehre,* 1886, p. 12). Christians, however, know and believe that the Holy Ghost was in Paul as an inspired Apostle of Christ.

It goes without saying that it is entirely improper to offer Luther's distinction between homologumena and antilegomena as proof for his "free" attitude toward inspiration. Voigt, for instance, says that "Luther could not have regarded Holy Scripture word for word as the product of the Holy Ghost," since "he felt at liberty to express the most liberal views on whole books of the Bible" (*Fundamentaldogmatik*, p. 536). And in Nitzsch-Stephan the remark occurs: "The Revelation of St. John displeases Luther so thoroughly that he regards it as neither Apostolic nor Prophetic."[98] This is an illogical identification of two things that have nothing in common. In the doctrine of the inspiration of Scripture we are not concerned with the extent of the canon, that is, whether the so-called antilegomena (the Epistles of James and Jude and the Revelation of St. John) belong in the canon, but we are concerned with the question whether the books which are canonical beyond a doubt (Luther calls them "the right certain, chief books") are inspired, are God's infallible Word. This Luther maintains from first to last, as we saw in the first part of this chapter. But as to the extent of the canon, Luther (as also Chemnitz, etc.) abides by the distinction which, according to the report of Eusebius (*Church History* III, 25), the Early Church made in regard to the certain or uncertain Apostolic origin of the books of the New Testament (St. L.

---

theless spoke only with one." Luther judges of this: "As far as this text is concerned, we grant that its historical meaning disproves no contention of the Jews; however, at times also the figurative and symbolic meaning is in place." Then follows Luther's remark on the allegory Gal. 4:21 ff: "For Paul does just that (Gal. 4:22). Having proved in a masterly manner the doctrine of faith [namely, "by other certain and clear passages of Scripture"] and, so to say, won it with the sword, he then adds the allegory of Sarah and Hagar, which, though it is too weak in controversy [that is how our St. Louis edition translates "*in acie minus valet*"], for it departs from the historical sense, nevertheless makes the matter of faith very clear and embellishes it" (St. L. I:1150).

[98] *Ev. Dogmatik*, p. 269. Seeberg argues along the same lines, *Dogmengesch.*, 2d ed., II, 287.

XIV:132). Luther states his position in his preface to the Epistle to the Hebrews in these words: "Hitherto we have had the right certain chief books of the New Testament. The four following [Hebrews, James, Jude, Revelation] had, in ancient times, a different reputation." (St. L. XIV:126.) Hoenecke writes (*Dogmatik*, I, 362): "One must distinguish well between the extent of the canon and the inspiration of the books which are canonical without question. Here W. Walther [Professor in Rostock, *Das Erbe der Reformation im Kampfe der Gegenwart*, Section 1, p. 42 ff.] says correctly that for Luther the extent of the canon was an open question, but the books that were canonical were absolutely authoritative for him as the inspired Word of God. But this distinction is always being overlooked. Modern theologians always want to draw conclusions from Luther's remarks concerning individual books as to his attitude towards the Word and its inspiration and thus make Luther share their liberal views regarding inspiration. It is rather an established fact that Luther regarded the Word as inspired. And the dogmaticians of the 17th century could with all reason appeal to him as the constant voice of the Church; and hence their doctrine is by no means an innovation over against Luther." On the same matter Walther of St. Louis voiced this sentiment: "Those who here draw attention to Luther's judgment on the antilegomena, how he, e. g., calls the Epistle of James 'a very strawy epistle as compared with them' (the Epistles of Paul and Peter – St. L. XIV:91), and who thus mean to prove Luther's allegedly liberal views on inspiration, we here pass up, since even the weakest mind can see without much reflection how foolish it is to conclude from an adverse verdict of Luther on a book which he did not regard as canonical that he held liberal views on the inspiration of those books which he regarded as canonical; just the opposite ought to be concluded from his verdict" (*Lehre und Wehre*, 1886, p. 8).

A further contention of modern theologians is to the effect that Luther limited the divine authority of Scripture to whatever in Scripture "deals with Christ"; that according to what "deals with Christ" in Scripture he determines whether the rest of Scripture is divine truth or not; that Luther assumes "a canon within the canon"; hence Luther could not possibly have assumed that all statements in Scripture were inspired by the Holy Ghost.[99] For this contention principally two pas-

---

[99] Cp. Dorner, *Geschichte der prot. Theologie*, p. 246; Luthardt, *Kompendium*, 10th ed., p. 328; Seeberg, *Dogmengesch.*, 2d ed., II, 288 ff.; Nitzsch-Stephan, p. 269. Even earlier Hase, *Ev. Dog.*, 4th ed., p. 394. Grimm (*Institutio Theologiae Dogmaticae*, 2d ed., p. 118) states the case of the critics thus: "Though Luther taught that in the controversies fought concerning the Lord's Supper one must

sages from Luther are cited. First, these words from Luther's preface to the Epistles of James and Jude: "Whatever does not teach Christ, that is not Apostolic, even though St. Peter or Paul taught it; again, what preaches Christ would be Apostolic, even though Judas, Annas, Pilate, and Herod did it" (St. L. XIV:129). And, second, the 49th thesis of Luther's "Disputation on Faith," which reads: "If our adversaries urge Scripture, we urge Christ against Scripture" (St. L. XIX:1441).

These words – to begin with the second passage – do have a strange sound. Taken out of their connection, they do give the impression as though Luther set "Scripture" and "Christ" in opposition to each other, with the idea that Christ, conceived as the substance of the Scriptures, must be used to correct the words of Scripture. But we can get that impression only if we neglect to consult the context of these words in Luther. By "Scripture," which the adversaries urge and against which Luther urges Christ, Luther means the Scripture as misused by the adversaries (the Papists), the falsely understood and falsely applied Scripture. Luther is thinking of the abuse of Scripture perpetrated by the Romanists in urging Scripture passages that speak of the Law and of human works against Christ, that is, against the Gospel and faith. That is Luther's own explanation of his use of the term "Scripture," in the preceding theses 42–48! There Luther castigates the Papists for introducing such Scripture passages as "Thou shalt keep the commandments" (Deut. 8:6), "Thou shalt love the Lord, thy God" (Matt. 22:37), "This do, and thou shalt live" (Luke 10:28), "Break off thy sins by righteousness, and thine iniquities by showing mercy to the poor" (Dan. 4:37), against Christ and faith, while these passages are to be understood in favor of Christ, since the works mentioned can be done only in Christ, that is, they always presuppose Christ and faith in Him. And in thesis 41, which begins this section, Luther expressly states that by "Scripture," against which he urges Christ, he means the falsely understood Scripture. The thesis reads: "One must not understand Scripture contrary to, but in favor of Christ; therefore one must bring it into relation with Christ or not regard it as true Scripture."

---

cling tenaciously to the letter of the Holy Scriptures and brought forward the individual words of Scripture with grandiloquent [!] praises, he nevertheless at other times made the divinity of the sacred books depend on the vigor and fervor with which the merit of Christ was preached and commended to the hearts, and thus, in a way, he established a canon within the canon." Somewhat differently, though rather hazily, Gottlob Mayer, *Das religioese Erkenntnisproblem*, 1897, I, 65 ff.

In passing, it may be said that it is futile on the part of modern theologians to seek cover for their attitude toward Scripture behind the alleged statement of Luther that only what "deals with Christ" is true in the Scriptures. For since practically all modern theologians deny the *satisfactio vicaria,* they teach nothing whatever of that in Scripture which "deals with Christ." The Christ who is the theme of Scripture is always the Christ who has reconciled mankind with God through His *satisfactio vicaria.*

Also what Luther says in the theses following thesis 49 has, contrary to its connection, been used to deny that Luther had "the strict conception of inspiration." Luther then expands the thought, which he also voiced on other occasions, that all who have Christ and thus the Holy Ghost can also make a decalog (*decalogum quendam*) and judge all things correctly. Theses 55—57 read: "For if the Gentiles, with their corrupt nature, could adopt statutes regarding God and be a law unto themselves, Romans 2, how much more can Paul or a mature Christian, filled with the Holy Ghost, arrange a sort of decalog and judge all things most correctly, just as all the Prophets and Fathers from the same Spirit of Christ spoke everything we have in Scripture." Because Luther here places "the mature Christian" and "the Fathers" beside Paul and the Prophets as speaking from one and the same Spirit, it has been argued that Luther assumes not a specific difference, but only a difference in degree between the illumination of the Christian and the inspiration of the writers of Holy Scripture and that as the Christians through their illumination do not become infallible but remain fallible, so do also the writers of Holy Scripture. But here again it is obvious that all who ascribe such a view of Scripture to Luther have failed to look at the context. For in the theses immediately following (58—60), Luther most emphatically denounces the thought that faith in Christ qualifies or entitles a Christian or even a theologian to take a "free" attitude toward the words of Scripture, to regard himself as not bound by the words of Scripture because the words might possibly contain an error. In this very place Luther draws a very sharp line of distinction between the inspired Prophets and Apostles on the one hand and all Christians and all later teachers on the other hand. The attitude of an independent lord over against the words of Scripture he designates as the characteristic of the "roving spirits" who by introducing thoughts not contained in the Word of the Apostles and Prophets cause divisions in the Church of God. The fact that all of us, Christians as well as Christian theologians, are strictly bound to the Scriptures of the Prophets and Apostles and are not permitted to criticize them is due, as Luther points out, to this great difference between us and the Apostles: the Apostles are appointed by God as infallible teachers and could not err; we, however, are subject to error. The words of Luther are very clear; they read: "Because we are meanwhile of an unequal spirit [though one and the same Spirit dwells in us and the Apostles] and the flesh wars against the spirit, it is necessary, also because of the roving spirits, to adhere to the certain commandments and Scriptures of the Apostles in order that the Church be not divided. For we are not all Apostles, who were sent to us by a firm decree of God as infallible teachers. Hence they cannot err, but we can, and we can be deceived in our faith, because we lack such a decree of God."

As to the words of Luther quoted in the first place: "Whatever does not teach Christ is not Apostolic, even though St. Peter or Paul taught it; again, what preaches Christ would be Apostolic, even though Judas, Annas, Pilate, and Herod did it," the use of the subjunctive indicates that Luther is here speaking not of an actual, but of a supposed case. Besides, as to the Apostle's preaching of Christ, Luther expressly states that "no one can do the like, neither Annas, nor Caiaphas, nor any man on earth" (Erl., 2d ed., V, p. 183).

The rest of the alleged proofs for Luther's liberal attitude have been taken care of in the first part of this chapter. From the *Chronikon* we add this additional thought that Luther prefers to ascribe the error "to the copyist" rather than to the original. We have reference to these words in the *Chronikon* (St. L. XIV:600): "The time of the Judges from the death of Moses until Samuel is 357 years, including Joshua, as you see. And this calculation is not wrong, since in the First Book of Kings (ch. 6) 480 years are counted from the Exodus to the temple of Solomon. Therefore there is an obvious error in Acts 13, through the fault of the copyist. And the Latin translation is doubly wrong, because it places 450 years before the Judges, during the distribution of the land, and thus forces Lyra to go back into the years of Isaac. The Greek text, however, is corrupted through an error of the copyist, which could easily occur by his writing τετρακοσίοις for τριακοσίοις." [100]

---

[100] Thus also Beza; cp. *Lehre und Wehre,* 1886, p. 72, note. The question here is not whether other solutions of the difficulty are not possible or even lie nearer at hand, but what is Luther's attitude toward the inerrancy of Scripture — which he definitely holds. Other solutions are found in the Weimarer Bibel, the Hirschberger Bibel, also in Calov. See the commentaries of Meyer, Lange-Schaff, and Bloomfield. Bloomfield, after offering two possible solutions, remarks: "Thus no error will attach to either passage [1 Kings 6:1 and Acts 13:20] and only different modes of computation be supposed to be adopted."

But one other argument of those who seek to hide behind Luther for their liberal attitude should be considered, since it has been much employed again in recent years. The argument runs thus: Luther teaches that the Holy Scriptures can be understood and "experienced inwardly" as divine authority only through the Holy Ghost; therefore Luther cannot possibly have assumed that the words of Scripture are the words of the Holy Ghost. Among the proofs that Luther cannot have maintained the "divinity" (*divinitatem*) of Holy Scripture, Grimm adduced this one: "Luther considered the illumination of the Holy Ghost necessary for a mind correctly to understand Scripture" (*Institutio*, p. 119). In the same manner also Seeberg argues when he says that Luther demanded that "man recognize the authority of Scripture not because the Church has recognized it, but because he has experienced its truth" (*Dogmengesch.*, 2d ed., II, 288) and quotes as first proof the words from the Erlangen edition of Luther (28:340): "Every man must believe solely for this reason that it is the Word of God and that he in his heart finds that it is the truth." Everyone will admit that an argument of this kind: Since Holy Scripture can be understood or experienced only through the Holy Ghost, therefore the words of Scripture cannot be inspired by the Holy Ghost, has no basis in logic whatever. Therefore Luther does not place the experiencing of the truth of Scripture in opposition to the inspiration of Scripture, but he teaches in this very place most powerfully "the inspiration in its strictest sense." On the following page (p. 341) he calls it "blasphemy" if anyone should say: "Nevertheless St. Matthew, Paul, Peter were also men; therefore their doctrine is also the doctrine of men. . . . If you hear such thoroughly hardened and blinded blasphemers, turn from them or plug your ears; they are not worthy to be spoken to. . . ." Page 342: "It is one thing if man himself speaks, another thing if God speaks through men. What the Apostles spoke, God commanded them to speak and confirmed and witnessed it by great miracles." Furthermore Luther says, in this place, of Scripture that "in it the uniform Word of God has been taught since the beginning of the world." And finally Luther declares on page 343: "The doctrine of men we do not condemn because men have spoken it, but because it is lies and blasphemies against Scripture, which, though it also has been written through men, is not of or by men but by God."

It is thus evident that the modern theologians who claim Luther as patron of their liberal attitude toward Scripture either have not read Luther at all, but have copied from compilations of others without verifying them, or, if they have actually read Luther, were unable to understand him, because their wish to have Luther as their protector was stronger than their sense of historical truth. Kahnis may serve as an example of the first class. In his sharply polemical writing against Hengstenberg *Zeugnis von den Grundwahrheiten des Protestantismus* he asserts that Luther took the same liberal attitude toward Scripture as he (Kahnis) takes and offers this as proof: "Walch has collected such statements in his edition of Luther, in Vol. 14. Let him who desires to be quickly oriented read the articles 'Inspiration' (by Dr. Tholuck) and 'Neutestamentlicher Kanon' (by Dr. Landerer) in Herzog's *Realencyklopaedie* (VI, p. 695 ff.; VII, p. 295 ff.)." Kahnis then offers from Tholuck's catalog the quotation which he regards as the most clinching one – the "hay, straw, and stubble" passage, which, as we have seen, and also Luthardt finally admits, does not speak of the inspiration of Scripture at all. But the fact that he copies Tholuck's quotation without correcting Tholuck's blunder proves that he did not verify the quotation.[101] In his *Dogmatics* Kahnis offers a lengthy catalog of opinions on Luther as proof of his assertion that "Luther takes a liberal stand" and adds in a footnote: "We are not verifying these statements, which are for the most part known to everyone, but for this verification direct the reader to the compilations mentioned." He had mentioned the compilations of Rudelbach, Tholuck, and Koestlin.

Other neologists have, indeed, read Luther, but in such a way that they read their attitude toward Scripture into Luther, ignoring the plain sense of Luther's statements. Seeberg, for instance, in his *Dogmengeschichte,* 2d ed., II, 289, refers to the Erlangen edition, 30, p. 313 f., 331, to prove "the censuring statements of Luther on some thoughts in Biblical books" and Luther's "admission of slips" in particular. Consulting Luther, we do find that Luther says "that Matthew and Mark do not observe the strict order, but Luke does." But Luther does not "censure" Matthew and Mark on that account; he says that both have not "promised" to do this (namely, to observe the chronological order); in Luke's case it was different: he had promised "that he would set forth these things from the beginning and in order; and that he proves, for his Gospel follows a fine order to the end." The predicate "censuring" Seeberg has read into Luther's statement. Luther finds it entirely in order that Matthew and Mark follow an order other than the chronological one. Again, at the other place (page 331), Luther indeed says that Matthew and Mark describe the Lord's Supper

---

101 The same thing happened to Dr. Briggs, as his trial showed.

"imperfectly." But with this "imperfectly" Luther is not charging Matthew and Mark with errors. He has only this in mind that Matthew and Mark do not report that "Christ has commanded us [the Church of all ages] to repeat His act and keep this Supper in like manner," as Luke and Paul do when they report the command to the Church of all ages: "This do in remembrance of Me!"

8

A Brief Critique of Modern Theology in So Far As It Denies the Inspiration of Scripture

We are summarizing what has already been said elsewhere. In Hastings' *Encyclopedia*, VII, p. 346, Strahan correctly describes the difference between the old theology and the modern theology as to their attitude toward Scripture thus: the old theologians aim to present in the article "De Scriptura Sacra" not their own notions, but God's views and teachings as He revealed them in His Word. Modern theologians, however, regard the opposite method as the only correct one. They assume a critical attitude over against Scripture. They do not propose to teach what the Scriptures say of themselves, but they judge of Scripture on the basis of the impression which Scripture makes upon them, the theologians. By this procedure, which they call the "scientific" one, they arrive at the result that the Scriptures are not the Word of God and that accordingly the old doctrine of inspiration must be discarded. Strahan declares: "Protestant scholars of the present day, imbued with the scientific spirit, have no *a priori* theory of the inspiration of the Bible." By the "*a priori* theory," rejected by "Protestant scholars of the present day," Strahan means nothing else than that these theologians do not propose to teach what Scripture says of itself. Strahan himself explains his words in this way when he continues: "They do not open any book of the Old or New Testament with the feeling that they are bound to regard its teaching as sacred and authoritative. They yield to nothing but what they regard as the irresistible logic of facts. They feel that, if they are not convinced of the inspiration of the Bible by its intrinsic merits, they cannot be legitimately convinced in any other way. And if in the end they formulate a doctrine of the divine influence under which the Scriptures were written, this is an inference from the characteristics which, after free and fair investigation, they are constrained to recognize."

The result of this method of ascertaining "the worth of Scripture" Strahan states in these words: "To sum up: the old doctrine of the equal and infallible inspiration of every part of the Old Testament . . . is now rapidly disappearing among Protestants. There is, in reality, no clear dividing line between what is and what is not worthy of a place in the Scriptures." Just as unfavorable, according to Strahan's report, is the result of the scientific investigation of the New Testament: "There are not a few passages in the Bible which cannot be regarded by Protestants as in any true sense inspired."

This portrayal of the attitude of modern theology toward Scripture in distinction from the old theology is absolutely correct. Take Theodore Kaftan as a representative. When he writes: "We are realists," he means thereby: What the Scriptures teach of themselves is not authoritative for us, but only that is authoritative which we, according to the impression which Scripture makes upon us, regard as the divine truth. By this method Kaftan also has arrived at the result that Verbal Inspiration must be "definitely abandoned" (*Moderne Theologie des alten Glaubens*, 2d ed., pp. 108, 113, 116).

The question why people do not recognize the Scriptures, which are the Word of God, as the Word of God, is clearly answered by the Scriptures. Jesus is dealing (John 8) with people who would not recognize His Word as the Word of the Son of God. Jesus indicates this when He says (v. 37): "My Word hath no place in you," and when He asks them (v. 43): "Why do ye not understand My speech?" and then supplies the answer: "Even because ye cannot hear My Word." And the cause of the Jews' inability to understand His speech and hear His Word, Jesus says, is the fact that they are not children of God, have no communion with God. Positively and negatively Jesus declares (v. 47): "He that is of God heareth God's words; ye therefore hear them not because ye are not of God." It is obvious from the context that the term "hear" is here used in the pregnant sense, denoting not merely the external hearing with the ears, but also the "internal" hearing, the reception of the word as God's Word. With the external ear the Jews heard Christ's Word, but since they were not children of God, they could not recognize Christ's Word as God's Word, but revolted against it. Christ here establishes the fact that acceptance of His Word as God's Word is confined to the Christians. Again, in John 10:4, in the Parable of the Good Shepherd, Christ says that His sheep follow Him, "for they know His voice," and in v. 26 He gives as the reason why the Jews would not accept His Word: "Because ye are not of My sheep." Luther, too, remarks on John 8: "Hence the Jews have no other ground for their unbelief than that they are not God's children" (St. L. XI:568). But, now, why does Christ deny that the Jews who were disputing with Him were God's children and declare that they were consequently unable to receive His Word as God's Word? The Jews based their divine sonship on their natural descent from Abraham, saying: "Abraham is our father," John 8:39. Thus they revealed that they did not recognize Christ as the Savior of sinners, as the One who had come to give His life as a ransom for many (Matt. 20:28). Expressed in theological terms, they did not recognize Christ's *satisfactio vicaria,* although His *satisfactio vicaria* had been clearly pictured to them by Isaiah: "He was wounded for our transgressions, He was bruised for our iniquities; the chastisement of our peace was upon Him; and with His stripes we are healed" (ch. 53:5), and though Christ Himself had reminded them of this *satisfactio* when He told them: "If you believe not that I am He, ye shall die in your sins" (John 8:24). In short, the Jews' rejection of the Word of Christ as not being the Word of God was but a symptom of a deeper-seated disease, namely, that they did not believe in Christ's vicarious satisfaction.

Even so the fact that the modern theologians do not perceive Scripture (which verily is Christ's own Word, given us through His Prophets and Apostles) to be the Word of God, is but a symptom of a deeper-seated disease, namely, that they have quite generally discarded the doctrine of the *satisfactio Christi vicaria.* For this reason all their theological thoughts move outside the Christian sphere. Without "the cost" ("*Koeste*"), that is, without Christ's *satisfactio vicaria,* doctrine and faith remain Turkish and Jewish, as Luther expresses it in his powerful sermon on John 3:16-21. "I have often said before this that faith in God is in itself not sufficient, but the cost must also be there. The Turk and the Jew, too, believe in God, but without the means and the cost." (St. L. XI:1085.) "*Iustus fide vivet, sed fide Crucifixi*" – the just lives by faith, by faith in the Crucified One (XXI a:1514). Where the *satisfactio vicaria* is not taught and believed, there is also no Holy Ghost, for only through this doctrine, through faith in this doctrine, does the Holy Ghost enter into the heart (Gal. 3:2; John 16:14); and He is the Spirit of truth, who teaches me to recognize His Word which He spoke through the Prophets and Apostles (1 Pet. 1:10-12) as His Word. Modern theology must therefore return to the Scriptural teaching of the *satisfactio vicaria.* Without this return it will never attain the Christian attitude toward Scripture, but will continue, in its teaching on Scripture, to contradict Christ and His Apostles to their face. – That is not to say that everyone who from the security of the rostrum or in his "scientific" writings criticizes the *satisfactio vicaria* cannot have faith in Christ. We like to think of a "double bookkeeping," or inconsistency, according to which a person in his heart and before God does not rely on what he defends as truth *in disputationibus,* as Luther and Chemnitz express it.

Furthermore, in order to understand the nature of modern theology as far as it attacks the inspiration of Scripture, the following should be noted: It lies in the nature of the case, and it is generally admitted, that truth cannot be fought with truth, but only with untruth. Now, since the inspiration of Scripture is the truth, all who attack this truth are compelled to operate with untruths. We see this clearly when we test the quality of the arguments which are adduced against inspiration. These arguments can adequately be called a large collection of historical and logical untruths. Let us recall here the facts which we have established above.

To refer, first, to historical untruths:

1. Nearly all opponents of the doctrine of inspiration insist that it was the later dogmaticians who invented the "artificial theory" that every word of Scripture is the infallible Word of God ("identification of Scripture with the Word of God"), while Luther had preserved an attitude of freedom over against Scripture. The historical truth is, as we have seen, that Luther presented in all its details the doctrine found in the dogmaticians and that he did it so much more powerfully than the dogmaticians could do it. 2. If we examine the quotations from Luther which are brought forward in the attempt to make Luther the protector of the neologists in their fight against inspiration, we find that these passages either do not speak of inspiration at all (as, e. g., the "hay, straw, and stubble" passage) or say the opposite of what is ascribed to Luther. This includes the passages which are adduced to show that Luther admitted contradictions, etc., in the Scriptures. 3. To discredit Verbal Inspiration in the eyes of the public, the assertion is rather generally made that the dogmaticians had entirely "mechanical conceptions" of the inspiration of Scripture. The historical truth is that the dogmaticians expressly reject all mechanical conceptions; they teach that the Holy Ghost *suavi operatione* (by a suave operation) so influenced the intellect and will of the writers that they wrote *volentes scientesque* (willing it and conscious of it), not *citra et contra voluntatem suam, inscii ac inviti* (without and contrary to their will, un-

knowingly and unwillingly). 4. To discredit Verbal Inspiration, it is further asserted that the verbal-inspirationists regarded Holy Scripture as "a codex of laws fallen from heaven," as "a paper pope," etc. The truth is that such a thought never entered the minds of the defenders of Verbal Inspiration. Rather they teach very clearly that Scripture did not fall from heaven, but was written here on earth by men, in a human tongue, through the inspiration of the Holy Ghost. And the advocates of Verbal Inspiration do not set up Scripture as a "paper pope," which demands external subjection without internal conviction, but to them Scripture is a book that – by virtue of its being God's own Word – itself works faith and *eo ipso* willing and joyous acceptance through the operation of the Holy Ghost inherent in it.

Furthermore, it is evident that modern theology in the heat of its battle against inspiration has been led into alogisms (absurdities), paralogisms (formal fallacies), self-contradictions, that is, into logical untruths. It betrays a total absence of logic when, as we have seen, 1) the distinct style of each writer, the reference of the writers to their historical investigation or to communications of facts by other persons, their use of existing records and documents, the variant readings in the copies of the Bible, are advanced against the doctrine of inspiration. 2) Also the fact that the holy writers were and remained sinners does not contradict the inspiration but rather calls for it if it is granted that the Church is not built on the fallible word of men, but is built to the end of time on the foundation of the Apostles and Prophets. 3) It is a paralogism to use Luther's "liberal opinions" on the antilegomena, which he, together with the Early Church, did not consider a part of the fixed canon, as proof that he took a "liberal attitude" toward Scripture in general, also toward the homologumena, and doubted their inspiration. 4) That the opposition to the truth of inspiration leads to the predicament of logical untruth is apparent from the self-contradictions in which these men involve themselves. On the one hand we have the assertion that in presenting the Christian doctrine one must not proceed from the "word revelation," that is, from Holy Scripture, but from "faith" in the "revelation by deed" or in the "facts of salvation," a faith which the Christian or theologian has in his heart. On the other hand, these same men admit, and they are right in doing this, that God's "revelation by deed" without God's revelation in the Word, remains an "undecipherable hieroglyph." The latter assertion entirely cancels the former, since it establishes that without God's revelation in the Word no faith whatever in God's "revelation by deed" is possible; nothing would be left from which to proceed. Similarly, Theo. Kaftan is so set on doing away with Verbal Inspiration that he, too, asserts two things that cancel each other. On the one hand he asserts that all theologians know that "there is no authentic text" of the Holy Scriptures since the number of variant readings is "legion." On the other hand he (Kaftan) is sure that he can determine on the basis of Scripture what is and what is not the objective Word of God in the Bible. (*Moderne Theol. d. Alten Glaubens,* 2d ed., p. 96 f., p. 113.) That this would be impossible on the supposition that "there is no established text" of the Holy Scriptures did not dawn on him.

In the foregoing paragraphs we have passed harsh judgments on the deniers of the inspiration of Holy Scripture. But while doing this, we do not forget – to use a drastic term of Luther – to "take hold of our own nose" and charge ourselves that we are not always as "serious as we should be" in taking the Bible to be the very Word of God. We confess that when we open our Bible, we do not always consider that the Bible is the book in which not men, but the great God Himself, the Creator and Lord of the universe, is speaking to us in matters of our salvation. We further confess that we do not read the Holy Scriptures as diligently as is proper for those who by God's grace are convinced that the Holy Scriptures are "God's letter" addressed to us. Luther says repeatedly, in various forms of expression: "Letters of lords and princes should be read twice and thrice, for they are carefully worded. But, verily, the letters of our Lord God – for thus St. Gregory calls the Holy Scriptures – one should read three times, seven times, yea, seventy times seven, or, to make it still stronger, without end. But we do not do it. I myself do not do it; therefore I hate myself, *ego odi me.* But when I get at it and read it, I derive strength from it; I feel that it is a power and not a mere story." (St. L. I:1055; XXII: 544, 1069.)

9

The Consequences of the Denial of the Inspiration of Holy Scripture

Though the earlier modern theologians, such as Kahnis, Luthardt, and others, denied the inspiration and together therefore necessarily the infallibility of Scripture, they nevertheless asserted that the Protestant principle of the sole authority of Scripture must stand. Nothing must be placed above the Bible in matters of the Christian faith. The Bible must remain the "final norm" of Christian knowledge and doctrine. Kahnis wrote: "Protestantism stands and falls with the principle of the sole authority of Scripture. This principle is independent of the dogmaticians' doctrine of inspiration."[102] These men were reminded at the time, here and abroad, that they were deceiving themselves. If the Scriptures are not the pure divine truth, but also contain error besides the truth, the theologian, whose task it is to separate the truth from the error according to his "faith consciousness" or his "Christian Ego," is necessarily made the ultimate and highest norm within Protestantism, is placed above the Scriptures. And this degrading of Scripture to a *norma normata* was very soon quite generally practiced and declared to be the only correct thing. Thus Seeberg, for instance, who declared that the "testimony of Christ and His salvation" in Scripture must act as the corrective of the Word of Scripture, even citing Luther as authority for such a procedure, writes: "From this viewpoint the Scriptures must *not* be co-ordinated as *the second principle* [Seeberg's emphasis] of Protestantism with justifying faith. The controlling fundamental thought is faith. And since faith alone understands Scripture and Scripture is intended only for faith, it [Scripture] must be *subordinated* [our emphasis] to the principle of faith." We see here what happens to Protestantism when it relinquishes the truth that Scripture is the infallible Word of God. The principle of Protestantism, "the sole authority of Scripture," is turned upside down. The faith of the Christians is no longer based on the Scriptures, on the Word of the Apostles and Prophets, but the order is inverted: the Scriptures, the Word of the Apostles and Prophets, are based on faith. Protestantism has degenerated into out-and-out "enthusiasm," as we have it in Quakerism. We point to Robert Barclay, the dogmatician of the Quakers, who likewise says that Scripture is not the "adequate primary rule of faith and morals," but is merely to be regarded as "a secondary rule, subordinate to the Spirit" (*regula secundaria, subordinata Spiritui*). "The last resort" and "the sure and immovable foundation of the entire Christian faith" is not the Holy Scriptures, but the inner, immediate revelation of the Holy Ghost, which brings with it its own certainty.

Seeberg fully agrees with Barclay; he merely substitutes "faith" for Barclay's "inner, immediate revelation," to which as first principle

[102] *Der innere Gang des deutschen Protestantismus*, 2d ed., p. 241, quoted in Baier-Walther, I, 103.

the Scriptures are to be "subordinated" as second principle (today it is no longer the fashion to speak of "inner, immediate revelations"). And the entire modern theology, in so far as it denies the inspiration of Scripture, agrees with Seeberg in principle and usually also in form. It is not Scripture which is the source and norm of faith, but faith is the source and norm of theology.

The results of the denial of the inspiration of Scripture are the following:

1. The knowledge of Christian truth is lost and in its place we get human illusion and ignorance. For if any man teach otherwise and consent not to the wholesome words of our Lord Jesus Christ, as we have them in the words of His Apostles and Prophets, he is bloated and ignorant, sick (νοσῶν) about questions and strife of words (1 Tim. 6:3-4; John 8:31-32; John 17:20). If those who deny the inspiration of Scripture are not entirely engulfed in human opinions and ignorance, it is because inconsistently they disown their false principle and still cling to portions of the truth revealed in Scripture.

2. Faith, in the Christian sense, is relinquished, since Christian faith can exist only vis-à-vis the Word of God. Faith comes by hearing the Word of God (Rom. 10:17).

3. Prayer must be given up, since Christian prayer presupposes the continuing in Christ's words. "If ye abide in Me and My words abide in you, ye shall ask what ye will, and it shall be done unto you" (John 15:7).

4. Victory over death is rendered impossible. "If a man keep My saying, he shall never see death" (John 8:51).

5. If we deny inspiration, we relinquish the one effective means of doing mission work, which consists in teaching men to observe all things whatsoever Christ has commanded His Church (Matt. 28:19). Whoever does not bring the doctrine of Christ should not be received or treated as a Christian teacher (2 John 9-10).

6. We lose the true Christian unity of the Church, which consists in faith in the Word of Christ (John 8:31-32; Matt. 28:19; Eph. 4:3). Luther: "The Word and the doctrine must effect the Christian fellowship and unity" (St. L. IX:831).

7. We relinquish intercourse with God, since God, remaining invisible to us in this life, approaches us only through His Word. He that does not commune with God solely by means of His Word is holding intercourse only with his own fantasies, with "projections of his human Ego" (1 Cor. 13:12; 1 Tim. 6:3-4).

8. We turn the Christian religion, which is the wisdom from above, the σοφία θεοῦ which has not "entered into the heart of man" and is a "mystery which was kept secret since the world began but now is made manifest by the Scriptures of the Prophets, according to the commandment of the everlasting God" (1 Cor. 2:9; Rom. 16:25-26) – this wisdom from above we turn into a wisdom "of this world," since we let men decide for us what in the Scriptures of the Apostles and Prophets is God's truth and what is not God's truth, and how much of Scripture is to be accepted and how much rejected. We demolish the divine Jacob's ladder, the bridge and the path, which unites heaven with this earth. In short, everything that makes Christians of us and keeps us Christians, we renounce in principle if we depart from the truth that the Holy Scriptures are by inspiration God's own infallible Word.

Walther, therefore, in 1886, a year before his death, induced by the attempt of modern theologians to make Luther the protector of their "liberal" attitude toward Scripture, wrote the following: "Suppose that Luther actually regarded the Bible as a book containing all manner of error, out of which only the scholars could lift the kernel of divine truth, that position would rob the Bible Christians only of Luther. But it is a most horrible thing that the theologians of the Modernist faith, including the Modernist Lutherans (without exception, it would seem), declare it to be a fact no longer debatable that the Scriptures contain, besides the 'good thoughts' of their authors, also 'hay, straw, and stubble,' which 'the fire consumes.' That stand robs the Bible Christians not only of a man whom they had heretofore regarded as a faithful witness of the truth, but it robs the Bible Christians of the Bible itself, a lamp to their feet and a light on their path forever, their rod and their staff in the dark valley of affliction, in short, of God's Word, their consolation in the terrors of sin, their hope in the darkness of their last hour! . . . We must say of this so-called 'divine-human nature of Scripture,' as the term is understood by modern theologians: Beware, beware, I say, of this 'divine-human' Scripture. It is a devil's mask, for at last it manufactures such a Bible according to which I certainly would not care to be a Bible Christian; namely, that henceforth the Bible should be no more than any good book, a book which I would have to read with constant scrutiny in order not to be led into error. For if I believe that the Bible also contains errors, it is to me no longer a touchstone, but itself stands in need of one. In a word, it is unspeakable what the devil seeks with this 'divine-human' Scripture." (*Lehre und Wehre*, 1886, p. 76 f.)

10

The Properties of Holy Scripture

Since Holy Scripture is God's Word by inspiration, it possesses, as a matter of course, also divine properties, or attributes (*affectiones vere divinae*), namely, divine authority (*auctoritas divina*), divine efficacy (*efficacia divina*), perfection (*perfectio*), and perspicuity (*perspicuitas, sive claritas*). And naturally, since modern theology surrenders the inspiration of Scripture, it also surrenders or, as it is often expressed euphemistically, "limits" [103] the divine properties of Scripture.

1. THE DIVINE AUTHORITY OF HOLY SCRIPTURE

Holy Scripture possesses divine authority, that is, in all that it says it is entitled to the same faith and obedience that is due God. We have seen that Christ and His Apostles took this position toward the Scripture of the Old Testament (Luke 24:25): "O fools and slow of heart to believe all that the Prophets have spoken." (Luke 24:25-27; 44-47; John 10:35; 2 Tim. 3:16-17; Matt. 4:4-7.) And Christ and His Apostles demand that we give the same obedience to their own Word in the New Testament (John 8:31-32: "If ye continue in My word, then are ye My disciples indeed"; 1 Cor. 14:37-38; Gal. 1:8). He that rejects, or even only criticizes Scripture, affronts the very Majesty on High; he is committing a *crimen laesae maiestatis divinae*. Hence Christ's warning: "The Word that I have spoken, the same shall judge him in the Last Day" (John 12:48).

This divine authority of Scripture is absolute. It is not founded on the personal repute of the holy writers nor on the endorsement of Scripture by individuals, or any number of men, or even by the Church Universal. The divine authority of Scripture rests solely on its nature, on its theopneusty. It is a correct theological axiom: "Scripture is αὐτόπιστος (worthy of credence on its own account) because it is θεόπνευστος." [104]

---

103 Cp., e. g., Zoeckler, *Handbuch d. theol. Wissenschaften*, 2d ed., III, p. 151.

104 Baier-Walther, I, 119: "The authority of Holy Scriptures is founded in its theopneusty, in its having God as its author. It does not depend on a *causa minus principalis*. Even as other writings do not get their authority from the amanuenses, just as little does Sacred Scripture get its authority from the Church, since the Church was not the author, or efficient cause, of it."

If it is asked how the divine authority of Scripture is recognized by us, or how the Scriptures became a divine authority for us, we distinguish between Christian certainty (*fides divina*) and natural, or scientific, certainty (*fides humana*).

Christian certainty is created solely by the self-testimony of Scripture, by the Word of Scripture, which through the power of the Holy Ghost operating in it, not by the employment of human proofs, creates faith in itself and *eo ipso* secures its acceptation. This is clearly taught in 1 Cor. 2:4-5. The Apostle there reminds the Corinthians how they came to believe the divine preaching (τὸ μαρτύριον τοῦ θεοῦ) which they heard from him. First he says negatively: "My speech and my preaching was not with enticing words of man's wisdom"; then he adds in positive form: "but in demonstration of the Spirit and of power," and finally points out the purpose of using such a method, of refraining from all human proof: "that your faith should not stand in [be based upon] the wisdom of men, but in the power of God." Christ employs the same method. He says of His preaching in the days of His flesh: "If any man will do His [the Father's] will [namely, to hear Christ's Word and to believe on Him, John 6:40], he shall know (γνώσεται) of the doctrine whether it be of God or whether I speak of Myself" (John 7:17). We may express this important truth in this form: The Word of Scripture, being the Word of God, is an object of perception that creates its own organ of perception, faith, and thus Scripture itself bears witness to its divine authority.

This is the so-called *testimonium Spiritus Sancti internum.* It is a mistake to assume that a person hears this testimony of the Spirit only when his emotions are stirred. It is already present in and with the Spirit-wrought faith in the Word of Scripture. By working faith in the Word of Scripture, which faith has its seat in the spirit of man, the Holy Ghost bears witness of the divinity of the Word of Scripture to the spirit of man. According to 1 John 5:9-10, he who believes God's witness of His Son has God's witness in him (ἐν αὐτῷ). Furthermore, the words of 1 Thess. 2:13: "When ye received the Word of God, which ye heard of us, ye received it not as the word of men, but, as it is in truth, the Word of God," state that the Thessalonians already by their reception of the Word, i. e., by their faith in the Word, became convinced of the divinity of the Word. That is the reason why Scripture calls faith in the Word of God a seal, or confirmation, of the truthfulness of God (John 3:33: "He that hath received His [Christ's] testimony, hath set to his seal that God is true"). For this reason Scripture says of him who does not believe God's witness: "He that believeth not God hath made Him a liar, because he believeth not the record that God gave of His Son" (1 John 5:10). – This truth that Christian certainty of the divinity of Scripture springs from the self-authentication of Scripture is of the greatest practical importance. When Christians are assailed by doubts as to the divinity of Scripture, they must have intercourse with Scripture, that is, they must read, hear, meditate on Scripture and thus permit it to act on themselves. Then the self-testimony of the Scriptures, the *testimonium Spiritus Sancti internum,* will dispel all doubts.

True, objections are raised against this self-attestation of Scripture. Rome, in the interest of the supremacy of the Pope over Scripture, and modern theologians, in the interest of severing faith from the written Word, accuse us here of arguing in a circle (*idem per idem*).[105] This objection is groundless, for the method objected to, that we become certain of a thing through perceiving it, is in universal practice. He who seriously questions this method has become a hopeless agnostic. Now, faith in the written Word is nothing more or less than the perception, called forth by the Word itself, through the operation of the Holy Ghost, of this Word as being the Word of God. Philippi (*Glaubenslehre,* 3d ed., I, 136) mentions the fact that Strauss calls the doctrine of the *testimonium Spiritus Sancti internum* "the Achilles' heel of the Protestant system" and also speaks of an argument in a circle. Philippi answers: "That is the same thing as when a blind man accuses his seeing neighbor of arguing in a circle, claiming that the sun shines, since he sees by its light." That is the answer which the old Lutheran theologians gave. Gottfried Hoffmann (d. 1728) writes: "As the first principles are known of themselves and shine in their own light, and as in the realm of nature light bears witness of itself and has no need of an outside light, so, too, the testimony of the Holy Ghost has no need of outside testimony, but shines in its own light and abundantly proves itself to be divine by its own divine efficacy and power, in which it rejoices, although another cannot be persuaded of this unless he himself attentively reads Scripture and thus shares in this internal testimony" (*Synopsis Theologiae Purioris,* p. 86).

Besides the Christian certainty (*fides divina*) of the divinity of Scripture, which is produced by the self-attestation of Scripture, there

---

105 Compare the chapter "Theology and Certainty."

is also a purely human conviction (*fides humana*, or "scientific certainty") of the divine authority of Scripture, which is based on arguments of reason. Our old theologians call these arguments of reason "arguments which show that the divine origin of Scripture is recognizable by, or credible to, human faith" (Baier-Walther, I, 121). All divine works bear the divine stamp, by which reason can see that they are not the product of man. One will hardly mistake an artificial flower for a natural one. Now, Scripture is as much a work of God, "God's Book," as is the created universe. And as a natural, rational observation of the creation reveals God as its Creator (Rom. 1:18 ff.), so, too, a natural, rational study of Holy Scripture points to God as its author. When we compare the Holy Scriptures according to content and style with other "Bibles" in the world, e. g., with the Koran, the other Sacred Books of the East, etc.,[106] when we think of the victorious march of Christianity through the world, though its teaching is an offense to the Jews and foolishness to the Greeks,[107] when we recall the astounding effects of the religion taught in the Scriptures on individuals[108] and whole nations,[109] then a reasonable reason cannot do otherwise than conclude that the Scriptures must be divine and confess that it is more reasonable to grant the divinity of Scripture than to deny it. This is the domain of apologetics.[110]

As to the value of the arguments that produce a human, or scientific, conviction of the divinity of Scripture, a twofold extreme must be avoided: overestimation and underestimation. It would be overestimation if we imagined that any one could be converted by such rational

---

106 See the lengthy quotation from the Koran in Baier-Walther, I, 130 f. Max Mueller on the contents of the "Sacred Books of the East": "One refrain through all — salvation by works. . . . Our own holy Bible, our Sacred Book of the East, is from beginning to end a protest against this doctrine. . . . It contains that faithful saying, worthy to be received by all men, women, and children, and not merely by us Christians — that Christ Jesus came into the world to save sinners." On the style or manner of expression consult Luthardt, *Apol. Vortraege*, I, 208 f.; Rousseau and Pascal, quoted by Luthardt, pp. 263, 265.

107 Baier-Walther, I, 129. Luthardt, *op. cit.*, p. 175 ff.

108 The assurance of being reconciled with God by faith in Christ's *satisfactio vicaria*, the holy life, patience in suffering, readiness to depart. Max Mueller: "Let us teach Hindus, Buddhists, Mohammedans, that there is only one Sacred Book of the East that can be their mainstay in that awful hour when they pass all alone into the unseen world."

109 It is generally admitted that nothing civilizes nations more quickly and more surely than Christianity.

110 See *Proceedings of the Western District*, Missouri Synod, 1865; also the extensive compilation of the arguments producing the *fides humana* in Baier-Walther, I, 121–131.

arguments. A man becomes a Christian, in every single case and until the Last Day, only in one way: by way of *contritio* and *fides;* that is, he must experience the divine judgment of condemnation, which the Law, speaking through Scripture, produces (*terrores conscientiae*) and believe in the remission of his sins through the Gospel, proclaimed in Scripture. This way of coming into His kingdom is taught by Christ when He instructs His disciples "that repentance and remission of sins should be preached in His name among all nations" (Luke 24:47), and when He Himself proclaimed: "Repent ye, and believe the Gospel" (Mark 1:15). Only after a person has in this manner become a sheep of Christ's fold, only after the Holy Ghost has entered his heart by faith in the forgiveness of sins, does he know that the Scriptures are God's Word, the voice of the Good Shepherd; in other words, only then does he have the Christian certainty, the *fides divina,* the *testimonium internum Spiritus Sancti* as to the divinity of the Holy Scriptures (John 8:37, 43, 47).

The arguments which call forth only a human faith (*fidem humanam*) would be underestimated if we declared them to be utterly worthless. Also Christ and His Apostles used them on occasion.[111] Such rational arguments serve to show how frivolous are the judgments of unbelief against the divinity of Scripture. These arguments may be used to good advantage also in the case of Christians who are afflicted with doubts as to the divine character of Scripture. These doubts arise from the unbelieving flesh of the Christians, and through these rational arguments the flesh of the Christians is outwardly checked and subdued.[112] Arguments of reason, historical arguments, etc., can also be of service in the conversion of a person by inducing those outside the Church to read or hear the Word of God itself and so come to faith in the Word by the operation of the Holy Ghost through the Word. – But we must not imagine that the presentation of such arguments of reason is a necessary prerequisite for the proclamation of the Word of God. The assertion that the

---

111 Christ tells the Sadducees, who declared the resurrection to be impossible: "Ye do err, not knowing the Scriptures nor the power of God" (Matt. 22:29). Christ is appealing not only to the Scriptures, but also to something which is known even to natural reason – to the omnipotence of God. He thereby declares that the doctrine of the Sadducees contradicts not only Scripture, but also reason. Paul tells the Corinthians the same thing (1 Cor. 15:34). Also Peter (Acts 2:15) operates with an argument of reason. Paul (Acts 17:28) appeals to "certain of your own poets."

112 Gerhard, *locus "De Scriptura Sacra,"* § 20: "When in their temptations believers begin to doubt the authority of Scripture, then one must deal with them as with those who deny it. For doubt is very close to denial."

"Christian assurance of truth" goes hand in hand with the "other truths possessed by mankind" is part of the basic error of modern theology. It is based on the erroneous opinion, as Ed. Koenig correctly remarks, "as though Holy Scripture were incapable of exerting an authority in consequence of which men yield ready assent to its statements" (*Der Glaubensakt des Christen,* 1891, p. 118 f.). We must always bear in mind that the self-attestation of Scripture as the Word of God is entirely independent of all rational arguments and of all human witness, whether coming from individuals or from the "Church." The objection that the self-attestation of Scripture pertains only to its contents, not to its words, has already been refuted as unscriptural and senseless (see the chapters "Theology as Doctrine" and "The Verbal Inspiration of Holy Scripture").

The question has frequently been raised how one can know whether he has the faith wrought by the Holy Spirit or only a human conviction of the divine authority of Scripture. Christians, too, are bothered about this matter. And it must be conceded that people are often self-deceived. Those who do not have the testimony of the Holy Ghost often think they have it; and those who fear they lack it actually may possess it. Now, who has this witness and who does not have it? We again draw attention to the following:

1. Since according to Scripture the witness of the Holy Ghost is never given without the Word of the Apostles and Prophets, but always through this Word, it is manifest that all opinions concerning the Scripture on the part of those who actually sever themselves from the Word of Scripture are not the witness of the Holy Ghost, but merely human fabrication and fiction.

2. Likewise those lack the internal testimony of the Holy Ghost as to the divine authority of Scripture who are prompted merely by arguments of reason or by human authority – such as the authority of the pastor, the parents, or other men – to regard Scripture as the Word of God.

3. Nor can those have the *testimonium Spiritus Sancti* who persistently deny the vicarious satisfaction of Christ, since the Christian faith is *fides Christi "crucifixi,"* and only with this faith does the Holy Ghost enter the heart of man, to enable him to judge correctly concerning divine things, and that includes Scripture. Philippi says on this point (*Glaubenslehre,* 3d ed., I, 135): "It is only the faith in the plenary sacrifice, brought in lowliness on the Cross for our sins by Him who is our Lord and our God, which brings the Spirit of sonship and the assurance of our inheritance and imbues us with the powers of

eternal life. And since the Church teaches men to find the righteousness of God and of life solely by faith in the propitiatory blood, it has appealed to the Word of God as attested by the Holy Ghost and to the absolute and exclusive authority of this Word, which has its infallible seal in the Spirit." Our missionaries in heathen countries, our home missionaries, and our institutional workers do not therefore begin with rational arguments for the divinity of Holy Scripture, but they preach "to one and all" ("*in den Haufen hinein*") repentance and remission of sins. And when faith in *Christum "crucifixum"* has once been created, there is no need to worry about securing faith in the divinity of Holy Scripture. — This covers the case of Johann David Michaelis (d. 1791), whose contention that "during his entire life" he never once perceived the witness of the Holy Ghost as to the divinity of Scripture has gained him a nearly world-wide renown in theological circles. We may leave the question undecided whether "during his entire life" fits his case. But it is clear that in his later life he did not have, and could not have had, the testimony of the Holy Ghost, for then he denied the Scripture doctrine of the *satisfactio Christi vicaria* and based the divine remission of sins on the moral improvement of man. The Holy Ghost does not confirm pagan work-righteousness, but testifies externally in the written Word and within the heart by working faith in the written Word that Christ died for our sins according to the Scriptures.[113]

4. But everyone who believes Scripture for its own sake, accepts as divine truth what Scripture says because Scripture says it, has the inner testimony of the Holy Ghost. And note well, *faith itself is the witness of the Holy Ghost.* It is just at this point that those who actually have the witness of the Holy Ghost, but imagine that they lack it and sigh for it, make their mistake. As those who pretend to have this witness without faith in the external Word err, so also do those dear Christians who indeed believe Scripture, hold what Scripture teaches as the incontestable truth, but nevertheless imagine that they lack the witness of the Holy Ghost. They err by not identifying faith in the Holy Scriptures with the inner testimony of the Holy Ghost that Scripture is divine. Both things must be identified, because they actually amount to the same thing. It is a fact that no man believes the Word of God of himself. The natural man neither believes the terrible judgment of the Law, as it is pronounced in Scripture, nor the

---

[113] On the case of Michaelis consult R. E., 2d ed., IX:746 ff.; Meusel, IV, 597. Also Knoes in *Inst. Theol. Practicae,* Holmiae, 1768, pp. 66–71, quoted in Baier-Walther, I, 136, deals with the case of Michaelis and men of his ilk.

comforting judgment of the Gospel concerning the forgiveness of sins, as it is likewise pronounced in the Scripture. Especially the Word of the Gospel telling of the forgiveness of sins *propter Christum "crucifixum"* is to every natural man an offense and foolishness. But when a man believes both: the Word of Scripture that consigns him to eternal damnation and the Word of Scripture which assures him of the forgiveness of his sins for the sake of the crucified Christ, such faith is solely the work of the Holy Ghost; the Holy Ghost has convinced him internally, by working this faith in his heart, that the Word of Scripture is not foolishness, but divine truth. In other words, the objective witness of the Holy Ghost, which we have in the Word of Scripture, external to us, becomes the inner witness of the Holy Ghost when our hearts say Yea and Amen to the objective witness in the Word of Scripture. This is expressly taught, as we have seen, in 1 John 5:9-10. V. 9 speaks of "the witness of God which He hath testified of His Son," of God's Word. But in v. 10 the Apostle adds: "He that believeth on the Son of God" – namely, on the basis of the witness that God has testified of His Son – "hath the witness in himself," ἐν ἑαυτῷ, in his heart.[114]

According to Scripture, then, the witness of the Holy Spirit is present not only when it is felt. There is such a thing as joyous feeling. A Christian has periods (days, hours, at times only moments) when he feels the truth, the sublimity, the majesty, the divinity, of Scripture so strongly that joyous emotions well up and flood his heart. But not only in these special periods of joy is the witness of the Holy Ghost to the divinity of Scripture present. This sensation of joy, strictly speaking, rather belongs to the effects and fruits of faith in the truth of the Word of God and thus to the external witness of the Holy Ghost (*testimonium Spiritus Sancti externum*). The inner witness of the Holy Spirit, in its first and proper sense, coincides, according to 1 John 5:9-10, with the Spirit-wrought faith in the written Word. It is present even when faith is not felt, but when the heart clings to the Word of Scripture, longs and reaches out for it with an inner yearning. Luther elaborates the point that the witness of the Spirit coincides with faith in the Word of Scripture thus: "We make no distinction between the Holy Ghost and faith, nor does He

[114] Huther: "Instead of ἑαυτῷ Tischendorf, following A. G. K., has αὑτῷ, which is merely another way of writing it." Huther adds in explanation: "ἔχει ἐν ἑαυτῷ, that is, for him the witness is no more merely an external one, but through his faith he has it in himself; what was external has become for him internal."

oppose faith; for He Himself is the certainty in the Word, who makes us certain of the Word, so that we do not doubt it, but without any doubt most certainly believe that it is just as God's Word tells and reports it. But the Spirit is given to no one without and outside the Word; He is given only through the Word. . . . Without the oral Word the Holy Ghost does not operate." (Erl. 58, 153 f.) The situation, then, is this: The Holy Ghost, who originally spoke His Word through the Apostles and Prophets, remains united with His Word until Judgment Day and through His Word works that faith which believes on the basis of the Word itself and not on the basis of rational arguments or human authorities. This is the Christian, or divine, faith (*fides divina*) in contrast to a mere human opinion, or conviction (*fides humana*).

2. THE DIVINE EFFICACY OF HOLY SCRIPTURE

The modern theologians, who refuse to "identify" Scripture with the Word of God, not only give Scripture, God's own and inviolable Word, all sorts of abusive names ("paper pope," "a codex of laws fallen from heaven," etc.), but they also ascribe to the Scriptures evil results, which they comprehend under such terms as "intellectualism," etc. They say the "psychological connection" is lacking if Scripture is brought into contact with man so directly as is done when Scripture is made the only source and norm of doctrine. But as a matter of fact, since the Scriptures alone among all books of the world are God's Word out and out, they alone have the *vis vere divina* outright. What the Church proclaims (the "Word of the Church") also has divine power and efficacy, but always only in so far as the Church remains true to its commission and proclaims only God's Word (Matt. 28:19; Rom. 3:2; 1 Tim. 6:3 ff.; 2 John 9-10). The Church has no word of its own. Whatever is not taken from Scripture is not the "Word of the Church," but what Luther bluntly calls "prattle." Also other books can exert a divine power and efficacy, but always only inasmuch as they have absorbed God's Word. Of Scripture Luther says: "No book teaches anything concerning eternal life except this one alone" (St. L. XIV:434). This dictum in his instruction how to acquire the theological aptitude will remain true. Whatever other books teach correctly concerning eternal life has been taken from Holy Scripture.

Wherein does the divine efficacy of Holy Scripture consist? In its effecting in man such things as far exceed human power.

The Word of the Law (νόμος πνευματικός), as it is revealed in Holy Scripture, has the inherent power to work such a knowledge of sin that man realizes his eternal damnation and despairs of all self-help (*contritio, terrores conscientiae*). Rom. 3:20: "By the Law is the knowledge of sin." True, man may arrive at a partial knowledge of his sinfulness by virtue of the divine Law as it is written in the heart of natural man also after the Fall. But while this knowledge suffices to give man an evil conscience, it is not sufficient to effect a complete collapse of man before God and to cause him to despair of all self-help. Natural man rather turns from one form of self-help to another, even to suicide. For this reason Christ has commanded in Luke 24:47 that in His name not only "remission of sins" should be preached among all nations, but, preceding that, "repentance."

The Word of the Gospel has the inherent power to work faith in the Gospel. Rom. 10:17: "Faith cometh by hearing and hearing by the Word of God." Thus it creates in man the assurance that his sins are forgiven. Rom. 5:1: "Therefore, being justified by faith, we have peace with God through our Lord Jesus Christ." Human strength and human learning, even at their best, do not suffice to work faith in the Gospel, as Scripture teaches clearly when it says that the crucified Christ is "unto the Jews a stumbling block and unto the Greeks foolishness" (1 Cor. 1:23) and that the natural man, the ψυχικὸς ἄνθρωπος, "receiveth not the things of the Spirit of God, for they are foolishness unto him, neither can he know them" (1 Cor. 2:14). All the children of God in the Old and the New Testament have experienced this truth. They know that their faith is not dependent on their own choice, their "self-assertion," their "self-determination," their "self-decision," etc., but is the result of God's power and efficacy, which is just as effective as the creative omnipotence by which God made the natural light shine forth out of darkness (Ps. 51:10-12; 2 Cor. 4:6).

The Word of the Gospel, presented in Scripture, has the inherent power to write God's Law into the heart of man, that is, so to change man inwardly that he gladly subjects himself to God's Law and willingly and with delight walks in the ways of God according to the new man, which is created in him through faith in the Gospel. Human strength and human training cannot accomplish this change. Rom. 8:7: "The carnal mind is enmity against God; for it is not subject to the Law of God, neither indeed can be." "*Lex praescribit, evangelium inscribit.*" (Jer. 31:31 ff.)

The Word of the Gospel, presented in Scripture, has the inherent power to deliver man from the fear of death and thus to make him the victor over death. This victory is beyond human power, as Scripture and experience testify. Scripture teaches expressly that all men by nature were all their lifetime subject to bondage through the fear of death (Heb. 2:15) and had no hope. But he who believes the Gospel rejoices: "O Death, where is thy sting?" (κέντρον – the deadly sting.) "Death cannot destroy forever," etc. (Stanzas of "Why Should Cross and Trial Grieve Me?") This is essentially the *vis vere "divina"* inhering in the Word of Scripture, since it is God's Word.

The divine power does not operate outside or alongside the Word, but through the Word and therefore inheres in the Word; that is the plain statement of Scripture, Rom. 10:17 (ἐκ), 1 Pet. 1:23 (διά), and must be maintained over against the Reformed, as will be shown in detail in the doctrine of the means of grace. The truth that the *efficientia vere divina,* exerted through the Word of God, is *resistibilis* (Matt. 23:37) will be presented more fully in the doctrine of conversion.

3. THE PERFECTION, OR SUFFICIENCY, OF HOLY SCRIPTURE

Modern theology denies also the perfection, or sufficiency, of Holy Scripture. Zoeckler, for example, asserts concerning the "use of the Bible as normative or judicial authority in doctrinal controversies" that "the possibility must be admitted that the appeal to Scripture very often results in a partial and incomplete settlement of the respective controversy." [115] The modern theologians are here consistent in applying their principle. For if Scripture is a book in which the line of demarcation between truth and error cannot be clearly drawn,[116] it certainly cannot serve as judge between truth and error. – The sufficiency of Scripture according to its own definition consists in its teaching everything that men must know to obtain salvation. To elaborate:

a. Scripture does not treat everything a man can know, for example, the things pertaining to the sphere of earthly or civil life. Scripture is certainly not, as some have put it, "a general encyclopedia of human knowledge." It is not a textbook of agriculture or architecture or of medical science. It is not "a manual of history and geography." Natural reason teaches these things, as Luther often reminds us, if men will only use their reason. But remember: When Scripture incidentally treats a scientific subject, it is always right, let "science" say what it pleases; for πᾶσα γραφὴ θεόπνευστος. Thus Luther says concerning the chronological data of Scripture that the Bible is the

[115] *Handbuch,* 2d ed., III, 151. *Lehre und Wehre,* 32, p. 4 f.

[116] See the chapter "The Relation of the Holy Ghost to the Holy Writers."

only book in which historical errors cannot occur (St. L. XIV:491). And when the "enthusiasts" of ancient and particularly of modern times assert that wine is under all circumstances "poison," we know from Scripture that this is not true. (John 2:1-11; 1 Tim. 5:23; etc.) Nevertheless, it must be maintained that the Bible is not a textbook of "universal human knowledge." There is a large area of human knowledge that is based on natural reason and human experience.[117]

b. The Scriptures do not reveal all divine matters. Concerning the knowledge of divine things attainable in this life it declares: "Now I know in part" (1 Cor. 13:12), and: "How unsearchable are His judgments and His ways past finding out! For who hath known the mind of the Lord?" (Rom. 11:33-34.) [118] When modern theologians contend that the Christian religion is perfect or absolute in that it constitutes "a logical, complete system" in the eyes of reason, they are in error and are setting up a false principle, which, consistently applied, would abolish the entire Christian religion.[119]

c. But Scripture teaches perfectly whatever we need to know to obtain eternal life.[120] It says concerning "the Holy Scriptures" (2 Tim. 3:15) that they "are able to make thee wise unto salvation through faith which is in Christ Jesus." Not only for Christians in general is Scripture a sufficient source of knowledge, but also for the teacher of the Church, who is perfect (ἄρτιος) through Scripture; he is "thoroughly furnished," fully equipped for his duty, "for doctrine, for reproof," etc., and so perfectly equipped that he is strictly commanded to continue in the words of Christ, which we have in the words of the Apostles (John 17:20), and not to take the liberty to change or add to these words (John 8:31-32; 1 Tim. 6:3 f.; 2 Tim. 1:13; Rom. 16:17; Gal. 1:6-9). It is certain, then, that the Scriptures, in order to attain their purpose of making men wise unto salvation, do not in any way need to be supplemented with any outside material, be

---

117 See *Lehre und Wehre*, 1901, p. 289 ff.: "Ueber die Grenzen der menschlichen Wissenschaft."

118 Quenstedt, *Systema* I, 147: "The Holy Scriptures are perfect, not in the sense of absolute perfection, embracing every knowable divine and supernatural thing; for that would not befit the Church Militant on earth, for whom the Scriptures are intended."

119 Cp. the chapters "Christianity the Absolute Religion" and "Theology and System."

120 Quenstedt (I, 147 *sq.*): "Holy Scripture is perfect . . . in the sense of a restricted perfection, in so far as it teaches all things that a Christian needs to know in order to believe correctly and to lead a saintly and pious life here on earth."

that tradition, church decrees, Pope, the experience of the theologian, science, or what not.[121]

It is self-evident that if the *perfectio,* or *sufficientia,* of Scripture be surrendered, the Scripture principle is given up. If a deficiency in the Bible must be supplied from some outside source, the Christian Church is *eo ipso* moved off its foundation, the Word of the Apostles and Prophets, and based on the Ego of the alleged supplementers. It is the old talk of Rome about a *perfectio implicita Scripturae Sacrae* – Scripture is perfect when supplemented by the "Church," that is, of course, by the Pope. In the same sense Roman theologians have called Scripture a *norma "remissiva"* – it is perfect inasmuch as it calls upon the Church, that is, the Pope, to supply the deficiencies. Our theologians have answered: "A *norma remissiva* is no norm at all, but the authority to which one is referred. According to this notion it would have been sufficient if Scripture had simply told us: 'Hear the Church,' or rather, according to the Roman interpretation: 'Hear the Pope!' But the Pope is not the man of whom Scripture says: 'Hear ye Him,' Matt. 17:5." (Quenstedt, I, 147.) And in regard to the Roman *perfectio implicita* our old theologians remark: "Then every beggar would be rich *implicite,* since he can state where the riches are; and every dolt would have to be regarded as learned, since he can point out a university where learned men teach; and he would be richly provided with food who can point others to a table richly covered with sumptuous food" (Quenstedt, I, 148). It amounts to a similar mockery and abolition of Scripture when the neologists place the Scriptures under the control of the "experience" of the theologizing individual. And we know what is back of this. In the words of Luther, "they speak such things only in order to lead us away from Scripture and make themselves masters over us, that we should believe their dream sermons ('*Traumpredigten*')." (St. L. V:334 f.)

4. THE PERSPICUITY OF HOLY SCRIPTURE

According to the Roman doctrine, Scripture becomes clear through the light emanating from the "Church," that is, from the Pope. According to the doctrine of the "enthusiasts" of all ages, it is illumined by the "inner light," which is communicated immediately. According to the view of modern theology, the Bible is "divine-human" in the sense that Scripture presents a mixture of truth and error, and it is the business of "the self-consciousness of the theologizing subject" to

[121] Cp. the chapter "Holy Scripture the Only Source and Norm of Christian Doctrine for the Church Today."

shed light upon this confusion — by means of his "experience" he separates the truth from the error and thus clarifies Scripture. All these views regarding the "perspicuity" of Scripture have one common feature: It is man who must illumine Holy Scripture. According to the teaching of Scripture, however, exactly the opposite relation obtains. Not men illumine Scripture, but Scripture illumines men. "Thy Word is a lamp unto my feet and a light unto my path" (Ps. 119:105).

According to Scripture, the perspicuity of Scripture consists in this, that it presents, in language that can be understood by all, whatever men must know to be saved. By way of elaboration:

a. This perspicuity is presupposed, as a matter of course, since not only those who are specially gifted, but *all* Christians are to read the Scriptures, are to believe on the basis of Scripture and to judge truth and error on the same basis. The perspicuity of the Old Testament is taken for granted in Luke 16:29: "They have Moses and the Prophets; let them hear them." In like manner Christ tells the Jews who would not believe His Word: "Search the Scriptures" (John 5:39), and we are told Acts 17:11 concerning the Bereans: "They searched the Scriptures daily whether these things were so." The same applies to the writings of the New Testament. Paul admonishes the Thessalonians: "Therefore, brethren, stand fast, and hold the traditions which ye have been taught, whether by word or our epistle" (2 Thess. 2:15). The fact that most of the Apostolic epistles were addressed to whole congregations and were to be read in their meetings (Col. 4:16; 1 Thess. 5:27) presupposes their perspicuity.

b. But the perspicuity of Scripture is not only presupposed as self-evident, but Scripture teaches it also very expressly; it most emphatically protests against ever regarding Scripture as an obscure book, as do not only the unbelievers, but also some within external Christendom; at times even devout Christians are disturbed. Scripture says of itself that it is a "light shining in a dark place" (2 Pet. 1:19) and that it "is a lamp unto our feet and a light unto our path" (Ps. 119:105). It is clear even for the unlearned, "making wise the simple" (Ps. 19:7). Even children can understand it, for "from a child thou hast known the Holy Scriptures" (2 Tim. 3:15). Even the writings of St. John, which have been singled out as being particularly obscure,[122] were understood not only by the "fathers," not only by the "young men," but also by the "little children" (1 John 2:12-13).

---

122 The Unitarian Enjedinus, quoted in Baier-Walther, I, 176, says: "If abrupt, halting obscurity, if a speech with utter lack of cohesion and consisting of allegories is to be called sublime, then I admit that John is sublime."

For Whom the Clear Scriptures Are an Obscure Book

1. For all those to whom the language of Scripture is altogether unknown or at least unfamiliar. On the first point Luther says: "A Turk's speech must needs be obscure to me; a Turkish child of seven would easily understand him, whereas I do not know the language" (St. L. X:473). To him who does not understand German the German Bible is dark. One who does not command the English tongue cannot understand the English Bible. But, in the second place, it is necessary that we become accustomed to the language of the Bible by diligent study. Like with any other book, we must penetrate into the Bible by reading it diligently ("*einlesen*"); to use Luther's phrase, we must familiarize ourselves ("*gewohnen*") with it, or it will remain unintelligible to us. If we read the Bible as diligently as we read the newspaper, it would be clearer to us than the newspaper is, since the language of the Bible is the simpler of the two. But to one who reads a thousand words in the newspaper to ten in the Bible, the words of the Bible will appear more or less strange and obscure. For this reason some accuse the Bible of obscurity, at least in their hearts, though they may not voice this charge publicly. Just so the knowledge of, and familiarity with, the Hebrew and Greek is needed in order to understand the Scriptures in the original tongues. Whoever commands but a meager knowledge of these tongues will find the Scriptures more or less unintelligible. In short, Scripture will be clear to him who, as Luther reminds us,[123] knows the languages and trains himself in the languages by the diligent reading of Scripture. And this diligent reading of Scripture is directly enjoined in the Old and the New Testament. (Ps. 1:2; Deut. 6:6-9; John 5:39; Col. 3:16; 1 Tim. 6:3 f.)

2. Scripture itself expressly says that its Word remains hidden to those who in their heart maintain a hostile attitude toward the Scriptures, i. e., who do not care to learn from the Scriptures, but aim to set Scripture right and criticize it with their own human notions. To the "wise and prudent" the divine Word will appear obscure. By the righteous judgment of God they see darkness where there is light: "Thou hast hid these things from the wise and prudent and hast revealed them unto babes" (Matt. 11:25). Likewise 2 Cor. 4:3-4: "But if our Gospel be hid, it is hid to them that are lost, in whom

---

[123] He does that at length in his treatise *"An die Ratsherren aller Staedte Deutschlands,"* St. L. X:473 ff.

the god of this world hath blinded the minds of them which believe not, lest the light of the glorious Gospel of Christ, who is the image of God, should shine unto them." God has given us His Word in order to deliver us from our own perverse thoughts of God and divine matters. But if we will not give up our own thoughts, but oppose them to God's thoughts and thus condemn God in His Word, the dread judgment will come upon us: We will look upon God's Word as obscure and offensive. (Is. 6:9-10; Acts 28:25-27; Rom. 9:31-33; 10:21; 11:7-10; Matt. 13:13 ff.)

3. Scripture remains dark also to those whose prejudice against certain Scripture doctrines keeps them from even externally taking note of the respective words of Scripture. Thus Christ's words regarding the Lord's Supper remain hidden to some of the Reformed because of the false interpretation of these words which they have heard since their youth. When they hear or read the words of Christ: "This is My body," they at once substitute in their thought the words: "This signifies My body," or: "This is a symbol of My body." They paste over the words of Scripture a human interpretation. The same thing is done by later Lutheran dogmaticians who teach an election *ex praevisione fidei finalis,* though the Bible in the passages that speak of the state of faith here in time represents the faith of the Christians as a consequence and result of their eternal election, as also the theologians of the 16th century and the Formula of Concord teach.[124]

Objections Raised Against the Perspicuity of Scripture

1. If the Scripture were clear, the office of the public ministry would be superfluous. We answer: One does not exclude the other. The public ministry is not superfluous, because it is a divine ordinance,[125] and Scripture is, according to its own statements, clear, as has been shown above. And this clarity is furthermore evident from the fact that Christians are able to judge on the basis of Scripture whether pastors are true or false prophets, whether they depart from the Word of the Apostles or continue in it (Matt. 7:15; Rom. 16:17). But the divine institution of the ministry alongside the clear Scripture shows us how earnestly God is concerned about our salvation.

---

[124] See the fuller discussion in the chapter "The Relation of Faith to the Election of Grace," in Vol. III.

[125] That will be shown fully in the chapter "The Public Ministry Not a Human, but a Divine Institution," in Vol. III.

He is so much concerned about it that He, so to say, went out of His way for it. Every one of us can come to faith and persevere in faith only by means of Scripture (John 5:39). But in order that no man fail to reach his life's goal, God, in addition, has appointed watchmen who are officially to watch over our souls with doctrine, admonition, reproof, and consolation from Scripture and with Scripture (Heb. 13:17; Ezek. 3:18).[126]

2) At all times, and particularly in our day, the great disagreement among theologians in the interpretation of the words of Scripture has been advanced against the perspicuity of Scripture. Unfortunately this disagreement is a fact. However it is not caused by the obscurity of Scripture, but by the departure of the theologians from the Word of Scripture and by their substituting for it and peddling their own thoughts concerning God and divine matters and taking these thoughts to market. God has so constituted Holy Scripture that one cannot err in the Christian doctrine as long as one continues in simple faith in His Word. Christ teaches that Scripture is a safe guide when He says: "If ye continue in My Word, then . . . ye shall know the truth" (John 8:31-32). Likewise the Apostle Paul declares (1 Tim. 6:3) that all error in doctrine can be traced to the refusal of the teacher to continue in the wholesome words of Christ. This refusal prompted Luther's constant warning against substituting an interpretation (gloss) for the Scripture words themselves, for the "*nuda Scriptura.*" "Be it known, then, that Scripture, without any gloss, is the sun and sole light from which all teachers receive their light, and not the contrary." (St. L. XVIII:1292 ff.) "The Word they still shall let remain." It is a characteristic of the Lutheran Church that it does not base its doctrine on any exegesis, not even on the exegesis of Luther, but on the bare words of Scripture, while the Papists and the Reformed in all doctrines in which they differ from the Lutheran Church do not stand on the word of Scripture, but on an "exegesis" of the Pope, Zwingli, Calvin, etc.[127] And modern theology, because of its denial of the inspiration of Scripture, declares openly that it does not stand on the Word of Scripture, but on the so-called "Christian experience."

3. Especially the occurrence of dark, difficult passages in Scripture has been urged against the perspicuity of Scripture. "It is indeed

---

[126] This will be further discussed in the chapter "Holy Scripture and Exegesis."

[127] See the chapter "The Cause of Divisions Within Visible Christendom."

true," says Luther, "some passages in Scripture are obscure" (St. L. V:335). But alongside this fact is, of course, the other fact, so clearly attested in Scripture, that Scripture is perfectly clear and is in regard to doctrine and life "a lamp unto our feet and a light unto our path." To state it more fully, these obscure passages either do not pertain directly to the Christian doctrine, but give chronological, topographical, archaeological, etc., data, or, if they do pertain to doctrine, the same matter is elsewhere in Scripture set forth clearly and explicitly. Augustine, Luther, Chemnitz, Gerhard, regard it as a well-established axiom that all Christian doctrines are revealed in passages that need no explanation whatever. Augustine: "In the clear passages of Scripture everything is found that pertains to faith and life" (*De Doctrina Christiana* II, p. 9). Chemnitz: "Many passages of Scripture are couched in clear and lucid words, which need no far-fetched explanation but explain themselves. Access to these passages is, as Augustine says, open to the learned and the unlearned. And these clear passages of Scripture contain everything pertaining to faith and life." (*Examen,* Geneva, 1667, p. 57.) Luther: "If you encounter an obscure passage in Scripture, do not doubt that it certainly contains the same truth which is elsewhere stated in clear language" (St. L. V:338). Then Luther adds: "If you cannot understand the obscure, then stay with the clear." That sounds dictatorial. Still, it is true and Scriptural. How could Christians carry out the imposed mandate to judge all teaching and all teachers if the faith of Christians were based in part on obscure passages, which are, more or less, intelligible only to professional theologians? The obscure passages have a different purpose than to serve as a basis for the Christian doctrine. Their purpose is indicated by Augustine as follows: "The Holy Ghost has arranged Holy Scripture in such a magnificent and wholesome way that through the clear passages He appeases the hunger and through the dark passages He prevents loathing. For hardly anything is derived from those obscure passages but what is stated elsewhere most clearly." (Quoted in Baier-Walther, I, 168.) Luther says: "Scripture without any gloss is the sun and the whole light" (St. L. XVIII:1293 f.) Luther indeed knows of "another study of the Scriptures, namely, the interpretation of obscure passages and allegories." But this he calls "a merry chase, in which certain entertaining meanings are the game that is hunted and caught. But the study that makes one fit for warfare is to be at home in Scripture and, as St. Paul says, able to contend with abundant clear passages without any glosses or commentaries, as with a bared and drawn sword. . . . Then the adversary, convinced by the clear light, must see and confess that the words of God stand alone and need not the explanation of man." [128]

It has been said, formerly as now, that Luther, to be consistent, would have to admit the obscurity of the words of Scripture, since he continually and powerfully taught that without the illumination of the Holy Ghost not one letter of Scripture could be understood. On this point, Luther has verily expressed himself clearly enough. He distinguishes between the spiritual or inner understanding of Scripture, which is found only in Christians, and the external clarity or external understanding, of which also the unbelievers are capable. He writes: "If you speak of the inner clearness, no man sees one iota in the Scriptures but he that hath the Spirit of God. All have a darkened heart, so that, even if they know how to speak of, and set forth, all things in the Scripture, yet they cannot feel them or know them; nor do they believe that they are the creatures of God or anything else, according to Ps. 14:1: 'The fool hath said in his heart, God is nothing.' For the Spirit is required to understand the whole of the Scripture and every part of it. If you speak of the external clearness, nothing whatever is left obscure or ambiguous; but all things that are in the Scriptures are by the Word brought forth into the clearest light and proclaimed to the whole world." (St. L. XVIII:1683 f.) So strongly does Luther insist on the external clarity of the words of Scripture that he is ready to make a Turk, a Jew, or a heathen the judge whether his [Luther's] doctrine or Zwingli's doctrine of the Lord's Supper is expressed in the words of Scripture on the Lord's Supper. He writes: "Even if I were a Turk, a Jew, or a pagan, who thought nothing of the faith of the Christians, but heard or read these Scripture passages on the Sacrament, I should have to say: I do not believe the doctrine of the Christians, but this I feel constrained to say: If they want to be Christians and hold to their doctrine [on the basis

---

128 See Quenstedt (*Systema* I, 173) on the purpose of the dark passages in Scripture. Luther's dicta on dark and on clear passages (St. L. V:336 f.) read in their entirety: "That indeed is true, some passages of Scripture are dark, but they contain nothing that is not found in other places in clear, open passages. And now come the heretics, explain the obscure passages according to their own mind, and contend with them against the clear passages, the foundation of our faith. Then the Fathers fought them with the clear passages, threw light with these on the dark passages, and showed that the dark passages taught the very same thing as the clear passages. Be assured and doubt not that there is nothing brighter than the sun, that is, the Scriptures. Even when a cloud has drifted before it, there is nothing else behind it than the same bright sun. Therefore, if you encounter an obscure passage in Scripture, do not doubt; it certainly contains the same truth which is elsewhere stated in clear language, and if you cannot understand the obscure, then stay with the clear."

of what Scripture says], they will have to believe that Christ's body and blood are eaten and drunk orally in the bread and wine" (St. L. XX:1093). As all men know, that is also the unanimous teaching of the dogmaticians.[129] The inner, or spiritual, understanding of Scripture consists according to Luther *primo loco* in faith in Christ. Christ is the true content of Scripture. "Take Christ out of the Scriptures, and what will you find remaining in them?" But the faith in Christ, which the Holy Ghost works through the Scriptures, is always faith in the *Christus crucifixus*, that is, faith in the vicarious satisfaction of Christ, the faith that "Christ suffered for us" (St. L. XVIII:1681). Without this faith the so-called faith is on a level with the faith of the Turks or Jews, who believe in God "without the cost"; here the spiritual understanding of Scripture and a genuine "experience of Christ" are entirely out of the question.

4. A familiar argument against the perspicuity of Scripture runs thus: Scripture contains matters that are incomprehensible to human reason; in this respect Scripture can and must be called dark. Erasmus argued thus against Luther. (St. L. XVIII:1681.) Erasmus points, for example, to the doctrines of the Trinity and of the Person of Christ, "the obscurity of which," he says, "has never been cleared up." One cannot see the sense of this argument. Of course the doctrine of the Holy Trinity is an inscrutable mystery to human reason. No man can comprehend how there can be three distinct persons and still only one undivided and indivisible God. And it is wholly unfathomable how in Christ God and man, Creator and creature, can form one person. But these facts, incomprehensible to narrow human reason, are so clearly revealed in Scripture that faith, which relies on the Word of Scripture, can apprehend them. He who is foolish enough to try to comprehend and fathom the articles of faith with his limited human reason, let him accuse himself of folly instead of charging Scripture with obscurity. Luther answers Erasmus: "Scripture simply confesses the Trinity of God, the humanity of Christ, and the unpardonable sin. There is here no obscurity or ambiguity whatever. But how these things are, Scripture does not say, nor is it necessary to be known. The sophists employ their dreams here; attack and condemn them,

[129] See the quotations in Baier-Walther, I, 169 ff. In the controversy with Rathmann the question was raised "whether an unconverted Jew without the added light of grace could understand the letter of Scripture and from it could get the *sensus literalis*." The faculty of Jena gave this opinion: "Quite a few have the correct sense of the words, but nevertheless lack the blessed understanding of the mysteries pertaining to faith; therefore one must guard also here against equivocations."

and acquit Scripture." (St. L. XVIII, 1682 ff.) Like Luther, our theologians distinguish in the doctrines of faith between the *that* (τὸ ὅτι) and the *how* (τὸ πῶς). The former is clearly revealed in Scripture; the latter we should not attempt to fathom.

5. Several Scripture passages have been used to call in question the perspicuity of Scripture and thus to destroy, practically, the authority of Scripture. Particularly 2 Pet. 3:16 and 1 Cor. 13:12 have been so misused. The first passage reads: "As also in all his [Paul's] Epistles, speaking in them of these things; in which are some things hard to be understood, which they that are unlearned and unstable wrest, as they do also the other Scriptures, unto their own destruction." Quenstedt remarks (*Systema* I, 180): "This passage speaks for the perspicuity of Scripture." Our old theologians have stressed the following in their polemics against Rome: 1) This passage does not say that all things, but that some things in Paul's Epistles are hard to understand. 2) The context shows what kind of things these are. They pertain to the Last Things, the destruction of this universe and the new heaven and the new earth, a matter of which the context immediately preceding speaks. These things are, of a truth, difficult to understand, embody mysteries for us, inasmuch as we have but an imperfect conception of the great change to be effected by the destruction of the world and of the new heaven and the new earth.[130] 3) What Paul and the other holy writers say of these mysterious things is wrested and perverted, not by intelligent and well-read Christians, but by the unlearned and unstable. For in the sentence: "which [things] they that are unlearned and unstable wrest," the unlearned and unstable are the active subject [also in the German], the predicate is "wrest" (στρεβλοῦσιν – pervert), and "which" is the object which they pervert. Not Paul's Epistles are here accused, but the unlearned and unstable who pervert unto their own destruction what Paul and the other holy writers had written. Quenstedt remarks (*loc. cit.*): "Peter mentions two reasons for this

130 Also those who prefer the reading ἐν οἷς to ἐν αἷς cannot but see in περὶ τούτων a reference to the previously mentioned Last Things. Thus the *Expositor's Greek Testament:* "Where he touches on these subjects (Mayor)" . . . "περὶ τούτων indicates a widening of the reference to include Paul's treatment of the whole question of the second coming." Bloomfield comments: "Instead of the vulg. οἷς several versions and some Fathers have αἷς, 'the Epistles,' which is preferred by Beza, Mill, Benson, and Dr. Malthy. . . . Yet the weight of authority is decidedly in favor of οἷς, which is retained by all the editors and preferred by most of the commentators." But Bloomfield makes too much of the various readings when he says: "Here some difference of opinion exists as to the sense, which mainly depends on the reading." Also those preferring αἷς must refer περὶ τούτων to the Last Things, the destruction of the world and the new heaven and the new earth.

perversion: the one is ignorance, the other instability. Neither results from Scripture."

When 1 Cor. 13:12: "For now we see through a glass, darkly," is adduced against the perspicuity of Scripture, the contrast immediately following is disregarded: "but then face to face." The Apostle compares our knowledge of God and divine things in this life with that in yonder life. In this life God does not come to us visibly, but in an αἴνιγμα, riddle, image, that is, in the cloak of His Word, and we know Him only by faith in His Word. In eternal life, however, the cloak of the Word will be removed, and faith will cease. Then the seeing face to face will take the place of the knowledge by faith. Compared with this seeing face to face, our present seeing of God by faith in His Word is indeed a seeing "through a glass, darkly." [131] Quenstedt's remark (*Systema* I, 180) is to the point: "The Apostle applies the knowledge 'through a glass' and 'in an image' to all pilgrims [to eternal life]; he does not even except himself and the other Apostles. For he does not say: 'Now ye see,' but 'Now we see through a glass in an image.' Were, then, the Scriptures dark even to the Apostle when he wrote this?"

We might add here some of the telling remarks our old theologians made in reply to the assertion of their Roman opponents that Scripture could be called clear inasmuch as the Church, that is, the Pope, explained and interpreted it – a perfect *reductio ad absurdum*. Quenstedt, for instance, remarks: "In that way also the riddles of the Sphinx could be called clear and lucid, since Oedipus could solve them." Quenstedt also quotes Dannhauer, who says: "Then there is no difference between the written declarations of God and those of Delphi, and our Scriptures will be the Sphinx and the Pope our Oedipus." When the Jesuit Gretser said: "Everything which illumines the spirit when it is explained may be called a lamp and a light," Dannhauer answered (*Hodosophia*, Phaenomenon I, p. 43): "In that way nothing remains obscure in all the sciences, in the whole world, and outside the world; even the Egyptian darkness would be a light, yea, even the 'outer darkness,' hell."

Of a kind with the Roman attitude toward Scripture, according to which Scripture becomes a "light" only by the interpretation of the "Church," that is, the Pope, is the attitude into which modern theology has drifted because of its denial of the inspiration of Scripture. As according to the Roman view the Scriptures become a "light" only

---

131 Also Meyer acknowledges that Luther rendered the sense of the term ἐν αἰνίγματι correctly with his *"in einem dunkeln Wort."*

through the interpretation of the Pope, so according to the view of modern theology the Scriptures receive the light needed to distinguish the truth from the error in Scripture from the "Christian Ego," the "self-consciousness of the theologizing subject," from "faith" which stands on its own feet. Only the "Oedipus" who interprets Scripture is changed. Likewise it is apparent that modern theology agrees fully, in principle, with the "enthusiasts" of all ages. The "enthusiast" Oedipus was and is the "inner light," which is independent of Scripture; Luther points out in the Smalcald Articles that at bottom Pope and the "enthusiasts" are in full agreement. The Pope has "all rights in the shrine of his heart," according to which he judges and interprets Scripture. And the "enthusiasts" are "spirits who boast that they have the Spirit, without and before the Word, and accordingly judge Scripture or the spoken Word and explain and stretch it at their pleasure, as Muenzer did and many still do at the present day who wish to be acute judges between the Spirit and letter and yet know not what they say or declare." (*Trigl.* 495, 3-4.)

It is but natural that modern theology, just like Rome and the "enthusiasts," should exhibit a deep interest in the obscurity of Scripture. If the Scriptures are dark, they are a fitting object to be illuminated by the product of the "self-consciousness of the theologizing subject." A dark Scripture is the vital element, as for Rome and the enthusiasts, so also for modern theology. Shady characters do not thrive in the light. Zoeckler is more restrained, as befits his Protestant surroundings, when he speaks of the obscurity of Scripture. He says: "The modern believer in inspiration self-evidently" judges concerning the attributes of Scripture – its authority, perspicuity, perfection, and efficacy – "in more than one respect differently than the adherent of the old conception of inspiration. Thus, with respect to the Bible as normative and judicial authority, where the possibility of a merely partial and incomplete settlement of the respective controversy through the appeal to Scripture must often be admitted. Likewise with regard to the questions of perspicuity, where the extant hermeneutical difficulties are appreciated with less bias." (*Handbuch*, 2d ed., III, 151.) Volk of Dorpat uses plainer language: "To enquire of Scripture is not so easy a matter" (*loc. cit.*, I, 745). Without any such reserve our American representative of Rome, Cardinal Gibbons of Baltimore, expresses the Roman fundamental tenet concerning the obscurity of Scripture: "The Scriptures are not of themselves clear and intelligible even in matters of the highest importance." [132]

---

[132] *The Faith of Our Fathers*, 1894, p. 111.

11

The Witness of History for Scripture

(*Homologoumena* and *Antilegomena*)

Besides Scripture's own testimony as to its divine authority, we have, through the gracious providence of God, ample historical testimony to that effect. For the Scriptures of the Old Testament we have the testimony of the Jewish Church and of Christ and His Apostles. Christian theologians of all ages are right in saying: If the Jews had been mistaken as to their canon or had falsified it, Christ would not have so unconditionally and without limitation pointed to the Scripture in the hands of the Jews and asserted their inviolability, as He does, e. g., in the words: "They have Moses and the Prophets; let them hear them" (Luke 16:29); "All things must be fulfilled which were written in the law of Moses, and in the Prophets, and in the Psalms, concerning Me" (Luke 24:44); "Search the Scriptures; for in them ye think ye have eternal life, and they are they which testify of Me" (John 5:39); "The Scripture cannot be broken" (John 10:35). – There is, however, no historical witness for the Apocrypha of the Old Testament. Neither the Jewish Church nor Christ recognized them as canonical.[133]

For the Scriptures of the New Testament we have the historical witness of the Early Church (*ecclesia primitiva*). Its witness is unanimous as to the Four Gospels, the Acts of the Apostles, the thirteen Epistles of Paul, the First Epistle of John, and the First Epistle of Peter (*homologoumena*). But as to the canonicity of the Epistle to the Hebrews, the Second Epistle of Peter, the Second and Third Epistles of John, the Epistle of James, the Epistle of Jude, and the Apocalypse, doubts, more or less strongly expressed, were entertained (antilegomena). Eusebius in his *Church History* lists the homologoumena and the antilegomena.[134] The historical fact that the Early Church

---

[133] Baier-Walther, I, 149. Gerhard, *Loci (locus "De Scriptura Sacra,"* § 75 *sqq.)*, furnishes much material on the refusal of the early Christian Church to receive the Apocrypha into the canon. Cf. Keil, *Einleitung*, § 216; H. L. Strack, R. E., 2d ed., VII, 442 ff.

[134] *Church History* III, 25. On the Epistles of James and Jude particularly, II, 23. He reports, VI, 25, on the canon of Origen and the latter's opinion of the Epistle to the Hebrews. Cp. for further detail Baier-Walther, I, 150, note b. Baier says: "It can certainly not be denied that in the ancient Church there was so much doubt as to their writers that they were denied the authority proper to inspired books." Cp. the comprehensive article "Kanon des Neuen Testaments," by Theodor Zahn, in R. E., 3d ed., IX, 768–796.

differentiated between the homologoumena and the antilegomena cannot be changed by a resolution of the later Church. Luther, too, abides by this judgment of the primitive Church; he says, appealing to Eusebius (*Church History* III, 25), that in ancient times the Epistle to the Hebrews, the Epistles of James and Jude, and the Apocalypse "had a different reputation." He finds much excellent instruction in the antilegomena, grants that the offensive passages may be explained acceptably by "glosses," and will keep no one from appraising them as he sees fit. But he will not class them with the "right certain chief books of the New Testament." As for himself, he will let the doubt entertained by the Early Church remain.[135] Chemnitz denounced the action of the Roman Catholic Church in declaring the Apocrypha of the Old Testament and the antilegomena of the New Testament a part of the canon of Scripture by a mere decree and in anathematizing all those who refused to accept the canon fixed in the Vulgate, as anti-Christian.[136]

Also the fathers of the Missouri Synod recognized the distinction between the homologoumena and the antilegomena. They did, however, leave it to the individual to form his own views regarding any of the antilegomena, for they were divided in their opinion regarding, e. g., the Apocalypse. In the second volume of *Lehre und Wehre* (1856, p. 204 ff.) the question regarding the homologoumena and the antilegomena is thoroughly ventilated in the article entitled: "Is He Who does Not Receive or Regard as Canonical All Books Contained in the Collection of the New Testament to be Declared a Heretic or Dangerous False Teacher?" Walther writes: "What induces us to discuss this question is the fact that Pastor Roebbelen in connection with the glosses on the Revelation of St. John published in the *Lutheraner* also stated that with Luther he does not regard the Apocalypse as canonical. This has, we are informed, given great offense in some quarters. Now, we do not agree with our dear brother Roebbelen on this point; we are convinced that this precious book, so rich in comfort for the Christians and the Church, belongs to the canon. Still, we be-

---

135 See Luther's prefaces to the epistles mentioned, St. L. XIV:126–139. On the Second and Third Epistles of St. John, Luther says: "They are not doctrinal epistles, but examples of love and faith and breathe a truly Apostolic spirit," *loc. cit.*, p. 126 f.

136 *Tridentinum*, Sess. IV: "But if anyone receive not, as sacred and canonical, the said books [the Old Testament plus the Apocrypha, the New Testament, including the antilegomena] entire with all their parts, as they have been used to be read in the Catholic Church, and as they are contained in the old Latin Vulgate edition . . . let him be anathema."

lieve that it is not fair – probably it is due to ignorance of the facts of the case – to stamp an otherwise unimpeachable theologian as a dangerous false teacher, who renders the very Word of God suspect, one who sincerely receives as canonical all homologoumena (universally accepted books), but who has his doubts as to the canonicity of one or the other of the antilegomena (disputed books). This would be thoroughly un-Lutheran. For our dear fathers in the faith, with hardly an exception till after the time of the Formula of Concord, regarded and declared all or at least some of the antilegomena as not belonging to the canon; and they did that not from hastiness or levity toward the Word of God, but, on the contrary, because they were very conscientious with regard to the Word of God. Luther's opinions on the antilegomena are not a 'blot' on our Church, but they rather bear witness how careful our Church once was in determining the standard and norm of our faith and life. The summary decrees of the Papists and the Reformed that all the antilegomena must be received as canonical by all Christians on pain of losing their salvation are so little a testimony for the high regard of these denominations for the Word of God that they rather demonstrate how easy it is for those to add something to the canon who hold that the Scriptures are to be interpreted either, in a blind collier's faith, according to the whim of the Church (that is, of the Pope) or according to the principles of reason. It will therefore not be improper to submit here the testimony of our fathers, particularly of the 16th and the first half of the 17th century; not that we personally hold these opinions, but in order to show that doubts as to the canonicity of the disputed books were held also by men whose orthodoxy no Lutheran would dare to deny, and thus to clear a man like Luther of the suspicion that he had brazenly, in his subjective pleasure, passed judgment on books which had been received into the New Testament Canon." Walther concludes his article with the words: "If this question be treated in a Christian manner, if the poor laymen are not confused by a dishonest presentation of the real issue, by a partisan exploitation of a matter which the common people find it hard to grasp – which may easily be done here – the discussion of the question can only serve to arouse the Christians to a serious investigation and thus to deepen and strengthen their knowledge and their faith. If any periodical takes cognizance of this our discussion, we herewith state beforehand that we shall not deem any foolish babbling, parading in the guise of a defense of God's Word, worthy of an answer; but any pertinent ventilation of this important subject will receive our attention, even though it pronounce ever so sharp a verdict on our old teachers, Luther, Brenz, Chemnitz, Veit Dietrich, Conrad Dietrich, etc."

In this article, Walther quotes extensively from Chemnitz, who in his *Examen Concilii Tridentini* exposes, in clear and powerful language, the Antichristian and insane character of the above-mentioned papal decree with its appended anathema. Because this presentation is considered a "classic" even today, we here submit it in its salient points.[137] "The third question is whether the Church of our day can make those Scriptures, regarding which there was doubt in the Early Church because of the contradiction of some, canonical, catholic, and equal to those of the first order. The Papists not only claim that they can do this, but they actually usurp this authority; they abolish entirely the necessary distinction which the primitive and early Church made between the canonical books and the apocryphal, or ecclesiastical, books. But the Church very manifestly does not have this authority; else it could for the same reason reject canonical books or canonize spurious books. For this entire matter hinges on the assured testimonies of that Church which existed in the days of the Apostles, which testimonies the Church that immediately followed preserved in trustworthy reports. . . . What an insolent audacity it is to decree: Though the primitive and the following early Church had its doubts regarding those books because of the contradiction of many churchmen, . . . *hoc tamen non obstante* we decree that these books must be received with the same certainty as of equal authority with those which have been always adjudged genuine. . . . But why, then, do they not impart this authority to the fables of Aesop or the true stories of Lucian? Not that I would compare those controverted books to the fables of Aesop (for with Cyprian and Jerome I assign them the honorable place which they have always held in the ancient Church), but by an ἐπαγωγῇ εἰς ἀδύνατον [by adducing the impossible] I want to show that the Church has not the power to make of spurious writings genuine ones; of genuine, spurious; of doubtful and uncertain, certain, canonical, and legitimate. . . .

"Our question pertains to those books which are found together in the Vulgate edition of the Bible and which are read in the churches by the faithful. . . . Of the writings of the Old Testament the Book of Wisdom, Sirach, etc., are listed with the Apocrypha, as not being in the canon. Of the books of the New Testament these are mentioned

---

137 *Examen,* 1667, p. 48 *sqq.* Walther gave a German translation of it, *op. cit.,* pp. 205–210. It is given in the original in Baier-Walther, I, 150 *sqq.*

by Eusebius in the Third Book, chapter 25, as not having had in the first and ancient Church sufficiently sure, firm, and consentient testimonies of their trustworthiness and authority: 'The writings which are not regarded as indubitable, but against which there is contradiction, though they are known to many, are these: The Epistle of James, of Jude, the Second Epistle of Peter, the Second and the Third Epistle of John; the Apocalypse of John some reject, while others pronounce it one of the certain and incontestable Scriptures.' And in chapter 3 he says: 'It is known that in the Roman congregation some rejected the Epistle to the Hebrews, asserting that its Pauline authorship has been disputed.' . . .

"The reasons why there was doubt about these writings should be noted: 1) There were not found among the ancients sufficiently certain, firm, and consentient testimonies that these books were approved by the Apostles and commended to the churches. 2) It did not appear certain from the testimony of the primitive and ancient Church whether these books had been written by those under whose names they were issued, but it has been judged that they have been issued by others under the name of the Apostles. 3) Because some of the most ancient writers attributed some of these books to the Apostles, while others disputed this claim, this matter has been left in doubt, since it was not indubitably certain. . . . Over against these very manifest testimonies of antiquity the Council of Trent decreed: 'If anyone receive not as sacred and canonical the said books entire with all their parts, as they have been used to be read in the Catholic Church, and as they are contained in the old Latin vulgate edition . . . let him be anathema.' But whence do they bring proof and confirmation for this their decree against the testimony of antiquity? Do they now produce some unassailable and clear documents, taken from the testimony of the primitive, Apostolic, ancient Church, which show that these controverted books bear the same certainty and the like authority with the others about which there never was any doubt? By no means; nor can they do this. But they arrogate to themselves the power that the Pope with his prelates can impart, as Pighius states, to these and perhaps also to other books canonical authority, which they do not merit of themselves or because of their authors, and which they did not have at the time of the Apostles and the primitive Church. Why do they not openly state their case? They say, in effect: 'Though it cannot be proved that those books were either written or approved by the Prophets or by the Apostles, and were received certainly and constantly by the primitive and ancient Church, yes, though the contrary is proved by the most evident testimonies of antiquity, which are clearer than the midday sun, *hoc tamen non obstante* we determine and decree that this is certainly to be believed; though no documents pertaining to this case have been produced by us, we assert that (if it please the gods) the plenitude of this Antichristian power lies buried in the shrine of the Pope's heart.'

"They pronounce the anathema on all who do not receive the apocryphal books as of the same certainty and authority as the canonical. Cursed, then, will be Eusebius, Jerome, Origen, Melito, and the entire primitive Apostolic Church, from whose testimony is taken what we adduced above about these books.

"This entire dispute, then, resolves itself into the question whether it is certain and indubitable that these books are the divinely inspired Scriptures. The entire antiquity responds that this is not certain, but has been doubtful because of the contradiction of so many. The Tridentine arrogance, however, threatens with an anathema anyone who does not receive them as of equal certainty and authority with the rest of the books about which there has never been any doubt. Is it astonishing, then, that some popish parasites have contended that the Pope could institute new articles of faith, since here he does not shrink from fabricating a new canonical Scripture? There is no longer any doubt who it is that, sitting in the temple of God, exalts himself above everything that is called God, 2 Thess. 2.

"Does this mean that these books are simply to be rejected and condemned? We are by no means seeking this. Then of what use is this dispute? I answer: To make sure the rule of faith or sound doctrine in the Church. For the ancients held that the authority of the Church dogmas rests solely on the canonical books. It was held that only by the authority of the canonical books could those things be established about which any dispute arose. The rest of the books which Cyprian calls ecclesiastical, Jerome apocryphal, were to be read in the Church for the edification of the people, but not to prove the dogmas of the Church. . . . No dogma which does not have a certain and clear foundation in the canonical books dare be constructed from these books. Nothing that is in controversy may be proved from these books if there are no other proofs and confirmations in the canonical books. But what is said in these books must be explained and understood according to the analogy of what is clearly set down in the canonical books. There can be no doubt that this is the meaning of the ancient Church. But the Council of Trent will hear nothing of this necessary and most true distinction of the ancient Church, subverts and abolishes it, for the reason that (as my Andradius says) they do not want to be confined to these narrow limits; they do not want to be so destitute of all other helps that they must derive their faith solely from the canonical Scriptures. For the Tridentine Synod says that it makes canonical books out of the apocryphal books in order to show what testimonies and helps it intends to use in confirming doctrines and restoring morals." Walther adds (Baier-Walther, I, 153): "The same position is taken by A. Osiander (d. 1617), Aeg. Hunnius, Hafenreffer, C. Dietrich, F. Balduin, Th. Thummius, and others."

It has been stated that this distinction between homologoumena and antilegomena has been dropped by the later Lutheran dogmaticians. Philippi (*Glaubenslehre* I, 108) mentions particularly Gerhard, whom he pronounces the "most renowned dogmatician" of the Lutheran Church after Chemnitz. True, in one form or another the later dogmaticians state that the Church today (*hodie*) observes no distinction between the various books of the New Testament.[138] As for Gerhard, he makes the statement that he believes the Apocalypse to be canonical. However, he adds this remark: "In the meantime, however, because there was at times doubt in the primitive Church on the part of some about the author of this book, we for this reason refer it to the canonical books of the second rank; not indeed detracting from its canonical authority, still not simply and in all respects classifying it with the rest of the canonical books about which there never was any doubt; and by the fairest right we demand that the interpretation of such a book in no manner conflict with the canonical books of the first rank." [139] This, however, as a matter of fact, amounts to the distinction between homologoumena and antilegomena. As we cannot speak in the doctrine of God of a Godhead of the second rank (as old and modern subordinationists indeed do), so we cannot, without a certain self-contradiction, speak of deutero-canonical writings in the doctrine of Holy Scripture, which are God's inviolable Word.

Some have argued that since there are antilegomena, we cannot determine exactly the extent of the canon and hence cannot know exactly what is the *principium cognoscendi* and *norma* of the Christian doctrine, but such have got their accounts mixed. We know that the Church of the New Testament possesses a fixed and firm canon,

---

138 Thus Baier, I, 150, 153.

139 *Disputatt. Theologic.*, Ienae, 1655, p. 1015; quoted in Baier-Walther, I, 153.

with no uncertainty attaching to it. For when Christ asks us (John 8:31-32; 17:20; and Eph. 2:20) to continue in His and His Apostles' doctrine, He presupposes the continued existence and possession of this doctrinal basis.

In this connection the question has been asked whether the distinction between the homologoumena and the antilegomena has any "sweeping dogmatical significance." We for our part answer No, assuming that the meaning is that he who regards and treats the antilegomena as canonical thereby obtains more and other doctrines. On the one hand we observe the distinction made by the ancient Church between the writings of the New Testament; on the other hand we are convinced that the antilegomena, even when taken by themselves, neither contain false doctrine nor yet a doctrine which goes beyond the doctrine contained in the books that have the unanimous testimony of the *ecclesia primitiva.* We are convinced that Rome and certain sectarians misuse the Epistle of James when they make it the protector of their doctrine of work-righteousness. We must simply keep in mind that James is speaking of faith not in so far as it justifies before God, but in so far as we are, according to God's will and ordinance, to evidence our faith to men, which can be done only by works. (See the chapter "Justification on the Basis of Works," in Vol. II.) James is addressing not so much the new man as the old man in the Christian. And the Apocalypse does not contain an inkling of that chiliasm with which old and modern chiliasts have disturbed and plagued the Church. The correctness of this judgment will be demonstrated in the chapter "The Second Advent of Christ," in Vol. III.

All this talk about the number of the Christian doctrines increasing with the number of the Biblical books is nonsense. It has been correctly pointed out that the single Gospel according to Matthew contains the entire Christian doctrine and that missionaries among the heathen for years got along, or rather had to get along, with a translation of this one Gospel and from it taught all the articles of the Christian faith. Anyone can convince himself that the Gospel according to Matthew contains the revelation of all doctrines that our Lutheran Church confesses in the Book of Concord. At the same time we thank the Lord for the fuller exposition of the saving doctrine which He gave us in the remaining books of the New Testament. What was written of the Old Testament: "Whatsoever things were written aforetime were written for our learning" (Rom. 15:4), applies also to the New Testament, and we praise God's grace and providence in having the saving doctrine recorded for us by so many divinely appointed witnesses. Having this manifold testimony, the Christians dwell "as in a paradise," and their assurance is mightily strengthened. Paul writes to the Philippians (3:1): "To write the same things to you, to me indeed is not grievous, but for you it is safe."

12

The Integrity of the Biblical Text

In the chapter "Objections to the Doctrine of Inspiration," where we treated the argument that the *variae lectiones* disprove the inspiration of Scripture, we had come to the conclusion that the integrity of the Biblical text is assured both *a priori*, by the promise of Christ, and *a posteriori*, by scientific investigation. This chapter adds some particulars and emphasizes what has already been said.

1. Whether the original Hebrew text contained the vowel points, as most of the older Lutheran dogmaticians assume,[140] or was written only in consonants, as Luther very emphatically asserts,[141] is a historical question which does not affect either the inspiration of Scripture or the integrity of the text. It is no ingenious argument when modern theologians quite generally claim that the assumption of Verbal Inspiration necessarily drove the Lutheran dogmaticians to the further assumption of the original writing of the vowel points.[142] Luther, as we have seen, emphatically teaches Verbal Inspiration in the fullest form and still denies just as emphatically that the vowel points were in the original text.

2. We would draw particular attention to the manifest care with which God kept watch over the integrity of the Biblical text of the

---

140 Gerhard, *Loci, locus "De Scriptura Sacra,"* defends this position at length, § 334–353.

141 Luther says of the *puncta vocalia:* "They are a recent invention . . . therefore I do not bother about these their grammatical superstitions. However, the grammar is on our side if the right vowel points are used." (St. L. VI:195.) In his Genesis Commentary (St. L. II:1838) he says: "I care little for the 'above' and 'below' of the rabbis; it would be better to read the Scriptures according to the 'internal.' And the New Testament gives us that right internal sense, not the 'upper' or the 'lower.'" Previously Luther had said: "At the time of Jerome, it seems, the vowel points were not yet in use, but the entire Bible was read without them." Luther evidently fears that the assumption "that the vowel points are of the same age with the text" might make something outside Scripture the principle of interpretation.

142 Thus Nitzsch-Stephan, p. 251; Cremer, R. E., 2d ed., VI, 755.

New Testament. Verily, we are face to face with a miracle of divine preservation of the text if only half of that be true which, according to L. Schulze, endangered the transmission of the original text. He writes (*Handbuch der Theol. Wissenschaften* I, 489): "The negligence of the copyists, which Cicero already deplored in his day (*Ad Quint.*, fr. 3, 5), Clemens Alexandrinus (*Str.* 4, 6) and Origen (*In Matt.* 19, 19, t. XV.) also deplore. The variants are: 1) accidental; since the fact that it was literally God's Word was not stressed in those days [143] and particularly in private use precise exactness was not demanded, the variants occurred partly through the negligence of the copyists (omissions, reduplications, transposition of words, confounding of letters, the latter being favored by the uncials and the *scriptio continua*); partly through the misunderstanding of the dictation (iotacism, e. g., ἰδέ for εἰ δέ, Rom. 2:17; πρόσκλησιν for πρόσκλισιν, 1 Tim. 5:21; in enumerations there occurred omissions or transposition or substitution of synonyms; e. g., Rom. 1:30-31 and Gal. 5:18-23); and partly through misunderstanding of what was heard or read, e. g., in the case of abbreviations. Add 2) the variants were intentional. Through the application of scientific methods the attempt was made to improve the language according to definite grammatical rules, or to clarify dark passages by additions or changes (particularly of unfamiliar expressions), or to guard against (dogmatic) misconceptions, or to correct statements held to be erroneous, or to harmonize passages by additions from oral tradition or from a comparison with the parallel passages (particularly in the Gospels and in the case of quotations from the LXX). This was done both by the copyists and often also by the correctors. From these learned transactions there resulted 3) glosses, which, first placed on the margin, later got into the text, either with or instead of the original words; likewise from the liturgical supplements of the lectionaries, where changes became necessary because of the unsuitable beginning or end of the pericopes. And, in addition, the text was 4) arbitrarily altered according to the established translations." Now, if in spite of all this, as L. Schulze himself remarks, the original form of the text, often as it was copied, was not corrupted "in essential points," we see in such preservation, as Philippi pointed out (*Glau-*

---

143 This is historically incorrect. As the Apostles claimed divine authority for the Word which they preached and wrote, so there is also sufficient evidence in the writings of the Church Fathers of the first centuries — and this is acknowledged also by recent theologians, for example Ihmels (*Zentralfragen*, p. 56) — that the "Primitive Church" identified "Scripture with the Word of God." That is the very thing for which the Early Church is criticized. Compare Ihmels, *loc. cit.*

benslehre I, 115 f.), a miracle of divine providence. The fact is that the changes in the text which occurred in the course of eighteen centuries are so insignificant that in the seminary we can use the various modern critical editions and the *textus receptus* side by side without any difficulty. Even if we did not have the results of modern textual criticism and had to rely solely on the *textus receptus,* on which practically all of Luther's translation and the Authorized Version are based, the Christian Church would not be the poorer in the knowledge of the divine truth. What the Church lacks in our day is not a reliable text of the Bible, but the faith in the sufficiently reliable text.

3. The following remarks are intended to allay somewhat the animosity which the discussion of questions of textual criticism usually produces. In the case of professional textual critics, who disagree for "scientific reasons," this animosity is readily explained. Even racial prejudices contribute toward such animosity. Tischendorf should not be blamed much for exaggerating somewhat the importance of his Sinaitic find (א). Some belonging to other nationalities have acted similarly. Also the English text critics, and the text critics in general, disagree among themselves. Bruce says: "Experts in modern criticism . . . in many cases do not accord, and their results cannot be regarded as final." [144] But also among the theologians who are considered to be "laymen" in textual criticism (Bruce counts himself as such, *op. cit.,* p. 56), some have become unduly – and we think quite unnecessarily – perturbed, especially in connection with the passage 1 John 5:7-8. All are agreed that this passage is not needed to establish the doctrine of the Holy Trinity. There is more than ample proof for this doctrine in numerous other passages. Tischendorf himself says: "It is a very grave error if some imagine that what the Church of Christ teaches on the Holy Trinity depends for the most part on these veiled words of John" (quoted in *The Exp. Greek Test.,* on our passage). In our opinion the decision as to the authenticity or spuriousness of these words depends on the understanding of certain words of Cyprian, which are about two hundred years older than our oldest codices. We find these words in Cyprian's *De Unitate Ecclesiae* (in my edition: Erasmus, Basle, 1525, p. 164): *"Dicit Dominus: 'Ego et Pater unum sumus'"* ("the Lord says: 'I and the Father are One'"). Cyprian is quoting John 10:30. And he immediately adds: *"Et iterum de Patre et Filio et Spiritu Sancto scriptum est: 'Et tres unum sunt'"* ("and again it is written of the Father and the Son and the Holy Ghost: 'And the

[144] *The Expositor's Greek Test.,* I, Introduction, p. 55, 4. That is one of the reasons why this commentary uses the *textus receptus.*

Three are One'"). Now, those who assert that Cyprian is here not quoting the words 1 John 5:7, are obliged to show that the words of Cyprian: "*Et tres unum sunt,*" applied to the three Persons of the Trinity, are found elsewhere in the Scriptures than 1 John 5. Griesbach counters that Cyprian is here not quoting from Scripture, but giving his own allegorical interpretation of the three witnesses on earth: "The Spirit, the water, and the blood; and these three agree in one." That will hardly do. Cyprian states distinctly that he is quoting Bible passages, not only in the words: "I and the Father are one," but also in the words: "And again it is written of the Father and the Son and the Holy Ghost." These are, in our opinion, the objective facts.

Others, like Huther in Meyer's Commentary, say that the words of Cyprian "appear" to refer to 1 John 5:7. But we obtain the right to speak of a mere "appearance" only by showing that the words referred to are found at some other place in Scripture. Huther offers no further proof for his assumption of an "appearance" than the bare statement: "The singular quotation in Cyprian finds its explanation in interpreting the words 'The Spirit, the water, and the blood' symbolically of the Trinity." But no matter how much Cyprian otherwise allegorizes in the doctrine of the Trinity, in these words he does not allegorize, but he quotes Scripture: "*Et iterum . . . scriptum est.*" Now, since the words of Cyprian are about two hundred years older than the oldest preserved codices (B and א), it is not fair to say that those are out of date who consider the words referring to the three witnesses in heaven to be genuine (e. g., Besser, Stoeckhardt, Sander, Mayer, and others).

The further assertion has been made that when Cyprian used the words "*Et iterum de Patre et Filio et Spiritu Sancto scriptum est: 'et tres unum sunt,'*" he was quoting v. 8. But v. 8 does not have the words: ἕν εἰσιν, "*'unum' sunt,*" but εἰς τὸ ἕν εἰσιν, "*'in unum' sunt,*" "they agree in one." But since Cyprian knew his Greek, the assumption that he might have rendered the εἰς τὸ ἕν εἰσιν with "they are one" is farfetched.

While we have always deplored the necessity of spending so much of the time of our regular dogmatical course on the textual discussion of 1 John 5:7-8, it has resulted in a twofold practical benefit. For one thing it gave us an opportunity to point out, with Tischendorf, that the doctrine of the Trinity is in no wise dependent on the genuineness of this passage, since there is more than enough proof for this doctrine in other passages. In the second place, it gave us the opportunity to inculcate the rule, never to attempt to use this passage in disputing with Unitarians. If this were done, the Unitarians would at once shift the discussion over to the field of textual criticism, with the result that the *status controversiae*, the doctrine of the Trinity, would be lost sight of and the public would receive the impression that the Scriptural foundation for this doctrine is rather weak.

May we be permitted to make a final remark that no theologian is risking his scientific reputation by whatever position he takes in the question of the genuineness of our passage. The "notoriously spurious," which modern theologians are quick to use in connection with this passage, does not prove their scientific superiority, but rather the opposite. Whoever is somewhat familiar with the true state of affairs cultivates a more modest language. Bloomfield remarks in his commentary that on this passage "volumes have been written by some of the most eminent scholars." He gives the names of the men who stand for the "*pro*" and the "*contra*" in this matter; then he comments, as Luther also did, on both versions; and finally he takes the well-known position of Bengel. He closes with the words: "On again examining, for this second edition of the present work, the evidence for and against the words, I still think that much of the mystery in which Bishop Middleton considers the passage as enveloped has yet to be cleared away; and my impression is . . . that, from the peculiar character of the evidence, external and internal (even after all that has been effected to strengthen the internal evidence, by the very learned Bishop Burgess), [145] we are neither authorized to receive the passage as indubitably genuine, nor, on the other hand, to reject it indubitably as spurious, but to wait for further evidence." But "waiting for further evidence" does not appeal to most modern theologians, including most of the recent textual critics. They want to consider the question as closed. But the hope voiced by Bengel that old documents might still be discovered that would throw further light on our text might not be so foolish in view of recent discoveries.

But whether new discoveries are made or not, the Church of God stands on a sufficiently firm Scripture text, as we know *a priori* from Christ's promise (John 8:31-32; 17:20) and *a posteriori* by scientific investigation. In every age the Church of God, which is built on the foundation of the Apostles and Prophets, had in its possession the Bible text which enabled it to carry out its commission to teach all nations all things that Christ had commanded. Luther could say in his day: "The Word they still shall let remain." Athanasius and

[145] Bishop Burgess is one of the theologians who based their arguments for the authenticity of the passage on text and context. Stoeckhardt also belongs in this class. Others of our circle voiced the opposite opinion.

Augustine could say the same thing in their days. We say the same thing in our day. One is saddened by the frivolity, the product of ignorance, with which nowadays the results of modern textual criticism are made accessible to the general public in so-called "scientifico-popular" writings. We read in one such book: [146] "We have been dwelling in the traditional text as in an ancient, comfortable house; the spirit of our fathers ruled there and made it comfortable and cozy. Now come the building inspectors and condemn the building and demand that it be vacated. But are the building inspectors responsible for its dilapidated and decayed condition? Should we not rather thank them for getting us out alive from the tumbledown building? Saving lives is the business of textual criticism." When the old Bible text is thus compared to a dilapidated house, from which speedy flight is necessary to save the life of the Church, this must cause great confusion among the general public, which is not in a position to investigate the matter. It seems that the true state of affairs was entirely hidden from this writer. On occasion he calls the text on which Luther based his translation the "corrupted text of Erasmus." He does not consider that the newer or the newest critical editions of the text differ so little from the "corrupted text of Erasmus" that both texts can be used side by side without any real conflict. We have grave misgivings about *The Expositor's Greek Testament*, because its theology is thoroughly modern, but we take great satisfaction in these two things: First, that in this commentary of five volumes the *textus receptus* has been made the basis of the exposition. That will in a measure check the irresponsible talk that we must at once move out of the "dilapidated" house of the old text if we do not want to lose the foundation of our faith. The second is the declaration of the editor in chief that he would rather await the "final results" of modern textual criticism before he discards the *textus receptus.*

13

The Original Text of Holy Scripture and the Translations

Since Scripture is intended for the use of all Christians, of whatever station, sex, age, etc. (Deut. 6:6-9; Joshua 1:8; Is. 34:16; Neh. 8:2-8; 2 Kings 23:1-2; Luke 16:29 ff.; John 5:39; 20:31; Acts 17:11:

---

[146] *Der Text des Neuen Testaments nach seiner geschichtlichen Entwicklung.* By August Pott, 1906, p. 14, one of a series of "Scientifico-popular Studies. . . ."

"They searched the Scriptures daily"; 2 Thess. 2:15; 1 John 1:4; 2:13-14; 2 Tim. 3:15; Col. 4:16; 1 Thess. 5:27: "I charge you by the Lord that this epistle be read unto all the holy brethren"),[147] it is God's will that the Scriptures be translated into the various human languages. And accordingly the Church, from its beginning, made it a point to furnish translations of Scripture into foreign languages.[148] We do not say that it is absolutely necessary that one must read the Scriptures in order to be saved. What is absolutely necessary is the knowledge of those fundamental articles of the Christian faith through which repentance and faith in the remission of sins purchased by Christ is brought about in man (Luke 24:46-47), and this knowledge may be obtained by the mere hearing of a Scriptural sermon or instruction. The dogmaticians teach that a man may come to faith and thus become a member of the Christian Church without as much as knowing that there is a Holy Scripture. Gerhard: "It is not simply and absolutely necessary to salvation to believe that there are any divine Scriptures if this unbelief issues from simple ignorance, for many have been saved who have grasped the essentials, or fundamentals, of the Christian faith."[149] But after men have become Christians, it is indeed God's will that they read the Scriptures, search the Scriptures, and judge according to the Scriptures, as is evident from the passages quoted above and as will be set forth more fully later.

The contention of the Papacy that the reading of Scripture cannot be permitted to all Christians because that would expose the "laymen" to the danger of interpreting Scripture according to their own thoughts and thus introducing false doctrine is beside the point, for experience has shown that it is, above all, the clergy and, *primus omnium*, the Pope who have interpreted the Scripture according to their own mind and filled the world with the most horrible heresies.[150]

---

147 The dogmaticians say: *"Finis cui Scripturae Sacrae omnes sunt Christiani, imo omnes homines."*

148 Detailed information on this point in Gerhard, *Loci*, *"De Scriptura Sacra,"* § 494 *sqq*. See the articles *"Bibeluebersetzungen"* in R. E., 2d ed., II, 437 ff., in Meusel I, 429 ff., or in any larger encyclopedia; also Fuerbringer, *Einl. in das N. T.*, 1914, p. 14 f.

149 *Loci*, *"De Ecclesia,"* § 121; so also Quenstedt, *Systema*, I, 313.

150 Rome treats the Bible as a dangerous book. Permission to read it is to be granted only to certain laymen, namely, to those to whom, in the opinion of the parish priest or confessor, it would not be harmful. The fourth rule of the Congregation of the Index of Prohibited Books, approved by Pius IV, states: "Since it is manifest by experience that if the Holy Bible in the vulgar tongue be suffered to be read everywhere without distinction, more evil than good arises, let the judgment of the bishop or inquisitor be abided by in this respect, so that, after consulting with the parish priest or the confessor, they may grant per-

The Relation of the Original Text to the Translations

It is self-evident that the original wields canonical authority also over the translations. The vernacular versions have authority only in so far as they correctly render the original text. All translations must submit to the test whether they reproduce the original correctly. When the Church of the Pope declares the Vulgate to be absolutely authoritative,[151] it commits an Antichristian outrage. However, the disparity

---

mission to read translations of the Scriptures, made by Catholic writers, to those whom they understand to be able to receive no harm, but an increase of faith and piety from such reading, which permission should be given in writing. But whosoever shall presume to read these Bibles, or have them in possession without such permission, shall not be capable of receiving absolution for their sins, unless they have first given up their Bibles to the bishop. The booksellers, however, who sell Bibles in the vulgar tongue to someone who has not this permission, or make a concession in any other way, are to lose the price of the books, which is to be converted to a pious use by the bishop or be subject to other punishments commensurate with their transgression according to the judgment of the bishop. The regular clergy, however, dare neither read nor buy them unless they have obtained the permission from their prelates." (In Smets, p. 224.) To this rule Clemens VIII added the note: "It is to be well noted in regard to the above described Rule of the Index of Pope Pius IV, of blessed memory, that through this impression and edition no right is given anew to the bishops, or inquisitors, or superiors of the regular clergy to grant permission to buy, read, or possess the Bible in a vulgar tongue edition; since so far this right has been taken away from them by the command and usage of the holy Roman and universal Inquisition, namely, the right of granting such permission of reading and having Bibles in the vernacular, or parts of the Holy Scriptures, be it of the New or of the Old Testament, in whatever vernacular they may be published, or even historical summaries or compends of the Bible or the books of Holy Scripture, in whatever vulgar idiom they may be written; all of which is inviolably to be observed." (*Observatio circa Quartam Regulam.* Cf. Index, etc. Coloniae sumpt. B. Gualtheri, 1602.) Earlier, Gregory VII had written Duke Wratislaw of Bohemia, who had asked for divine worship, and of course for the use of Scripture, in the national tongue: "Since your Honor has asked that the divine office be celebrated among you in the Slavonic tongue, know that we can by no means comply with this your petition. To us who are familiar with the Scriptures it is clear that the omnipotent God was not without reason pleased to have the Holy Scriptures dark in some places, in order that they might not, if they were clear unto certainty for all and everyone, become worthless and despised, or, falsely understood by the common people, lead into error. Neither does that serve as an excuse that certain religious men have patiently borne or left uncorrected what the people simply demand; for the primitive Church has overlooked much which, after Christianity had taken firm root and religion was spreading, was after thorough examination corrected by the holy fathers. We therefore prohibit by the authority of the blessed Peter that which is imprudently demanded by your people, and we command you to resist this ill-considered temerity with all your power, to the honor of omnipotent God." (Mansi XX, 296. Gieseler, *Kirchengeschichte* II, 1, p. 257.) Compare the thorough article by Walther: "Das antichristische paepstliche Verbot, die Heilige Schrift in der Muttersprache zu lesen," *Lutheraner* 29, 73–90. Guenther, *Symbolik,* p. 112.

[151] *Tridentinum,* Sess. IV, *decretum de editione,* etc.

between the original of Scripture and its translations must not be unduly stressed. Modern theologians engage in this erroneous and dangerous talk when they argue against the inspiration of Scripture along these lines: Even if Scripture were entirely God's Word, that would be of no benefit to the Church, since the Church, with the exception of a small minority of its members, can use the Scriptures only in translations, and the translations must be regarded as merely human views. With this argument Dr. Briggs sought to confuse the Presbyterian Board of Investigation at his trial.[152] Also Henry E. Jacobs declared: "It is only the Scriptures as written in the original languages that are inspired. Even the best translation is only a human explanation or interpretation of the inspired words, however well the inspired thought may be conveyed in other language." [153] These words could convey the thought that Bible colporteurs could offer an English or German Bible to prospective customers not as being the Word of God, but merely as being the translator's understanding of the Word of God. Over against this view it must be maintained: Of course even the best translators of the Bible are not inspired as were the infallible Apostles and Prophets, and for that reason their translations must remain under the control of the original text and in so far are *norma normata.* Our dogmaticians emphasized this over against Rome. On the other hand it must not be forgotten: Whatever is God's Word in Greek, is God's Word also in German and English if only the German or the English is a faithful translation of the Greek. We should here keep in mind the nature of the Holy Scriptures. The language of Holy Scripture is so simple, particularly in the *sedes doctrinae,* that every translation which at all deserves the name of a "translation" must reproduce the original. One who understands the New Testament Greek and commands the language into which he is translating must take particular pains if he is minded to produce a translation which does not reproduce the original text.

Place side by side the Greek text of John 3:16, the German, the English, and the Latin translation: will anyone say that the translations do not reproduce the original? that we cannot say of the translated passage that it is the Word of God? that we must say that it is merely "a human explanation or interpretation" of the inspired text? John 3:16: Οὕτως γὰρ ἠγάπησεν ὁ θεὸς τὸν κόσμον, ὥστε τὸν υἱὸν τὸν μονογενῆ ἔδωκεν, ἵνα πᾶς ὁ πιστεύων εἰς αὐτὸν μὴ ἀπόληται, ἀλλ' ἔχῃ ζωὴν αἰώνιον; *"Also hat Gott die Welt geliebt, dass er seinen eingebornen Sohn gab,*

---

[152] Cp. Dr. S. A. Farrand, *The Other Side,* p. 17 ff.

[153] *Elements of Religion,* 1898, p. 31 f.

auf dass alle, die an ihn glauben, nicht verloren werden, sondern das ewige Leben haben"; "God so loved the world that He gave His only-begotten Son, that whosoever believeth in Him should not perish, but have everlasting life"; "*Sic Deus dilexit mundum, ut Filium suum unigenitum daret, ut omnis qui credit in eum non pereat, sed habeat vitam aeternam*" (Vulgate). And – to meet an objection – it is not only John 3:16 which is so clear that the translator could not go astray, but, as the greatest theologians of all ages (Augustine, Luther, Chemnitz, Gerhard, and others) have pointed out, the whole Christian doctrine is revealed in Scripture passages that need no exegesis, but are an open book alike to the learned and the unlearned and can be so readily translated that the translator cannot go wrong unless he has made up his mind to depart from the original. We are confronted by the fact that there is not one among the common versions of the Bible in which the Christian doctrine in all its parts is not plainly stated and the opposing errors are not rejected.

This holds true even of the Vulgate of the Roman Catholic Church. The "*ipsa conteret caput tuum*" of Gen. 3:15 is rejected through the correct translation of the many passages which present Christ as the sole Savior from the guilt of sin and death, e. g., 1 Tim. 2:5-6: "*Unus enim Deus, unus et Mediator Dei et hominum, homo Christus Iesus, qui dedit redemptionem semetipsum pro omnibus*"; and Gal. 3:16: "*Abrahae dictae sunt promissiones et semini eius. Non dicit: 'Et seminibus,' quasi in multis, sed quasi in uno: 'Et semini tuo,' qui est Christus.*" Also justification alone by faith without the deeds of the Law is clearly taught in the Vulgate, e. g., Rom. 3:28: *Arbitramur enim iustificari hominem per fidem, sine operibus legis;* and Gal. 2:16: *Scientes autem, quod non iustificatur homo ex operibus legis, nisi per fidem Iesu Christi.* In its official Confession, the Tridentinum, the Roman Catholic Church, in several canons, anathematizes justification by faith without the deeds of the Law, but this curse is directed against the doctrine which is clearly taught in its own official Bible translation, the Vulgate. If one should agree, *disputandi causa,* to discuss the doctrines with the Papists on the basis of the Vulgate, he would still retain the weapon with which to vanquish the opponent.

The same thing applies to making the Authorized Version the basis of the dispute with the Reformed. Though the Reformed sects which follow in the footsteps of Zwingli and Calvin teach an immediate operation of the Holy Ghost, without and alongside the means of grace – "efficacious grace acts immediately" – their Bible nevertheless teaches the correct doctrine: Rom. 10:17: "So, then, faith cometh by hearing, and hearing by the Word of God"; 1 Pet. 1:23: "Being born again, not of corruptible seed, but of incorruptible, by the Word of God, which liveth and abideth forever"; and Titus 3:5: "According to His mercy He saved us by the washing of regeneration." Also the real presence of Christ's body and blood in the Lord's Supper is clearly stated in the Authorized Version: Matt. 26:26-28: "Jesus took bread, and blessed it, and brake it, and gave it to the disciples, and said: Take, eat; this is My body. And he took the cup and gave thanks and gave it to them saying: Drink ye all of it; for this is My blood of the new testament, which is shed for many for the remission of sins." The parallel texts of Mark, Luke, and Paul teach the same. The Reformed sects have separated from the Lutheran Church and are maintaining their separation by the rejection of doctrines taught unmistakably in their own Bible translation.

Thus Holy Scripture checks, so to speak, by its clear and simple mode of speech, false translations. It is by God's arrangement a light that no translation can extinguish easily. This confirms what Luther says of Holy Scripture: "There is no clearer book written on earth than Holy Scripture" (St. L. V:334). We should, then, not say that even the best translations are but a human view, or opinion, of God's Word. On the contrary, in so far as the translations are faithful translations – and exact translations are hard to avoid particularly in the *sedes doctrinae* – they are likewise the very Word of God. Walther therefore is right in saying: "One may be unacquainted with the original languages of the Bible and still be divinely assured that his German Bible is God's Word, for through it he receives the witness of the Holy Spirit."[154] As Scripture in the original tongues proves itself to be God's Word, so also the translation – if it be a real translation – has the same power.

There is ample Scripture proof for the fact that translating does not deprive Scripture of its character of being the infallible Word of God. According to Scripture the infallible Word of the Apostles and Prophets will to the end of time, at all places, among all nations and tongues, be the foundation of faith for all Christians and the norm and standard according to which all Christians judge whether the doctrine is true or false. Since, however, the vast majority of Christians possess the written Word of the Apostles and Prophets only in translations, it is clear that Holy Scripture does not lose its character of being the infallible Word of God by being translated. God's pro-

---

154 *Proceedings of the Northern District,* 1867, p. 34.

tecting hand has guarded not only the original text, but also the translations. As we have a firm and fixed Word of God in the original despite the *variae lectiones,* so the current versions of the Bible present a firm and fixed Word of God, and this despite the fact that every existing translation contains occasional mistakes and is subject to continuous correction in the light of the original.

The continuous demand for "revised" translations calls for two additional remarks. 1) As all theologians who deny the substitutional satisfaction of Christ and the inspiration of Scripture are according to God's order excluded from the teaching office of the Christian Church, so all such theologians should realize that they have no call to translate the Scriptures. 2) We shall always have to be content with versions which in the translation of difficult passages do not introduce false doctrines, but offer a translation which is "according to the analogy of faith" (what the analogy of faith, or the *regula fidei* is, will be shown in the chapter "Holy Scripture and Exegesis"). In that case the translator may have had, as Luther says, the correct thoughts at the wrong place. Such translations will do no harm. They do not in any way militate against the clarity of Scripture, as has been shown in the chapter on "The Perspicuity of Scripture."

14

The Use of Scripture in Deciding Doctrinal Controversies

It is a familiar assertion of the Roman Catholic Church that Holy Scripture is incapable of deciding doctrinal issues; hence for the establishment and preservation of unity in teaching the Church needs a visible head (*caput visibile*), a visible vicar of Christ (*vicarium Christi*), who will determine by virtue of his personal authority the meaning of the Scriptures. Also modern theology, through its denial of the infallible divine authority of Scripture, has been driven into renouncing the principle of the Christian Church that Scripture is the *iudex controversiarum.* Neologists have declared with Zoeckler: "With respect to the Bible as normative and judicial authority, the possibility of a merely partial and incomplete settlement of the respective controversy, through the appeal to Scripture, must often be admitted" (*Handbuch,* 2d ed., III, 151). And Volck of Dorpat said, as we heard: "To inquire of Scripture is not so easy a matter" (*op. cit.,* I, 746).

Scripture teaches the contrary. It requires the teachers of the

Church, and in particular also all Christians, to make use of Scripture as *iudex controversiarum.* For this direction we have the normative example of Christ. When He was tempted to follow after a false faith, he overcame the devil with His "It is written" and obtained the victory by adducing the pertinent Scripture passages. As for the teachers of the Church, it belongs to their office to stop the mouths of the vain talkers (Titus 1:10-11), not, of course, with the fist or similar carnal weapons (2 Cor. 10:3 ff.), but by "holding fast the faithful Word, as he hath been taught" (Titus 1:9), by "holding fast the form of sound words" which they heard and learned from the Apostles (2 Tim. 1:13). Scripture nowhere recognizes either the Roman position that the Scriptures are entirely unsuited to decide controversies or the claim of modern theology that Scripture "often fails" as norm of doctrine. It never fails when wielded by men who are "apt to teach." And as for the Christians in general, Scripture not only finds that they are competent to judge in matters of Christian doctrine (John 6:45: "They shall be all taught of God"), but impresses upon them the duty of distinguishing between true and false prophets (Matt. 7:15; Rom. 16:17) and to keep a watchful eye on the ministry of their own teachers (Col. 4:17: "And say to Archippus, Take heed to the ministry which thou hast received in the Lord, that thou fulfill it"). And they are to do this not according to the norm of their own thoughts, but are bound to judge, just as their teachers are, by God's Word (John 8:31-32: "If ye continue in My Word"; 1 Pet. 4:11: "If any man speak, let him speak as the oracles of God"). It is an established truth of Scripture that all Christians, every one of them, can and should use Scripture as *norma doctrinae* and as *iudex controversiarum.* Luther: "The right to judge, and pronounce on, matters of doctrine belongs to each and every Christian, so much so that he is doing an accursed thing who impairs this right by a hairbreadth" (St. L. XIX:341).

To settle a doctrinal controversy, two rules, to which also our old theologians constantly call attention, must be observed. 1) Define exactly the question at issue (*status controversiae*); and 2) when that has been done, let those Scripture passages speak which treat of the controversial point. Then Scripture itself will decide the matter with the greatest clearness and certainty. It will, of course, not force the external acceptance of its decision and externally stop the mouth of the gainsayer, but it will either inwardly convince and persuade him, as was the case with the servants of the Sanhedrin (John 7:46), or it will confront him who tenaciously clings to his error with the dire possibility of becoming an αὐτοκατάκριτος (Titus 3:11: "knowing that he that is such is subverted and sinneth, being condemned of himself"). Baier's statement is to the point: "Though Holy Scripture does not force men by external power to acquiesce in its decision according to the λόγον τὸν ἔξω, or so that they do not raise any objection by external act, nevertheless since the meaning of Scripture as the divine voice is plain, it is certain that the hearts of men will be convinced according to the λόγον τὸν ἔσω, so that they cannot contradict except against the protest of their conscience" (Baier-Walther, I, 186). It is for this reason that Scripture says of Scripture that it speaks, testifies, accuses, judges, concludes under sin, stops the mouth, etc. (John 19:24; Rom. 3:21; John 5:45; 12:48; Gal. 3:22; Rom. 3:19).[155]

When the Papists raised the objection that Scripture is a "dumb book," which cannot speak, judge, and decide, our old theologians would answer: Only in the Papacy is the Bible a "dumb book," because there it is prohibited from speaking ("*Scriptura Sacra non muta nisi in papatu, ubi prohibetur loqui*"). In addition, they put it up to the Roman theologians, who held Scripture to be God's Word, why the words of Scripture could not make decisions as well as the words or epistles of the Pope – unless they seriously held that "God's letter" to mankind (Scripture) had less power than the epistles of the Pope. – With particular vehemence the Roman theologians denounced the Scripture teaching that also "laymen" could and should judge doctrine on the basis of Scripture. They appealed to the Scripture passages which figuratively call the Christians "sheep," such as John 10:16: "And other sheep I have, which are not of this fold," and particularly to John 21:16-17, where Christ says to Peter: "Feed My sheep." Our theologians replied: The Christians are indeed compared to sheep; however, not to foolish sheep, but to wise sheep, that know how to distinguish the voice of Christ from the voice of the stranger and of the pseudo shepherd. John 10:4-5: "When he putteth forth his own sheep, he goeth before them, and the sheep follow him; for they know his voice. And a stranger will they not follow, but will flee from him; for they know not the voice of strangers." And v. 27: "My sheep hear My voice, and I know them, and they follow Me."[156]

---

155 Holtzmann (*Neutestamentl. Theologie* II, 297) correctly remarks that the Apostle Paul evidently "personifies" Scripture and lets it speak "directly to present-day Christendom." He ascribes this to the "Jewish opinion" of the Apostle, "according to which theopneusty is ascribed directly to Scripture."

156 Gerhard, *Loci, "De Ministerio Eccles.,"* § 88: "We do not make shepherds of the sheep, but demand that they be and remain sheep; however, we do not want them to be brute sheep, which neither can nor should distinguish between shepherds and wolves." Gerhard in this paragraph convincingly refutes

the chief arguments of Rome against the ability and right of the "laity" to judge doctrine on the basis of Scripture. "Bellarmine objects: 'The uneducated people cannot judge the doctrine of their shepherds otherwise than by comparing it with the doctrine of their predecessors and the regular shepherds.' I answer: the example of the Bereans shows that this is wrong; they daily searched the Scriptures, inquiring carefully whether these things were so that were proclaimed by Paul and Barnabas (Acts 17:11); they set up as norm of judgment not the doctrine of the regular shepherds, but the Holy Scriptures, and for this they were commended by the Holy Spirit. The ignorance of the people in the Papacy, of which Bellarmine speaks, arose from the prohibition to read Holy Scripture, for which sacrilege its authors will some day have to give strict account. But we invert Bellarmine's argument: If the ignorance does not keep them from comparing the doctrine of their shepherds with the doctrine of their predecessors or regular shepherds, it will also not keep them from comparing the doctrine of their shepherds with the doctrine of Christ, the Prophets, and the Apostles, presented in Scripture, and from distinguishing according to this norm the true prophet from the false one. If the former be true, the latter also is true. The major premise is proved by the fact that Christ, the Prophets, and the Apostles can teach and did teach as clearly as the ordinary shepherds. When Christ, the Prophets, and the Apostles performed their ministry of teaching here on earth, they preached not only to the learned, but also to the unlearned, in such a manner that they were understood by all; why, then, should the writings of the Prophets and Apostles be so obscure and perplexing that the unlearned people could not in any way judge from them? Certainly the Prophets and Apostles did not write anything else than they preached *viva voce.* – 'But,' says Bellarmine, 'if the people could of themselves pass judgment on the doctrine of the shepherd, they would not need preachers.' I answer: That is an illogical conclusion. Both things are commanded by God; that the people pass judgment on the doctrine of the shepherd – which Bellarmine a while ago in definite words conceded to the people – and that there are to be nevertheless ministers in the Church, 'they are not all teachers' (1 Cor. 12:29; Eph. 4:11). It is one thing to inquire into the truth of the doctrine and know the difference between heresy and orthodoxy, between false prophets and true teachers; this is the general call, which belongs to all Christians. It is another thing to teach publicly in the Church; that is the special call. We do not make shepherds of the sheep, but demand that they be and remain sheep; however, we do not want them to be brute sheep, which neither can nor should distinguish between shepherds and wolves. The Papists make of their hearers brute sheep, which follow a shepherd without discretion, not asking whether he leads them to noxious pastures or changes himself into a wolf; they make of the hearers parrots which hang on the nod of the prelates, and of the prelates they make angels, which are infallible and accountable to no one. . . . The reason which Bellarmine adds is plainly Antichristian: 'When the appointed shepherd and one who is not called teach things which are contrary to each other, the people should by all means rather follow their shepherd than him who is not a shepherd, even if it should chance that the shepherd erred.' But it is wrong that the people ought to follow the appointed shepherd when he errs; for this would be nothing else than to command the sheep to follow their shepherd also to noxious pastures, to ask the Christians to prefer darkness to light, error to truth, human regulations to divine authority. Bellarmine indeed submits 'that it is not credible that God should permit an appointed shepherd so to err that he deceives the simple people.' But in vain does he argue whether a thing can occur of which it is manifestly certain that it has occurred. He cannot without brazen impudence deny that appointed shepherds have often erred and deceived the simple people. Here we put Bellarmine into a dilemma and ask him whether the people should follow

Since Scripture is plain on the point that all doctrinal issues can and should be decided by Scripture, the question arises why doctrinal debates and colloquies so seldom achieve the desired end. The answer is intimated in the beginning of this chapter. If the *status controversiae* either is not at all defined – or as happens still oftener – is again lost sight of, the result is that the two parties are talking of two different things, and an agreement is out of the question. Nor can an agreement be reached if the controverted point is not placed in the light of Scripture. This happens when an "interpretation" takes the place of Scripture or passages are quoted which treat of a different doctrine. The latter case is of frequent occurrence. Thus the proposal has been made that the doctrine of the Lord's Supper be taken not from the words of institution, but from John 6, or that the doctrine of our eternal election to salvation be taken not from the Scripture passages which treat of election, but from John 3:16; etc. Modern theology even goes so far as to demand that each doctrine be derived from "the whole of Scripture." This senseless and impossible method, recommended and adopted by the "Reformer of the nineteenth century" (Schleiermacher), is declared to proceed from a "deeper understanding of Scripture," while the old theologians are said to have cut up Scripture by insisting that each doctrine be taken from the passages in which it is revealed. It is clear that in all these cases Scripture is not heard at all, but its mouth is stopped by a principle foreign to Scripture, exactly as is done in the Papacy. Any agreement in cases like these is, of course, out of the question. This subject will be taken up again in the chapter "Holy Scripture and Exegesis."

---

appointed shepherds when they err. If he answers affirmatively, he will make it plain that he is lending his venal support to him who in '*Si papa*,' dist. 40, thus bellows: 'If the Pope, unmindful of his and his brethren's salvation, is found negligent, incompetent, and remiss in his labors, and in addition silent as to the good, which will harm him and all, and leads innumerable nations in multitudes with him to hell, as its first property, to be punished with him by many plagues throughout eternity: let no mortal presume to accuse him of guilt in this case; for he who himself will judge all can be judged by none.'" (Quoted in Baier-Walther, I, 188.) – Luther's well-known words (St. L. X:1542 f.) belong here: 'All warnings uttered by St. Paul, Rom. 16:17-18; 1 Cor. 10:15; Gal. 3:4-5; Col. 2:8, and at all other places, likewise all passages in the Prophets instructing us to avoid the doctrines of men, take the right and power to judge doctrine away from the teachers and place it, with earnest commands and threatening the loss of salvation, upon the hearers; they have not only the right and power to judge whatever is preached, but it is made their duty thus to judge on pain of incurring the disfavor of the divine Majesty. It will be seen how the tyrants have dealt with us in a most unchristian manner, taking this right, which we are commanded to exercise, from us and appropriating it to themselves."

15

The Authority of Scripture and the Confessions

In adopting its Symbols, or Confessions, the Lutheran Church did not adopt doctrines which are foreign to Scripture, but confessed its faith in the doctrines *revealed in Scripture.* The attempts to spread unscriptural doctrines in the Church under the guise of Scriptural teaching forced the Church to set forth in its own words what the Scriptures actually do teach. The Symbols, or Confessions, of the orthodox Church are simply its affirmation of the Scriptural doctrine over against the denial of it by heretics.

This same truth – that the Lutheran Church does not set up in its Symbols a second norm alongside Scripture – is evidenced by its insistence on the *quia* form of subscription. It binds its teachers to the doctrine contained in the Confessions not because it is the doctrine of the Confessions, but because it is the doctrine of Scripture. There are many who insist on the *quatenus* form of subscription – "in so far as" the symbols teach the Scripture truth. One wonders whether these people take a serious view of the obligation involved. J. G. Walch aptly remarks that with the restrictive *quatenus* one could place his signature under the Koran or the Racovian Catechism.[157] A person who seeks to justify the *quatenus* by saying that he is not yet certain what is the Scriptural truth and how far the Symbolical Books give expression to this truth must be told that he is not yet ready for the ministerial office. And if he complains that the *quia* subscription would entail the coercion of his conscience, he must be told that nobody is coercing him to take up the office of pastor or teacher. As a rule, only such people speak of coercion here as have gotten away from God's Word and still want to find purchasers of their own thoughts at the expense of the congregation. Walther writes in his *Pastoraltheologie,* p. 52: "The minister who is called by a congregation must obligate himself to teach according to God's Word and the Church's Confession; he owes this to the congregation as a guaranty that he will not dispense his own wisdom, but will preach publicly and privately the pure Christian doctrine and not attempt to be master of their faith." The *quatenus* subscription annuls the Symbols as a Confession of faith.

The *quatenus* pledge has appeared in several forms.

---

[157] *Introductio in Libros Symb.* II, 2, § 11.

1. It is said that the Symbols "offer an essentially correct" presentation "of the chief doctrines." It is left to the whim of the individual what is to be regarded as "chief doctrines" and what is "an essentially correct" presentation of these fundamental doctrines.[158]

2. It has been said that the Symbols must be interpreted "historically." This is to say, not all doctrines contained in the Symbols are binding, but only those which the Church was compelled to discuss by reason of a doctrinal controversy in its midst. Everything in the Confessions which has not been "historically occasioned" must be regarded as not belonging to the substance of the Confessions. It is plain that this conception of the Symbols lets the subjective judgment of the individual decide how much of the Symbols he will accept as "historically occasioned." If only so much of the Symbols obligates us as has been the result of a controversy within the Church, we might have to cancel Article XI of the Formula of Concord as not binding upon us. For concerning this article the Formula says that "among the theologians of the Augsburg Confession there has not occurred as yet any public dissension whatever concerning the election of the children of God that has caused offense and has become widespread." It was only "to prevent disagreement and separation on its account *in the future* among our successors" that the article is here presented. (*Trigl.* 1062.) Again, under this "historical" view of the Symbols someone might get the notion to put even the doctrine of the inspiration of Scripture on the free list, for this doctrine had not been in controversy; and there is no special article on it in the Confessions; it is only incidentally that Scripture is "identified" with God's Word, etc. We have previously stated that modern theologians seek indulgence for their denial of the inspiration of Scripture in these facts.

3. Again, there are those who are ready to subscribe to the Confessions with the understanding that they be interpreted "according to Scripture," or "correctly." In this sense, Reformed theologians, including Calvin, have signed the Unaltered Augsburg Confession.[159] And a Lutheran pastoral conference in Germany proposed to the fathers of the Missouri Synod that the Lutheran Confessions be "understood according to Scripture and in the light of the error specifically

---

158 Cp. F. Bente, *American Lutheranism,* II, p. 39 ff., on the doctrinal basis of the General Synod prior to 1864.

159 See Walther: "*Warum sind die symbolischen Buecher unserer Kirche von denen, welche Diener derselben werden wollen, nicht bedingt, sondern unbedingt zu unterschreiben?*" (St. L., 1858, p. 6 ff.)

rejected" (*Lutheraner*, Vol. X, p. 90). That has a pious and Scriptural ring, but in fact it completely overlooks and does away with the purpose of the Symbols. By subscribing to the Symbols a man does not declare his readiness to interpret them "according to Scripture," but the minister or candidate in question makes the solemn declaration to the congregation that he has already discovered what Scripture teaches and he finds the Lutheran Confessions to be the expression of his own faith and confession.

4. It is a *quatenus* form of subscription when men profess to follow, not the "letter," but the "spirit," of the Confessions. The rationalists of the eighteenth century were very willing to sign the Confessions with this restriction. By "spirit" they meant their own spirit, which transformed the essence of Chistianity into heathen morality.

All these and other *quatenus* forms frustrate the purpose of the confessional obligation. The congregation can never know how much of the doctrine contained in the Confessions is being accepted. These *quatenus* forms are, at bottom, in conflict with common honesty and uprightness. And experience shows that behind the demand for a conditional subscription lies the refusal to accept certain doctrines of the Confessions. That applies also to those Lutherans of our day who insist on some form of the *quatenus* subscription because they are not in accord with the doctrinal position of the Confessions in the doctrines, e. g., of the Church, of the Ministry, of the Last Things (Chiliasm), and of Antichrist.

Arguing against the unconditional subscription, the *quatenus* men ask whether they are supposed to subscribe to all the historical, scientific and purely external remarks that are found here and there in the Confessions. Nobody asks them to do this. They are simply beclouding the issue. The confessional pledge covers only the doctrine. It is the confession of the Church, and the Christian Church is concerned about the doctrine. They also make much of the argument that no one can expect them to subscribe to "all exegetical proof" offered in the Confessions. No one expects them to do this. We readily grant that together with the passages that prove a doctrine passages are occasionally quoted which belong elsewhere. But what we do claim is that there is no doctrine found in the Confessions for which there is not ample Scripture proof offered. And we add this: the Confessions may serve as a model of Scripture proof in that they employ little "exegesis" – as this term is usually understood – but, to speak with Luther, are satisfied to let the *nuda Scriptura*, without much explanation, speak for itself. More of this in the next chapter, "Scripture and Exegesis." [160]

---

[160] On the question what the unconditional pledge means and what it does not mean, Dr. Walther in his essay "Why Are the Symbolical Books . . . to be Signed Unconditionally?" says the following: "Since the Symbols are confessions of the faith, or doctrine, of the Church, and are to be and desire to be nothing else, an unconditional subscription to them can mean nothing else than the solemn affirmation and oath, given to the Church by him who is entering on its service, that he has found the doctrinal content of the Symbols of our Church, without any exception whatever, as not conflicting, neither in a fundamental nor in a secondary point of doctrine, with Holy Scripture; that he, accordingly, sincerely believes in this doctrine as the divine truth and hence is resolved to preach this doctrine without adulteration. No matter, therefore, what place any doctrine may occupy in the doctrinal system of the Symbols and in what form it may occur there, whether it be the subject discussed *ex professo* or whether it occurs as an incidental reference, the unconditional subscription pertains to every one of them; none of them is excepted by the signer. Some doctrines, for example, are used in the Symbols merely to support the line of argumentation; but far from declaring these doctrines immaterial, our Church treats them as the irrefutable foundations of doctrine and takes for granted that they are gladly accepted by those who subscribe to the Symbols.

"On the other hand, since the Symbols were never intended to be anything else but confessions of faith and doctrine, the confessional pledge does not cover things which do not pertain to doctrine. As little as he who unconditionally signs the Symbols of the Church, his Symbols, thereby declares them to be the norm of German or Latin orthography or of a perfect style, so little does his signature pertain to things which belong in the domain of the human sciences. When, e. g., Art. VI of the Augsburg Confession quotes a passage from an old commentary on the First Epistle to the Corinthians, and Art. XX (of the Latin text) quotes a passage from the *De Vocatione Gentium* as statements by Ambrosius, and when Art. XVIII quotes a statement from the ancient writing *Hypognosticon* as a statement by Augustine, he who subscribes to the Augsburg Confession unconditionally self-evidently does not obligate himself to regard Ambrosius and Augustine as the authors of those books simply because they are attributed to them in the Confessions; and this would be the case even if it were not well known that the writer of this our fundamental Confession himself knew that these writings were customarily cited as written by these men, without directly ascribing the authorship to them. And as anything that is properly a subject for criticism does not bind the servant of the Church, so in general nothing in the Symbols binds him that belongs into the realm of history.

"This applies also to the interpretation given in the Symbols to individual Scripture passages. As an absolutely necessary requirement of an unobjectionable 'prophecy' or interpretation of Scripture the Apostle Paul himself names this: 'Having prophecy, let us prophesy according to the proportion of faith' (Rom. 12:7). From this Johann Gerhard draws this exegetical canon: 'Even though we may not arrive at the true and particular meaning of all passages, it suffices if in our interpretation we offer nothing conflicting with the analogy of faith.' Granted that the exegete did not succeed in finding the particular meaning of some Bible passage, but nevertheless gave it a meaning which is supported by other clear passages, he would indeed be mistaken in finding that particular truth in this passage, but he would not be erring in the doctrine. One who therefore subscribes to the Symbolical Books unconditionally is simply declaring that the interpretations found in them are 'according to the analogy of faith.' —

To show the relation between Holy Scripture and the Symbols of the orthodox Church, the following terms have been used: *norma* and *norma normata, norma primaria* and *secundaria.* Both terms express the truth that the Symbols are a norm, but not by themselves (*absolute*), but only in a certain respect (*secundum quid*), namely, a derived norm, because the doctrines confessed in our Symbols are taken from Scripture.[161] The purpose of the Symbols is brought out in the terms *norma decisionis* and *norma discretionis* (deciding norm and distinguishing norm). Scripture alone decides which doctrine is true, which is false; but from the attitude which one takes toward the Symbols of the Lutheran Church we learn whether he knows and accepts the Scripture doctrine or does not accept it (*norma discretionis discernit orthodoxos ab heterodoxis*).[162]

Mylius (d. 1607) and Hutter (d. 1616) and some later Lutheran theologians spoke of an inspiration of the Lutheran Symbols. They did not mean, of course, to place the Symbols on a plane with Scripture, but they merely wanted to state that the Symbols were produced under the special guidance and assistance of the Holy Ghost; Hollaz has shown from their own words that Mylius and Hutter used the term *inspiration* in a wider sense (*sensu latiori*).[163] But even with these precautions the Symbols should not be called "inspired." It is certainly better to reserve the term for the writings of the Apostles and Prophets. Walther adds to the words of Hollaz: "Shelvigius and I. G. Neumann likewise claim that the Symbolic Books might be called θεοπνεύστους, while Loescher, Carpzov, and others justly express their dissent." [164]

Since, furthermore, the argumentation in favor of a doctrine may be faulty (though the doctrine to be proved, or the conclusion, rests on an immovable, divine foundation and the auxiliary doctrines used to prove it, or the major and the minor, are perfectly correct), the unconditional subscription does not imply that the line of argumentation is not subject to improvement; in other words, that the form, the method, and the process of the argumentation is perfect and that hence every faithful servant of the Church would be held to use the method followed in the Symbols and no other. In this way our fathers understood the unconditional confessional pledge."

161 Chemnitz *Loci*, Wittenb., 1623, III, 235: "The Symbols are not something alongside or contrary to Scripture, but are the very marrow of Scripture. And so we also say that we accept Scripture in the sense which is delivered to us in the true and proved Symbols of the ancient Church."

162 A list of the terms is given in Walch, *Introd. in Libr. Symb.*, Jena, 1732, p. 932 *sqq.;* Baier-Walther, I, 139 *sqq.*

163 *Examen*, Proleg. II, qu. 27.

164 The treatise of Walther: "Why Are the Symbolical Books . . . to be Signed Unconditionally?" an essay adopted at the Western District Convention

16

Holy Scripture and Exegesis

All exegesis, whether it be in general the unfolding of the sense of Scripture [165] or in particular the explanation of (or rather the attempt to explain) the more difficult passages of Scripture,[166] is based on the fact that the entire Christian doctrine is revealed and set forth in Scripture passages so clear that the learned and unlearned alike can understand them; they do not stand in need of "exegesis" for explanation. If Scripture did not have this quality, it would not be for all Christians "a lamp unto their feet and a light unto their path," nor would all Christians be able to establish the truth of their faith by

---

of 1858, deals in its twenty pages more thoroughly with the question at issue than any other publication known to us. The same matter is treated in the "*Gutachten der Dorpater theologischen Fakultaet ueber die von der Deutschen Ev.-Luth. Synode von Iowa in Nordamerika ihr vorgelegten Fragen den kirchlichen Lehrkonsensus betreffend*" of 1866, signed by the Professors T. Harnack, Kurtz, v. Oettingen, M. von Engelhardt, W. Volck. *Lehre und Wehre* reviewed the "Dorpat Opinion," 1867, p. 257 ff. See also *Oeffentliches Kolloquium, abgehalten vom 13. bis 19. November 1867 zwischen den Vertretern der Synode von Missouri, Ohio u. a. St. und der Synode von Iowa."* – The nature and authority of the Symbols is treated from the modern theological viewpoint, e. g., in Nitzsch-Stephan in the chapter: "*Das Verhaeltnis des Protestantismus zur Tradition,*" p. 282 ff. The terminology *norma,* used of Scripture, and *norma normata,* used of the Symbols, does not mean anything to modern theology. Since it has renounced Scripture as the infallible Word of God, it has thereby in principle renounced the difference between Holy Scripture and the Symbols and other religious books. It has made of Scripture a *norma normata.* Its *norma normans* is the "Christian experience," the pious self-consciousness of the theologizing subject. It would be downright mockery if the modern theologians, who deny the inspiration of Scripture and the *satisfactio vicaria,* consented to subscribe to the Symbols of the Lutheran Church, because the entire doctrinal content of the Symbols rests on those two fundamental doctrines. – The article on the confessional obligation by Dr. von Burger, in the *R. E.,* 2d ed., XV, p. 86 f., agrees in most points with Dr. Walther's essay. Dr. Burger attacks especially the theological professors whose object in demanding "academic freedom" is to assail the Confessions of the Church. He also refutes the senseless assertion that the confessional obligation involves coercion.

165 The so-called *enarratio,* as, for instance, Luther's *Enarrationes in Genesin.* Thus old regulations for the examination of candidates for the ministry demand that the candidate be examined as to whether he possesses, besides the sound knowledge of all articles of the Christian faith, also the gift of "expounding the Scripture," the δύναμις ἑρμηνευτική, that is, the "gift and aptitude to teach others," the ability to proclaim the Scripture doctrine in the public ministry.

166 In this narrow sense, Quenstedt employs the term: "Scripture is interpreted when the genuine sense of the more difficult passages, in agreement with the mind and intention of the Holy Spirit and with the help of hermeneutical methods and rules, is aptly sought and shown" (*Systema* I, 199).

Scripture and in the light of Scripture to mark and avoid false teachers. The great teachers of the Church, Augustine, Luther, Chemnitz, etc., have always insisted that God gave His people a Bible which presents the entire Christian doctrine in all its parts in passages which need no clarification on the part of the exegetes. We have brought the proofs from Augustine under the heading of the perspicuity of Scripture. As Luther expresses it: "If you cannot understand the obscure, then stay with the clear" (St. L. V:338). No one need fear that if he follow this course, he may be deprived of one or the other doctrine of faith or life.

Good Papists and poor Protestants object here that in that case the special gift of explaining the Scriptures, which God gives to some Christians in preference to others, would be of no use. The objection is not valid. There is a wide territory open for the profitable exercise of the gift of interpreting Scripture in spite of the perfect clarity of Scripture in the sense just described. In the first place, Harless declares in his preface to Luther's explanation of John 17: "Even though the Word of God in itself does not need interpretation, still our hard hearts and deaf ears stand in need of the voice of the heralds and the preachers in the wilderness. And this again not as though Christ's words were too high and deep, too obscure and mysterious, but because, as Luther correctly saw, we human beings in our perverse desire to reach false heights, like blind idiots, take no notice of the divine simplicity of the words of Christ."[167] The first and foremost duty of the exegete consists in holding the flighty spirit of man to the simple word of Scripture and, where he has departed from it, to lead him back to the simple word of Scripture. Luther says that the sole purpose of all his writings and particularly of his exegetical works is to lead back into Scripture, to get every Christian and every teacher to base his faith on the bare Scripture, on the *"nuda" Scriptura,* minus any "gloss," the good glosses no less than the false interpretation. Luther therefore, as is well known, frequently uttered the wish that also his books might perish in order that Christians might base their faith on the *"nuda" Scriptura,* without any interpretation; every interpretation is less clear than Scripture, and every interpretation must be examined in the clearer light of Scripture. "No clearer book has been written on earth than Holy Scripture. Among all other books it is like the sun among all lights." (St. L. V:334.)

Fortunately Luther's wish that all his books might disappear was

---

[167] Leipzig, 1857, p. V.

not fulfilled. For the writings of Luther cannot but lead the flighty spirit of man to the bare Scriptures, without interpretation, and keep it there, so that every Christian and particularly every public teacher in the Church can say with Luther: "The Word they still shall let remain," the "*nuda*" *Scriptura.* This *manuductio ad nudam Scripturam* was necessary not only in Luther's day. The Church in all ages, up to the Last Day, needs it; for men will always be inclined, "in their perverse desire to reach false heights, like blind idiots, to take no notice of the divine simplicity of the words of Christ." Thus our day, too, needs exegetes – they do not have to be in every case professional theologians – who by God's grace possess principally four qualities: 1) they know Scripture to be God's own Word and treat it accordingly; 2) they have learned, from Scripture's own testimony, that Scripture is clear; 3) they concentrate their efforts upon the *manuductio ad nudam Scripturam;* 4) they uncover the deceit practiced when men propose, under the good name of exegesis, to shed light on Scripture by means of their human opinions. Zwingli asserted that "the most precious words concerning the eternal deity and the true manhood of Jesus Christ" must "by figures and tropes be made to agree with the right sense which faith demands." [168] Also modern theologians assert that Scripture must be "subordinated" to "faith" as the highest principle in theology; "faith" meaning the pious self-consciousness of the theologizing individual (Seeberg, *Dogmengesch.*, 2d ed., II, p. 289).

And this constitutes the second part of the work of the true exegete: he must be able to expose the abuse connected in ancient and modern times with the "exegesis according to the faith" or "according to the analogy of faith." Scripture must certainly be interpreted "according to the analogy of faith." But this term is used in a twofold, contradictory sense, with totally different results. Rightly used, it serves the proper interpretation of Scripture. Wrongly used, it serves utterly to pervert Scripture. Luther and the old theologians, who with him took the right course, understand by analogy of faith the clear Scripture passages that require no interpretation, but are lucid in themselves. The sum of these passages constitutes the "analogy," or the "rule of faith." The Apology defines the "rule of faith" when it says: "Besides, examples [as the life of the Rechabites] ought to be interpreted according to the rule, i. e., according to certain and clear passages of Scripture" (*Trigl.* 441, 60). And Luther reminds us:

---

[168] Quoted from Zwingli's answer to Luther's book *Dass diese Worte,* etc. (St. L. XX:1196.)

"Therefore you are to know that Scripture without any gloss is the sun and the whole light, from which all teachers receive their light; they do not shed light on the Scriptures" (St. L. XVIII:1293). He teaches that both the instructing and the refuting of error must be done "with clear passages, as with a bared and drawn sword, without any glosses or commentaries." These clear passages are the rule according to which the faithful teacher is to explain obscure passages, as far as this lies in his power. "The holy fathers," Luther says, "explained Scripture by taking the clear, lucid passages and with them shed light on obscure and doubtful passages" (St. L. XX:856). These "clear, lucid" passages are, of course, to be found in those places in Scripture which deal with a doctrine *ex professo*, in the so-called *sedes doctrinae*. Quenstedt says: "It is to be observed that every article of faith has its proper and native seat, from which it is determined" (*Systema* I, 349). Only in this way the principle is maintained: *Scriptura ex Scriptura explicanda est*. Luther: "In this manner Scripture is its own light. It is a fine thing when Scripture explains itself. Therefore do not believe the Pope's lies; freely regard as dark whatever is not approved by clear passages of Scripture. Thus we have first had to remove the error that the Scriptures are obscure and must be illuminated by the doctrines of men; this had taken a deep hold. It is certainly a capital error and a blasphemy; in fact, it amounts to taking the Holy Ghost to school and teaching Him how to speak." (St. L. XI:2335 f.)

Diametrically opposed to this view is the false conception of "faith," or the "analogy of faith," held by all those who do not permit the "*certae et clarae Scripturae*," the "clear, lucid passages of Scripture," to constitute the rule, or analogy, of faith, but substitute for it a "faith" which, with complete disregard of the clear and lucid passages, they have constructed out of their own notions. This "faith" is to be the light with which to elucidate the clear passages of Scripture, which need no elucidation whatever! The Sacramentarians were exegetes of this type. In order to evade Scripture and retain their own thoughts concerning the Lord's Supper, they proposed that Luther should disregard all passages dealing with the Lord's Supper and, like themselves, construct the doctrine of the Lord's Supper from John 6. The modern theologians belong in the same class of exegetes. In order not to be instructed and reproved by Scripture, but to be able, undisturbed by Scripture, to make the "pious self-consciousness" the source and norm of theology, they take recourse under the leadership of Schleiermacher and of Hofmann to the "whole of Scripture." And the old method of taking the Christian doctrines from the passages which treat of these doctrines they seek to discredit with the cry that this outmoded method converts Scripture into a "collection of proof-texts."

Exposing the fraud perpetrated by the "enthusiasts," who, under the guise of interpreting Scripture, by referring to John 6 entirely did away with Scripture, Luther wrote: "It is the arrogance and fatuous malice of the wicked devil who would in this serious matter make fools of us through these 'enthusiasts' by pretending a readiness to accept the instruction of Scripture if only he be first permitted to get rid of Scripture or twist it to suit his prejudice. Just as if I would deprive my opponent of his weapons by cunning words and gave him in place thereof painted paper weapons – just like his – and then would dare him to vanquish me with them and fight me off. Oh, that would be a daring hero – fit to be spit upon!" (St. L. XX:780.) Back of the proposal of the "enthusiasts" to explain the words of institution with John 6 lay the thought, more or less clearly expressed, that the sense of all Scripture passages, including the clear ones, must be determined by comparing them with other passages. Luther had no use for such an exegetical method. He wrote: [169] "The result of this method will be that no passage in Scripture will remain certain and clear, and the comparison of one passage with another will never end. . . . To demand that clear and certain passages be explained by drawing in other passages amounts to an iniquitous deriding of the truth (*nequiter veritatem illudere*) and the injection of fog into the light (*nebulas in lucem vehere*). If one set out to explain all passages by first comparing them with other passages, he would be mixing up Scripture into an uncertain and wild chaos (*totam Scripturam in infinitum et incertum chaos confundere*). Is not this plain enough? No doubt you will see that this is the case." Luther is unalterably convinced that God gave Holy Scripture such a form that the entire Christian doctrine is revealed and submitted in passages which need no "exegesis" (exegesis in the sense of removing obscurities). He who would determine the meaning of the clear passages through still other passages engages in a work of interminable adjustments, makes the entire Scriptures uncertain and obscure, and converts them into an inextricable chaos. Yes, there is the rule: "One passage must be explained by another," but, as Luther adds immediately: "Namely, a

---

[169] In a letter to Carlstadt, reprinted in De Wette, Luther's *Briefe*, etc., III, 231–240, translated by Dr. Hoppe in St. L. XX:325 ff.

doubtful and obscure passage (*locus ambiguus et obscurus*) must be explained by means of a clear and certain passage." The clear passage needs no further explanation. Shall we adopt the senseless exegetical method of illuminating the light by darkness and explaining the clear matter by the obscure? This method has been fostered carefully by the errorists of all times. After Luther had stated that in the obscure passages of Scripture nothing else is found "than what is found at other places in the clear passages," he adds: "Then the heretics come forward and explain the obscure passages according to their own mind and contend with them against the clear passages, the foundation of our faith." (St. L. V:335.)

These severe strictures of Luther apply in even a higher degree to the modern theologians who would explain the whole Bible and in particular also all clear passages of Scripture according to the "whole of Scripture." If anything is pure "human self-conceit" (*Menschenduenkel*), the very antithesis of "Scripture," it is this "whole of Scripture," which, introduced by Schleiermacher, has penetrated, particularly through Hofmann's influence, into the modern so-called Lutheran theology. This "whole of Scripture" lies entirely outside Scripture. It is the product of the illusion that the Christian doctrine forms a whole or a system agreeable to human reason and the several doctrines of Scriptures must be adjusted to fit into this system. Before us lies the proof that this exegetical method makes a mockery of the entire Christian truth and turns the entire Scriptures into a shapeless ruin. Modern theologians admit that Schleiermacher by means of the "whole of Scripture" cast the entire Christian doctrine overboard. And Hofmann, too, denied, as the result of his system, the inspiration of Scripture, the *satisfactio vicaria,* original sin, etc., and, by principle, the entire Christian doctrine, though he for his person did not draw this final conclusion. In short, exegesis according to the "whole of Scripture" does not permit Scripture to be its "own light," but this "whole of Scripture," which Schleiermacher, Hofmann, etc., extract from their own Ego, is made the light of Scripture.

Exegesis, in its double function of the *enarratio* of the Scriptural content and of the removal of obscurities by means of the clear passages, is a most serious and sacred occupation. The Scriptures are the Word of God, and adding to them or subtracting from them is strictly forbidden to everyone (Deut. 4:2). Whoever attempts to shed more light on dark passages of Scripture than Scripture itself offers in its clear passages is adding to God's Word. And whoever obscures clear passages by bringing in obscure passages is taking away from

God's Word. Let the exegete particularly study the words εἴ τις λαλεῖ, ὡς λόγια θεοῦ (1 Pet. 4:11). What he cannot speak as God's Word, he should leave unuttered. If he is not certain that he is speaking God's Word, he should say so and – following Luther's advice – leave the passage unexplained. If the exegete wishes to hold the right course and keep the fountain of the Christian doctrine clear, he must ever bear in mind the divine truth (Ps. 119:105; 2 Pet. 1:19) that "the Scriptures are a light in themselves," that *Scriptura sua radiat luce.* He must reject every interpretation which is based on something outside Scripture.

This principle takes in both the linguistic usage and the historical circumstances of the text. Interesting and important for apologetics as it is, e. g., to compare the New Testament Greek with the earlier Greek of Homer and with the contemporary Greek of Philo and Josephus and the monuments, etc., in the last analysis the linguistic usage of the New Testament alone decides the matter. We would be violating the fundamental tenet: *Scripturam ex Scriptura explicandam esse,* and introducing an element of uncertainty into our understanding of Scripture if we invested a word or a phrase with a meaning which it does not bear in Scripture itself. This is generally admitted. Our theologians lay particular stress upon it. As Homer, Plato, Aristotle, Athanasius, Jerome, etc., must be understood according to the linguistic usage which is peculiar to each, so Scripture, as it emphatically declares, demands the same treatment; otherwise we would be practicing eisegesis instead of exegesis. Compare, e. g., the chapter in Quenstedt: *An Sacra Scriptura seipsam interpretetur?* [170]

The same applies to the historical statements and circumstances. All historical and chronological data which are needed to the end of time for the correct understanding of Scripture are furnished by Scripture itself. The study of the Old and New Testament contemporary history has been given an undue importance in our day. Recently an essayist at a sectarian conference in St. Louis took occasion to assert that the layman could never be positively sure of the meaning of Scripture because the meaning of Scripture depended on the "historical background" with which only the experts were familiar. There you have again the Roman fundamental article of the obscurity of Scripture; only instead of the Pope you have the experts in Old and New Testament contemporary history to "hatch the eggs and become our idol" (Luther). To be sure, acquaintance with contemporary history,

---

170 *Systema* I, 199 *sqq.;* Calov, *Syst. Locorum Theol.* I, 469 *sqq.*

as it is based on what secular writers, historical monuments, etc., say, is important; important, for instance, for apologetics, with which we cannot entirely dispense. It enables us to show that the historical, etc., data of Holy Scripture are not fables but are largely confirmed by secular history. But, on the other hand, it must be maintained that the sure understanding of Scripture in no wise depends on the acquaintance with its secular-historical background, since the entire "historical background" necessary for a correct understanding of the meaning of Scripture is given in Scripture itself.

In fact, we go astray in our exegesis of Scripture as soon as we think that the historical background given in Scripture needs to be supplemented by material from secular history and permit this supplementation to have any decisive influence on our exegesis. Such a procedure, too, would be an infraction of the truth that Scripture shines in its own light and would introduce also an element of uncertainty into the interpretation of Scripture, for who will guarantee the correctness of the background taken only from secular history? The Bible is the only book in the world in which no historical errors can occur. – The most flagrant misuse of contemporary history is committed when men undertake to correct, or cast doubt upon, the historical data of Scripture on the basis of "contemporary history." We have pointed out above how modern theologians, who do not accept the Bible as God's Word, correct, or at least cast doubt upon, the historical statements of Scripture by means of the contemporary history furnished by Josephus.

We close this chapter with Luther's oft-repeated admonition never to substitute a human interpretation for the "text," i. e., for the words of Scripture themselves. He says: "With the text and from the foundation of the Holy Scriptures I have silenced and slain all my opponents. For whoever is well founded and practiced in the text will become a good and fine theologian, since a passage, or text, from the Bible has more weight than many commentators and glosses, which are not strong and round and do not help in the controversy." (Erl. 57, p. 7.) Again: "When the fathers teach anything, they do not trust their teaching, fearing it to be too obscure and uncertain, but they go to the Scriptures and take a clear passage out of it to shed light on their teaching. How should they have overcome the heretics if they had fought with their own glosses? They would have been regarded as fools and madmen; but when they brought forward clear texts which needed no glosses, so that reason was brought into captivity, the evil spirit himself with all his heresies was completely routed." (St. L.

XVIII:1293.) And so Luther further admonishes: "It must be the prime concern of a theologian to be well versed in the text, a *bonus textualis,* as it is called" (St. L. V:456). He complains about the many "commentaries and books," through which "the dear Bible is being buried and covered up so that no one takes note of the text." He refers to his own experience: "When I was young, I familiarized myself with the Bible, read it often, and became well acquainted with the text; so well acquainted that I knew where every passage that was mentioned was to be found; thus I became a *good textualis.* Not till then did I read the commentators. But finally I had to disregard them all and put them away because the use of them did not satisfy my conscience, and I had to take my stand again on the Bible; for it is much better to see with your own eyes than with another's." (St. L. XXII:54 f.) Thus Luther and his conscience stood on the bare text of Scripture, excluding all human interpretation.

The talk common in our day that all church bodies stand on Scripture and differ only in their interpretation of it is not in accordance with the facts. The Roman Catholic Church does not stand on Scripture, but on the papal interpretation of Scripture. The Reformed Churches, as far as they differ from the Lutheran Church, do not stand on Scripture, but on Zwingli's, Calvin's, etc., interpretation of Scripture. The Lutheran Church, however, does not stand on an interpretation of Scripture, but on Scripture itself. This is not a mere assertion. It can be proved by induction in the face of universal contradiction.

The Doctrine of God

(DE DEO)

THE only source of man's knowledge of God is God's self-revelation. There can be no absolute knowledge of God independent of God's self-revelation, because God dwells in the light which no man can approach, 1 Tim. 6:16, φῶς οἰκῶν ἀπρόσιτον. God has revealed Himself in a twofold manner: a) In creation, or in the realm of nature, and b) in His Word, or in Holy Scripture, the only source and norm of Christian doctrine. Accordingly we distinguish between a natural and a Christian knowledge of God.

1

The Natural Knowledge of God

(Notitia Dei naturalis)

Man knows by nature not only that there is a personal, eternal, and almighty God, the Creator, Preserver, and Ruler of the universe, but also that this God is holy and just, who demands and rewards the good and condemns and punishes the evil. This natural knowledge of God is derived

a. From the divine works of creation (ποιήματα τοῦ θεοῦ, *creaturae Dei*), which bear the unmistakable stamp of being God-made. Rom. 1:20, "The invisible things of Him from the creation of the world are clearly seen, being understood by the things that are made, even His eternal power and Godhead." This text states that though God is invisible, He can nevertheless be seen by man. Man need only observe the works of creation (τὰ ποιήματα τοῦ θεοῦ), and he will clearly see (καθορᾶται) God's invisible Being (τὰ ἀόρατα τοῦ θεοῦ), more particularly, His eternal power and Godhead (ἥ τε ἀΐδιος αὐτοῦ δύναμις καὶ θειότης).[1] It is noteworthy that heathen philosophers, using their reason (νοῦς), employ almost identical language, as when, for example, Aristotle says of God: "Though God is invisible to every mortal creature, He is visible from His very works."[2] Likewise Cicero: "You

---

[1] Concerning the use of ἀπό in ἀπὸ κτίσεως κόσμου: The New Testament employs ἀπό to denote the cause or source from which something is known, as in Matt. 7:16: "By their fruits (ἀπὸ τῶν καρπῶν αὐτῶν) ye shall know them"; and also as a temporal preposition, as in Matt. 19:4: "Which made them at (ἀπό) the beginning." Luther takes ἀπό in the first sense: *"an der Schoepfung der Welt."* We accept Luther's rendition because it fits well into the context, and classical Greek suggests it, as, for example, Aristotle. The exegetes are not agreed.

[2] *De Mundo,* cap. VI.

do not see God, and yet you learn to know God from His works."[3] (The cosmological argument for the existence of God.)

b. From God's continuous operation both in the realm of nature and in human history. From Acts 14:15-17 we learn that although God suffered the heathen to walk in their own ways, He nevertheless gave them abundant witness of Himself in the realm of nature. The manner of this divine self-manifestation is described by St. Paul: "He did good and gave us rain from heaven and fruitful seasons, filling our hearts with food and gladness." And from Acts 17:26-28 we learn that God manifests Himself also in the history of mankind. God made the human race stem from one progenitor and occupy the entire world according to the chronological and geographical boundaries fixed by Him. The purpose of the history of the human race in both its unity and its diversity is that men should seek (ζητεῖν) the Lord, if they might feel and find Him (ψηλαφεῖν . . . εὑρίσκειν). God's guiding hand is evident not only in the history of the nations, but also in the life of every individual; for St. Paul adds: "He is not far from every one of us, for in Him we live and move and have our being." And thus "the history of the world is also the judgment of the world." (Historico-theological argument for the existence of God.)

c. From the divine Law written into the heart of all men. In the realm of nature and in history God approaches man through things outside man. By writing His Law in the heart of man, however, God confronts man directly from within man's nature. He manifests Himself as the holy and righteous God, who demands and rewards the good and condemns and punishes the evil. St. Paul says that the Gentiles know the judgment of God, τὸ δικαίωμα τοῦ θεοῦ (Rom. 1:32), and even without the written Decalog they "show the work of the Law written in their hearts, their conscience also bearing witness, and their thoughts the meanwhile accusing or else excusing one another" (Rom. 2:14-15). The text states that man's conscience is God's tribunal within man and is recognized as such by man. This explains the attempts of the heathen to propitiate God by idol worship, sacrifices, asceticism, etc., and thus to silence their accusing consciences. (Moral argument for the existence of God; the proof from the fact of the Moral Law; proof from "practical reason.")[4]

It is evident therefore that atheism of all shades – crass atheism,

---

[3] *Deum non vides, tamen Deum agnoscis ex operibus eius. Tuscul. Disputt.* I, 28.

[4] For other proofs for the existence of God see Baier-Walther, I, p. 26 ff.

or pantheism, or polytheism, or agnosticism — is neither rational nor scientific. On the contrary, atheism springs from the suppression and denial of the natural knowledge of God. And this suppression has its source in man's love of immorality. St. Paul describes the representatives of atheism as men "who hold down the truth in unrighteousness," τὴν ἀλήθειαν ἐν ἀδικίᾳ κατέχειν (Rom. 1:18). Only he who suppresses his reason (νοῦς) can assert that there are no proofs for the existence of God. Scripture says that God's invisible nature and His eternal power and deity are clearly perceived from the things that have been made, τοῖς ποιήμασιν νοούμενα (Rom. 1:20).

In its sphere the natural knowledge of God is ἀλήθεια, the truth (Rom. 1:18). The Apology says: "*Ius naturale vere est divinum, quia est ordinatio divinitus impressa*" (*Trigl.* 366, 12). This leads to the question whether man can suppress the natural knowledge of God so completely that it fails to function or disappears entirely. Hollaz is undoubtedly right when he denies this: "It is possible that in theory men become atheists. By nature they are not atheists, but they become such when God in His justice forsakes them and the devil blinds them; not by a total eradication of the light of nature, but by the suppression of its function and exercise; nor is man ever an atheist throughout life and permanently, but only when the paroxysm comes upon him. For the law of nature will never permit anyone to entertain as his deliberate and settled conviction the conclusion that there is no God. Though the mind of a wicked person may be put to sleep and fall into a stupor, so that it no longer thinks about God, it is impossible to conceive of anyone whose conscience will not finally assert itself and in the very hour of death accuse man of having ignored God." (*Examen* I, cap. I, qu. 5.) This raises another question: Is the natural knowledge of God innate (*innata*) or acquired (*acquisita*)? It is both. That it is innate is evident from Rom. 2:15: "The Gentiles show the work of the Law written in their hearts," τὸ ἔργον τοῦ νόμου γραπτὸν ἐν ταῖς καρδίαις αὐτῶν. But man can exercise and increase his innate knowledge by contemplating the universe, and thus it becomes *notitia Dei acquisita* (acquired knowledge of God). Quenstedt says: "The natural knowledge of God is twofold; partly ἔμφυτος or by nature impressed upon the minds of men in their very origin, innate and implanted, by which men recognize God through certain principles born within them, by certain fragments, as it were, and remains of the divine image, without any research or operation of the mind; partly ἐπίκτητος, or acquired, because it is evolved through the inborn principles of nature through a process of reasoning and the accurate contemplation of created things, or gathered from the works of God in creation and those traces of divinity which are scattered throughout the universe." (*Systema* I, 366.)

As to the practical result of the natural knowledge of God, Scripture teaches two things:

a. In man's present condition the natural knowledge of God is entirely insufficient to attain salvation. It arouses the conscience of man, but it cannot quiet the awakened conscience; it shows man that there is a God and a divine Law, but it does not enable man to keep this Law. The natural knowledge of God leaves man with an evil conscience and under the curse (Rom. 1:19, 21; 1:32; 2:14-15). Without faith in the Gospel, man remains *extra ecclesiam Dei* and in a state of hopelessness and despair (Eph. 2:12: "Being strangers from the covenants of promise, having no hope and without God in the world").

b. Nevertheless the natural knowledge of God has a positive value. First, it is the foundation of civil righteousness (*iustitia civilis*); which is indispensable for the maintenance of all social relations. The Apology quotes Aristotle to that effect and sets forth the great value of the "righteousness of reason" (*iustitia rationis*). (*Trigl.* 127, 22—24.) For this reason statesmen, also among the heathen, have raised the question whether it is advisable to grant the right of citizenship to avowed atheists. — The natural knowledge of God is of value also for the Church. For one thing, the Church has its temporary home in the body politic; and civil righteousness, which maintains order and peace, thus serves the Church indirectly. (1 Tim. 2:1-2.) Furthermore, the Law written into the heart of man serves as the point of contact when the Church preaches the Law. Luther: "If the Natural Law had not been inscribed and placed by God into the heart, one would have to preach a long time before the consciences are touched; to a donkey, horse, ox, cow, one would have to preach 100,000 years before they would accept the Law in spite of the fact that they have ears, eyes, and heart, as man has; they can also hear it, but it does not touch their heart. Why? What is at fault? Their soul is not so constituted and formed that this preaching would take hold. But when the Law is propounded to man, he soon says: Yes, it is so; I cannot deny it. Of this validity he could not be convinced so quickly were it not for the fact that the Law is written in his heart. Since, however, it is already in his heart, although completely blurred, it is aroused by the preaching of the Word, so that the heart cannot help confessing that we must, as the Commandments read, honor, love, and serve God, for He alone is good and does good not only to the pious, but also to the wicked" (St. L. III:1053). Our Lutheran theologians are very careful when they discuss the natural knowledge of God. On the one hand, they set forth its value in great detail;[5] on the other hand, they stress its inadequacy and utter insufficiency in bringing man to salvation.[6] They

---

[5] Speaking of the value of the Natural Law and warning against identifying it absolutely with the written Law, the Decalog, Chemnitz enumerates the following points: 1) Paul discusses this matter *ex professo* in Romans 1 and 2 and ascribes honorable terms to the Natural Law. He calls it God's truth (Rom. 1:18); God's manifestation (v. 19); God's judgment (v. 32); the work of the Law written into the heart at man's very creation (Rom. 2:15). And even the term *lex naturae* is taken from Scriptures: "The Gentiles do by nature the things of the Law" (Rom. 2:14). And we gratefully acknowledge the blessing that God did not permit the light of the Law to be totally extinguished through the Fall, but wanted certain remnants of it to remain, so that among men there might be a political society in which God through the Gospel could gather His Church. The terms employed by Paul show that these remnants are indeed to be considered highly. 2) The comparison between the natural and the written Law has the useful purpose of teaching us to respect and praise all those pronouncements which philosophers, poets, historians, legislators, etc., made on moral issues and which agree with the Natural Law, for they are the divine right and the divinely revealed truth of God. Paul does not hesitate to quote even in a most important theological discussion the pagan author Menander's sentence: "Evil communications corrupt good manners" (1 Cor. 15:33). 3) It is also helpful to the end that we recognize the testimony of the conscience in the unregenerate as a genuine testimony, lest man deaden the accusing thoughts (Rom. 2:15) under the pretense that the testimony of the conscience is an empty fantasy, causing worry only to women, whereas in reality it is the judgment of God convicting man of his sin. 4) The comparison of the unwritten with the written Law enables us to observe in which points the natural knowledge of the Law is obscured, where the judgment is corrupt, and which acts, both good and evil, are unknown to reason and revealed only in the Law. (*Loci,* II, 103 f.; ed. Viteb.)

[6] Chemnitz: "What is the natural knowledge, what is its character, its extent, and its efficacy? Strictly speaking, it is non-existent, or imperfect, or inactive. It is *non-existent,* because in the entire realm of philosophy there is no knowledge whatsoever of the gracious promise of the forgiveness of sin. This has been revealed to the Church by the Son of God, who is in the bosom of the Father (John 1:18; Matt. 11:27; 1 Cor. 1:21; 2:7). – It is imperfect, because the Gentiles knew only a part of the Law. Concerning the worship of the heart commanded in the First Table, reason knows nothing definite; at best, the heathen philosophers can give some instructions concerning outward conduct. It is inactive, for although the knowledge that there is a God, and that He prescribes an obedience which carefully distinguishes between good and evil, is inscribed in the human heart, nevertheless man's assent to this knowledge is not only weak, but is frequently suppressed entirely by horrible doubt. This fact is exemplified in *Tuscul.,* where Cicero, in a discussion on the immortality of the soul, says to Anthony: 'Examine carefully Plato's book concerning the soul; you can find nothing better.' Anthony answered: 'I have often done it. But I cannot understand that while I am reading it, I agree; and when I lay it aside and begin to meditate concerning the immortality of the soul, all assent disappears.'" (*Op. cit.,* I, 20 *sq.*)

condemn those who deny that there is a natural knowledge of God as well as the great number of those who admit men to heaven on the basis of their natural knowledge of God. And in this criticism they spare neither friend nor foe.[7]

2

The Christian Knowledge of God

The Christian knowledge of God, which is derived from God's Word, the Holy Scriptures, is Trinitarian; in other words: the Christian knows that the one true God is Father and Son and Holy Ghost. Luther's thesis is correct: "The Holy Scriptures teach that God is absolutely one and that He is also three persons, absolutely distinct" (St. L. X:177).

First, Holy Scripture, both the Old and the New Testament, teaches that God is *one* (monotheism). Deut. 6:4: "The Lord, our God, is one Lord"; 1 Cor. 8:4: "There is none other God but one." The entire Scriptures may fittingly be called a mighty protest against polytheism. In the Old Testament the gods of the heathen are called non-gods (לֹא אֱלֹהִים, Jer. 2:11), nonentities, vanities without existence (אֱלִילִים, Lev. 19:4; 26:1); and in the New Testament "nothing" (1 Cor. 8:4), "vanities" (Acts 14:15). They can neither harm nor help man, because there is no breath in them (לֹא רוּחַ בָּם), and they are a vanity, a dream (הֶבֶל הֵמָּה) (Jer. 10:5, 14-15). Scripture therefore demands

[7] Gerhard in *Loci, locus "De Natura Dei,"* § 63, lists those who err *in defectu:* the Socinians, who in denying that the first man was created in the image of God naturally deny that remnants of the divine image remain in fallen man; Flacius, who held that no true rudiments of the knowledge of God remain in man, and others. In § 81 he lists those who err *in excessu:* a) Certain Church Fathers and Scholastics, who held that "philosophy at one time by itself justified the Greeks; for many are the ways to salvation" (Clemens Alexandrinus). Thus also Justin Martyr, Irenaeus, Tertullian, Epiphanius, Jerome, Chrysostom, etc. b) Certain Papists, such as Andradius and Erasmus, who held that Cicero is leading a quiet life among those in heaven. c) Some among the Calvinists, as, for instance, Zwingli, who placed "Numa, Aristides, Socrates, etc., among the blessed dwellers in heaven" *(Expos. Fidei)* and declared: "A heathen, if he nurses a pious mind within himself, is a Christian, even though he is ignorant of Christ." (Vitus Winshemius: "Beware, my hearers, of the heaven of the Zwinglians: I should not like to live in that heaven; I should be afraid of the club of Hercules.") d) The Photinians, who hold that the heathen could by nature reach the knowledge of things necessary unto salvation. The Racovian catechism (pp. 25–26) teaches that it is sufficient to salvation to know "that God is, that He is only one, that He is eternal, that He is perfectly just, that He is perfectly wise and perfectly powerful."

of man a monotheistic worship. Ex. 20:3: "Thou shalt have no other gods before Me"; likewise Mark 12:29-30, where the command to worship the Lord with all our heart, all our soul, all our mind, and all our strength follows immediately upon the great monotheistic sentence: "Hear, O Israel, The Lord, our God, is one Lord." A plurality of gods would of necessity require a division of our adoration according to the number of gods. The polytheistic worship is in no wise a worship of God, *cultus divinus.* The sacrifices of the Gentiles are offered not to God, but to devils (1 Cor. 10:20). If the Gentiles really desire to worship God, they must discard their gods and turn to the one true God. Paul and Barnabas summarize the irreconcilable conflict between polytheism and monotheism in their address to the heathen of Lystra: "We preach unto you that ye should turn from these vanities unto the living God" (Acts 14:15). Thus Scripture teaches monotheism and denounces polytheism in no uncertain terms.

But Scripture just as definitely teaches that the one God is Father, Son, and Holy Ghost. There are three Persons in the one God. For the terms *Father, Son,* and *Holy Ghost* denote Persons. The Christian Baptism is Trinitarian, a Baptism in the name of the Father and of the Son and of the Holy Ghost (Matt. 28:19). The Christian benediction likewise is Trinitarian: "The grace of the Lord Jesus Christ, and the love of God, and the communion of the Holy Ghost" (2 Cor. 13:14). And at Christ's Baptism God revealed Himself as the Triune God. "Go to the Jordan, and there learn the Trinity" (Matt. 3:16-17), where, as Luther says, "the Divine Majesty reveals itself as follows: The Father in the voice, the Son in His humanity, and the Holy Spirit in the form of a dove: three distinct Persons and yet only one God, one almighty, eternal, divine essence" (St. L. XII:1133). The fact that God clearly revealed Himself as the Triune God also in the Old Testament – though not so clearly as in the New Testament – will be treated in a special chapter.

This Christian knowledge of God is brought to us and is wrought in us not by God's self-revelation in nature, history, and man's conscience, but solely by God's self-revelation in His Word. For in Holy Scripture, which is God's Word, God speaks to us and with us and there reveals His innermost being and His loving heart. The natural knowledge of God, as Luther says (St. L. XII:629 ff.), enables us to know God, as it were, from without, from His works, just as we learn something of the character of the builder from the quality of the house he builds. Holy Scripture, however, which is God's Word to man, gives us the Christian knowledge of God; it reveals God's inner being, the gracious purposes in the mind of God, just as one man reveals his true nature, his feelings, and the thoughts of his heart to another by his spoken words. Modern theology attempts to erase this vast difference between the natural and the Christian knowledge of God. And this difference would indeed disappear if the Bible were no more than the record of human concepts of God as they were developed under Jewish and Christian influence. But, thank God! this Modernist claim is entirely groundless. Christ and the Apostles "identify" Scripture with God's Word without any restrictions. If, therefore, we abide in the Scriptures, we hear what God declares about Himself. We learn that the one true God is the Father, the Son, and the Holy Ghost as well as what kind of thoughts He has entertained from eternity toward fallen mankind. This brings us to a discussion of the practical value of the Christian knowledge of God.

The natural knowledge of God cannot deliver us from an evil conscience. The Christian knowledge of God, however, calms the troubled conscience. In fact, it is our salvation. Scripture does not propose the doctrine of the Trinity as an academic question or a metaphysical problem. With the proclamation that in the one eternal God there are three Persons of one and the same divine essence Scripture combines the further gracious message that God so loved the world that He gave His only-begotten Son into death as the Savior from the guilt of sin and death; that in the fullness of time, the eternal Son became incarnate and by His vicarious satisfaction reconciled the world to God and that the Holy Ghost engenders faith and thus applies to man the salvation gained by Christ. When the Christian confesses, "I believe in God the Father, Son, and Holy Ghost," he is saying, "I believe in that God who is gracious to me, a sinner."

Throughout the history of the Christian Church, men have taken offense at the prolonged and sometimes acrimonious battle which the Church fought to preserve the doctrine of the Trinity. But the stakes in this controversy were high: the preservation of the Christian knowledge of God and man's salvation. The Church of the Reformation, too, confesses in the first article of the Augustana the doctrine of the Trinity and renounces any and all fellowship with the deniers of the Trinity. The Apology maintains that all Anti-Trinitarians who have arisen within the Church are outside the Christian Church.[8] Turning to

---

[8] Article I, *Trigl.*, p. 103: "The First Article of Our Confession our adversaries approve, in which we declare that we believe and teach that there is *one divine essence, undivided,* etc., and yet that there are three distinct *persons,* of the same divine essence, and coeternal, Father, Son, and Holy Ghost. This

Luther, we find that he likewise zealously maintained the doctrine of the Trinity as he did the central doctrine of the Christian faith, justification by faith. The two doctrines are found side by side in Luther's writings, not only in carefully and precisely drawn theological theses,[9] but in all his writings,[10] and especially in his sermons. We call attention especially to two sermons for Trinity Sunday, in which Luther sets forth in popular language the difference between the natural and the Christian knowledge of God and the indivisible connection between the doctrine of the Trinity and justification. (St. L. XII:628 ff.; XIII:664 ff.) Every theologian will derive benefit from these sermons. In the first sermon Luther says in part: "This is the revelation and knowledge Christians have of God; they not only know Him to be one true God, who is independent of and over all creatures, and that there can be no more than this one true God, but they know also what this one true God is in His essential, inscrutable essence. The reason and wisdom of man may go so far as to reach the conclusion, although feebly, that there must be one eternal divine Being, who has created, and who preserves and governs, all things. Man sees such a beautiful and wonderful creation in the heavens and on the earth, one so wonderfully, regularly, and securely preserved and ordered, that he must say: It is impossible that this came into existence by mere chance or that it originated and controls itself; there must have been a Creator and Lord from whom all these things proceed and by whom they are governed. Thus God cannot but be known by His creatures, as St. Paul says: 'For the invisible things of Him from the creation of the world are clearly seen, being understood by the things that are made, even His eternal power and Godhead (Rom. 1:20).' This is the knowledge (*a posteriori*) that we have when we contemplate God from without, in His works and government; as one, looking upon a castle or house from without would learn something about its lord or keeper. But from within (*a priori*) no human wisdom has been able to conceive what God is in Himself or in His internal essence. Nor can anyone know or give information of it except it be revealed to him by the Holy

---

article we have always taught and defended, and we believe that it has, in Holy Scripture, sure and firm testimonies that cannot be overthrown. And we constantly affirm that those thinking otherwise are outside of the Church of Christ, and are idolaters, and insult God."

[9] Cp. *Opp. v. a.* IV, 470 ff.: "*Disputatio theologica de mysterio sanctae trinitatis,*" of 1544, and "*Disputationes duae de unitate essentiae divinae et de distinctione personarum in divinitate,*" of 1545. The German translation: St. L. X:177 ff.

[10] See especially *Exposition of the Last Words of David,* St. L. III:1884 ff.

Spirit. For no one knoweth, as Paul says (1 Cor. 2:11), the things of a man save the spirit of man which is in him, even so the things of God knoweth no man, but the Spirit of God. From without I may see what you do, but what your intentions are and what you think, I cannot see. Again, neither can you know what I think unless I enable you to understand it by word or sign. Much less can we know what God in His own inner and secret essence is until the Holy Spirit, who searcheth and knoweth all things, yea, the deep things of God – as Paul says above – reveals it to us. He revealed it in this article, in which He teaches us the existence in the Divine Majesty of the one undivided essence, but this in such manner that there is, first, the Person who is called the Father; and of Him the Second Person called the Son, born from eternity; and proceeding from both of these is the Third, namely, the Holy Ghost. These three Persons are not of separate essence from each other, as individual brothers or sisters are, but they have one and the same eternal, undivided, and indivisible essence in common. This, I say, is not discovered or reached by human reason. It is revealed from heaven above. Therefore only Christians can intelligently speak of what the Godhead essentially is, and of His outward manifestation in His creatures and of His will toward men concerning their salvation. For all this is told them by the Holy Spirit, who reveals and proclaims it through the Word.

"Those who have no revelation and who judge according to their own wisdom, such as the Jews, Turks, and heathen, must consider this teaching the greatest error and rankest heresy; they must say that we Christians are mad and foolish in setting up three gods, when, according to all reason – yea, even according to the Word of God – there can be but one God. It would not be reasonable, they will say, that there should be more than one householder over the same house, more than one lord or sovereign over the same government; much less reasonably should more than one God reign over heaven and earth. They imagine that thus with their wisdom they have completely overthrown our faith and exposed it to the derision and scorn of all the world. As if we were all blockheads and egregious fools and could not see their logic as well as they! But, thank God, we have understanding equal to theirs and can argue as convincingly, or more so, as they with their Alkoran and Talmud, that there is but one God. . . . Now, we Christians have the Scriptures, which we know to be the Word of God. The Jews also have them, from whose fathers they have descended to us. From these Scriptures, and from no other source, we have obtained all that is known of God and divine works, from the beginning of the world.

Even among the Turks and the heathen all their knowledge of God — excepting what is manifestly fable and fiction — came from the Scriptures. And our knowledge is confirmed and proved by great miracles, even to the present day. These Scriptures declare concerning this article that there is no God, or Divine Being, save this one alone. They not only manifest Him to us from without, but they lead us into His inner essence and show us that in Him there are three Persons; not three gods, or three different kinds of deity, but the same undivided, divine essence. . . . And what help will it afford you if you are not able to say more than that God is merciful to the pious and will punish the wicked? Who will assure you that you are pious and that you please God with your papistic or Turkish monkery and holiness? Is it enough that you say: God will reward with heaven such as are faithful to the order? No, dear brother, you may not order this matter according to your whims and imagination. I could do that as well as you. Such peculiar ideas are indeed widespread. One devises a black, and another a gray monk's cowl. Instead, we should hear and know what God's counsel is, what is His will and mind. This none can know of his own wisdom, and no book on earth can teach it except the Scriptures. These God Himself has given, and they make known to us that He sent His Son into the world to redeem us from sin and the wrath of God and that whosoever believes in Him should have everlasting life."

3

The Trinitarian Controversies

It is a mistaken idea that the doctrine of the Trinity and the deity of Christ were developed by the church councils of the fourth and fifth centuries. On the basis of the oral and written Word of the Apostles the Apostolic Church knew and accepted these doctrines. (Acts 2:42; Eph. 2:20; 2 Thess. 2:15). Luther therefore is right when he says that the doctrines formulated by the Councils of Nicaea, Constantinople, Ephesus, and Chalcedon are presented "far more abundantly and powerfully" in the Holy Scriptures themselves (St. L. XVI:2248). Nevertheless, the Christian Church has been compelled to fight bitter wars not only against professed Anti-Trinitarians outside the Church, against heathen, Jews, Mohammedans,[11] but also against

[11] The Koran says: "Believe in God and in His messenger [Jesus], but say nothing of the Triad. Avoid that, and you will be better off. There is only one God. Far be it from Him to have a son! . . . How can the Creator of heaven and earth have a son, since He has no wife?" (Quoted in Baier-Walther, I, 131.)

those in her own borders who disturbed and disrupted the Church by teaching a doctrine of God which was nothing but the result of their own speculation. Some maintained that the Church must discard the three Persons in order to retain the unity of God; others, however, renounced the unity of God (the εἷς θεός) in order to maintain – so they claimed – the three distinct Persons in the divine essence. Modernism, which rejects Scripture, naturally also rejects the doctrine of the Trinity. In line with the Koran's ridicule of this doctrine ("Triad – the Creator has no wife") the doctrine of three Persons in one God has been represented as "establishing a heavenly family."

Since the Christian knowledge of God consists in this, "that we worship one God in Trinity and Trinity in Unity, neither confounding the Persons nor dividing the Substance," the Christian Church must necessarily take an uncompromising position a) against all such as deny the three Persons and b) against all who deny the one God, or the one divine essence.

A. THE CHRISTIAN CHURCH AND UNITARIANISM

Unitarianism – known also as Monarchianism and Anti-Trinitarianism – has appeared in various forms. For practical purposes the Monarchians have been divided into two classes, modal and dynamic. The Modalists of the third century held that God is a Unity (μονάς) and therefore unipersonal. This unipersonal God has revealed Himself successively in three different modes, or forms: In the Father as Creator, in the Son as Redeemer, and in the Holy Ghost as Sanctifier. Father, Son, and Holy Ghost are not three distinct Persons, or hypostases, but merely three roles, or parts (πρόσωπα), played by the one divine. Person. Modal Monarchianism as advocated by Noetus of Smyrna, the Patripassian Praxeas, and especially Sabellius (excommunicated 260), at first appealed to many because it not only upheld monotheism over against pagan polytheism, but also taught a certain trinity in God's mode of revelation and apparently also emphasized the deity of Christ. Dynamic Monarchianism, on the other hand, teaches that Jesus was a mere man, who was pre-eminently endowed by the indwelling of the *Logos*, a power [*dynamis*] emanating from the unipersonal God. Likewise the Holy Spirit is only a divine power operative in Moses, the Prophets, and particularly in Jesus. The three divine names are therefore actually no more than the personification of such divine attributes as omnipotence, love, grace. Jesus may be called the Son of God because, under the Logos influence, He was able to establish a moral union with God, i. e., His will was in perfect agreement with God's will. As a result of the indwelling of the Logos and the Holy Spirit, Jesus was "adopted" as God's Son (Adoptionism), received the power to perform miracles, and ultimately attained a permanent oneness with God. Dynamic Monarchianism was repudiated by the Church when its chief representative, Paul of Samosata, was excommunicated in 272. While Modalism and Dynamism differ in many important points, they are agreed in their categorical denial of the three distinct Persons in God. The Photinians, adherents of Photinus (bishop of Sirmium, d. 366 A. D.) were anti-Trinitarians; their teaching was revived by the Socinians of the 16th century. In our day all those Protestant theologians who reject the doctrine of "the two natures" in Christ, or the "*enhypostasia*" of the human nature of Christ, holding that the human nature of Christ is a person by itself, distinct from the Person of the Son of God, are to be classed with the Unitarians. When Seeberg, e. g., says (in *Grundwahrheiten,* p. 115): "This eternal energy of love [God's] so filled the human soul of Jesus that it became its content. This is the deity of Christ," he might be classed as a Dynamic Monarchian.[12] Most of the English, American, and German Unitarians are Dynamic Monarchians.

The Christian Church has always successfully met and overcome Unitarianism by the following three Scripture proofs:

a. The names Father, Son, and Holy Ghost can denote only three self-subsisting persons, *drei Ich.* No one who hears these names of God will think of three modes of appearance or three activities of the same person.

b. Personal actions, such as knowing, willing, teaching, reproving, speaking, are ascribed to each of the three, Father, Son, and Holy Ghost. Scripture says that the Father and the Son "know" (γινώσκειν, Matt. 11:27); that the Son "declares" (ἐξηγεῖσθαι, John 1:18), and "wills" (θέλειν, John 17:24; Luke 22:42); that the Holy Ghost "teaches" (διδάσκειν, John 14:26); "reproves" (ἐλέγχειν, John 16:8); "speaks" (λαλεῖν, Acts 28:25). All these predicates denote personal acts. Here the axioms apply: *Actiones semper sunt personarum sive suppositorum intelligentium. Opera sunt personis propria.*

c. Scripture expressly describes the relation between Father, Son, and Holy Ghost as ἄλλος καὶ ἄλλος καὶ ἄλλος. In His relation to the Son, the Father is expressly called ἄλλος; [13] and again, in His relation to the

12 See further, in Vol. II, "The Personal Union and the Christological Theories of Modern Theology."

13 John 5:32: "There is another (ἄλλος) that beareth witness of Me; v. 37: "And the Father Himself, which hath sent Me, [He, ἐκεῖνος] hath borne witness of Me."

Father and the Son, the Holy Ghost is expressly called ἄλλος παράκλητος (John 14:16). The Athanasian Creed therefore says correctly: *Alia est persona Patris, alia Filii, alia Spiritus Sancti.* The Augustana reproduces the ecclesiastical *usus loquendi* of "person" fully when it states: "And the term 'person' they use as the Fathers have used it, to signify not a part or quality in another, but that which subsists of itself" (Art. I).[14]

B. THE CHRISTIAN CHURCH AND TRITHEISM AND SUBORDINATIONISM

The unity of God is denied by the Tritheists and the Subordinationists, both of whom ascribe to the one and indivisible Divine Being, in addition to the three Persons, also three divine essences, or natures. Tritheism assumes that these alleged three essences are of equal quality, while Subordinationism teaches that they are of unequal quality. The chief representatives of Tritheism were John Philoponus, toward the end of the sixth century, and Roscellin, in the eleventh century.[15] Subordinationism is taught by the Arians and Semiarians, Arminians,[16] and even some modern Lutherans, especially Kahnis, who speaks of the Son and the Holy Ghost as "God in the second and third sense of the word."[17]

---

[14] There is no foundation for the claim of modern theologians that they have filled the term "person" with a richer meaning than the ancient Church was able to do. This will be discussed in chap. 8, B.

[15] Both of these men attempted to harmonize the Scripture doctrine of the Trinity with human reason in the interest of apologetics. They imagined that what holds true of human persons: *"Quot personae, tot essentiae,"* must also be applied to the three Persons in the Godhead: *"Quot personae divinae, tot essentiae divinae."* But certainly neither God's actions nor His essence are subject to human reasoning. Scripture — and the Christian Church — teaches *"tres personas et unam numero essentiam in divinitate."* — Roscellinus renounced his error at the Synod of Soissons, 1092. Roscellinus (a nominalist) was right in denying the objective existence of the genera and species; he erred in applying to the three Persons in the one God what was true of three human beings. (Cp. R. E., 2d ed., XVI, p. 47 ff.; XIII, p. 52 ff.)

[16] The Arminian Limborch is willing to grant that the divine essence belongs to the Son and the Holy Ghost, but he vitiates the Trinitarian doctrine by adding: "It is evident that with respect to these three persons a certain subordination obtains. . . . There is a certain superiority *(supereminentia)* of the Father over the Son, and of the Father and the Son over the Holy Ghost. It is more exalted to beget than to be begotten, to send than to proceed; the One who sends has power over the One that is sent, but not the One that is sent over Him who is sending." *Theol. Christ.*, II, 17, 25-26. Similarly the Arminian Episcopius, *Inst. Theol.*, IV, 2, 32.

[17] See Baier-Walther, II, 53 ff., for pointed quotations from Kahnis' *Dogmatik* and also from Hofmann's *Schriftbeweis*. G. Stoeckhardt discusses the position of Modernist Lutherans in "Der moderne Subordinationismus im Licht der Schrift," *Lehre und Wehre*, 40, 17–323 *passim*.

In opposition to Tritheism (three equal divine essences) and Subordinationism (three unequal divine natures), the Christian Church maintains that the Divine Being cannot exist in three essences, or natures, because the Scriptures ascribe to the Father, to the Son, and to the Holy Ghost the one divine essence (*eadem numero essentia*).

Scripture teaches, in the first place, that there is no division of the divine essence. On the basis of 1 Cor. 8:4 ("there is none other God but one," εἰ μὴ εἷς) we must maintain the indivisibility of the Godhead. There is, as it were, only one sample of the divine essence. We must also maintain that each of the three Persons possesses this one undivided and indivisible divine essence in its entirety. A division of the Divine Being which would ascribe to the Father the first third of the Godhead, to the Son the second, and to the Holy Spirit the third, is contrary to the very essence of God. The Divine Being is infinite, and infinitude precludes the possibility of division. Any division of the divine essence is also contrary to the express teaching of God's Word, which ascribes the entire divine essence to the Father as well as to the Son and to the Holy Ghost. In Col. 2:9 we read of the Son: "In Him dwelleth all the fullness of the Godhead bodily." And addressing Ananias, St. Peter said with reference to the Holy Ghost (Acts 5:4): "Thou hast not lied unto men, but unto God" (τῷ θεῷ); and ὁ θεός certainly denotes the entire Godhead and not one third of it. The fact that the divine name is given to each of the three Persons shows clearly that the entire divine essence is the property of each Person. In the baptismal formula (Matt. 28:19), the Father and the Son and the Holy Ghost have only one name (τὸ ὄνομα). Again, the Old Testament name Jehovah is given to each of the three Persons. The name Jehovah is that distinctively divine name which denotes the immutable being of God, the absolute essence. God Himself defines this name as to its etymology and meaning: "I am that I am" (Ex. 3:14), i. e., *semper idem*. Luther: "God has no beginning nor end . . . and His name can never be 'has been,' or 'will be,' but it must always be 'Is,' 'Being,' 'Jehovah.'"[18] The term אֱלֹהִים (God) is ascribed also to

[18] *Treatise on Shem Hamphoras*, St. L. XX:2057 ff. This treatise deserves to be read again and again. ". . . Now, as to the pretense of Jews that His name is unutterable, they do not know what they are babbling. If they refer to the letters, it cannot be true, for it is pronounced Jehovah. But if they do it to honor this name, then they ought to do it also in the case of all other names [of God] and let them also be too sacred to utter. Scripture indeed says that God's essence, power, wisdom, benevolence, is unspeakable, immeasurable, infinite, incomprehensible, etc., not as though the letters or syllables were unutterable, but what those letters and syllables mean is beyond utterance. . . . God has no

creatures in so far as they actually or allegedly performed divine functions and enjoyed divine authority (e. g., judges, Ps. 82:6; idols, Deut. 4:28). The term "Jehovah," however, is used only of God and has therefore been designated as *nomen Dei essentiale et incommunicabile.* And this specifically divine name is ascribed not only to the Father, but also to the Son and to the Holy Ghost. The "Angel of the Lord" in Ex. 3:2, that is, the messenger of the Lord, par excellence, the Son of God, is, according to vv. 4, 7, 15, Jehovah Himself, the God of Abraham, Isaac, and Jacob. Likewise the Holy Spirit is known in the Old Testament as Jehovah. In Ps. 85:8 the Psalmist says: "I will hear what God the Lord [Jehovah] will speak," but this Lord, or Jehovah, is the "Spirit of the Lord," who spoke through David (2 Sam. 23:2), and the "Spirit of Christ," who foretold the future glory of the New Testament Church through the Prophets (1 Pet. 1:11). The Holy Spirit is therefore the Lord Jehovah. The New Testament calls Christ not only ὁ κύριος καὶ ὁ θεός (John 20:28), but also ὁ ἀληθινὸς θεός (1 John 5:20), ὁ μέγας θεός (Titus 2:13), ὁ ὢν ἐπὶ πάντων (Rom. 9:5). Likewise the Holy Ghost, in contrast to men, is expressly called ὁ θεός (Acts 5:3-4).

Scripture teaches, secondly, that there is no division or limitation of the divine attributes, works, or worship among the three Persons, but that the three Persons share in them without any distinction of rank. 1) Scripture nowhere indicates that the divine attributes are distributed among the three Persons, as though the divine omnipotence, omniscience, or omnipresence could be divided into three parts and one part assigned to the Father, another to the Son, and the third to the Holy Ghost. On the contrary, Scripture ascribes these attributes without any division or limitation not only to the Father, but just as absolutely to the Son (John 10:28, omnipotence; John 21:17, omniscience; Matt. 28:20, omnipresence) and to the Holy Ghost (Ps. 33:6, omnipotence; 1 Cor. 2:10, omniscience; and Ps. 139:7, omnipresence). 2) Scripture ascribes the same divine works (*opera ad extra*) to the Son and the Holy Spirit as well as to the Father. The creation of the world is the work of the Son (John 1:3; Col. 1:16; Heb. 1:10) and also

---

beginning or end, but is from eternity, in and of Himself, His name can never be 'has been' or 'will be,' but it must always be 'Is,' 'Being,' 'Jehovah.' . . . Hence, as His 'Is,' 'Am,' and 'Being' is incomprehensible, so it is also inexpressible, for no creature can comprehend that which is eternal. . . . In the Divine Being there is Father, Son, and Holy Ghost, three Persons in one eternal, incomprehensible being, or essence. Who will undertake to name, to fathom, fully to express, fully to describe such a marvelous being, or essence? . . . God *is* from eternity and is called three Persons."

the work of the Holy Ghost (Ps. 33:6; Job 33:4). 3) Since all three Persons possess the same divine essence, attributes, and works, therefore one and the same divine worship is due each Person. ***Trium personarum unus est cultus divinus.*** Concerning the worship of the Son the Scriptures state expressly that "all men should honor the Son even as they honor the Father" (John 5:23). While the Scriptures do not say in express words that men must worship the Holy Ghost,[19] it is nevertheless taught very definitely in all those Scripture passages where divine majesty, attributes, and works are ascribed to the Holy Ghost. That the Holy Spirit is entitled to the same worship as the Father and the Son is expressed also in the baptismal formula. By being baptized into the name of the Father, the Son, and the *Holy Ghost,* the Christian adores the Holy Spirit with the same divine worship which is accorded to the Father and the Son. The Christian Church therefore worships the Trinity in Unity and the Unity in Trinity.[20]

4

Objections to the Unity of the Godhead

The First Objection: In His sacerdotal prayer, Christ addresses the Father as "the only true God" (John 17:3) and thereby disclaims essential equality with the Father *(homoousia). Answer:* The fact is that Christ very emphatically claims nothing less than this essential equality. In John 10:30 (ἐγὼ καὶ ὁ πατὴρ ἕν ἐσμεν) He declares in unmistakable words that there is absolute unity of essence between Him and the Father. Any other interpretation of these words is out of the question, because Christ makes this statement to prove that it is as impossible to pluck the sheep out of His hand as out of the Father's. But if Christ claims unity of essence with the Father, why does He demand in John 17:3 that men must know not only the Father, but that in distinction from, and in addition to, the Father they must also know the Son? The answer is found in the immediate context. First (in v. 2), Christ claims unity of essence with the Father by ascribing to Himself the divine work of giving eternal life. Second, the real scope of John 17 is to answer the practical question how men can come to the saving knowledge of the one true God. And Christ answers this question

---

19 Cardinal Gibbons says that the worship of the Holy Ghost cannot be proved from Scripture, but has been established as doctrine through the traditions and the authority of the Pope. *Faith of Our Fathers,* p. 111.

20 Athanasian Creed, *Trigl.,* 33, 25.

when He says: "I have glorified Thee on earth" (v. 4); "I have manifested Thy name unto men" (v. 6); "I have given them Thy Word" (v. 14). In other words, the "only true God" is revealed only in the incarnate Son of God, whom the Father has sent (v. 4). Christ is the only way by which men can come to the Father (John 14:6-11). Accordingly, it is not sufficient for salvation to know the Father, but men must also know the Son if they would be saved. Luthardt is essentially correct when he says: "Men can find life only in God, who has revealed Himself as the God of our salvation only in Christ. Hence He is not the only true God to the exclusion of Jesus Christ, as Arians, Socinians, and Rationalists teach." [21] In a masterful way Luther shows that the Arians pervert Christ's words (John 17:3) "as though Christ excluded Himself and ascribed the deity only to the Father." The Arians press the word "only," superficially look at the text, and ignore the context entirely. They refuse to see that Christ "makes our salvation dependent on knowing both the Father and the Son and makes of the two one knowledge." Luther continues: "These words [John 17:3] are most powerfully directed against the Arians and all heretics, Jews, and unchristians, who claim to believe, and pride themselves on believing, in only one God, who made heaven and earth, and on account of that article condemn us Christians as people setting up another God. For He [Christ] means to indicate that they do not know the right, true God, though they think so and boast of it; for they do not discover Him as the one He is, nor do they know how they must learn to know Him, namely, that He is this one true God who has sent Jesus Christ. Which amounts to saying: Whoever wants to discover the one true God, he must seek Him alone in the Lord Christ, for there is in truth no other God but the One who sent Christ. Now, whoever has not Christ, must also miss the right, true God, even though he knows and believes that there is but one true God. For he does not believe in Him who has sent Christ and through Him gives eternal life. Therefore the important word is 'Thee' ("that they might know Thee, the only true God"). Which 'Thee'? Thee who hast sent Jesus Christ. As though He said: The Jews and others also have only one God, as they think; but Thee, who alone art the true God, they do not know, because they do not know Christ sent by Thee, and in the meantime imagine a god according to their own thoughts, who is in truth no god, but pure nothing. Hence you see that Christ does not use the little word 'only' to separate Himself from God according to the divine

---

[21] Quoted *ad locum* in Strack-Zoeckler's *Commentary*.

essence (since this is amply prevented through the other words), but rather to show the intimate union between the Father and Himself against those who seek God outside of Christ." (St. L. VIII:759 ff.) In the eleventh sermon on the Gospel of John (St. L. VII:1702 ff.) Luther calls the knowledge of God which does not know Christ "a knowledge of the wrong side of God," a knowledge in which God does not show His real face to man, but "turns His back to man." The knowledge of God outside Christ leads man no farther than to the knowledge of the Law of Moses, which shows us that God will give eternal life to those who keep the Law, while He will condemn those who transgress it. But that is not the true and complete picture of God, for God has not sent His Son into the world to condemn the world, but to save it (John 3:17; 1 Tim. 1:15). "Therefore," says Luther, "face about, and see what the true countenance of God is." The true face of God is He whom God has sent into the world, Jesus Christ. He is the "Angel of His presence" (Is. 63:9) and God's πρόσωπον (2 Cor. 4:6). On the face of Jesus is emblazoned the gracious truth that God does not desire to condemn one sinner, but to save all sinners for Christ's sake. The inscription on Christ's face reads: "God so loved the world that He gave His only-begotten Son," etc. (John 3:16), and the Father directs all mankind to look upon this face of Jesus Christ (Matt. 17:5). Whoever has a different God cannot have the "one true God." He has painted a god according to his own fancy; his god is a caricature, a nonentity, an idol. Hence St. John's earnest warning: "Little children, keep yourselves from idols" (1 John 5:21), for, as he said in the preceding verse, the Christian knowledge of God consists in this, that "we know that the Son of God is come and hath given us an understanding that we may know Him that is true, and we are in Him that is true, even in His Son, Jesus Christ. This is the true God and eternal Life." These words state as expressly as do the words in John 17:3, that there is no knowledge of the true God outside the incarnate Son of God. The only difference between the two statements is that the implied *homoousia* of John 17:3 is here stated *expressis verbis*. "This [the Son, Jesus Christ] is the true God." [22]

Second Objection: Because the Son is of the Father (παρὰ πατρός) and the Holy Spirit of the Father and of the Son (τὸ πνεῦμα τοῦ πατρός and τοῦ υἱοῦ), the Son must be inferior to the Father and the Holy Ghost inferior to both the Father and the Son.[23] *Answer:* This objec-

---

[22] G. Stoeckhardt in *Lehre und Wehre,* 40, 293 ff., shows that οὗτός ἐστιν ὁ ἀληθινὸς θεός must refer to the immediately preceding "His Son, Jesus Christ."

[23] Arminians, modern Lutherans, and others.

tion is puerile. Even in the natural realm a son is not necessarily inferior to his father in physical stature, intellectual endowments, position, and prestige. Theologians who raise this objection lack not only discernment in the realm of nature, but are void of spiritual insight. According to God's own self-revelation in His Word it is impossible for the Son to be inferior to the Father and for the Holy Spirit to be inferior to the Father and the Son. As shown above, each Person possesses the entire divine essence as well as the divine attributes and works, which do not exist in three "sets," but only in one "set." In other words, each Person in the Deity is the entire God, and not a third of God. Luther: "Of these Persons each one is the *entire* God, outside which [Person] there is no other God." [24] And the Christian congregation sings with Luther in the "battle hymn of the Reformation": "Jesus Christ it is. . . . And there's none other God."

Franz Delitzsch raised the question: "Is it permissible to call Jesus Christ the Lord Sabaoth, the one God, besides whom there is none other?" (*Allgem. Ev.-luth. Kirchenzeitung*, 1884, No. 49). But Delitzsch raised the question only to deny it and thereby manifested that his spiritual insight had fallen far below the Christian level, for he actually denied the clear statement of Col. 2:9. If Delitzsch really followed the implications of his denial, then he thought of the Son of God only as a half-god or third-god. Every form of Subordinationism and modern Kenoticism is nothing less than a relapse into pagan polytheism.

Zoeckler straddles the issue. He states: "We cannot classify as heretical that form of subordination which maintains the essential equality of the three Persons while subordinating the Son and the Spirit to the Father and which was taught by many ante-Nicene Fathers, the Arminians, Episcopius, Curcellaeus, Limborch, a large part of the supranaturalist dogmaticians, likewise Kahnis, the more positive theologians of the Ritschlian School" (*Handbuch der theol. Wissenschaften* III, 91). Whoever takes the term "Subordinationism" in its native and accepted sense is compelled to deny the unity of essence and to say with Kahnis that "the Son is God only in a secondary sense of the word" (*Dogmatik*, 2d ed., I, 361).

The following argument of the Subordinationists also renounces the Christian knowledge of God: Since the Son is of the Father, He is younger than the Father, and the Holy Spirit is inferior to the Son and the Father regarding time, because He proceeds from them. This

---

[24] Theses *De unitate essentiae divinae et de distinctione personarum in divinitate, Opp. v. a.*, IV, 474; St. L. X:178.

argument presumes that the concept of time with all its implications can be predicated of timeless eternity and of the immutable and eternal God. Such an assumption is a denial of eternity and of the eternal God. Whoever uses this specious argument renounces the Christian knowledge of God, yes, even the natural knowledge of God, for the eternity of God's power and Godhead is clearly understood by the things that are made (Rom. 1:20). Accordingly the Athanasian Creed states: "And in this Trinity none is before or after other; none is greater or less than another, but the whole three Persons are coeternal together and coequal" (*Trigl.* 33, 24-25).

The ecclesiastical terminology "the Father is the First, the Son is the Second, and the Holy Spirit is the Third Person" is Scriptural. According to the Scriptures, the Father is called the First Person, because He is not of another, but of Himself. The Son is called the Second Person, because He has the divine essence from the Father. The Holy Spirit is called the Third Person because He is not of Himself, but has the divine essence from the Father and the Son and because another does not proceed from Him. The dogmaticians call this an order of natural enumeration (*ordo naturalis enumerationis*). It is the best way in which the divine mode of subsistence in the Holy Trinity can be expressed (*ordo in modo subsistendi*). The argument that this order implies subordination either as to time or dignity is suggested by the unscriptural and irrational assumption that human and temporal standards apply to the eternal God.

Third Objection: Scripture itself teaches subordination when it states that the divine works in nature and in the Church are wrought through (διά, ἐν) the Son and the Holy Spirit. *Answer:* True, Scripture states that all things were made by the Son (John 1:3; Col. 1:16); that "by the Word of the Lord were the heavens made and all the host of them by the Breath [Spirit] of His mouth" (Ps. 33:6); that "God hath chosen us in Him [the Son]" (Eph. 1:4); "God hath from the beginning chosen you to salvation through sanctification of the Spirit" (2 Thess. 2:13). But it is a fallacy to infer from this a subordination of the Son and of the Holy Ghost. As there is an order of Persons, without subordination, so there is also an order of operation (*ordo in modo operandi*). As the Son has His divine essence from the Father, so also His operation: "the Son can do nothing of Himself but what He seeth the Father do" (John 5:19). Likewise the Holy Spirit has from the Father and the Son both His Godhead and His operation, for the Holy Ghost "shall not speak of Himself, but whatsoever He shall hear, that shall He speak. . . . He shall receive of Mine" (John

16:13-15). The fact that there is an order of operation does not imply a division of the divine activity, for the Scriptures ascribe the one operation (*una numero actio*) to the Son and the Holy Ghost as well as to the Father. Jesus not only says that He can do nothing of Himself, but adds immediately that He does the same work in the same manner (ὁμοίως) as the Father, thereby declaring that the work of the Father and the Son is numerically identical, that is, the operation belongs to the entire Trinity without any division among the three Persons (John 5:19).[25] This is evident from such passages as ascribe a divine work to one Person without even mentioning the others, e. g., Heb. 1:10 (the work of creation is ascribed to the Son) and 1 Cor. 12:11 (as He wills, the Holy Spirit distributes the special spiritual gifts).

Fourth Objection: Christ says expressly that the Father is greater than the Son (John 14:28-29). *Answer:* Christ is here speaking of an inferiority to the Father which is to cease at His glorification and return to the Father; in other words, Christ is inferior only according to the human nature in the State of Humiliation. The Savior tells His disciples to rejoice that He will go to the Father, because this event marks His entrance into the State of Exaltation according to the human nature and will therefore terminate His inferiority. This is the only possible meaning of the Savior's words in the light of His high-priestly prayer: "O Father, glorify Thou Me with Thine own Self with the glory which I had with Thee before the world was" (John 17:5). In a sermon on the Gospel for Pentecost Sunday, Luther says: "What He says – 'the Father is greater than I' – is not said of the personal, divine essence of His own nature, nor of His Father's, as the Arians have falsely interpreted this passage, not wishing to see why or whereof Christ so speaks here; but concerning the difference between the Kingdom which He shall have with His Father and His service or servile state in which He was before His resurrection. Now I am small, He wishes to say, in My work and station as a Servant; as He says in Matt. 20:28: 'The Son of Man came not to be ministered unto, but to minister and to give His life a ransom for many.' That is making Himself little, and, as St. Paul says in Phil. 2:8, humbling Himself, or casting Himself beneath all things and letting sin, death, devil, and world tread upon Him. But this littleness shall not continue, He says, for that would be a complete undoing; it shall be only a passageway,

---

25 Commenting on John 5:19, the old dogmaticians say correctly: "These words ascribe to the Son not impotence, but rather the identical divine majesty of the Father, because numerically the Father and the Son possess one and the same power and operation."

the way and means by which I come to the Father, where I shall no longer be little, but great and powerful, as He is, and where I shall rule and reign with Him forever." (St. L. XI:1079 f.)

In his exposition of John 14:28-29 Luther discusses this same point in greater detail. He points out that the Arians used these words to mislead the simple Christians; that even some Church Fathers, as Hilary, missed the real meaning when they taught that Christ's inferiority to the Father was not one of essence, but one of authority. Luther points out that it is necessary to understand the words if one is not to misunderstand the subject matter; otherwise he may, as the proverb says, "take a cow for a horse." But it is just as important to know the subject matter; otherwise one may understand the words but fail to comprehend the subject matter under discussion. Luther then proceeds to show from the context that Christ is not speaking of Himself according to the divine nature, nor according to the human nature in general, but according to the human nature in the State of Humiliation. "The Father is greater than I, because now I am a Servant; but when I return yonder to My Father's, then shall I become greater, namely, as great as the Father, that is, I shall rule with Him in equal power and majesty. . . . Thus Christ goes out of this temporary hovel into the infinite heaven, out of this dungeon into His great, glorious kingdom, where He is much greater than before. Formerly He was the poor, miserable, suffering, and dying Christ; now, however, being with the Father, He is the great, glorious, living, almighty Lord over all creatures." (St. L. VIII:477 f.)[26]

5

The Doctrine of the Trinity in the Old Testament

This is a highly controverted matter and deserves special discussion. Luther's position may be summarized as follows: Although the doctrine of the Trinity is not revealed as clearly in the Old as in

---

[26] Thus also Philippi, Hengstenberg, Keil, Noesgen, Luthardt, Stoeckhardt. Any other interpretation violates the text. Meusel (VI, p. 476) says that Meyer arrived at his Subordinationism by way of "exegesis." "Exegesis" should be stricken out and "eisegesis" substituted. Meyer is here employing "dogmatical" exegesis, under the spell of which the prominent leaders of modern theology refuse to find the *satisfactio vicaria* and the inspiration of Scripture and the deity of Christ and the Trinity and the Christian doctrine of justification and the Christian doctrine of the Church taught in the clearest texts.

the New Testament, nevertheless this doctrine is unmistakably set forth in the Old Testament (St. L. X:1019). "Thus at the very beginning of the world the doctrine of the three Persons in the Godhead was indicated, later clearly understood by the Prophets, and finally fully revealed in the Gospel" (St. L. I:274). In his exposition of Gen. 35:7 Luther says that the greater part of the Jews, of course, did not believe this doctrine, just as in his own time the Jew and the Turk rejected the Trinitarian doctrine. Yes, even many in visible Christendom do not heed or believe this doctrine. The same thing happens to them that Isaiah says of his hearers (6:10), namely, that their heart is fat, their ears are heavy, and their eyes shut, so that they do not see nor hear nor understand. (St. L. II:940.) The Lutheran theologians of the sixteenth and seventeenth centuries are agreed that the doctrine of the Trinity is revealed to such an extent in the Old Testament that the believers were able to perceive and believe the doctrine of the Trinity. The Helmstedt school of George Calixt, however, held that "the mystery of the Trinity was not contained in the Old Testament, but was given to the patriarchs and the Prophets by immediate and special revelation; that neither the Old Testament believers nor we today could learn it without the help of the New Testament; that the Old Testament contains only vestiges or intimations, but no clear and convincing statements of this doctrine" (Quenstedt I, 510). And Luthardt declares: "The Old Testament at best only prepares for the Trinitarian knowledge of God, because it contains only the germs of a Trinitarian revelation. The New Testament alone brings the Trinitarian knowledge, because it alone contains the Trinitarian revelation." Luthardt condemns the Scripture proof of the Lutheran theologians: "It rests mostly upon a false and forced exegesis and in general on an unhistorical approach, which ignores the gradual and progressive development of revelation" (*Kompendium,* 10th ed., pp. 111–112). Kirn makes the sweeping statement: "Today no theologians will turn to the Old Testament for prooftexts in support of the doctrine of the Trinity" (R. E., 3d ed., XX, p. 112).

The question whether the Old Testament teaches the doctrine of the Trinity is settled once and for all in the Christian Church by the fact that Christ and His Apostles prove the divine personality of the Son and of the Holy Spirit from the Old Testament. From Ps. 110:1 Christ proves to the Pharisees that the Messiah is not only David's Son, but also David's Lord. (Matt. 22:41 ff.) Everyone will admit that the term "David's Lord" does not denote the symbol or the germ of a personality, but a full and complete personality. And from the same

Old Testament text Jesus incidentally also teaches the divine personality of the Holy Spirit when He says that David called the Messiah his Lord through the Holy Spirit (ἐν πνεύματι). The Savior thereby is confirming what David declares 2 Sam. 23:2: "The Spirit of the Lord (רוּחַ יְהוָה) spake by me." In Hebrews 1, the deity of Christ, and that can only mean His divine personality, is proved from six Old Testament texts: Ps. 2:7; 2 Sam. 7:14; Ps. 97:7; 45:7; 102:26-28; 110:1. As we examine these Old Testament texts concerning the Messiah (e. g., He laid the foundation of the world, loves righteousness, hates iniquity, rules, is worshiped), we see that the Messiah is not a Platonic idea, a mere concept, a symbol, a germinal personality, but that the Messiah is a real, living, and complete personality. The personality of the Messiah is evident particularly in Psalm 110, where He is described as the Ruler of both the universe and His Church, and as the Priest who reconciles God and man. Likewise the Old Testament clearly teaches the divine personality of the Holy Spirit in predicating of Him such activities (*actiones et passiones*) as creation (Gen. 1:2), reproving man (Gen. 6:3), speaking through David (2 Sam. 23:1-3), being vexed and embittered by Israel (Is. 63:10). And, finally, the doctrine of the Trinity is taught also in those passages which, like the New Testament in Matt. 28:19 and 2 Cor. 13:14, enumerate the three Persons of the Trinity side by side and as three separate Persons. This is obviously the case in Is. 63:8-10: "For He [Jehovah] said, Surely they are My people, children that will not lie; so He was their Savior. In all their affliction He was afflicted, and the Angel of His presence saved them; in His love and in His pity He redeemed them; and He bare them and carried them all the days of old. But they rebelled and vexed His Holy Spirit; therefore He was turned to be their enemy, and He fought against them."

Thus the Old Testament unmistakably teaches the divine personality of the Son and the Spirit by ascribing to each of them divine names, properties, and works. It is therefore only natural to regard also those passages as a reference to the Trinity a) in which God speaks of Himself in the plural (Gen. 1:26; 3:22; 11:7), and b) in which God is worshiped in a threefold hymn of petition or praise, e. g., the Aaronic blessing (Num. 6:24-26), which significantly is followed by the explanation: "They shall put My *name* upon Israel" (v. 27), and the Trisagion (Is. 6:3).

A treatise on the doctrine of the Trinity in the Old Testament is incomplete without a discussion of those passages from Genesis (22:11 f.) to Malachi (3:1) in which divine names and attributes are ascribed to the Angel of the Lord: מַלְאַךְ יְהוָה. In Gen. 22:11-12 we read: "The Angel of the Lord called unto him out of heaven and said, Abraham, Abraham, and he said, Here am I. And He said, Lay not thine hand upon the lad, neither do thou anything unto him; for now I know that thou fearest God, seeing thou hast not withheld thy son, thine only son, from Me." Aside from any other consideration, the phrase "from Me" (Luther: *"um meinetwillen"*) is in itself sufficient reason to reject the idea that a created angel is here speaking. But more: not only does Abraham call the name of the place *Jehovah jireh* (the Lord shall see), but in the subsequent address the Angel of the Lord calls Himself the Lord who has sworn by Himself to bless Abraham and multiply his seed (vv. 15-18). No created angel could make that statement. The story of Moses at Mount Horeb (Ex. 3:1-15) reveals in great detail the identity of the Angel of the Lord. The Angel who appeared to Moses in the burning bush could not have been a created angel, because in v. 4 the Angel of the Lord identifies Himself with Jehovah. But more: the Angel of the Lord describes Himself as the God of Abraham, Isaac, and Jacob, and of His people Israel, which Moses is to liberate from the Egyptian bondage. Upon Moses' insistent pleas for a more precise identification the Angel of the Lord identifies Himself as the essential and unchanging God, the אֶהְיֶה אֲשֶׁר אֶהְיֶה, "I AM THAT I AM." There is absolutely no ground for Luthardt's claim that as Jehovah's ambassador a created angel could identify himself with Jehovah. Imagine the English ambassador at Washington introducing himself as "His Majesty, the King of England!" He would be recalled at once as an impostor.

There are many passages in which the Angel of the Lord is identified with Jehovah. Gerhard furnishes a list of these passages and interprets them (*Loci, locus "De Natura Dei,"* § 36, 37). On Gen. 48:15-16: "The God which fed me. . . . The Angel which redeemed me from all evil," etc. Luther says in a sermon for Trinity Sunday: "Jacob here distinguishes the Persons in the Holy Trinity. He applies the term 'Angel of the Lord' to Christ, not as though He were an angel by nature, for it would be manifest idolatry to pray to an angel and invoke his blessing. By his prayer Jacob actually ascribes deity to the Person whom he designates as the Angel. Jacob, however, calls Him Angel to indicate that this divine Person shall not always remain the invisible God, but shall be sent into the world, be clothed in our flesh, and be sacrificed for our sins. Christ uses the same language when He says, 'The Father hath sent Me.' Again, in the Prophet

Isaiah: 'The Lord hath sent Me to bind up the brokenhearted' (61:1); also: 'and the Angel of His presence saved them' (63:9). And Malachi calls Christ 'the Messenger of the covenant' (3:1). The two names 'God' and 'Angel' as used by Jacob therefore designate two distinct Persons and yet one and the same divine essence." (St. L. XIII:670 f.) Similarly Philippi: "The Angel of the Lord is different from Jehovah in regard to His Person, and yet one with Him in essence." He adduces the following prooftexts: Gen. 16:7-14; chaps. 18—19; 21:17-19; 22:11-18; 31:11-13, cp. 28:11-22; 33:25-30, cp. Hos. 12:5; 48:15 f.; Ex. 3:1-7; 13:21, cp. 14:19; 23:20 f.; 33:14 and Is. 63:8-9; Joshua 5:13; 6:2; Judg. 6:11-24; 13:3-25. Philippi says: "In their native sense these passages teach that the Angel of the Lord is the uncreated angel, identical with Jehovah, to whom divine attributes, works, names, and worship are ascribed. If we found in these passages only Oriental hyperbolism, then we would sacrifice the solid basis for Scripture interpretation, and, following such a course consistently, would with the rationalist dissolve and cancel even the firmest and most indestructible revelation." [27]

What Scripture teaches concerning the "Angel of Jehovah" confirms what Luther says concerning the doctrine of the Trinity in the Old Testament in general: "In the New Testament everything is clearly and powerfully attested of the holy, divine Trinity that in the Old Testament is not so clearly set forth, though it is strongly indicated also there" (St. L. X:1019). And here we have Kirn claiming that in our day no reputable theologian will any longer seek prooftexts for the Trinity in the Old Testament! That does not speak well for the theology of today. These theologians are ready to cast doubt on the theological ability of Christ and His Apostles, who, as we have seen, proved the Holy Trinity from the Old Testament.[28]

---

[27] Philippi, *Glaubenslehre*, 3d ed., Vol. III, 191. Other theologians who take the same position are Hengstenberg, Keil, Thomasius, Rohnert. So also Joseph Addison Alexander, on Is. 63:9: "The old Christian doctrine is that the Angel of God's presence was that Divine Being who is represented in the New Testament as the brightness of the Father's glory and the express image of His Person, the image of God, in whose face the glory of God shines and in whom dwelleth all the fullness of the Godhead bodily. . . ." (Commentary on Isaiah, Vol. II, p. 394.)

[28] In refuting the claim that the Old Testament does not teach the Trinity, our Lutheran dogmaticians agree with Luther in saying, on the one hand, that the Old Testament does not teach the doctrine of the Trinity as fully as the New Testament; but, on the other hand, they all agree with Quenstedt (I, 516) that Christ and the Apostles confuted the Jews by the testimonies from the Old Testament and set forth this mystery (of the Trinity) on the basis of the Old

6

The Trinity and Human Reason

On the one hand, we dare not differentiate between a divine Person and the Divine Being, because the Scriptures ascribe the entire Godhead not only to the Father, but also to the Son (Col. 2:9) and to the Holy Ghost (Acts 5:4). Luther (St. L. X:178): "It is not the function of reason to inquire in what manner the Person differs from the Deity itself; not even the angels understand this mystery. In fact, to assume some kind of distinction is a dangerous procedure and must be avoided because each Person is the entire and the very God." [29] The proposition advocated by Scholastics, e. g., Scotus, which would establish a so-called formal distinction is, as Luther says, vain and fatuous. "No matter how subtle this distinction of Doctor Subtilis appears to be, reason does not see how a formal distinction differs from a material or a real distinction." (*Loc. cit.*)

On the other hand, we must not make a notional, but a real distinction between the Persons, because the Holy Scriptures speak of three Persons as ἄλλος καὶ ἄλλος καὶ ἄλλος and because only the Son – not the Father nor the Holy Ghost – was incarnate. We are confronted by the fact which Luther describes in the following words: "Reason cannot comprehend that one thing contains no distinctions and at the same time is three distinct things." This mystery compels us to admit with Luther: "Metaphysics and every speculation on the part of a creature must be excluded in the doctrine of God." The warning against making the doctrine of the Trinity plausible to reason cannot be made too emphatic. There are two attempts to explain the mystery of the Trinity.

1. It is not wrong when the Christian finds in certain phenomena of nature a reminder of the fact that there are three Persons in one

---

Testament writings (Matt. 22:46; Acts 18:24, 28) and that either the argument of Christ and the Apostles was sufficient and the Jews could be convinced from the writings of the Old Testament alone or Christ and the Apostles based their argument on an inadequate and untenable foundation, which would be an impious statement. And they agree with Kromayer: "It is surprising that not so many years ago some professed adherents of the Augustana challenged the statement that the Trinity is proved from the Old Testament. It certainly could not escape them that in the controversies with the Jews, who do not accept the New Testament, this doctrine was defended so conclusively from the Old Testament that until now it stands without successful contradiction." (*Theol. Pos.-pol.* I, 146.)

[29] Two disputations concerning the unity of the essence and distinction of the Persons, St. L. X:178.

divine essence, but the Christian dare not use such analogies as proof for the Trinity, yes, not even as a confirmation of this mystery.[30] Man cannot perceive, still less prove, the doctrine of the Trinity from the divine works in the realm of nature (*opera ad extra*), because these works are common to all three Persons. Every blade of grass bears the inscription "God has made me" so plainly that every rational being can see and understand it. But no creature in the entire realm of nature bears this inscription: "The three Persons of the Godhead have made me." In fact, it cannot bear such an inscription, because there is only *one* divine omnipotence, *one* divine operation. Only in His Word does God tell us that the one divine Creator and Preserver of the universe is the Father, the Son, and the Holy Ghost. Only in His Word, not in the realm of nature, does God reveal to us the nature of His internal essence. Therefore we are to seek no proofs for the Trinity in the realm of nature.

2. Nor is it possible by a process of rationalization to derive the doctrine of the Trinity from the divine essence itself (e. g., the divine intellect or the will) or the divine attributes (e. g., love).[31] Even the later Melanchthon erred on this point when he taught in the *Corpus Misnicum:* The Son of God is born of the Father by reflection, or cogitation, because, when the Father studies and considers His own being, He brings forth an image which has real and permanent existence, just as our mind produces an image of God, which, however, is only accidental and ephemeral. The Reformed philologist and theologian Barthol. Keckermann (d. 1609) says: "We shall make clear to the anti-Trinitarian that a Trinity of Persons logically follows from the very

---

30 In his *Commentary on Genesis* (I:1150 f.) Luther reminds us that the Church Fathers employed inapt and at times very weak arguments to establish the doctrine of the Trinity and thereby gave occasion to the Jews to claim that our entire doctrine is false. "But," says Luther, "after the doctrine of the Trinity has been established from clear words of Scripture, then it is permissible to explain and illustrate the doctrine with allegories and figures of speech. Augustine does not establish the doctrine of the Trinity on the fact that there are three powers in man (for example, *memoria, intelligentia, voluntas*). Nevertheless, it is a happy thought to seek reminders of the Trinity in man and in all creatures."

31 Augustine attempted to "prove" the Trinity from God's attribute of love. He argues that "there are not more than three Persons; if I love, then there must be three: I, the object of my love, and reciprocal love itself. Thus one sees the Trinity when one sees love." *De Trin.* VIII, 8–10; IX, 2. This Augustinian "trinity of love" was further developed by the mystic-scholastic Richard of St. Victor. In more recent times Ernst Sartorius (d. 1859) popularized this theory (*Die Lehre von der heiligen Liebe* I, 7 f.). Compare Philippi, *Glaubenslehre,* 2d ed. II, 172.

essence of God and that God could not be God unless He had three modes of existence or three distinct powers. After we have proved this, we shall also bring testimony from the Scriptures." [32] In their line of argumentation Melanchthon and Keckermann could, of course, appeal in part, or in whole, to a long list of predecessors.[33] But the Lutheran dogmaticians remind us very emphatically that the doctrine of the Trinity can be understood and proved only from the Word of God.

Quenstedt says that the proposition: "The generation of the Son of God is a result of the Father's reflection and the procession of the Holy Spirit a result of His will," has no support in Scripture, *destituitur autoritate Sacrae Scripturae* (*op. cit.*, p. 559). Against Keckermann, Quenstedt states: "He will never successfully maintain that the divine intellect reflecting upon itself brings forth from this reflection an image separate and distinct from the reflecting subject and that the divine will, reflecting, produces out of this self-contemplation, love as distinct from the will." Keckermann bases the mystery of the Trinity on the slippery foundation of reason and thereby accomplishes no more than that he exposes this mystery to the cavil of the opponents.[34] Whoever presumes to entertain his own man-made ideas in the doctrine of the Trinity actually assumes the right to play the role of the Holy Spirit. For only the Holy Spirit searches the deep things of God (1 Cor. 2:10). It is, therefore, the height of megalomania when finite and shortsighted man, who does not even understand the nature of his fellow men (1 Cor. 2:11), becomes so opinionated that he assumes to understand the majestic God, who dwells in a "light which no man can approach unto" (1 Tim. 6:16; John 1:18).

Modern theology, which in its rejection of Scripture has shifted from Scripture to the theological opinions of the individual, can present only human speculations concerning the doctrine of the Trinity. Naturally, there are as many theories and personal opinions as there are individual speculative theologians. Nevertheless, the many shades of theological opinion fall into two general categories:

---

[32] *Systema Theol.*, lib. 1, c. 3; quoted in Gerhard, *Loci, locus "De Sanctissimo Mysterio Trinitatis,"* § 27.

[33] Cp. Quenstedt, 1, 554, Antithesis.

[34] Philippi, *op. cit.*, 181, calls attention to Twesten's correct presentation, who says (*Dogmatik* I, 196) that it is hazardous to establish one's faith on specious philosophical arguments. Such a procedure undermines the ground for true assurance and misleads men to accept hypotheses as evidence in matters of faith; it prompts men to assign a secondary position to the only foundation of Christian truth; and, finally, to doubt a doctrine which requires such dubious arguments for its support.

1. The first class consists of those from whose theological "I" crass Unitarianism emanates like a miasma. They openly deny the deity of the Son and of the Holy Spirit. While they employ the terms Father, Son, Holy Ghost, they explain these terms as three divine powers, wills, operations, of one divine Person. We have here a revival of the errors – frequently even of the terminology – of ancient modal and dynamic Monarchianism and later Socinianism. These modern Monarchians contend that the orthodox doctrine of three distinct Persons must inevitably lead to tritheism. The eternal essential Trinity (ontological Trinity) is changed into a historical trinity, a trinity of divine economy. This is the position of modern Liberalism.

2. A second class comprises all those who are known as "conservative" modern theologians. These men, like the liberal theologians, have shifted from the Word of God to their own subjective theology and therefore attempt to fix the doctrine of the Trinity from their own religious experience. But from this subjective starting point, which is at best a trinity of the threefold divine economy, they expect to arrive at the Church's doctrinal position of an essential Trinity. In other words: they teach that the threefold divine operation which the Christian experiences corresponds to the antemundane metaphysical Trinitarian relation in God. In the feud between the radical and conservative Modernists the latter can easily charge the radicals with Unitarianism. But the radicals can also successfully charge that the conservatives in their line of argumentation and in their conclusions are at variance with the dogmaticians of the 16th and 17th centuries. In particular, the radicals are right when they say that the conservative party in Modernism endeavors to make the mystery of the Trinity plausible to human reason by developing the doctrine from the concept of love; that they teach a subordination of the Persons; and that they define the term "Person" not as an individual personality, but attempt to give a new meaning to this concept. This, say the radicals, is foreign to the theology of the Reformation and old genuine Protestantism.[35] This is correct. The conservative wing of modern theology will not teach the Scripture doctrine of the Trinity until it again believes with the Christian Church that Holy Scripture is God's infallible Word and renounces the theological Ego as the source of doctrine. Only then will it believe and teach concerning the Trinity what God Himself has revealed in His Word.[36]

---

[35] Cp. Nitzsch-Stephan, p. 432 ff.

[36] See the chapter "The Personal Union and the Christological Theories of Modern Theology" in Vol. II.

Is the Christian doctrine of the Trinity contrary to reason? Karl Hase's answer is very much to the point: "It is not the business of the Church to defend its doctrines with rational arguments. To do so would be a concession to the claim of reason that the doctrine of the Trinity is not only above reason, but also contrary to reason when reason is made the judge." [37] Hase should have added that when reason attempts to judge and to assail the doctrine of the Trinity, it ceases to be reason and actually becomes the climax of unreason. In presenting the doctrine of the Trinity, Luther again and again points out what folly it is for us poor mortals, who do not even understand the essence of our own nature, to presume to sit in judgment on God's being and even go so far as to deny the Trinity. He says, e. g.: "If it were proper to employ our human reason in this matter, I venture to say I would be able to speculate and rationalize with more skill than the Jews or the Turks. But I thank my God that He gave me grace to have no desire to dispute concerning this article, whether it be true or consistent; but because I find it well grounded and taught in the Scriptures, I believe God more than my own reason and thoughts, and care nothing for the objection that it is unreasonable to teach the existence of but one essence in which there are three distinct Persons, God the Father, God the Son, and God the Holy Ghost. The question here is not whether this doctrine is true, but whether it is found in the Word of God. If it is found there, then be assured that it is true, for God's Word is truth. Since the Holy Scriptures have this article of faith, as we have just now seen, and since our fathers so earnestly contended for its preservation and have handed it down to us in its purity, we should not attempt to investigate with our reason how Father, Son, and Holy Ghost can be one God. We poor human beings cannot even comprehend, though we have the help of ever so many wise men of this world, how it happens that we laugh, or can see a high hill many miles away, or how sleep overpowers us so that the body seems dead and is yet alive. If we are thus unable to understand matters pertaining to our own life and daily experiences, why, then, prompted by the devil, should we venture with our own reason to comprehend God in His majesty and divine essence! If we must speculate, let us begin with our own selves and find out what becomes of our eyes, ears, and other senses when we sleep. Speculation in this direction might at least be indulged in without harm." (St. L. XIII:664 ff.) Furthermore: "No, God be praised, we [Chris-

---

[37] Hase, *Hutterus Redivivus*, p. 180.

tians] clearly perceive such doctrine to be beyond the reason of man. No acute Jewish intellects are needed to demonstrate that to us; with full knowledge we consent to such assertion. Upon the strength of our own experience we confess that wherever the light of reason is not supplemented by that of the Holy Spirit, it will be impossible to apprehend, believe, and maintain this article of faith. What a proud, conceited, Jewish thing is reason that it dares to sit in judgment concerning the Deity, though it has never beheld the Divine Being; yes, is unable to behold Him. Reason does not know what it is talking about, for 'God dwells in an unapproachable light' (1 Tim. 6:16) and must come to us, though as light concealed in a lantern; and again, 'no man hath seen God at any time, the only-begotten Son, which is in the bosom of the Father, He hath declared Him' (John 1:18); and long ago Moses said: 'There shall no man see Me and live' (Ex. 33:20). . . . What uncouth louts are we to prize our poor, blind reason more highly than the testimony of Scripture! The Scriptures are God's testimony concerning Himself; reason can know nothing of Deity itself, and yet it ventures to judge what is beyond its ken. That, surely, means to make a blind man the judge of color." (St. L. X:1007, 1018.)

In this connection we must refer to several unwarranted charges and aspersions whereby Unitarians endeavor to discredit the Christian doctrine of the Trinity.

1. The first charge is that the traditional Trinitarian doctrine is an "artificial theory," a "philosophical speculation developed by the ancient Church Fathers." Thus Horst-Stephan.[38] Ritschl even went so far as to claim that Luther and his adherents retained the doctrine of Christ's person and of the Holy Trinity in the interest of church politics.[39] Such wild talk, which virtually turns historical facts topsy-turvy, finds a ready ear just because it is so daring. The historical facts, however, are that the old dogmaticians were opposed to every philosophical construction, such as the *somnium Philippi* (see above), not only in theory, but in fact as well. Whatever they taught concerning the inner-Trinitarian revelation, they had received from God's self-revelation in Scripture. Lutheran dogmaticians, therefore, agree with Luther: "In order to become better grounded in knowledge and faith as regards the Trinity of Persons in the unity of the Godhead, we ourselves and they ought to unite in the study of the Scriptures. We have not invented this doctrine, nor could we have done so." (St. L. X:1017.)

---

[38] *Glaubenslehre*, 1921, p. 193.

[39] *Die christl. Lehre von der Rechtfertigung u. Versoehnung*, 3d ed., II, 18.

After bringing the Scripture proof for the deity of Christ and the Trinity from the Old and the New Testament, Luther adds: "Let him who can, puncture this proof; I can't" (St. L. X:669).

2. A second contention of Unitarianism is that the orthodox doctrine encumbers the mind with dead formulas and actually proves to be a detriment to true piety; it is sufficient if men accept Christ as the great Revealer of God's love. The fact is that the Unitarian teaching concerning Christ as the "Revealer of God's love" remains a "dead formula" and has absolutely no dogmatic or religious value. The Son of God is indeed "the Revealer of God's love" toward sinful mankind. But He is the Revealer only by His vicarious atonement; only as the Lamb of God which taketh away the sins of the world; only as the Son of God who in the fullness of the time became man and in the stead of man assumed the obligations and punishment of the divine Law (John 1:29; Gal. 4:4-5; 3:13). And the Holy Spirit will glorify the Son of God in the hearts of men by creating faith in Him as such a Revealer of God's love, John 16:14. The Unitarian talk of a "God of love" without Christ's vicarious satisfaction is a lie, and the Holy Spirit as the Spirit of Truth will never glorify and confirm lies. Because Unitarianism denies the deity of Christ and His vicarious atonement, their pious-sounding phrase of the fatherhood of God is nothing but human speculation and self-delusion. And sooner or later the Unitarians experience that their favorite formula is without spirit and without life, for in spiritual anguish or in the hour of death the voice of conscience, which had been violently suppressed, will no longer be silenced, as the cases of Horace Bushnell, A. Ritschl, W. R. Harper, and others prove.[40]

Even the "aesthetic" rationalist Karl Hase, who did not accept the essential deity of Christ and the essential Trinity, has no sympathy for the shallowness displayed by the vulgar rationalists and the modern theologians in their criticism of the orthodox doctrine of the Church. In his *Hutterus Redivivus* he takes Hutter's position (though not always quite successfully) and from this standpoint attacks rationalism. He disposed of the glib remarks of the rationalist Klein in a most telling way. Klein had stated that the orthodox formulation of the doctrine of the Trinity is "empty words," only negations, containing nothing definite, and that it is impossible to understand what good effect faith in the mystery of the Trinity could possibly have for our bliss and our morality. Hase answers (*op. cit.*, p. 181): "It is true, in-

[40] See "Some Modern Theories of the Atonement Examined," in Vol. II.

deed, that the dogma [of the Trinity] has no significance for a this-worldly bliss and for a virtue which in Kantian fashion requires only such a God as will reward man's beggarly works. But more is necessary to attain a bliss which consists solely in peace with God and to acquire a virtue which in spite of its noblest works considers itself so impoverished that it can be satisfied only by faith in justification and sanctification. For such a bliss and such a virtue, faith in a redeeming and sanctifying God takes on so great a significance that without it true bliss and genuine virtue are impossible."

3. Finally, the opponents of the orthodox doctrine of the Trinity claim that this doctrine must inevitably lead to tritheism. They say that if three persons were postulated in the one God, then we must also divide our worship among Father, Son, and Holy Ghost and thus deny the unity of the divine worship. We answer, in the first place, that Scripture teaches, and therefore demands, that we worship the one God in three Persons. The Christian Baptism must be performed in the name of the Father and the Son and the Holy Ghost. Scripture, furthermore, demands that all men must honor the Son even as they honor the Father, and adds that he that honoreth not the Son, honoreth not the Father (John 5:23). The aphorism of the ancient Church is correct: *Trium personarum est unus cultus divinus.* In the second place, there can be no division of the divine worship, because each Person is the entire God and not one third of God. The entire majesty is in the Father (by virtue of His eternal fatherhood – *agennesia*), in the Son (by His eternal generation) and in the Holy Spirit (by His eternal procession from the Father and the Son). Luther: "Each Person is the entire and the very God" (St. L. X:178). "The fullness of the Godhead" dwells in the Son (Col. 2:9), and the Holy Spirit is ὁ θεός (Acts 5:4). Even Hase admits that "all the trickery of liberal exegetes is incapable of expunging from the New Testament the evidence for Christ's deity. While it may be possible to explain away this doctrine when isolated passages are viewed separately, the deity of Christ is ineradicable when the New Testament passages are studied collectively." (*Op. cit.*, p. 181.) Finally, whoever worships God as the Father worships also the Son and the Holy Ghost. God is our Father only for the sake of Christ's vicarious atonement and the Holy Spirit's revelation. Whoever honors the Son honors also the Father, which hath sent Him (John 5:23), and the Holy Ghost, who glorifies the Son in the hearts of men (John 16:14). Whoever prays to the Holy Spirit thereby prays to the Father and the Son, for the Holy Spirit is the Spirit of both the Father (Matt. 10:20) and the Son (Gal. 4:6).

7

Ecclesiastical Terminology and the Christian Knowledge of God

Scripture does not reveal the doctrine of the Trinity as a metaphysical speculation or an academic problem, but as an exceedingly practical article of faith necessary for our salvation. Scripture establishes an indissoluble nexus between the doctrines of the Trinity and soteriology. (Rom. 16:25 f.) In accord with the Holy Scriptures, the Constantinopolitanum presents the doctrine of the Trinity as to its soteriological meaning and import. It not only confesses, "I believe in one God, the Father Almighty; and in one Lord Jesus Christ; and I believe in the Holy Ghost," but with its confession of the deity of Christ it unites the confession of the saving truth, that the second Person became man and was crucified and died for us; and to its confession of the deity of the Holy Ghost it adds a statement concerning His soteriological work, calling Him "the Life-giver," and "divine Revealer." Luther likewise points to the integral unity between the three Persons in God and God's plan for man's salvation. He says: "Such revelation (of God's most inner being, as three Persons in one divine essence) is in accord with God's highest work and indicates His divine counsel and will, for God has decreed from eternity and accordingly revealed in the many Messianic promises that His Son should become man and die to reconcile lost mankind to God. Nothing could redeem us from the dreadful fall into sin and from eternal death except an eternal Person who has the power to destroy sin and death and to give eternal righteousness and life instead. For this no angel nor any other creature was sufficient. Only God Himself could accomplish this." (St. L. XII:632.)

Self-righteous and conceited man rejects the doctrine of the Trinity; he has no use for the soteriological import of this revealed doctrine. And man's enmity is directed primarily against the essential deity of Christ, whom self-righteous and conceited man will not accept as the only Mediator between God and man. The words of 1 Tim. 2:6: "He gave Himself a ransom for all," are, as Luther says, "nothing but thunderclaps and fire from heaven against the righteousness of the Law and the doctrine of works. The wickedness, error, darkness, ignorance, of my will and intellect was so great that only an inexpressibly great ransom could free me." (St. L. IX:236 f.)

But the Christians realize the seriousness of the attacks upon the essential deity of Christ. They know that a denial of Christ's deity destroys the theanthropic work of redemption and thus of the object of saving faith. And the Lord has always raised stanch defenders of the deity of Christ and of the Holy Ghost. He did so in the life-and-death struggle of the Christian Church during the Trinitarian controversies of the third and fourth centuries (Athanasius in 325 at Nicaea; the Cappadocians in 381 at Constantinople). Today the controversy of the Church with Modernism is no less serious and difficult. In the interest of its self-righteousness modern theology has reduced Christianity to an ethical religion; in the interest of the alleged omnicompetence of reason, Modernism has adopted the so-called scientific method in religion. This is an open disavowal of divine revelation, of Christ's vicarious atonement, and of the Scriptural doctrine of the Trinity. In view of man's hatred against this doctrine and the persistent attack upon this article, it is, indeed, a miracle of divine grace that the Christian doctrine of the Trinity and with it the Christian knowledge of God and the Church itself have survived. A study of the history of dogma reveals, as Luther points out, that God has guarded this doctrine with special care (St. L. XIII:675). Even a man like Wilhelm Augusti, who struggled valiantly to steer his ship out of the fog of rationalism, wrote: "History introduces us to outspoken opponents as well as to men who attempted to explain and modify the doctrine of the Trinity. But it is a striking phenomenon that from the beginning of the Christian Church down to our day neither the outspoken opponents nor the compromising theologians have been able to suppress this doctrine, confident though they were of their anti-Trinitarian position. Nor has faith in the Trinitarian God ever proved to be an obnoxious error; on the contrary, both in theory and in practice it has proved to be a salutary doctrine. These facts speak louder for the doctrine than all the prating about its incomprehensibility speaks against it." [41]

The ecclesiastical terminology is not of absolute necessity. The terminology employed by the Church during the first five centuries against the opponents of the Trinity is found in the Athanasian Creed, also known as the *Quicunque*. [42] Though many Christians are not acquainted with the terminology, they nevertheless believe and accept the correct doctrine on the basis of clear Scripture passages. An

---

[41] *System der christl. Dogmatik*, 1809, p. 128.

[42] The history of the Athanasian Creed as well as of the other two ecumenical creeds is discussed by Bentė, *Trigl.*, "Historical Introductions to the Symbolical Books," p. 9 f.

examination of the content of the ecclesiastical terms reveals that they constitute an epitome (Luther: "*Summarienwort*") of what Scripture teaches of the Trinity more clearly than the sun (*sole clarius*). It is therefore desirable that Christians become thoroughly familiar with the Church's terminology. For this reason our hymnal very properly contains the three Ecumenical Creeds. Luther did not hesitate to employ ecclesiastical terminology in his sermons and to quote, for example, the Athanasian Creed (St. L. X:1007). Modern Unitarians thoroughly despise it, but Luther said: "I doubt whether the New Testament Church has a more important document since the Apostolic Age" (St. L. VI:1576).

Among the terms which the Church has employed in presenting the Christian knowledge of God, the following are the most significant: 1) Trinity; 2) Person; 3) Essence; 4) *Homoousia;* 5) *Filioque;* 6) *Perichoresis;* 7) *Opera divina ad intra et ad extra.*

1. *Trinity.* This term does not occur in the Holy Scriptures,[43] but summarizes everything which God has revealed in Scripture concerning Himself, namely, that He is one (1 Cor. 8:4) and yet the Father, the Son, and the Holy Ghost (Matt. 28:19).[44] In their rejection of the Church's Trinitarian formulation, modern theologians have appealed to Luther. But this appeal to Luther's authority is as invalid as when the same theologians claim Luther as a champion of the denial of Verbal Inspiration. True, Luther said that neither the Latin word *trinitas,* nor the German *Dreifaltigkeit* are adequate terms (*"lauten nicht koestlich"*), but he adds that human language is too limited to express adequately the lofty article of the Trinity; this doctrine so far surpasses human understanding that God as a kind Father will condone stammering and prattling of His children so long as their faith is correct; this term expresses the Church's faith as well as can be done in human language, for the word *Trinity* conveys the Christian knowledge of God, namely, that the Divine Majesty is three distinct Persons in one divine essence. (St. L. XII:628 f.)

---

43 Tertullian is credited with being the first to use this term. Cp. Zoeckler, *Handbuch der theol. Wissenschaften,* III, 88.

44 "Our Churches, with common consent, do teach that the decree of the Council of Nicaea concerning the Unity of the Divine Essence and concerning the Three Persons, is true and to be believed without any doubting; that is to say, there is one Divine Essence which is called and which is God: eternal, without body, without parts, of infinite power, wisdom, and goodness, the Maker and Preserver of all things, visible and invisible; and yet there are three Persons, of the same essence and power, who also are coeternal, the Father, the Son, and the Holy Ghost" (Augbsurg Confession I. *Trigl.* 43).

2. The word *person* (*persona*, πρόσωπον, ὑπόστασις) has been and still is being employed by the Christian Church to disavow the Unitarian heresy which considers the Father, the Son, and the Holy Ghost only three manifestations and modes of operation or three powers and divine attributes. Luther points out that the term *person* was used by the Early Church to refute the folly of the Monarchian heretics as though the three names could denote one and the same Person in three successive manifestations (St. L. XIII:674). Like the ancient Unitarians, so also our modern Unitarians make fools of themselves when they reduce the three Persons to three powers, operations, and divine attributes. The term *person*, however, is employed not only antithetically, but also positively, for it clearly sets forth that in the one God there are three individual personal agents ("*Ich*"), or self-subsisting subjects ("*Selbstaendige*"). Luther: "Because Christ is born of the Father, He must be a Person distinct from the Father. You may use whatever term you will, we use the term *person*. We realize, of course, that our terminology is inadequate and is really only a stammering. But we cannot do justice to this truth, for we have no better term." (St. L. XIII:669.) The definition of the Augsburg Confession is fully satisfactory. "And the term *person* they use as the Fathers have used it, to signify, not a part or quality in another, but that which subsists of itself." [45]

Modern theologians of the so-called conservative wing claim that the concept *person* has changed in the course of the centuries. Seeberg states: "At one time the word *person* denoted an individual being; today, however, this term designates the soul-life ["*das geistige Wesen*"] of an individual being." [46] Even Ihmels says that the term *person* when applied to the inter-Trinitarian life of God dare not be understood in the sense of an individual personality.[47] But the term *person*

---

[45] Dogmaticians have defined *person* also as *suppositum intelligens* (a thinking self-existing being), *substantia individua intelligens incommunicabile*.

[46] *Grundwahrheiten*, 5th ed., p. 115.

[47] The difficulties arising from the inadequacy of human language became apparent in the discussions between the Eastern and the Western Church Fathers. The Greek Fathers objected to the Latins' use of *persona*, because in its basic meaning this Latin word denotes the mask, role, character of an actor, and it was alleged that when applied to the Trinity, it fails to express the real distinction between the Father, the Son, and the Holy Ghost. The Latins countered that the Greeks' term *hypostasis* means an essence, and that its use in the doctrine of the Trinity makes of the three *hypostases* three essences. After many conferences it was agreed that the Greeks should use the term *persona*, and the Latins the term *hypostasis*. See Baier, Vol. II, p. 57. Cp. Augustine, *De Tr.*, Vol. VII, 4. Chemnitz summarizes the salient points of this doctrine, *op. cit.*, 38.

as a designation of the inter-Trinitarian relation, or "internal essence," has not undergone and will never undergo a change, because God and His Word can never change. As was shown above, every Christian believes on the basis of the Holy Scriptures that God is three Persons, three distinct Persons, and the concept of *person* has not changed. But today we are confronted by a "theology" which follows the strange method of seeking God not in His Word, but in the subjective experience of the theologian. These modern theologians have changed the terms *Father, Son,* and *Holy Ghost* to denote three divine energies, operations, and wills. Seeberg: "The eternal dynamic love of God filled the human soul of Jesus, and this constitutes its essence. In this the deity of Christ consists." (*Loc. cit.*) But this is really nothing new. We find that the Dynamic Monarchians of the third century attempted to transform the Father, the Son, and the Holy Ghost into mere powers. By God's grace, however, the Church of the 20th century will abide by that definition of the word *person* which is clearly taught in Holy Scripture. In bold defiance of every type of Unitarianism, we declare with Luther: "This article of the Holy Trinity has been maintained, first, with the Word of God; then, through the valiant stand of the Apostles and the Church Fathers; and, finally, with miracles against the devil and the world. And with God's help this doctrine shall be maintained." (St. L. XIII:679.)

But while Luther and the dogmaticians with the ancient Church Fathers retain the term *person* – because they have no better term – they do not fail to point out the unique *usus loquendi* of the word in this doctrine. Ordinarily three persons have three essences, three wills, three distinct operations. But in the Trinity the three Persons have one and the same essence, not three; one set of divine attributes, not three; one operation in divine works (*ad extra*), not three. Three human persons are said to have one essence, but only in kind (*secundum speciem*); the three Persons in the Trinity have one essence in number (*secundum numerum, eandem numero essentiam*). For this reason the doctrine of the Trinity is an inscrutable mystery. Hence human reason also cannot comprehend how only the Second Person became man without the Father and the Holy Ghost at the same time becoming man. The fact is clearly stated in Holy Scripture (John 1:14; Gal. 4:4; Col. 2:9); the manner surpasses all human comprehension. Luther: "I would presume to be as sagacious as any heretic if I would interpret the words 'the Word was made flesh' to suit my whim and fancy" (St. L. VII:2161). Chemnitz says in his *Loci* concerning the use of the term *person* in the doctrine of God: "The use of the term *person* differs from the ordinary *usus loquendi.* We know what the word *person* signifies among men or among angels. Peter, Paul, and John are three persons, who, while they have the one human nature in common, differ in many respects: personality, age, will (Gal. 2:11); influence (1 Cor. 15:10); fields of labor (Gal. 2:8). In the Trinity, however, the three Persons cannot be distinguished as one angel is distinguished from another, one human being from another. The entire Peter, for example, is separated locally from the entire Paul. Christ, however, says, 'I am in the Father, and the Father in Me' (John 14:10). While men have a common nature, it does not follow that all the other persons are where the one person is (cp. Dan. 10:13). The Son, however, says: 'He that sent Me is with Me'; the Father hath not left Me alone (John 8:29). Among men and angels the individual persons differ from one another regarding time, will, power, activity. Among the Persons of the Trinity, however, there is coeternity, one will, one power, one activity. This distinction must be observed. This mystery would not be so great if the one essence were three persons, as Michael, Gabriel, Raphael, are three persons who have in common the angelic nature. On the basis of these fundamental facts, the rule has been established: the Persons of the Trinity are different, not essentially, as in creatures, where each has its own peculiarity (*suum proprium esse*), nor is the distinction only notional, as Sabellius held, but there is a real distinction, though the manner is incomprehensible and unknown to us. If anyone raises the objection that the terms *essence* and *person* are not sufficiently restrictive to express the mystery of the unity in the Trinity, then we may answer with Augustine: 'Human language labors under a truly great paucity of words. We speak of three persons not in order to say just that, but rather so as not to be silent altogether *(De Trin.* V).'"

3. *Essence. Essentia,* οὐσία, φύσις. The term *essence,* like *person,* has singular meaning when used in the doctrine of the Trinity. It denotes the one divine essence which in its totality and without any division is the property of each of the three Persons. We sometimes say that three persons have the same essence. This is correct if we use the term as a universal proposition, an intellectual abstraction, or a philosophical (nominalistic) concept, to denote a characteristic which is common to everyone in an entire class or genus. This definition, however, does not apply to the doctrine of the Trinity. The one divine essence of the three Persons is a true reality, because there is only one such essence which belongs to each person wholly and without division, in fine, is the true God. This is the doctrine of the

teachers of our Church. Chemnitz, for example, points out that while the essence of man is said to be communicable, in reality it is only a universal concept, which does not actually exist *per se*, but is only inferred in the thought and conceived of by the intellect. The divine essence, however, is communicable, is not an abstract concept, a genus, or a species, but is a true reality. He refers to Augustine's excellent statement: "Essence is ascribed to the Father, Son, and Holy Ghost, but not in the common sense when various species are said to have a common genus, or a number of individuals are said to belong to the same species, or when that which is applied to the whole is applied also to its parts. Essence is ascribed to the three Persons in an ineffable and incomprehensible manner." Chemnitz reminds us also of Augustine's splendid rule: "If you cannot find out what God is, beware lest you make Him what He is not." The Church therefore does not use the term *essence* in the philosophical meaning of a universal term, but as the truly existing divine nature, which is communicable and is therefore common to all three Persons and is totally and entirely in each Person. Chemnitz concludes: "I do not know what the essence of God is unless we say that the divine attributes are God's essence itself." (*Loci*, I, p. 38 *sq.*) Gerhard defines the term *essence* in almost the same words as Chemnitz: "The 'essence of man' is a universal term, which does not actually exist *per se*, but is only inferred in thought and conceived by the intellect. But as used of the Godhead, essence is not an imaginary something, as genus or species, but actually exists, though it is communicable" (*Loci, locus* "*De Nat. Dei*," § 49).

Luther explains how we must view the numerical unity of the divine essence and the Trinity of Persons in the following words: "By his birth from another, man becomes not only an individual person, distinct from his father, but also an individual substance, being, or essence. There is no absolute identity between the being of the father and the son. But here [in the Divine Majesty] the Son is born as a Person distinct from the Father, and yet His being remains identical with the Father's. As to persons they are distinct, but as to essence they retain absolute unity. When one man is sent on a mission by another, then the two are separate not only as to their person, but also as to their essence. In the Trinity, however, the Holy Spirit proceeds from the Father and the Son, even as He is sent by the Father and the Son and assumes a distinct personality, but in such a way that He remains in the Father's and the Son's essence, and that the Father and the Son remain in the Holy Ghost's essence. In other words, all three Persons retain the absolute unity of one and the same

Godhead. The theologians define the Son's birth as an immanent generation, which in no way takes place outside the Divine Being, but originates in the Father alone and therefore remains in the deity. Likewise the procession of the Holy Spirit is known as an immanent procession, because it occurs alone within the Father and the Son and allows for no separation from the deity. The manner of this relation is a matter of faith. Even the angels, who constantly behold this majesty with joy, cannot fathom it. All who have tried to understand it have broken their necks." (St. L. X:1008 f.)

4. Ὁμοούσιος τῷ πατρί, *consubstantial,* or coessential, with the Father. The Nicene formula the Son is ὁμοούσιος τῷ πατρί, of the same essence with the Father, on the one hand condemns Arianism, which called Christ the first creature, κτίσμα ἐξ οὐκ ὄντων ("and made Him only a cosmic agent through whom God created the world"), and on the other hand expresses the Scriptural truth that the Son is of one essence, ***unius numero essentiae,*** with the Father. Luther declares emphatically and correctly that this term teaches no new doctrine, but expresses the doctrine of Scripture in opposition to the Arian heresy. Luther said: "The Council did not discover this article or set it up as something that was new and had not existed in the Church before, but only defended it against the heresy of Arius. . . . Otherwise what would have become of the Christians who, before the Council, for more than three hundred years, since the days of the Apostles, had believed and had prayed to the dear Lord Jesus and called upon Him as true God and had died for it and had been miserably persecuted?" (St. L. XVI:2188 f.) "*Homoousios* means 'of one essense, or nature,' not two, as the Church Fathers determined at Nicaea and as is sung in the Latin creed, *consubstantialis;* some *coexistentialis; coessentialis*" (St. L. XVI:2211). Athanasius understood the term *homoousia* to denote the numerical unity of the essence, because he rejected every division of the divine essence and maintained: "One They are, the Son and the Father, as to peculiarity and relation of the nature and as to the identity." [48]

Gieseler finds a contributory cause of Arius' heresy in the fact that he had been trained in the historico-exegetical school of Antioch under the Samosatanian Lucian (*Kirchengesch.* I, 369). The real cause of the Arian controversy, however, has been given by Luther: "Into this fair and peaceful paradise and peaceful time came the Old Serpent and raised up Arius, a priest of Alexandria, against

[48] *Contra Arianos* III, 4. See Seeberg, *Dogmengesch.*, 2d ed., I, 166.

his bishop. He wanted to bring up a new doctrine against the old faith and be a man of importance; he attacked his bishop's doctrine, saying that Christ was not God; many priests and great, learned bishops followed him, and the trouble grew in many lands, until at last Arius ventured to declare that he was a martyr, saying that he was suffering for the truth's sake at the hands of his bishop, Alexander, who did not countenance this teaching and wrote scandalous letters against him to all countries." (St. L. XVI:2186.) Gieseler's historical judgment as to the genesis of Arianism is strange, indeed, for it is impossible that a truly exegetical training will ever lead a person to the denial of the deity of Christ, the Trinity, the Vicarious Atonement, or the inspiration of Scripture. Liberal theology claims that deeper insights into the Scripture and a "recapture of the culture of the Bible" demand a re-interpretation and a re-definition of the Scriptural terms. This is only a subterfuge for the denial of the fundamentals of our Christian faith. The true exegetical training consists in this, that, as Luther says, we deal with Scripture in such a way as to remember at all times that God speaks to us, and that we continue in Christ's Word in spite of our human opinions (John 8:31-32). The genesis of Arianism and of every form of heterodox teaching – including the heterodoxy of our day – has been exposed in 1 Tim. 6:3 f.: the turning away from the wholesome words of our Lord Jesus Christ, and the resultant inflation, being bloated with one's own wisdom. Expressed in modern terms, the origin of heresy is the formulation of doctrine on the basis of the religious self-consciousness of the theologizing subject. According to Horst Stephan, Luther and Melanchthon "were too accustomed to view the Bible as the only source of doctrine and the old Confessions as a summary of Bible teaching." [49] In support of the charge that Luther was tradition bound, Stephan quotes Luther: "This article (concerning the Trinity as taught by the Fathers according to Moses and the Apostles and defended against the heretics) has come to us as a precious heritage, and God has preserved it until this day against all heretics. Let us in due simplicity retain it and not become wise in our own conceit." (St. L. XII:656.) There is no traditionalistic spirit in Luther's theology. On the contrary, Luther's theology is based on the principle that "our God will save those who do not profess to be wise, but simply believe the Word, while those who follow their reason and despise the Word shall go to their doom in their vaunted wisdom."

5. The term *Filioque* expresses the truth that the Holy Spirit

---

[49] *Glaubenslehre,* 1921, p. 192.

proceeds not only from the Father, but also from the Son. It is generally accepted that this term was added to the Niceno-Constantinopolitan Creed by the Synod of Toledo (589). But the term is later than the doctrine. Even though the Christians of the first centuries did not know the term, they believed the fact of the *Filioque* on the basis of Scripture, which called the Holy Spirit not only the Spirit of the Father (Matt. 10:20), but also the Spirit of the Son (Gal. 4:6). Scripture, furthermore, ascribes the sending of the Spirit to the Son (John 15:26; 16:7) as well as to the Father (John 14:16). In fact, it adds the significant expression that the Holy Spirit would not speak of Himself, but shall receive His message from the Son (John 16:13-14), and is therefore called the "breath of His [the Messiah's] lips" (Is. 11:4), and the "Spirit of His mouth" [the Word] (2 Thess. 2:8). The procession of the Spirit from the Son is also clearly indicated in John 20:22, when Christ breathed on His disciples and said, "Receive ye the Holy Ghost." [50]

6. Περιχώρησις, ἐνύπαρξις, *circumincessio,* interpenetration, immanence. These terms express the fact that each Person has the one divine essence and that therefore the three Persons are in one another and reciprocally interpenetrate, interpermeate, each other.[51]

This is clearly taught in John 14:11 ("I am in the Father and the Father in Me"); John 17:21. Nevertheless, according to Scripture, it does not follow from this mutual immanence that the Father and the Holy Spirit became man when the Son was made flesh. Only the "would-be-wise heretic," as Luther said, pretends to penetrate this mystery.

7. *Opera divina ad intra* and *opera divina ad extra.* It has been said, especially in our day, that in these technical terms the entire

---

[50] The *Filioque* became one of the points which caused the schism between the Eastern and the Western Churches. In the Orthodox Confession of 1643, p. 142, we read: "The Holy Spirit proceeds from the Father alone as the Foundation and Source of the Godhead" (Quoted in Plitt, *Grundriss der Symbolik,* 3d ed., p. 40). — The fact is, of course, that the *Filioque* in substance was taught in the public writings before 589. Augustine taught it. See Seeberg, *op. cit.,* I, 195. Cp. also Baier, II, 69, quoting Gal. 4:6; Rom. 8:9; 1 Pet. 1:11; John 20:22; Is. 11:4, compared with 2 Thess. 2:8. The Scripture proof ought to mean something to those modern theologians who admit that the economic (historical) divine acts presuppose eternal *("vorzeitliche")* or ontological relations in God. The Eastern Churches would hardly have denied the *Filioque* so tenaciously if they had not sought for a reason to separate from the Western Church.

[51] Quenstedt: "An inevitable result of the one essence is the mutual interpenetration and immanence by which because of the unity of essence the one Person is in a most peculiar manner in the other, John 14:11; 17:21" (I, 470).

apparatus of the ecclesiastical terminology in the doctrine of the Trinity has reached the climax of sophistry and is the apex of unintelligible and meaningless jargon.[52] But these terms are not based on sophistry, but rest on Scripture. Neither are they unintelligible and meaningless. As was pointed out previously, Luther did not hesitate to use these terms in sermons preached to the common man. The term *opera ad extra* denotes the divine works which relate to the world, which have the universe as their object, such as creation, preservation, building of the Church. These works, as was shown above, are common to all three persons, because there is only one divine essence, not three; only one set of divine attributes and works, not three. *Opera divina ad extra sunt indivisa. Opera divina ad intra* are those divine works which have no bearing upon the world, but take place within the Deity. Luther calls the *opera ad intra* works which "remain in the Deity," which do "not extend beyond the Deity." Such works are the eternal generation of the Son and the eternal spiration of the Holy Ghost. In designating the Son as the Only-Begotten of the Father (John 1:14), the Scriptures reveal an intertrinitarian act which emanates from the Father and affects the Son. Likewise the fact that the Holy Spirit is called the Spirit of the Father (John 15:26; Matt. 10:20) and the Spirit of the Son (Gal. 4:6; Rom. 8:9) is the revelation of an act within the Divine Majesty of which the Father and the Son are the subject and the Holy Spirit the object. By revealing these "intertrinitarian" divine works, Scripture reveals in unmistakable terms that there are three distinct Persons in the one divine essence. The names Father, Son, and Holy Ghost are *personal* propositions.

The *opera ad intra* are not common to all three Persons, as are the *opera ad extra,* but are ascribed only to one or two Persons. The generation of the Son is ascribed only to the Father, the spiration of the Holy Ghost only to the Father and the Son, and thereby the Father is revealed as a Person distinct from the Son, and the Holy Spirit as distinct from the Father and the Son. Each of these intertrinitarian acts belongs only to one Person (*opera ad intra divisa sunt*), and these acts are, therefore, very properly designated as personal acts within the Divine Majesty (*actus personales*). This additional terminology became necessary to defend and uphold the distinction of the three Per-

[52] Horst Stephan: "To this were added the ancient speculations concerning the *opera ad intra* (the two sets of personal acts, namely, the generation proceeding from the Father, and the spiration proceeding from the Father and the Son) which result in three personal properties (paternity, filiation, procession) and in the equally meaningless phrase *notiones personales.* In this way the ancient Church arrived at a very artificial theory." (*Glaubenslehre,* 1921, p. 193.)

sons against Unitarianism and to condemn any and every confusion of the three Persons. Because personal acts are predicated of each of the three Persons, we must also ascribe to each a specific personal attribute: to the Father, paternity; to the Son, filiation; and to the Holy Spirit, passive spiration, or procession. The term "personal properties" serves the purpose of maintaining the distinction of the Persons and prevents the confusion of them. From the personal properties flow the "personal notations," which amount to negative or passive attributes and are, in the case of the Father, the incapability of being born or proceeding, *innascibilitas et improcessibilitas;* in the case of the Son, *nascibilitas, sive generatio passive talis,* and in the case of the Holy Spirit, *processio sive spiratio passiva.* These terms express the same truth which is confessed in the Athanasian Creed, "The Father is made of none; neither created nor begotten. The Son is of the Father alone; not made, nor created, but begotten. The Holy Ghost is of the Father and of the Son; neither made, nor created, nor begotten, but proceeding." [53]

This terminology is not meaningless jargon, but necessary theological apparatus. Of course, Christians might wish that the Church would never have been troubled by Unitarians and therefore would have had no occasion to formulate this terminology. Christians say with St. Paul: "I would they were even cut off which trouble you" (Gal. 5:12). But, as Chemnitz points out (*Loci* I, 36 *sqq.*), this terminology became necessary on account of the errors and the treachery of the heretics. What effrontery when Stephan claims that this terminology is nothing but "human speculation," "artificial theory," and "meaningless"! This reckless statement finds its counterpart in the Modernist claim that Scripture does not claim inspiration and inviolability for itself. The fact is that the terminology used in connection with the *opera ad intra* is in full accord with the teaching of Scripture. Modern theologians are, of course, at liberty to refuse to believe the Bible. They may also charge Luther with being "Scripture bound" and traditionalistic and therefore unable to break with the ecclesiastical terminology which summarizes the Biblical doctrines. But honest scholarship should have kept them from making the assertion that this terminology is not in accord with the content of Scripture and is nothing more than human speculation. In reality this terminology expresses the simple faith

---

[53] *Trigl.*, p. 33. – Baier-Walther, II, 64: *Distinguuntur personae divinae actibus personalibus, proprietatibus et notionibus personalibus.* Loeber, *Ev.-Luth. Dogm.*, 1872, p. 201, explains the ecclesiastical terms personal acts *(Wirkungen)*, attributes *(Eigenschaften)*, and marks of recognition *(Kenntnisse)*.

which every Christian believes on the basis of clear Scripture passages even though he has never heard of these terms. Every Christian believes that the Son is the Only-Begotten of the Father and that the Holy Ghost is the Spirit of the Father and of the Son. Therefore he believes implicitly the *actus personales* (generation and spiration), the *proprietates personales* (paternity, etc.), and the allegedly meaningless *notiones personales* (innascibility, etc.).

But why – ask the less outspoken anti-Trinitarians – why encumber these self-evident truths with a whole battery of ecclesiastical terms? We have the heretics to thank for this situation. The Church did not invent these terms from an itch for novelty (Chemnitz says: "Not from any mischievous desire for innovation"), much less from a sort of malice to worry future generations. But the terminology has become necessary because the enemies of the Church have constantly devised new perversions of God's Word and devious subterfuges to attack God's self-revelation. In one way or another they have consistently endeavored to change the concept divine *persons* into operations or wills or powers. Even the so-called conservative wing of Modernist theology travels this evil road. An examination of the modern theologian's alleged "deeper insight into the concept *person*" shows that he also believes that the concept *person* is nothing more than divine power, will, or operation. The ecclesiastical terminology *opera ad intra* and *ad extra* is therefore far from "meaningless," and even today it is very much in order. The Church has always been compelled to fight Unitarianism. At Luther's time some labored under the delusion that in spite of their denial of the Trinity they could be members of the Christian Church. Luther was constrained, therefore, to emphasize the doctrine of the Trinity not only in his writings, but also in his sermons, and in his polemics against Unitarians he did not hesitate to employ the ancient ecclesiastical terminology, even the terms *opera ad intra* and *opera ad extra,* setting forth that these terms are in full accord with Scripture.

The question has been raised: Can we expect our people to understand the nature and manner of the Son's eternal generation from the Father and the Holy Spirit's eternal procession from the Father and the Son? Obviously the answer must be in the negative. But neither can the trained theologian understand the mystery of the Trinity. Every wise theologian will confess: *Quid sit nasci, quid processus, me nescire sum professus.* Baier says very correctly: "It is certain that there is a distinction between the Son's generation and the Spirit's procession, but it is impossible to define more fully the manner in which they differ" (*Compend.* II, p. 69). In other words, the difference between the Son's generation and the Spirit's procession is not abstract, transcendent, notional, but is real, because the terms employed by Scripture establish a real difference. The attempt to go beyond the fact of the distinction and to explain its nature is contemptible presumption. And whoever endeavors independently of God's self-revelation to penetrate the Divine Majesty, which dwells in a light to which no man can approach (1 Tim. 6:16), attempts the impossible. Luther reminds us that not even the angels can fathom this mystery, and all who have tried it have broken their necks. (St. L. X:1008 f.)

The destructive criticism and the deep-seated hatred with which modern theology approaches the term *opera ad intra* need not surprise us. Because there are eternal *opera ad intra,* that is, eternal personal acts, in the divine Majesty (the eternal generation of the Son and the eternal spiration of the Holy Ghost); and because there are also *proprietates* and *notiones personales* (there never was a time when the Father was not the Father, when the Son was not born of the Father, etc.), Unitarians, including the Subordinationists and the advocates of the so-called economic, or temporal, trinity, do not have a leg to stand on; on the contrary, the truth as expressed in Aug. Conf., Art. I, stands irrevocable: "There is one divine essence, and there are three Persons of the same essence and power, who also are co-eternal." No wonder that in this point – just as in the doctrine of inspiration – a theology which has turned its back on Scripture haughtily renders the verdict: "Artificial theories, human speculations, meaningless, noxious terms."

We believe it proper and beneficial to give the floor once more to Luther and Chemnitz on the terms *opera ad intra* and *opera ad extra.* In his commentary on *The Last Words of David* Luther offers a very detailed presentation of the doctrine of the Trinity, based on both the Old and the New Testament. (St. L. III:1884 ff.) Throughout this treatise Luther directs his warning against those who rely on their vaunted wisdom and attempt to judge this doctrine according to reason. He says: "Here Madam Wiseacre, our reason, which is ten times wiser than God Himself, takes offense." "Such highly intelligent people are the Jews, Mahomet, the Turks, and the Tartars; they claim to comprehend the incomprehensible essence of God in the spoon or nutshell of their reason and say: God has no wife; therefore He can have no Son. Shame, shame, shame upon you, the devil, with the Jews and Mahomet and all those who are the pupils of blind, foolish, miserable reason in these high matters which no one understands but

God Himself and which we can understand only to the extent in which the Holy Ghost has revealed them to us through the Prophets." It is noteworthy that Luther, throughout this treatise, employed ecclesiastical terminology, *opera ad intra,* etc. "Here every Christian must follow the Athanasian Creed and be very careful lest he confound the Persons into one Person or divide the one divine essence into three Persons. If in the realm of creation, that is, outside the Trinity [*ad extra*] I were to ascribe to each Person a specific work in which the other two would not share, then I would divide the one Godhead and posit three gods or creators. That is wrong. And again, if within the Deity, or outside and beyond creation [*ad intra*] I do not ascribe to each Person a distinct characteristic which cannot be said of the other two, then I have confounded the three Persons into one Person, and that, too, is wrong. St. Augustine's rule, therefore, applies: *Opera trinitatis ad extra sunt indivisa.* The divine works performed by God outside the Deity cannot be divided. In other words, the Persons dare not be divided according to their works, nor dare their specific work from without [*ad extra*] be ascribed to each Person. Within the Godhead [*ad intra*] the Person must be distinguished. But every work outside the Godhead must be assigned to all three Persons without distinction. For example: The Father is your and my God and Creator. But the Son has done the same work, and He also is your and my God and Creator as well as the Father. The Holy Spirit has also performed the same work which has brought you and me into existence and is therefore your and my God and Creator just as well as the Father and the Son. And yet there are not three gods, three creators, but only one God and Creator, who has made both you and me. This my confession is my bulwark against the Arian heresy which divides the divine essence into three gods and creators, whereas I confess that there is no more than one God and Creator. — On the other hand, when I step outside creation and into the inner, infinite being of the divine God, then – following Scripture and not reason – I find that in this one indivisible eternal Deity the Father is an entirely different Person from the Son. His distinctive property is that He is Father and therefore does not receive the deity from the Son nor from another. The Son is a Person distinct from the Father in the one divine Godhead of the Father. His distinctive personal attribute is that He is a Son, that He possesses the deity not from Himself, but only from the Father through the eternal generation. The Holy Spirit is a Person distinct from the Father and the Son in the same one Godhead. His personal attribute is that He proceeds from the Father and the Son and has the deity from no one but the Father and the Son. This relation is unchangeable from eternity to eternity.[54] And with this my confession (of my faith in the three distinct Persons) I take my stand against the Sabellian heresy, against Jews and Mohammedans, and all who would be wiser than God. I do not confound the Persons into one Person, but in the true Christian faith I retain three distinct Persons in the one, divine, eternal essence, even though these three Persons in their relation to us and to the entire creation [*ad extra*] are one God and Creator. This distinction may be too subtle and academic for us Germans and should be confined to the schools. Nevertheless, it is necessary to discuss this doctrine in theological terminology. We see that in these last times the devil switches his tail,[55] as though he would incite to all manner of new heresies. We hear how the world in its folly itches to hear something new, loathes sound doctrines (2 Tim. 4:3), and thus opens wide the door to the devil to introduce whatever he wills. It is therefore beneficial, yes, necessary, that there are more, both among the laity and especially among the clergy, who can present these articles of our faith in clear and precise terminology. Let him who finds this too difficult stay with the children's catechism and pray against Satan and his heretics, against the Jews and Mohammedans, that they may not lead him into temptation." Chemnitz presents the same views (*Loci* I, 40 *sq.*): As to the rule *Opera Trinitatis ad extra sunt indivisa,* he shows that Scripture teaches it. "Because Scripture says: 'Let us make' (Gen. 1:26) and John 5:19: 'What things soever He [the Father] doeth, these also doeth the Son likewise'; John 14:10: 'the Father that dwelleth in Me, He doeth the works'; and again, John 5:17: 'My Father worketh hitherto, and I work'; John 16:15: 'All things that the Father hath are Mine. . . . He [the Spirit] shall take of Mine and shall show it unto you.' These passages show in a fine way how the *opera ad extra* are common to all three Persons." As to the value of the Augustinian rule *Opera Trinitatis ad intra sunt divisa,* etc., Chemnitz points out that the formulations are not merely academic niceties and erudite distinctions. Since God wants to be known, invoked, and proclaimed only as He has revealed Himself, we

---

54 Thus Luther repudiated the theories of an economic Trinity, as successive revelation of God in three different persons, which is, of course, only another name for Unitarianism.

55 Today the devil does more than merely "switch his tail." During one period of the Arian controversy it was said that the world had become Arian. Today it can be said that the so-called Protestant world has become Unitarian. See Nitzsch-Stephan, *op. cit.*, p. 490 ff.

must make every effort that our thoughts concerning these mysteries are pious and our words reverent. We should therefore studiously emulate the care of the ancient Fathers in their controversy with the anti-Trinitarians and take to heart Jerome's words: "From inexact speech springs heresy."

But has the Church consistently observed the Augustinian rule: *Opera ad extra indivisa sunt?* Does not the Apostles' Creed ascribe to each Person a special *opus divinum ad extra:* to the Father, creation; to the Son, redemption; to the Holy Spirit, sanctification? Does not the second part of Luther's Small Catechism actually mislead Christian people to a "naive tritheism" by dividing the divine works among the three Persons? [56] This objection to the Church's terminology does not rest on fact. In the first place, no orthodox teacher speaks of a division and distribution of the *opera ad extra* unless the tongue or the pen has slipped. Furthermore, while the Church uses the terms *attribution* and *appropriation,* it does not use the term *distribution.* The former terms have Scriptural basis because Scripture attributes the work of creation especially to the Father. This is clearly taught in those passages which state that the Father created the world through the Son (Col. 1:15-16; Heb. 1:2); and through the Holy Ghost (Ps. 33:6). This is evident from all those passages which tell us that the Son became man, gave Himself for us, redeemed us from the curse of the Law (John 1:14; 1 Tim. 2:6; Gal. 3:13). Scripture attributes the work of redemption especially to the Son. And whenever the Scriptures say that the Holy Spirit convicts the world (John 16:8-11), that He glorifies Christ (v. 14), that He guides into all truth (v. 13), that He is the Spirit of adoption (Rom. 8:15-16), Scripture ascribes the work of sanctification especially to the Holy Ghost.

In other passages, however, Scripture teaches just as clearly that the three works are common to all three Persons. The work of creation is also the work of the Son and of the Holy Spirit. This becomes evident from such passages as speak of the world being created by the Son and by the Spirit (Ps. 33:6; Col. 1:16; John 1:3), and especially from those references where the work of creation is attributed to the Son and the Holy Ghost directly (Heb. 1:10; Job 33:4). Likewise the work of redemption is attributed also to the Father, because He gave His only-begotten Son and reconciled the world (John 3:16; 2 Cor. 5: 18-19); and also to the Holy Ghost, because Christ, according to His human nature, was conceived of the Holy Ghost (Matt. 1:20) and

---

[56] See Horst Stephan, *Glaubenslehre,* 1921, p. 193.

because the Holy Spirit rested upon Christ (Is. 61:1; Luke 4:18). Finally, the work of sanctification is also the work of the Father, and of the Son, for both sent the Spirit (John 14:16, 26; 16:7; 15:26; Acts 2:33); the Father has elected us unto sanctification (2 Thess. 2:13), and the Son sanctifies us through His Word (John 17:19), and He is made unto us sanctification (1 Cor. 1:2, 30). Scripture therefore teaches the twofold truth: 1) That each of the *opera ad extra* (creation, redemption, sanctification) must be attributed to one Person in particular; 2) that the same works must be ascribed to all Persons (*opera tribus personis communia*).

The *opera ad extra* are common to all three Persons because each of the Persons has the divine essence entirely and indivisibly. In relation to the creatures (*ad extra*) each Person has the same attributes and the selfsame works. The fact that Scripture, on the one hand, attributes the *opera ad extra* to each of the Persons, and, on the other hand, makes them common to the three Persons, is another proof (Luther would say "revelation") of the ontological, or essential Trinity. Luther treats this point at great length, though he realizes that this matter is profound and difficult. He raises the question: "Why does Scripture teach us to say, 'I believe in God the Father Almighty, Maker,' etc., and does not teach us to call the Son the Maker? Why, 'And in Jesus Christ, conceived by the Holy Ghost'? Why, 'I believe in the Holy Ghost, the Giver of Life, who spake by the Prophets'? In these words of the Creeds we ascribe to each Person externally [*ad extra*] a special and distinct work, even as the Persons are distinct, internally [*ad intra*]." (St. L. III:1923.) To make his point clear, Luther distinguishes between an "absolute" and a "relative" study of creation. Viewed absolutely, the works of creation tell us nothing of a Triune God because every work is the work of the one God. But we must study God's works also relatively, that is, in their relation to us, for in such study of His creatures God intends to illustrate the Trinity to us. God employs the dove to picture and reveal the Holy Spirit as an externally distinct Person. The dove may never be used as a picture of the Father or of the Son, but only of the Holy Spirit, in order to assure us that the eternal essence exists in three distinct Persons from all eternity (Luke 3:22). The Son is revealed to us in the form of man, a humble and obedient man (Phil. 2:7). Though the Father and the Son and the Holy Spirit have created this humanity, this specific creation, according to God's good pleasure, is the means to reveal in a specific way the Son. By coming in the fashion of man, the Son made Himself known as a distinct Person. Again, the Father has revealed Himself as a distinct Person in the voice, a revelation restricted to the Father. To illustrate his point, Luther refers to the analogy employed by such men as Bonaventura: If three girls put a dress on one of the three, each one would have a part in putting on the dress, and yet only the third one is actually being clothed. In like manner we must understand that all Persons in God, one in essential unity, have created a unique human nature and united it with the Son in His Person, but in such a manner that only the Son actually assumed the human nature. Likewise the dove and the voice are adopted by the Holy Spirit and the Father respectively as the means of the revelation. When we confess in the Creed, "I believe in God the Father,"etc., we do not mean to say that only the Father is almighty, the Creator, because we believe that also the Son and the Holy Spirit are the Creator. Yet there are not three Almighties, as little as there are three Saviors, or three Sanctifiers, though the Father and the Holy Spirit are also our Redeemer, and the Father and the Son are also our Sanctifier. *Opera ad extra indivisa sunt, sic cultus Trinitatis indivisa est.* We must, therefore, accept and believe the three Persons in the one divine essence, neither confounding the Persons nor dividing the essence. (St. L. III:1923–1929.)[57]

In this connection two specific questions must be answered:

1. Is the procession of the Holy Spirit from the Father (John 15:26), ἐκπορεύεται, temporal or eternal, or both? – Luther and the Lutheran dogmaticians consider it practically self-evident that John 15:26 teaches not the temporal, economic, but the eternal (ontological, Trinitarian) procession from the Father. The Athanasian Creed defines the ἐκπορεύεται as the eternal procession. Hofmann,

---

[57] Chemnitz presents the same views. (*Loci* I, 42 *sq.*) Among other things he says: "The Persons are distinct not only in their 'inner distinctions,' but also by their works to the outside, for while in the works *ad extra* the three Persons work jointly, nevertheless, the personal property of each Person must be observed. The three works of the Trinity according to Rom. 11:36 (of Him, through Him, to Him) are indivisible, for St. Paul does not add, 'To them be glory,' but, 'To whom be glory.'" Chemnitz summarizes as follows: We believe the unity of the essence and allow for no confusion of the Persons. The rule that the works *ad extra* are common to the three Persons must be understood so that the distinctions and properties of the Persons are not confounded. This rule must be observed especially in our worship, for while the divine worship is indivisible, the Christian prayer differs fundamentally from all non-Christian prayers inasmuch as the Christian does not invoke the three Persons indiscriminately *(confuse)*, but he is aware of the particular distinctions and blessings of each Person.

Meyer, Luthardt, Klostermann, say that the procession in John 15:26 refers only to temporal procession, while Olshausen, Stier, Lange, and Godet restrict it to eternal or inter-Trinitarian. De Wette's comments on this passage are entirely misleading and emanate from his false view of the Trinity. He says that the words "proceeded from the Father" do not pertain to the Spirit's essence, but only to His appearance in His activity within the Christian Church. De Wette's view, however, is false, for the words "whom I will send" speak of the temporal appearance, while the subordinate clause "which proceedeth," etc., clearly and definitely speaks of the eternal and essential relation of the Holy Spirit to the Father. Luthardt contradicts himself in his attempt to restrict the words "who proceedeth," etc., to the economic and temporal procession. He says that the statement "who proceedeth," etc., and "whom I will send" are parallel because in both instances the words "from the Father" are added. True, but we note that the tense changes: πέμψω, future; ἐκπορεύεται, present tense. When the Savior uses the future tense, He clearly and unmistakably is speaking of the economic and temporal activity, which the Holy Spirit would initiate after Christ's ascension. The same is true of μαρτυρήσει, "He will testify of Me." It is significant that the phrase in the present tense, "who proceedeth," is placed between the two phrases with the future tense. This change of tense prevents us from co-ordinating temporally the procession with the sending and testifying. On the contrary, we are compelled to accept the procession as an eternal and timeless act. If the procession referred only to the Spirit's activity, then the Savior would have used the future: ἐκπορεύσεται.[58]

2. As modern theologians appeal to Luther in defense of their denial of Inspiration, they also appeal to Luther with regard to their rejection of the terminology of the ancient Church. Did Luther sub-

---

[58] Quenstedt (I, 577) employs the same line of argument against the Socinians. Incidentally, Quenstedt also anticipates and refutes Luthardt, who in Zoeckler's *Commentary* on John 15:26 uses virtually the same arguments which the Socinians had employed at Quenstedt's time. Luthardt says: "The ancient Church understood this passage of the eternal procession; in fact, the Eastern Church used this passage in its opposition to the *Filioque* of the Western Church. However, the context [?] and the preposition παρά (from near by), not ἐκ (from within) compel us to understand the procession as a historical and temporal one." Quenstedt's refutation of the Socinian error is therefore applicable to Luthardt. He writes: "My answer is: 1) τὸ παρά does not exclude τὸ ἐξ of origin; 2) the Son is also called the Only-Begotten of (παρά) the Father by generation (John 1:14). In this mystery ἐκ τοῦ πατρός and παρὰ τοῦ πατρός are synonymous terms."

scribe *ex animo* to the ancient terminology, especially the terms *trinitas* and ὁμοούσιος? — This question is in order because Luther appears to speak quite disparagingly of these terms. We have already discussed Luther's attitude toward the term *Trinity* (*Dreifaltigkeit*). In his treatise against Latomus (1521) Luther says that "his soul loathed the word ὁμοούσιος" (St. L. XVIII:1182). The reference reads: "Assuming the case (*quod si*) that my soul loathes the word ὁμοούσιος and that I would not want to employ it, I would not thereby become a heretic, for who can compel me to use this term as long as I accept the doctrine which the Council [at Nicaea] formulated on the basis of God's Word?" Luther speaks conditionally, and his statement is no more than a protest against the substitution of human terminology for the clear Word of God. Under the same or similar conditions, we, too, would use similar language. As Philippi points out (*Glaubenslehre*, 2d ed., II, 156 f.), ecclesiastical terminology has only a hypothetical and relative, not an absolute, necessity. This was Luther's position to the end of his life. As late as 1543 he advised those who find the ecclesiastical terminology too difficult simply to retain the simple Catechism truths. (St. L. III:1920 f.) But in his condemnation of Arianism, Luther unequivocally accepted the term *homoousios*, as is evident from his treatise *Of Councils and Churches*. Luther says: "When they [the Church Fathers in their opposition to Arius] came to the heart of the matter, namely, that Christ is *homoousios* with the Father, the Arians could no longer find any trick or loophole or ruse or wile, for the plain fact is that the term *homoousios* adopted by the Fathers at Nicaea means, 'of one and the same essence, or nature,' and not, 'of two natures.' Christ is *consubstantialis* (so the Latin Creed), or *coexistentialis* and *coessentialis* (thus some of the Fathers). At Nicaea the Arians had accepted the term *homoousios* and employed it when they discussed the doctrine of the Trinity in the presence of the emperor and the Church Fathers. But in their own schools they attacked the word vehemently, their argument being that the word is not found in the Scriptures. They convened many councils, even as late as in the reign of Constantine, with the one design to weaken and undermine the Nicene Council. Their maneuvers caused untold confusion and so alarmed the men of our party that even Jerome in his perplexity petitioned Damason, bishop of Rome, to delete the word *homoousios*. 'I have no idea,' says Jerome, 'what kind of poison is in this word which makes it so objectionable to the Arians.' A dialog has come down to us in which Athanasius and Arius disputed about the word *homoousios* before an official named Probus. When

Arius insisted that the word is not in Scripture, Athanasius turned the tables on him and caught him in his own trap. 'Neither does Scripture contain the words *innascibilis, ingenitus Deus.*' And yet the Arians use these words to prove that Christ cannot be God because He was born, while God cannot be born. Probus decided against Arius. It is true, indeed, that in divine things we dare not teach anything outside the Scripture. This, however, does not mean that one dare not use more or other words than Scripture uses, especially in controversies when heretics employ subterfuges to distort the doctrine and to pervert Scripture. The Arians played a double game: In their own schools they perverted Scriptures by adding false comments, but before the emperor and the Council they would quote these passages without any comment. Therefore it became necessary to summarize the teaching of Scripture in one watchword and to ask the Arians whether they accepted Christ *homoousios* as the Scriptures so plainly teach in many instances. It is the same as when the Pelagians wanted to drive us into a corner because we employed the term 'original sin' or 'Adam's malady,' since these terms do not occur in Scripture. But Scripture mightily teaches what these terms designate when it says that we were conceived in sin (Ps. 51:5), are by nature the children of wrath (Eph. 2:3), and are all sinners by one man's transgression (Rom. 5:12)." (St. L. XVI:2211 f.)

8

God's Essence and Attributes

(De essentia et attributis divinis)

The doctrine of God is usually presented under two headings: "The Holy Trinity" and "God's Essence and Attributes." It is of no consequence in which order these two parts of the doctrine are treated, as long as the Scriptural principle is maintained, i. e., as long as no human opinions are injected into either doctrine. The fact is, of course, that neither doctrine can be studied without constant reference to the other. If we were to discuss God's essence and attributes independently of the Trinity, we could do so only on the basis of natural theology and by completely excluding the Christian knowledge of God. Chemnitz therefore very properly shows at the very outset (*Loci, locus "De Deo in genere"*) that without the knowledge of Christ and the Trinity man's knowledge of God is in reality *ignorantia Dei* as far as the practical result, viz., the worship of God, is concerned. (*Loci* I, 22 *sq.*)

But neither can we present the doctrine of the Trinity without a discussion of the doctrine of God's essence and attributes. We must constantly keep in mind that Scripture ascribes to each of the three distinct Persons the one and the same divine essence and the selfsame divine attributes.

In the course of years we have alternated the order of these two sections. In this volume we have discussed the doctrine of the Trinity first, so that at the very outset the attention is riveted upon the fundamental difference between the Christian and the natural knowledge of God – a difference which today is almost universally ignored. In this section we shall now present the Scriptural doctrine of God's essence and attributes under the following headings. A. "The Relation of the Divine Essence to the Divine Attributes and of the Attributes to One Another"; B. "The Classifications of the Divine Attributes"; C. "The Separate Divine Attributes."

A. THE RELATION OF THE DIVINE ESSENCE TO THE DIVINE ATTRIBUTES AND OF THE ATTRIBUTES TO ONE ANOTHER

On the basis of Scripture, two points must be maintained:

1. In God, essence and attributes are not separate, but the divine essence and the divine attributes are absolutely identical, because God is infinite and above space (1 Kings 8:27) and time (Ps. 90:2, 4). Were we to assume that there are parts in God, we would ascribe finitude to the infinite God and thereby erase the difference between God and man. Therefore the Augsburg Confession says: God is "without parts" (*Trigl.* 43, I, 3). On the basis of Scripture the Lutheran dogmaticians have maintained that objectively, that is, in God, essence and attributes are absolutely identical.

2. Since finite human reason cannot comprehend the infinite and absolute simplex, God condescends to our weakness and in His Word divides Himself, as it were, into a number of attributes which our faith can grasp and to which it can cling. Scripture itself teaches us to distinguish between God's essence and His attributes when it speaks of God's love (Rom. 5:8), God's wrath (Rom. 1:18), God's long-suffering (Rom. 2:4). It is only natural that when we hear of God's love or wrath, our mind thinks, first, of God's being and, secondly, of love or wrath as an attribute and characteristic of God. Because God employs our human language, He has also adopted our way of thinking and accommodated Himself to the laws of human thought processes,

or logic.[59] Scripture distinguishes not only between God's essence and attributes, but also between the various divine attributes in their relation to one another. Scripture ascribes the motives for particular divine acts to particular divine attributes or dispositions (*affectiones*). For example: Scripture ascribes the sending of God's Son to God's *love* (John 3:16); the sinner's justification to God's *grace*, through the redemption in Christ, without human merit (Rom. 3:24); the condemnation of the wicked to God's punitive *justice* (2 Thess. 1:6). In his prayer, Daniel distinguishes sharply between the attributes of God when he says: "We do not present our supplications before Thee for our righteousnesses, but for Thy great mercies" (Dan. 9:18).

The Lutheran dogmaticians follow Scripture also in this point. Baier: "Though in reality these perfections, or attributes, are not accidents nor in reality different from the divine essence, they are nevertheless distinguished from the divine essence and likewise from one another, because our finite and imperfect reason cannot comprehend the infinite perfection of God" (*Compend.* II, 11). Gerhard: "Although within God Himself the divine attributes are in reality not distinct one from the other nor from the divine essence, nevertheless the weakness of our mind requires that we deal with them one by one. 'God descends to us,' says Augustine, 'that we might mount upward,' and since we are men, He speaks to us after the manner of men." [60]

Dorner, of course, cannot understand how the old dogmaticians can teach both the objective oneness *(Ununterschiedenheit)* of the divine attributes and the distinction between the divine attributes.[61] But Dorner, as an empiricist and "*Ichtheologe*," has discarded Scripture as the source and norm of truth and therefore cannot follow the old dogmaticians, for they were Scripture theologians. They had learned from Scriptures that, on the one hand, God designates Himself as the infinite, indivisible God *(Deus impartibilis, ohne Stuecke* [Augsb. Conf. I]), and that, on the other hand, the indivisible God divides Himself, as it were, into parts. By describing Himself as the holy and the righteous and the gracious God, etc., He mediates to us a knowledge of Himself which, though not perfect, is sufficient for our sal-

---

59 Our dogmaticians express it thus: "By the term 'divine essence' that is understood which is conceived as being the first in God and which according to our mode of conception is the *principium* and *radix* of all perfections which are ascribed to God after the manner of *attributes*" (Baier, II, 11).

60 *Loci, locus "De Natura Dei,"* § 51 (Ed. Frankf. and Hamburg, 1657, I, 59).

61 *Geschichte d. protest. Theologie*, p. 563 f.

vation. And this is the reason why the dogmaticians maintain both the indivisibility of God and the distinction of the divine attributes, e. g., justice and mercy. And all theologians who claim to be Scripture theologians will follow the dogmaticians. For surely no Scripture theologian will seriously assume parts in God. On the other hand, every Scripture theologian desires to remain in agreement with St. Paul, who expressly describes the knowledge of God in Scripture as partial, fragmentary, piecemeal (1 Cor. 13:9: "We know in part, and we prophesy in part").

The doctrine that God's attributes, viewed "objectively," are indivisible has been misused, and two cautions are in order.

a. Under the pretense that all divine attributes constitute an indivisible unit, the distinction between the attributes has been ignored, and one attribute has been substituted for another. This procedure corrupts all theology, as Scripture teaches clearly by word and example. All who base the forgiveness of sin on God's remunerative righteousness which rewards civil righteousness, in other words, on the works of the Law and not upon God's grace through Christ's vicarious satisfaction, will receive not the forgiveness of sin, but God's curse (Gal. 3:10). Israel after the flesh forfeited its membership in the Kingdom of God because it substituted the righteousness of the Law (*iustitia Dei legalis*) for grace (Rom. 9:31-33; 10:1-3), and for the same reason the Pharisee remained unjustified before God (Luke 18:9-14). Twice the Apostle Paul pronounces a curse upon the Judaizing teachers in Galatia because they insisted on this substitution of divine attributes (Gal. 1:8-9). Therefore we must very carefully avoid substituting one divine attribute for another, for this leads to a false concept of God and *eo ipso* to apostasy from the God who is revealed in Scripture. To use only one illustration: A god who justifies sinners not by grace, but on the basis of His remunerative righteousness does not exist. All who deny Christ's vicarious atonement have painted a caricature of God and, like the heathen, who know not God, worship an idol.

b. An earnest warning must also be sounded against men's presumptuous attempt to describe the divine attributes according to their preconceived "theological" opinions and not according to God's Word. We have in mind especially Unitarians and Modernists, who deny the doctrines of eternal damnation and the vicarious atonement because in their opinion these doctrines are in direct conflict with God's justice and love. It is indeed a foolish and blasphemous undertaking when we men on an *a priori* basis (i. e., independent of God's self-revelation in His Word) presume to determine what God according to His love or righteousness can or ought to do, or what is or is not compatible with God's love or justice. This attempt rests on the false premise that finite man can comprehend the infinite God. The fact is that as God is infinite, so also His attributes are infinite and are therefore beyond our comprehension.

In our study of God's being on the basis of Scripture we find that the same attributes are predicated of both God and man. This seems to involve us in a difficulty, since God and His attributes are infinite, while human attributes are finite. It is true, Scripture ascribes to both God and man being (*esse*, existence) as well as a series of properties and works. Examples: Being (God is, Is. 48:12; men are, Acts 17:28); life (God lives, Ezek. 14:16; man lives, Gen. 3:20); love (God loves, John 3:16; man loves, 1 Kings 5:1); justice (God is just, Rom. 3:26; man is just, Matt. 1:19); sight (God sees, Gen. 1:31; man sees, Deut. 32:52); etc. This raises the question: In what manner can the same properties be ascribed both to God and to His creatures? Scripture supplies the answer: a) Not univocally, in the identical sense, as though the term and the matter apply to God and the creature in the same manner and degree (*univoce*); b) not equivocally, as though the terms when applied to God and to the creatures had no more in common than the sound, but in such case have an entirely different meaning (*aequivoce*); but c) analogically, similarly, because both being and attributes belong to God and the creatures, though not in the same manner or degree (*analogice*). We ascend (*consurgimus*, as Augustine says) from the imperfections of the creature (imperfect being, life, love, etc.) to the absolute perfection in God (absolute being, life, love, etc.). This analogous view is clearly taught in Scripture, e. g., Is. 49:15 ("Can a woman forget her sucking child . . . yet will I not forget thee"); Luke 11:13 ("If ye, then, being evil, know how to give good gifts unto your children [from natural love], how much more shall your heavenly Father give the Holy Spirit to them that ask Him?").

If we were to follow the Scotists, the later Nominalists, and others who ascribe being and attributes to God and the creatures in the same manner (*univoce*), then, strictly speaking, we would remove the essential difference between God and man. This would be tantamount to the deification of man. If, however, we were to go to the other extreme and ascribe being and attributes to God and man only "equivocally," we would practically destroy all knowledge of God. It would be impossible for us to know whether anything at all is in God, or what is in God, or what God's attributes actually mean, for example. His love, of which He assures us in John 3:16; 1 John 4:16. But, thanks be to God, the fact is that the majestic and transcendent God has adopted human language and condescended to our thought patterns in order thus to lift us up to Him and to reveal His loving affection for us. True, this knowledge is imperfect and fragmentary (1 Cor. 13:9); nevertheless it is true and reliable, so that we are able to know the things that are given us by God (1 Cor. 2:12). The Lutheran dogmaticians have discussed this point in considerable detail and have refuted every error which might endanger the Christian knowledge of God.[62]

The names of God (because they describe God) must also be listed among God's predicates. Some have counted ten such descriptive names of God. Luther disapproves of this number as not being sufficiently exhaustive. In his *Treatise on Shem Hamphoras* Luther refers to the Jewish custom of ascribing ten names to God, a custom

---

[62] Quenstedt, I, 422 *sq.*: "Essence, substance, spirit, and the remaining attributes which are ascribed alike to God and to creatures, cannot be predicated of God and the rational creatures in the same manner (συνωνύμως, *univoce*) nor in an equivocal sense (ὁμωνύμως, *aequivoce*), but only in an analogous way (ἀναλόγως, *analogice*), that is, they apply to God primarily (πρώτως) and absolutely, to the creatures in a secondary and derived manner. . . . In its proper and strict meaning, *univoce* is used when the things share fully both the name and the matter which is denoted by the name and when there is no inequality due to a dependence of the one upon the other. Things are said to agree *aequivoce* when they share the name, but not the matter which is designated by the name. We use the term *analogice* when things have both the name and the matter in common; however, in an unequal degree, the one having the name and the matter in a primary and absolute way, the other in a secondary and derived (*per dependentiam*) manner." In his antithetical section (*op. cit.*, 423) Quenstedt lists: 1) The Scotists and some nominalists, as Occam and Biel, who held that being, essence, spirit, etc., must be predicated of man and of God univocally. 2) Certain Scholastics, Keckermann and others, declared that essence, substance, spirit, can be ascribed to both God and rational creatures only equivocally. This means that in reality essence, etc., is not ascribed to the creatures at all. Thomas Aquinas (P. I, q. 13, Art. 5) shows that if essence and attributes are ascribed to God and the creatures only equivocally, then it is impossible to learn anything concerning God from nature. This is contrary to philosophy, which has proved many things concerning God *demonstrative*, and also contradicts St. Paul (Rom. 1:17-18). Quenstedt also shows that the idea of equivocation is absurd: "1) If the creatures share only in the name, but not in the reality of essence, they would be nonentities. Who would assert that God created mere nonentities? 2) If the creature were no more than a nonentity, how could it owe its existence as a dependent being to God? 3) In assuming the human nature, Christ would have assumed a nonentity." In the interest of their wrong Christology some Calvinists have asserted that the attributes in God are nonentities. Since God cannot communicate attributes which He does not possess, they could deny the communication of divine attributes to the human nature in Christ, *op. cit.*, p. 427.

which Jerome followed in his *Epistola ad Marcellum,* where he lists the following: *El, Elohim, Eloha, Tsebhaoth, Elyon, Ehye, Adonai, Yah, Yehovah* [*Yahwe*], *Shaddai.* Luther continues: "I do not think much of this. There certainly are more divine names in Scriptures, e. g., *Ab, Bore, Or, Chai,* etc., Father, Creator, Light, Life, Salvation, and many others. And can you think of anything good which must not be ascribed to God first of all, who is the Author and Source of good, as Christ says: 'God alone is good' (Luke 18:19), from whom we have received all that we have received, are, and possess"? (St. L. XX: 2057.) Immediately following this quotation is Luther's masterful exposition on the uniqueness of the name Jehovah, the *nomen Dei essentiale sive incommunicabile,* meaning "Pure Being" (Ex. 3:14).[63] Zoeckler justly condemns the childish manner in which the Papists, Jews, and Turks play with the number of divine names. He places the battology practiced in the Roman Catholic Church on the same level with the vain practice of pagan Buddhism and Islam and says that it is of no importance whatsoever for scientific theology and utterly devoid of any Christian value.[64] The reason for this vain babbling of the names of God as practiced by the Greek and Roman Catholic Churches, the Moslems, the heathen, is the fact that they do not know the name of Jesus, in whom we have the redemption through His blood, the forgiveness of sins. Steeped in work-righteousness (*opinio legis*), they hope to win God's favor by the mere recitation of God's names. – Though liberal theology claims to have studied scientifically and historically the meaning of the names of God, it has failed to understand the meaning of God's names and attributes. And how can they arrive at a correct definition of these since they do not accept the Scriptures as God's Word? The entire Scriptures are in reality nothing else than an elaboration of God's name (*"ein ausgebreiteter Name Gottes"*). By denying that Scripture is God's Word, men reject the only principle or source from which they can derive an understanding of God's name. This fact prompted Luther to remind us again and again that only the

---

[63] Let the vocalization of יהוה be what it may, on the meaning there can be no doubt, since God Himself has explained it etymologically and essentially (Ex. 3:14) as "Pure Being."

[64] *Handbuch der theolog. Wissenschaften* III, 85 f. Zoeckler lists such works as Raym. Lull, *De centum nominibus Dei;* Goerres, *Christliche Mystik,* who enumerates the 150 names with which St. Rosa of Lima addressed God; J. Blueher, *Die 100 biblischen Namen unsres Herrn Jesu Christi* (1870); the Spaniard Luis de Leon's three *Books of the Name of Christ* (Salamanca, 1583); Edwin Arnold, *Pearls of the Faith, or Islam's Rosary* (1882), where the 550 names of Allah are listed, 99 of which are said to be the sweetest and are recited according to the 99 pearls of the rosary.

true Scripture doctrine honors God's name and builds His Church, while false doctrine, springing from the heart of men, profanes God's name and destroys His Church. In his commentary on Ex. 20:7 Luther says of the Second Commandment: "In this Commandment the name of God is used correctly when the Word of God is rightly preached and rightly believed. And, again, God's name is blasphemed when preachers under the cloak of God's Word and name mislead the people." (St. L. III:1076.) For this reason faithful preachers are a blessing, while false teachers are a curse to their country and to the world. Of course, in teaching God's Word in its truth and purity, teachers run the risk of incurring opposition. Luther points to this: "The greatest and most difficult part of this Commandment is to defend this name against those who not only misuse it in spiritual matters, but also spread it [their false definition of God's name] among men. It is not enough that I praise the divine name in prosperity and call upon it in adversity for myself and in my own heart. I must also step into the open and for the sake of God's honor and name incur the enmity of all men according to Christ's word: 'Ye shall be hated of all men for My name's sake' (Matt. 10:22). Here we must provoke to anger even father, mother, and our best friends. . . . Here we must bear the charge of resisting the spiritual and civil government and of being disobedient. Here we must incense the learned, the saints, the wealthy, the mighty, and all who count for something in the world. That is what it means to be 'God's friend and all the world's enemy.' Though this is primarily the duty of preachers, every Christian is in duty bound to do this as time and occasion demand. When a person accepts God's Word, the Gospel, he must by all means keep in mind that he is running the risk of losing all his goods, home, real estate, business, farm, wife, children, father, mother, yes, his very life. Should danger and misfortune overtake him, he can bear it more readily, realizing from the outset that matters would take this course. Here such passages apply as Matt. 10:24: 'The disciple is not above his Master.'" (St. L. III:1078 ff.)

B. CLASSIFICATIONS OF THE DIVINE ATTRIBUTES

To facilitate the study of the divine attributes, we may classify them in various ways. Among Lutheran theologians the following two categorizations have principally been used: 1) quiescent and operative attributes; 2) negative and positive attributes. [65]

[65] Modern German theologians use the terms "*Weltabgezogenheit*" and "*Weltbezogenheit*."

Those who have employed the first classification define as quiescent those attributes in which no effect upon, and no relation to, the world is implied, but which are conceived as remaining within the Godhead and being apart from the world, such as eternity, simplicity, infinity. They are called, more or less appropriately, *attributa immanentia, quiescentia,* ἀνενέργητα. The words "absolute" and "remote" may also be employed. "Operative attributes" is the term for all those divine attributes which denote an operation on, or a relation to, this world, such as omnipotence, omniscience, omnipresence, justice, mercy. These attributes are also known as *attributa relativa, operativa, transeuntia,* ἐνεργητικά.[66]

Those who classify the divine attributes as negative and positive designate as negative such attributes as unity, simplicity, immutability, infinity, immensity, eternity; in other words, the imperfections of creatures cannot be ascribed to God. All those attributes which are found in man, but which are ascribed to God in a higher degree or in an absolute sense are known as positive attributes, such as life, knowledge, wisdom, holiness, righteousness, truth, power, love, goodness, grace, mercy.[67]

There is a great diversity among modern theologians in classifying the divine attributes. But they are agreed that the divisions of the old dogmaticians are in the pattern of Scholastic dialectics, lack religious value, and are contrary to the findings of modern psychology and religious experience. This judgment need not surprise us, for modern theology is in disagreement with the theological method of the old theologians who describe the divine attributes on the basis of, and according to, Scripture. Modern theologians believe that God can be discerned only in a "religious experience" of God in nature and history.[68] Though they retain the old classification of the attributes, they have given an entirely different sense to the meaning of the terms employed. In spite of differences in the classifications the old theologians were agreed that all divine attributes are identical with the

---

66 Quenstedt, I, 409: There are two classes of attributes: 1) Those which describe the divine essence viewed in its absoluteness *(absolute)* and by itself *(in se)* without any regard to any activity. These are called immanent, nonoperative, quiescent, *i. e.,* they do not concern themselves with certain acts of God. They are, e. g., immensity, eternity, spirituality. 2) Those which describe the divine essence in relation to an act of God *(relative),* or are operative, have an external effect and are directed toward certain operations, such as might, knowledge, justice, mercy.

67 Cp. Baier, II, 16, for this type of classification.

68 Nitzsch-Stephan, *op. cit.,* p. 452, describes the position of outstanding German theologians.

divine essence. There can be nothing accidental or adventitious, or mutable, or amissible in God — *in Deum non cadit accidens* — for in God the attributes are not distinct from the essence. Life, wisdom, grace, are God's very substance and cannot undergo change, as in man.[69] Modern kenotics, such as Thomasius, teach amissible attributes. They say that the relative attributes, such as omnipotence, omnipresence, omniscience, are not essential, but accidental, properties of God and can therefore be separated from God. But they maintain this view in the interest of their false Christology, claiming that only by divesting Himself completely of omnipotence, omnipresence, omniscience, could the Son of God become man.[70]

No classification of the divine attributes is fully adequate. It is, therefore, of no theological consequence which classification is adopted, so long as the various attributes are defined according to Scripture alone. We agree with Hoenecke (*Dogmatik* II, 72): "It may sound unscientific to say no more of this division [the division into immanent and transitive attributes] than that it seems to be more appropriate than the others. The fact is that none of the commonly accepted divisions are fully adequate and entirely unobjectionable." [71]

We shall follow the division into negative and positive attributes, though we have no special preference for this classification. But in this division, because it is based essentially on a comparison of God and His creatures, we have occasion to ascend from the level of human imperfection to the divine perfection, or, better still, to adore the divine perfection, which transcends all human comprehension. In making this comparison (between human and divine attributes) we dare never go beyond Scripture nor forget the infinite chasm between God and man, for all attributes, regardless of the division, belong to God in a unique manner *(modo singulari)*.

Before discussing the separate divine attributes we must make one more general observation. All divine attributes revealed in Scrip-

---

69 Chemnitz, *Loci*, I, 28.

70 Thomasius, *Christi Person und Werk*, 2d ed., I, 49 ff. For further details on kenoticism see "The Person of Christ."

71 The inadequacy of an absolute classification is evident in Quenstedt's definition. He divides the attributes into immanent and transitive and says that the immanent attributes have no relation to God's acts. But this is not true of immensity, the first in his list of the immanent attributes. God's immensity becomes active, if not directly, at least indirectly, in the transitive attributes. This is also indicated in Aug. Conf., Art. I, which speaks of God's infinite power, wisdom, and goodness. — See the chapter "All Divine Attributes are Communicated to the Human Nature" in Vol. II.

ture, such as unity, infinity, omniscience, omnipotence, omnipresence, could only fill our hearts with terror if Scripture had not also revealed God's free grace toward all sinful mankind for the sake of Christ's vicarious atonement. This attribute of God's grace is the center of the entire Scriptures, for the scope of all Scripture is Christ, the Savior of sinners, "who gave Himself a ransom for all, to be testified in due time" (1 Tim. 2:6). The attribute of God's grace, which is provided through the redemption that is in Christ Jesus, is also the God-intended center of all human history, for the only purpose of the world's existence is the proclamation of God's grace through the redemption in Christ (Matt. 24:14).

a. The Negative Attributes

1. *The Unity of God (Unitas Dei)*

God is in a class by Himself. Every creature has at least something in common with other creatures and exists in duplicate, triplicate, or multiple form. There can be no other God besides God. God is not *unus genere*, nor *unus specie*, but *unus numero*. Viewed in His entirety, He cannot be divided into several such entities as He is Himself. God is the absolute monad. The Scriptures, both of the Old and the New Testament, point to the unity of God as evidence of the divine majesty. "Understand that I am He; before Me there was no God formed, neither shall there be after Me" (Is. 43:10). The unity is stated very emphatically in Is. 45:5: "I am the Lord, and there is none else; there is no God beside Me." 1 Cor. 8:4: "There is none other God but one." It is God's will that His people acknowledge and proclaim the unity of God: "Hear, O Israel: The Lord, our God, is one Lord" (Deut. 6:4).

But are not creatures also called gods in Scripture? Yes, for rulers and governors are called gods according to a real and true analogy, because under God they exercise divine functions. (Cp. Ps. 82:6; John 10:35.) Also the idols are called gods, but according to a false analogy, because men erroneously ascribe existence and divine activity to idols (Deut. 4:28). At the same time Scripture distinguishes sharply between these so-called gods (λεγόμενοι θεοί, 1 Cor. 8:5) and the one God, who is in a class by Himself, besides whom there is none. He is the μόνος δυνάστης, the only Potentate, the ὁ μόνος ἔχων ἀθανασίαν, the only one who hath immortality (1 Tim. 6:15-16). God is the *ens summum*, the Absolute Reality, and therefore He cannot share being, activity, authority, glory, with anyone or anything. The gods of the heathen are absolutely impotent to harm or help men, because they are non-existent (Is. 41:23). The "creature gods," such as civil rulers, on the other hand, have existence and administrative powers, but only in a derived sense. Without God they are nothing and can do nothing. How important, therefore, our private and public intercessions that the one true God preserve the being and authority of these "gods"!

The doctrine of God's unity has great practical value: 1) The earnest admonition to cling only to this one God with undivided allegiance (Mark 12:30; Deut. 6:5), and 2) the comfort that no person and no event can harm us if God is on our side (Rom. 8:31).

Is it possible to formulate a precise definition of God, since He is in a class by Himself? The answer is negative if we attempt to define God as we define a creature, according to its genus, species, and distinctive characteristics. There is no genus under which the general concept "God" can be classified, nor are there specific characteristics by which God can be differentiated from others in the same genus, for the simple reason that there is no other God besides the one God. Baier: "There is no reason why one should demand or expect a carefully worded definition" (Baier-Walther, II, 14). Gerhard: "The concept genus cannot be used of God in the same sense (*univoce*) as other entities, for His absolutely simple being does not consist of a genus and specific differences" (*Loci, locus "De Nat. Dei,"* § 89). This is true even of the definition which has found favor among dogmaticians, namely, "God is an independent Spirit." As Gerhard points out, the term *"Spirit"* in Christ's statement "God is a Spirit" (John 4:24) cannot be applied to God in the same sense as to angels (*univoce*), but only in a highly unique manner, because an infinite and a finite essence, an uncreated and a created spirit, differ in every respect *plus quam toto genere.* (Gerhard, *loc. cit.*) Luther therefore says very correctly: "Who knows what God is? He is above body, spirit, yes, above everything that we can say, hear, or think" (St. L. XX:806.)

Strictly speaking, then, a definition of God is impossible. But we can and should formulate a description of God. In accord with the attributes which God ascribes to Himself in His Word, we can and should describe Him as the one, simple, immutable, almighty, omnipresent, just, gracious God, etc. In reality the entire Scriptures are a description of God. We subscribe to the maxim: *Deus non definiri, sed ex verbo suo revelato describi potest.* Would to God that we would at all times make diligent use of this description!

2. *The Simplicity of God (Simplicitas Dei)*

We can describe God's simplicity only in negative terms. It is that attribute according to which God exists entirely uncompounded and without parts. The infinitude of God permits of no parts. But does Scripture not ascribe to God members, e. g., eyes, mouth, hands, feet, and thereby teach that He is compounded of parts? The Scriptures compel us to understand such passages as Ps. 139:16 (eyes), Is. 55:11 (mouth), Ps. 119:73 (hands), Matt. 5:35 (feet), figuratively, anthropopathically, anthropomorphically. This is evident especially from John 4:24, where Christ corrects the Samaritan woman's external and corporeal concept of God by declaring: πνεῦμα ὁ θεός. God is *incorporeus, impartibilis* (Augustana, Art. I). We therefore reject anthropomorphism, which ascribes corporeity and materiality to God,[72] and also the dream of modern theosophists (Oetinger, d. 1782) of a spiritual body *(Geistleib)*, which was solidified in and by the creation of the world.[73] But does Scripture not become involved in a contradiction when it ascribes to God both simplicity and a plurality of attributes? True, God is one, indivisible, uncompounded, for, as was shown above, all the divine attributes are God's indivisible being. But this is simply beyond all human comprehension. Therefore God Himself has condescended to us, divided Himself, as it were, into component parts, and because of our finite intellect permits us to conceive of God's attributes, e. g., justice, omnipotence, grace, as following one after another or as existing alongside one another. This is a knowledge of God "in part," as St. Paul says 1 Corinthians 13.

Ancient and modern Unitarians charge that there is an irreconcilable conflict between the triad of Persons and the unity and simplicity of God. Scripture answers this objection by stating that the essence of God is not divided among the three Persons, but that the entire divine essence is without any division, or multiplication, or distinction in the Father, in the Son (Col. 2:9), and in the Holy Ghost (Acts 5:3-4). But the Unitarians contend that a real, and not only a

---

[72] Luther: "If the Anthropomorphites [a Syrian sect of the fourth century which ascribed a body to God] really entertained such crass opinions, they were justly condemned. . . . It seems to me, however, that they only endeavored to present the doctrines in a simple manner to the common people. For in His being, God is unknowable and inexpressible. We are at our wits' end when we try to define God." (St. L. I:487.)

[73] See the quotation in Baier-Walther, II, 18-19. The theosophists have the pantheistic conception of the emanation of the world from the essence of God.

notional, distinction between the Persons must lead to tritheism, and they therefore do away with the unity and simplicity of God. Our answer is: Here we are confronted with the mystery of the Holy Trinity. On the basis of Scripture we believe both the unity of God and the trinity of Persons (1 Cor. 8:4-6; Matt. 28:19). Subordinationists, indeed, by subordinating the Son to the Father and the Holy Ghost to the Father and the Son, deny the unity and simplicity of God and become polytheists.

3. *The Immutability of God (Immutabilitas Dei)*

The Psalmist brings into the sharpest possible contrast the change and decay to which all creatures are heir and the immutability of God when he says: "They shall perish, but Thou shalt endure; yea, all of them shall wax old like a garment; as a vesture shalt Thou change them, and they shall be changed; but Thou art the same, and Thy years shall have no end" (Ps. 102:26-27). God is unchangeable in His essence. He is immutable also in all His attributes, e. g., His kindness (Is. 54:10), His wrath (John 3:36), His will (Prov. 19:21: "The counsel of the Lord shall stand"). Scripture draws a twofold lesson from God's immutability: 1) To warn the wicked, because God's wrath is unchangeable (Mark 9:44); 2) to comfort the pious, because God's grace can never depart (Is. 54:10).

When Scripture ascribes to God change of mind (Gen. 6:6; 1 Sam. 15:11; Jonah 3:10) or change of place (Gen. 11:5), it does so to conform to our mode of thinking in terms of time and space, cause and effect. But God is above these, and therefore no change or mutation can be predicated of God's essence. Scripture teaches this very clearly in all those passages in which God and man are placed into sharp antithesis, for example, in 1 Sam. 15:29: "God is not a man that He should repent." God enters into time and space without becoming temporal or local in His essence (Jer. 23:24).

Scripture speaks of God in a twofold manner: 1) In His majesty as being above time and space (cp. especially Ps. 90:4: "A thousand years in Thy sight are but as yesterday"); 2) in accordance with our human views as being in time and space. Only in the latter manner is God comprehensible to us. We must so think of God that God, who in His being is immutable, is angry or merciful according to the difference in the object of His affection. We must so conceive of God that in spite of the immutability in His essence He is a gracious God to the humble, poor, and contrite sinners, but a jealous God to the proud and self-righteous (1 Pet. 5:5; Luke 18:9-14; Luke 1:52-53). God remains immutable, but there is mutability in the objects of His affection.

Two objections are frequently raised against God's immutability. It has been said that the creation of the world and the incarnation of the Son imply a change in God. The first objection can be raised only by theosophical pantheists, who view the world as an emanation from God and a part of God's being and deny the *creatio ex nihilo.* Indeed, the creation of the world implies a change, a change, however, not in God, but in relation to the creature. And the second objection can be made only by the kenotics. Scripture teaches that the Son of God without any change in His deity has assumed into His Person the human nature from the Virgin Mary.[74]

4. *The Infinity of God (Infinitas Dei)*

All creatures are finite, that is, they are subject to the limits and boundaries of their being and activity. God is infinite. The term *infinity* expresses the idea that God in His being and activity is in no way bound by the limitations of time and space. Scripture very emphatically ascribes infinity to God both according to His essence (Ps. 145:3: "His greatness is unsearchable") and according to His various attributes (Ps. 147:5: "His understanding is infinite"). Being and attributes in God are one; therefore as God's being is infinite, so are also all His attributes infinite, as will be seen in the discussion of omnipotence, omniscience, etc.

In so far as God cannot be measured according to human standards, the infinity of God is also called His immensity. By ascribing immensity to God, Scripture expressly reminds us that we dare not make our puny reason and intellect the yardstick to measure God's

---

[74] Gerhard answers this twofold objection as follows: In the creation two things must be considered: 1) the source of action; 2) the resultant effect. The source of action is the Divine Essence itself, which experiences no change by the creation, because in the creation God carried out in time what He had decreed from eternity in His immutable will. A change took place only in the resultant effect, a change from non-existence to existence, but there was no change whatsoever in God. – The same answer must be given to the question whether the work of incarnation made God changeable. Socinus answers affirmatively: 'If God truly became incarnate in the moment when Christ was conceived of the Holy Ghost in the womb of the Virgin Mary and born of her, who then can deny that something adventitious and new, and that of the most important significance, was added to God Himself and to His being?' (*Defensio animad. Posn.*, p. 66). But there remains the same Person, though it began to be the Person of another [besides His divine] nature. *Loci, locus "De Nat. Dei,"* § 154.

being and activity. Scripture says that God dwells "in the light which no man can approach unto" (1 Tim. 6:16) and that "His greatness is unsearchable" (Ps. 145:3), and our Confessions, in accord with Scripture, say: "God is of infinite power." But Unitarians simply ignore these passages and take the liberty to claim that reason cannot possibly accept three distinct Persons in the one indivisible God. It is very necessary that we constantly heed the Scriptural emphasis on God's immensity and infinity, lest we ignore the absolute difference between God and man, for we are only too prone to forget our limitations. Man is impressed with his own importance. But God's word (Is. 40:15-17): "Nations are as a drop of a bucket . . . as the small dust of the balance . . . as nothing," reduces us to our proper size. Finally, by ascribing infinity and immensity to God, Scripture precludes the notion that God may be confined within a given space in the universe. God is always above space, as Solomon confessed at the dedication of the Temple: "Will God indeed dwell on the earth? Behold, the heaven and heaven of heavens cannot contain Thee; how much less this house!" (1 Kings 8:27.) Accordingly, the axiom is correct and Scriptural: God enters into space and time and still always remains above space and time.

5. *Omnipresence of God (Omnipraesentia Dei)*

God alone is omnipresent. Man and all creatures are always limited to a specific locality. Not even the angels are omnipresent, for, as Chemnitz says on the basis of Dan. 10:13, one angel is in Persia, another in Greece (*Loci* I, 39). Over against the many erroneous views the Scriptural teaching on God's omnipresence may be summarized in three points.

1. God is omnipresent according to His essence, not only according to His operation (*immanentia Dei*). He is essentially, not only dynamically, omnipresent. In the interest of their false Christology some Reformed theologians have denied, and some modern theologians still deny, the essential omnipresence. Wherever God works, He is present. God never works *in absentia.* Luther: "God sends out no bailiffs or angels when He creates and preserves a thing, but all that is the direct work of His divine power. But if He is to create and sustain it, He must Himself be present and must form and sustain His creature, both in its innermost and its outermost parts. Therefore God must be present in every creature in its innermost and its outermost parts, on all sides, through and through, below and above, before and behind. Nothing can be more present and closer to the creature

than God Himself with His power." (St. L. XX:804.) In Jer. 23:24 God says: "Can any hide himself in secret places that I shall not see him? Do not I fill heaven and earth?" The point is: God sees everyone, because He is present according to His essence and not only according to His power. The Psalmist expresses this same fact: "If I ascend up into heaven, Thou art there; if I make my bed in hell, behold, Thou art there" (Ps. 139:8).

2. But God's omnipresence is of such a nature that while He is present in all creatures, He is at the same time outside the creature and never becomes the creature or even a part of the creature (*transcendentia Dei*). So intimately is God present to all creatures that only in Him can they have life, motion, and being (Acts 17:28), for in Him all things consist (Col. 1:17). But at the same time He is far outside, and distinct from the creature as the Infinite is distinct from the finite. God never partakes of the composite nature of the creature. Gerhard: "God is everywhere present, not συνεκτῶς, so that He is contained; but συνεκτικῶς, so that He comprehends and contains all things" (*Loci, locus "De Nat. Dei,"* § 172). In connection with the essential omnipresence the question has been raised whether it is proper to think of God as present in *unclean* places. Erasmus thought it inadvisable to discuss this point publicly (in his *Diatribe;* see St. L. XVIII:1605). Luther countered that while carnal and vain babblers could not speak of this without giving offense, pious preachers could discuss this in sermons with the proper decorum; in fact, with great benefit. The saints were cast into filthy prisons, even into public sewers. If God were not present there, they could not have called upon Him until they had been transferred from these revolting places into a beautifully decorated temple. But God is everywhere and fills all things. Whoever takes offense at God's presence in filthy places has human and childish ideas of God; he evidently imagines that God, whom the highest heavens cannot contain, is confined by spatial limits. (St. L. XVIII:1700.)

3. God is present everywhere without local extension, contraction, multiplication, or division. These concepts would be applicable to God only if He were subject to the laws of space. According to Scripture, God, though present and active in the world, transcends all space. The transcendence of God is clearly taught in 1 Kings 8:27; Is. 66:1. We would hardly expect that within the Christian Church anyone would ascribe local and corporeal extension to God. And yet Zwingli, Calvin, and modern Reformed theologians have actually done this. How else can we account for their apprehension that the human

nature of the body of Christ would not be sufficiently large to serve as the body for the fullness of the Godhead (Col. 2:9)? Luther assuages their needless fears: "The proud and conceited spirit reveals his crude and doltish ideas when he conceives of God's omnipresence, as though God were a huge, expansive being, which fills the universe and even extends beyond it like a straw sack stuffed so full that the straw sticks out at the top and the bottom; in other words, as though God were omnipresent according to the 'local mode,' in a physical and tangible manner. If this were so, then indeed Christ's body would have to be a phantasm or a monster, an immense straw sack, large enough to comprehend God with heaven and earth. Can anyone have such crude and coarse ideas of God? We refuse to say that God is such an extended, long, broad, thick, high, low being. We confess that God is a supernatural, unfathomable Being, who at one and the same time is entirely in every little kernel of grain and also in and above and outside all creatures. God cannot be fenced in, as the false spirit dreams. Let him observe this paradox: A human body is much, much too large for the Godhead; in fact, many thousand godheads could find ample room in one human body; on the other hand, one body is far too small for only one Godhead. Nothing is so small, God is still smaller; nothing so large, God is still larger; nothing so short, God is still shorter; nothing so long, God is still longer; nothing so wide, God is still wider; nothing so narrow, God is still narrower; in short, God's being is so far above and beyond words and thought that it is simply indescribable." (St. L. XX:960 f.)[75]

The omnipresence raises several questions: 1) Is there space outside of the universe? That is impossible, for space is part of the universe, a creature like the universe, and cannot extend beyond itself. Where the universe ends, space also ends. To assume space beyond the universe would imply an endless *progressus in infinitum* and ultimately identify God with the world. (Pantheism.) But where the universe ends, there God is. The universe (τὰ πάντα) is not in space, but in God (Col. 1:17), or, as Gerhard expresses it: "God is not confined by space. On the contrary, it is He who gives to space and the things contained in space their being." (*Loci, locus "De Natura Dei,"* § 172.) At Marburg, Zwingli made the claim that every true body must exist locally and spatially.[76] But Luther countered that the uni-

---

[75] This is probably the loftiest statement that has been written since the days of the Apostles on God's omnipresence.

[76] For details see "The Person of Christ."

verse is a true body and still is not in space. 2) Can we assume a special presence of God when He manifests His wrath or love in a special way (*specialis approximatio essentiae divinae*)? Quenstedt and others answer affirmatively (*Systema* II, 92); Baier and others negatively (Baier, *Compend.*, II, 24 *sqq.*). On the basis of Jer. 23:24 and similar passages which teach the essential presence of God in the entire universe, it is safer to side with Baier. If we assume a special presence of God also according to His essence, we run the risk of transferring the idea of local extension to God. But in any event we must maintain, as did Quenstedt and Baier, that not only God's gifts, but the Triune God Himself mystically dwells in the believers (John 14:23). This is the statement of the Formula of Concord (*Trigl.* 937, 65). 3) What did God do before the creation of the world? Luther calls this a foolish question and refers to Augustine's reply: "God prepared hell for all those who would pry into His secrets" (St. L. I:13).

The doctrine of God's omnipresence is a practical doctrine. 1) It is revealed for our warning, for there is no place where God does not see us (Jer. 23:24). No change of address can remove us beyond the reach of His omnipresence (Ps. 139:7 ff.). Gerhard: "Quite often such things are done under the cover of darkness from which we would recoil in the presence of any upright man. But God is present everywhere, He to whom nothing is hidden and whom no one can deceive. How, then, does it happen that His presence does not fill us with fear and caution lest we transgress?" 2) God's omnipresence is consoling. No place or space separates us from His loving protection. We need fear no evil even in the dark valley (Ps. 23:4). Christ is with His disciples unto the end of the world (Matt. 28:20). Gerhard: "Even though we are cast into the squalor and darkness of a dungeon for Christ's sake, we can say: The Lord, who is my Light and Salvation, is with me. 'Thus saith the Lord that created thee, O Jacob, and He that formed thee, O Israel: Fear not; for I have redeemed thee, I have called thee by thy name; thou art Mine. When thou passest through the waters, I will be with thee; and through the rivers, they shall not overflow thee; when thou walkest through the fire, thou shalt not be burned; neither shall the flame kindle upon thee' (Is. 43:1-2)." (*Loci, locus* "De Nat. Dei," § 189.)

6. *The Eternity of God (Aeternitas Dei)*

Scripture uses the term *eternity* in a modified and in an absolute sense. In a modified sense it denotes a long, indefinite period of time, e. g., the period of the Old Testament. The Children of Israel were to observe the Passover עַד עוֹלָם, "forever" (Ex. 12:24), and circumcision was called בְּרִית עוֹלָם, an everlasting covenant. Circumcision and the Passover were to be in force throughout the Old Testament, but to be abolished with the institution of Baptism and the Lord's Supper.[77] The term *eternal* is used in a modified sense also to denote an existence which, though it has no end, has a beginning. Men and angels are creatures and therefore have a beginning, but by the power of God they have no end, and all men and all angels will enter either eternal life or eternal punishment (Matt. 25:46).[78]

In its strict and absolute sense the word *eternity* denotes infinite, unlimited duration without beginning, without end, without succession. In this sense, eternity can be predicated only of God.[79] God is without beginning: "Before the mountains were brought forth or ever Thou hadst formed the earth and the world, even from everlasting to everlasting, Thou art God" (Ps. 90:2). He is without end: "Thou art the same, and Thy years shall have no end" (Ps. 102:27). The term *eternal* is used in Scripture to express God's majesty and is used as God's name: Gen. 21:33 (אֵל עוֹלָם, "the everlasting God"); Is. 40:28 (אֱלֹהֵי עוֹלָם, "everlasting God"); Rom. 16:26 (ὁ αἰώνιος θεός); 1 Tim. 1:17 (ὁ βασιλεὺς τῶν αἰώνων). God's transcendence of time, His eternal presence, is taught in Ps. 90:4: "A thousand years in Thy sight are but as yesterday when it is past and as a watch in the night." God is the Creator of time without becoming temporal. He accompanies time without becoming subject to time or its laws. God's relation to time is the same as His relation to space. For though God created space and place and is present everywhere, He does not become local, but remains exalted above space and place.

The eternity of God is used in Scripture for our warning and our comfort. There is a punishment "with everlasting destruction (ὄλεθρον αἰώνιον), from the presence of the Lord" (2 Thess. 1:9).[80]

---

[77] Col. 2:11-12; Matt. 28:19; Matt. 26:26-28 (blood of the new covenant).

[78] The good angels belong to the eternal heavenly family, Heb. 12:22-24; Eph. 1:21. The eternal fire is prepared *primo loco* for the devil and his angels, Matt. 25:41.

[79] Baier: "The eternity of God, absolutely and strictly speaking, denotes the permanent existence and duration of God without beginning, without end, without any succession or alternation (*op. cit.*, II, 27).

[80] Gerhard: "O soul, created for eternity, slough off the love for mundane and transitory things. Put your affections on the heavenly things, for they are eternal. . . . The world passes away, the earth perishes, all things in it are subject to perdition. But worse is the perdition of him who attaches his heart to the earthly and transitory things." (*Op. cit.*, § 149.)

But there is also an eternal (πάντοτε) presence "with the Lord" (1 Thess. 4:17), an eternal home in heaven (αἰώνιον ἐν τοῖς οὐρανοῖς, 2 Cor. 5:1).[81]

b. Positive Attributes

1. *Life (Vita)*

God alone has life in an absolute sense. Creatures also have life, but it is a derived life, a life in God (Acts 17:28). God, however, has life in Himself (John 5:26). The Scriptures call God the "living God" to set forth the majesty of the one true God in contrast to the pagan idols, who are only vanities (Joshua 3:10; Jer. 10:10; Acts 14:15), and in contrast to all created life, which has its origin in God, for He "giveth to all life and breath" (Acts 17:25).

According to Scripture the fact that God is the living God is a warning for the godless, for "it is a fearful thing to fall into the hands of the living God" (Heb. 10:31). But for the believers it is a comforting fact. The covenant people of the Old Testament, standing on the brink of Jordan, witnessed that God is indeed a living God (Josh. 3:10), and the New Testament Church as "the Church of the living God" (1 Tim. 3:15) places its trust in the living God (1 Tim. 4:10). In days of disaster and despair the Christian exclaims with Luther: *"Vivit!"*

2. *The Knowledge of God (Scientia Dei)*

Knowledge is an attribute common to both God and man. The heathen know God's righteousness, judgment, Law, for the work of the Law is written into their hearts (Rom. 1:32; 2:15). The Christian knows that he is not justified by the deeds of the Law, but only through faith in Jesus Christ (Gal. 2:16). Knowledge is an attribute of the evil and the good angels. The devils know a great many things: that there is a God; that Christ is God's Son; that an eternal doom awaits them (James 2:19; Mark 5:12; Matt. 8:29). The knowledge of the good angels is immense. They know "the manifold wisdom of God according to the eternal purpose in Christ" (Eph. 3:10-11). They place their intelligence into the service of the Christian Church. (Heb. 1:14; 1 Pet. 1:12; Matt. 4:11; Luke 16:22; Matt. 13:30, 39, 49.)

---

81 Hollaz: "Though the devil frightens us and the world oppresses us, we lift our hearts in the hope of eternal glory. 'Our light affliction, which is but for a moment, worketh for us a far more exceeding and eternal weight of glory; while we look not at the things which are seen, but at the things which are not seen; for the things which are seen are temporal, but the things which are not seen are eternal,' 2 Cor. 4:17-18." (*Examen, cap.* I, "De Deo," qu. 50.)

The knowledge of creatures is relative, imperfect. God's knowledge is absolute, perfect. The knowledge of God differs from that of creatures in two points: in its extent and in its manner.

a. God's knowledge is omniscience (John 21:17; 1 John 3:20) and comprises all things. It includes all future events, which are hidden to creatures and known only to God (*praescientia*) (Is. 41:22-23), and even the contingent events, as whether the people of Keilah would deliver David to Saul if he remained there (1 Sam. 23:12); what would have happened to Sodom if it had seen the miracles which Christ performed in Capernaum (Matt. 11:23). (*Scientia de futuro conditionata.*)[82]

b. Man's knowledge is acquired. He progresses from the known to the unknown and from one known fact to another. God's knowledge is not acquired, for He knows all things in one, simple, all-comprehensive act. Man acquires his knowledge mediately, for he can learn the nature of things only by a process of perception, induction, deduction, based on a study of observable characteristics and actions of the objects. God, however, knows and discerns the inner nature, the inherent essence of all objects directly and immediately. The old dogmaticians put it thus: "God discerns objects not by means of comprehensible characteristics (*per species intelligibiles*), but in their very nature and being. Man looks at things (*adspicit*); God sees through them (*perspicit*)."

Scripture therefore tells us that God knows the thoughts of men even though they do not reveal these thoughts by actions, words, or attitude. God knows the hearts of all the children of men (1 Kings 8:39); He is the true καρδιογνώστης (Acts 15:8); Christ sees (ἰδών) the thoughts of men (Matt. 9:4) and knows what is in man (John 2:25).

What Scripture teaches concerning God's knowledge serves for our warning and comfort. It is the prerogative of the Divine Majesty alone to know future events (Is. 41:22-23). All who consult fortunetellers and necromancers (spiritualistic mediums, palm-readers, astrologers) transfer God's glory to men and devils. They are an abomination to God and a curse to their country and were therefore put to death under the Old Testament theocracy (Deut. 18:9 ff.; Lev. 20:6, 27). It is furthermore the prerogative of God alone to know what is in God. "No man knoweth the Son but the Father, neither knoweth any man

---

[82] The Latin terms, especially *scientia de futuribili, scientia media,* to describe the divine knowledge of contingent or possible things, may not sound so well. But to challenge the fact itself reveals not wisdom, but opposition to the clear Scripture passages.

the Father save the Son, and he to whomsoever the Son will reveal Him" (Matt. 11:27). All who teach otherwise and consent not to the wholesome words of Christ (1 Tim. 6:3), but make their own reason or religious experience the source and standard of truth, dismiss the only competent Teacher in the Church and usurp His prerogatives. God warns against these self-appointed teachers: "Hearken not unto the words of the prophets that prophesy unto you; they make you vain; they speak a vision of their own heart and not out of the mouth of the Lord" (Jer. 23:16). And, finally, we are all only too prone to forget that the all-wise God knows all our thoughts, words, and deeds and that the darkness cannot hide us from Him, for "the night shineth as the day, and darkness and light are both alike to Him" (Ps. 139:12).

But Scripture shows us also how to employ God's omniscience for our comfort in spiritual and physical needs. God knows those who have a contrite heart, who tremble at His Word (Is. 66:2), and He delights to dwell with them in His grace (Is. 57:15; Ps. 34:18; 51:17). Our heavenly Father knows our physical wants and needs (Matt. 6:32). He knows the righteousness of our cause when the enemies of the truth malign and persecute us (Ps. 17:3).

A number of problems confront the philosopher who attempts to analyze the omniscience of God. The most vexing problem is: What is the relation of the infallible prescience of God to human freedom and responsibility? If there is an infallible foreknowledge of God, then everything must happen as God has foreknown it. If that is true, then there can be no human freedom of action and, of course, no human responsibility. This is the position of some pagan philosophers,[83] of the Socinians,[84] as well as some modern theologians. They have denied God's omniscience entirely, at least in reference to the wicked deeds of men.

In answering this problem Scripture teaches us to observe three things:

1. God's prescience extends over all things and is infallible. Everything happens as God has foreknown it. The opposite assumption would abolish the true conception of God.[85]

---

83 Such as Cicero. – See Gerhard, *op. cit.*, ¶248.

84 Socinus, *Prael. Theol.*, c. 8–11: "No argument nor Scripture testimony can be adduced from which it can be clearly gathered that even before they were committed God knew the wicked deeds which came solely from the will of men."

85 Nitzsch-Stephan, p. 459 f., discusses and dissents from the views of the Socinians and such modern theologians as Rothe and Weisse.

2. Though the omniscience of God extends over all things without exception, it is not the efficient cause of the things which it knows. In the light of Scripture, when God views a thing abstractly (*notionaliter*), He always views it as already existing. Thus we read in Ps. 139:1-4: "O Lord, Thou hast searched me and known me. Thou knowest my downsitting and mine uprising; Thou understandest my thought afar off. Thou compassest my path and my lying down, and art acquainted with all my ways, for there is not a word in my tongue, but, lo, O Lord, Thou knowest it altogether." When God through His messenger announces to the Laodicean congregation that He knows its works, that it is neither cold nor hot (Rev. 3:15), this divine knowledge does not effect the sad conditions at Laodicea, but views them as already existing. In describing God's omniscience the Formula of Concord says very correctly: "The foreknowledge of God *(praescientia)* foresees and foreknows also that which is evil; however, not in such a manner as though it were God's gracious will that it should happen. . . . However, the beginning and cause of evil is not God's foreknowledge (for God does not create and effect [or work] evil, neither does He help or promote it): but the wicked, perverse will of the devil and of men [is the cause of evil]." (*Trigl.* 1065, 6-7.) And the Epitome: "For the foreknowledge of God is nothing else than that God knows all things before they happen." (*Trigl.* 833, 3.)

But there is also a knowledge on the part of God which is causative. It differs from the omniscience in two respects: This unique and special knowledge extends over only a certain definite number of objects, not over all things, good and evil; and second, it causes and effects the object of God's foreknowledge. It was this knowledge which selected Israel as the chosen race ("You only have I known of all the families of the earth," Amos 3:2); which converted the Galatians, who were "known of God" (Gal. 4:9). This is the so-called *nosse cum affectu et effectu* or the "pregnant" use of the term "*to know.*" [86]

3. There seems to be an irreconcilable contradiction between the first and the second statement, even when we define "God's foreknowledge as nothing else than that God knows all things before they occur" (Formula of Concord). Can we maintain God's infallible foreknowledge and also human freedom and responsibility? Reason argues, if it is true – as indeed it is true – that all things must happen as God has foreseen them, then we must either join Cicero, the Socinians, *et alii*

---

[86] For further details see the "Eternal Election" in Vol. III.

and sacrifice the infallible and absolute omniscience or become Stoics and deny the freedom of human action and man's responsibility for his sin. But on the basis of Scripture we must maintain both, even though in this life we cannot harmonize the apparent contradictions. The Formula of Concord suggests the only possible mode of procedure: 1) We must firmly believe that everything must happen as God has foreknown it; 2) We dare not trouble ourselves with what God may have foreknown concerning ourselves and others, because we would then enter the realm of the unrevealed and inscrutable mysteries of God. 3) We must use the means of grace to which God has directed us. "Thus there is no doubt that God most exactly and certainly foresaw [*praeviderit*] before the time of the world, and still knows, which of those that are called will believe or will not believe; also which of the converted will persevere [in faith] and which will not persevere; which will return after a fall [into grievous sins], and which will fall into obduracy [will perish in their sins]. So, too, the number, how many there are of these on either side, is beyond all doubt perfectly known to God. However, since God has reserved this mystery for His wisdom, and has revealed nothing concerning it to us in His Word, much less commanded us to investigate it with our thought, but has earnestly discouraged us therefrom, Rom. 11:33 ff., we should not reason in our thoughts, draw conclusions, nor inquire curiously into these matters, but should adhere to His revealed Word, to which He points us." (*Trigl.* 1081, 54 f.) This practice is not a "scientific" solution of the problem. But is it not more scientific frankly to admit one's ignorance than to deceive oneself and others with a counterfeit solution or with the impossible promise of a final solution after further exploration?[87]

A second problem is stated as follows: Since there is no past or future with God, how can we speak of God's *praescientia*? Answer: God ascribes prescience to Himself (Is. 46:10), but He does so to conform to our mode of thinking. Being in time and subject to its laws of temporal sequence, we cannot conceive of timelessness, of God's eternal "today," of an ever-present moment. We think only in terms of the past, the present, the future, and therefore God condescends to our concepts of time. In this sense He with whom there is no future ascribes to Himself a knowledge which in distinction from all human wisdom extends also to future events.[88]

---

87 For further details see "Divine Providence" and "Eternal Election."

88 This was the view of Luther and other dogmaticians. Commenting on 1 Pet. 3:19-20, Luther says: "We are unable here on earth to view this life in

Finally, the question is frequently asked whether foreknowledge may not also be ascribed to man, his disembodied spirit, and angels. The Scriptural answer is a definite no. Foreknowledge is the exclusive property of the divine Majesty. Furthermore, Scripture expressly affirms that man does not know the future; for example, the time of the Last Judgment (Matt. 24:36). When men, as Daniel (Dan. 2:27-28, 45), or angels, as Gabriel (Luke 1:19), foretold future events, they did so by a special revelation for a specific purpose. Man's so-called prophecies are at best conjecture or a prognostication based on calculations. Fortunetellers who claim to foretell the future are the mediums of the devils, for the good angels will never become guilty of such a blasphemous encroachment upon God's prerogative.

3. *The Wisdom of God (Sapientia Dei)*

Scripture makes a distinction between God's wisdom and His knowledge, Rom. 11:33 (καὶ σοφίας καὶ γνώσεως, "the depth of the riches both of the wisdom and knowledge of God"). The two words are not synonymous when applied to God. From God's viewpoint there is no distinction between the various divine attributes, for they constitute His indivisible essence itself. Since the human mind cannot comprehend God in His absolute unity, God reveals Himself for our sake in separate attributes. This fact compels us to differentiate also between wisdom and knowledge, especially in view of the fact that καί . . . καί not only co-ordinate, but also differentiate the σοφία and the γνῶσις. Likewise in 1 Cor. 12:8 a distinction is made between the two gifts of the Holy Spirit: λόγος σοφίας and λόγος γνώσεως. In Scrip-

---

one glance, because it unfolds step by step until the Last Day. In God's sight, however, our life is a moment, for with Him a thousand years are as one day." "Therefore," says Luther, "we cannot comprehend this life [with God and before God]. We view things lengthwise, but God views them crosswise." (St. L. IX:1245.) Gerhard: "Prescience is ascribed to God for our sake. To God the things which lie in the future from our viewpoint are present." (*Op. cit.*, § 243.) John Adam Osiander: "As there is no 'postscience' [knowledge of the past] in God, though He knows the past, so, strictly speaking, no prescience can be predicated of God by which He knows the future." *Colleg. Theol.* I, 290. While God graciously condescends to our finite modes of comprehension and divides His knowledge according to our concept of time, He is nevertheless at the same time exalted above space and time, for in His presence a thousand years are as yesterday (Ps. 90:4). God will therefore not permit us to transfer the division of His knowledge to His essence. Gerhard: "The divine knowledge does not dwell in God by means of *(per modum)* an aptitude added to His essence, but it must be ascribed to God as an absolutely unconditioned act *(actus purissimus)*. By one simple act of understanding and in one single moment He perceives all things." *(Loc. cit.)*

ture the term *wisdom* – *sapientia*, σωφία – denotes a practical knowledge,[89] the ability to discern correctly the best ends and choose the best means for attaining these ends. And in this sense, Scripture ascribes wisdom to God. God reveals this wisdom not only in the realm of nature by the acts of creation and preservation (Ps. 104:24), but also in the realm of grace by His counsel and acts concerning our salvation. The Gospel of Christ Crucified is expressly called σοφία θεοῦ, the "wisdom of God," the "hidden wisdom which God ordained before the world unto our glory." (1 Cor. 2:6 ff.)

Since God is the "only wise God" (1 Tim. 1:17; Rom. 16:27) and since man is totally unable to fathom the depths of His unsearchable wisdom (Rom. 11:33), we dare never criticize God's wisdom, but must stand before it in adoration and praise. By nature we are only too prone to criticize God in His works and to elevate our own puny wisdom above God's unsearchable wisdom. This is true particularly of liberal theology, where a carping and censorious spirit – under the pretense of a scientifically critical method – has gained complete control. Modern theologians challenge God's wisdom especially a) in their claim that Scripture is not the inviolable truth of God, and b) in the rejection of the Vicarious Atonement as too mechanical, juridical, as unethical and even detrimental to morals.[90] Because of the old Adam even the Christian at times criticizes the ways of God. But in spite of the Modernist and the old Adam in the Christian, the Scriptural truth cannot be challenged that not only in a general way, but in every detail everything in this world is taking the right course. It cannot be otherwise, for all things are controlled by the expert hand of the all-wise God. (חָכְמָה, σοφία θεοῦ). This includes also all the punishments, e. g., famines, wars, depressions, earthquakes, floods, with which God allows mankind to be afflicted (Gen. 3:16ff.; Matt. 24:1ff.). They must serve God's gracious purpose and will to bring men to repentance and faith, as Christ expressly teaches on the basis of concrete examples in Luke 13:1 ff.

4. *The Attributes of the Divine Will*

The Scriptures ascribe to God not only mind (Rom. 11:34: "Who hath known the mind of the Lord"), but also will (1 Tim. 2:4: "who will have all men to be saved"; John 6:40; 1 Thess. 4:3: the will of God

---

89 2 Chron. 2:7: Solomon requested Hiram to send a man cunning (אִישׁ־חָכָם) to work in gold, etc.

90 See "Some Modern Theories of the Atonement Examined" in Vol. II.

concerning our salvation and our sanctification). The remaining positive attributes may be viewed as being related to God's will and include His *holiness, justice, truth, power, benevolence, mercy, love, grace,* and *long-suffering.*

Before we discuss the various attributes of God's will, two questions must be answered: 1) Do causes influence God's will? 2) Is a classification of the divine will permissible?

1. The first question must be answered as follows: a) Scripture, on the one hand, describes God in His majesty. As the God of majesty He is independent of all things, is absolute and unconditioned (Rom. 11:36: "Of Him and through Him and to Him are all things"). It is therefore impossible to ascribe to God in His majesty cause and effect as two separate and distinct concepts. *Non sunt in Deo causae formaliter causantes.* b) Scripture, on the other hand, compels us to make a distinction between cause and effect in God, because we are unable to comprehend the absolute God. Scripture therefore teaches us to view God's wrath as being caused by man's sin (Ps. 90:7-8; Jer. 2:19) and God's grace as resting upon Christ's merit (Rom. 3:24: "through the redemption that is in Christ Jesus"). *In Deo sunt causae virtualiter causantes.*[91]

2. There can be no division and classification of God's will as far as God's essence is concerned. In Him there is only one will, and this is identical with His essence. But because of our finite comprehension Scripture itself teaches us to observe the following classification and divisions.

a. We distinguish between God's first, or antecedent, and second, or consequent, will (*voluntas prima, sive antecedens, et voluntas secunda, sive consequens*). According to John 3:17 we must first think of God as not willing to condemn a single person, but that He earnestly wills the salvation of everyone. Then we must secondly think of God that He wills the condemnation of all who reject Christ, for in v. 18 we read: "He that believeth not is condemned already." The distinction between the antecedent and the consequent will has been misused

---

[91] The dogmatical statements, though inadequate, express the Scriptural truths that in God cause and effect are not two essentially (*formaliter*) different things, because there is nothing outside God which can cause something in the absolute God. But since we must progress in our thinking from cause to effect, Scripture permits us to view the effect as actually caused (*virtualiter*) by a preceding cause. Many theologians insist that we must not speak of a "change in the mind and disposition of God." See Vol. II, p. 367, Note 69.

in the interest of synergism since Chrysostom's days. But we must maintain this distinction because it is Scriptural and because Calvinism denies it by ascribing to God in His relation to lost mankind two independent and contradictory wills.

b. We must distinguish between an irresistible and a resistible will in God (*voluntas irresistibilis et voluntas resistibilis*). God in His majesty cannot be resisted. No one can resist Christ's will which will summon all men before the Judgment throne. There is a divine "must" (δεῖ) behind this will (John 5:28; Matt. 25:31 ff.; 2 Cor. 5:10: "We must [δεῖ] appear"). But Christ's will to bring men to faith through the preaching of the Gospel can be resisted (Matt. 23:37: "Ye would not"). This distinction has been misused by ancient and modern synergists, who argue that the ability to resist implies the ability to assist and who therefore ascribe to the natural man *facultas se applicandi ad gratiam,* self-determination.

c. God wills immediately and mediately (*voluntas absoluta et voluntas ordinata*). At Cana, Christ made wine without employing the usual means for making wine (John 2:1-11). In exceptional cases, so-called reserved cases, God works immediately even in the Kingdom of Grace, as is evident from the fact that John was endowed with the Holy Ghost in his mother's womb (Luke 1:15, 41). But God's usual order is that He works faith, preservation of faith, sanctification, etc., only through the means of grace which He has appointed and to which He has bound us (Rom. 10:17; Titus 3:5; 1 Pet. 1:23 ff.; Mark 16:15; Matt. 28:19-20). When "enthusiasts" appeal to Luke 1:15, they misapply this text. "Enthusiasm" in all its forms perverts the divine order.

d. God's will is unconditioned by any human effort as well as conditioned by human efforts (*voluntas gratiae et voluntas conditionata*). In the realm of grace, God's will is not contingent upon man's good works, for man is saved by grace without the deeds of the Law (Rom. 3:28), by grace alone (Eph. 2:8-10; Rom. 11:6). All who endeavor to supplement the will of grace by human effort will receive the curse (Gal. 3:10). In the realm of the Law, however, God's will is conditioned by man's work. "This do, and thou shalt live" (Luke 10:28; Gal. 3:12). But let no one who hopes to be saved in this way forget that the will of God is conditioned by nothing less than a perfect fulfillment of the entire Law, for "cursed is everyone that continueth not in all things which are written in the Book of the Law to do them" (Gal. 3:10).

e. Scripture distinguishes between God's revealed and His hidden will (*voluntas revelata, voluntas signi,* and *voluntas abscondita, voluntas beneplaciti*). On the one hand, Christians know God's will; they know "the things that are freely given us of God," "they judge all things" and "know the mind of Christ" (1 Cor. 2:12, 15-16). On the other hand, it is also true that no man "knows the mind of the Lord" (Rom. 11:33-34). In all matters of their salvation men are directed solely to the gracious will of God, which is revealed in Christ and clearly taught in all those passages which tell us that God can and will be known only in Christ (John 1:18; Matt. 17:5; John 6:40) and that salvation can be found only in Christ (Matt. 11:28). Theologians find fault with Luther because he first makes a distinction between the hidden and the revealed wills of God, and then in matters of salvation completely ignores the hidden will, since it is unsearchable, and directs our attention solely to the revealed will. This procedure, they say, is an act of violence in the realm of reason (*Gewaltakt*).[92] The fact is that Luther's procedure is that of the Scriptures (1 Cor. 2:12, 15-16; Rom. 11:33-34).[93]

We are now ready to discuss the positive attributes of God that may be viewed as relating to God's will.

a. The Holiness of God (Sanctitas Dei)

The holiness of God denotes 1) God's supreme majesty and absolute transcendence. The basic meaning of קָדוֹשׁ in the Trisagion (Is. 6:3) is separate, removed, exalted. God is the Holy One (Is. 43: 3, 14; etc.), the absolutely Remote. Though He permeates and fills all things, He is exalted above all creatures, sits upon a throne, high and lifted up, before whom the seraphim cover their face and feet. The New Testament equivalent of קָדוֹשׁ is δόξα θεοῦ (John 12:41). In its first meaning the holiness of God describes God in His essence and therefore includes all His attributes.[94] The "Holy One of Israel" and "the God of Israel" are unequivocal synonyms (Ps. 71:22). 2) The term *holiness* denotes also the absolute ethical purity of God. As the holy God He is separate from sin, and His holiness includes His contrast and opposition to man's sin. "Be ye holy, for I am holy" (1 Pet. 1:16; cp. Lev. 11:44-45; 19:2; 20:7). Isaiah was fully conscious of the fact that the revelation of God's holiness brought God's absolute purity into sharp contrast with his own and his people's sin. (V. 5: "Woe is

---

[92] Karl Hase, *Ev. Dogmatik,* 3d ed., p. 295.

[93] Cp. Vol. II, p. 34–49.

[94] This fact is brought out also in Nitzsch-Stephan, p. 399.

me! for I am undone," etc.) Modern theology denies in part or in whole this twofold definition of God's holiness.[95]

The revelation of God's holiness teaches us two important lessons. In the first place, we must enter into His presence with deep awe and great reverence. Jehovah's throne is an awe-full throne, before which we are, as Abraham said, nothing but dust and ashes. (Gen. 18:27 ff.) But, secondly, we can come into His presence with confidence and joy, because the holiness of God has been perfectly appeased through Christ's vicarious atonement (Rom. 5:1, 10; Eph. 3:11-12).

b. The Justice of God (Iustitia Dei)

The Scriptures ascribe justice to God and thereby exclude all unrighteousness from God's being, Ps. 92:15 ("The Lord is upright, and there is no unrighteousness in Him"), and especially Deut. 32:4, which abounds in predicates denoting justice ("He is the Rock, His work is perfect, for all His ways are judgment; a God of truth and without iniquity, just and right is He").

If we attempt to comprehend God's righteousness according to our mode of thinking, we encounter an insurmountable difficulty. Man is just when his actions conform to the Law of his divine Superior. But since God has no superior and therefore no fixed norm, can we really predicate righteousness of Him? This apparent difficulty is resolved in the Scriptural axiom coined by the Scholastics and used by Luther: *Deus est exlex.* God is outside the Law. "He is just, because He wills and does everything in conformity with His own Law." Luther: "God issues His Law to others, but He does not apply it as a norm to Himself.[96]

In its relation to man God's justice is 1) *iustitia legalis,* the divine righteousness revealed in the Law, and 2) *iustitia evangelica,* the right-

---

[95] The teaching of modern theologians on the holiness of God is summarized and reviewed in Ed. Koenig, *Theologie des Alten Testaments, kritisch u. vergleichend zusammengestellt,* 1922, p. 171 ff.

[96] "Gott gibt das Gesetz aus, aber er nimmt es nicht wieder hinauf." Luther's sermon on Ex. 9:16, St. L. III:811 ff. Luther points out that whoever makes God subject to the law of "a universal concept of good," loses God, destroys the concept of God, reduces God to an idol. The universal concept of good is subject to God. "A man is pious when he acts and lives according to the Law. In God's case you must invert the order: An act is good because God performs it. . . . Do not dare to apply a law or a standard to God, for He is not a creature; He is immeasurable. Man must live according to a norm. . . . Since God has no law, standard, or limit, He cannot transgress them." Prov. 16:4: "The Lord hath made all things for Himself," *i. e.,* according to His own pattern. — "*Exlex,*" by the way, is not "church Latin," but is found in "classical" Latin, as any larger Latin lexicon will show.

eousness revealed in the Gospel. The former is *legislative*, inasmuch as it is the standard for man's moral being and actions and demands absolute conformity with this norm (Matt. 22:37); it is *remunerativa*, inasmuch as it rewards the good; and it is *vindicativa* (*punitiva*, *ultrix*), inasmuch as it punishes the evil (2 Thess. 1:4-10). The *iustitia evangelica* is the very opposite. It consists in God's setting aside His *iustitia legalis* (χωρὶς νόμου), declaring the sinner righteous, forgiving his sin by grace for the sake of Christ's righteousness (Rom. 3:21-22: "The righteousness of God without the Law is manifested . . . the righteousness of God which is by faith of Jesus Christ"). Man's salvation rests solely on the *iustitia evangelica*, and faith in this "evangelical justice" constitutes the essence of Christianity. – Here we have the answer to the question whether God punishes sin adequately. According to Gal. 3:13; John 3:36, etc., Christ bore the adequate punishment of sin in our place, and whoever rejects this full and complete payment must pay it himself eternally.

c. The Truthfulness of God (Veracitas Dei)

Men put little faith in what God says. They believe neither God's threats in the Law (Ps. 90:11) nor His promises in the Gospel (Is. 53:1; John 12:38). But this distrust and disbelief frustrates God's gracious purpose to save man. Therefore God does not hesitate to assure us in His Word that He is not a liar like men, but the absolute truth. Rom. 3:4: "Let God be true, but every man a liar." According to God's record man's veracity score is zero. Not only does Scripture characterize some peoples and persons as past masters at lying, e. g., the Cretans (Titus 1:12), but Christ declares that the whole human race is inherently dishonest, deceitful, mendacious. Out of the heart, the inner being, proceed false witnesses and blasphemies (Matt. 15:19). And David states: "All men are liars" (Ps. 116:11). Over against this universal dishonesty of man, Scripture repeatedly places the absolute truthfulness of God into the sharpest possible antithesis (Titus 1:2: ὁ ἀψευδὴς θεός; John 3:33: ὁ θεὸς ἀληθής; Heb. 6:18: ἀδύνατον ψεύσασθαι θεόν; 1 Sam. 15:29; Num. 23:19). – God's words can therefore never pass away (Matt. 24:35); John 10:35: "The Scripture cannot be broken."

The absolute truthfulness of God in His wrath as well as in His grace should, on the one hand, arouse men from their carnal security, for God will not be mocked (Gal. 6:7) and, on the other hand, incite them to trust God's gracious promises unconditionally (Rom. 10:11; Titus 1:2: "Eternal life, which God, that cannot lie, promised.")

d. The Power of God (Potentia Dei)

The power of God differs from the power of creatures both in the manner and in the extent of its activity. Concerning the mode, Scripture teaches us to say that God effects His works by an act of the will.[97] God creates by His will, by His *fiat* (Gen. 1:3). God's will is God's power; what He wills, He does (Ps. 115:3). In regard to the extent of God's power the Scriptures say that "with God all things are possible" (Matt. 19:26), or, stated more emphatically in a double negative, "With God nothing shall be impossible" (Luke 1:37). God is omnipotent. How foolish to entertain the pantheistic and rationalistic idea that in the work of creation God exhausted His power and reached the limit of His creative capacity! But it is just as foolish when men take the liberty to determine not only what God's omnipotence may do, but also what it actually has done. God's Word alone answers that question, and man has no right to say that God in His omnipotence forgives sin without the Vicarious Atonement, because He has revealed to us that we have forgiveness only in Christ's redemption (Rom. 3:24).

Whatever God wills He accomplishes in one of two ways: either by His appointed means (*causae secundae, potentia ordinata*) or without them (*potentia absoluta, immediata*). In either case, however, the one and selfsame divine power is operative. The same divine omnipotence is at work when God according to His established order sustains life by food and drink or immediately, as He sustained Moses for forty days without meat or drink (Ex. 34:28). "Thou feedest us from year to year" (Hymn 569:8). All those works which God performs without employing the usual means (*causae secundae*) are defined in Scriptures as miracles (John 2:11: σημεῖα; Acts 2:43: τέρατα καὶ σημεῖα). Two points must be observed in considering miracles: 1) God is not bound to observe the distinction between *potentia absoluta* and *ordinata;* in other words, He can do without means what He ordinarily does through means (Ex. 34:28). God is above the laws of nature and can therefore dispense with them at will, as Christ teaches: "Man shall not live by bread alone, but by every word that proceedeth out of the mouth of God" (Matt. 4:4). Strictly speaking, there are no immutably fixed laws of nature. They exist only in the foolish minds of mechanistic philosophers and evolutionistic theorizers. In reality the laws of nature are nothing more than the will of God as applied to the creature. 2) God has bound us to the appointed means. We shall

---

[97] *Deus producit volendo.* Thus also Nitzsch-Stephan, *op. cit.,* p. 456.

leave the performance of miracles to God. Of course, there is a miracle-working faith (*Wunderglaube, fides heroica,* Matt. 17:20; 21:21; 1 Cor. 12:1, 10) which is not bound to rules. He that has this gift knows when to use it.[98]

The objection that God is not omnipotent because He cannot die, lie, steal, etc., does not emanate from genuine motives, such as spiritual afflictions or an honest quest for the truth. In the final analysis the objection is nothing but a sophistical denial of God's essence, in which will and power are one. It does not merit refutation.[99]

e. God's Goodness, Mercy, Love, Grace, Long-suffering, Patience (Bonitas, Misericordia, Amor, Gratia, Longanimitas, Patientia Dei)

The close relation of these attributes makes it advisable to treat them under one heading.[100]

On the basis of Scriptures the dogmaticians distinguish between the objective and subjective *goodness* of God. Viewed objectively, goodness is that quality in God whereby He is the absolute Good, the unconditioned and essential Perfection. Scripture ascribes goodness to creatures not only before the Fall (Gen. 1:31: "very good"), but also after the Fall (1 Tim. 4:4: "Every creature of God is good"). But creatures are good only in so far as they are God's creation. God alone is good of Himself and in Himself (τὸ αὐτὸαγαθόν), and in this sense "there is none good but One, that is, God" (Matt. 19:17). God's goodness and absolute perfection are the same. Gerhard: "God is really good, He alone is good, and He is the cause of all goodness" (*Loci, locus "De Nat. Dei,"* § 208).[101]

There is a very important lesson in the truth that God alone is good in Himself, whereas all human goodness is only a derived goodness. This truth will guard us against pride when we observe special

---

[98] Cp. Luther, St. L. XI:957 ("If it is necessary"); Walther, *Pastorale*, p. 294 [Fritz, *Pastoral Theology*, 1945, p. 210].

[99] *Sunt sophismata, quibus definitio rei tollitur.* Some dogmaticians have refuted the objection in detail. Scherzer, *Systema*, p. 55: "If God were to lie, to die, to sin, He would not be God. If the creature had infinite perfection, it would not be a creature. If yesterday had not passed away, it would not be yesterday; if tomorrow existed today, there would be no today."

[100] Nitzsch-Stephan, 472 ff., correctly calls attention to this advisability.

[101] Baier: "Goodness belongs to God absolutely and essentially *(absolute et in se)* and is therefore God's perfection itself or His essence, in so far as His goodness comprises all divine perfections." The only difference between perfection and goodness is that the former is viewed only as a remote attribute, while the latter is both remote and relative. *Compend.* II, 44.

gifts in ourselves not bestowed on others, and against envy when the situation is reversed. Scripture and experience teach us that pride and envy have always been the great troublemakers in the Church and in the State. Scripture warns against pride (1 Cor. 4:7) and against envy (1 Pet. 2:1). Gerhard: "All good gifts come down to us and our neighbors from God. Whoever therefore is envious of the neighbor has a quarrel with God, the Giver of the gifts, and is in reality a θεομάχος [one who picks a fight with God]." *(Op. cit.,* § 215).

God's goodness is not only "remote," "objective," an attribute within the divine essence, but it is also "subjective," "relative," an attribute which describes God's benevolence and beneficence toward His creatures.[102] Scripture contains many references concerning God's goodness toward all creatures, rational and irrational: The Lord is good to all (Ps. 145:9), has pity even on animals (Jonah 4:11), helps both man and beast (Ps. 36:6); and especially Psalm 136, with its refrain: "For His mercy endureth forever." For this reason the Psalmist calls on all creatures to praise God (Psalm 148).

But Scripture focuses our attention in particular on God's goodness toward man, more specifically, toward man as a sinner. It does so by using the terms *mercy, love, grace, patience, long-suffering.* These terms are, of course, synonyms, inasmuch as they all describe God's goodness. But from our viewpoint they present various aspects of God's goodness, and these synonymous terms bring God's goodness into full view, just as the various facets refract and reflect the brilliance of the diamond.

The *mercy* of God is goodness as compassion upon man, whose sin has brought him into untold misery. "Through the tender mercy of God [διὰ σπλάγχνα ἐλέους θεοῦ] . . . the Dayspring [Christ] hath visited us, to give light to them that sit in darkness and in the shadow of death" (Luke 1:78-79). The *love* of God shows us that facet of God's goodness which reveals Him as being deeply attached to sinful mankind and anxious to restore men to communion with God, John 3:16 God is the Philanthropist, whose love toward man (φιλανθρωπία) has appeared, Titus 3:4. The *grace* of God is goodness in so far as man in no wise has deserved it, but God is good toward the sinner only for the sake of Christ's vicarious satisfaction (Titus 3:5: "Not by works of righteousness which we have done"; Rom. 3:24: "freely, by His grace, through the redemption that is in Christ Jesus"). The terms *patience* and *long-suffering* reveal that phase of God's goodness which prompts

102 Quenstedt, *Systema,* I, 418.

Him not to punish immediately, but to wait for the sinner's repentance. He waited for 120 years before the Flood (1 Pet. 3:20), and the postponement of the world's final Judgment is due not to God's slackness, but to His long-suffering, which earnestly desires that all should come to repentance (2 Pet. 3:9). God characterizes Himself as "the Lord God, merciful and gracious, long-suffering and abundant in goodness and truth" (Ex. 34:6).[103]

The repeated occurrence of great catastrophes, such as earthquakes, floods, wars, panics, is viewed by some as denying God's goodness. But these ravages are employed by God in the interest of His saving goodness. They are a call to repentance to all men (Luke 13:3, 5). Therefore we observe a day of penitence after such catastrophes. Unfortunately the vast majority remains impenitent and compels God to complain: "Why should ye be stricken any more? Ye will revolt more and more; the whole head is sick, and the whole heart is faint" (Is. 1:5).

God's goodness must be reflected in His children. "Be ye therefore merciful, as your Father also is merciful" (Luke 6:36). Christians are taught of God to love one another (1 Thess. 4:9). They love, bless, help, and intercede for their enemies that they may be children of their heavenly Father (Matt. 5:44-45). They are kind to one another, forgiving, tender-hearted, even as God for Christ's sake has forgiven them (Eph. 4:32; Col. 3:13). God's goodness toward the dumb creatures must also reflect itself in the Christian, for "a righteous man regardeth the life of his beast, but the tender mercies ["the heart": marginal reading] of the wicked are cruel" (Prov. 12:10).

Among all the attributes of God, Scripture assigns a unique place to God's goodness as grace in Christ. We must always keep in mind that the true scope of the Bible is none other than to reveal God's grace. For Scripture reveals Christ the Savior of sinners, and in Christ's redemptive work God turns His gracious countenance toward sinners. "For God sent not His Son into the world to condemn the world, but that the world through Him might be saved" (John 3:17). Also the Old Testament has no other scope than to reveal the forgiveness of sins in Christ, i. e., God's grace, as St. Peter testifies: "To Him give all the Prophets witness that through His name whosoever believeth in Him shall receive remission of sins" (Acts 10:43). If Scripture had

---

[103] A detailed discussion of the attributes of mercy, love, etc., in their unity and divergence will be offered under the heading "Concept of Saving Grace" in Vol. II.

revealed all the divine attributes except God's grace, then Scripture would be of no value to us. Our knowledge of God would fill our hearts with terror if Scripture had not revealed that the one, indivisible, immutable, infinite, omnipresent, eternal, living, all-knowing, all-wise, omnipotent, holy, just, truthful God is also the gracious God – gracious in Christ and for Christ's sake. "All sins Thou borest for us, Else had despair reigned o'er us." This is God's true countenance.

Let us take heed lest we deface God's gracious countenance. Rome defaces it in a very coarse way by coldly making the doctrine of work-righteousness its central doctrine and by expressly pronouncing the anathema on the doctrine of justification through faith in God's grace for Christ's sake.[104] In the Papacy, God's gracious countenance is transformed into the countenance of an angry judge. Luther complains that as a result of the papal system of work-righteousness he had feared Christ more than the devil. – God's gracious countenance is distorted also in some sections of the Protestant Church, though not so patently as in Rome, yet just as seriously. Calvinism emphasizes the sovereignty of God in such a one-sided manner that the countenance of grace is virtually obliterated. Synergism, ancient and modern, in so far as it makes man's salvation depend on some good quality in man, thereby actually places the mask of a cruel and vindictive judge over the loving face of our gracious Father. – The same is done by the modern theologians who deny the *satisfactio vicaria.*[105] But only too often even Christians who clearly understand the doctrine of God's grace and are also able to state it correctly, deface God's gracious countenance. This occurs when they attempt to determine God's gracious attitude toward themselves on the basis of their subjective feelings and emotions and not on the basis of the objective Word of God.[106]

In concluding our discussion of the doctrine of God we must once more point out that all who deny the Holy Trinity know nothing of God's gracious countenance. If there is no Trinity, then there is no eternal Son of God, no incarnation of the Son of God in the fullness of time, no Vicarious Atonement, no justification by faith, no peace with God through our Lord Jesus Christ; then there is only the Law, with its obligations, demands, threats, and curses. The Triune God is the gracious God – and the gracious God is the Triune God.

---

[104] See "The Papacy and the Doctrine of Justification" in Vol. II.

[105] "Modern Protestant Theology and the Doctrine of Justification" in Vol. II.

[106] See "The Denial of the Means of Grace in the Personal Life of the Christians" in Vol. III.

The Creation of the World and of Man

(DE CREATIONE)

1

The Record of Creation

SINCE no human being observed the creation of the world, we have no other authentic account of the creation than the one given by God Himself in the Scriptures. The statements: "All Scripture is given by inspiration of God" (2 Tim. 3:16) and "The Scripture cannot be broken" (John 10:35) include, of course, also the report of the creation in Genesis 1 and 2. We human beings can indeed know *a posteriori* (reasoning from effect to cause) that all things were created by God. All creatures bear the divine stamp; God's invisible nature, that is, His eternal power and Godhead, are clearly seen (καθορᾶται) from the creation of the world, from the creatures (Rom. 1:20). But our knowledge of the particular circumstances of the creation (e. g., of the time in which creation was completed and of the order of creation) is derived solely from God's revelation in Scripture. Men who presume to correct God's record of the creation through conclusions drawn from the present condition of the world are playing the role of scientific wiseacres, a procedure unworthy of Christians, as well as of men in general. The discord among professional geologists, for example, as to the age of the earth and of man is so great that only he will speak of "assured results" of geology who has completely renounced the use of what reason is left to man after the Fall.[1]

2

The Definition of Creation

While heathen pantheism assumes that the world is an emanation from God and is therefore God Himself, and heathen dualism assumes an eternal matter (ὕλη, ὕλη ἄμορφος, τὸ μὴ ὄν) of which the deity

[1] On the disagreement among the geologists see Luthardt, *Apologie,* I, 68 ff. Luthardt himself makes concessions that are out of place. In our own publications this subject has often been dealt with, e. g., *Lehre und Wehre,* 44, p. 364 ff: *"Ueber das Alter der Erde."* For Geikie's discussion of "palaeontological problems," which so far have not been solved and whose certain solution cannot be expected in the future, see *Lehre und Wehre,* 59, p. 71.

(ὁ νοῦς, τὸ ὄν) formed the world (κόσμος),[2] Holy Scripture teaches that the Triune God created everything outside God, the universe, through His mere will, out of nothing. And "nothing" does not mean a *materia ex qua*, a *nihil positivum* (Plato's μὴ ὄν, chaos), but it means absolutely nothing, *nihil negativum, materiam excludens;* for, as Gen. 1:1 tells us, before the creation of the world nothing at all was in existence except God. "In the beginning" means that then the things outside God had their beginning. According to Scripture, God alone, in distinction from all things outside Himself, had no beginning. That is the emphatic declaration of Ps. 90:2: "Before the mountains were brought forth or ever Thou hadst formed the earth and the world, even from everlasting to everlasting Thou art, God," and of Col. 1:17: "He is before all things." Men are bound by the rule: *De nihilo nihil fit*, but not so God. God follows the rule given Rom. 4:17: "God calleth those things which be not as though they were." Accordingly, only he knows God who knows that He created the world from nothing.[3]

3

The Hexaemeron

The time in which creation was completed was six days, as Gen. 1:31 and Gen. 2:2 expressly state (*hexaemeron*). These six days are neither to be shortened, for pious reasons (to set forth God's omnipotence), to a moment (Athanasius, Augustine, Hilary), nor are they to be extended, for impious reasons (to bring Scripture into agreement with the "assured results" of science), to six periods of indefinite length (thus almost all modern theologians). Scripture forbids us to interpret the days as periods, for it divides these days into evening and morning. That forces us to accept the days as days of twenty-four hours.[4]

---

[2] Cp. Philippi, *Glaubenslehre*, II, 225 f., quoted in Baier-Walther, II, p. 98.

[3] We read in Nitzsch-Stephan, p. 427: "A creation out of nothing is not immediately taught in the canonical books of the Bible, not even Heb. 11:3 (and Rom. 4:17); there only the raising from non-existence to existence is spoken of." It is clear that the second sentence abolishes the first. Raising from non-existence to existence constitutes creation out of nothing. Compare on the "nothing" Twesten, *Vorlesungen ueber die Dogmatik der ev.-luth. Kirche*, II, *Abteil.* I, 75 f., quoted in Baier-Walther, II, 97 f.

[4] Luther: "Hilary and Augustine, two great lights in the Church, believed that the world was made of a sudden and all at once (*subito et simul*), not successively during the space of six days. Augustine plays with these six days in a marvelous manner. He considers them to be mystical days of knowledge in the

4

The Order Observed in Creation

Genesis 1 teaches clearly that God, in creating, progressed from the simple and the inorganic to the organic, or from the imperfect to the perfect. God first created the rudiments of heaven and earth, matter in a chaotic condition ("*Weltstoff*"; Luther, *moles coeli et terrae*). Then He created, one after the other: 1) the light (vv. 3-5); 2) the visible firmament (vv. 6-8); 3) the sea and the dry land, together with the plant life on the earth (vv. 9-13); 4) the sun, the moon, and the stars in the heavens (vv. 14-19); 5) fish and fowl (vv. 20-23); 6) land animals and, finally, man (vv. 24-28).

This order observed by God cannot be interpreted as a self-development of the creature (evolution), for in the various stages of the order recorded everything depends on the divine monergism. The earth, for instance, does not produce grass and herbs (v. 11) and living creatures (v. 24) by way of self-development, but by the word of the Almighty: "Let the earth bring forth," the earth causes plant life and animal life to spring forth. The theory of "two factors" must be rejected as evolutionism. Luthardt indeed declares: "Scripture tells us that two factors co-operated in the progressive steps of the formations: the spontaneous activity of the powers of nature and the creative influence of God" (*Apologie* I, 70). But he is mistaken. According to Scripture, grass and animals do not come into existence in part through God's operation and in part through the "spontaneous activity" of the earth, but they owe their existence entirely to God's operation. The earth is

---

angels *(mysticos dies cognitionis in angelis)* and not six natural days. . . . As Moses is not instructing us concerning allegorical creatures or an allegorical world, but concerning natural creatures and a world visible and capable of being apprehended by the senses, he calls, as we say in the proverb, 'a post a post,' he calls the thing by the right name, day and evening; his meaning is the same as ours when we use those terms, without any allegory whatever." (St. L. I:6.) Vilmar, too, admits: "The manner in which these 'six days' in Gen. 2:2-3 and later in the Law are used shows that days of twenty-four hours are meant, and the wording used (evening and morning, the first day, the second day, etc.) seems to speak in favor of it" (Vilmar, *Dogmatik*, I, 247, quoted in Baier-Walther, II, 79). But later he adds: "On the other hand, the description of God given in Ps. 90:4 and 2 Pet. 3:8, according to which a thousand years are as one day and one day as a thousand years with the Lord, favors the assumption of periods in the creation." But it is utterly impossible to parallel Ps. 90:4 and 2 Pet. 3:8 with the record of the creation. These passages state that in God and with God there is no time. But the record of the creation announces by its very first words: "In the beginning," that it deals with time, that is, it is a historical report. Both Luther and the dogmaticians stress this point. Quenstedt, I, 613.

merely, as the dogmaticians say, the *materia ex qua*. God alone creates the plant and the animal. Luthardt proposes that the lines separating the Bible and the natural sciences be sharply defined and observed (*"Grenzregulierung"*). This is a good suggestion. But he does not observe the lines when he says (*op. cit.*, p. 53): "Religion tells us that it is God who gives us our daily bread; but natural science teaches us how the grain grows in the field." This is so crass an error that Luthardt two pages later corrects himself: "Even today the origin of life is an impenetrable mystery. How something comes into being no man can tell, and we shall never discover it." This statement is certainly correct. The truly scientific study of nature, which is based on experience and observation, knows of no development of organic creatures from the inorganic (*generatio aequivoca*) and no evolution of a higher species from a lower.[5] – And, as the creation of the creatures is God's work, so, too, their continued existence, their activity, and their propagation depend solely on the continued operation of God, not on a "spontaneous activity" of the creatures, nor partly or entirely on evolution. For Col. 1:17 tells us: "By Him all things consist," and Acts 17:28: "In Him we live, and move, and have our being."

5

The Work of the Six Days

The First Day: The phrase "In the beginning" refers to things outside God. When they came into existence, time and space began. – "Heaven and earth" is usually employed in Scripture to denote all created things, the universe, *das Weltall* (Gen. 2:1; Is. 37:16; Jer. 32:17; Acts 4:24; 14:15). Col. 1:16: "For by Him were all things created that are in heaven and that are in earth, visible and invisible." But since

---

[5] See the quotations concerning the *generatio aequivoca* in Luthardt, *Apol.* I, 236 f., and Charles Hodge, *Systematic Theology,* II, 5 ff., on the attempts in England to produce life from dead matter – unsuccessful attempts. Dr. Walther was accustomed to say, somewhat drastically, in connection with Ex. 8:18: "The dabblers in natural science may acquire lice, but make them they cannot." Huxley admits that evolutionism presupposes the generation of life from dead matter. See *Lehre und Wehre,* 59, p. 71. The fact that there is no scientific proof for the evolution of a higher species from a lower and that in this respect true natural history is in agreement with Scripture (everything "after his kind") is often presented in our periodicals, for example, *Lehre und Wehre,* 44, 303; 46, 233; 54, 559; 59, 75. Evolutionism and all that is involved is thoroughly treated and refuted in *Lehre und Wehre,* 46, 8–239 *passim;* 55, 289–550 *passim.*

the following verses describe heaven and earth as we know them today, as being formed out of the original substance, we rightly understand this original substance, "heaven and earth" of Gen. 1:1, to be the "*rudis moles coeli et terrae*" (St. L. I:9), or, in modern phraseology, the "*Weltstoff*." – The water was created with the crude material, since it was present on the first day (Gen. 1:2) and surrounded the earth (v. 9). – The term תֹהוּ וָבֹהוּ is used Jer. 4:23 to describe a devastated country, but in Gen. 1:2 it designates a chaotic condition in which things are still a formless mass.

The theory, held by Kurtz, Delitzsch, Rudelbach, and Guericke, that this תֹהוּ וָבֹהוּ denotes the remains of an earlier world which perished when a part of the angels fell and that the creation described in Genesis 1 is merely the restitution of a prior creation has no foundation whatever in the text.[6] – Nor does anything in the text indicate that "heaven" refers to the empyrean (*coelum empyrium*), a supposed region of pure fire in which God dwells with the angels and the saints, as was held by Scholastics, Romanists, Calvinists, and Arminians.[7] The heaven of the angels and saints is not a created locality, but the condition of the blessed vision of God. Matt. 18:10 teaches that the angels, while attending the "little ones" on earth, at the same time always behold the face of God in heaven. (For further details see "Eternal Life," p. 553, Note 84.)

The light which God created on the first day was the "elemental light," which, on the fourth day, was concentrated in the celestial bodies. According to the clear statement of Scripture there was light before sun, moon, and stars existed. Nobody will object to this as long as he believes in an omnipotent God.[8]

The Second Day: The expanse, or "firmament" (רָקִיעַ), is not the atmosphere surrounding the globe (as Baier and others have thought), but the visible vault of the sky (Luther and others); v. 8: "God called

---

6 See the long quotation from Kurtz' *Bibel und Astronomie*, 2d ed., pp. 94, 96, in Baier-Walther, II, 83. Zoeckler, too, rejects the "restitution theory," R. E., 2d ed., XIII, 645 f.

7 Quenstedt, I, 623: "A sweet daydream and a mere figment."

8 What is light? Is it rarefied matter (emanation theory, or emission theory) or undulations of the "molecules of the ether" (undulation theory)? Baier (II, p. 84) takes it to be "a certain luminous body produced by the substance of the heaven." Chemnitz, *Loci*, I, 120: "Because Paul says 2 Cor. 4:6: 'God commanded the light to shine out of darkness,' that is, while it was dark, the light suddenly appeared at God's word and command, it seems that the light, too, was immediately created out of nothing." *The Century Dictionary*, IV, p. 3445, *s. v.* "light," does not define the status of the controversy exactly; it says that Newton's "emission theory" has been abandoned in our day.

the רָקִיעַ heaven," v. 14: "the רָקִיעַ of heaven." According to vv. 6-8 this firmament divides the waters above and below it. Is it not dangerous to place waters above the firmament? They are no more dangerous than the waters in the sea, which are also kept in their place only by God's omnipotence.[9]

The Third Day: God gathered the waters under the heavens together at one place and let dry land appear. At God's command the land then brought forth the plant life. The plants appeared before the seed: God created the plants, which "yielded seed." This fact answers the famous question: Which was first, the oak or the acorn?

The Fourth Day: God created the celestial bodies, sun, moon, and stars. We are not told of what (*materia ex qua*) they were created, but it is stated for what purpose (*finis cuius*) and for whose good (*finis cui*) they were made. They are to serve as the dispensers of light and the indicators of the time and seasons (Gen. 1:14-18). The Bible does not teach any so-called astronomical "system," but it does teach clearly the following facts: The earth came into existence before the sun, and the light was before the sun. The earth does not serve the sun, but the sun was made to serve the earth. The existence and activity of the sun, moon, and stars are dependent on the existence of the earth. When the earth has run its course, having fulfilled its purpose, which is to provide a habitation for men to hear the Gospel of the crucified Savior of sinners, then the sun, moon, and stars will disappear with this present earth. Matt. 24:14 speaks plain language: "And this Gospel of the Kingdom shall be preached in all the world for a witness unto all nations; and then shall the end come." With the end of this world the end of all things, of the universe, πάντων τὸ τέλος (1 Pet. 4:7), is come. No matter what size, compared with the earth, men may ascribe to sun, moon, and stars, these celestial bodies have no independent history and no independent meaning and function, but

---

[9] Luther: "Now, this is a most wondrous thing, that Moses with clear words makes three parts and puts the firmament between the waters. I would like to think and speculate in this wise, that the firmament is the highest above all things and the waters would not be above, but below the heavens, namely, the clouds, which we see; that is to say, the waters which are divided from the waters are the clouds, which are separated from the waters which are in the earth. But Moses declares in plain words that the waters are above and below the firmament. Therefore I must take my thoughts captive and bow to the Word, albeit I do not comprehend it." (St. L. I:32.) John Meissner remarks, *Phil. Sobria* (P. I, p. 819): "The majority of theologians have always held it to be real water, which, they maintained, God in a singular and miraculous manner really and truly placed above the firmament, or stellar heavens."

their history and significance or function are dependent upon the earth. These facts are positively taught in Holy Scripture.

As to the astronomical systems constructed by men, every Christian, and particularly every Christian theologian, must keep these four things in mind: 1) Scripture is errorless, also in physical matters. Scripture is indeed "no textbook of the natural sciences." Its purpose is to teach the way to heaven by faith in Christ (2 Tim. 3:15; John 17:20; 20:31; Eph. 2:20-22). But when, even though only in passing, it does teach matters of natural science, its statements are the inviolable truth (John 10:35). 2) Scripture accommodates itself to our human conception of things (e. g., when it speaks of a *praescientia Dei* or of a *descensus Dei*), but never to erroneous human conceptions. We are not entitled to limit John 10:35: "The Scripture cannot be broken," and John 17:17: "Thy Word is truth" by saying that this "self-evidently" does not refer to the historical, geographic, scientific, etc., statements of Scripture. 3) Our human knowledge of astronomical matters is naturally limited much by our inability to view them from a position outside this globe and the universe. Even the geographer Daniel, who is himself a Copernican, reminds us of this fact. "The cosmic systems, all of them without exception, are not based on experience, for this would demand a position outside the earth, but on conclusions and combinations. All of them therefore are and remain hypotheses." [10] 4) It is unworthy of a Christian to interpret Scripture, which he knows to be God's own Word, according to human opinions (hypotheses), and that includes the Copernican cosmic system, or to have others thus to interpret Scripture to him.[11]

---

[10] Dr. H. A. Daniel, *Handbuch der Geographie*, 3d ed., 1877, p. 9.

[11] The Copernicans particularly have the bad habit of offering their "view of the cosmos" as the "assured result of science." The Lisco vs. Knack affair (1868) is a case in point. Pastor Lisco had asserted in an "ecclesiastical report" to the Berlin District Synod that science had forever demolished "the world view of the Biblical writers" and that not one of the "modern orthodox" theologians would believe with the Bible that the earth stands still and the sun revolves about it. Pastor Knack answered this challenge by saying: "Indeed, I believe that. I know no other world view than that of Holy Scriptures." This declaration raised the ire of the "scientific" Copernicans. And *Lehre und Wehre* (1868, p. 325) gives the following report of these repercussions: "The aged *Oberkonsistorialrat* Twesten said in his classroom: 'Do not imagine that you as theologians have the pitiful prerogative to be narrow-minded.' And Stroebel answered in the '*Zeitschrift fuer luth. Theol. und Kirche,*' 1868, p. 734: 'As long as man keeps his head, he will not accept the dream of a revolving earth as the finding of science, but as a madness indicating lack of thought or lack of reason.'" Stroebel wrote these words in a review of a pamphlet by Pastor J. L. Fueller, in which he praises the writing, but classes as a flaw the assertion: "We adherents of the Copernican system know what Joshua and his army did not know," and

Fifth Day: God created the aquatic animals and the birds (vv. 20-22). Gerhard calls the fifth day the "birthday" of the fish and the fowls (*Loci, locus "De Creatione,"* § 32). In regard to the *materia ex qua* of the fowls the opinion among Lutheran theologians is divided. They all agree that in the so-called *creatio mediata,* i. e., in the creation of the creatures from the existing matter, every form of self-activity of matter (evolution) is to be rejected. The matter existing since the first day comes into consideration merely as the material from which (*materia ex qua*) the infinite power of God produced the creatures, each one after its kind. The matter is *principium passivum, non concurrit* (as a second factor) *cum Deo ad aliquid creandum.*[12] But as to the substance from which the fowls were created, Luther and Calov say: *Ex aqua;* Baier and Hollaz: *ex terra.* Hollaz appeals to Gen. 2:19: "Out of the ground the Lord formed every beast of the field and every fowl of the air." And Gen. 1:20 the water is not expressly indicated as the matter from which the fowls were made. But Hollaz overlooks that Gen. 2:19 the words: "out of the ground" are connected with, and apply to the creation of, the beasts and need not pertain to the fowls. Walther quotes both sides but leaves the matter undecided. So we, too, hold the matter in abeyance and admire the creative power of God in either case. This is what Chemnitz, who accepts the *ex aqua,* stresses (*Loci* I, 122).

Sixth Day: God created the land animals out of the ground (Gen. 1:24; 2:19). If it be asked whether the scavengers, maggots, and the like, and the predatory animals, which are now at war with man, were also created by God on this day, we should answer that (a) these animals also are a part of creation, but (b) they had a different sphere of activity. Before the Fall there was no φθορά (decay) in nature, nor had the animals risen against man. The poisonous plants either had

---

says: "But the words 'And the sun stood still' (Joshua 10:13) are not the words of the son of Nun and the Children of Israel, but the words of the Holy Ghost; and must the Holy Ghost first go to Copernicus' school before He can speak on this matter? Why did not Pastor Fueller apply his correct principle also to the Copernican system: 'I do not think that anyone need be disturbed who has not yet entirely renounced all independence of thinking and investigating and does not yet in a blind collier's faith accept all unproved and unprovable assumptions and assertions as the results of science!'" This is what we meant when we said above: "It is unworthy of a Christian to interpret Scripture, which he knows to be God's own Word, according to human opinions (hypotheses)." Luther, we know, objects to all astronomical systems which are palmed off as objective truth beyond what experience teaches. (St. L. I:33; XI:300 f.) – By the way, the newspapermen threatened about a year ago that Einstein's theory of relativity would give Copernicanism the death blow.

[12] Hollaz, *Examen* I, c. 3, qu. 26; Quenstedt, I, 607.

a different nature before the Fall, or they were not harmful to man in his uncorrupted state. Thus Luther and the dogmaticians.[13]

Finally, on the *sixth day,* God created man. The fact that man is the crown of creation, superior to the other creatures, is indicated by the following circumstances: 1) Before He made man, the Triune God held a consultation: "Let Us make man" (Gen. 1:26). 2) God did something special when He created man. He did not simply speak, as He did when He created animals: "Let the earth bring forth," but He molded the body of man out of the clay and by a special act breathed into his nostrils the breath of life (Gen. 2:7). 3) The fact that God breathed into man the breath of life indicates that man was given a life principle different from that of the animals, namely, a rational and immortal soul.[14] However, the human soul is not an efflux of God's essence or a part of God (pantheism). 4) Of special importance is the creation of man in God's own image (בְּצַלְמֵנוּ and כִּדְמוּתֵנוּ, Gen. 1:26). Man was endowed with the knowledge of God and perfect righteousness and holiness. (This matter will be more thoroughly presented in the chapter "Man Before the Fall.") 5) The installation of man as ruler over the earth and its inhabitants (Gen. 1: 26-28).[15]

---

[13] See the quotations in Baier-Walther, II, 87 *sq.* Luther, St. L. I:249 ff. Gerhard, *Loci, locus "De Creatione,"* § 33: "If someone asks as to the poisonous plants, the predatory animals, etc., we answer with Augustine (*De Gen. ad literam* III c. 15): 'The noxious animals would not have harmed man if he had not sinned. To punish the vices and to test and perfect the virtues of the dwellers on earth, they began to be noxious; hence they were created harmless, but because of sin they became harmful.'" This matter seems ridiculous to Andrew White. He says in *The Warfare of Science* I, 30: "Luther, who followed St. Augustine in so many other matters, declined to follow him fully in this" [namely, that there are "superfluous" animals]. "To him [Luther] a fly was not merely superfluous, it was noxious – sent by the devil to vex him when reading." White takes everything taught by Scripture concerning the Creation, the Fall, and the consequences of the Fall to be myths.

[14] In his *Bibelwerk,* Lucas Osiander comments on Gen. 2:7: "Man was made a living, but a rational, 'animal,' not a brute; for it is not said that God breathed life into the rest of the animals, as He did into man."

[15] Luther on Gen. 2:7: "Moses here returns to the work of the sixth day and shows whence the cultivator of the earth came, namely, that God formed him out of the ground, as the potter with his hand forms the vessel out of clay. He did not say in this case as in that of the other creatures: 'Let the earth bring forth man,' but: 'Let Us make man.' In this case, Moses describes God as thus speaking in order that he may set forth the excellency of the human race and make manifest the peculiar counsel of God according to which He created man, although afterwards man grew and multiplied, as all the other animals multiply. . . . But with reference to their first creation Moses shows that there was the greatest possible difference, since the human nature was created by a peculiar divine counsel and wisdom and formed by the finger of God. The difference which

DICHOTOMY AND TRICHOTOMY

The assumption that man consists of three essentially different parts: of the σῶμα (body) as the material part; the ψυχή (soul) as the lower, or animal, principle of life, which man has in common with animals; and the πνεῦμα (spirit) as the higher, or spiritual, principle of life, which distinguishes man from the animals, is not sufficiently supported in Luke 1:46-47 and 1 Thess. 5:23. In Luke 1:46-47 ("My soul doth magnify the Lord, and my spirit hath rejoiced in God, my Savior") "soul" and "spirit" are plainly synonymous, according to the parallelism of Hebrew poetry. The thought: "My lower principle of life" magnifies the Lord, and "my higher principle of life" hath rejoiced in God, my Savior, is foreign to the context. In 1 Thess. 5:23 the words "Your whole spirit and soul and body" refer to the progressive sanctification of the Christians in view of the approaching Judgment Day, and it is certainly better to take "spirit" not as a natural part of man, but as designating the entire spiritual nature of a regenerate person, and the καὶ ἡ ψυχὴ καὶ τὸ σῶμα as specifying the ὁλόκληρον ὑμῶν τὸ

God made in the original creation of man and of cattle likewise shows man's immortality. And though all the other works of God fill us with wonder and are truly magnificent, yet that man is the most excellent creature is evident from the fact that God in creating him had recourse to His deep counsel and proceeds in a new manner. For God does not leave it to the earth to bring forth man, as it brought forth the beasts and the trees. For God Himself forms man in His own image to be a participator of God and one designed to enjoy the rest of God. Hence Adam, before he is formed by the Lord, is a mere lifeless lump of earth, lying on the ground; God takes that lump of earth into His hand and forms out of it a most beautiful creature, partaking of immortality. If Aristotle were to hear these things, he would burst out into a loud laugh and would say that this whole matter is a fable, a very pleasant one indeed, but a very absurd one, namely, that man, who was originally a lump of earth, was formed by divine wisdom and designed for immortality. For although some of the philosophers, as Socrates and others, asserted the immortality of the soul, they were laughed at and almost cast out by their fellows. But how great is the folly of reason to be offended at this fact, when it beholds that the generation of man to this very day fills us with wonder! For who would not judge it an absurdity to suppose that man, who is designed to live eternally, should be born from one single drop of seed, as it were, from the loins of the father? This is just about as absurd as the statement of Moses that man was formed from a lump of earth by the finger of God. But reason shows by all this folly that it understands nothing of God, who by the efficacy of His thought makes out of a lump of earth not only the seed of man, but man himself, and makes also, as Moses afterwards says, the woman out of the rib of man. This, then, is the origin of man. Having thus been created male and female, man is generated out of their blood by the divine blessing. And although this generation is common to man and beasts, this similarity by no means detracts from the glory of our original formation, that we are vessels of God, fashioned by His own hand, that He is our Potter and we His clay, as Isaiah says in his 64th chapter." (*Opp. exeg.*, Erl. I, 104 *sqq.*; St. L. I:101 ff.)

πνεῦμα, so that the meaning is: May your whole spirit, your soul as well as your body, be preserved blameless. Dichotomy is favored decidedly by passages like Matt. 10:28: "Fear not them which kill the body, but are not able to kill the soul; but rather fear Him which is able to destroy both soul and body in hell." Man is here described according to his entire essence (his "totality"), and still only "body" and "soul" are mentioned. Matt. 16:25-26 is also conclusive: "What shall a man give in exchange for his soul?" That "soul" and "spirit" are essentially the same and are interchangeable terms is also evidenced by the fact that the departed, after having laid aside the body, are called both "spirits" (πνεύματα) and "souls" (ψυχαί) (1 Pet. 3:19 and Rev. 6:9). Recent theologians are divided on the question;[16] nearly all the older Lutheran dogmaticians teach dichotomy.[17]

THE UNITY OF THE HUMAN RACE

There were no pre-Adamites,[18] nor were there co-Adamites (contemporaries of Adam),[19] but all men are Adamites, i. e., Adam is the first man and the progenitor of all mankind. This is no theological problem, but a doctrine clearly revealed in Scripture. Gen. 1:26-28: one set of parents; Acts 17:26: "And hath made of one blood all nations of men"; Rom. 5:12: "By one man sin entered into the world." This is the conclusion also reached by recent anthropologists.[20] God did not create the woman independently of Adam, by forming her of the dust and breathing into her the breath of life, but built her out of a part of man, a rib. Woman (אִשָּׁה) is derived from man (אִישׁ), and that according to body and soul.[21]

---

16 See Luthardt, *Komp.*, 11th ed., p. 166 f. (13th ed., p. 194.)

17 See the antithesis in Quenstedt, I, 738 *sq.*, and the quotations in Baier-Walther, II, 91 *sq.*

18 Isaac La Peyrere (d. 1676) and others held that Adam was the forefather only of the Jews. Baier-Walther, II, 93, antithesis. Schelling, E. v. Bunsen, M'Causland, Zoeckler, *R. E.*, 2d ed., IX, 383, held the same view.

19 Polygenesis, autochthonism. The Greeks disclaimed a common origin with the "barbarians." Zoeckler, *loc. cit.*

20 Luthardt, *Apologie*, I, 76. Zoeckler, *op. cit.*, p. 583 ff.

21 Thus Luther, Quenstedt, etc. Luther, *Opp. exeg.*, Erl. I, 162; St. L. I:157: "Therefore my view of the passage is that the Lord did not take the bare rib, but the rib clothed with flesh, as Adam himself says: 'This is now bone of my bone and flesh of my flesh.' And be it observed that God did this by His Word; we are not to suppose that God did any cutting, after the manner of a surgeon." Quenstedt, I, 731: "The rib out of which the woman was formed was not dead or inanimate, but animate, since it was taken by the divine hand from a living body. And thus Eve was produced, soul and body, out of that rib. The soul of Eve

SPECIAL QUESTIONS REGARDING THE BIBLICAL ACCOUNT OF CREATION

1. Did Moses receive the account of creation by direct divine revelation, or was it handed down to him by oral transmission from our first parents, who received it from the Lord? (See Luther on Gen. 25:5-6, St. L. I:1758.) That is immaterial, for in either case the Biblical report is God's own report, since all Scripture is given by inspiration of God. Besides, the Biblical record, especially if it is compared with the creation myths of other nations, bears the divine stamp so unmistakably that even natural reason can recognize it. (Zoeckler, R. E., 2d ed., XIII, 631 f.) – Because the modern theologians do not receive Scripture as God's Word and will therefore not recognize the Biblical account of creation as God's account, the compliments which at the outset they shower on the Biblical account naturally end with a criticism, which arises from the impious Ego of speculating theologians.[22]

---

was not created by God immediately out of nothing and put into her by divine power, but the rib of Adam was the bearer *(tradux)* of the human soul to Eve, that is, it did not come into existence by immediate creation, but by propagation and traduction. Out of the living rib the living woman was formed (Gen. 2:22)."

[22] Zoeckler, for example, says on p. 629 ff. of Volume XIII of the R. E., 2d ed., *s. v. "Schoepfung"*: "If there is a living, personal God, nothing in this world can have originated except through the working of the absolute power and love of this one God. . . . That is the only true conception of creation, and the two records of the Biblical monotheism, the Old and the New Testament, present this concept in its purity." But on pages 644 ff. this same Zoeckler criticizes the Biblical account. He represents "the strictly literalistic understanding of the six days as a period of exactly six times twenty-four hours, which since Luther's day had become customary in Lutheran dogmatics . . . as aftereffects of the abstractly monotheistic conception of creation as held by early Jewry." He demands adjustment "with the incontestable facts of geological and astronomical science." He calls for "the indeterminate long periods of evolution that were at work on our globe before the human race appeared." He gets rid of the idea that light was created before the sun and the sun later than the earth "by assuming that the description in Gen. 1:14-19 is optical or merely phenomenological." In order to harmonize the Mosaic account of the creation with "the results of scientific investigation," Godet, who does not belong to the radical party of modern theology, resorts to the vision theory and draws a "picture" of the hexaemeron which has all the marks of a romance. He writes in his *Bibelstudien* (on the Old Testament, 1875, p. 101 f.): "We are sitting on a mountain with the man of God. . . . The prophetic instinct, which is natural with us, stirs in us, and we envision the beginning of the universe. . . . This darkness is not that of the grave, but that of the fertile night which is the cradle of all life. And into this darkness, lasting only a moment, are crowded together innumerable centuries, all the ages that have passed from the creation of matter to the formation of a firm surface of the earth. Suddenly a voice breaks the silence of this long night: 'Let there be light!' . . . The rays of light gradually lose their brilliancy, fade more and more, and finally have again become entirely extinct. Darkness envelops us. In this one day we have seen the story of

2. Genesis 1 and 2 are not two essentially different stories of the creation, but Genesis 2 is plainly seen to be a fuller report of the creation and of the first dwelling place of man. The reason why "*Elohim*" of Genesis 1 is changed to "*Jehovah Elohim*" of Genesis 2 is that from here on God's activity pertaining to man is the subject of the story. Hence we have in Genesis 2 the beginning of the history of mankind. [23]

3. The controversy as to the best world. We know that the world as created by God was good. Gen. 1:31: "And God saw everything that He had made, and, behold, it was very good." Could God not have created a better world? This is a foolish question, since God's will is the standard of all things, therefore also of goodness and beauty. The creatures were good because they were exactly as God desired them to be. Axiom: *Causam exemplarem* (pattern) *creationis ideae divinae rerum creandarum constituunt.* (Baier-Walther, II, 96.)

THE ULTIMATE PURPOSE OF THE WORLD

God made all things for His own sake (Prov. 16:4: "The Lord hath made all things for Himself") or for His glory (Psalm 104: The work of creation shows how "very great" He is, "clothed with honor and majesty"). Therefore not only men (Ps. 104:1 ff.), but also the irrational creatures are called on to praise God (Psalm 148). Scripture mentions particularly the glory of His power (Ps. 115:3: "Our God is in the heavens; He hath done whatsoever He hath pleased"); of His wisdom (Ps. 104:24, בְּחָכְמָה and Ps. 136:5, בִּתְבוּנָה); and of His goodness (Psalm 136, with the refrain: "for His mercy endureth forever"). The idea that it would be ascribing selfishness to God to declare that God made all things for Himself and for His praise is (1) unscientific, since it applies human standards to the majestic God, and (2) atheistic, since it assigns to creatures an independent existence alongside God.

CLOSING REMARKS

Creation as an *opus Dei ad extra* is the work of the Triune God; that has been demonstrated in the doctrine of God. To speak of three Creators, or of a "division" of the work of creation among the three

---

thousands of days that broke over our earth before there was a human eye to observe them. The voice sounds forth anew: 'Let there be an expansion in the midst of the waters, and let it divide the lower from the upper waters.' Again it becomes day," etc.

[23] See Fuerbringer, *Introduction to the Old Testament,* the entire chapter: "The Pentateuch," p. 16 ff. Also *Lehre und Wehre,* 25, p. 321 ff. Jean Astruc, a French physician (d. 1776), is "the father of the source theory." His book appeared in Brussels, in 1753, with the title *Conjectures,* etc.

Persons, is contrary to Scripture and offends Christian thought. As each Person possesses the whole divine essence, which is one in number (*una numero essentia*), so all *opera ad extra*, including the creation, are wholly and entirely the work of each Person. They are *eaedem numero actiones*.[24] Even Philippi slipped up when he said: "We see here [in the creation] the activity quite equally divided among all three Persons." [25] The Lutheran theologians emphatically reject the idea as though there were a "creation corporation," *causae sociae creationis*.[26] Luther emphatically refuses to speak of three Creators (see Vol. I, page 424).

Creation is a free act of God, not necessary on His part (Ps. 115:3: "He hath done whatsoever He hath pleased"). Declaring the creation to be a necessary act of God would amount to pantheism and nullify the concept of a personal God. As God was a *causa libera* in the redemption through the incarnation of the Son of God, so also He was a *causa libera* in the creation.[27]

---

[24] See the chapters "The Trinitarian Controversies," p. 381, and "Objections to the Unity of the Godhead," p. 387.

[25] *Glaubenslehre*, 3d ed., II, 126. It was shown above (p. 391, "Third Objection") that Philippi's terminology cannot be justified by the use of the so-called *particulae diacriticae* ἐκ, διά, ἐν. Referring to these diacritical particles, Luther says: "Scripture uses this manner of speaking: The world is created through Christ, by the Father, in the Holy Ghost, for all of which there is a reason, though we cannot sufficiently explore or express it. But this much we know, that Scripture uses this manner of speaking in order to indicate that the Father does not derive His divine essence from the Son, but the Son has it from the Father, and that the Father is the first and original Person in the Godhead. For this reason the Bible does not say that Christ made the world through the Father, but that the Father made it through Him, so that the Father remains the first Person and that from Him, but through the Son, all things have their being. Also John uses this manner of speaking, chapter 1:3: 'All things were made by Him.' And Col. 1:16: 'By Him were all things created,' and [v. 17] 'by Him all things consist.' And Rom. 11:36: 'Of Him and through Him and to Him are all things.'" (St. L. XII:157 f.) We summarized this relation, on page 391, thus: "As there is order," etc.

[26] Baier-Walther, II, 95: "There is, I say, one efficient cause of creation, not three associated causes. For the creative power of the three Persons is one." Quenstedt treats the question exhaustively whether the three Persons may be called associated causes of creation. He answers the question negatively on the basis of the *una numero essentia* and the *eaedem numero actiones divinae ad extra*.

[27] Quenstedt, I, 593: "Nor had there been any prevenient cause of creation except solely the pleasure of God, who communicated Himself not from a necessity of nature, but of His free will." Baier, II, 96: "See Ps. 136:5 *sqq.*, where the formula is added to every work of creation mentioned: 'For His mercy endureth forever.'" Kirn, in his *Grundriss der Evangelischen Dogmatik*, 3d ed., p. 59, presents the matter correctly: "According to the Biblical viewpoint the world came into existence not by a necessary emanation from God, not through evolution of an eternal world substance, but through God's free creative will."

Divine Providence, or the Preservation and Government of the World

(DE PROVIDENTIA DEI)

1

Definition of Divine Providence

GOD, who created the world, also preserves it. Col. 1:16-17: "All things were created by Him . . . by Him all things consist." We call this act, by common consent, the divine providence (the Greek terms are πρόνοια and διοίκησις), which means that God actually preserves and governs the universe and all individual creatures through His omnipresence and His omnipotence. The close relation between the creation and the preservation of the world is indicated in Col. 1: 16-17. After creating the world, God did not withdraw from it, neither entirely nor half nor in the least degree, but He remains in contact with the world and sustains everything in it, the greatest and the least, by His divine power. The sustaining power of God, and this alone, insures the continued existence of the world. If God would desert this world, it would at once disappear. If God would withdraw His presence from any part of the world, that part would cease to exist. This is clearly stated in the words: "By Him all things consist."

The clearest exposition of the teaching of Scripture on preservation over against false views is without doubt that of Luther. In support of the thesis that God has entirely or partially withdrawn from the world and put it under the rule of the "laws of nature," men maintain that according to Gen. 2:2 God rested on the seventh day from all the works which He had made. Luther expounds the passage thus: "The Sabbath, or the rest of the Sabbath, means that God so rested that He did not design to create another heaven and another earth. It does not mean that God ceased to preserve and govern the heaven and the earth which He had created. Concerning the manner of creation, Moses has given us the fullest information in the preceding chapter, where he says that God created all things by the Word: 'Let the sea bring forth fishes; let the earth bring forth the green herb, the beasts, etc.' Now, all these words of God remain unto the present day in their full force. We see that creatures multiply without cessation or end. If the world were to last untold years, the power and efficacy of this Word would not cease, but there would still continue to be a perpetual increase, by virtue of the power and efficacy of this Word, or, if I may so express it, of the first creation. The solution of the question is thus plain: 'God rested from all His works' means that

God was content with the earth and the heaven which He had created by the Word, He did not create a new heaven or a new earth or new stars and new trees; but God nevertheless still works, since He has not deserted the creatures, which He made in the beginning, but governs and sustains them by the power of His Word. He ceased from the work of creation. He does not cease from preserving and governing." (St. L. I:91 f.)

Hence Luther also says explicitly: "We Christians know that creating and preserving is one and the same thing with God (*idem est creare et conservare*)" (St. L. I:1539). Do we entertain scruples about calling the divine providence a continuous creation (*creatio continuata*)? That would indicate pretty strongly that we entertain wrong conceptions of the creation as well as of the preservation of the world. Perhaps we have given room to the thought that the world, at least to some extent, rests in the hands of the "laws of nature." More on this later.

Our reason can and should be aware of the fact of divine providence. Nature proclaims it (Acts 14:17: "Nevertheless He left not Himself without witness," etc.), and history tells of it (Acts 17:26-28: "And hath made of one blood all nations of men for to dwell on all the face of the earth and hath determined the times before appointed," etc.). But because of the blindness and perversity of the human heart divine providence is also taught in many places of the Holy Scriptures. Christ teaches it at length Matt. 6:25-32: "Take no thought for your life what ye shall eat or what ye shall drink. . . . Behold the fowls of the air; for they sow not, neither do they reap, nor gather into barns; yet your heavenly Father feedeth them. . . . Consider the lilies of the field, how they grow. . . . Wherefore, if God so clothe the grass of the field," etc. Matt. 5:45: "He maketh His sun to rise . . . and sendeth rain." Paul and Barnabas at Lystra bear witness to the Gentiles: "Nevertheless He left not Himself without witness in that He did good and gave us rain from heaven and fruitful seasons" (Acts 14:17). And Paul declares at Athens: "For in Him we live and move and have our being" (Acts 17:28). Scripture teaches furthermore that the preservation and government of the world, as an *opus ad extra*, is a work of the Triune God. In speaking of the preservation of the world, the Son of God says (John 5:17): "My Father worketh hitherto, and I work." And Scripture particularly emphasizes, for the comfort of Christians, that the incarnate Son of God rules and keeps all things according to His human nature, as our Brother. Eph. 1:22: "And hath put all things under His feet." Eph. 4:10: "He that descended is the same also that ascended up far above all heavens, that He might fill all things." (See the chapter "Communicated Omnipresence," in Vol. II.)

According to Scripture the objects of divine providence are both τὰ πάντα (Col. 1:17) and the individual things that constitute the universe: the plants (Matt. 6:28-30), the animals (Matt. 6:26), and men (Acts 17:25-28). Divine providence centers in the Church. Scripture teaches expressly that all things and all occurrences in heaven and on earth must serve the Church. According to Rom. 8:28 "all things work together for good to them that love God." According to Matt. 24:14 the world exists solely for the Church. And according to Heb. 1:14 the angels are ministers in the service of the Church.

OBJECTIONS RAISED AGAINST THE DIVINE PROVIDENCE

As an argument against divine providence extending over all things, men have contended that such activity would burden God too heavily and would give the trivial things of life undue prominence over against the great things. It is apparent that this argument does away with the true concept of God. It measures the almighty and omniscient God with a human yardstick. It changes the glory (δόξα) of the uncorruptible God into an image made like to corruptible man (Rom. 1:23). It need not surprise us that atheistic pagans like Democritus, Epicurus, and others have derided divine providence and called it an old wives' fable.[1] But it jars us that a Christian, like Jerome, could write the following: "As for the rest, it is an absurd detraction of the majesty of God to say that God knows every moment how many gnats are born and how many die; how many bedbugs, fleas, and flies there are on earth, what number of fishes live in the water. We are not such fatuous sycophants of God that while we make His power concern itself with most insignificant creatures, we are unfair to ourselves by assuming a like providence extending over rational and irrational creatures." [2] Gerhard tries in vain to put a good construction on Jerome's words.[3] Jerome was nodding here, as has happened to him on other

[1] See Quenstedt, I, 768 *sqq*.

[2] *Com. in Habac.* 1; quoted in Quenstedt, I, 769.

[3] He intimates, in *Loci, locus "De Provid.,"* §58, that Jerome may have merely wanted to say that God does not take cognizance of things step by step, but that everything is present to His mind at once. But it is impossible to put that construction on Jerome's words. Jerome fears that men might not receive the attention due them if God concerned Himself also about the small irrational creatures individually. — Gerhard points out in this very passage that Scripture explicitly teaches what Jerome's words seem to deny.

occasions. But who are we to pass harsh judgment on him? He only expressed in words the thoughts which we only too often harbor in our hearts. Our natural, God-estranged mind does not realize that God provides for us, His children. The Savior needs to remind us continually: "Take no thought for your life. . . . O ye of little faith!" (Matt. 6:25-32.) "But the very hairs of your head are all numbered" (Matt. 10:30). The entire question whether divine providence extends even to the minutest creatures, the Church Fathers and orthodox theologians settled with the Scriptural axiom: "If it was not unworthy of, and improper for, God to create even the minutest creatures, much less can it be improper for Him to rule what He created."[4]

---

[4] Quenstedt furnishes the quotation from the Church Fathers, *op. cit.*, § 59. Walther reproduces (in the *Compendium*) these words of Rambach's *Schriftmaessige Erlaeuterung der Grundlegung der Th.*, 1738, p. 157 f.: "Objects of the divine providence are all created things, none excepted, visible and invisible, living and lifeless, heaven, earth, and sea, and all that is in them. As He has created all things, so also His providence extends over all. He preserves 1) the invisible creatures, the angels; the good angels cannot govern themselves without His wisdom nor preserve themselves without His power; the evil angels cannot do harm without His permission, and He set limits to their malevolence; 2) the visible creatures, not alone man, the noblest creature, but also all irrational animals. In Egypt, frogs and lice must execute His commands. And this providence extends over every genus, over every species, even over all individuals of every genus. For instance, God cares not only for the genus of birds, but for every species, storks, swallows, and sparrows, and even for every single individual of every species, for every single stork, swallow, and sparrow. He not only takes care that the trees grow and are preserved, but He provides for every single tree and branch and leaf. Every one of them is under His government, as Christ teaches Matt. 10:29. A sparrow is one of the most insignificant and (apparently) useless birds; nevertheless Christ says that not one of them perishes, is shot, or hurt against the Father's will. Luke 12:6: 'Not one of them is forgotten before God.' The smallest, most insignificant, and most useless thing is under God's government and providence. Christ assures us of this Matt. 10:30: 'But the very hairs of your head are all numbered,' so that not one of them can fall out without the Father's will. What we prize we count. It indicates an exact knowledge and the care to preserve. As the light of the sun does not disdain the lowliest worm, so also God's providence does not turn away from it. We should well note this, that God's providence extends to the lowliest things. God does not rule like an earthly king, who provides by a general edict for all and every one of his subjects in general, though there are thousands whom the king does not know. God knows the smallest and provides for it, as Christ, the Mouthpiece of truth, assures us. Reason indeed holds that it is beneath divine Majesty to condescend also to the lowliest of His creatures. The heathen Pliny holds that it would defile divine Majesty if He took care of the despised things. However, these are foolish thoughts, which were entertained also by the great teacher of the Church Jerome. But this redounds to the glory of God. 1) The glory of His unlimited goodness, that with the arms of His providence He embraces the lowliest worm as well as the most exalted angel. If it is not improper for God to create them, why should it be improper for Him to preserve them? 2) It redounds to the glory of His power and wisdom. The power of God is no less

2

The Relation of Divine Providence to the Causae Secundae

The *causae secundae* (second causes) are the means through which divine Providence operates. God operates, and the means operate. Ps. 127:1: The Lord builds the house, and the builders build the house. But the relation between the operation of the means and the operation of God is this: The operation of the means is not coordinate with the operation of God, but subordinate to it, and subordinate to that extent that the means work only that which God works through them, and they work only as long as God works. For "except the Lord build the house, they labor in vain that build it."

We speak indeed of the natural constitution, movement, power, and working of the creature. But what the creatures do naturally, e. g., that the worm crawls, man walks, the sun shines, the tree grows and bears fruit after its kind, medicine heals, bread nourishes, the watchman protects, etc., they do because of God's influence on the creatures (*Dei in creaturas influxus*). Gerhard elaborates on this point (*Loci, locus "De Provid.,"* § 62. 63): "What is more natural to man than that he moves? And still we move in God (Acts 17:28). What is more natural for the sun than that it rises day by day? And yet 'God maketh His sun to rise' (Matt. 5:45). Though the creatures possess these attributes by nature, it is only by divine power that they, so to express it, have their being and life (*essentientur et vegetentur*). Ps. 104:29-30: 'Thou hidest Thy face, they are troubled; Thou takest away their breath, they die and return to their dust. Thou sendest forth Thy spirit, they are created; and Thou renewest the face of the earth.' Deut. 8:3 and Matt. 4:4 we are told that 'man shall not live by bread alone, but by every word that proceedeth out of the mouth of the Lord.' This not only tells us that God may nourish and sustain man without means, but it also informs us that the power to nourish does not so inhere in the bread that it could nourish man if the Word, by

---

evident in the creation of a gnat than in that of an elephant; and the same applies to His providence. The excellence of His wisdom is seen when He directs and guides the creatures to fulfill the purpose of their existence, which they themselves do not know. There is furthermore no difference among the creatures in themselves; the difference arises from their relation to us; e. g., it is commonly held that a worm deserves less consideration than a lion. The latter is, of course, better than a worm in our evaluation; but aside from this, the least worm is in its nature as remarkable as the lion. – Finally, it does not overburden God, as one might think. His infinite intellect knows no weariness."

which it was originally created and was given the power to nourish, were retracted. The continuous influence of the Word, which creates, as it were, and sustains life, is needed if the bread is to exert the nourishing power given to it. The same obtains in the sphere of medicine. Man is not healed through the herbs, but through the Word of God which originally gave the herbs their healing property and day by day maintains their power." Our table prayer ("Speak Thy blessing on the gifts," etc.) and the prayer we utter when taking the medicine have the same meaning. It was the meaning expressed by the doctor who said concerning his patient: "I bandaged him, but God healed him."

Maintaining this truth, our Lutheran teachers say that the operation of God and the operation of the second causes are not *"duae" actiones,* but *"una" numero actio.* This one operation must not be divided in extent, as though God performed one half of the action and the secondary cause the other half; nor separated in time, as though God first exerted His influence, and then afterwards and later the means or the creatures wrought by means of a power which was given them.[5] To ward off the conception of operations separated by time, the dogmaticians explicitly say that the operation of the *causae secundae* is not the result of an *actio Dei praevia* (a preceding action of God), but the result of a *continuus Dei in creaturas influxus* (of an uninterrupted operation of God on the creatures and through the creatures). (Quenstedt I, 780.) If we know this, we shall say with Job (ch. 10:8): "Thine hands have made me and fashioned me together round about" and confess with Luther in the Small Catechism: "I believe that God has made me [not only Adam] and all creatures, has given me my body and soul, eyes, ears, and all my members, my reason and all my senses, and still preserves them." We received our soul and body with all their members from our parents as the *causae secundae,* and at the same time we know that God is our Creator and Father. Luther expresses it thus: "It is God that makes the skin; it is He who makes also the bones; it is He who makes the hair on the skin; it is He also who makes the marrow in the bones; it is He who makes every particle of hair; it is He who makes every particle of marrow; He must make everything, both the particles and the whole" (St. L. XX:804). Again: "He who made a man out of the ground also creates men to this day from the blood of the parents" (St. L. I:155). And to guard against the thought as though God, working through means,

[5] It was so held by Durandus (d. 1334), Taurellus (d. 1606), and by some Arminians. See Quenstedt, I, 782.

is by these means separated from the world, Luther says: "God does not send out bailiffs or angels when He creates or preserves a thing, but all that is the direct work of His divine power. But if He is to create and sustain it, He Himself must be present and must form and sustain His creature both in its most inward and its most external parts." (St. L. XX:804.)

Quenstedt expresses the same truth when he writes against the deists, who separate God from the operation of the means through the interposition of the "laws of nature": "It is wrong to say that the second cause [the means through which God works] separates the first cause [God] from the effect, since the effect is the immediate result both of the first cause and of the second cause" (*Systema* I, 781). The so-called "laws of nature" are not something which differs from God's will and operation, but are God's will and operation itself in its relation to the existence and operation of the creatures.[6]

3

Divine Providence and Sin

Concerning the *concurrence* of God in the actions of moral beings (men and angels) we must distinguish between good and evil actions. As to evil actions, Scripture, in the first place, tells us 1) that God is unalterably opposed to them: "Thou shalt have no other gods before Me." "Thou shalt not kill," etc.; 2) that God often prevents their occurrence, as in the case of Abimelech of Gerar (Gen. 20:1 ff.); and 3) that when they occur, they must serve His good purposes, as when Joseph was sold into Egypt (Gen. 50:20).

But now, in the second place, the question arises: How far does God concur in the performance of sinful actions? The Scriptural teaching on this point may be thus summarized: God concurs in evil

---

[6] Baier, II, 169: "God makes it manifest that He is not bound to the workings of nature and the order freely established by Him." He refers to the following examples: "Secondary causes, the operation of which is not yet fixed by nature, are made to operate by divine command; see 1 Kings 18:44, on the accelerated rain. At times God confers on the secondary causes either plainly supernatural power or He restores or augments the natural power which was either lost or debilitated; see Judges 16:28-29 on the restored and augmented strength of Samson; Gen. 17:16-17, 19 on the reproductive power conferred on the centenarian Abraham and the nonagenarian and sterile Sarah. Finally, God impedes the secondary causes which are set by nature to perform their operations so that the effect does not follow, as when He threatens (Deut. 28:23) that He will withdraw the rain from the disobedient people."

actions in so far as they are acts (*quoad materiale*), for Scripture says that men live and move and have their being in God (Acts 17:28). But God does not concur in the evil actions in so far as they are evil (*quoad formale*), for Scripture says of God: "Thou hatest all workers of iniquity. Thou shalt destroy them that speak leasing; the Lord will abhor the bloody and deceitful man" (Ps. 5:6-7). – We are well aware that this distinction between the *materiale* and the *formale peccati* does not remove the difficulty our mind finds in this co-operation of God. But we also know that for the present, during our life here on earth, we human beings must confine our thinking to the limits set by this distinction. All explanations that go beyond these limits are based either on self-deception or on a denial of the two factors that enter in here. We shall have to deny either the concurrence of God in the evil acts, as far as they are acts (Pelagius, according to Jerome, did this; he declared that he could move his hand, bend his finger, sit, stand, and walk without God's concurrence – see Quenstedt, I, 782), or we shall have to deny that there is anything evil in the human action; we make God responsible for it and deny human responsibility. Both are against Scripture and against human experience. It is contrary to Scripture. For Acts 17:28 clearly teaches the thief or the murderer cannot perform his acts without God's concurrence; it states that all men, including the thieves and murderers, live in God, move in God, have their being in God. It is contrary to experience, for inevitably the conscience of the thief and of the murderer holds them responsible for their evil actions. All pantheistic phrases which say that man is not responsible for his acts since God is responsible for his existence and movements are refuted by the fact of the evil conscience. Rom. 2:15: "Their conscience also bearing witness and their thoughts the meanwhile accusing or else excusing one another." (Rom. 1:32; Ps. 14:1, 5.) [7]

4

Does God Permit Men to Sin?

This question has often been put. Scripture answers in the affirmative. It describes God's relation to sin also as a sufferance of sin, a *permissio*. Ps. 81:12: "So I gave them [the Jews] up unto their own

---

[7] Dr. L. T. Townsend relates the following in *Bible Theology and Modern Thought*, 1883, p. 162: "A friend of Voltaire once wrote him these words: 'I have succeeded in getting rid of the idea of hell.' Voltaire replied: 'Allow me to congratulate you; I am far from that.'"

heart's lust; and they walked in their own counsels." Acts 14:16: "Who in times past suffered all nations [the Gentiles] to walk in their own ways." The phrase: "God permits men to sin" is therefore not subject to criticism. It is based on Scripture. But this does not fully describe God's activity in connection with the sins of men. According to Scripture, God in His righteous judgment punishes sin with sin. We read Rom. 1:24-28: "Wherefore [because of their idolatry] God also gave them up to uncleanness . . . unto vile affections . . . to a reprobate mind." And 2 Thess. 2:11-12 describes this activity of God in these words: "And for this cause [because they received not the love of the truth] God shall send them strong delusion, that they should believe a lie; that they all might be damned who believed not the truth, but had pleasure in unrighteousness." Cp. Formula of Concord, *Trigl.*, 1091, 83.

THE CONCURRENCE OF GOD IN GOOD ACTS

Scripture teaches 1) that God works the good acts unbelievers do as citizens (*iustitia civilis*), according to His general government of the world, through their conscience. Rom. 2:14: The Gentiles, who do not have God's [written] Law, do by nature the things contained in the Law. This civil righteousness is of great value in the kingdoms of this world; it is the foundation of the well-being of the community and the State (1 Tim. 2:1-2; Rom. 13:1-4). (See the section "The Good Works of the Heathen," under "Sanctification," Vol. III.) 2) The spiritually good actions (*iustitia spiritualis*) God works in the Kingdom of Grace, that is, by the special operation of the Holy Ghost in the Word. This concurrence of God is found only in the believers, and in them God creates not only the ability to perform the good (*potentiam agendi*), but also the act itself (*ipsum agendi actum*). Phil. 2:13: "It is God which worketh in you both to will and to do." According to 2 Cor. 3:5 God produces also the λογίζεσθαι [the thinking] needed for the proper performance of the ministry. We learn from Rom. 8:13 that the actual mortification of the deeds of the body takes place through the Spirit of God.

5

Divine Providence and Free Will

The fact that men live, move, and have their being in God does not make them automata; they remain moral beings, free from coercion (*libertas a coactione*), i. e., beings personally responsible to God, or, in other words, persons. That is the teaching 1) of Scripture. Acts 17:31: God will judge the world in righteousness, and judgment presupposes the responsibility of man. It is 2) also the teaching of experience, of the conscience of man. Rom. 2:15: The thoughts accuse or excuse one another. Rom. 1:32: The sinners know that they which commit such things deserve death. The responsibility of man, his freedom from coercion, is a fact. How these facts agree with the fact that God works all things, we do not know.

In this connection the special question comes up for consideration: Must all events in the world occur just as they do occur (*necessitas immutabilitatis*), or could they happen otherwise (*contingentia rerum*)? Scripture compels us to maintain both the necessity and the contingency. From the viewpoint of the divine providence the necessity obtains, from the human viewpoint the contingency. Examples illustrating the necessity: Scripture says that the betrayal of Christ by Judas and His crucifixion by the Jews and Gentiles had to occur according to the determinate counsel of God. Acts 4:27-28: Against Thy holy Child Jesus, Herod and Pontius Pilate with the Gentiles and the people of Israel were gathered together, to do what Thy counsel determined before to be done. And when Christ was apprehended, He said (Matt. 26:54): "Thus it must be." But these same events are also represented in Scripture as contingent from the human viewpoint. By warning Judas, the Jews, and Pilate, Christ sought to keep them from committing betrayal and murder. Matt. 26:24: "The Son of Man goeth as it is written of Him; but woe unto that man by whom the Son of Man is betrayed. It had been good for that man if he had not been born." And Jesus did what He could to keep Pilate from pronouncing an unjust sentence. The words of the Lord: "He that delivered Me unto thee hath the greater sin" warn Pilate that he would be committing a wrong if he would comply with the demand of the Jews. These words made an impression on Pilate, for "from thenceforth Pilate sought to release Him." (John 19:11-12.) So those old theologians who carefully weigh their words say: "According to the law of divine providence, which rules all things, it is correctly said that all things happen of necessity; from the standpoint of man everything in human affairs is done freely and contingently." [8]

It is necessary to teach both of these Scriptural truths, the necessity and the contingency, in order to safeguard the Christian religion

---

[8] Cp. Heerbrand, *Compendium*, pp. 214–216; quoted in Baier-Walther, II, 176.

against Epicureanism and atheism (things happen without God, by chance) on the one hand, and fatalism and Stoicism (disregard of the divinely ordained means) on the other. The following rule of life must be observed: We should in all our ways, in the Kingdom of Power and of Grace, diligently make use of the means which God supplies. In sickness, for example, we call in the doctor and the nurse; and in seeking salvation we make use of the means of grace, through which God creates and sustains faith. – It is a foolish undertaking to attempt to penetrate the divine providence *a priori* while setting aside the God-appointed means. We would be entering a domain which is beyond the reach of our present understanding. Shall the creature make bold to explore God in His bare majesty (Luther: "*nuda maiestas*")?

Apply this to another special question: Is the *terminus vitae* subject to change or unchangeable? Scripture teaches, on the one hand, that the end of our days is immovably fixed. Job 14:5: "Seeing his days are determined; the number of his months are with Thee; Thou hast appointed his bounds that he cannot pass." On the other hand, Scripture teaches just as clearly that human life may be prolonged or shortened. Hezekiah prayed God that his life might be prolonged, and his prayer was heard (Is. 38:1 ff.; 2 Kings 20:1 ff.). Others, again, shorten their lives. Ps. 55:23 says of the bloody and deceitful men that they shall not live out half their days. Both of these truths, the immovably fixed *terminus vitae* and life's prolongation or shortening, must be maintained as divine truths. The former is true as viewed from God's standpoint, the latter is true as viewed from our human standpoint. And when God condescends to speak from our human standpoint, He directs us to use the means which sustain our earthly life.

It is folly to study the *terminus vitae* from God's standpoint while disregarding the divinely appointed means; that is beyond the powers of comprehension with which we are equipped for this present life. Therefore it is God's will and order that we use the means which He has appointed for sustaining and prolonging our lives (the exceptions, i. e., that God can also sustain our lives without means, we leave to Him, Ex. 34:28). As God-appointed means Scripture mentions: work (Ps. 128:2: "Thou shalt eat the labor of thine hands"; 2 Thess. 3:10: "If any would not work, neither should he eat"); food (Acts 27:33-36: Paul directs the sailors and passengers to take food to sustain them); if need be, a little wine (1 Tim. 5:23); especially a pious life (Eph. 6:2-3: "That it may be well with thee and thou mayest live long on the earth"); prayer (Hezekiah, Is. 38:1 ff.); also flight from danger

(Acts 9:23-25: Paul's flight from Damascus when the Jews threatened his life); etc. Since these means are appointed by God, they have been made part of the divine providence. That is emphasized Acts 27:31: "Except these [seamen] abide in the ship, ye cannot be saved" — God has made the saving of your lives dependent upon the use of these means. Through the use or the refusal of these means we reach the *terminus vitae* which God has immovably fixed.[9]

---

[9] Compare here what was said above under the "Omniscience" of God regarding the infallible divine prescience of all things and the right attitude towards this fact. See also, in Volume III the chapter "Election in Its Proper Setting." We also call attention here to the diametrical opposition between Luther's and Calvin's teachings, while both speak of a "hidden" and a "revealed" God. This will be fully treated in Volume II, in the chapter "The Theological Terminology Regarding the Divine Will of Grace."

Angelology

(DE ANGELIS)

IF further proof is needed that modern theology has made the *I* of the theologizing subject the *principium cognoscendi* of theology, its more or less skeptical attitude toward the teaching of Scripture on the existence of good and evil angels offers that proof. The degree of the skepticism depends on the consistency with which it applies the Ego viewpoint. The attitude of the liberal wing may be thus summarized: The existence of good angels may be possible, but there is no convincing proof of it; at all events, the existence of a personal devil cannot be proved.[1] The more conservative wing does not want "the idea of the angels banished from the language of religious contemplation," but it does insist that what Scripture says about the angels does not entitle us to speak of a "doctrine" of the angels; to get a "dogmatic" rating, its "inner necessary connection with the experience of salvation found in the theologian must be shown." Kirn declares. (*Ev. Dogmatik,* 3d ed., p. 72): "Since the angels have no inner necessary connection with the saving truth and the experience of salvation, it is not the business of dogmatics to set up a particular doctrine of the angels." – There are modern theologians who have become convinced of the existence of good and evil angels through their own investigations.[2] But we need to remind ourselves that the

---

[1] Nitzsch-Stephan correctly presents (p. 441 ff.) the "older Lutheran doctrine" concerning the angels, but adds under "Examination and Results": "One cannot, on the one hand, declare the reality of the angels impossible, but, on the other hand, there is no proof for it." And concerning the devil we read on page 364: "The entire theory of the devil being the first fallen angel is nothing but a dogmatic hypothesis." – Karl Hase, an aesthetic rationalist, relegates the doctrine of the angels to the sphere of poetry, superstition, and church art. (*Ev. Dogmatik,* 4th ed., p. 192 f.) – David Friedrich Strauss, the infidel, makes sport of the modern theologians who want to convert the personal devil into the "idea" of evil (rationalists, Schleiermacher, also Kirn) in these words (quoted in Luthardt, *Komp.*, 10th ed., p. 155 (13th ed., p. 234): "The demons must be taken as necessary components of the world view of Jesus and the Apostles. . . . If Christ came to destroy the works of the devil, there was no need of His coming if there was no devil; if there is a devil only as the personification of the principle of evil – all right, then also a Christ as an impersonal idea will suffice."

[2] Nitzsch-Stephan mentions particularly Kaehler and Schlatter (p. 445): "Kaehler holds that, having reached the conviction that our own personal existence is independent of this sensuous life, our eyes are ready to see the supernatural realm of personal creatures whose existence and participation in the history of mankind counterbalances the weight of evidence supplied by our material existence. . . . (*Lehre,* p. 267 f.) Schlatter finds that the idea of angels points to the glory of God; God must be greater than the world we are capable of

Christian doctrine of the angels can be ascertained only from Scripture as God's infallible Word. We are laboring under a delusion if we imagine that we can disregard Scripture and evolve with "inner necessity" the Christian doctrine of the angels either in whole or in part from our Ego.

A word on the argument that since the doctrine of the angels does not occupy a central position in the order of salvation, it should not be called a "doctrine" at all. Kirn says (*loc. cit.*): "We cannot regard the idea of angels as being essential to the revelation of salvation and so must leave the use of the conception of angels to religious tact." Now, we have already seen (under "Non-Fundamental Doctrines") that and why the doctrine of the angels must not be classified as a fundamental article. We are brought into communion with the grace of God not by believing in the existence of angels and their services, but by believing in Christ the Crucified, in His *satisfactio vicaria* (1 Cor. 2:2; 15:3); in all ages men have become Christians who did not know that there were angels. But when a man has become a Christian and reads the Bible, he will find in it, from Genesis to Revelation, the doctrine of the angels, side by side with the central article of Christ, the Savior of sinners. And it certainly requires a great deal of inconsistency for him to accept the doctrine of Christ and reject the doctrine of the angels. – The idea of modern theologians that the denial of the Christian doctrine of the angels can easily be harmonized with the "Christian experience of salvation" is due largely to their wrong conception of the Christian experience of salvation. This Christian experience is, in the nature of the case, *terra incognita* to all who deny the *satisfactio Christi vicaria.*

1

The Existence of Angels and the Time of Their Creation

From Genesis to Revelation Scripture bears witness to the existence of angels. On the basis of this testimony of Scripture, and not on the basis of reasons of probability, we believe that there are

experiencing. Being reminded of this fact urges us to 'assume a display of the creative power' that is not confined to nature and mankind. 'And what Scripture says entitles us to go beyond the thought of a mere possibility.' . . . (*Dogma*, p. 92 f.)" P. 361: "Conservative theology is even today teaching a doctrine of Satan. It does this out of loyalty to Jesus . . . and, besides this, in the conviction that the origin of human sin becomes comprehensible only after and through the assumption of a satanic background." All of this argumentation is too subjective.

angels. On the basis of Scripture the Christian Church has a doctrine of the angels.

They were created within the hexaemeron. They were not created before the universe, because before the universe there was only God (John 1:1-3). They were not created after the universe, because after the creation of the universe God "rested from all His work" (Gen. 2:2-3).[3] On which day of the hexaemeron they were created cannot be determined with certainty, because Scripture is silent on this point.[4]

2

The Name "Angel"

"Angel" (מַלְאָךְ, ἄγγελος) is an official title (*nomen officii*); it does not describe the essence of the angels. That is described by the term "spirit" (πνεῦμα); see next chapter. That the term "angel" is an official title, designating an ambassador or messenger, is clear from the fact that Scripture also calls men, in particular the preachers of God's Word, angels. Mal. 2:7: "The priest's lips should keep knowledge, and they should seek the Law at his mouth; for he is the messenger (מַלְאָךְ) of the Lord of Hosts." Likewise John the Baptist is called an "angel." Mal. 3:1; Matt. 11:10: "Behold, I send My messenger (τὸν ἄγγελόν μου) before Thy face." Christ Himself bears the name "the Messenger of the Covenant" or the Messenger of God κατ' ἐξοχήν. Mal. 3:1: "And the Lord whom ye seek shall suddenly come to His temple, even the Messenger of the Covenant" (John 3:17, 34; 6:40; Gal. 4:4-6). The question when the term "angel of the Lord," used in the Old Testament, denotes the *Angelus increatus* has already been answered. (See "The Doctrine of God," chapter 5.) [5]

---

[3] Gerhard, *Loci, locus "De Creatione et Angelis,"* §39, takes issue with those Church Fathers who assumed that the angels were created before the world. "By antemundane time, Scripture always means eternity, as appears from Psalm 90, Proverbs 8, John 1, and other passages. But certainly the angels are not eternal."

[4] See Luther on Gen. 1:6; St. L. I:27 f.: "Not one word is found in all the Scriptures concerning their creation, their battle, or their fall, except that one word of Christ, John 8:44. . . . It is wonderful that Moses is wholly silent on things of such great interest." Gerhard, *loc. cit.*, § 40: "On which day the angels were created is a question more subtile than useful."

[5] Gerhard, *Loci, locus "De Creatione et Angelis,"* § 37: "When either the name Jehovah or divine works or divine worship is attributed in Scripture to an angel, then this Angel must be understood to be the Son of God."

3

The Nature and the Properties of the Angels

The angels are spirits (πνεύματα), that is, immaterial beings. Luke 24:39 forbids us to ascribe to the angels even an ethereal corporeity. "A spirit hath not flesh and bones, as ye see Me have." Here we are told that being a spirit is the direct opposite (*oppositio adequata*) to every form of corporeity, including the glorified form. The same applies to the evil angels: "We wrestle not against flesh and blood" (Eph. 6:12). The idea of some Church Fathers and also of recent theologians who clothe the angels with some kind of ethereal body, a refined material fabric and the like, has no basis in Scripture.[6] The human bodies in which angels, incorporeal by nature, appeared on certain occasions (see Genesis 18 and 19) were therefore only assumed forms (*unio accidentalis*), by which the invisible angels rendered themselves temporarily visible. The consumption of food (Gen. 18:8 and Gen. 19:3), by the way, was a real eating; it was not necessary for the nourishment of these assumed bodies, but it convinced men of the reality of the presence of these angels. The food was consumed in a manner incomprehensible to us; perhaps, as some dogmaticians say, as food is consumed by fire.[7]

---

[6] See Quenstedt, I, 658 *sqq.*, on the antithesis. Also Hollaz, *Examen*, P. I, c. IV, qu. 3, under the thesis: "Angels are spirits, free from all matter, coarse as well as fine." Walther against the modern theologians who invest the angels with corporality, *Lehre und Wehre*, 22, 166 ff. The statement of Kurtz (*Bibel und Astronomie*, pp. 78—84), at which Walther's criticism is especially aimed, is given in Baier-Walther, II, 108. Kurtz had asserted: "In creatures corporality is the condition of all existence, the organ of all activity, the reflector of the spirit; from it the creature derives its limitation, its distinct character, and its stability; lacking this support, the creature would melt away and dissolve." Kurtz has left the almighty God out of his calculations. A related matter is the "intermediate body" of the departed souls (see "Eschatology" chap. 2; also Philippi, *Glaubenslehre*, II, 296 ff.; he rejects the idea of the corporality of the angels).

[7] Joh. Adam Osiander: "Men eat and drink from necessity; but the angels are able to consume food in the manner of a flame" (*Colleg. Theol.* II, 165; quoted in Baier-Walther, II, 109). Brochmand: "Men here make difficulties where there are none. They contend that the angels did not really engage in vital functions in the assumed bodies, but only seemingly did so, so that to Abraham and Lot the angels only appeared to be eating when in fact they did not eat at all. . . . The example of Christ (Luke 24:41-43) proves abundantly that a true eating can take place without the food being digested in the stomach and converted into the lifeblood; after His resurrection He ate before His disciples to convince them of the truth of His resurrection, but the food was not converted into nourishment, for the nature of a glorified body did not permit this (Luke 20:36). It is therefore contended in vain that the bodies assumed by the angels were not really living. For though they were not vivified by the soul,

The difference between God as πνεῦμα (John 4:24: "God is a spirit") and the angels as πνεύματα (Heb. 1:14: "Are they not all ministering spirits?") is the difference between God as the Creator and the angels as finite spirits, finite creatures. (This has already been set forth in the chapter "The Unity of God.") — As distinct from the immaterial human soul, the angels are complete beings (*spiritus completi*), while the human soul is a *spiritus incompletus,* since the body belongs as an integral part to man; soul and body make the complete man.

The properties of the angels. Scripture ascribes to them intellect (*intellectus*) and will (*voluntas*). The good angels know "by the Church the manifold wisdom of God" (Eph. 3:10) and gladly minister to them who shall be heirs of salvation (Heb. 1:14). The temptation of Eve (Genesis 3) as well as that of Christ (Matthew 4) by the devil shows that the evil angels likewise possess intelligence and will. Scripture informs us further that the angels possess the power to react to material things. Angels take Lot and his wife and daughters by the hand (Gen. 19:16) and the devil takes Christ into the holy city and sets Him on a pinnacle of the Temple (Matt. 4:5). This influence is analogous to the one our immaterial soul exercises on our material body. How it is accomplished is beyond our comprehension. (More on this matter in the chapters on the activity of the good and evil angels.) — Let us recall here that since only God has *omniscientia* and *praescientia,* the angels do not know all things, and particularly they have of themselves no knowledge of future things. They also do not know the thoughts of men, since this likewise is a prerogative of God. 1 Kings 8:39: "Thou only knowest the hearts of all the children of men." Baier, II, 111: "On the hidden thoughts of men the angels can form only a conjectural opinion, based on the signs and effects."

The power of the angels is very great. Scripture speaks of them as "His angels, that excel in strength" (Ps. 103:20) and as "His mighty angels" (2 Thess. 1:7). And the devil is described as "the strong man" (Matt. 12:29). It is a power far transcending human power. The good angels, our guardians, are stronger than we, whom they guard (Ps. 91:11-13). The evil angels are stronger than men; the devil holds all unbelievers securely captive in his kingdom (Luke 11:21-22), while the believer can withstand the attacks of Satan only in the power of

---

they were enabled by the singular power of the angels to perform the works of living beings, such as to speak and touch and move. As to the question in dispute among the fathers and the Scholastics whether the bodies in which the angels appeared were created by God out of nothing or were formed out of preexistent matter by the angels themselves, I freely confess my ignorance." (*System. Univ. Theol.,* p. 98; quoted in Baier-Walther, II, 113 *sq.*)

God (Eph. 6:10-17). However, the power of the angels is not unlimited, but is rather at all times subordinate to the power of God.

In this connection the question has been raised whether the devils can perform miracles. The dogmaticians here make a distinction. The devils cannot perform real miracles, e. g., they cannot create new things, raise the dead, etc., for Scripture ascribes this to God alone (Ps. 72:18: "Blessed be the Lord God, the God of Israel, who only doeth wondrous things"). But under God's sufferance and according to His decree the devils can do things which to men appear as miracles. Men lack an all-embracing understanding of the realm of spirits and particularly of the might and ability of the spirits. Scripture expressly states that Antichrist will secure a following among men by "the working of Satan with all power and signs and lying wonders" (2 Thess. 2:9). And that this occurs according to God's decree is stated in the words that follow: "For this cause [because they received not the love of the truth] God shall send them strong delusion, that they should believe a lie: that they all might be damned who believed not the truth, but had pleasure in unrighteousness." The dogmaticians distinguish between *miracula* and *mirabilia seu mira* (wonderful or amazing things).[8]

The story that angels can and did contract marriages with human beings, which is retold by some modern theologians, is pure fiction. They base this fable on Gen. 6:2: "The sons of God saw the daughters of men that they were fair; and they took them wives of all which they chose." Scripture, however, names this as a characteristic of the angels, that "they neither marry nor are given in marriage" (Matt. 22:30).[9]

---

[8] Quenstedt deals at length with the power of the angels in a special "question": "What and how great is the power of angels." I, 666 *sqq*.

[9] For the teaching of modern theologians on this point see Kurtz: *Die Ehen der Soehne Gottes mit den Toechtern der Menschen*, 1857, pp. 1, 11 ff. – August Pfeiffer (*Dubia Vexata*, 2d ed., p. 59 *sq.*) is right in stating that Matt. 22:30 proves two things: 1) that the married estate among men belongs to the mundane life and has no place in the life to come, and 2) that in this respect they will be like the angels, "they neither marry nor are given in marriage"; and that certainly states clearly that as it is against the nature of the angels to marry, so "in the resurrection" men will no longer live in marriage. *"Repugnat naturae angelicae."* Pfeiffer is also right in adducing Acts 17:26, which states that all men that have lived, are now living, and will live to the end of days are "made of one blood," the descendants of Adam. But on the assumption that angels contracted marriages with human beings the human race would have an admixture of "angel blood" and would be some sort of a half-breed race. – To escape the force of this argument some would make Gen. 6:2 speak only of an occasional intercourse of angels with men. But that, too, would introduce "angel blood" into the human race and contradict the "made of one blood." However, the

The angels are illocal, that is to say that while they may be at a definite place (as the angel was with Peter in the prison, Acts 12:7), they are, as immaterial beings, independent of space; they occupy no space – they can be in the space occupied by another body. Quenstedt: *"Coexistunt loco corporeo vel corpori"* (*Systema* I, 633). They are not, of course, omnipresent, for at any particular time they are only at some one place. They are, as the dogmaticians express it, somewhere (πού), which "somewhere" can be determined. A case in point is the human soul. The immaterial soul fills no space, and still we can say where it is. In a living person it is not outside his body, but "in him" (Acts 20:10).[10]

---

words "they took them wives" (נָשִׁים) denote regular and permanent matrimony. Defenders of angel marriages who do not want to go so far have no right to appeal to Gen. 6:2. – But also the context of Gen. 6:2 entirely excludes angel marriages. In the preceding and in the following words only men are mentioned: "When men began to multiply on the face of the earth." "My Spirit shall not always strive with man." "And God saw that the wickedness of man was great in the earth." "I will destroy man, whom I have created." In the entire context only men are mentioned, never angels or angel-men (half-breeds). – But does not the term "sons of God" prove the angel marriages? As to the linguistic usage of בְּנֵי הָאֱלֹהִים, Stroebel gives the facts as follows in his review of Kurtz's treatise: "Moses very frequently mentions angels, but never calls them 'sons of God.' Also he often speaks of 'sons (children) of God,' but always means men. . . . The designation of angels as 'sons of God' is an entirely unknown usage before the days of David and after the days of Daniel, and to claim that this designation is used already in the book of Genesis is an anachronistic *petitio principii.*" (Quoted in *Lehre und Wehre,* 5, 188, from Rudelbach-Guericke's magazine, 1859.) Compare also the full presentation of Philippi, *Glaubenslehre,* 3d ed., pp. 182–192, who arrives at this conclusion: "In our mind the context seems to demand incontrovertibly that the *Bne Elohim* refers to the sons of Seth [not to angels]. Even Delitzsch acknowledges this (see *Genesis,* p. 225; 3d ed., p. 232), though he personally prefers to refer it, with several exegetes of the first centuries and of modern times (cf. especially Hofmann, *Schriftbeweis,* 2d ed., I, p. 424 f., and Kurtz, *Die Ehen der Soehne Gottes,* etc.), to the angels." August Pfeiffer arrived at the same result as Philippi: "The 'sons of God' who took wives and begat children are not good angels, neither are they evil angels, but pious men and their descendants who, though they have here fallen away, are nevertheless called 'sons of God,' either from their former state or because of their external association with the true Church."

[10] Quenstedt, I, 134: "The angels have a πού, or *ubi,* in which they are *definitive.* The angels are in a certain space, which is designated or defined, that is, they are present in a certain space according to their substance and not according to the effect they produce, so that they are there and not in other places, much less everywhere." They can also change their πού. Baier-Walther II, 117: "We do not say that the angels are everywhere, but they are in some certain and definite πού, as it is called, so that they can also move from some *ubi* to another *ubi,* and can also move material things elsewhere. See Matt. 8:32, where the devils, ejected out of the possessed man, in whom they had been for some time, entered into the herd of swine and hurled the whole herd into the sea."

4

Number and Ranks of the Angels

The number of the angels is very large. Dan. 7:10: "Thousand thousands ministered unto Him, and ten thousand times ten thousand stood before Him." Luke 2:13: "A multitude of the heavenly host." We cannot compute the number of them exactly; Scripture itself tells us as much when it speaks of "an innumerable company of angels" (Heb. 12:22) and uses the expressions "thousand thousands" and "ten thousand times ten thousand" (Dan. 7:10). Keil in his *Commentary* on this passage: "A term for the innumerable host of the angels who surround God and serve Him; cp. Deut. 33:2; Ps. 68:17."

That there are orders or classes among the angels is clear from the different appellations given them in Scripture. Scripture mentions *Cherubim* (Gen. 3:24; Ps. 80:1), *Seraphim* (Is. 6:2), "thrones, dominions, principalities, powers" (Col. 1:16), "archangel" (1 Thess. 4:16). Also among the evil angels there are greater and lesser spirits (Matt. 25:41: "The devil and his angels"; Luke 11:15, 18, 19: "Beelzebub, the chief of the devils"). But we are unable to determine the number of the ranks and their precise difference, since Scripture does not give us sufficient information. Luther and the dogmaticians reject the nine orders, or choirs, of angels with the subdivisions (*terniones*) as uncertain.[11] It has been rightly pointed out that Scripture changes the order of enumeration in naming the several ranks of the angels; cp. Col. 1:16 with Eph. 1:21.

5

Good and Evil Angels

Originally all angels were positively good, not merely morally indifferent or even with a proclivity toward evil. Since the angels were

[11] Luther: "Hence it is that men, there being nothing certain recorded upon the subject [in Scripture], invented the nine choirs of the angels and said that there were so many of them that they were nine whole days falling from heaven. . . . But so it is ever: where there are no plain and sure testimonies of Scripture, impertinent and presumptuous men consider themselves at liberty to imagine and invent what they please." (St. L. I:27.) Quenstedt I, 681: "That there are definitely nine orders, or choirs, of angels, and that these are divided into three classes, or *terniones,* which they call *hierarchies* – about which the Scholastics and Papists, above all Becanus, philosophize much on the basis of the Pseudo-Dionysius Areopagita – this we reject as uncertain and false."

created within the six days, God's verdict of "very good" (Gen. 1:31) necessarily applies also to the angels. The existence of two classes of angels, good and evil, is due to the fact that some of the angels did not remain in the *status originalis,* but fell away from God into sin. Even if we do not translate the ἕστηκε in John 8:44 with "The devil abode not in the truth," but with "He stands not in the truth," the fall is not denied, but presupposed as self-evident.[12] The good angels are those who, when the rest fell, remained good and were by the gracious action of God so confirmed in the good (*in bono confirmati*) that they can no longer sin and fall away. Let others declare this state of *non posse peccare* to be a "fiction"; our faith is greatly strengthened by it. For God would not have appointed the angels to minister to us, the heirs of salvation, if the angels were not perfectly safe ministers and protectors. The evil angels are those who by their defection from God became evil and can nevermore become good (*in malo confirmati*). The opinion has been voiced in practically every age that also the devils might be converted and saved from eternal damnation; but this opinion is not shared by the devils themselves. They declared Matt. 8:29: "Art Thou come hither to torment us before the time?" The fire prepared for the devil and his angels is "the everlasting fire" (Matt. 25:41).

We cannot determine the exact time when some of the angels fell. We know, however, that the fall of the angels occurred before the fall of man, since man fell through the seduction of the devil (Gen. 3:1-14). John 8:44: "He was a murderer from the beginning"; the devil is the ἀνθρωποκτόνος. As to the particular sin by which the defection of these angels from God took place, we cannot offer more than a surmise. The majority assume that pride was the original sin.[13]

---

[12] So also Luthardt in Zoeckler's *Commentary* of this passage.

[13] Quenstedt, I, 729: "We may assume that pride was the first sin of the angels. We make this deduction 1) from 1 Tim. 3:6: 'Lest, being lifted up with pride,' τυφωθείς (Vulg.: '*in superbiam elatus*'), 'he fall into the condemnation of the devil,' that is, that he may not incur the same condemnation which Satan brought upon himself through arrogance. Thus Chrysostom, Gerhard, and others. . . . 2) From the temptation in which Satan undertook to instill the sin of pride into our first parents, the pride of arrogating to themselves equality with God; 'Ye shall be,' he said, 'as gods' [as God]. 3) From his perpetual endeavor to transfer the glory of God to himself. . . . This opinion is approved also by our sainted Luther, on Genesis 1. Basilius Magnus, Cyprian, and Bernard join envy with the pride."

6

The Good Angels and Their Activity

The good angels are confirmed in the good (see above) and are in the state of bliss. Their bliss consists in the beatific vision of God. During their ministrations on earth they always behold the face of God (Matt. 18:10). With the vision of God is most intimately united the most fervent love of God; whoever beholds God cannot but love Him as the highest good. And so the will of the good angels coincides constantly and perfectly with the will of God; the sole object of their entire activity is the accomplishment of the good. – Men raise the objection that the good angels could not enjoy "moral freedom" if they cannot sin. This objection is based on a wrong conception of moral freedom, as though moral beings could be morally free only if they are as free to do evil as to do good (*posse peccare aut non peccare*). According to this principle there would be no "moral freedom" in heaven and in eternity, since the blessed in heaven, hallowed and glorified by the glory of God ("Then shall the righteous shine forth as the sun," Matt. 13:43), can no longer sin.

Because Scripture also speaks of "elect angels" (1 Tim. 5:21), we may also speak of an election of the angels, though Scripture does not define this election in detail. What we do know from Scripture is 1) that the good angels were not elected because of the merits of Christ, since they never became sinners (Heb. 2:16), and 2) that the evil angels were not rejected because of an absolute decree, but solely because of their apostasy (2 Pet. 2:4: "God spared not the angels that sinned"). – There is no Scriptural basis for extending Christ's work of redemption also to the angels, as some Papists and some Calvinists do (see Vol. II: "To Whom and for Whom Did Christ Render Satisfaction?").

The functions of the good angels are to praise God (Is. 6:3; Luke 2:13) and to be His ministers in the world and in the Church (Ps. 103:20-21: "Bless the Lord, ye His angels . . . that do His commandments, hearkening unto the voice of His word"; Ps. 104:4; Heb. 1:14), not as though God stood in need of their service, but because it pleased God to have it so (*non ex quadam Dei indigentia, sed ex voluntate Dei libera*).[14] In particular, Scripture reveals that God sends the angels

---

[14] Hofmann has the notion that God needs the angels "to make Himself present to His world." See his *Schriftbeweis*, I, 282 ff., quoted in Baier-Walther, II, 163 f.

to serve the children (Matt. 18:10), the believers in their work and calling (Ps. 91:11-12: "He shall give His angels charge over thee, to keep thee in all thy ways"), and the dying (Luke 16:22: "The beggar died and was carried by the angels into Abraham's bosom"). Does every Christian have his particular guardian angel? The theologians are not ready to give a definite answer, since passages like Matt. 18:10 and Acts 12:15 ("then said they: It is his angel") are not conclusive.[15] But Scripture teaches very clearly that the angels are deeply interested in all that occurs in the Church. Not only do they admire and adore the mystery of the Redemption (Luke 2:13; 1 Pet. 1:12: "Which things the angels desire to look into"; Eph. 3:10: "To the intent that now unto the principalities and powers in heavenly places might be known by the Church the manifold wisdom of God"), but they also rejoice over every repenting sinner (Luke 15:10: "There is joy in the presence of the angels of God over one sinner that repenteth"). Scripture also notes the presence and ministrations of the angels at all the chief events in the Kingdom of God. Angels are present at the giving of the Law on Mount Sinai (Deut. 33:2; Gal. 3:19). They proclaim the conception, the birth, the resurrection, the return of Christ (Luke 1:26; 2:11; 24:5 ff.; Acts 1:10 ff.). They will attend Christ at the Last Judgment (Matt. 13:41 f.; 24:31; etc.). Scripture also reveals that the angels are present in the public worship of the Christians (1 Cor. 11:10). Their activity in promoting the welfare of the family and preserving law and order in the State is described in passages such as Gen. 24:7; Matt. 18:10; Dan. 10:13.

While modern theologians regard the doctrine of the angels as "superfluous," we should rejoice and take comfort in their service and carefuly avoid grieving them (1 Cor. 11:10; 1 Tim. 5:21: "I charge thee before God and the Lord Jesus Christ and the elect angels that thou observe these things").[16] But we must not render them religious service (*cultus religiosus*), pray to them, etc., for they are and remain creatures. They themselves protest against it (Rev. 22:8-9: "See thou do it not").[17]

---

[15] Quenstedt I, 686: "Is a certain angel assigned by God to every believer for his protection? That not only one, but many good angels are given to the individual believers for their protection is clearly stated in Scripture. However, whether a certain angel is assigned to every single believer from the day of his birth as his guardian . . . likewise, whether the guidance and government of the Church is assigned to certain angels, and also whether a special angel presides over every province, is partly uncertain and partly false."

[16] Cp. Baier-Walther, II, 128, on these passages.

[17] Cf. Quenstedt, I, 686 *sqq.*, especially the *Antithesis Scholasticorum et Pontificiorum*. Also Guenther, *Pop. Symbolik*, p. 266 f. [*Popular Symbolics*,

7

The Evil Angels, Their Activities, and Their Eternal Punishment

The reason why God did not provide a Savior for the fallen angels, as He did for fallen man, lies hidden in the "unsearchable judgments" of God. Quenstedt (*Systema* I, 829) suggests probable reasons (*probabiles rationes*), among which perhaps the most familiar is that the devil fell without seduction, while man fell by seduction. But here we must be on our guard lest we impugn the free compassion that induced God to provide salvation for mankind. – Another question which has been much ventilated is what we are to make of the devil's intelligence (*vis intelligendi, intellectus*), since Scripture, on the one hand, credits him with great cunning (Gen. 3:1 ff.; 2 Cor. 11:3: "As the serpent beguiled Eve through his subtilty"; Eph. 6:11: "the wiles of the devil"), and, on the other hand, tells of his great stupidity in promoting the death of Christ, by which he was cast out of his kingdom. Christ expressly stated that His death would have that effect: "Now shall the prince of this world be cast out" (John 12:31). It is also undeniable that the devil was not unfamiliar with the prophecies of the Old Testament from Gen. 3:15 on to Isaiah 53 and beyond; he must have known how the death of the Messiah would affect his rule. A probable explanation of the folly of the devil is that his hatred of everything that is of God or divine is so great that it blinded his reason. His will was so taken up with evil that his intellect failed to function. (More on this point in Vol. II, under "The Sinlessness of the Human Nature of Christ.") We have an analogy for such folly in the hatred of men for the Gospel, which has its seat principally in the love of evil (John 3:19-20: "Men loved darkness rather than light, because their deeds were evil") and directs the mind, that is, deprives it of its capacity to act. All opposition to the divine truth, including the opposition to the *satisfactio vicaria* and the inspiration of Scripture (Verbal Inspiration), can clearly be shown to be unreasonable.

The activities (*operationes*) of the evil angels are, as we have just said, evil throughout. Scripture describes them, for our informa-

---

pp. 141, 197.] The term προσκυνεῖν (worship) is used in Scripture to designate both civil reverence, *cultus civilis*, and worship of God, *cultus divinus*. The Papists turn this homonymy (identity of name with diversity of sense) to account in the interest of their *veneratio* and *invocatio angelorum*. By this, too, the Papacy proves itself pagan.

tion and warning, very clearly and in full detail. All endeavors of the wicked angels are aimed at harming man in his body (Luke 13:11, 16: the woman bound by Satan eighteen years), in his temporal possessions (Job 1:12 ff.; Matt. 8:31-32: the herd of swine), and particularly in his soul (1 Pet. 5:8: "Your adversary the devil, as a roaring lion, walketh about, seeking whom he may devour"). The entire state of unbelief (*status incredulitatis*) – among heathen nations as well as in external Christendom – is a work of the devil (Eph. 2:1-2: "And you hath he quickened, who were dead in trespasses and sins; wherein in time past ye walked according to the course of this world, according to the prince of the power of the air, the spirit that now worketh in the children of disobedience"). All who do not believe the Gospel are thinking and doing what the devil wills; they are completely in his power (Acts 26:18; Col. 1:13: "Who hath delivered us from the power of darkness and hath translated us into the kingdom of His dear Son"). And the fact that men do not know this, yes, even deny the existence of the devil, is likewise due to the operation of the devil. It is Scriptural to describe the status of all those who do not believe that the blood of Jesus Christ cleanses us from all sins as *obsessio spiritualis.* We may reserve this term for particular cases and persons, using it to describe an intensified operation of the devil in individuals.[18] But while doing this, we must never forget that every unbeliever is completely in the power of Satan, until God's grace and power delivers him from the power of Satan and translates him into the kingdom of His dear Son (Col. 1:13). This spiritual possession does not relieve man of personal responsibility (Matt. 25:41), nor does it destroy the free will of man (taken as freedom from coercion), since the unbeliever of his own will rejects the Gospel and gladly does what is evil.

Bodily possession (*obsessio corporalis*) presents an entirely different case. Also children of God may suffer this affliction (Mark 5:6, 18, 19; Luke 8:28, 38, 39); [19] by it the devil, under God's sufferance, takes possession of a man by personally (κατ' οὐσίαν) dwelling in him,

---

[18] As in Judas Iscariot (Luke 22:3: "Then entered Satan into Judas"), and in the incumbent of the Papal office, as the man of sin and the son of perdition in his function as the ἀντικείμενος κατ' ἐξοχήν, who sitteth in the temple of God, setting himself forth as God (2 Thessalonians 2). The French Revolution, which is often adduced as an example of an intensified *obsessio spiritualis,* is matched by occurrences of more recent date, such as the activity of the Communists and many Socialists, the deliberate falsehoods of the statesmen and their allies of the press during and since World War I. The "scientists" who rave against the Christian Church and the Word of God as though they were insane might also be listed here.

[19] See Noesgen on these passages, in Zoeckler's *Commentary.*

so that the demoniac, bereft of the use of his reason and will, becomes the involuntary instrument of Satan. The human personality no longer functions; the devil in person (αὐτοπροσώπως) becomes the acting subject.[20] The demoniac is no longer responsible for his actions.[21]

The activity of the evil angels against the Church is portrayed fully in Scripture. According to Matt. 16:18 "the gates of hell" are continually waging war against the Church, and it is Christ alone who preserves the Church against the onslaughts of the powers of hell. Behind everything that harms the Church are the evil spirits. They bring about the inattention of the hearers of the Word (Luke 8:12: "Then cometh the devil and taketh away the Word out of their hearts") and the falsification of the divine doctrine, which Christ would have His Church maintain in purity (Matt. 13:25: "But while men slept, his enemy came and sowed tares among the wheat"; 1 Tim. 4:1 ff.: "the doctrines of devils"). Especially the Papacy is described in Scripture as the devil's masterpiece in the Church, 2 Thessalonians 2. We have lost the Biblical judgment on false doctrine if we do not regard it as the work of the devil. Also persecution and oppression of the Church by the State and organizations within the State is a result of the activity of the evil spirits.[22]

As Satan unceasingly wages war on the Church, so he is also in arms against the divine order of the State and the family. He persuades David to take a census of the nation (1 Chron. 21:1) and Ahab to wage war against the Syrians (1 Kings 22:21-22). It is the devil who forbids to marry (1 Tim. 4:1-2) and who tempts married people to infidelity (1 Cor. 7:5). Scripture also tells us that God uses the evil angels not only to punish the godless (2 Thess. 2:11-12), but also to try the believers, as was the case with Job (Job 1:7 ff.) and the Apostle Paul (2 Cor. 12:7).

The punishment of the evil angels is eternal torment in the fire of hell (Matt. 25:41: "Depart from me, ye cursed, into everlasting fire, prepared for the devil and his angels"). The question as to the nature

---

20 On the *obsessio spiritualis* and *corporalis* see Baier-Walther, II, 136 ff. On the nature, symptoms, and treatment of bodily possession see Walther's *Pastorale*, p. 293 ff.

21 Fecht therefore (quoted in Walther's *Pastorale*, p. 295) says that "the possessed person, if he is a believer, should be reminded, when he is in his right mind, that he is not accountable for the blasphemies uttered in his paroxysms by Satan." [See John H. C. Fritz, *Pastoral Theology*, 2d ed., p. 209 f.]

22 Among other things we are thinking of the bills in various legislatures aimed at our Christian schools. In spite of the favorable decision by the Supreme Court these attempts are being renewed.

of this fire (whether material or immaterial) need not be answered (see the chapter "Eternal Damnation," in Vol. III). So also the question how fire can take effect upon spirits. Scripture teaches the fact! — Whoever denies the eternal punishment of the evil angels and of those who are *finaliter* seduced by them will have to deny, if he would be consistent, also eternal life (Matt. 25:46: "And these shall go away into everlasting punishment; but the righteous into life eternal") and thus the entire Christian religion (1 Cor. 15:19: "If in this life only we have hope in Christ, we are of all men most miserable"). To conceive of the eternal fire as purifying or annihilating the wicked and the evil angels contradicts Scripture.

Finally, we should bear in mind that all that the Bible says of the evil angels and their eternal punishment serves the ends of divine compassion. Its purpose is to impress on men the necessity of repentance and of faith in Him who by His blood ransomed mankind not for hell, but for heaven.

The Doctrine of Man

(ANTHROPOLOGIA)

In conformity with the data we shall consider man (A) before the Fall *(in statu integritatis)* and (B) after the Fall *(in statu peccati).*

A. MAN BEFORE THE FALL

(De Statu Hominis Ante Lapsum)

1

Man Created in the Image of God

The original state of man is described in the general term "very good" (Gen. 1:31), a term which covers all creatures. The specific feature of goodness which characterized man in distinction from all other creatures is named in the statement that God created man in His [God's] image. Gen. 1:26-27: "And God said, Let Us make man in Our image, after Our likeness. . . . So God created man in His own image."

"Image" (צֶלֶם) and "likeness" (דְּמוּת) are synonyms. Some assume that "image" signifies man's mind and will, and "likeness" a mind which knows God and a will which is in agreement with God's will. This interpretation contradicts Scripture, for in v. 27, which reports the execution of v. 26, only "image" is used. Now, since the divine execution surely agrees with the divine resolution, "image" by itself includes the whole of the divine image and likeness. The two terms are used in v. 26 simply to stress the divine likeness and aptly translated by Luther: *"Ein Bild, das uns gleich sei."* Baier (II, 143): *"Imago simillima."* So also Gerhard, *Loci, locus "De Imagine Dei."* [1]

Owing to the difference between God the Creator and man the creature, the divine aseity [self-existence] and eternity could not have been communicated to man, and the other divine attributes, for instance, the wisdom, lordship, etc., were only reflected in man. God is wise, and man is wise; God rules, and man rules. But God possesses unlimited, man only limited wisdom, dominion, etc. (See the doctrine of God.)

One more remark on Gen. 1:26-27. This passage gives no support

---

[1] At one place in his *Commentary on Genesis* (St. L. I:410 ff.) Luther distinguishes between the two terms.

whatever for the thesis that man was created after the image of the human nature of Christ (thus Origen and Andrew Osiander) or after the image of the divine nature of Christ. On the contrary, the plural possessive suffix: "in Our image, after Our likeness," shows that man was created in the image of the Triune God, of the glorious divine essence belonging to the three Persons. In the language of the dogmaticians: *Causa exemplaris imaginis divinae non una divinitatis persona, sed Deus triunus est.* In addition, making the human nature of Christ the pattern for man's nature contradicts clear passages of Scripture. According to 1 Cor. 15:45 f., Christ is "the last Adam" (man) and Adam "the first man." And, according to Heb. 2:14, Christ assumed the flesh and blood of man; men were not patterned after the flesh and blood of Christ.[2]

2

What Constituted the Image of God

The image of God in man consisted in much more than in his possession of intellect and will, in his personality; it consisted in the right disposition of his intellect and will, in his knowledge of God and

---

[2] All erroneous notions on this point, past and present, are refuted by Quenstedt. He says (I, 861 *sq.*): "The opinion of the Origenists and Osiander, who affirm: 'Adam was created after the likeness of the human nature of Christ, preconceived in the divine mind,' is refuted 1) by Gen. 1:26, where the Father, speaking with the Son and the Holy Spirit, does not say: 'Let Us make men in Thy image,' namely, of the Son, who was to become man, but: 'in Our image'; 2) by 1 Cor. 15:45, where Christ is called 'the second Adam'; but if the idea or form of the human nature of Christ, preconceived in the divine mind, after the likeness of which Adam is supposed to have been created, preceded the creation of Adam in the order of things, Christ should be called the first Adam rather than the second Adam; we need not mention that in this sense we were not made like unto Christ, but Christ was made like unto us, sin excepted, Heb. 2:14. 3) Nowhere in Scripture is it said that man was created κατὰ τὸν υἱόν, according to the Son, but κατὰ τὸν θεόν, according to God in general. *Per contra*, the Son of God is said to have been ἐν ὁμοιώματι σαρκὸς ἁμαρτίας, in the likeness of sinful flesh, Rom. 8:3, and to have taken upon Him μορφὴν δούλου, the form of a servant. 4) The order of the divine decrees is opposed to it. For the decree to make man in the image of God preceded (logically) the decree to send the Son of God into the flesh for the restitution of this image after its loss, and accordingly the Son of God, who was to become incarnate *in posteriori*, could not *in priori* be the pattern of the divine image to be created in man. 5) The very mission of the Son is opposed to it, which took place not for the sake of the likeness, but for the sake of restoring the bliss of man, 1 Tim. 1:15. 6) The image of God consists in the knowledge of God, righteousness, and holiness, as Col. 3:10 and Eph. 4:24 demonstrate; not, however, in the members of the body, in the figure or stature of the body. 7) Through the Fall the image of God was lost, but the bodily members were not lost."

the will to do only God's will. And his sensuous desires *(appetitus sensitivus)*, in his eating, etc. – if we wish to distinguish this from the intellect and will – were free from all ungodly propensity. This is clear not only from Gen. 1:31 ("very good") and from Gen. 2:25: "And they were both naked, the man and his wife, and were not ashamed,"[3] but also from two additional facts mentioned in the record of the original condition of man. 1) God gave man commandments to keep (Gen. 2:16-17: "Of every tree of the Garden thou mayest freely eat; but of the Tree of the Knowledge of Good and Evil, thou shalt not eat of it"). 2) Man is presented as living in intimate intercourse and peaceful communion with God (Gen. 2:19 ff.; 3:2-3). All these facts show that man knew God and was endowed with a holy disposition. This truth is corroborated in the New Testament. Col. 3:10 describes the new man as "renewed in knowledge after the image of Him that created him," and Eph. 4:24 as "created after God in righteousness and true holiness."[4]

We must therefore reject as anti-Scriptural the notion that man originally was a brute, without language, or that he was a being "morally indifferent," neither good nor bad, or that he was even then infected with an ungodly inclination towards gratification of his desires ("*Sinnlichkeit*"). According to Scripture, man was not created a brute, but the lord of the animal kingdom. And he was not merely capable of culture, but was truly cultured, endowed not only with the gift of speech, but with an intelligence that, besides knowing God, had such a grasp of the natural sciences as is unattainable today even by the most diligent study. Luther is right in saying that only Adam, as he was before the Fall, really deserves the title of philosopher.[5] But,

---

[3] Cp. Luther's remarks on this nakedness before and after the Fall, St. L. I:170.

[4] The old teachers are agreed that these passages contain a direct reference to the original state of man. Meyer and others deny it; but when at the same time they admit that the Apostle Paul "had in mind, according to the analogy of Adam's creation, the divine image which the first man possessed," and that we have in the words of the Apostle "a parallel with the creation of Adam after the image of God," they are contradicting themselves. The "parallel" with the creation of Adam after God's image would disappear if there were no direct statement here regarding the original condition of man. Philippi (*Glaubenslehre*, 3d ed., III, 372 ff.) and other recent theologians take the right view. Ellicott, for instance, writing on Eph. 4:24 against Jul. Mueller, says: "From this passage, compared with that from Colossians, we may appropriately deduce the great dogmatic truth: 'that what we had lost in Adam, i. e., our being made in the image and likeness of God, has been restored to us in Christ Jesus.'"

[5] Luther: "If we would speak of a great and excellent philosopher *(insignis philosophus)*, let us speak of our first parents when they were yet free from sin. . . . Adam and Eve understood the senses, nature, powers, of all the animals." (St. L. I:80–81.)

above all things, man was not originally in a state of moral indifference or endowed with a mere aptitude for what is good,[6] but he was positively good (*sanctae Dei voluntati conformis, amore et fiducia Dei praeditus*), without any trace of sensuality or propensity toward evil. Frequently a false conception of what moral goodness means lies at the bottom of the opposition to the Scriptural doctrine of the concreated divine image or the *iustitia originalis concreata.* Men imagine that only that is morally good which man himself produces by way of evolution (self-activity, self-decision, self-determination), not that which God has concreated in men, given to man.

Luther occasionally calls the original state of man *status medius.* He is then not speaking of man as being morally indifferent, but as not yet so confirmed in welldoing that he could not fall. He distinguishes (St. L. I:135 ff.) between "childlike" and "manly" innocence (*innocentia puerilis* and *virilis*). "Childlike innocence" is the state in which men could still be deceived by Satan, "manly innocence" the state which the angels, confirmed in holiness, enjoy and which the blessed in heaven will enjoy (*inamissibilis innocentia et immortalitas*). But Luther was far from conceiving this state of "childlike" innocence as a state of "indifference." He castigates the idle talk of the Scholastics, who described the original state as a mere capability (*qualitas*) of doing good. And he describes the original righteousness thus (St. L. I:138): "If we wish to follow Moses, we can say that the original righteousness consisted in this, that man was righteous, true, and upright, not only in his body and externally, but, above all, inwardly in his soul, and that he knew God, was obedient to Him with the utmost pleasure, understood the works of God without any instruction concerning them. . . . The original righteousness also consisted in Adam's loving God and God's work with all his heart, in a pure spirit."

3

Image of God in the Wider and in the Proper Sense

The Lutheran theologians are agreed that the image of God, which consists in the knowledge of God and holiness of the will, is lacking in

---

[6] Ritschl takes the divine image to have been the predated [i. e., to be attained] ideal of life, not as that which God gave to man at the creation, but as that which man makes of himself through evolution. See his *Rechtfertigung und Versoehnung*, 3d ed., III, 314 ff.

man after the Fall, since Col. 3:10 and Eph. 4:24 distinctly state that it is being restored in the believer. They differ, however, on the question as to whether in Gen. 9:6 ("Whoso sheddeth man's blood, by man shall his blood be shed; for in the image of God made He man") and James 3:9 ("With the tongue . . . curse we men, which are made after the similitude of God") a divine image is still ascribed to man after the Fall. Some deny this and take the passages to describe man as the noble creature who once bore the image of God and in whom God would recreate this image through faith in Christ. Thus Luther (on Gen. 9:6, St. L. I:600 f.), Philippi (*Glaubenslehre,* 3d ed., II, 371 f.), Gottfried Hoffman (*Synopsis,* p. 291). Others say that these passages describe man as he is after the Fall, a creature endowed with intellect and will, and contend that this constitutes a certain similitude with God. Thus Baier (II, 146), Quenstedt (*Systema* I, 876, 901 ff.), and others. The latter distinguish between the image of God in a wider sense, according to which man, in distinction from the animals, is still a rational being even after the Fall, and the divine image in the proper sense, consisting in true knowledge and service of God, which was lost through the Fall. It will be seen that these two interpretations do not differ materially, since Luther and those who agree with him do not deny that man after the Fall retains his intellect and will, and Baier and those who agree with him do not deny that man has through the Fall completely lost the *sapientia* and *iustitia originalis.* However, the interpretation of Luther is to be preferred.

It has been maintained that not a lost image of God, but only a still extant image could be a sound reason why we are not to shed man's blood or curse him. But Luther and those who share his position see in these texts not only the lost image, but the image that is to be restored again in Christ. Luther (*loc. cit.*): "While it is true that man has lost this image through sin . . . yet it remains true that it can be again acquired through the Word of the Holy Ghost." This interpretation presents a thought which is found throughout Scripture from Gen. 3:15 on. The only reason why God still concerns Himself with fallen mankind and preserves it — and for its sake also the world — is that, according to Scripture, He desires to renew fallen mankind to the image in which He originally created it (Col. 3:10; Eph. 4:24). This viewpoint is of great practical importance. The truth that God gave His Son to the world and would renew the world in Christ to the original image of God will shield us against the misanthropy which the deceitfulness and malice of men in the spiritual domain (in fighting against the Gospel) and in secular affairs (as in the World War) would create in us. – To call man the image of God because he possesses reason and will and leave out of consideration what he is to become in Christ is to stretch a point. Reason and will of fallen mankind is "an idling motor"; fallen man's reason does not recognize salvation, but operates entirely in spiritual darkness (1 Cor. 2:14: "neither can he know them"), and his will does not cling to God, but is enmity toward God (Rom. 8:7: "The carnal mind is enmity against God").

4

The Relation of the Divine Image to the Nature of Man

The divine image, that is, the true knowledge of God and the conformity of the human will to the will of God, was not subsequently and externally added to man at the creation, as the Papists contend, who regard the divine image (holiness and righteousness) as a *donum superadditum*, a superadded gift.[7] Rather was man created with the divine image, as Gen. 1:26 shows: "Let Us make man in Our image, after Our likeness." The divine image was a *donum concreatum, donum naturale, donum intrinsecum.* It follows that now, after the Fall, the human nature is no longer perfect (*natura integra* or *in puris naturalibus*), as the Papists and modern theologians and philosophers teach, but thoroughly and in its innermost parts corrupt (*natura corrupta, natura sauciata*).[8] It is true, the *iustitia originalis* did not con-

[7] Catechismus Romanus I, 2, 18: "God formed man of clay of the earth, so composed and constituted in his body that he was, not by the strength of his nature, but by divine gift immortal and not subject to suffering. But as to the soul, God formed it after His image and similitude and granted it the free will; besides, He tempered all emotions *(motus)* of the soul and the appetites (desires) in him so that they always obeyed the rule of reason. Then He added the wonderful gift of original righteousness and furthermore willed that he rule the rest of the living creatures." See also Guenther, *Pop. Symbolik*, pp. 137, 142 (*Pop. Symbolics*, p. 166). Quenstedt, I, 889.

[8] Luther on the relation of the divine image to the human nature: "The Scholastics argue that the righteousness in which Adam was created did not form a part of Adam's nature, but was, as it were, an ornament or gift which was bestowed on him in his first estate; just as a garland is placed on the head of a beautiful maiden, which garland does not belong to the nature, but is something added from without and might be taken away again without harming the nature. They argue therefore that although men and devils have lost the righteousness in which they were created, yet their natural powers remained pure, in their original state. Since this doctrine detracts from the magnitude of

stitute the nature of man. Even after the Fall, man is still ἄνθρωπος (Rom. 5:12), inasmuch as the original righteousness was not the substance, but a non-essential attribute, an accident.[9] But the *iustitia originalis* belonged to the nature of uncorrupted man, of man as he should be, as God created him, and as he is to become through Christ. According to Scripture it is certainly an abnormal thing that man, created for God and conscious of the existence of God (Rom. 1:19 ff.), does not and cannot serve God (Rom. 8:7: "The carnal mind . . . is not subject to the Law of God, neither indeed can be"), but lives his life on earth as a practical atheist. Eph. 2:12 says of all heathen: "Having no god and without God (ἄθεοι) in the world." And the worship of the heathen is described in the words: "The things which the Gentiles sacrifice, they sacrifice to devils, and not to God" (1 Cor. 10:20).

The real seat of the divine image is not the body, but the soul of man, since the knowledge of God and holiness inhere in the soul. But, naturally, the divine image was manifested also in the body, since the body is the organ of the soul and an essential part of man. Apology: "Therefore original righteousness was to embrace . . . an even temperament of the bodily qualities [perfect health and, in all respects, pure blood, unimpaired powers of the body]" (*Trigl.* 109, 17).

5

Immediate Consequences of the Possession of the Divine Image

1. Man was immortal (able not to die). According to Scripture, death and its forerunners (illness, debility) entered into the world by sin. Gen. 2:17: "In the day that thou eatest thereof, thou shalt surely die"; Rom. 5:12: "And death by sin"; Rom. 6:23: "The wages of

---

original sin, it is to be shunned as deadly poison. We must rather conclude that original righteousness was not a superadded gift, separate from the nature of man, but belonged to the nature of man, so that it was natural for Adam to love God, to believe in God, to know God. These things were as natural for Adam as it is natural for the eye to behold the light. When the eye is injured and hurt, you may well say that the nature is harmed and injured. . . . For as it is the nature of the eye to see, it was natural for Adam's reason and will to know God, to trust in God, and to fear God." (St. L. I:201 f.)

[9] Luther: "Nature does indeed remain, but it is corrupted in various ways" (*Opp. ex.*, Erl. I, 211).

sin is death." It is a pagan opinion that death is bound up with the material substance of the body; some modern theologians share that opinion. (See the chapter "Temporal Death" in Vol. III.)

2. Man exercised dominion over the creatures. That was an immediate consequence of possessing the divine image, for we read: "Let Us make man in Our image, after Our likeness; and let them have dominion," etc. (Gen. 1:26-28.) It was a real dominion; willingly all creatures rendered man service. After the Fall, man retained only a caricature of his original dominion; he must now employ cunning and force to assert some kind of mastery over the animals. With man's innocence also the dominion over the creatures, as described Gen. 1:28, was lost. All that is left of this dominion, Luther calls a "mock sovereignty" (*speciem dominii* and *nudum titulum dominii*). It is true that man succeeds by cunning and coercion in subduing the creatures partially. But in spite of all the creature remains in revolt against its sinful master. The beasts harass, harm, kill, and eat their former lord; in the air he breaks his neck; the water drowns him; the earth becomes his tomb, etc. Such considerations, says Luther, serve a useful purpose. They teach us what an abomination before God sin must be, since it has so thoroughly deranged the relationship between man and the rest of the creatures.[10]

---

[10] Luther: "Adam and Eve are made rulers of the earth, the sea, and the air. This dominion is committed to them not only by the counsel of God, but also by an express mandate. . . . So, then, the naked man, without arms and walls, yea, without any garments, ruled in his bare body over all birds, beasts, and fishes. . . . Who can understand this part of the divine nature (if we may use this expression) that Adam and Eve understood and knew all about the senses, nature, and powers of all the animals? For they could have exercised no rule if they had not known these things. . . . If we would therefore speak of a great and excellent philosopher, let us speak of our first parents when they were yet free from sin. . . . They also had a sure knowledge of the stars and of all astronomy. What we accomplish in our life is accomplished through industry and art, not by that dominion which Adam had. For we see that birds and fishes are caught by cunning tricks; the beasts are tamed by our skill. For those animals which are most domesticated, like geese and hens, are by their nature wild animals. Hence, even our leprous body, by the grace of God, has some show of a dominion over the other creatures. But it is very paltry and far inferior to that dominion in which there was no need of art and cunning, where the animals simply obeyed the divine voice and Adam and Eve were commanded to rule over them. So we now retain the mere name and word of dominion or the bare title; the matter itself has been completely lost. And yet it is good to know and think of these things, so that we may long for that day in which all the things which we have lost in Paradise shall be restored to us. For we look for that life which Adam also had been expecting. And well indeed may we wonder and render thanks unto God that we, so deformed by sin, so dull, so

6

The Purpose of the Divine Image

Here, too, we do not have to resort to guessing. The nature of the divine image clearly shows its purpose. God created man in His own, in the divine image, in order that one of His creatures 1) would know Him, live in conformity with His will, and in communion with Him enjoy bliss, and 2) would rule over the other creatures as His representative. After this original purpose has been frustrated by the sin of man, God revives it again in Christ. For the sake of Christ's substitutionary satisfaction He cancels the guilt of man and restores in believers in Christ the knowledge of God and the holiness of will (Col. 3:10; Eph. 4:24).

The knowledge of God which the saved sinner has after the Fall is thus changed as to its object, since now the object of his knowledge of God is *primo loco* the God who for Christ's sake and through faith in Him, without the deeds of the Law, forgives sins. Luke 1:77: "To give knowledge of salvation . . . by the remission of their sins." Whether, when, and how God would have effected a change in man's status (his "paradisiacal state") if he had not fallen, is altogether conjecture. But we know that the concept of salvation by redemption, σωτηρία, *salus,* does not apply to man in his original state, since the σωτηρία gained by Christ presupposes the Fall. Luke 19:10: "The Son of Man is come to seek and to save that which was lost."

7

Woman and the Divine Image

The Encratites, a Gnostic sect of the second century, later known as Severians, were led by their false asceticism to deny that Eve possessed the divine image (Eusebius, *History of the Church,* 4, 29). But Gen. 1:26-27 expressly states that the woman, too, was created in the image of God: "Let Us make man in Our image. . . . So God created man in His own image . . . male and female created He them." This is corroborated in the New Testament. The restitution of the divine

---

stupefied, so dead, as it were, should be enabled through the merits of Christ to look for that same glory of a spiritual life which Adam would have looked forward to if he had remained in the earthly life which possessed the image of God." (*Opp. ex.,* Erl. I, 82 *sqq.;* St. L. I:80–82.)

image in Christ (Col. 3:10 and Eph. 4:24) takes place in women as well as in men, for there is no difference made between male and female in regard to participation in the gifts of Christ. We read Gal. 3:28: "There is neither Jew nor Greek, there is neither bond nor free, there is neither male nor female; for ye are all one in Christ Jesus." The woman shared with man also the dominion over the creatures. The plural form is used: "God blessed them, and God said unto them . . . have dominion . . . over every living thing that moveth upon the earth" (Gen. 1:28). Baier's opinion that Eve had less knowledge of nature than Adam cannot be substantiated from Scripture.[11]

On the other hand, Scripture teaches that woman in her relation to man occupied a position of subordination even before the Fall. This fact is expressed in the term used in Gen. 2:18: "an helpmeet for him." The same thought is voiced in the New Testament. 1 Cor. 11:9: "Neither was the man created for the woman; but the woman for the man." Hence woman is forbidden to exercise dominion over man. 1 Tim. 2:12: "I suffer not a woman to teach, nor to usurp authority over the man." There are two reasons for this: a) Adam was created first, then Eve (v. 13), and b) the woman introduced a disastrous innovation – sin (v. 14: "Adam was not deceived, but the woman, being deceived, was in the transgression"). It is the plain teaching of Scripture that in relation to the man, the woman is in a position of subordination. Both the order of creation and the order established after the Fall assign her that position.

People in our day are becoming more and more oblivious to this divine order, and this for two reasons. In spite of its wide circulation the Bible exerts less influence on human society than formerly, and good common sense, in spite of all advances in technical science, is rapidly diminishing among men. – We find in Luther two different sets of statements on the position of woman in human society. On the one hand, he says: "God did not set up womankind to rule, neither in the Church nor in secular offices" (St. L. II:687). Again: "The Holy Ghost has excluded women from the government of the Church" (St. L. XVI:2280). On the other hand, Luther requires men to show special reverence (*reverentia*) to woman, because the woman is the mother and educator of the human race. "*Mulier ut est creatura Dei, cum reverentia spectanda est; ad hoc enim est creata, ut circa virum sit, ut filios nutriat et educet honeste et pie*" (*Opp. ex.*, Erl. XXI:170;

---

[11] Baier-Walther, II, 158: "In regard to her knowledge of nature, Eve seems to have ranked below Adam."

St. L. V:1516). ("Since woman is a creature of God, she is to be regarded with reverence; for this purpose, indeed, she was created that she should be with man, that she should nurture and train children in honesty and piety.") Luther maintains consistently that God's creation of man and woman with a different sex appoints and fits them for a separate sphere of activity. He says: "Each one functions best as he has been created. 'A woman with her little finger does better by a child than a man with both his fists.' Let everyone stick to that work to which God has called and appointed him." (St. L. V:1517.) This is the Scriptural position. Scripture makes the home the sphere of the woman; it distinguishes sharply between the forbidden public and the permitted and commanded domestic activity of woman. It forbids the public speaking and teaching of women. It states: "It is a shame for women to speak in the church" (1 Cor. 14:35). Women are not even to ask questions in the public assemblies and thus start discussions, but they should ask their own men *at home* (ἐν οἴκῳ). Also 1 Tim. 2:12: "I suffer not a woman to teach," pertains according to the context to the public teaching of women. On the other hand, Scripture declares the home to be the sphere of woman's dominion and teaching activity. 1 Tim. 5:14: "I will therefore that the younger women [R. V.: "widows"] marry, bear children, guide the house" [οἰκοδεσποτεῖν: R. V.: "rule the household"]. The matrons should be, according to Titus 2:3, "teachers of good things"; "teach the young women . . . to love their husbands, to love their children, to be . . . stewards of the home" (οἰκουροί, keepers of the house; another reading, οἰκουργοί, homemakers). Perhaps no teacher of the Church has so frequently and so eloquently extolled the glory of woman as wife and mother as Luther. Rome exalts the state of monks and nuns, but Luther says: "What better and more profitable thing can be taught in the Church of God than the example of a pious housemother, who prays, sighs, cries, thanks God, rules the home, does what the office of a pious wife entails, desires to have children, in great chastity, gratitude, and piety" (St. L. II:540).

We hear people decry as "Oriental" the Biblical view that the home is the sphere of woman's activity. Men have asserted in all seriousness that if the Apostle Paul had written to American congregations, he would not have said: "It is a shame for women to speak in the church," and "Let the woman learn in silence with all subjection. But I suffer not a woman to teach," but because of the changed conditions he would have written somewhat in this wise: "Women to the front!" "Get on the platform!" "It is not shameful for a woman to speak in the church." These men are deluding themselves. 1 Corinthians 14 and 1 Timothy 2 are not dealing with a temporary "Oriental" order, but with a universal, permanent order, for Paul gives as the reasons for his vetoing any public teaching of the women in the church 1) the order of creation, that Adam was made first, after him Eve; and 2) the role that woman played in the Fall: "Adam was not deceived, but the woman, being deceived, was in the transgression" – facts which remain the same in the Occident as in the Orient and at all times, and the order based on these facts remains the same.

One other point should be mentioned in this connection. Woman ought not be dragged from her place of honor into public life, for it is universally acknowledged that woman is the most influential teacher of the human race. If women prove themselves good teachers in the home (Titus 2:3), they thereby wield a greater influence on the coming generation than the men, including the pastors and schoolteachers.

B. MAN AFTER THE FALL

(De Statu Peccati)

A revival of the tenets of the ancient Gnostic sect of the Ophites ("the brotherhood of the serpent") [12] represents sin as the exaltation of mankind. This is the very interpretation of sin by which Satan seduced our first parents. Gen. 3:5: "Ye shall not surely die . . . ye shall be as gods [R. V.: God], knowing good and evil." Schiller sees in the Fall "the most fortunate and the greatest event in the history of mankind." [13] Hegel expressed it in these words: "The state of innocence, this paradisaic state, is the brutish state. Paradise is a park where only beasts, and not men, can abide. The fall into sin is therefore the eternal myth telling how man becomes a man." [14] Similar views regarding the Fall and sin are voiced here in America. Strong furnishes ample evidence for this from the writings of Emerson, Hawthorne, Schurman, and others. From the humanistic and pantheistic viewpoint, sin is regarded as the necessary transitional stage

---

12 On the Ophites see *R. E.*, 2d ed., V, 240 ff.

13 Quoted in Nitzsch-Stephan, p. 322 f., from Schiller's *Etwas ueber die erste Menschengesellschaft, Uebergang des Menschen zur Freiheit und Humanitaet.*

14 Quoted in Luthardt, *Komp.*, 10th ed., p. 165, from Hegel's *Philosophie der Geschichte,* p. 233. Nitzsch-Stephan, p. 322: "Hegel regards sin as the necessary period of transition through which the finite spirit rises from the bondage of nature to liberty."

or the background for virtue. Sin, even in the form which it took in the infidel Thomas Paine, is, taken as a whole, necessary for the perfection of the world.[15] These men have reached the general conclusion that, as Strong remarks, "the Fall was a fall up and not down" and, we say it again, repeat Satan's lie as to the effect of sin (Gen. 3:5).

According to Scripture, sin is not the exaltation of man which produced his happiness, but is the deepest degradation and the one great calamity that has come upon mankind; all other evils are solely the consequence of sin. And man's experience confirms this truth. All this humanistic-pantheistic talk about sin as the necessary transitional stage leading to "moral freedom" and to the evolution of "true humanity" is disproved by the voice of man's conscience. The human conscience has properly been called the invincible foe of pantheism and every other form of atheism. Man simply is unable to convince himself that sin was the passageway to "true humanity," representing "advancements" and constituting "the most fortunate event in the history of mankind." For, on account of his sin, man has an evil conscience before God; because of his sin he feels just as "happy" as Adam and Eve were when after the Fall they "hid themselves from the presence of the Lord God amongst the trees of the Garden" (Gen. 3:8). But by the grace of God an exceedingly great and fortunate "event in the history of mankind" has come to pass for us fallen sinners – the incarnation of the Son of God, the purpose of which is to richly restore to us, by His substitutionary satisfaction, what we have lost through the devil's seduction in the fall of our first parents. And in this divine restoration only he will share who will not permit Satan to deceive him again in the matter of the Fall and of sin, but who gains the right view of these things from God's Word. The Christian doctrine therefore necessarily contains the *locus de peccato.*

This doctrine will be treated under the three heads: a) *de peccato in genere,* b) *de peccato originali,* c) *de peccatis actualibus.* We shall have occasion to meet also the modern antitheses.

---

[15] Augustus H. Strong, *Systematic Theology,* p. 563: "Emerson's view of Jesus is found in his *Essays,* 2, 263: 'Jesus would absorb the race; but Tom Paine, or the coarsest blasphemer, helps humanity by resisting this exuberance of power.' " "In his *Divinity School Address,* Emerson banished the Person of Jesus from genuine religion. He thought 'one could not be a man if he must subordinate his nature to Christ's nature.' " Page 565: "Hawthorne hints, though rather hesitatingly, that without sin the higher humanity of man could not be taken up at all, and that sin may be essential to the first conscious awakening of moral freedom and the possibility of progress."

a. ON SIN IN GENERAL

(De Peccato in Genere)

1

Definition of Sin

According to Scripture, sin is nonconformity to the divine Law (νόμος), which is given to man as a norm; and this norm pertains both to man's condition (*status, habitus*) and to his individual internal or external actions (*actiones internae et externae*), as Scripture states, 1 John 3:4: "Sin is the transgression of the Law," ἀνομία [R. V.: "Sin is lawlessness"]. 'Ανομία (lawlessness) is, etymologically considered, a negative concept, expressing a lack of conformity to the divine Law (*carentia conformitatis cum lege*). But according to Scripture usage ἀνομία is also a positive concept and denotes opposition to the Law, a breaking and violating of the Law. Scripture clearly states that he that doeth sin "doeth also lawlessness," 1 John 3:4 (R. V.), and: "Depart from me, ye that work iniquity" (τὴν ἀνομίαν ποιεῖν). That this lack of conformity to the divine Law is a positive evil is also evident from the following truths set down in Scripture: 1) Man as a moral being, endowed with intellect and will, is in duty bound to conform to the divine will in every moment of his life. The answer to the question as to the foremost commandment in the Law (Matt. 22:37-40) admits no restrictions or qualifications: "Thou shalt love the Lord, thy God, with all thy heart and with all thy soul and with all thy mind. . . . Thou shalt love thy neighbor as thyself." Where this full agreement with the divine Law is lacking, there is opposition to the Law, or wickedness. To use an analogy: The servant who fails to carry out the duties incumbent on him would be condemned by his own conscience if he pleaded that he had done no wrong, but simply had taken a neutral position over against his duties. 2) It is psychologically impossible for man, endowed with intellect and will, to remain neutral even for a moment. If his mind and will are not attached to God, they are attached to some creature, and that is apostasy from God, as Christ expressly states Matt. 6:24: "No man can serve two masters."

It is a grave error to say that only conscious and deliberate action against God's will constitutes sin. According to Scripture, the evil condition in which man is born and which he cannot change is sin, as is clearly shown in Eph. 2:3: "And were by nature the children of wrath." And Scripture further bears witness that this evil condition does not lose its sinful character even when the Christian detests it.

The Apostle declares: "The evil which I would not, that I do. . . . O wretched man that I am! who shall deliver me from the body of this death?" (Rom. 7:19, 24.) Over against this prevalent error the Lutheran Church adheres strictly to Scripture. The Apology designates the teaching that consciousness, deliberation, voluntariness, belong to the essence of sin as a pagan error. "In the schools they transferred hither from philosophy notions entirely different, that, because of passions [inborn evil inclinations] we are neither good nor evil, we are neither deserving of praise or blame. Likewise, that nothing is sin, unless it be voluntary. (Inner desires and thoughts are not sins, if I do not altogether consent thereto.) These notions were expressed among philosophers with respect to civil righteousness, and not with respect to God's judgment." (*Trigl.* 117, 43.) These papistical views have been taken over by modern theologians like Hofmann, who says: "As long as the Ego is still in a stage of development, one cannot say in like manner as later that it is the subject committing the sin; it becomes such a subject in the measure in which it becomes a true Ego, beginning to determine itself consciously or rather permitting itself to be determined by the innate sin." [16]

2

The Divine Law and Sin

Since sin is ἀνομία (lawlessness), we must, if we would properly know the doctrine of sin, clearly see what the νόμος is, the trans-

---

[16] *Schriftbeweis,* 2d ed., I, 562. *Lehre und Wehre,* 24, 248. Also the later Lutheran theologians take the position of the Lutheran Confession that "τὸ *voluntarium*" [conscious volition] is not a part of the essence of sin. Baier II, 275: "The philosophers indeed hold that nothing may be called sin unless there appears in it some kind of voluntariness, so that the things which are against the Law are called sins only in so far as they participate in them voluntarily. In Scripture, however, sin has a much wider meaning. St. John covers the case when (1 John 3:4) he defines sin as 'ἀνομία' and does not mention voluntariness." Quenstedt, I, 967: "Antithesis: 1) of certain Papists, like Andradius, lib. 3, *Defens. Conc. Trid.,* who denies that all ἀνομία is sin. . . . 2) of the Pelagians . . . who contend that original sin is not sin, because in infants it is involuntary; 3) of the Papists, who assert that voluntariness belongs to the nature of sin, so that nothing is sin unless in some degree the will consents to it. Thus Bellarmine. . . . 4) of the Socinians, such as Socinus, Ostorodus, Smalzius, who openly deny original sin for the same reason (scilicet, because it is not voluntary). . . . 5) of the Arminians, who in *Actis Synodal. Def.,* art. 4, and in Apol. Conf., ch. 7, assert that conscious volition belongs to the nature of sin. . . . 6) of Zwingli and Calvin, who, writing on Genesis 3, deny original sin for the same reason, namely, that it is involuntary."

gression of which constitutes ἀνομία. The definition of the Law given by the Formula of Concord is Scriptural in every detail: "We unanimously believe, teach, and confess that the Law is properly a divine doctrine, in which the righteous, immutable will of God is revealed, what is to be the quality of man in his nature, thoughts, words, and works, in order that he may be pleasing and acceptable to God" (*Trigl.* 957, 17). It is pointed out here, in the first place, that the power to decree laws for men rests solely with God, with God's will. That belongs to the dignity of man. Every man is subject to God's Law. Laws enacted by men are a norm binding our consciences only when God sanctions them and thus makes them His precepts. God does that in the case of the laws of civil government (Rom. 13:1 ff.: "Let every soul be subject unto the higher powers") and of the parents (Col. 3:20: "Children, obey your parents in all things"), and He sanctions here only such laws as do not contradict the divine Law (Acts 5:29: "We ought to obey God rather than men").

The so-called "laws of the Church" cannot bind our consciences. Christ has not given His Church any legislative power (*potestas legislatoria*); on the contrary, He has forbidden His Church to exercise any such power. Matt. 23:8: "One is your Master, even Christ; and all ye are brethren." What Christ has not commanded is regulated in the Church not by command, but by mutual agreement of the Christians themselves. Even the abuse of this liberty must not lead the Church to command things which God has not commanded. In short, we must maintain from first to last that only God's Law is the norm, the transgression of which constitutes a sin. "The Pope," Luther declares, "has filled the world with satanic obedience. For the Pope does not command what God has enjoined, but what he himself invents; whence it has come about that his whole religion is not true, but is his own fabrication and choice, and, in short, pure hypocrisy." (St. L. I:765.)

In the second place, God's Law is authoritative not only in part, but in its every detail. God demands in His Law the purity of the human nature (therefore Eph. 2:3 says of the inborn corrupt state of nature: "And were by nature the children of wrath") and consequently also the purity of all internal and external acts which belong to a righteous and pure nature. He demands purity of thoughts (Matt. 5:22: "Whosoever is angry with his brother without a cause shall be in danger of the judgment," and v. 28: "Whosoever looketh on a woman to lust after her hath committed adultery with her already in his heart"); of words (Matt. 12:36: "But I say unto you that every idle word that men shall speak, they shall give account thereof in the Day of Judgment"); and of works (Eph. 5:5: "For this ye know that no whoremonger, nor unclean person, nor covetous man, who is an idolater, hath any inheritance in the Kingdom of Christ and of God"). There has always been opposition, public, and even more so, secret, to the truth that the divine Law pertains to all internal and external acts of men. People have been saying at all times: "God hath forgotten; He hideth His face; He will never see it" (Ps. 10:11). And in particular there always was and still is today a universal protest against declaring the inborn depravity of human nature to be truly sin and bearing the "character of guilt." "Guiltless sin," men say, is the proper term to be used here. (See the section *De Peccato Originali.*) But men cannot nullify God's Law; the Lord will enforce it to its full extent. And no matter what attempts they make to remove guilt from sin, the Lord holds man accountable for every transgression of His Law. And – we say it again and again – man's own conscience holds him accountable.

The Formula of Concord correctly defines the Law as the righteous, immutable will of God as to "what is to be the quality of man in his nature, thoughts, words, and works, in order that he may be pleasing and acceptable to God." The correctness of this definition is clearly confirmed by the fact that our Substitute, who in our stead assumed the obligation to fulfill the demands of the Law and bear its punishment, thus to make us "pleasing and acceptable to God," had to be a most unique, miraculous person, namely, "holy, harmless, undefiled, and separate from sinners" (Heb. 7:26), one "who knew no sin" (2 Cor. 5:21).

3

How the Divine Law is Made Known to Man

Though the Gospel remains hidden to the natural heart of man (1 Cor. 2:9: "Eye hath not seen, nor ear heard, neither have entered into the heart of man, the things which God hath prepared for them that love Him"), man has a natural knowledge of the Law. Also after the Fall the conscience (συνείδησις, *conscientia*) of man still bears witness of the divine will, or Law. Man's conscience functions in two ways: a) it reveals and demands (Rom. 2:15a: The heathen, who do not have the written Law, "show the work of the law written in their hearts, their conscience also bearing witness"); and b) it judges and condemns (Rom. 2:15b: "Their thoughts the mean while accusing or else excusing one another").[17]

But since the Fall the conscience does not give a fully reliable testimony concerning the will of God. There is such a thing as an *erring* conscience (*conscientia erronea*). Fallen man regards certain things as permitted, yea, even commanded, which God has forbidden. He will commit idolatry (Gal. 4:8: "When ye knew not God, ye did service unto them which by nature are no gods"), submit to the Antichrist (2 Thess. 2:11: "that they should believe a lie"), murder Christians (John 16:2: "Whosoever killeth you will think that he doeth God service"). And fallen man regards as forbidden what God has permitted. He will, for instance, abstain from certain foods (Rom. 14:1 ff.). Therefore since the Fall the knowlėdge of God's immutable will is gained with certainty only from God's revelation in the Word, namely, in Holy Scripture. While the real scope of the Scriptures is the Gospel (John 5:39; Acts 10:43; 1 Cor. 2:2), they nevertheless also contain a complete revelation of the immutable will of God. Matt. 5: 18-19: "Till heaven and earth pass, one jot or one tittle shall in no wise pass from the Law till all be fulfilled. Whosoever therefore shall break one of these least commandments," etc.

Holy Scripture also determines exactly which laws applied only temporarily and locally, for instance, only to the Jews under the covenant of the Law, and are therefore not the divine norm for all men of all times. A great and harmful confusion of the consciences of men is, even to our day, caused by generalizing temporary and local laws. With reference, for instance, to the commandment given Ex. 31: 14-15: "Ye shall keep the Sabbath . . . everyone that defileth it shall surely be put to death," and Lev. 19:26: "Ye shall not eat anything with the blood," and Leviticus 11 and Deuteronomy 14 (the catalog of clean and unclean beasts), the New Testament distinctly says: "Let no man therefore judge you in meat, or in drink, or in respect of an holy day, or of the new moon, or of the Sabbath days" (Col. 2:16). We get this result: Only that is divine Law for all men which is taught in Holy Writ as binding on all. Not even the Ten Commandments in the form in which they were given to the Jews (Exodus 20) are binding on all men, but only the Ten Commandments as set down in the New Testament, as we have them, e. g., in Luther's Catechism.[18] — Commandments given to individuals (*mandata specialia*), e. g., the

---

[17] *Lehre und Wehre*, 22, 231 ff. See the quotations in Baier-Walther II, 269.

[18] See Luther's presentation of this matter, St. L. XX:146 ff.

commandment received by Abraham to sacrifice Isaac, do not obligate others. In general, the rule to be applied to the life and acts of the saints is, in the words of the Apology: "Examples ought to be interpreted according to the rule, *i. e.*, according to certain and clear passages of Scripture, not contrary to the rule, that is, contrary to Scripture" (*Trigl.* 441, 60).

4

The Cause of Sin

There is in fallen man a strong tendency to make God or other creatures responsible for his sinfulness and thus to remove the blame for his sin, either in whole or in part, from his own person. We see Adam and Eve doing this after the Fall. Gen. 3:12-13: "The woman, whom Thou gavest to be with me, she gave me of the tree, and I did eat. . . . The serpent beguiled me, and I did eat." This sort of excuse is typical of the entire fallen human race. In doctrinal discussions and in practical life we are repeatedly confronted with questions like the following: "Why did God create man with the ability to fall?" And: "Why does God today permit man to be tempted when according to His all-governing providence He could keep temptation away from men?" Such and similar questions tend to confuse the question as to the *causa peccati.*

According to Scripture the cause of sin in man is a) the devil. He sinned first and then seduced man. And he is still the power impelling unbelievers to sin and tempting believers to sin. Christ tells the unbelieving Jews, John 8:44: "Ye are of your father the devil," and those who are delivered from the power of darkness (Col. 1:13) Paul warns in 2 Cor. 11:3: "But I fear, lest by any means, as the serpent beguiled Eve through his subtilty, so your minds should be corrupted from the simplicity that is in Christ." Because he seduced men to sin, the devil is called "a murderer from the beginning," John 8:44 (ἀνθρωποκτόνος, "manslayer"); and since he is the *prima causa peccati,* the inventor of sin, we call sin, with good reason, a work of the devil, even in the case of sins committed by believers. That such is the case is clearly indicated by Christ when He says to Peter, who sought to keep Christ from suffering and dying: "Get thee behind Me, Satan." [19]

---

[19] The relation of the serpent to Satan (Gen. 3:1 ff.) has been defined by the old theologians in the words: "*Serpens verus, sed instrumentum diaboli.*" That definition should never have been called into question. Gen. 3:1, 14 clearly

The cause of sin in man is b) sinning man himself. Seduction by the devil does not do away with the fact that man perpetrates the sin; it does not relieve him of the responsibility for it. That is the clear teaching of Scripture. Though Adam and Eve were seduced by the devil, they are guilty and are punished by God (Gen. 3:16-18). According to 2 Thess. 2:9-12 those who are seduced by Satan and by Antichrist with all power and signs and lying wonders remain responsible to God and are judged by God. The same judgment is expressed in Matt. 18:7: "Woe unto the world because of offenses"; men are punished because they fall prey to the offenses. And man's conscience bears testimony to the same effect: It reproves him after sinning. We see Adam and Eve hiding from God after they had sinned (Gen. 3:8). On the *causa peccati* the Augsburg Confession states: "Although God does create and preserve nature, yet the cause of sin is the will of the wicked, that is, of the devil and ungodly men" (*Trigl.* 53, Art. XIX).[20] Hence man remains, as the dogmaticians express it, the *subiectum quod peccati,* active and responsible, even though he was originally seduced by Satan and is today (as long as he is without faith in Christ) wholly ruled by Satan (Col. 1:13) and cannot refrain from sinning (Rom. 8:7).

The true seat of sin in man, the true seat (*subiectum quo*) of the ἀνομία, is man's soul. In the soul the νόμος (the inscribed Law) had, and should still have, its seat. The body becomes a seat of sin inasmuch as it is the organ of the soul. The contrary opinion, that the body, and not the soul, is the seat of sin, the soul being the innocent captive, is a heathen concept. Christ clearly teaches Matt. 15:19: "Out of the heart proceed evil thoughts, murders, adulteries, etc." The heart is the true seat of sin, the birthplace of all internal and external sinful acts.

---

describes a real serpent, and v. 15 names the devil as active in the serpent; he it is whose head the Seed of the woman would crush. Thus also in 1 John 3:8, 2 Cor. 11:3, and also in Rev. 12:9 ("That old serpent, called the devil"), the devil is the active agent.

[20] Neither God's all-sustaining and governing providence nor the fact that He punishes sin with sin makes God the efficient cause of sin (see above). The Formula of Concord says: "Moreover, it is to be diligently considered that when God *punishes sin with sins,* that is, when He afterwards punishes with obstinacy and blindness those who had been converted, because of their subsequent security, impenitence, and willful sins, this should not be interpreted to mean that it had never been God's good pleasure that such persons should come to the knowledge of the truth and be saved" (*Trigl.* 1091, 83). Contrary to Scripture and the Confessions, Fecht says (*Syllog. Controv.,* p. 109; in Baier-Walther II, p. 274): "The statement of some: 'God punishes sins with sins,' is improper, not to be imitated, and even charges God with injustice."

5

The Consequences of Sin

Since God has forbidden sin, that is, the deviation from His νόμος, sin makes man guilty before God (Rom. 3:19: "All the world may become guilty before God"; *reatus culpae*) and subjects him to the punishment imposed by God on sin (Gal. 3:10: "Cursed is everyone that continueth not in all things which are written in the Book of the Law"; *reatus poenae*). Furthermore, since the νόμος is given by God, not by any human authority, the nature and extent of the punishment cannot be determined by human sentiment, but must be determined solely by God's revealed Word. And according to God's revealed Word, sin is in every case a capital crime, that is, makes man guilty of death, as both the Old and the New Testament declare. Gen. 2:17: "In the day that thou eatest thereof, thou shalt surely die." Rom. 5:12: "And death by sin."

On the basis of Scripture, death may be said to be threefold.

1. It is the death of the soul, or "spiritual death," i. e., the disruption of the communion of the soul with God. Only by the communion with God, for which it was created, does the soul live – by cleaving to, believing, trusting, and loving God. But sin breaks this communion abruptly. The evil conscience cannot but flee from God. Sin separates the soul from God. By the sin which Adam had committed he was separated from God inwardly, in his soul, to such an extent that he also fled from God outwardly when he heard the voice of the Lord in the Garden. And, as Luther remarks, when Adam fled from God, "he was in the midst of death and hell" (on Gen. 3:11, St. L. I:215). He was brought back from death and hell into spiritual life only by hearing and believing the Gospel of the Seed of the woman, only by having his good conscience restored. In his exposition of the words that the Seed of the woman should bruise the head of the serpent (Gen. 3:15), Luther says: "This text it was that restored Adam and Eve to life and raised them again from death to the life which they had lost by their sin" (St. L. I:240). "This text is the absolution acquitting him and us all. For if this Seed is so strong that He crushes the head of the serpent, He also crushes all its power; so, then, the devil is conquered, and all damage which Adam suffered is repaired. Adam enters again the estate in which he was before." (St. L. III:66.) This theme, Gen. 3:15: "He shall bruise thy head," is taken up again in 1 John 3:8: "For this purpose the Son of God was manifested that

He might destroy the works of the devil." And that the works of the devil have been destroyed through the atoning death of Christ is clearly stated John 12:31 and John 16:11: "The prince of this world is judged."

There can thus be no doubt about what Scripture means by "spiritual life" and "spiritual death." After the Fall man gains spiritual life when by faith in Christ's work of reconciliation he finds healing for his evil conscience, finds peace with God. And he is in the state of spiritual death when on account of his sin he has an evil conscience before God, inwardly flees from God. Scripture describes the death of the soul, or spiritual death, as someone's being dead while living (1 Tim. 5:6: "She that liveth in pleasure is dead while she liveth").

2. Spiritual death carries in its wake a fearful catastrophe; the only reason why we do not fully realize its enormity is its daily occurrence among us. That is temporal death (*mors corporalis, sive temporalis*). Bodily death is nothing less than a tearing asunder of man, the separation of the soul from the body, the unnatural disruption of the union of soul and body which have been created by God to be one. This event, so terrifying in itself, loses its terrors for Christians only because through faith in Christ they have already in this life been raised from spiritual death into spiritual life; death translates their souls into Paradise (Luke 23:43) to be with Christ (Phil. 1:23).

3. Spiritual and temporal death will be followed, unless the guilt of sin is removed from the heart and conscience by faith in Christ, by eternal death (*mors aeterna*). Eternal death is not the annihilation of man, the cessation of his existence, but his eternal existence in torments. 2 Thess. 1:9: "Who shall be punished with everlasting destruction from the presence of the Lord." Matt. 25:46: "These shall go away into everlasting punishment." Hollaz, *Examen, "De Peccato,"* qu. 20: "Spiritual death is followed by bodily and eternal death."

The Scripture teaching on the guilt and punishment of sin needs to be constantly set before men, because depraved man, following the example of the devil and our first parents (Gen. 3:4-5, 12-13), is continually arguing against it. The temporal punishments (the disorders in the realm of nature: wearisome work, pain, calamities caused by storms, floods, and earthquakes, wars, temporal death), though they are before men's eyes, are regarded not as God's judgments over sin, but as natural phenomena.[21] And the eternal punishment is called in

---

[21] Luther on this point: "All the creatures are against us, prepared and armed to bring about, if possible, our destruction. How many are there whom fire and water destroy? How much peril threatens us from wild and venomous beasts, which harm not only our bodies but also our food, intended for our

question as being contrary to God's love and mercy (see the chapter on "Eternal Damnation" in Vol. III). – Also Christians, as far as they still are flesh, are in constant danger of forgetting the guilt and punishment of sin. The passage Mark 9:43-48 (threatening "eternal fire") is, according to the context, addressed, and particularly so, to the Christians. They need this preaching; they must ever bear in mind what would be the inevitable consequence of their sins, too, if they did not by daily repentance continue in spiritual life and crucify the flesh with its affections and lusts. Believers daily pray: "So teach us to number our days that we may apply our hearts unto wisdom" (Ps. 90:12).

Here would be the place to discuss the nature of the sufferings which befall believers here in this life (Ps. 73:14). Since their sins are not charged against the believers (Rom. 4:8) – they are free from the guilt and punishment of sin (Rom. 8:33: "Who shall lay anything to the charge of God's elect? It is God that justifieth"; Is. 53:5-6) and they have peace with God, Rom. 5:1 ff. – Scripture calls these punishments, on the one hand, a judgment of God upon the sins of the believers (1 Pet. 4:17: "The time is come that judgment must begin at the house of God"); on the other hand, Scripture teaches just as clearly that these punishments are intended as fatherly chastisements (*castigationes paternae*) and that their purpose is to keep us from apostasy (1 Cor. 11:32: "But when we are judged, we are chastened of the Lord, that we should not be condemned with the world"). Luther therefore calls these sufferings "a gracious and joyous punishment" (St. L. I:243).[22]

---

nourishment? Not to mention that we ourselves fall upon each other and murder each other, just as if there were not enough pestilence and other calamities to threaten us. . . . What are thorns, thistles, water, fire, caterpillars, flies, fleas, lice, bugs, etc., what are all these, jointly and severally, but messengers which preach to us of sin and of the wrath of God? . . . Therefore, though we know better and our eyes see it, we are living in a more than Egyptian darkness. Though all creatures ever remind us of the wrath of God, so that we cannot avoid seeing it, yet we do not pay any attention to it, but love this earthly life and cling to it as our only delight." (St. L. I:249 ff.; 254; 255.)

[22] See the Apology (*Trigl.* 299, 53 ff.) on these punishments that come upon the believers; they do not expiate for sin, as the Romanists teach. – The dogmaticians distinguish between τιμωρία and παιδεία. By τιμωρία they mean the just punishment of sin which is meted out to those who despise the reconciling blood of Christ (Heb. 10:29) and which consists in nothing less than eternal damnation. By παιδεία they mean the *castigationes paternae*, which are not punishments in the strict sense *(non ad vindicandam culpam iniuriamque Deo illatam compensandam inferuntur)*, but have the purpose to preserve from eternal damnation those whose guilt and punishment has been remitted by faith in the substitutionary satisfaction of Christ (1 Cor. 11:32).

b. ORIGINAL SIN

(De Peccato Originali)

1

Definition of Original Sin

Original sin, which is the sin which is not committed but which is inborn in man since Adam's Fall, embraces two things: a) hereditary guilt (*culpa hereditaria*), the guilt of the one sin of Adam which God imputes to all men; and b) hereditary corruption (*corruptio humanae naturae hereditaria*), which by imputation of Adam's guilt is transmitted to all his descendants through the natural descent from the first fallen pair. The Scripture proof for the original guilt is Rom. 5:18: "By the offense of one, judgment came upon all men to condemnation," and v. 19: "By one man's disobedience many were made sinners." The Scripture proof for the hereditary corruption, which is transmitted by natural birth, is Ps. 51:5: "Behold, I was shapen in iniquity, and in sin did my mother conceive me," and John 3:6: "That which is born of the flesh is flesh." The word "flesh" (σάρξ) here denotes, as the context shows, not merely the body, but the entire sinful man, particularly also the soul, with all its powers and activities. It describes the man who is outside the Kingdom of God and can enter into the Kingdom only by means of regeneration (vv. 3, 5). A parallel passage using the term "flesh" in this sense is Rom. 8:7: "The carnal mind is enmity against God."

It is particularly the doctrine of the original guilt which has aroused the antagonism of man. Pelagians, Socinians, Arminians, Quakers, and even some modern Lutherans insist that only that can be charged against man as a transgression which he has himself committed.[23] The antagonism runs the whole gamut, from simple denial to outright blasphemy.[24] Now, we frankly admit that human sentiment, because

---

[23] Quotations from the writings of the Pelagians, Socinians, and Arminians are given by Quenstedt, I, 995. On American sects (Socinians, Unitarians, Arminians, Quakers, Shakers, Mormons, Seventh-Day Adventists, etc.) see Guenther, *Pop. Symbolik,* p. 152 ff. [and *Popular Symbolics,* p. 89, and Index]. – On modern Lutherans, e. g., Vilmar, see Baier-Walther, II, p. 291 *sq.* – For a brief and correct presentation of the teaching of the dogmaticians on original guilt, see Nitzsch-Stephan, p. 315 f.; on the denial of original guilt on the part of modern theologians, including most of the conservatives, see p. 327 ff.

[24] The Pelagian Julianus: "The sin of another cannot be imputed by God to the little ones" (see Quenstedt, I, 995). Socinus: "It is wrong to say that

of the blindness of our heart (Eph. 4:18), rises in rebellion against the fact of the imputation of hereditary guilt. But that does not in the least change the fact which is set before us in God's Word, in Rom. 5:18-19, namely, that by the offense of one man judgment came upon all men to condemnation (κατάκριμα) and that by one man's disobedience the whole multitude of mankind (οἱ πολλοί) was placed before God in the category of sinners (ἁμαρτωλοὶ κατεστάθησαν). And there is the further fact that all men since Adam's fall are born with hereditary corruption (*corruptio hereditaria*) for the sole reason that they are guilty of Adam's sin.[25] As to the justice of this action of God, we must bear in mind the further fact that Scripture parallels the imputation of the sin of Adam and the imputation of the righteousness of Christ to all men. Rom. 5:18-19: "Therefore as by the offense of one, judgment came upon all men to condemnation; even so by the righteousness of One the free gift came upon all men unto justification of life. For as by one man's disobedience many were made sinners, so by the obedience of One shall many be made righteous." Those who reject the imputation of Adam's sin as an injustice are compelled, if they would be consistent, to declare the imputation of Christ's righteousness to be an injustice and to reject it; thus they take their stand outside the pale of Christianity.

In adducing proofs for the justice of the imputation of hereditary guilt, we must observe due caution. We may indeed point to the fact

---

Adam's transgression and disobedience has been imputed to mankind." The Socinian Volkelius: "We firmly deny that the sin of Adam is imputed to his descendants." (Quenstedt, *loc. cit.*) The Arminians in their Apology *Contra Censuram Leydensium*, p. 84: "Neither Scripture nor divine truthfulness, wisdom, and goodness, nor the nature of sin, nor the character of justice and equity, will permit them to say that Adam's sin has been imputed to Adam's descendants." (Quenstedt, *loc. cit.*) The Quakers in the *Declaration of Faith*, 1887: "We rejoice in believing that sin is not imputed to anyone until he transgresses the divine Law after having received sufficient ability to understand it" (Guenther, p. 153). The Quaker Barclay declares in his *Apology* (th. 4–5) that the doctrine of original guilt is an "unscriptural barbarism." (Guenther, *loc. cit.*)

[25] Following old dogmaticians, Hoenecke writes in his *Ev.-luth. Dogmatik* II, 413: "The sole reason why all men born since Adam are already at their birth in the state of corruption, into which Adam plunged by the Fall, is this, that God regards the deed of Adam as their deed, charges them with its guilt, and sentences them to be born in the miserable state of hereditary corruption as one deserved by themselves." And on p. 408 f. he has this: "The fall of Adam brings guilt and punishment to all men, not only because the corruption which is acquired through the Fall and is thereby inherited *(peccatum originis originatum)* renders them damnable before God *(imputatio mediata)*, but also because Adam's fall itself *(peccatum originis originans)* is imputed to them as their fault *(imputatio immediata)*.

that since Adam was the moral and physical head of all mankind, that one sinful act of his is therefore justly charged to his descendants.[26] But this argument is met by the counterargument: Is it right that the son should bear the iniquity of the father? Israel thus argued with its God (Ezekiel 18). Again, we may argue: "*Adami voluntas erat 'interpres' voluntatis omnium hominum*" (Adam's will was the interpreter of the will of all men), that is to say: God foresaw that we, in similar circumstances, would have acted the same as Adam. But here the objection has been raised today as well as formerly that it would seem fairer to let each person "interpret himself." Hence in the end we must take our stand on the one reason that silences all opposition. It is the reason to which Quenstedt, after having brought forward several other reasons, points in the words: "God as Judge, in accord with His supreme judicial authority, punishes the crime of lese majesty also in the descendants" (I, 994). God's imputation of Adam's guilt to his posterity is one of the "stubborn facts" against which all arguing is vain, foolish, godless. God is always just, also where His justice is beyond our comprehension. We may not and dare not measure the justice of God with a human yardstick.[27] And, in studying the imputation of Adam's sin, may we never forget the other fact which is published also in Scripture, the fact that the same God who condemned all men because of Adam's sin has also justified all men for the sake of Christ's righteousness. This is the truth set forth at length by the Apostle in the section Rom. 5:12-21. To ward off every misunderstanding of this passage, the Apostle himself summarizes his extended presentation with ἄρα οὖν (so then) in v. 18: "Therefore [so then] as by the offense of one, judgment came upon all men to condemnation; even so by the righteousness of One the free gift came upon all men unto justification of life." Christians are well aware of these facts, and therefore they sing: "As by one man all man-

---

[26] Thus Meisner in his *Anthropologie*, as quoted in Quenstedt, I, 995: "In any body, whether it be a physical or political or mystical body, that which the head does, as far as it is the head, is rightly imputed to the whole body. . . . The acts of the magistrate are imputed to the whole commonwealth, the acts of the *pater familias* to the whole family, to such an extent that the children are justly despoiled of all goods by the ruler because of the crime of rebellion, or lese majesty, though this was committed solely by the father."

[27] Baier points out this truth, though rather timidly: "It is not necessary, neither, perhaps, is it wise, that we should pryingly inquire how God could so impute the sin of our first parents to their posterity, not yet in existence, that for this reason they should necessarily be born destitute of original righteousness and as sinners. It is enough that τὸ ὅτι [the fact] is revealed, although τὸ πῶς [the explanation of it] be unknown." (II, 290.)

kind fell And, born in sin, was doomed to hell, So by one Man, who took our place, We all received the gift of grace" (*Hymnal* 369, 5). "Adam and Eve by their fall brought me death's ruination. Jesus, Thy life and Thy suffering gave me salvation. God of all grace, All grief and woes of my race Ended with Thy incarnation." (*Gesangbuch* 27, 2.)

There is not so much doubt about hereditary corruption (*corruptio hereditaria*). Human reason perceives something of it. Even pagan writers note a natural inclination of man toward evil. Horace writes: "For without faults no one is born; the happiest one is he who is oppressed by the least." (*Satir.* I, 3, 68 *sq.*) Again: "Even if you drive nature away with a pitchfork, still it continually returns" (*Epist.* I, 10, 24). Cicero: "As soon as we are born into the light, we are taken up immediately with all depravity and cast about in the utmost perversities of opinion; we seem to have imbibed error almost with our mother's milk" (*Tuscul. Disp.* III, 1). But the full understanding of the depth of the innate corruption and its origin in the fall of our first parents is gained only from the revelation of Holy Scripture. The Smalcald Articles point out this fact in the words: "This hereditary sin is so deep and horrible a corruption of nature that no reason can understand it, but it must be learned and believed from the revelation of Scripture" (*Trigl.* 477, I, 3). How little, e. g., Cicero knew of the depravity of human nature, in spite of his remark "we seem to have imbibed error almost with our mother's milk," is evident from the fact that both in the preceding and the following words he declares human nature to be basically good and traces the prevailing vices back to the wicked influence of nurses, teachers, and listening to and reading the poets. Hence the Formula of Concord declares that "no philosopher, no Papist, no sophist, yea, no human reason, however acute it may be, can give the right explanation [of the depth of the hereditary corruption], but all understanding and every explanation of it must be derived solely from the Holy Scriptures" (*Trigl.* 879, 60). Rolle says on the point that the hereditary corruption originated in the fall of our first parents: "Without the divine revelation no one can know that the propensity to evil arises from the fall of the first parents, is truly sin, and that on its account man is subjected to eternal damnation" (quoted in Baier-Walther, II, 281).

With regard to hereditary depravity erroneous views are held a) by all those who deny it altogether when they assert that children do not inherit the corruption from their parents through their birth (*generatione*), but learn it by following the evil example (*exemplo*), which is contrary to John 3:6: "That which is born of the flesh is flesh";[28] b) by all who admit a measure of corruption, but deny that it is sin, asserting that *peccatum* is always *voluntarium*, must be done deliberately, willfully, etc., which is contrary to Eph. 2:3: "And were by nature children of wrath"; [29] and c) by all those who minimize the hereditary corruption, which is done by the Semi-Pelagians and synergists of all ages. They do not regard fallen man as dead (νεκρός) in trespasses and sins (Eph. 2:1, 5), but ascribe to him, in varying degrees and under various designations, sufficient strength in spiritual matters to co-operate in his conversion; his obtaining God's favor and salvation does not depend solely on the grace of God for Christ's sake, but

---

[28] Thus the Pelagians: "Sin passes from the first man to other men not by propagation, but by imitation." (See Seeberg, *Dogmengeschichte*, I, 263, from Augustine's *De Peccator. Meritis et Remiss.* I, 9, 9; Quenstedt, I, 999, has a similar quotation from Augustine's *De Nat. et Gratia*, c. 9: "That all have sinned in Adam is [according to the Pelagians] said not because it is contracted through the natural birth, but because of imitation.") Exactly as expressed among the heathen by Seneca: "You err if you think that the faults are inborn in man; they befall us, are carried in" (*Epist.* 69. See Quenstedt, I, 999). The Socinians teach the same; see Guenther, *Pop. Symbolik*, p. 148 [*Pop. Symbolics*, pp. 396, 403]; Quenstedt, I, 1000; Plitt, *Grundriss der Symbolik*, 3d ed., p. 154.

[29] Thus Zwingli in *Fidei Ratio*, Niemeyer, p. 20: "Whether we like it or not, we are forced to admit that original sin, as we find it in the children of Adam, is not properly sin, as has already been shown; it is not an act done against the Law. It is therefore properly a disease and a condition." Rome teaches, *Trid.*, Sess. V, 5, that the inclination to sin *(concupiscentia, fomes)* which remains after Baptism is no longer sin, although Scripture sometimes calls it sin. "With regard to this concupiscence, which the Apostle sometimes calls sin (Rom. 6:7-8; Colossians 3), the holy Synod declares that the Catholic Church has never understood it to be called sin, as being truly and properly sin in those born again, but because it is of sin and inclines to sin." The Catechismus Romanus, "*De Baptismo*," qu. 32, says: "These desires (the appetites of the heart, which in their nature are contrary to reason) are far from the real nature of sin, unless the consent of the will or negligence is connected with them." It has previously been pointed out that among modern theologians also Hofmann makes "conscious" self-determination an integral factor of sin and as a result denies that this hereditary corruption is sin. Concerning the American sects which deny that original sin is sin, see Guenther, p. 152 ff. Concerning the Methodists, Guenther says, p. 151: "The Methodists, whose Confession of Faith is an excerpt from the 39 Articles of the Episcopal Church, omit in the article of original sin the important words: 'And this infection of nature doth remain, yea, in them that are regenerated. . . . And although there is no condemnation for them that believe and are baptized; yet the Apostle doth confess that concupiscence and lust hath of itself the nature of sin.' The doctrine that concupiscence is truly sin also in the regenerate does not fit in with their doctrine of perfection." Wesley said: "Such [involuntary] transgressions you call sins, if you please; I do not." (More on this in the chapter "The Imperfection of Sanctification," in Vol. III.)

depends also on his self-determination, or self-decision, on his proper conduct, on his lesser guilt in comparison with others, etc.[30]

Every minimizing of the hereditary corruption, whether in the crass Papist-Arminian form or in a finer or the finest form, in which it has crept into the Lutheran Church, involves a denial of the *sola gratia* and accordingly of the whole Christian religion. This fact calls for a separate chapter on the effect of original sin on the mind and will of man.

2

The Effect of Hereditary Corruption on the Mind and Will of Man

While natural man, after the Fall, still retains a certain amount of intelligence in natural things (Augustana, Art. XVIII), he is utterly

[30] The popish sect teaches that in fallen man the ability to do good, that is, to obtain justification and salvation, is not entirely lost, but only weakened. *Trid.*, Sess. VI, can. 4: "If anyone saith that man's free will, moved and excited by God, by assenting to God exciting and calling, nowise co-operates toward disposing and preparing itself for obtaining the grace of justification, . . . let him be anathema." Can. 5: "If anyone saith that, since Adam's sin the free will of man is lost and extinguished . . . let him be anathema." Sess. VI, can. 1, declares that the *liberum arbitrium* of Gentiles and Jews, "attenuated as it was in its powers, was by no means extinguished in them." The Arminian position is essentially the Catholic one. The Catholic J. A. Moehler gives them credit for this: "Their [the Arminians'] articles of belief on these points are nearly identical with the Catholic; and therefore, like the Council of Trent, they speak of a resuscitating grace, which only awakens the dormant powers still existing in fallen man, in opposition to the Lutheran theory, according to which the higher faculties must first be created anew in them" (*Symbolik*, 5th ed., p. 634). Quenstedt quotes (I, 1103) from the Arminian *Collatio Hagiensis* (1610): "There are two causes of faith and conversion: One is the so-called prevenient and exciting grace of God, the second is the will of man, sequent and co-operative. For the gift of faith is not given without the co-operation of the human will. We affirm that man co-operates in his regeneration." In the *Apologia pro Confessione Remonstrantium* (Leyden, 1630, p. 162) it is stated that the divine grace "without the co-operation of the free human will" would accomplish nothing. On the Arminian sects, Methodists, Mennonites, etc., see Guenther, *Symbolik*, p. 159 (*Popular Symbolics*, pp. 284, 260, 270, 280). — The synergistic Lutherans, too, from the later Melanchthon on down to the most recent days, minimize the Scripture teaching of the hereditary corruption. That will be shown in the *locus* on conversion, Vol. II. When they speak of a *facultas se applicandi ad gratiam*, of a *liberum arbitrium* given to man before his conversion, enabling him "to determine himself," "decide himself" *pro* or *contra*, and declare that actual conversion depends on man's proper conduct or on his lesser guilt in comparison with others, they presuppose that man after the Fall is not dead, but only half dead, seemingly dead. The synergists with their doctrine of hereditary depravity do not belong in the Lutheran, but in the Roman and the Arminian camp.

incapable of understanding spiritual matters, the things that have to do with the obtaining of God's grace and salvation. In his natural condition, man regards the Gospel, his only salvation after the Fall (John 3:16-18; Acts 4:12, etc.), as foolishness, and he cannot do otherwise. 1 Cor. 2:14: "They are foolishness unto him, neither can he know them." And he turns to the Law, which denounces the wrath of God and damnation against him (Gal. 3:10-12), as offering him a way of salvation. Therefore Scripture gives the intelligence of all natural men this rating: "Having the understanding darkened" (Eph. 4:18); "Ye were sometimes darkness" (Eph. 5:8); "The people that walked in darkness" (Is. 9:2); "The darkness shall cover the earth" (Is. 60:2); "Are ye so foolish?" (Gal. 3:3.) Nor can any human schooling or culture remove this lack of intelligence. Scripture tells us very plainly that the σοφία θεοῦ, the Gospel of Christ, crucified for the sins of the world, remains hidden even from the aristocrats of mankind. 1 Cor. 2:7-8: "The wisdom of God . . . which none of the princes of this world knew." Col. 2:8: "Beware lest any man spoil you through philosophy."

The will of natural man gets the same rating. According to Scripture the will is not only opposed to the Law of God, but it cannot change its condition; *non potest non peccare*. Rom. 8:7: "The carnal mind is enmity against God; for it is not subject to the Law of God, neither indeed can be." Even when natural man desires to do things externally good, e. g., feed the hungry, clothe the naked, etc., he is not moved by love of God, but he acts, at best, from natural compassion. Such works are praiseworthy in the natural domain or in the civil domain, and they have, as the *iustitia civilis* in general, their temporal reward; [31] but they remain sinful before God because they do not comply with the demands which God's Law makes on every man. God's Law is νόμος πνευματικός, a spiritual Law (Rom. 7:14). It is not satisfied with works that are performed from any kind of motive, but demands very definitely that love of God be the motive of every act of man. Matt. 22:37: "Thou shalt love the Lord, thy God, with all thy heart and with all thy soul and with all thy mind." And natural

[31] See further the chapter on "The Good Works of the Heathen," in Vol. III. We have an example for this in the hospitality extended to Paul and his shipwrecked companions by the heathen inhabitants of the Island of Malta. "The barbarous people showed us no little kindness [φιλανθρωπία, love of men], for they kindled a fire and received us everyone, because of the present rain and because of the cold" (Acts 28:2). The temporal reward is also mentioned. After Paul had healed the sick father of the governor of the island, "others also which had diseases in the island came and were healed" (v. 9).

man will never come to love God. Because of his transgressions he has an evil conscience and can do nothing but flee from God. He lives without hope and without God (as an ἄθεος) in the world, as Paul convinces all heathen from their own experience (Eph. 2:12). That being the case, how can he love God and do his works for God's sake? The more God's Law presses him with its demands, the more it becomes evident that "the carnal mind is enmity against God" (Rom. 8:7). Luther's oft-repeated remark that "he wished there were no God" is no exaggeration.

In short, man's inner attitude toward God's Gospel (1 Cor. 1:23) and toward God's Law (Rom. 8:7) is one of enmity. This is the effect of original sin on the mind and will of man.

How completely the Fall ruined the mind and will of man may be seen from the behavior of Adam and Eve after they had transgressed God's commandment. As Luther says in his exposition of Gen. 3:10, "Adam is totally changed and has become quite another man" (St. L. I:213. Opp. ex., Erl. I, 220). The intelligence of Adam suffered an eclipse, and his will is changed into an evil will. Luther's entire exposition of this point should be read again and again (St. L. I:199–223). Taking issue with Rome's teaching according to which the loss of the divine image, merely a *donum superadditum*, left the natural powers of man essentially unimpaired, Luther says: "Since this doctrine detracts from the magnitude of original sin, it is to be shunned as a deadly poison."

Luther proceeds to show how the conduct of Adam and Eve after the Fall reveals their folly and wickedness. Their flight from God proves their foolishness: "We can entertain no doubt that the understanding had become corrupt, seeing the device by which Adam and Eve hoped to accomplish their safety. Was it not the very extreme of folly (*extrema stultitia*): first, to attempt the impossible in trying to flee from Him whom no one can escape or avoid; and, in the next place, to attempt the flight in such a foolish way (*stulto modo*), thinking thc trees would afford them safety, when they must have known that no iron wall, no great mountain could save them? . . . As it was folly (*stulte*) for Adam to attempt to flee from God, so he answers Him in the utmost folly (*stultissime respondet*). So utterly is he bereft by sin of all wisdom and counsel." The reason Adam gives for fleeing from God is that he heard the voice of God. But that reasoning was utterly foolish. "Had he not heard the voice of the Lord before, when the Lord forbade him to eat of the fruit of the tree? Why did he not then also fear and hide himself? How was it that then he stood with joy and with uplifted countenance, seeing and hearing God? He is no longer the same Adam; he is totally changed (*mutatus*) and has become quite another man; he now looks about for a lie and a false cause for his defense." As a further reason for his flight Adam mentions his nakedness. "The poor wretched man never thinks that he had no such fear before and was not ashamed of his nakedness then. For as God had thus created him, why should he be ashamed of that which God had made? He then walked in his nakedness before God and all creatures in Paradise, for he knew that God loved him and he loved God. But now he is ashamed of his nakedness, flees from God, and hides himself."

Moreover, when God faces Adam with the true and only reason for his flight and shame because of his nakedness, namely, that he had eaten of the tree in spite of God's commandment: "Thou shalt not eat of it," Adam more than ever manifests the corruption of heart and will that had set in. He pleads: "The woman whom Thou gavest to be with me, she gave me of the tree, and I did eat." The state of Adam's heart, which caused him to make such a defense, Luther describes thus: "When Adam was convinced of the sinfulness of his sin in what he had done, he attempts to defend his act as right (*iure*) and says: 'If Thou hadst not given me this woman, I should not have eaten the fruit.' Thus he lays all blame for his sin on God, and he charges God therewith." And as to Eve, Luther says: "Now behold the example of Eve, who, being corrupted by sin, is seen to be in no degree better than Adam (*nihilo melior est quam Adam*). Adam wanted to appear innocent and laid the blame on God, because He had given him a wife. And so also Eve attempts to excuse herself and puts the blame on the serpent, which also was a creature of God. She confesses indeed that she had eaten of the apple, but, says she, the serpent, which Thou hast created and which Thou permittedst to walk about in Paradise, has deceived me. Is that not blaming the Creator and disavowing one's own guilt?"

Luther drew this description of the corruption wrought by the Fall in human nature, in man's intellect and will, not from his own notions, but on the basis of God's own Word (Gen. 3:7-13). It is therefore entirely correct. And this depravity has been transmitted through natural propagation from the first fallen pair to all their descendants, as Christ affirms in John 3:6: "That which is born of the flesh is flesh," and all statements of the Scriptures of the Old and New Testaments tell the same story. The record of every man is set down Gen. 6:5: "Every imagination of the thoughts of his heart was only evil continually." We have in Rom. 3:10-18 a comprehensive description of the corrupt state of human nature, as to both intellect and will, made up of statements of the Old Testament: "There is none righteous, no, not one. There is none that understandeth, there is none that seeketh after God. . . . And the way of peace have they not known. There is no fear of God before their eyes." And Paul here stresses in particular that this description takes in all of mankind and fits both Jews and Gentiles equally.

The Lutheran Church has embodied this description of the hereditary corruption fully and completely in the Second Article of the Augsburg Confession: "Of Original Sin": "Also they teach that since the fall of Adam, all men begotten in the natural way are born with sin, that is, without the fear of God, without trust in God, and with concupiscence; and that this disease, or vice of origin, is truly sin, even now condemning and bringing eternal death upon those not born again through Baptism and the Holy Ghost. They condemn the Pelagians and others who deny that original depravity is sin and who, to obscure the glory of Christ's merit and benefits, argue that man can be justified before God by his own strength and reason." (*Trigl.* 431.)

3

The Negative and the Positive Side of Original Corruption

Holy Scripture describes the original corruption not only as a defect, that is, a lack of the concreated righteousness, but also as evil lust (*concupiscentia*), that is, the habitual inner inclination to evil. Gal. 5:17: "The flesh lusteth against the spirit"; Rom. 7:23: "I see another law in my members, warring against the law of my mind." Both the positive and the negative side are mentioned in Art. II of the Augsburg Confession: "All men begotten in the natural way are born with sin, that is, without the fear of God, without trust in God, and with concupiscence" (*Trigl.*, p. 43).[32] In so far as original corruption is concupiscence, we may call it something positive.

---

[32] In defending this statement, the Apology says: "We, therefore, have been right in expressing, in our description of original sin" [in Art. II of the Augsburg Conf.], "both, namely, these defects: the not being able to believe God, the not being able to fear and love God; and, likewise: the having concupiscence, which seeks carnal things contrary to God's Word, i. e., seeks not only the pleasure of the body, but also carnal wisdom and righteousness, and, con-

This is not to say that original sin is something positive in the sense of being a substance if by substance we mean *substantia materialis, quae proprie subsistit,* i. e., a thing existing by itself, having a separate existence. If we distinguish between substance and accident in this manner that by substance we mean a thing having a separate existence, and by accident something inherent in a thing as a separable attribute, then certainly original corruption is an accident; for human nature, also after the Fall, still remains God's creation and as such is good in itself and remains good. This distinction must be maintained against every form of Manichaeism, which assumes two substances, one good, the other evil. The Formula of Concord declares in Art. I, "Of Original Sin": "We believe, teach, and confess that there is a distinction . . . between the nature [itself], which even after the Fall is and remains a creature of God, and original sin. . . . For God created not only the body and soul of Adam and Eve before the Fall, but also our bodies and our souls after the Fall, notwithstanding that they are corrupt, which God also still acknowledges as His work, as it is written, Job 10:8: 'Thine hands have made me and fashioned me together round about.'" To assume that the human nature as such, or according to its substance, is sin, would conflict with the articles of the Christian faith concerning creation, redemption, sanctification, and resurrection. For the Son of God assumed the human nature, without sin, indeed, but according to its substance, its essence, into the unity of His person. He has also "redeemed it as His work, sanctified it as

---

temning God, trusts in these as good things. Not only the ancients [like Augustine and others], but also the more recent [teachers and scholastics], at least the wiser ones among them" *(cordatiores)* "teach that original sin is at the same time truly these, namely, the *defects* which I have recounted, and *concupiscence.*" (*Trigl.* 111, 27 f.) As for the Scripture proof, "Paul sometimes expressly calls it a defect [a lack of divine light], as 1 Cor. 2:14: 'The natural man receiveth not the things of the Spirit of God.' In another place, Rom. 7:5, he calls it concupiscence, working in our members to bring forth fruit unto death." (*Loc. cit.,* § 30.) Over against the calumnies of the Papists, Luther's doctrine of the original corruption is thus presented: "He [Luther] always wrote thus, namely, that Baptism removes the guilt of original sin [the hereditary guilt], although the material, as they call it, of the sin, i. e., concupiscence, remains. . . . In the same manner, Augustine also speaks, who says: 'Sin is remitted in Baptism, not in such a manner that it no longer exists, but so that it is not imputed.'" (*Loc. cit.,* § 36.) The positive character of the original corruption is proved from the fact that this corruption is a part of the punishment *(poena)* laid upon Adam's fall. "The defects and the concupiscence are punishments and sins. Death and other bodily evils, and the dominion of the devil, are properly punishments. For human nature has been delivered into slavery and is held captive by the devil, who infatuates with wicked opinions and errors, and impels it to sins of every kind." (*Loc. cit.,* § 47.)

His work, raises it from the dead, and gloriously adorns it as His work. But original sin He has not created, assumed, redeemed, sanctified; nor will He raise it, will neither adorn nor save it in the elect, but in the blessed resurrection it will be entirely destroyed." (*Trigl.* 779 f.)

On the other hand, we maintain against Pelagianism and synergism that original sin is an "accident" which has infected the entire substance of the human nature. It has so totally corrupted human nature that man is become incapable of any spiritual good and inclined to all evil. Rom. 7:18: "I know that in me (that is, in my flesh) dwelleth no good thing." And we maintain, furthermore, that this inherited corruption clings so firmly to our nature that no human power or endeavor, but only God's grace and almighty power, exercised for Christ's sake, can free us from it. Rom. 8:3: "The Law could not do" it. The Formula of Concord summarizes it thus: "We believe, teach, and confess that original sin is not a slight [*levis*] but so deep a corruption of human nature that nothing healthy or uncorrupt has remained in man's body or soul, in his inner or outward powers, but, as the Church sings: 'Through Adam's fall is all corrupt, Nature and essence human.' This damage is unspeakable, and cannot be discerned by reason, but only from God's Word. And [we affirm] that no one but God alone can separate from one another the nature and this corruption of the nature." (*Trigl.* 781, 8–10.)

While the First Article of the Formula of Concord was prompted by Flacius' wrong and tenaciously defended expression that original sin is the substance of fallen man, this article is at the same time directed against Pelagianism, Semi-Pelagianism, and the synergism of Strigel and all Philippists, as the antitheses (*Trigl.* 781, 1–6) clearly demonstrate.[33]

---

[33] See Carpzov's remark on Flacius (*Isagoge in Libros Symbolicos,* p. 1160): "If he only had corrected his language, this great quarrel would never have arisen, and the orthodox party could easily have come to an understanding with him." Flacius called original sin the *forma substantialis,* but distinguished that from the *forma "materialis"*; original sin is not the *forma materialis.* It seems that by *forma materialis* Flacius understood what other people call substance, and by *forma substantialis* what we call accident. Carpzov: ". . . Flacius did not by *essentia* and *forma essentialis* understand the substance itself in so far as it signifies a thing subsisting by itself, but rather that essence which is man's not in so far as he is a man *(homo),* but in so far as he is . . . a corrupt man, namely, the accidental form, which, together with the subject itself, is . . . essential to the corrupt man, so that, so long as and so far as he is corrupt, corruption and wickedness cannot, even in thinking, be separated from him." See the thorough discussion of "The Flacian Controversy" by F. Bente in the "Historical Introductions to the Symbolical Books." (*Trigl.* 144 f.) Plitt is right in remarking that Flacius has been "habitually and from ignorance" condemned beyond all measure (R. E., 2d ed., IV, 563 ff.).

4

The Subject of Hereditary Corruption

Subiectum quod of the hereditary depravity are all men, all natural descendants of Adam. We have sufficiently treated this point above. The one exception is Christ. He is exempt from original sin because He assumed the human nature not by natural generation, but through the operation of the Holy Ghost. Matt. 1:20: "That which is conceived in her is of the Holy Ghost." *Conceptus est de Spiritu Sancto. Natus ex Maria virgine.* Therefore, according to His human nature, Christ is called "that holy thing which shall be born of thee" (Luke 1:35).[34]

The Virgin Mary does not form an exception. Not Scripture, but the decretal of Pius IX, 1854, took her, in the interest of Mariolatry, out of the category of sinners and ascribed to her an immaculate conception.[35]

In defining the subject of original sin it is also of great importance to determine exactly where in man the hereditary corruption has its true seat *(subiectum quo peccati originalis, subiectum proprium,* πρῶτον δεκτικόν). The dogmaticians answer: The soul is the primary, the body the secondary, seat of original corruption, since the body is the organ of the soul. Baier: "*Subiectum quo primarium* of original sin is the soul with its faculties, namely, the intellect, the will, and the sensuous appetite; secondarily, however, and as a consequent, also the members of the body must be mentioned" (Baier-Walther, II, 295). Elucidating this point, the dogmaticians say: As the body before the Fall partook in the original righteousness as the organ of the righteous soul, serving the soul in performing the works of righteousness and holiness, so now, after the Fall, it participates in the unrighteousness, since it is the organ of the totally depraved soul and as such is placed with all its members into the service of sin. Scripture teaches this

---

[34] See the section entitled "Peculiarities of Christ's Human Nature," in Vol. II.

[35] The decretal reads: "We declare, pronounce, and define that the doctrine which holds that the most Blessed Virgin Mary, in the first instant of her conception, by a special grace and privilege of Almighty God, in view of the merits of Jesus Christ, the Savior of mankind, was preserved free from all stain of original sin, has been revealed by God and therefore is to be firmly and steadfastly believed by all the faithful. Wherefore, if any shall presume, which may God avert, to think in their heart otherwise than has been defined by us, let them know and, moreover, understand that they are condemned by their own judgment, that they have made shipwreck as regards the faith, and have fallen away from the unity of the Church."

truth expressly. It speaks of "eyes full of adultery" (2 Pet. 2:14) and lists, so to say, the members of the body in their evil activity, Rom. 3:13-18: "Their throat is an open sepulcher; with their tongues they have used deceit; the poison of asps is under their lips; whose mouth is full of cursing and bitterness; their feet are swift to shed blood; destruction and misery are in their ways." And when the Apostle adds (vv. 17-18): "And the ways of peace have they not known, there is no fear of God before their eyes," he is tracing the wickedness performed by the member of the body back to its primary seat, the soul, to the highest faculties of the soul, to the intellect and will. When Papists and others, including some modern theologians, make the lower powers (*"Sinnlichkeit," appetitus sensitivus*) the true seat of sin, they are not in harmony with Scripture. The Formula of Concord expresses the Scriptural truth when it says "that we all by disposition and nature inherit from Adam such a heart, feeling, and thought as are, according to their highest powers and light of reason, naturally inclined and disposed directly contrary to God and His chief commandments, yea, that they are enmity against God, especially as regards divine and spiritual things" (*Trigl.* 863, 11).

5

The Effects of Original Corruption

We have already shown at length that original corruption includes spiritual death, the condition of being dead in trespasses and sins (Eph. 2:1, 5), of being alienated from the life of God (Eph. 4:18), and that if this spiritual death is not removed through faith in Christ, who blots out sin, it will be followed by temporal death and by eternal death, eternal damnation. We now add some particulars.

With regard to temporal death, the question has been ventilated much, from the days of the Church Fathers down to our day, whether the words: "In the day that thou eatest thereof thou shalt surely die" (Gen. 2:17) meant that death would ensue at a later period or whether it would set in immediately with the sinning. It would seem that the latter is meant. The expression "in the day that," etc., links the dying closely with the act of sinning. The final total separation of body and soul is simply the culmination of the dissolution which began at once. All men are in the process of dying from their birth, because they are Adam's children and thus sinners. The infirmities and sicknesses to which we are subject are the gradual loosening of the bond uniting body and soul; they are the early stages of the complete separation that will come to pass sooner or later.[36]

Of far greater importance is the question just why the eating of the forbidden fruit brought death to Adam and Eve. Modern theologians, such as Delitzsch and Hofmann, have expressed the view that death was not caused by the transgression of the divine commandment (Gen. 2:17), but rather was caused by the fact that the devil had taken possession of the forbidden tree, in consequence of which the eating had such an evil effect on "the physical nature" of Adam and Eve that their sensual desire was focused on "a material thing." This strange notion, inspired by the determination to take from the first sin the stigma of ἀνομία, of a direct violation of God's Word,[37] is in conflict with the Biblical report and turns it topsy-turvy. The devil begins his seductive work not by calling Eve's attention to the edibility and beauty of the fruit, but by creating, first and foremost, doubt of God's Word. He suggests to Eve that God could hardly have given such a strange commandment. Eve, well-informed as to God's command and the punishment placed by God on its transgression, responds: "God hath said, Ye shall not eat of it, neither shall ye touch it, lest ye die." But when the Tempter perceives that Eve does not indignantly turn from him, but finds that she is beginning to doubt the truth of the divine Word, he openly contradicts the Word of God and answers her that eating of the forbidden fruit will not result in death, but in great progress in knowledge. This argument against God's Word pleases Eve, and now she sees the tree in a new light, as "a tree to be desired to make one wise." Then "she took of the fruit thereof, and did eat, and gave also unto her husband with her, and he did eat." Such was the origin of the first sin: it bore the nature of ἀνομία. Eve

---

[36] Gerhard, *Loci, locus "De Morte,"* § 17: "Because we, their [the first parents'] descendants, always carry with us in this life that venom of sin in our bodies, we also always carry with us our death; we do not meet death suddenly, but approach it step by step."

[37] See Delitzsch, in his commentary on Genesis, first edition, quoted in Baier-Walther, II, 305; the third edition maintains the same interpretation. Also Hofmann, *Schriftbeweis,* I, 465 ff. Hofmann agrees with Delitzsch also in asserting that the fruit of the tree was evil in itself: "The fruit directly caused a corruption of the body, in so far as it serves propagation, and it did that through a power inherent in the fruit itself" (p. 477). He will not have death regarded as a result of the wrath of God over sin, but as "an evil which befell man through the eating of the fruit." He accordingly translates טוֹב וָרָע not with "good and evil," but with "good and harmful" (*"gut und schlimm"*). Kliefoth is right in saying: "If sin does not begin with enmity against God, neither does redemption begin with *reconciliation*" (*Der Schriftbeweis des D. von Hofmann,* p. 287). And, as is well known, Hofmann did deny the *satisfactio vicaria* Christi.

clearly knew, but deliberately set aside the divine νόμος. The fruit of the forbidden tree did not kill because it was in itself harmful or evil, but because it was forbidden.

Luther goes into this matter thoroughly. He epitomizes his presentation with the words: "Adam did indeed force his teeth into this apple; but in reality his teeth struck upon the sting in this apple, which was God's prohibition and disobedience to God. This was the real and true cause of this tragedy, that Adam sinned against God and despised His command and obeyed the devil. The tree of the knowledge of good and evil was good and bore the most noble fruit; but since the prohibition of God was attached to it and man disregarded it, the tree became more deadly than poison. . . . *Arbor scientiae boni et mali occidit virtute verbi prohibentis.*" (St. L. I:117 f. Opp. ex., Erl. I, 120 *sq.*)

We are here strongly reminded of the analogous way by which modern theology has arrived at the denial that Scripture is the Word of God. Their thought processes are about as follows: Are the Scriptures, which speak in so human a manner, in the human tongue, indeed God's Word? True, this has been assumed by the primitive Church, then by the Church of the Reformation, and particularly by the dogmaticians. And there is a certain excuse for this assumption; at that time the sense for "reality" was still undeveloped. But since, because of the great progress in all branches of science, the "well-developed sense of reality" has become the special endowment of our day, it is wholly impossible for men today to "identify" Scripture with the Word of God. At this point they form the definite judgment: Scripture is not the Word of God, and they regard it as imperative to flee away from Scripture into the "pious self-consciousness of the theologizing subject." The final result is: All theologians who practice theology in this manner are actually become as God, yea, superior to God, for now they know how much of God's Word is good, how much evil. One cannot fail to see here an analogy to the first deception of the devil.

In connection with the Fall, which occurred as a result of eating of the forbidden tree, the question is again and again raised, why the *lex paradisiaca* (the law given to man in Paradise) turned on such an unimportant, yea, arbitrary matter; would it not have been more appropriate if the "paradisiacal law" had embraced the entire Decalog? Similar thoughts have arisen in the hearts of many Christians in reading the story of the fall. "I ask you," says Brenz,[38] "what the idea is

---

[38] Quoted in *Lehre und Wehre*, 24, p. 193 f.

in God's prohibiting the eating of the fruit of a tree and not rather some other kind of sin? . . . Why does He not rather recite to Adam the Decalog, which later in the desert of Sinai He recited to the Israelites?" Brenz answers: 1) The Decalog as natural Law was already inscribed in the hearts of Adam and Eve and therefore stood in no need of a special proclamation; and 2) it therefore pleased God to give them a commandment for the exercise and proof of their obedience which was not written in their hearts. Luther stresses the point very much. We take the proper attitude toward God only when we freely and willingly subject ourselves to His Word also when we do not understand why God speaks, commands, and acts just in this way and not in another. Luther says: "After all things had been delivered to Adam, that he might use them according to his pleasure for his need or for his enjoyment, God finally (*tandem*) demands of him that he prove his reverence and obedience in this tree of the knowledge of good and evil and thus, in a way, exercise divine worship." At this point, Luther goes on to say, the matter becomes "theological"; the preceding regulations concerned only things of nature or of the family or civil government.

The theologians especially should note this point. Modern theology lies prostrate with this grievous malady that instead of taking the Christian doctrine from Scripture alone, they would obtain the doctrine by way of investigation (*erkenntnismaessig*) and according to their findings either accept or reject it. Against this pestilence – the expression is not too sharp – also they must be on their guard who sincerely accept the word: "If any man speak, let him speak as the oracles of God" (1 Pet. 4:11). This pestilence forms a part of the original corruption, which clings to us throughout our life on earth; for a characteristic of this corruption is not only the *propagabilitas a parentibus ad liberos,* but also the *"tenacitas" seu pertinax inhaerentia per omnem vitam.*[39]

One of the consequences of the hereditary corruption is the loss of free will in spiritual matters. This is really no new subject, for all that can be said in this matter is already contained in the statement of Scripture that every man is "dead in trespasses and sins." But since the term "free will" does not always mean the same thing and this ambiguity of meaning has been used for the purpose of denying the "death in trespasses," a special treatment is called for. Where ambiguity prevails, the rule applies: *Bene docet, qui bene distinguit.* In accordance with this rule, the following is to be said:

---

[39] Thus the dogmaticians. See Baier-Walther, II, 305 *sq.*

a. If by "free will" is meant that man in distinction from the irrational creatures still has a will of his own and wills things, we shall have to say that man also after the Fall has a free will. Though fallen man is dead in sins and cannot but sin, *non potest non peccare* (Eph. 2:1, 5; Col. 2:13; Rom. 6:13; 8:7), he nevertheless sins voluntarily and gladly. The desire to sin is innate in him. John 3:6: He is σάρξ by birth; the state of this σάρξ is described Rom. 8:7: "The carnal mind is enmity against God"; also Gen. 8:21: "The imagination of man's heart is evil from his youth." We call this freedom of the will *libertas a coactione* or formal freedom. Coercion contradicts the very nature of the will. Therefore Gerhard correctly states that freedom of the will, conceived as freedom from coercion, and the servitude of sin, whereby man cannot but sin, agree very well. "There exists in man freedom of will along with the servitude of sin; for he both sins and cannot refrain from sinning (*non potest non peccare*), and nevertheless he sins freely and delights in sin; although he is moved to nothing but evil, yet he chooses it freely, i. e., willingly and spontaneously, not unwillingly or under coercion, and is moved to it with all his energy" (*Loci, locus "De Libero Arbitrio,"* § 29).[40]

b. If by free will is meant the ability to will or desire what is spiritually good, to believe the Gospel of Christ and out of love of God to keep God's Law, we deny that since the Fall man has a free will. He cannot know the Gospel as the truth, but regards it as foolishness (1 Cor. 2:14; 1:23), and he cannot subject himself to God's Law, but can only hate it (Rom. 8:7). We are speaking only of free will in this sense when we say that man after the Fall and before regeneration has no free will, cannot decide for the Gospel, but can only reject it. Lest the *status controversiae* be shifted, it must be borne in mind that we are here not concerned with the will of man in itself, but with the object of his will.[41]

c. To be sure, fallen man, to a certain extent, still can render

---

[40] The *toto impetu* ("with all his energy") is exemplified by the exceeding readiness of the Unitarians, the lodges, Communists, a part of the Socialists, etc., to reject the Christian religion, of Rome to anathematize in the Tridentinum the Christian doctrine of justification, and of modern Lutherans to assail both Scripture as the Word of God and the *satisfactio vicaria*.

[41] Gerhard, *Loci, locus "De Libero Arbitrio,"* § 32: "The whole question turns on the liberty in regard to the object with which the will is occupied." On Bellarmine's willful beclouding of the issue, Gerhard says in Par. 8: "Away therefore with those frightful accusations which Bellarmine in the preface of the books on free will hurls against our churches, as though we abolished the freedom of the will, do violence to nature itself, and declare ourselves to be similar not only to brutes, but to brutes bereft altogether of reason."

an external, or civil, righteousness (*iustitia carnalis, operum, carnis*). But we are constrained to add the qualification "to a certain extent." This civil righteousness does not amount to much. The innate concupiscence and the enticement of the devil, who exercises dominion over the non-Christians (Eph. 2:2; Col. 1:13; Acts 26:18), is so strong that the restraining power of natural probity, education, culture, and other props of civic righteousness proves itself but a spider's web. All these points are brought out by the Apology, in the article *"De Libero Arbitrio"*: "The human will has liberty in the choice of works and things which reason can comprehend by itself. It can to a certain extent render civil righteousness or the righteousness of works; it can speak of God, offer to God a certain service by an outward work, obey magistrates, parents; in the choice of an outward work it can restrain the hands from murder, from adultery, from theft. Since there is left in human nature reason and judgment concerning objects subjected to the senses, choice between these things and the liberty and power to render civil righteousness are also left. For Scripture calls this the righteousness of the flesh which the carnal nature, i. e., reason, renders by itself, without the Holy Ghost. Although the power of concupiscence is such that men more frequently obey evil dispositions than sound judgment. And the devil, who is efficacious in the godless, as Paul says, Eph. 2:2, does not cease to incite the feeble nature to various offenses. These are the reasons why even civil righteousness is rare among men, as we see that not even the philosophers themselves, who seem to have aspired after this righteousness, attained it." (*Trigl.* 335, 70 f.)

The list of specious arguments for the free will of natural man in spiritual matters is quite imposing. 1. Faith in Christ, or conversion, and the observance of the commandments of God, is demanded of men. 2. Unless man co-operates (*facultas se applicandi at gratiam*, etc.), conversion would imply coercion. 3. God works only the power to believe, not the act of faith. 4. Without human co-operation the subject who believes would not be man, but the Holy Ghost. 5. Since the reason for man's non-conversion lies in man, the decisive reason for the conversion of man must "according to invincible logic" also lie in man. 6. Conversion must be conceived as a "moral" process. 7. *Homo "libere" se convertit;* faith is "free obedience." 8. The *iustitia civilis*, education, culture, science, etc., also have a part in the conversion of man. 9. Natural man still has the power to use the means of grace, to go to church, listen attentively, etc. These arguments are examined and refuted in Volume II, under the "Doctrine of Conversion," and material from history of doctrine is there given. The true reasons which lead men to assert the freedom of will in spiritual matters — self-righteousness and self-conceit — are fully set forth there.[42]

d. The hereditary corruption results, finally, in the various sinful acts, the actual sins (*peccata actualia*). Scripture definitely declares the innate evil condition to be the source of the individual sinful acts. Thus Psalm 51 traces the actual sin of adultery ("he had gone in to Bathsheba") to its evil source: "Behold, I was shapen in iniquity; and in sin did my mother conceive me "(v. 5). According to John 3:5 men are by their natural birth σάρξ (flesh), and according to Gal. 5:19-21 "adultery, fornication, uncleanness, lasciviousness, idolatry, witchcraft, hatred, variance, emulations, wrath, strife, seditions, heresies, envyings, murders, drunkenness, revelings, and such like," are the works of the flesh, actions proceeding from the hereditary corruption. That leads to the chapter on the actual sins (*peccata actualia*).

c. ACTUAL SIN

(De Peccato Actuali)

1

Definition of Actual Sin

By actual sin (*peccatum actuale*) we understand the ἀνομία which is done or committed by man. We distinguish it from the ἀνομία which, being innate in man, is not done by man, but is present before

[42] Note on the history of the doctrine. First of all one should read Erasmus' *De Libero Arbitrio* Διατριβή, 1524 (translated in St. L. XVIII:1600 ff.) and Luther's answer *De Servo Arbitrio* (translated in St. L. XVIII:1668 ff.). The arguments of Erasmus for a free will in spiritual matters are identical with the arguments with which the Lutheran doctrines of conversion and election have been attacked as Calvinistic in the past and the present century. Luther's *De Servo Arbitrio* has been quite universally misunderstood; see in Vol. II the chapter "The Theological Terminology Regarding the Divine Will of Grace" and in the chapter "The Pernicious Character of Synergism" the section dealing with the assertion that the "later" Luther receded from the position he took in *De Servo Arbitrio*. See also in Baier-Walther, II, 300 ff., the antithesis from Quenstedt (Pelagians, Semi-Pelagians, Scholastics, Papists, Arminians, Lutheran synergists of the 16th and 17th centuries), together with the false teaching of modern Lutherans; also the long treatises on *De Libero Arbitrio* in Chemnitz, *Loci*, I, 174 ff., and in his *Examen Conc. Trid.;* in Gerhard, *Loci*, II, 238, Quenstedt, *Systema*, I, 1076 ff., Hollaz, *Exam.*, I, 615 ff. — Historical matter on Luther's controversy with Erasmus is given in the St. Louis Edition of Luther's works, XVIII, Preface, p. 47 ff. See also F. Bente, "The Synergistic Controversy" in the "Historical Introductions to the Symbolical Books" (*Trigl.* 124 *sqq.*).

any activity and consists of the *imputatio peccati Adamitici* and of the *corruptio hereditaria, quae in omnes homines per carnalem generationem derivatur.* Luther on this distinction between original sin and actual sin: "Original sin, or nature sin, or person sin, is truly the principal sin. If this sin did not exist, there would be no actual sin either. This sin is not committed as all other sins are: but it is the living power which commits all sins." (St. L. XI:287.)[43]

In defining "actual sin" we must always bear in mind that actual sins are not only those sins committed *agendo,* by doing what is prohibited, but also those committed *non agendo, omittendo,* by failing to do what is enjoined. A still shorter definition is: *Peccatum actuale* is the commission or omission of any act which constitutes ἀνομία, that is, which is in conflict with the will of God. Scripture stresses the sinful character of the sins of omission because it is so easily lost sight of. When Christ calls the servant who had hid his talent in the earth an "unprofitable servant" and pronounces upon him the verdict: "Cast ye the unprofitable servant into outer darkness: there shall be weeping and gnashing of teeth" (Matt. 25:30), many a Bible reader will, at first sight, consider this a harsh verdict. But how gravely that servant sinned *non agendo* will become apparent when we consider that when God gives men His gifts, spiritual or physical, small as well as great, He does so with the express command that we employ them faithfully in His service; it is a transgression of His command to let them lie idle. He that defaults in this service is an unfaithful steward. Nor dare we overlook that mighty word: "Unto whomsoever much is given, of him shall be much required; and to whom men have committed much, of him they will ask the more" (Luke 12:48). We are thereby taught that here, too, a *peccatum actuale omissionis* is committed when the measure of the service does not correspond to the measure of the gifts.

But in uncovering and reproving the *peccata omissionis* let us be on our guard lest we become legalistic taskmasters; we should rather, as behooves a Christian teacher, invite and encourage Christians with the mercy of God in Christ, which they have experienced (Rom. 12:1), so that they take pleasure in performing the will of God and, to use

---

[43] With Luther the terms "original sin," "nature sin," "person sin," "principal sin," are synonyms, "original sin" signifying that it is transmitted to us from the first [original] sin of Adam through carnal birth; nature sin, because it inheres in our corrupt human nature; person sin, because it is found wherever there is a person, also in the child in the mother's womb (St. L. V:752), and principal sin *(Hauptsuende),* because it is the evil source of all other sins.

Luther's phrase, "walk as in a paradise" in doing the works of their Christian calling. "Make duty a pleasure!"[44]

It is understood, of course, and has also been previously stated, that all wicked thoughts and volitions which rise in our hearts against the Christian doctrine and life are actual sins. Matt. 15:9: "Out of the heart proceed evil thoughts." Eph. 2:3: ". . . fulfilling the desires of the flesh and of the mind."[45] – In the chapter "The Inner Motions of Sanctification," Vol. III, the necessity of the *Initiis obsta* [Resist the beginnings] will be pointed out.

2

The Causes of Actual Sin

There are, as Scripture plainly indicates, causes within and causes outside man.

CAUSAE PECCATI ACTUALIS INTRA HOMINEM

The general cause of actual sin within man is the depraved nature, or the hereditary corruption. Paul declares (Rom. 7:17) that the "sin that dwelleth in me" does the evil which I would not do. As special causes Scripture mentions

a. The ignorance produced by the hereditary corruption. Paul sinned "ignorantly in unbelief" (1 Tim. 1:13). But sin does not because of this, either wholly or in part, lose the character of sinfulness, for Paul adds (v. 15): "of whom [sinners] I am chief." Christ, too, states that ignorance is the cause of actual sin when He prays (Luke 23:34): "Father, forgive them; for they know not what they do," as also Peter (Acts 3:17): "I wot that through ignorance ye did it, as did also your rulers."

b. Actual sins are caused by violent emotions and passions (*affectus, passiones, παθήματα*), such as fear, violent rage, natural love, etc. Examples: Peter walking on the water (Matt. 14:30), in the

---

[44] See further the chapters on "The Quality and the Quantity of Good Works," in the doctrine of sanctification and good works, Vol. III.

[45] Chemnitz: "In Matthew 5, in a long sermon, Christ shows that the Law condemns not only actual sins, but also original sin, and that actual sins are not only the external actions, but also the internal affections which conflict with the Law of God. And Paul gives one common appellation to the internal and external vicious actions. Gal. 5:19-21 he mentions among the works of the flesh not only fornication, drunkenness, but also heresies, idolatry, wrath, etc." (*Loci* I, 255.)

palace of the high priest (Mark 14:66 ff.), in Antioch (Gal. 2:12: "Fearing them which were of the circumcision"). That the *affectus* and *passiones* do not make the sin sinless we see from Luke 22:62: "Peter went out and wept bitterly."

c. The evil habits, developed by repeating the sinful act, become a cause of actual sins. The dogmaticians speak, on the basis of Scripture, of an *inclinatio ad malum acquisita,* of a *peccatum habituale acquisitum,* of a *habitus vitiosus acquisitus.* Jer. 13:23: "Accustomed to do evil." There is such a thing as being trained to do evil, just as men are trained to practice righteousness.

CAUSAE PECCATI ACTUALIS EXTRA HOMINEM

Scripture names as the external cause of sin

a. The devil and thus portrays to us the realm of sin in its true colors. Scripture teaches that Satan is active not only in the unbelievers (Eph. 2:2: "The spirit that now worketh in the children of disobedience"; 1 Cor. 10:20), but also is the cause of the sins of the children of God. He provoked David to take the census of Israel (1 Chron. 21:1), induced Peter to deny the Lord (Luke 22:31), and through Peter sought to keep Christ from going up to Jerusalem (Matt. 16:23: "Get thee behind Me, Satan"). The causal relation of the devil to the actual sins of the children of God is illustrated in his temptation of Christ, though in this case the diabolical *causa* failed.

It has been asked whether the devil exercises only a moral influence or whether he also produces a physical effect. We dare not exclude the latter utterly (Matt. 4:5: "The devil setteth Him on a pinnacle in the Temple").

b. Other men become the external causes of actual sin. They seduce by word or by acts or by both. They deceive the hearts of the simple by false doctrine (Rom. 16:17-18: "Mark them which cause divisions and offenses contrary to the doctrine which ye have learned"; 2 Tim. 2:17: "Their word [the denial of the bodily resurrection] will eat as doth a canker," and by godless and immoral speech, songs, publications.[46] They seduce by wicked acts, e. g., through the example of an ungodly life, through unchaste gestures and pictures, especially nudities.[47]

---

[46] 1 Cor. 15:33: "Evil communications corrupt good manners." It is most deplorable that the works of the most popular writers are filled with immoral, wicked matter. Cicero already deplores the evil influence of the poets on the morals of the people, *Tuscul.* III, 2, 3.

[47] 2 Sam. 11:2. After the Fall, clothing is the divine ordinance (Gen. 3:21).

God is not, because of His immanence and concurrence, the cause of the sins that are actually committed. This was shown under "Divine Providence." (On the "hardening of the heart" see in Vol. II, pages 28 to 31.) That the evil in the sense of suffering comes from God, who absolutely controls every occurrence, is the clear teaching of Scripture (Is. 45:7: "I make peace and create evil"). That is to be maintained over against Manichaeism and is very comforting for the children of God. When troubles overtake us, we do not have to deal with Satan, who knows no mercy, but we turn in true contrition and faith to the one true God and Father. Luther: "God is good, just, and merciful, also when He smites us. Whoever will not believe this fact forsakes the unity of faith that there is but one God and invents for himself another god, who is not consistent with himself, but is now good, then evil." However, Luther adds: "But it is a signal gift of the Holy Ghost to believe that God, when He sends evil, is still reconciled to us and merciful." (On Ps. 51:10. *Opp. ex.*, Erl. XIX, 106; St. L. V:570.)

3

The Scripture Doctrine of Offense

Seducing others to sin the Scriptures call "giving offense," σκάνδαλον ποιεῖν (Rom. 16:17). We may define it thus: To give offense means to teach or to do something by which we lead another not to believe or to believe error or to lead a wicked life and thus cause him, as far as we are involved, to perish eternally. Hence the solemn warnings of Scripture against giving offense (Matt. 18:6: "But whoso shall offend one of these little ones which believe in Me, it were better for him that a millstone were hanged about his neck and that he were drowned in the depth of the sea"; Mark 9:42 ff.; Luke 17:1-2, etc.). Scripture teaches in addition that offense is given not only by doing evil (false doctrine and wicked life), but also through the inconsiderate use of permissible things (e. g., eating meat and drinking wine, Romans 14 – adiaphora); for, by our example, Christians who are weak in knowledge may be induced to do things which in their erring conscience they regard as wrong and thus endanger their faith. For (v. 20): "All things indeed are pure; but it is evil for that man who eateth with offense"; (v. 23): "He that doubteth is damned [κατακέκριται] if he eat"; (v. 15): "Destroy [ἀπόλλυε] not him with thy meat for whom Christ died." We note that the Apostle in Romans 14 does not censure those who feel free in regard to food, drink, or days; they occupy the correct theological position (v. 14: "There is nothing unclean of itself"; v. 22: "Happy is he that condemneth not himself in that thing which he alloweth"). But we must be willing to restrict this correct theological knowledge in practical use in every case where our use of the right knowledge would induce the brother who is weak in knowledge to act contrary to his erring conscience.

The general rule to be observed is this: We must waive the use of our Christian liberty unless the truth of the Gospel is at stake. And that is the case when the weak brother insists that his error be acknowledged as the true doctrine and judges him who has the right knowledge, declaring him to be a transgressor of God's commandment. In this case the weak brother becomes a false teacher, and then Col. 2:16 applies: "Let no man therefore judge you in meat or in drink or in respect of an holy day," etc., and Gal. 5:1: "Stand fast therefore in the liberty wherewith Christ hath made us free." It may happen that by the commanded use of the Christian liberty weak Christians are offended, that is, are induced to act contrary to their conscience; but the responsibility for the offense rests on those who, by demanding recognition for their error [by their κρίνειν] have forced us to make use of our Christian liberty.[48]

From offense which is given we must distinguish offense which is taken. Offense is taken when one who is spiritually blind and wicked takes occasion to sin from the words or acts of another without the other's fault. Christ the Crucified One becomes a "stumbling stone and rock of offense" to the self-righteous Jews (Rom. 9: 30-33), and to the Greeks seeking after wisdom He is foolishness (1 Cor. 1:22-23). Both Jews and Greeks insisted on, and persisted in, their false notion of the way of salvation over against Christ's way of saving men. Men will continue to the end of time to take offense at Christ and His Church.[49] Even Christians take offense at Christ when

---

[48] Keeping this in mind, we understand why Paul had Timothy circumcised (Acts 16:3) and refused definitely to have Titus circumcised (Gal. 2:4-5). In the case of Timothy he respected the weakness of those who had not yet been sufficiently instructed; in the case of Titus he defended the truth of the Gospel against the κρίνοντες. Likewise Peter (Galatians 2) was *in statu confessionis*. Paul reproves Peter for denying the truth of the Gospel by his conduct in refusing to eat with the Gentile Christians when they that were of the circumcision put in their appearance. Compare the quotations in Baier-Walther, II, 313 *sqq*.

[49] Modern theologians are offended at Christ because He expects them to give up their Ego theology, to continue in His Word, to receive the Scriptures as the infallible Word of God. (John 8:31-32; 17:20; 10:35; Eph. 2:20; 1 Tim

they fall away from Him because they are not willing to follow Him on the way of suffering. Matt. 24:10-11; "Then shall many be offended. . . . And many false prophets shall rise and shall deceive many." Matt. 13:21: "When tribulation or persecution ariseth because of the Word, by and by he is offended." For this reason, Christ so earnestly warns: "Blessed is he whosoever shall not be offended in Me," etc. (Matt. 11:6, 25, 26.)

4

The Scripture Doctrine of Temptation

There is a) a temptation to evil, and b) a temptation to good. The temptation to evil comes from the devil, from other men, and from our own depraved nature. Its object is the seduction into sin (*tentatio seductionis*). The temptation to good comes from God, and its purpose is the testing and strengthening of faith (*tentatio probationis*). Examples of the *tentatio seductionis* are Christ's temptation by the devil (Matt. 4:1 ff.) and the Christians' temptations by their evil flesh (James 1:14: "Every man is tempted when he is drawn away of his own lust"). Examples of the *tentatio probationis* are God's tempting of Abraham by the command to sacrifice Isaac (Gen. 22:1-18) and God's permitting false prophets to come with signs and wonders to put the people to the test whether they will continue in the Word of God (Deut. 13:3: "The Lord, your God, proveth you to know whether ye love the Lord, your God, with all your heart and with all your soul"). Also in the New Testament God permits heresies (αἱρέσεις) to arise, not to bring about the apostasy of the Christians, but "that they which are approved may be made manifest among you" (1 Cor. 11:19), and Paul tests (δοκιμάζων) the love of the Christians whether it be sincere (2 Cor. 8:8).

When men criticize the *tentatio probationis* by saying that it makes God the *causa peccati*, they commit the *crimen laesae maiestatis divinae*. To ward off any such thoughts, God tells us plainly in Scripture that He will not suffer us "to be tempted above that ye are able, but will with the temptation also make a way to escape" (1 Cor. 10:13). The Scriptural axiom is: Whoever succumbs to temptation

6:3 ff.) Another stumbling block for them is the *satisfactio vicaria*. Therefore they ascribe to unconverted man the *facultas se applicandi ad gratiam* in its various forms: self-determination, *Selbstsetzung*, self-decision, liberty of choice *in utramque partem*, etc.

falls by his own fault, namely, through self-confidence, i. e., defection from grace, as was the case with Peter (Matt. 26:33-36). All Christians are warned: "Let him that thinketh he standeth take heed lest he fall" (1 Cor. 10:12). But he who overcomes temptation owes the victory not to his own merit and own power, but solely to God's grace.[50]

5

Classification of Actual Sins

Scripture presents the *peccata actualia* under various classifications, which are not useless and should not bore us. They serve the purpose, as Chemnitz points out (*Loci*, I, p. 259), of guarding Christians against carnal security and showing how many wild beasts are slumbering in their own flesh and must be fought. "Every true Christian will therefore, together with Paul (1 Cor. 9:27), discipline his own body and keep it in subjection, lest he become a reprobate." We will fervently implore God "that He would deign to endow us richly with the grace of His Holy Spirit, so that we may truly know our sins, sincerely deplore them, by firm faith seek forgiveness of them solely by the merit of our Savior Jesus Christ, and so in Him ultimately reach eternal blessedness. Amen."

a. VOLUNTARY AND INVOLUNTARY SINS

The will of man plays a part in every sin, whether he is aware of it or not, and in that sense we might call all sins voluntary sins. But the will of man participates in the sin in varying degrees. In some cases the participation of the will is so pronounced that man plans the sin, though he may hide behind all manner of excuses, and executes it with heart and soul. Examples: Judas' betrayal (Matt. 26:14-16); Absalom's rebellion (2 Samuel 15). In this sense we speak of *peccata voluntaria, proaeretica, malitiae* (willful, premeditated, malicious sins). In other instances the will of man so recedes into the background that the sin is called forth by ignorance, by passions, such as fear, by natural love, by partisanship, etc. Examples: the two hundred who went with Absalom in ignorance of his evil plan (2 Sam-

---

50 Paul warns the Gentile Christians who overcome temptation ("thou standest by faith") not to look down upon the Jews who fell (Rom. 11:20-22). Therefore 2 Cor. 12:9 tells us that the power of God "is made perfect in weakness," that is to say: "In temptation the strong are weak, and the weak strong."

uel 15); Peter and his Gentile fellow Christians denied Christ out of fear (Luke 22:55 ff.; Gal. 2:12 ff.). In this sense we speak of *peccata involuntaria, ignorantiae, praecipitantiae* (involuntary sins, sins of ignorance, of rashness).

The term "sins of weakness" (*peccata infirmitatis*) should be reserved for Christians, since unbelievers do not sin from weakness, but because they are dead in sins and are wholly in the power of the devil (Eph. 2:1-2). We classify the evil thoughts, desires, and feelings which suddenly arise out of the flesh of Christians against their will as sins of weakness. Luther: "When you have wicked thoughts, you should not on this account despair; only be on your guard lest you be taken captive by them. . . . Wherever faith comes into being, there come a hundred evil thoughts and a hundred temptations more than before. Only see to it that you act the man; do not suffer yourself to be taken captive; continue to resist and to say: I will not, I will not." (St. L. IX:1032.)

With regard to the sins of infants the statement of the baptismal act must stand: ". . . that there may be drowned and destroyed in him all that he hath inherited from Adam and himself added thereto." (*Liturgy and Agenda*, p. 320.) While infants do not commit *peccata proaeretica*, premeditated sins (Deut. 1:39: ". . . your children, which in that day had no knowledge of good and evil"; Jonah 4:11), they do commit *peccata actualia*. Just as by the working of the Holy Ghost true faith and works of faith are found in infants (Ps. 8:2: "Out of the mouth of babes and sucklings hast Thou ordained strength"), so we dare not, on the other hand, deny that since they are "flesh born of flesh" (John 3:6), their flesh stirs within them, though they are not conscious of these evil strivings. – The *peccata actualia* in infants are, of course, denied by all who, contrary to Scripture, make the *voluntarium*, or the conscious self-determination, an essential part of sin.

b. THE RELATION OF PECCATA ACTUALIA TO THE CONSCIENCE

The old division of actual sins into *peccata contra conscientiam* (a) *veram*, (b) *erroneam*, (c) *probabilem*, (d) *dubiam* may appear at first glance rather mechanical, but it serves a real need. Whoever sins against a correctly informed conscience (*conscientia recta*) sins most grievously. He sins as an αὐτοκατάκριτος ("being condemned of himself," Titus 3:10); he is approaching the condition of a man who is determined to espouse error and faces the danger of committing the sin against the Holy Ghost.[51] – One who has an erring conscience (*conscientia erronea*), who regards it, e. g., as his duty to pray to the saints, is in a predicament. He sins when he obeys his conscience, and he sins when he does not obey his conscience. In the first case he does what God has forbidden. In the second case he sins because he fails to do something which he feels conscience bound to do as commanded by God.[52] It is therefore of great importance to correct an erring conscience by proper instruction from God's Word. – "Against the probable conscience he sins who neglects the safer way" (Hollaz, *Examen, "De peccatis actualibus,"* qu. 11). This somewhat infelicitous expression – *conscientia probabilis, opinativa, Wahrscheinlichkeitsgewissen* – conveys an important truth. He sins who, instead of inquiring conscientiously which of two or more possible or proposed modes of procedure is the best and safest one, treats the whole question lightly. That holds true in the secular as well as in the religious domain. In all things that are left to their decision, Christians are so much concerned about choosing the best that they implore God to lead them to choose the safest and the best way. – In the case of a doubting conscience (*conscientia dubia*) Christians must wait until the doubt is cleared up before they act. Rom. 14:23: "He that doubteth is damned if he eat, because he eateth not of faith." [53]

c. SINS AGAINST GOD, AGAINST THE NEIGHBOR, AND AGAINST ONESELF

Scripture names as the persons against whom sin is committed: God, the neighbor, and oneself. Gen. 39:9: "How, then, can I do this great wickedness and sin against God?" Lev. 19:17: "Thou shalt not hate thy brother in thine heart; thou shalt in any wise rebuke thy neighbor, and not suffer sin upon him." 1 Cor. 6:18: "He that committeth fornication sinneth against his own body." But we must remember that the sins against the neighbor and against oneself are

---

[51] Cp. what was said on the danger of clinging to the error in doctrinal controversies (Vol. I, p. 90).

[52] See the quotation, in Baier-Walther, II, p. 269, from Ad. Osiander's *Colleg. Theol.-system,* p. 288 *sq.*: "An erring conscience . . . does not obligate [*obligat*], but it binds [*ligat*]. But to bind is to constrain one that he cannot justly act according to such a conscience, if it lasts, so that he sins if he acts contrary to it and also sins if he acts in accordance with it."

[53] Cf. *Lutheraner,* 34, p. 129 ff.: *"Habt ein gutes Gewissen."* We find in our pastoral practice that, e. g., the parties to a marriage in the prohibited degrees may, before the marriage, delude themselves into believing that they have a *conscientia recta,* only to have it become evident soon after marriage that they had a *conscientia dubia.*

sins only because they are transgressions of God's commandment. The general canon is: *Omne peccatum in Deum committitur.* That is stated Ps. 51:4: "Against Thee, Thee only, have I sinned." David is not denying his sin against Uriah and Bathsheba; he is setting forth its enormity.[54]

d. GRIEVOUS AND LESS GRIEVOUS SINS

As to their degree, Scripture itself distinguishes between grievous and less grievous sins. On the one hand, Scripture teaches that every sin, being ἀνομία, or rebellion against God, merits damnation. Gal. 3:10: "Cursed is everyone that continueth not in all things which are written in the Book of the Law to do them." On the other hand, Scripture clearly distinguishes degrees in sinning. Christ says of the Jews (John 19:11) that, compared with Pilate, they were committing "the greater sin." Children who have not reached the *anni discretionis* (the years of discretion) are less guilty than mature men. Deut. 1:39: "Your children, which in that day had no knowledge between good and evil, they shall go in thither" (Canaan). Scripture teaches that sinning against better knowledge of the will of God is more grievous than sinning in ignorance. Luke 12:47-48: "That servant which knew his lord's will and prepared not himself, neither did according to his will, shall be beaten with many stripes. But he that knew not and did commit things worthy of stripes shall be beaten with few stripes. For unto whomsoever much is given, of him shall be much required; and to whom men have committed much, of him they will ask the more." Accordingly Scripture also teaches degrees in the eternal punishment of sin (see the *locus* of "Eternal Damnation," in Vol. III).

The most grievous of all sins is despising the Gospel of grace, of the *sola gratia.* In the Gospel of the *sola gratia* God reveals His innermost heart, His true will toward all mankind. He sent "not His Son into the world to condemn the world, but that the world through Him might be saved" (John 3:17). It spells enmity against the Gospel if, like the Pharisee, we set ourselves above other men and lay claim to a greater righteousness or a lesser guilt before God. This claim is a complete rejection of the gracious will, which knows only the *sola gratia,* and was the national sin of carnal Israel. Therefore Paul calls himself, after his eyes have been opened, "the chief of sinners" (1 Tim. 1:15), and the Reformer of the Church warns all that bear the glorious name of Christians, including himself, against harboring any such

---

[54] Cf. Hengstenberg in his *Psalmenkommentar* on the passage.

thoughts: "In that Christ says, 'The first shall be last,' He strips you of all presumption and forbids you to exalt yourself above the whore, even if you were like Abraham, David, Peter, or Paul. And when He says, 'The last shall be the first,' He asks you never to despair and forbids you to place yourself beneath any saint, even if you were Pilate, Herod, Sodom, and Gomorrah" (St. L. XI:515).[55]

When we divide sins into *peccata cordis, oris, operis* (thoughts, words, deeds), we classify them, as a rule, according to the degree. But that is not always the case. A secretly harbored implacability may be a more grievous sin than a word or deed prompted by a sudden burst of passion.

e. PECCATA MORTALIA ET VENALIA

As to their effect, sins are divided into mortal sins and venial sins. Mortal sins are those which result in the death of the sinner. This term takes in all the sins of the unbelievers. In the case of the believers those sins are called mortal which force the Holy Spirit to depart from one's heart, which destroy faith. Venial sins are sins which, though they in themselves merit eternal death, are daily forgiven to the believer.[56] They are also called sins of weakness. They do not drive the Holy Spirit from the heart, do not extinguish faith.

The Romanists teach that certain actual sins are venial in themselves and do not deserve eternal, but only temporal punishments.[57] The Arminians hold essentially the same view as the Catholics.[58] The Calvinists teach that in the case of the elect even *peccata enormia*

---

[55] This truth does not contradict those Scripture passages in which a distinction is made between greater and lesser sins. Scripture teaches that all men are equally and totally depraved (Eph. 2:1-5; John 3:6). Scripture, moreover, teaches, and all Christians know it by experience, that in their flesh there dwells no good thing and that it is due solely and alone to the grace of God if in their case the original depravity did not produce all its natural results, even including eternal damnation. If, then, we take credit for the things which we owe entirely to God's preservation and grace and seek to deal with God on the basis of our lesser sin and guilt (in comparison with others), such action is an unreasonable and direct refusing and despising of the Gospel of grace. Therefore Luther warns us against exalting ourselves before God above any whore, etc., in which case the first shall be the last.

[56] See Luther's Explanation of the Fifth Petition.

[57] See the statement from the Catechismus Romanus (II, 5, qu. 46) and from the catechism of Bishop Henni (pp. 75–76) in Guenther, *Symbolik*, p. 155 [*Pop. Symbolics*, p. 168]. Luther shows in the Smalcald Articles (*Trigl.* 485, 21 ff.) that Rome's teaching that certain sins deserve only temporal punishment lies at the basis of its business of satisfactions, indulgences, and purgatory.

[58] See their *Confession* VII, 6, in Guenther, *op. cit.*, p. 156; Quenstedt, I, 1048; Baier-Walther, II, 325 *sqq*.

do not destroy faith nor deprive them of the Holy Ghost.[59] The Scholastics enumerate seven sins as mortal sins: ***superbia, avaritia, luxuria, ira, gula*** [gluttony], ***invidia, acedia.***[60] This list is misleading; any sin may become a mortal sin if we persevere in it against the admonition of our conscience.

f. DOMINANT AND NON-DOMINANT SINS

This division is practically the same as the division into mortal and venial sins. In unbelievers the sins are always dominant, even though individual sins do not become acts. All unbelievers are dead in sins, and Satan is the ruling power in them (Eph. 2:1-3; Col. 1:13; Acts 26:18). The state of grace in which sin no longer rules is found only in the believers. Rom. 6:14: "Sin shall not have dominion over you; for ye are not under the Law, but under grace." When in the lives of erstwhile believers the struggle of the spirit against the flesh has ceased and the sins have again become dominant, then these believers have fallen from faith. Hence the admonition: "Let not sin therefore reign in your mortal body" (Rom. 6:12).

g. PARTAKING OF OTHER MEN'S SINS

Scripture warns us emphatically against this species of *peccata actualia:* "Neither be partaker of other men's sins" (1 Tim. 5:22). It names specific instances. One who practices church fellowship with those who in their doctrine depart from God's Word becomes guilty of their sin. 2 John 11 states explicitly: "He that biddeth him [who does not bring the doctrine of Christ] Godspeed is partaker of his evil deeds."[61] And in order to preserve Christians from this sin, Paul instructs all Christians (Rom. 16:17) to "avoid them," namely, all those who deviate from the Apostolic doctrine. We share in the sins of others also when we take pleasure in the evil they do. As a mark of extreme wickedness of the Gentiles, Paul specifies (Rom. 1:32) that they not only "do the same" [things worthy of death], but they "have pleasure in them that do them." Pleasure in the sins of others is experienced particularly in a) reading books which glorify immorality

---

[59] See the statements from the Canons of the Synod of Dort and from the *Confession of Faith* of the Presbyterians in the section "Re-Conversion," in Vol. II, p. 468, note 24 [*Pop. Symbolics*, p. 225].

[60] That *acedia* (ἀκηδία), satiety in regard to God's Word, is correctly classed with the mortal sins, Luther shows in his Large Catechism, *Trigl.* 608, 99.

[61] We are not forbidden to hold friendly, civil intercourse with him. What is forbidden is to greet such a one, and deal with him, as a brother in the faith.

and b) reading books which glorify false doctrines or false teachers. The various ways in which one participates in the sins of others are set down in the old Latin verse:

Consulo, praecipio, consentio, provoco, laudo,
Non retego culpam, non punio, non reprehendo,
Non obsto, sed praecipio et defendo aliena

(I counsel, teach, consent to, provoke, laud, do not reveal the guilt, do not punish, do not reprehend, do not resist, but teach and defend the sins of others.)[62]

h. SINS CRYING TO HEAVEN (PECCATA CLAMANTIA)

Certain sins cry out to God for public vengeance. As such, Scripture lists murder (Gen. 4:10: "The voice of thy brother's blood crieth unto Me from the ground"); the slaying of Christians (Rev. 6:10: "They cried with a loud voice, saying, How long, O Lord, holy and true, dost Thou not judge and avenge our blood on them that dwell on the earth?"); withholding from hired laborers their wages (James 5:4); the oppression, in general, of the helpless, strangers, widows, orphans, the poor, the enslaved, etc., who cannot help themselves and therefore cry to God that He would intervene. (Ex. 22:21-24; Is. 3:14-15; Ex. 3:7-9; etc.) Chemnitz (*Loci*, I, p. 258): "In the schools they call them *peccata clamantia* because Scripture says that these sins, even though men remain silent, cry to God and call for His vengeance." Referring to Gen. 4:10; 18:20; Ex. 3:7; 22:23; James 5:4, he quotes the old memory verse:

Clamitat ad coelem vox sanguinis et Sodomorum,
Vox oppressorum mercesque retenta laborum

(To heaven cries the voice of the blood and of the Sodomites, The voice of the oppressed and the withheld wage of the laborers.) — At the same time we bear in mind that unbelief, the refusal to accept Jesus as the Savior of the world, is the greatest and most grievous sin. John 16:9: "Of sin, because they believed not on Me" (John 15:22). It may be called *peccatum clamantissimum.* Christ reproved the unbelief of the Pharisees, who objected to the "Hosannah" at His entrance into Jerusalem, with the words: "I tell you that if these should

---

62 In Chemnitz, *Loci*, I, 258; Baier-Walther, II, 322. Also numerous examples from the Bible are given. The "*non retego culpam*" ("I do not reveal the guilt") refers, of course, to cases where the revelation of the guilt is demanded by our calling and duty; otherwise Prov. 11:13 applies: "A talebearer revealeth secrets." The question in which case publishers and bookdealers become guilty of another's sin is treated in *Lutheraner*, 27, p. 172 ff.

hold their peace, the stones would immediately cry out" (Luke 19:40; cp. Heb. 12:22-25).

When some dogmaticians speak of *peccata non clamantia,* they do not mean to say (as some neologists do) that there is a class of "guiltless sins," but they are pointing out that God in His patience and long-suffering is withholding His judgment of sin, giving room for repentance, or that according to His reckoning the measure of their sin is not yet full (Gen. 15:16: "The iniquity of the Amorites is not yet full"). As for us Christians, we thank God that He also recognizes *peccata non clamantia.* For while we know and experience, on the one hand, that we harbor a multitude of sins, which certainly merit God's wrath and eternal damnation, we know, on the other hand, that these sins no longer cry to God for vengeance; God daily and richly forgives them because we have an Advocate with the Father, Jesus Christ the Righteous, who has made full propitiation for our sins, and we can pray with the full assurance of being heard: "Hide Thy face from my sins, and blot out all mine iniquities" (Ps. 51:9).

i. THE SIN AGAINST THE HOLY GHOST

If we would separately classify those sins for which pardon may be obtained (*peccata remissibilia*) through repentance and distinguish them from those which are unpardonable (*peccata irremissibilia*) because there is no longer room for repentance, the latter class would comprise only one sin, the sin against the Holy Ghost.

The Scripture passages treating of this sin (*sedes doctrinae*) are Matt. 12:22-32 and its parallels, Mark 3:22-30 and Luke 12:10. Also 1 John 5:16 is correctly referred to the sin against the Holy Ghost. In these passages the sin against the Holy Ghost is set apart from all other sins; it is declared to be the one sin which is never remitted. Matt. 12:31: "All manner of sin and blasphemy shall be forgiven unto men; but the blasphemy against the Holy Ghost shall not be forgiven unto men." And Scripture further stresses the unusual character of this sin by distinguishing it from the sin against the Son of God. Matt. 12:32: "Whosoever speaketh a word against the Son of Man, it shall be forgiven him; but whosoever speaketh against the Holy Ghost, it shall not be forgiven him, neither in this world, neither in the world to come." Mark 3:28-29 has the same statement: "All sins shall be forgiven unto the sons of men, and blasphemies wherewith soever they shall blaspheme [as many, ὅσας, blasphemies as they may utter]; but he that shall blaspheme against the Holy Ghost, hath never forgiveness, but is in danger of eternal damnation." Likewise Luke 12:10.

In 1 John 5:16 ("If any man see his brother sin a sin which is not unto death, he shall ask, and He shall give him life for them that sin not unto death. There is a sin unto death; I do not say that he shall pray for it.") the "sin not unto death" and the "sin unto death" are distinguished. The distinction is that we should, of course, intercede for one who sins "not unto death," but in the case of the sin "unto death" there is to be no intercession: "I do not say that he shall pray for it." It is clear that the sin unto death cannot be simple unbelief, for it is our duty to pray for the unbelievers (1 Tim. 2:1, 4; the First and Second Petition; the example given us by Christ and Stephen). Nor does the Apostle refer to those who on account of their manifest apostasy are excluded (excommunicated) from the Christian congregation. For such men intercession is to be made, since the purpose of excommunication, the last sharp remedy, is to bring them to faith and save them (1 Cor. 5:5; 2 Cor. 2:6-11). But since in the case of the "sin unto death" intercession is excluded, this term can be only another appellation for the sin against the Holy Ghost.[63]

What is the nature (*forma*) of the sin against the Holy Ghost as distinguished from all other sins? a) It does not consist in final impenitence (*impoenitentia finalis*). The vast majority of men die in unbelief, and Scripture does not charge them with the unpardonable sin. b) Nor does every kind of resistance against the Holy Ghost constitute this sin. For then all men who hear and read the Gospel would be guilty of it, since all men by nature regard the Gospel as foolishness and therefore resist until the Holy Ghost through the Word changes their resisting will into a consenting will. c) Nor does the sin against the Holy Ghost consist in the blasphemy against the truth resulting from spiritual blindness. Paul confesses that he had been "a blasphemer and a presecutor and injurious," ignorantly, in unbelief, but that nevertheless he "obtained mercy" (1 Tim. 1:13). Nor does he who denies the truth from fear or other strong emotions commit the unpardonable sin. Peter did that, and he was again converted (Luke 22:61-62).

But the case of the Pharisees whose conduct induced Jesus to warn against the sin was entirely different. These Pharisees were powerfully impressed by the miracle performed by Jesus. It had the same effect upon them as it had upon the common people, of whom it is said: "All the people were amazed [ἐξίσταντο] and said, 'Is not this the Son of David?" (Matt. 12:23.) And yet these Pharisees, though

---

[63] Luther, in his *"Sermon von der Suende wider den Heiligen Geist"* (St. L. X:1205), and most of the dogmaticians take this view.

they had the inner conviction that this was a divine miracle, blasphemed with the worst possible blasphemy: They declared it to be a satanic work. They blasphemed: "This fellow doth not cast out devils but by Beelzebub, the prince of the devils" (Matt. 12:24). Hereupon Christ warned against the one great sin which, unlike other sins, is not forgiven. Accordingly we must give this definition: The sin against the Holy Ghost is committed when, after the Holy Ghost has convinced a person in his heart of the divine truth, that person nevertheless not only rejects the truth he is convinced of, but also blasphemes it. Hollaz thus describes this sin: "The sin against the Holy Ghost is the malicious denial of the divine truth which a person has clearly understood and approved in his conscience, a hostile assault on it, horrible blaspheming, and an obstinate rejection of all the means of grace, which lasts to the end." (*Examen, "De Pecc. Act.,"* qu. 38.)[64] The sin against the Holy Ghost is committed not against the person, but against the office of the Holy Ghost; it is the willful and determined suppression of the inner conviction wrought by the Holy Ghost. It is therefore specifically distinguished from the sin committed against the Person of the Son of God ("whosoever speaketh a word against the Son of Man, it shall be forgiven him," Matt. 12:32).[65]

Several questions related to this matter need to be investigated.

1. Does the sin against the Holy Ghost still occur today? Some Arminians have held that it was confined to the days of the Apostles.[66] We must answer the question affirmatively. The passages Matthew 12, etc., are too general in their scope. Nothing in them indicates that the sin occurred only in the days of Christ and the Apostles. They are without doubt words of warning addressed to the Christians of all times.

2. Can it be established *in concreto* whether a person has committed the sin against the Holy Ghost? The correct answer to this question is of great practical importance to the individual Christian and for pastoral practice. It has been correctly stated concerning this sin that those who have not committed it often torture themselves with

---

[64] In his *"Sermon von der Suende wider den Heiligen Geist"* (St. L. X:1203), Luther distinguishes between the "veiled Holy Ghost," as was the case with Paul before his conversion, and the "revealed Holy Ghost," as was the case with the Pharisees whom He inwardly convinced of the truth. "Here the Holy Ghost is manifest and uncovered, breaks forth and shines like lightning, so that His brightness penetrates the heart. . . . This they formerly called *impugnationem veritatis agnitae* [assault on the realized truth]."

[65] See further on this point Walther, *Law and Gospel,* p. 393.

[66] Thus Episcopius in *Resp. ad 64 qu.,* 14; quoted in Quenstedt, I, 1072.

the despairing fear of being guilty of it, while those who have actually committed it are not concerned about it, this being the natural result of the state of extreme obduration, which is a concomitant of this sin. Now, one who is worried about his sins and fears that they are an indication of his having committed the unpardonable sin, while at the same time his heart is filled with the longing not to be excluded from the remission which Christ has purchased with His blood – in him the Holy Ghost is carrying on His mighty work, as is clearly attested by this worry and this desire. He is a believer. The Formula of Concord is entirely right in saying that all "who feel and experience in their hearts a small spark of longing for divine grace and eternal salvation" can and should "know that God has kindled in their hearts this beginning of true godliness, and that He will further strengthen and help them in their great weakness to persevere in true faith unto the end" (*Trigl.* 885, 14). For this claim the Formula of Concord brings irrefutable Scripture proof; it shows that a desire for God's grace in Christ is not found in the natural heart of man, but is in every case God's operation in "godly Christians." Most Lutheran dogmaticians therefore held that the Italian jurist Francesco Spiera (d. 1548) had not committed the sin against the Holy Ghost, but that he had died in despair because he *thought* he had committed it. Thus Quenstedt, I, 1064: "Spiera must by no means be regarded as having committed the sin against the Holy Ghost, because 1) he fell away to the Papacy not maliciously, but from weakness, not of his own will and initiative, but through the persuasion of friends; and 2) he did not antagonize and blaspheme the doctrine of the Gospel, but highly deplored that he had fallen away from the truth. It was therefore a kind of despair, but not blasphemy against the Holy Ghost, as the sainted Meisner says; or he merely thought he had committed this sin." This does not fully describe the historical case of Spiera, but in our opinion Quenstedt's judgment is correct.[67]

Now for our question: Can the sin against the Holy Ghost be recognized in a concrete case? Two things should be borne in mind: a) Let us not be hasty (*temere*) in charging someone with this sin.

---

[67] The case of Spiera is described in R. E., 2d ed., XIV, p. 799 ff. and in Meusel, VI, p. 354, but not always with a sound theological judgment. The R. E., for instance, says (p. 801): "Spiera had wantonly trifled with the Word of God and his knowledge of it; else he could not so easily and quickly have apostatized." One should bear in mind how quickly Peter fell as a result of fear of men and of death. Also Calvin's judgment of this case should carry no weight, since he, denying God's universal will of grace, could not have formed a correct judgment concerning the sin against the Holy Ghost.

Luther, too, is very cautious here. "Do not rashly charge anyone with this sin. There are poor, burdened consciences which the devil is driving to despair by causing them to think they have committed the unpardonable sin" (in his "Sermon," St. L. X:1209). b) On the other hand, those who assert that this sin can in no case be detected go too far. From 1 John 5:16 we learn two things: 1) The sin does occur and is discernible, because it frees from the obligation of interceding: "There is a sin unto death; I do not say that he shall pray for it." 2) While John employs the plural in the context preceding and following, and there describes a knowledge common to all Christians, he uses the singular in v. 16: "If any man see." He is speaking of a special case, and by the singular number he indicates that in order to distinguish between "sin not unto death" and "sin unto death" a discernment and knowledge is required which is confined to one or several persons, perhaps to the pastor or to one or the other Christian who has the special gift of discerning the spirits.

3. Most Lutheran theologians assume that only a regenerate person can commit the sin against the Holy Ghost. Quenstedt in his θέσις is rather cautious in voicing this opinion. "The opinion of those who ascribe the sin against the Holy Ghost only to the truly reborn, justified, and renewed seems more probable to us" (*Systema* I, 1060); others, such as Baier, Balthasar Meisner, Feurborn, hold that also unregenerate persons can commit this sin in the moment when the Holy Ghost is about to convert them. At any rate, an internally convincing testimony of the Holy Ghost must precede this sin; that is contained in the term "against [εἰς, κατά] the Holy Ghost."

4. The passages Heb. 6:4-8 and Heb. 10:26-27 can be harmonized with Matthew 12, etc., only by assuming that they, too, deal with the *peccatum in Spiritum Sanctum.* They, too, clearly deny the possibility of a renewed repentance in the case of those "who were once enlightened and have tasted the heavenly gift," but then sin "willfully" (ἑκουσίως). — As to Heb. 12:17, where it is said that Esau "was rejected; for he found no place of repentance, though he sought it carefully with tears," the evidence favors the opinion that the "repentance" is not Esau's, but the change of mind of his father Isaac with respect to the blessing of the first-born. Among recent exegetes, Luenemann, Ebrard, Moll hold this view. How he sought to bring about the change of mind in the father, "carefully with tears," is recorded Gen. 27:34 ff.

5. How does the fact that the sin against the Holy Ghost is not forgiven agree with that other fact that Christ gained forgiveness for all sins, therefore also for the sin against the Holy Ghost? Unscriptural

solutions of this difficulty are offered by the Calvinists and by the Papists and the synergists. The Calvinists solve the difficulty by declaring, in the end, that the gracious will of God and the merit of Christ extend not over all men, but only over a part of mankind. They say that those who commit the unpardonable sin belong to the class of those whom God never intended to save, whom Christ has not reconciled to God. This solution is wrong, for according to Scripture Christ is the Propitiation (ἱλασμός) "for the sins of the whole world" (1 John 2:2). They furthermore claim that the converting operation of the Holy Ghost does not extend to those who sin against the Holy Ghost. The very description of this sin shows that this claim is a pure human fiction. This sin is precisely, according to Scripture, the malicious revolt against the internally convincing operation of the Holy Ghost.

Roman theologians solve the difficulty in a different way. They hold that those who commit the sin against the Holy Ghost belong in the class that has failed to acquire the needed merit to obtain salvation. And the synergists of all shades hold that, as in the case of the unbelievers and the obdurate, so also in the case of those who sin against the Holy Ghost, there is a lack of the required self-determination; they do not reduce the resistance and the guilt of sin to the degree needed for conversion and salvation. But that this co-operation in conversion and in the obtaining of salvation is fiction, Christ shows in that very connection in which he warns against committing the sin against the Holy Ghost. Christ teaches in this very context that all men remain under the power and dominion of Satan until the Stronger One, Christ, overcomes him and robs him of his spoils. In short, we must say also in regard to this sin: a) If a person does not commit it, it is due solely to God's grace and in no wise to a good human quality or accomplishment, call it what you will. And b) If a man does commit the sin against the Holy Ghost, it is entirely his fault; it was not caused by a lack of God's grace or of Christ's merit or of the saving operation of the Holy Spirit. Here, too, it is either, on the one hand, the *sola gratia Dei* or, on the other, the *sola culpa hominis*.

We face this situation also in the case of obduration. The Formula of Concord reminds us: "One is hardened, blinded, given over to a reprobate mind, while another, who is indeed in the same guilt, is converted again, etc. — in these and similar questions Paul (Rom. 11:22 ff.) fixes a certain limit to us how far we should go, namely, that in the one part we should recognize God's judgment. For they are well-deserved penalties of sins . . . in order that we may live in the fear of God, and acknowledge and praise God's goodness, to the exclusion of, and contrary to, our merit in and with us, to whom He gives this Word, and with whom He leaves it, and whom He does not harden and reject." (*Trigl.* 1081 f., 57 ff.) And where is the Christian who, when he honestly examines himself, would dare to say: The reason why I have not committed the sin against the Holy Ghost lies in me? Therefore Luther says in his "Sermon": "For this let us pray that we do not fall into this sin that will not endure the plain truth; for in that case there is no counsel, or help, or excuse, but the final wrath of God has set in." And at the close of the "Sermon," Luther repeats the prayer: "May God keep us from this sin" (St. L. X: 1206, 1209).

Concluding Remark. There is only one thing that will deliver us from the fear of having committed the sin against the Holy Ghost. We must turn our heart, mind, and thoughts wholly to the absolutely universal and the absolutely free grace of God in Christ, which is revealed in Scripture *sole clarius* (clearer than the sun). Sorry comforters in this case are the Papists and the synergists and also the Calvinists. The Reformed theologian Schneckenburger shows conclusively that a Calvinist must first become a Lutheran if he would deliver anyone from the fear of having committed the unpardonable sin.[68] Therefore it behooves us to maintain the *universalis gratia* and the *sola gratia.* That will be demonstrated further in the first section of Volume II.

---

[68] *Vergleichende Darstellung des luth. und des ref. Lehrbegriffs,* I, p. 260 ff.: "The only thing that will avail here is to point with Luther to the objective merit of Christ, the promise of God's Word, and the faithfulness of Him who calls, who will not give up the work begun, but will preserve us. The Reformed Christian will simply have to forget that the merit of Christ, etc., does not concern all, perhaps does not concern him."

